Interdisciplinary Advances in Information Technology Research

Mehdi Khosrow-Pour
Information Resources Management Association, USA

Managing Director: Lindsay Johnston
Editorial Director: Joel Gamon
Book Production Manager: Jennifer Yoder
Publishing Systems Analyst: Adrienne Freeland
Assistant Acquisitions Editor: Kayla Wolfe
Typesetter: Christy Fic
Cover Design: Jason Mull

Published in the United States of America by
Information Science Reference (an imprint of IGI Global)
701 E. Chocolate Avenue
Hershey PA 17033
Tel: 717-533-8845
Fax: 717-533-8661
E-mail: cust@igi-global.com
Web site: http://www.igi-global.com

Library of Congress Cataloging-in-Publication Data

Interdisciplinary advances in information technology research / Mehdi Khosrow-Pour, editor.
pages cm
Includes bibliographical references and index.
Summary: "This book explores multiple fields and the research compiled, to compare how they differentiate and relate to one another"--Provided by publisher.
ISBN 978-1-4666-3625-5 (hardcover) -- ISBN 978-1-4666-3626-2 (ebook) -- ISBN 978-1-4666-3627-9 (print & perpetual access) 1. Information technology--Research. 2. Management information systems--Research. I. Khosrowpour, Mehdi, 1951-
T58.5.I5652 2013
004.072--dc23

2012045940

British Cataloguing in Publication Data
A Cataloguing in Publication record for this book is available from the British Library.

Editorial Advisory Board

List of Reviewers

Table of Contents

Chapter 5
Self-Organizing Tree Using Artificial Ants 60
Hanene Azzag, Université Paris 13, France
Mustapha Lebbah, Université Paris 13, France

Chapter 6
Co-Evolutionary Algorithms Based on Mixed Strategy 75
Wei Hou, Harbin Engineering University & Northeast Agricultural University, China
HongBin Dong, Harbin Engineering University, China
GuiSheng Yin, Harbin Engineering University, China

Chapter 7
A Hyper-Heuristic Using GRASP with Path-Relinking: A Case Study of the Nurse Rostering Problem 89
He Jiang, Dalian University of Technology, China
Junying Qiu, Dalian University of Technology, China
Jifeng Xuan, Dalian University of Technology, China

Chapter 8
Pareto Artificial Life Algorithm for Multi-Objective Optimization 100
Jin-Dae Song, Hyosung Ebara Engineering Co., Korea
Bo-Suk Yang, Pukyong National University, Korea

Chapter 9
An Optimization Model for the Identification of Temperature in Intelligent Building 116
ZhenYa Zhang, Anhui University of Architecture & University of Science & Technology of China, China
HongMei Cheng, Anhui University of Architecture, China
ShuGuang Zhang, University of Science & Technology of China, China

Chapter 10
Research of Biogeography-Based Multi-Objective Evolutionary Algorithm 125
Hongwei Mo, Harbin Engineering University, China
Zhidan Xu, Harbin Engineering University, China

Chapter 11
The Effects of Investments in Information Technology on Firm Performance: An Investor Perspective 136
Jeffrey Wong, University of Nevada, Reno, USA
Kevin E. Dow, University of Alaska, Anchorage, USA

Detailed Table of Contents

CADIAG-2 is a well known rule-based medical expert system aimed at providing support in medical diagnose in the field of internal medicine. Its knowledge base consists of a large collection of IF-THEN rules that represent uncertain relationships between distinct medical entities. Given this uncertainty and the size of the system, it has been challenging to validate its consistency. Recent attempts to partially formalize CADIAG-2's knowledge base into decidable Gödel logics have shown that, on formalization, the system is inconsistent. In this paper, the authors use an alternative, more expressive formalization of CADIAG-2's knowledge base as a set of probabilistic conditional statements and apply their probabilistic logic solver (Pronto) to confirm its inconsistency and compute its conflicting sets of rules under a slightly relaxed interpretation. Once this is achieved, the authors define a measure to evaluate inconsistency and discuss suitable repair strategies for CADIAG-2 and similar systems.

In intensive care units (ICUs), clinicians must monitor patients' vital signs and make decisions regarding the drugs they administer. The patients' lives depend on the quality of these decisions but experts can make mistakes. Recent technological strategies and tools can decrease these errors. In this paper, the authors describe the development of a knowledge based system (KBS) to provide support to clinicians with respect to the drugs they administer to patients with cardiopathies in ICUs to stabilize them. To develop the system, knowledge from medical experts at the Meixoeiro Hospital in Vigo (Spain) has been extracted and formally represented as an ontology. As a result, a validated KBS has been obtained, which can be helpful to experts in ICUs and whose underlying knowledge can be easily shared and reused.

The complexity of problems has led to a shift toward the use of modular neural networks in place of traditional neural networks. The number of inputs to neural networks must be kept within manageable limits to escape from the curse of dimensionality. Attribute division is a novel concept to reduce the problem dimensionality without losing information. In this paper, the authors use Genetic Algorithms to determine the optimal distribution of the parameters to the various modules of the modular neural network. The attribute set is divided into the various modules. Each module computes the output using its own list of attributes. The individual results are then integrated by an integrator. This framework is used for the diagnosis of breast cancer. Experimental results show that optimal distribution strategy exceeds the well-known methods for the diagnosis of the disease.

Information technology and, more precisely, the internet represent challenges and opportunities for medicine. Technology-driven medicine has changed how practitioners perform their roles in and medical information systems have recently gained momentum as a proof-of-concept of the efficiency of new support-oriented technologies. Emerging applications combine sharing information with a social dimension. This paper presents DISMON (Disease Monitor), a system based on Semantic Technologies and Social Web (SW) to improve patient care for medical diagnosis in limited environments, namely, organizations. DISMON combines Web 2.0 capacities and SW to provide semantic descriptions of clinical symptoms, thereby facilitating diagnosis and helping to foresee diseases, giving useful information to the company and its employees to increase efficiency by means of the prevention of injuries and illnesses, resulting in a safety environment for workers.

In this paper, the authors propose a new approach for topological hierarchical tree clustering inspired from the self-assembly behavior of artificial ants. The method, called SoTree (Self-organizing Tree), builds, autonomously and simultaneously, a topological and hierarchical partitioning of data. Each ''cluster'' associated to one cell of a 2D grid is modeled by a tree. The artificial ants similarly build a tree where each ant represents a node/data. The benefit of this approach is the intuitive representation of hierarchical relations in the data. This is especially appealing in explorative data mining applications, allowing the inherent structure of the data to unfold in a highly intuitive fashion.

Chapter 6
Co-Evolutionary Algorithms Based on Mixed Strategy 75
Wei Hou, Harbin Engineering University & Northeast Agricultural University, China
HongBin Dong, Harbin Engineering University, China
GuiSheng Yin, Harbin Engineering University, China

Inspired by evolutionary game theory, this paper modifies previous mixed strategy framework, adding a new mutation operator and extending to crossover operation, and proposes co-evolutionary algorithms based on mixed crossover and/or mutation strategy. The mixed mutation strategy set consists of Gaussian, Cauchy, Levy, single point and differential mutation operators; the mixed crossover strategy set consists of cuboid, two-points and heuristic crossover operators. The novel algorithms automatically select crossover and/or mutation operators from a given mixed strategy set, and improve the evolutionary performance by dynamically utilizing the most effective operator at different stages of evolution. The proposed algorithms are tested on a set of 21 benchmark problems. The results show that the new mixed strategies perform equally well or better than the best of the previous evolutionary methods for all of the benchmark problems. The proposed MMCGA has shown significant superiority over others.

Chapter 7
A Hyper-Heuristic Using GRASP with Path-Relinking: A Case Study of the Nurse Rostering Problem 89
He Jiang, Dalian University of Technology, China
Junying Qiu, Dalian University of Technology, China
Jifeng Xuan, Dalian University of Technology, China

The goal of hyper-heuristics is to design and choose heuristics to solve complex problems. The primary motivation behind the hyper-heuristics is to generalize the solving ability of the heuristics. In this paper, the authors propose a Hyper-heuristic using GRASP with Path-Relinking (HyGrasPr). HyGrasPr generates heuristic sequences to produce solutions within an iterative procedure. The procedure of HyGrasPr consists of three phases, namely the construction phase, the local search phase, and the path-relinking phase. To show the performance of the HyGrasPr, the authors use the nurse rostering problem as a case study. The authors use an existing simulated annealing based hyper-heuristic as a baseline. The experimental results indicate that HyGrasPr can achieve better solutions than SAHH within the same running time and the path-relinking phase is effective for the framework of HyGrasPr.

Chapter 8
Pareto Artificial Life Algorithm for Multi-Objective Optimization 100
Jin-Dae Song, Hyosung Ebara Engineering Co., Korea
Bo-Suk Yang, Pukyong National University, Korea

Most engineering optimization uses multiple objective functions rather than single objective function. To realize an artificial life algorithm based multi-objective optimization, this paper proposes a Pareto artificial life algorithm that is capable of searching Pareto set for multi-objective function solutions. The Pareto set of optimum solutions is found by applying two objective functions for the optimum design of the defined journal bearing. By comparing with the optimum solutions of a single objective function, it is confirmed that the single function optimization result is one of the specific cases of Pareto set of optimum solutions.

Chapter 9
An Optimization Model for the Identification of Temperature in Intelligent Building 116
ZhenYa Zhang, Anhui University of Architecture & University of Science & Technology of China, China
HongMei Cheng, Anhui University of Architecture, China
ShuGuang Zhang, University of Science & Technology of China, China

Methods for the reconstruction of temperature fields in an intelligent building with temperature data of discrete observation positions is a current topic of research. To reconstruct temperature field with observation data, it is necessary to model the identification of temperature in each observation position. In this paper, models for temperature identification in an intelligent building are formalized as optimization problems based on observation temperature data sequence. To solve the optimization problem, a feed forward neural network is used to formalize the identification structure, and connection matrixes of the neural network are the identification parameters. With the object function for the given optimization problem as the fitness function, the training of the feed forward neural network is driven by a genetic algorithm. The experiment for the precision and stability of the proposed method is designed with real temperature data from an intelligent building.

Chapter 10
Research of Biogeography-Based Multi-Objective Evolutionary Algorithm 125
Hongwei Mo, Harbin Engineering University, China
Zhidan Xu, Harbin Engineering University, China

Biogeography-based optimization algorithm (BBO) is an optimization algorithm inspired by the migration of animals in nature. A new multi-objective evolutionary algorithm is proposed, which is called Biogeography-based multi-objective evolutionary algorithm (BBMOEA). The fitness assignment and the external population elitism of SPEA2 are adapted to ensure even distribution of the solution set. The population evolutionary operators of BBO are applied to the evolution of the external population to ensure the convergence of the solution set. Simulation results on benchmark test problems illustrate the effectiveness and efficiency of the proposed algorithm.

Chapter 11
The Effects of Investments in Information Technology on Firm Performance: An Investor Perspective 136
Jeffrey Wong, University of Nevada, Reno, USA
Kevin E. Dow, University of Alaska, Anchorage, USA

Analyzing the beneficial effects of investments in information technology (IT) is an area of research that interests investors and academics. A number of studies have examined whether investments in IT have a positive effect on some measure of earnings or other form of financial return. Results from these studies have been mixed. This paper extends the literature by adopting an investor's perspective on firm performance when IT investments are made, using the preservation of capital as a performance measure. The authors examine companies that made public announcements of their investments in technology to see if they were able to mitigate losses to investors by reducing their downside risk to investors. This study further discusses whether different types of IT investments have different impacts on firm risk from an investor's viewpoint. Findings suggest that IT investments impact a firm's downside risk, and the authors offer an alternative perspective on the benefits of IT investments, particularly where no positive incremental financial results are evident.

Due to the unprecedented growth of outsourcing ICT projects by the Iranian government, a critical need exists for the proper execution and monitoring of these projects. In this paper, the authors propose a web-based project management system to improve the efficiency and effectiveness of the management processes and accelerate decision making. Based on the requirements and information flow between various units involved in the complete life-cycle of ICT project management, a functional model and system architecture with various underlying structures has been designed. The functional model contains two sub-systems: process management and information service. The proposed system structure is based on a four-layer client-server computing model. As a part of a publically available ICT system, it must be secure against cybercrime activities. This system can bring efficiency in managing the projects, improve decision making, and increase the overall management process with total accounting and management transparency. The proposed system overcomes the problems associated with a central system and traditional management processes, as is currently the case in Iran.

This paper incorporates the concepts of aspects and software reuse in archetype driven architecture. The proposed work develops the software by partitioning the whole system into different independent components and aspects to facilitate component reuse. The authors illustrate the ease of modeling the components separately and emphasize concerns that the OOP paradigm has failed to address. This paper places emphasis on designing and modeling the software rather than coding. Identification of reusable components is carried out using the hybrid methodology and aspects are identified by domain experts. Along with the components, the PIM and aspects developed are stored in separate repositories to be used in development of other software of similar requirements and basic structure.

In this paper, the authors investigate the professional practices of software developers from two different cultures—Norway and India. The authors examine if systematic differences exist between Norwegian and Indian software developers in their professional practice. Using Hofstede's cultural dimensions, the authors expected to find cultural differences between the two groups of professionals. Building on a survey among software developers in the two countries, the authors have the following conclusions. Firstly, the main finding is that there are surprisingly few differences between the two groups, giving support to the view of a common professional culture. Secondly, the few differences that are observed cannot easily be explained by Hofstede's cultural dimensions.

Wireless technologies have lately been integrated in many types of environments; their development is able to provide innovative services minimizing costs and the time necessary to identify the necessary information. However medical information is very sensitive since it contains critical personal data. Security and privacy preservation are very critical parameters. Lately, innovative technologies such as software agents' technology have been utilized to support distributed environments. Presented is an architecture that allows secure medical related information management using software agents; this work expands previous research (Belsis, Skourlas, & Gritzalis, 2011). The authors present a security oriented solution and also provide experimental evidence about the capability of the platform to operate in wireless environments with large number of users.

Currently, organizations are increasingly aware of the need to protect their computer infrastructure to maintain continuity of operations. This process involves a number of different concerns including: managing natural disasters, equipment failure, and security breaches, poor data management, inadequate design, and complex/impractical design. The purpose of this article is to delineate how virtualization of hosts and cloud computing can be used to address the concerns resulting in improved computer infrastructure that can easily be restored following a natural disaster and which features fault tolerant hosts/components, isolates applications security attacks, is simpler in design, and is easier to manage. Further, because this technology has been out for a number of years and its capabilities have matured an attempt has been made to describe those capabilities as well as document successful applications.

The adoption of mobile technologies for emergency management has the capacity to save lives. In Australia in February 2009, the Victorian Bushfires claimed 173 lives, the worst peace-time disaster in the nation's history. The Australian government responded swiftly to the tragedy by going to tender for mobile applications that could be used during emergencies, such as mobile alerts and location services. These applications have the ability to deliver personalized information direct to the citizen during crises, complementing traditional broadcasting mediums like television and radio. Indeed governments have a responsibility to their citizens to safeguard them against both natural and human-made hazards and today national security has grown to encapsulate such societal and economic securitization. However, some citizens and lobby groups have emphasized that such breakthrough technologies need to be deployed with caution as they are fraught with ethical considerations, including the potential for breaches in privacy, security and trust. The other problem is that real world implementations of national emergency alerts have not always worked reliably and their value has come into question as a result. This paper provides a big picture view of the value of government-mandated location-based services during emergencies, and the challenges ensuing from their use.

Preface

The chapters in this book provide insight into the latest research and advances in information science (IS) and technology (IT). IS and IT have applications in nearly every field and profession, necessitating a comprehensive understanding of knowledge management tools in order to successfully navigate uncertainty in disciplines ranging from the physical sciences to entrepreneurship, education, and medicine. Serving as a scholarly compendium of emerging breakthroughs in information science research, this book will provide researchers, academics, students, and practitioners with a fresh perspective into methodologies best suited to meet their various personal and organizational goals.

Chapter 1, "The Consistency of the Medical Expert System CADIAG-2: A Probabilistic Approach" by Pavel Klinov *et al.* defines CADIAG-2 as a well known rule-based medical expert system aimed at providing support in medical diagnosis in the field of internal medicine. Its knowledge base consists of a large collection of IF-THEN rules that represent uncertain relationships between distinct medical entities. Given this uncertainty and the size of the system, it has been challenging to validate its consistency. Recent attempts to partially formalize CADIAG-2's knowledge base into decidable Gödel logics have shown that, on formalization, the system is inconsistent. In this chapter, the authors use an alternative, more expressive formalization of CADIAG-2's knowledge base as a set of probabilistic conditional statements and apply their probabilistic logic solver (Pronto) to confirm its inconsistency and compute its conflicting sets of rules under a slightly relaxed interpretation. Once this is achieved, the authors define a measure to evaluate inconsistency and discuss suitable repair strategies for CADIAG-2 and similar systems.

Next, Ana Torres Morgade *et al.*, in "Development of a Knowledge Based System for an Intensive Care Environment Using Ontologies," explain how clinicians in intensive care units (ICUs) must monitor patients' vital signs and make decisions regarding the drugs they administer. The patients' lives depend on the quality of these decisions but experts can make mistakes. Recent technological strategies and tools can decrease these errors. In this chapter, the authors describe the development of a knowledge based system (KBS) to provide support to clinicians with respect to the drugs they administer to patients with cardiopathies in ICUs to stabilize them. To develop the system, knowledge from medical experts at the Meixoeiro Hospital in Vigo (Spain) has been extracted and formally represented as an ontology. As a result, a validated KBS has been obtained, which can be helpful to experts in ICUs and whose underlying knowledge can be easily shared and reused.

The complexity of problems has led to a shift toward the use of modular neural networks in place of traditional neural networks. The number of inputs to neural networks must be kept within manageable limits to escape from the curse of dimensionality. Attribute division is a novel concept to reduce the problem dimensionality without losing information. In "Breast Cancer Diagnosis Using Optimized Attribute Division in Modular Neural Networks," Rahul Kala *et al.* use Genetic Algorithms to determine the optimal distribution of the parameters to the various modules of the modular neural network. The attribute set is divided into the various modules. Each module computes the output using its own list of attributes. The individual results are then integrated by an integrator. This framework is used for the diagnosis of breast cancer. Experimental results show that optimal distribution strategy exceeds the well-known methods for the diagnosis of the disease.

"DISMON: Using Social Web and Semantic Technologies to Monitor Diseases in Limited Environments," by Ángel Lagares-Lemos *et al.*, presents DISMON (Disease Monitor), a system based on Semantic Technologies and Social Web (SW) to improve patient care for medical diagnosis in limited environments, namely, organizations. Information technology and, more precisely the internet, represent challenges and opportunities for medicine. Technology-driven medicine has changed how practitioners perform their roles, and medical information systems have recently gained momentum as a proof-of-concept of the efficiency of new support-oriented technologies. Emerging applications combine sharing information with a social dimension. DISMON combines Web 2.0 capacities and SW to provide semantic descriptions of clinical symptoms, thereby facilitating diagnosis and helping to foresee diseases, giving useful information to the company and its employees to increase efficiency by means of the prevention of injuries and illnesses, resulting in a safety environment for workers.

In "Self-Organizing Tree Using Artificial Ants," Hanene Azzag and Mustapha Lebbah propose a new approach for topological hierarchical tree clustering inspired from the self-assembly behavior of artificial ants. The method, called SoTree (Self-organizing Tree), builds, autonomously and simultaneously, a topological and hierarchical partitioning of data. Each cluster associated to one cell of a 2D grid is modeled by a tree. The artificial ants similarly build a tree where each ant represents a node/data. The benefit of this approach is the intuitive representation of hierarchical relations in the data. This is especially appealing in explorative data mining applications, allowing the inherent structure of the data to unfold in a highly intuitive fashion.

Inspired by evolutionary game theory, "Co-Evolutionary Algorithms Based on Mixed Strategy" by Wei Hou *et al.* modifies previous mixed strategy framework, adding a new mutation operator and extending to crossover operation, and proposes co-evolutionary algorithms based on mixed crossover and/or mutation strategy. The mixed mutation strategy set consists of Gaussian, Cauchy, Levy, single point, and differential mutation operators; the mixed crossover strategy set consists of cuboid, two-points, and heuristic crossover operators. The novel algorithms automatically select crossover and/or mutation operators from a given mixed strategy set, and improve the evolutionary performance by dynamically utilizing the most effective operator at different stages of evolution. The proposed algorithms are tested on a set of 21 benchmark problems. The results show that the new mixed strategies perform equally well or better than the best of the previous evolutionary methods for all of the benchmark problems. The proposed MMCGA has shown significant superiority over others.

He Jiang *et al.* then describe "A Hyper-Heuristic Using GRASP with Path-Relinking: A Case Study of the Nurse Rostering Problem." The goal of hyper-heuristics is to design and choose heuristics to solve complex problems. The primary motivation behind the hyper-heuristics is to generalize the solving ability of the heuristics. In this chapter, the authors propose a Hyper-heuristic using GRASP with Path-Relinking (HyGrasPr). HyGrasPr generates heuristic sequences to produce solutions within an iterative procedure. The procedure of HyGrasPr consists of three phases, namely the construction phase, the local search phase, and the path-relinking phase. To show the performance of the HyGrasPr, the authors use the nurse rostering problem as a case study. The authors use an existing simulated annealing based hyper-heuristic as a baseline. The experimental results indicate that HyGrasPr can achieve better solutions than SAHH within the same running time and the path-relinking phase is effective for the framework of HyGrasPr.

Most engineering optimization uses multiple objective functions rather than a single objective function. To realize an artificial life algorithm based multi-objective optimization, "Pareto Artificial Life Algorithm for Multi-Objective Optimization" by Jin-Dae Song and Bo-Suk Yang proposes a Pareto artificial life algorithm that is capable of searching Pareto set for multi-objective function solutions. The Pareto set of optimum solutions is found by applying two objective functions for the optimum design of the defined journal bearing. By comparing with the optimum solutions of a single objective function, it is confirmed that the single function optimization result is one of the specific cases of Pareto set of optimum solutions.

"An Optimization Model for the Identification of Temperature in Intelligent Building" by Zhen-Ya Zhang *et al.* investigates methods for the reconstruction of temperature fields in an intelligent building with temperature data of discrete observation positions. To reconstruct temperature field with observation data, it is necessary to model the identification of temperature in each observation position. In this chapter, models for temperature identification in an intelligent building are formalized as optimization problems based on observation temperature data sequence. To solve the optimization problem, a feed forward neural network is used to formalize the identification structure, and connection matrixes of the neural network are the identification parameters. With the object function for the given optimization problem as the fitness function, the training of the feed forward neural network is driven by a genetic algorithm. The experiment for the precision and stability of the proposed method is designed with real temperature data from an intelligent building.

Next, Hongwei Mo and Zhidan Xu describe their "Research of Biogeography-Based Multi-Objective Evolutionary Algorithm." Biogeography-based optimization algorithm (BBO) is an optimization algorithm inspired by the migration of animals in nature. A new multi-objective evolutionary algorithm is proposed, which is called Biogeography-based multi-objective evolutionary algorithm (BBMOEA). The fitness assignment and the external population elitism of SPEA2 are adapted to ensure even distribution of the solution set. The population evolutionary operators of BBO are applied to the evolution of the external population to ensure the convergence of the solution set. Simulation results on benchmark test problems illustrate the effectiveness and efficiency of the proposed algorithm.

Analyzing the beneficial effects of investments in information technology (IT) is an area of research that interests investors and academics. A number of studies have examined whether investments in IT have a positive effect on some measure of earnings or other forms of financial return. Results from these studies have been mixed. "The Effects of Investments in Information Technology on Firm Performance: An Investor Perspective" by Jeffrey Wong and Kevin E. Dow extends the literature by adopting an investor's perspective on firm performance when IT investments are made, using the preservation of capital as a performance measure. The authors examine companies that made public announcements of their investments in technology to see if they were able to mitigate losses to investors by reducing their downside risk to investors. This chapter further discusses whether different types of IT investments have different impacts on firm risk from an investor's viewpoint. Findings suggest that IT investments impact a firm's downside risk, and the authors offer an alternative perspective on the benefits of IT investments, particularly where no positive incremental financial results are evident.

Due to the unprecedented growth of outsourcing ICT projects by the Iranian government, a critical need exists for the proper execution and monitoring of these projects. In "Design of an Integrated Project Management Information System for Large Scale Public Projects: Iranian Case Study," Mona Taghavi *et al.* propose a Web-based project management system to improve the efficiency and effectiveness of the management processes and accelerate decision making. Based on the requirements and information flow between various units involved in the complete life-cycle of ICT project management, a functional model and system architecture with various underlying structures has been designed. The functional model contains two sub-systems: process management and information service. The proposed system structure is based on a four-layer client-server computing model. As a part of a publically available ICT system, it must be secure against cybercrime activities. This system can bring efficiency in managing the projects, improve decision making, and increase the overall management process with total accounting and management transparency. The proposed system overcomes the problems associated with a central system and traditional management processes, as is currently the case in Iran.

The next chapter, "An Aspect Oriented Component Based Archetype Driven Development," by Rachit Mohan Garg and Deepak Dahiya, incorporates the concepts of aspects and software reuse in archetype driven architecture. The proposed work develops the software by partitioning the whole system into different independent components and aspects to facilitate component reuse. The authors illustrate the ease of modeling the components separately and emphasize concerns that the OOP paradigm has failed to address. This chapter places emphasis on designing and modeling the software rather than coding. Identification of reusable components is carried out using the hybrid methodology and aspects are identified by domain experts. Along with the components, the PIM and aspects developed are stored in separate repositories to be used in development of other software of similar requirements and basic structure.

In Chapter 14, "Software Developers in India and Norway: Professional or National Cultures?" Gheorghita Ghinea *et al.* investigate the professional practices of software developers from two different cultures—Norway and India. The authors examine if systematic differences exist between Norwegian and Indian software developers in their professional practice. Using Hofstede's cultural dimensions, the authors expected to find cultural differences between the two groups of professionals. Building on a survey among software developers in the two countries, the authors have the following conclusions. Firstly, the main finding is that there are surprisingly few differences between the two groups, giving support to the view of a common professional culture. Secondly, the few differences that are observed cannot easily be explained by Hofstede's cultural dimensions.

Next, Petros Belsis explores "Secure Electronic Healthcare Records Management in Wireless Environments." Wireless technologies have lately been integrated in many types of environments; their development is able to provide innovative services minimizing costs and the time necessary to identify the necessary information. However medical information is very sensitive since it contains critical personal data. Security and privacy preservation are very critical parameters. Lately, innovative technologies such as software agents' technology have been utilized to support distributed environments. Presented is an architecture that allows secure medical related information management using software agents; this work expands previous research (Belsis, Skourlas, & Gritzalis, 2011). The authors present a security oriented solution and also provide experimental evidence about the capability of the platform to operate in wireless environments with large number of users.

Currently, organizations are increasingly aware of the need to protect their computer infrastructure to maintain continuity of operations. This process involves a number of different concerns including: managing natural disasters, equipment failure, and security breaches, poor data management, inadequate design, and complex/ impractical design. The purpose of the next chapter, "Enhancing the Disaster Recovery Plan through Virtualization" by Dennis C. Guster and Olivia F. Lee, is to delineate how virtualization of hosts and cloud computing can be used to address the concerns, resulting in improved computer infrastructure that can easily be restored following a natural disaster and which features fault tolerant hosts/components, isolates applications security attacks, is simpler in design, and is easier to manage. Further, because this technology has been out for a number of years and its capabilities have matured, an attempt has been made to describe those capabilities as well as document successful applications.

The final chapter is "The Value of Government Mandated Location-Based Services in Emergencies in Australia" by Anas Aloudat *et al.* The adoption of mobile technologies for emergency management has the capacity to save lives. In Australia in February 2009, the Victorian Bushfires claimed 173 lives, the worst peace-time disaster in the nation's history. The Australian government responded swiftly to the tragedy by going to tender for mobile applications that could be used during emergencies, such as mobile alerts and location services. These applications have the ability to deliver personalized information direct to the citizen during crises, complementing traditional broadcasting mediums like television and radio. Indeed governments have a responsibility to their citizens to safeguard them against both natural and human-made hazards and today national security has grown to encapsulate such societal and economic securitization. However, some citizens and lobby groups have emphasized that such breakthrough technologies need to be deployed with caution as they are fraught with ethical considerations, including the potential for breaches in privacy, security, and trust. The other problem is that real world implementations of national emergency alerts have not always worked reliably, and their value has come into question as a result. This chapter provides a big picture view of the value of government-mandated location-based services during emergencies, and the challenges ensuing from their use.

Chapter 1
The Consistency of the Medical Expert System CADIAG-2:
A Probabilistic Approach

Pavel Klinov
The University of Manchester, UK

Bijan Parsia
The University of Manchester, UK

David Picado Muiño
Institut für Diskrete Mathematik und Geometrie, Austria

ABSTRACT

CADIAG-2 is a well known rule-based medical expert system aimed at providing support in medical diagnose in the field of internal medicine. Its knowledge base consists of a large collection of IF-THEN rules that represent uncertain relationships between distinct medical entities. Given this uncertainty and the size of the system, it has been challenging to validate its consistency. Recent attempts to partially formalize CADIAG-2's knowledge base into decidable Gödel logics have shown that, on formalization, the system is inconsistent. In this paper, the authors use an alternative, more expressive formalization of CADIAG-2's knowledge base as a set of probabilistic conditional statements and apply their probabilistic logic solver (Pronto) to confirm its inconsistency and compute its conflicting sets of rules under a slightly relaxed interpretation. Once this is achieved, the authors define a measure to evaluate inconsistency and discuss suitable repair strategies for CADIAG-2 and similar systems.

INTRODUCTION

CADIAG-2 (Computer Assisted DIAGnosis) is a well known rule-based expert system aimed at providing support in diagnostic decision making in the field of internal medicine. Its design and construction was initiated in the early 80's at the Medical University of Vienna by K.P. Adlassnig (Adlassnig et al., 1985, 1986; Adlassnig, 1986; Leitich et al., 2002) for more on the origins and design of CADIAG-2.

DOI: 10.4018/978-1-4666-3625-5.ch001

CADIAG-2 consists of two fundamental pieces: the inference engine and the knowledge base. The inference engine (for alternative formalizations and analyses of CADIAG-2's inference see Ciabattoni et al., 2010; Picado Muiño, 2010) is based on methods of approximate reasoning in fuzzy set theory, in the sense of (Zadeh, 1965, 1975). In fact CADIAG-2 is presented in some monographs as an example of a fuzzy expert system (see for example Klir et al., 1988; Zimmermann, 1991).

The knowledge base consists of a set of *IF-THEN* rules –also known in the literature as *production* rules– intended to represent relationships between distinct medical entities: symptoms, findings, signs and test results (*S*) on the one hand and diseases and therapies (*D*) on the other. The vast majority of them are binary (i.e., they relate single medical entities) and only such rules are considered in this paper. The one that follows is an example of a binary rule of CADIAG-2 (Adlassnig et al., 1986):

```
IF suspicion of liver metastases by
liver palpation
THEN pancreatic cancer
with degree of confirmation 0.3
```

The *degree of confirmation* refers, intuitively, to the degree to which the conditioning event (i.e., '*suspicion of liver metastases by liver palpation*' in the example above) confirms the uncertain event (i.e., '*pancreatic cancer*' above). How these degrees of confirmation are to be *formally* interpreted will be discussed later.

In this paper we present a formalization of a coded version of the binary fragment of CADIAG-2's knowledge base (i.e., that contains only codes for the identification of the distinct medical entities) as a probabilistic logic theory. We then check the satisfiability of that formalization with *Pronto*, our probabilistic description logic solver, which we briefly introduce. We find that CADIAG-2 is *highly* unsatisfiable (confirming the results of an alternative, weaker formalization, Ciabattoni et al., 2010) and analyze the sources of unsatisfiability.

To our knowledge, the probabilistic version of CADIAG-2 is the largest PSAT (Probabilistic SATisfiability) problem to be solved by an automated reasoner and is certainly the largest non-artificial one. This is, perhaps, a bit misleading as it is comparatively easy to detect unsatisfiability by first heuristically detecting small but likely unsatisfiable fragments and then performing a satisfiability check on each fragment. While this might suffice to validate that CADIAG-2 is unsatisfiable it is not sufficient, without further qualification, to detect all conflicting sets of rules, nor can it ensure that a satisfiable fragment is so in the context of the entire knowledge base.

As CADIAG-2 is too large (the number of rules in the binary fragment we are concerned with is over 18000) we describe an approach to split the knowledge base into comparatively large fragments that can be tested independently and prove that such methodology is complete, i.e., is guaranteed to find all conflict sets. With this methodology we are able to determine that CADIAG-2 contains numerous sets of conflicting rules and compute all of them for a slightly relaxed interpretation of the knowledge base.

We complete the paper with the introduction of an inconsistency measure aimed at evaluating CADIAG-2-like databases and a brief account of suitable repair strategies for CADIAG-2 and similar systems. The measure presented attempts to quantify *how far* the knowledge base is from consistency and its computation, in as much as it yields an adjustment in the degree of confirmation or uncertainty of each conditional statement, provides the modeler with a possible repair of the database.

NOTATION AND PRELIMINARY DEFINITIONS

Throughout we will be working with a finite propositional language $L = \{p_1, ..., p_l\}$, for some $l \in \mathbb{N}$. We will denote by *SL* its closure under Boolean connectives. Within the context of CADIAG-2 the language *L* will represent the set of medical entities $S \cup D$ in the system.

We will use the abbreviations $\bot$ and $\top$ for classical *contradiction* and classical *tautology* respectively. For $\Gamma \subset SL$ finite, we will use the abbreviations $\wedge\Gamma$ and $\vee\Gamma$ to refer to the conjunction and disjunction of all the sentences in Γ respectively. For the next definition and throughout $\models$ will be classical entailment.

Definition 1: Let $\omega : SL \to [0,1]$. We say that ω is a probability function on *L* if the following two conditions hold, for all $\theta, \phi \in SL$:

- If $\models \theta$ then $\omega(\theta) = 1$.
- If $\models \neg(\theta \wedge \phi)$ then $\omega(\theta \vee \phi) = \omega(\theta) + \omega(\phi)$.

We can restrict probability functions to the set $[0,1] \cap \mathbb{Q}$. Such probability functions will be called *rational*.

A probability distribution ω on *L* can be characterized by the values it assigns to the expressions of the form $\pm p_1 \wedge ... \wedge \pm p_l$, which we call *states* or *worlds*, where $+p$ and $-p$ stand for *p* and $\neg p$ respectively. We denote the set of states in *L* by *W* and define, for $\phi \in SL$, W_ϕ as follows: $W_\phi = \{\alpha \in W \mid \alpha \models \phi\}$.

We will be assuming that *W* is an ordered set.

We can characterize ω by 2^l-coordinate vectors in $\mathbb{D}_{2^l}$, where

$$\mathbb{D}_{2^l} = \{(x_1, ..., x_{2^l}) | x_i \geq 0, \sum_i x_i = 1\}.$$

Sentences in *SL* can also be identified with 2^l-coordinate vectors. Let $\phi \in SL$ and define the 2^l-coordinate vector $\vec{r}_\phi$ as follows: for each $i \in \{1, ..., 2^l\}$ and $\alpha_i \in W$, $r_\phi^i = 1$ if $\alpha_i \models \phi$ and $r_\phi^i = 0$ otherwise.

We define probability on conditional statements in *SL* from the notion of unconditional probability in the conventional way.

We will be dealing with conditional probabilistic statements of the form '*the probability of* ϕ given θ is equal to η', for $\phi, \theta \in SL$ and $\eta \in [0,1]$. Notice that statements of the form '*the probability of* ϕ is equal to η' correspond to the case when $\theta \equiv \top$.

Let us set $\mathcal{K} = \{\phi \mid \theta \mid \phi, \theta \in SL\}$, the set of conditional statements in *SL*. Notice that $\mathcal{K}$ is, up to classical equivalence, a finite set. For most of this paper we will be interested in the subset $\mathcal{K}_L = \{q \mid p \mid p, q \in L\} \subset \mathcal{K}$.

We will denote the collection of intervals in [0,1] by $\Im$.

Let us consider $\Delta \subseteq \mathcal{K}$ and *v* a map from Δ to $\Im$. We call *v* an *assignment* on Δ and denote the set of such maps by V_Δ.

We set $\mathcal{PK} = \{(\Delta, v) \mid \Delta \subseteq \mathcal{K}, \Delta \neq \varnothing, v \in V_\Delta\}$. For the set of conditionals $\mathcal{K}_L$ we will have $\mathcal{PK}_L = \{(\Delta, v) \in \mathcal{PK} \mid \Delta \subseteq \mathcal{K}_L\}$.

We will sometimes write $(\Delta, v) \in \mathcal{PK}$ in compact form; i.e., as $\{v(\phi \mid \theta) = \Omega \mid (\phi \mid \theta) \in \Delta\}$, with $\Omega \in \Im$ or, for CADIAG-2 settings, as $\{\langle \phi \mid \theta, \Omega \rangle \mid (\phi \mid \theta) \in \Delta,\ v(\phi \mid \theta) = \Omega\}$.

Intervals of the form $[\eta, \eta] \in \Im$ (i.e., point values) will normally be denoted by η itself (so, for example, instead of writing $v(\phi \mid \theta) = [\eta, \eta]$ we will write $v(\phi \mid \theta) = \eta$).

Let $\Delta = \Delta_1 \cup \Delta_2 \subseteq \mathcal{K}$ and $(\Delta, v) \in \mathcal{PK}$. We denote by $v_{|\Delta_1}$ and $v_{|\Delta_2}$ the restriction of *v* on Δ_1 and Δ_2 respectively.

Definition 2: We say that the probability function ω on L *satisfies* $(\Delta, v) \in \mathcal{PK}$ if, for all $\phi \mid \theta \in \Delta$, we have that $\omega(\theta) > 0$ and $\omega(\phi \mid \theta) \in v(\phi \mid \theta)$.

In that sense, we say that (Δ, v) is *satisfiable* or *consistent* (we use both words interchangeably) if there exists a probability function ω on L that satisfies (Δ, v).

Definition 3: We say that (Δ, v) is a *minimal unsatisfiable set* (or minimal inconsistent set) if (Δ, v) is not satisfiable and, for all $\Delta' \subset \Delta$, $(\Delta', v_{|\Delta'})$ is satisfiable.

The words '*satisfiable*' and '*consistent*' will be used interchangeably throughout this paper.

In order to prove some results and characterize the meaning of *degree of consistency* in CADIAG-2 we will regard *L* as a collection of unary predicates or sets in a first-order language and *SL* the closure of predicates in *L* under boolean combinations.

Definition 4: An interpretation $\mathcal{I}$ of *L* is a pair $(D^{\mathcal{I}}, \nu^{\mathcal{I}})$ where $D^{\mathcal{I}}$ is a finite non-empty domain and $\nu^{\mathcal{I}}$ is a map from $L \times D^{\mathcal{I}}$ to [0, 1].

An interpretation $\mathcal{I}$ is said to be *classical* if $\nu^{\mathcal{I}}(p,a) \in \{0,1\}$ for all $(p,a) \in L \times D^{\mathcal{I}}$. It is said to be *rational* if $\nu^{\mathcal{I}}(p,a) \in [0,1] \cap \mathbb{Q}$ for all $(p,a) \in L \times D^{\mathcal{I}}$.

Given an interpretation $\mathcal{I}$ of *L*, we will refer to the elements in $D^{\mathcal{I}}$ by Latin characters a, b, c…

THE KNOWLEDGE BASE OF CADIAG-2

We can classify CADIAG-2's binary rules (Φ_{CB}) into three different types: rules in which both conditioning and uncertain event are medical entities in S (*symptom-symptom*, $\Phi_{S|S}$), rules in which both conditioning and uncertain event are medical entities in D (*disease-disease*, $\Phi_{D|D}$) and those in which the conditioning event is a medical entity in S and the uncertain event an entity in D (*symptom-disease*, $\Phi_{D|S}$). The degree of confirmation in a rule of the first two types is a value in the set $\{0,1\}$ and it is in this sense that we say that rules of these types are *classical*.

The knowledge base of CADIAG-2 formally contains relationships where the conditioning event is a medical entity in D and the uncertain event an entity in S. However, such rules are never used by CADIAG-2's inference mechanism and are not taken into account in this paper.

Let $\langle q \mid p, \eta \rangle \in \Phi_{CB}$ be a rule in CADIAG-2's binary knowledge base, with $p, q \in L$ and $\eta \in [0,1] \cap \mathbb{Q}$. The value η is intended to quantify the *degree* to which p (the conditioning event) *confirms* q (the uncertain event), claimed in most of the literature on CADIAG-2 (see Adlassnig et al., 1985, 1986) to have been calculated from a certain database or interpretation $\mathcal{I}$ as follows:

$$\frac{\sum_{a \in D^{\mathcal{I}}} min\{\nu^{\mathcal{I}}(p,a), \nu^{\mathcal{I}}(q,a)\}}{\sum_{a \in D^{\mathcal{I}}} \nu^{\mathcal{I}}(p,a)} = \eta. \qquad (1)$$

We say in *most* of the literature. There are some references in which the interpretation suggested for η in $\langle q \mid p, \eta \rangle$ is different. For example in Adlassnig, (1986) it is claimed that η can be interpreted as a frequency and thus $\langle q \mid p, \eta \rangle$ as a probabilistic conditional statement.

Throughout we will use the expression $(q \mid p)_{\mathcal{I}} = \eta$ to abbreviate (1). Sometimes, in order to generalize results, we will be considering an interval, say $\Omega \subseteq [0,1]$, instead of a single value (i.e., η in (1)) and we will be using the expression $(q \mid p)_{\mathcal{I}} \in \Omega$ to abbreviate the corresponding modification of (1). Such modification is motivated by the possibility of alternative, suitable interpretations of the rules in Φ_{CB} that one could consider interesting in the view of some theoretical or practical aspects. Among these alternative interpretations we consider replacing η in Equation (1) by the interval $[\eta, 1]$ (i.e., consider η a lower bound for the degrees of confirmation instead of a precise one) or replacing η whenever $\eta \in (0,1)$ by an interval of the form $[\eta-\delta, \eta+\delta]$, for δ small (i.e., a slightly relaxed interpretation of Φ_{CB}).

For the next definition let $\mathcal{I}$ be an interpretation of L and $\Phi \in \mathcal{PK}_L$.

Definition 5: We say that $\mathcal{I}$ is a model of Φ (denoted $\models_{\mathcal{I}} \Phi$) if $(q \mid p)_{\mathcal{I}} \in \Omega$ for all $\langle q \mid p, \Omega \rangle \in \Phi$.

Proposition 1: $\Phi \in \mathcal{PK}_L$ has a classical model if and only if it has a rational model.

Proof: The right implication follows trivially from the fact that every classical interpretation is also rational. In order to prove the left implication let us assume that $\mathcal{I} = (D^{\mathcal{I}}, \nu^{\mathcal{I}})$ is a rational interpretation such that $\models_{\mathcal{I}} \Phi$.

Let C be the set given by the values $\nu^{\mathcal{I}}(p,a)$, for $(p,a) \in L \times D^{\mathcal{I}}$. It is assumed that all the values in C are rational. Let us consider the minimum common multiple of the denominators of all the elements of C, say $Q \in \mathbb{N}$. We next construct a new interpretation $\mathcal{J}$ from $\mathcal{I}$ such that $\models_{\mathcal{J}} \Phi$.

We first define $D^{\mathcal{J}}$ from $D^{\mathcal{I}}$. For each element $a \in D^{\mathcal{I}}$ we set Q elements in the domain $D^{\mathcal{J}}$, labeled as follows: $\{a_1, \ldots, a_Q\}$. Let us consider now $p \in L$ and $a \in D^{\mathcal{I}}$ and assume that $\nu^{\mathcal{I}}(p,a) = P / Q$. We define $V^{\mathcal{J}}$ on $L \times D^{\mathcal{J}}$ from $\nu^{\mathcal{I}}$ as follows, for $i \in \{1, \ldots, Q\}$:

$$V^{\mathcal{J}}(p, a_i) = \begin{cases} 1 & i \leq P \\ 0 & otherwise \end{cases}$$

It is easy to see that $\mathcal{J}$ thus defined is such that $\models_{\mathcal{J}} \Phi$.

For what follows we will be considering the collection of intervals $\Im^*$ in the set [0, 1]. $\Im^*$ differs from $\Im$ in that an interval $\Omega \in \Im^*$ needs to have its maximum and/or minimum in $\mathbb{Q}$, provided it has a maximum and/or a minimum.

We define the set

$$\mathcal{PK}_L^* = \{(\Delta, v) \in \mathcal{PK}_L \mid v(q \mid p) \in \Im^* \text{ for all } q \mid p \in \Delta\}$$

and consider $\Phi \in \mathcal{PK}_L^*$ for the next proposition.

Proposition 2: If Φ has a model then it has also a rational model.

Proof: Let $\mathcal{I}$ be an interpretation such that $\models_{\mathcal{I}} \Phi$. We then have that, for all $\langle q \mid p, \Omega \rangle \in \Phi$, $(q \mid p)_{\mathcal{I}} \in \Omega$.

For each $(q \mid p)_{\mathcal{I}} \in \Omega$ we consider the inequalities

$$\sum_{a \in D^{\mathcal{I}}} \eta_1 \nu^{\mathcal{I}}(p,a) < \sum_{a \in D^{\mathcal{I}}} min\{\nu^{\mathcal{I}}(p,a), \nu^{\mathcal{I}}(q,a)\} < \sum_{a \in D^{\mathcal{I}}} \eta_2 \nu^{\mathcal{I}}(p,a),$$

where Ω is assumed to be of the form $(\eta_1, \eta_2) \in \Im^*$ (for $\Omega \in \Im^*$ of any other form we replace '<' in the inequalities above by '$\leq$' as required) and with $min\{\nu^{\mathcal{I}}(p,a), \nu^{\mathcal{I}}(q,a)\}$ replaced by $\nu^{\mathcal{I}}(p,a)$ or $\nu^{\mathcal{I}}(q,a)$ accordingly.

Let us also consider, for each $(q \mid p)_{\mathcal{I}} \in \Omega$, the inequalities

$$0 \leq \nu^{\mathcal{I}}(p,a), \nu^{\mathcal{I}}(q,a) \leq 1,$$

$$\sum_{a \in D^{\mathcal{I}}} \nu^{\mathcal{I}}(p,a) > 0$$

and, for $\nu^{\mathcal{I}}(p,a)$ greater than $\nu^{\mathcal{I}}(q,a)$, the inequality $\nu^{\mathcal{I}}(q,a) \leq \nu^{\mathcal{I}}(p,a)$ (the inequality $\nu^{\mathcal{I}}(q,a) \geq \nu^{\mathcal{I}}(p,a)$ otherwise).

The solution set of the linear system above with unknown values $\nu^{\mathcal{I}}(p,a)$, $\nu^{\mathcal{I}}(q,a)$ is not empty, since $\mathcal{I}$ is assumed to be a solution, and needs to contain rational solutions due to the form of the intervals in $\Im^*$. Therefore, there has to exist a rational interpretation of L that satisfies Φ.

Corollary 1: Φ has a model if and only if it has a classical model.

By Corollary 1 we have that Φ_{CB} has a model if and only if it has a classical model.

For the next proposition let $\Phi = (\Delta, v) \in \mathcal{PK}_L^*$.

Proposition 3: Φ is satisfiable if and only if it has a classical model.

Proof: That Φ is satisfiable if and only if it has a rational model is clear. We need to prove that if a probability function satisfies Φ then there exists a rational probability function that satisfies Φ.

Let us consider the linear system with variables the 2^l-coordinates of the vector $\vec{x}$ given by the inequalities

$$\eta_1 \vec{r}_\theta \cdot \vec{x} < \vec{r}_{\phi\wedge\theta} \cdot \vec{x} < \eta_2 \vec{r}_\theta \cdot \vec{x},$$

for all $\phi \mid \theta \in \Delta$, with $v(\phi \mid \theta)$ assumed to be of the form $(\eta_1, \eta_2) \in \Im^*$ (for $v(\phi \mid \theta)$ of any other form we replace '$<$' in the inequalities above by '$\leq$' as required).

Along with these inequalities we also consider the constraints $\vec{x} \in \mathbb{D}_{2^l}$ and $\vec{r}_\theta \cdot \vec{x} > 0$ for each $\phi \mid \theta \in \Delta$.

We assume that this linear system has a solution (i.e., that there exists a probability function that satisfies Φ). By an argument similar to that in the proof of Proposition 2 we can conclude that if a probability function satisfies Φ then there has to exist a rational probability function that satisfies Φ.

Proposition 3 implies that Φ_{CB} can be regarded, for consistency-checking purposes, as a knowledge base formalized in propositional probabilistic logic (or PPL).

CHECKING SATISFIABILITY OF CADIAG-2

One of our main goals is to determine satisfiability or unsatisfiability of Φ_{CB} and, therefore, solve the PSAT problem (Probabilistic SATisfiability) for Φ_{CB}. Provided that Φ_{CB} is unsatisfiable (which turns out to be the case) we also want to compute all its minimal unsatisfiable subsets. Despite the fact that Φ_{CB} is formalized as a propositional knowledge base and the existence of propositional PSAT algorithms we use *Pronto*, our PSAT solver designed for our purposes (for more expressive probabilistic description logics see Klinov et al., 2010; Lukasiewicz, 2008). We do so for several reasons.

- First, unlike propositional solvers, it treats classical (i.e., certain) and probabilistic knowledge separately and scales well with respect to the amount of the former. Φ_{CB} contains many classical rules (for example, the number of rules in $\Phi_{D|D}$ is over 200) and so, given the scalability limits of PPL solvers (about 1000 statements), they are likely to be unable to handle a sufficient number of uncertain *symptom-disease* rules in addition to $\Phi_{D|D}$ and (a fragment of) $\Phi_{S|S}$.
- Second, *Pronto* has *pinpointing* capabilities for finding all minimal unsatisfiable subsets in an unsatisfiable knowledge base. This feature is critical in the context of this work given the size of Φ_{CB} and, as we will see shortly, the number of potentially overlapping inconsistencies. It must be noted

that finding *all* minimal unsatisfiable subsets is by no means a trivial extension of the PSAT algorithm (for example, its naïve implementation using a PSAT solver as a black-box reasoner is not practical due to the hardness of PSAT). Even with our implementation, the number of unsatisfiable subsets in a range of fragments of Φ_{CB} presents a significant challenge to the reasoner.

- Last but not least, we are interested in evaluating our algorithms (see the next subsection) on such a large and naturally occurring knowledge base as Φ_{CB}.

ALGORITHMS

In this subsection we briefly sketch the PSAT and conflict-finding algorithms implemented in *Pronto* within the frame of classical propositional logic (since for Φ_{CB} a formalization in terms of the probabilistic description logic language is not necessary).

Probabilistic Satisfiability Algorithm

For the sake of clarity and brevity we will consider the case of PSAT for sets of probabilistic statements of the form $\langle \phi \,|\top, \eta \rangle$ on L (a finite propositional language), with $\phi \in SL$ and where η represents the probability assigned to it (i.e., all probabilistic statements considered are unconditional and assigned point-valued probabilities. It is straightforward, but technically awkward and space consuming, to generalize the procedure to handle conditional interval statements (see Klinov et al., 2010 for a more detailed account).

We say that a collection of probabilistic conditional statements of such form, say Φ, is satisfiable if and only if the objective value of the following linear program is equal to 1:

Maximize $\sum_{\alpha \in W} x_\alpha$ given the following constraints: (2)

- $\sum_{\alpha \in W_\phi} x_\alpha = \eta \times \sum_{\alpha \in W} x_\alpha$, for each $\langle \phi \,|\top, \eta \rangle \in \Phi$,
- $\sum_{\alpha \in W} x_\alpha \leq 1$ and all $x_\alpha \geq 0$,

where x_α is the assignment to the possible world $\alpha \in W$.

Let A denote the matrix of linear coefficients in (2). At every step of the simplex algorithm, A is represented as a combination (B, N) where B and N are the submatrices of the *basic* and *non-basic* variables, respectively. Values of non-basic variables are fixed to zero and the solver proceeds by replacing one basic variable (i.e., column in A) by a non-basic one until the optimal solution is found. As the size of A is exponential in the size of our language L, one should determine the entering column without representing A explicitly. This is done using the column generation technique in which entering columns are computed by optimizing a subproblem, sometimes referred to as the *pricing-out problem* (or POP). Observe that the above system of linear inequalities always admits a solution (e.g. $x_\alpha = 0$ for all $\alpha \in W$), even if Φ is unsatisfiable, which facilitates the column generation process. Note, however, that the actual linear programs solved in *Pronto* are considerably more involved (in particular, they include slack and stabilization variables to improve convergence).

The critical step is to formulate linear constraints for the pricing-out problem such that every solution (a column) corresponds to a possible world in W. In the propositional case this can be done by employing a well known formulation of SAT as a mixed-integer linear program (Hooker, 1988). In the case of expressive languages, such as those in description logics, there appears to be no easy way of determining a set of constraints H for the pricing-out problem such that its set of solutions is in one-to-one correspondence with W. *Pronto* implements a novel *hybrid* procedure to compute H iteratively via interaction with a description logic reasoner.

The main idea of the algorithm is that every column produced as a solution to the pricing-out problem is converted to a description logic concept expression which is then checked for satisfiability by the description logic reasoner. If the expression is satisfiable, it means that the column corresponds to a possible world (in W in our context) and can be added to (2). Otherwise, the justifications of unsatisfiability –see (Horridge et al., 2008)– are converted into linear constraints and added to the pricing-out problem, which is then re-optimized. Finally, either an entering column is found or the pricing-out problem becomes infeasible (which implies that the system (2) is optimal).

A detailed description of the PSAT algorithm is beyond the scope of this paper and is left as the core of a future publication.

Conflict-Finding Algorithm

A satisfiability algorithm is generally not sufficient for a comprehensive analysis of an inconsistent knowledge base (either classical or probabilistic). Typically users need to identify those fragments of the knowledge base which cause the inconsistency in order to repair them. Such fragments are typically required to be *minimal* so that the user can choose a repair strategy with minimal impact on the rest of the knowledge base.

We are interested in determining the minimal unsatisfiable subsets of a certain collection of probabilistic conditional statements in L, say Φ.

We apply the classical approach to finding minimal unsatisfiable sets based on hitting sets which dates back to Reiter (1987). Reiter's hitting set tree (HST) algorithm requires, as a subroutine, a satisfiability procedure which can extract one minimal unsatisfiable set from the knowledge base. It then systematically removes each axiom from that minimal unsatisfiable set and applies the satisfiability procedure again to generate a new minimal unsatisfiable set. By being systematic in the 'repairs', the procedure finds all minimal unsatisfiable sets in the knowledge base. We reduce the problem of finding a single minimal unsatisfiable subset of Φ to the problem of finding a minimal infeasible subset of inequalities in the corresponding linear system of the form (2) above. Such subsets are known as *irreducible infeasible systems* (IIS) in the linear programming literature (see Parker et al., 1996). However, given that the system (2) is never represented in its full version the application of the Ryan and Parker's algorithm is far from straightforward. If the optimal value of the system (2) is less than 1 then some inequalities have non-zero dual values. Such inequalities correspond to conflicting constraints in Φ but are not guaranteed to be minimal (though is typically quite small and close to the minimal set). We then do a brute force trial and error search to remove all superfluous constraints.

Decomposition of Φ_{CB}

To our knowledge, none of the existing probabilistic solvers can solve PSAT for Φ_{CB} taken as a whole within a reasonable amount of time (see Table 1 for a precise account of the size of Φ_{CB}). However, Φ_{CB} has a certain structure that allows splitting it into fragments that can be examined independently. A crucial property of our probabilistic formalization is that Φ_{CB} is satisfiable if and only if all of the fragments are individually satisfiable, as we show in Table 1.

We can regard Φ_{CB} as a directed graph where the nodes are the medical entities in L and the edges are given by the rules in Φ_{CB} (i.e., a rule of the form $\langle q \mid p, \eta \rangle$ in Φ_{CB} would correspond to an edge directed from p to q).

Let $p \in L$. We denote by $\Phi_p \subseteq \Phi_{CB}$ the set of rules that yield a directed edge in a path from

Table 1. Number of symptoms, diseases, and rules

Number of distinct symptoms	1761
Number of distinct diseases	341
Number of *symptom-symptom* rules	720
Number of *disease-disease* rules	218
Number of *symptom-disease* rules	17573

p to any other medical entity in L or a directed edge in a path from any medical entity in L to p.

For the next two results let us consider two medical entities $p_1, p_2 \in S$ and assume that there is no path from p_1 to p_2 in Φ_{CB} or vice versa and that there is no medical entity $p \in L$ from which there exists a path to both p_1 and p_2.

Proposition 4: If Φ_{p_1} and Φ_{p_2} are satisfiable then $\Phi_{p_1} \cup \Phi_{p_2}$ is satisfiable.

Proof: Let $\mathcal{I}_1$ and $\mathcal{I}_2$ be models of Φ_{p_1} and Φ_{p_2} respectively. We can assume without loss of generality that $D^{\mathcal{I}_1} \cap D^{\mathcal{I}_2} = \varnothing$. We can construct a model $\mathcal{I}$ of $\Phi_{p_1} \cup \Phi_{p_2}$ from $\mathcal{I}_1$ and $\mathcal{I}_2$ in a pretty trivial way by setting $D^{\mathcal{I}} = D^{\mathcal{I}_1} \cup D^{\mathcal{I}_2}$ and $\nu^{\mathcal{I}}(p,a) = 1$ if and only if $\nu^{\mathcal{I}_1}(p,a) = 1$ or $\nu^{\mathcal{I}_2}(p,a) = 1$ and 0 otherwise, for all $(p,a) \in L \times D^{\mathcal{I}}$. In can be easily seen that $\mathcal{I}$ thus defined satisfies $\Phi_{p_1} \cup \Phi_{p_2}$.

Corollary 2: If Φ is a minimal unsatisfiable set of rules in $\Phi_{p_1} \cup \Phi_{p_2}$ then Φ needs to be contained in Φ_{p_1} or Φ_{p_2}.

Proof: It follows trivially from Proposition 4. Notice that if Φ were a minimal unsatisfiable subset of $\Phi_{p_1} \cup \Phi_{p_2}$ and that it were neither contained in Φ_{p_1} nor in Φ_{p_2} then we could define satisfiable subsets from Φ_{p_1} and Φ_{p_2} of the same structure (possibly by removing rules from other minimal unsatisfiable subsets of Φ_{p_1} and Φ_{p_2}, but none from Φ).

Although trivial, it is worth mentioning that the previous propositions also hold for any alternative interpretation of the rules in terms of probabilistic intervals (i.e., by taking certain real intervals in place of point-valued probabilities).

Φ_{CB} has the following properties which will enable us to decompose it into a set of fragments:

- All conditional statements contain only atomic medical entities (i.e., entities in L).
- *Uncertain* rules (i.e., non-classical, $\Phi_{D|S}$) condition only on symptoms.
- The graph of $\Phi_{S|S}$ contains many disconnected subgraphs.

We split Φ_{CB} into a set of fragments of the form Φ_p, where $p \in S$ is a symptom such that there is no rule in Φ_{CB} of the form $\langle p \mid q, \eta \rangle$. For simplicity we include the entire $\Phi_{D|D}$ in each fragment since it is decomposable to a much less extent than $\Phi_{S|S}$. The largest fragments have around 200 conditional statements that normally relate two or three connected symptoms to diseases.

Corollary 2 guarantees that all minimal unsatisfiable sets of rules in Φ_{CB} can be found by computing such sets for each fragment. Thus our methodology is simply a systematic analysis of the sets of the form Φ_p, which involves a PSAT test and (if the fragment is unsatisfiable) the computation of all minimal unsatisfiable sets in it (see the algorithms in the two previous subsections).

Related Approaches in the Literature

Consistency-checking methods and algorithms for large-scale databases have long been of relevance in scientific computational research. In relation to expert systems and in particular to CADIAG-2 it is worth referring to Moser et al. (1992) as an example of research of this nature.

In this paper, a classical first-order logic theorem prover was used to analyze the predecessor of CADIAG-2 (CADIAG-1), which did not contain any uncertain rules, and that helped to detect some inconsistent sets of rules. Consistency-checking in CADIAG-2 by means of formal methods is much harder mostly due to the necessity of an appropriate formalism for representing degrees of confirmation in rules (in particular in *symptom-disease* rules). Very recently the first such attempt (Ciabattoni et al., 2010) was made using a specific fragment of monadic infinite-valued Gödel logic extended with classical, involutive negation (denoted by $G^{\sim}$).

In Ciabattoni et al. (2010) a sentence in $G^{\sim}$ is associated to each rule of the form $\langle q \mid p, \eta \rangle$ in Φ_{CB}. It is proved that, for $\langle q \mid p, \eta \rangle \in \Phi_{CB}$ and θ the sentence in $G^{\sim}$ associated to it, the following holds:

- If $\eta \in (0,1)$ then θ is satisfied by a certain interpretation $\mathcal{I}$ of L if and only if $(q \mid p)_{\mathcal{I}} \in (0,1)$.
- If $\eta \in \{0,1\}$ then θ is satisfied by a certain interpretation $\mathcal{I}$ of L if and only if $(q \mid p)_{\mathcal{I}} = \eta$.

In (Ciabattoni et al., 2010) the problem of checking satisfiability of the set of sentences in $G^{\sim}$ associated to the rules in Φ_{CB} is proved to be equivalent to the problem of satisfiability in classical first-order logic for such sentences (i.e., equivalent to determining whether there is a classical interpretation of L that satisfies the sentences associated to the rules).

The relation between our approach and that in Ciabattoni et al. (2010) is clear in the light of the results stated in the third section. We will have that a certain collection of rules $\Phi \subseteq \Phi_{CB}$ will be found to be inconsistent according to the approach defined in Ciabattoni et al. (2010) if and only if there is no probability function ω on L such that $\models_{\omega} \Phi^{*}$, where Φ^{*} is defined from Φ by replacing η in each rule $\langle q \mid p, \eta \rangle \in \Phi$ by the interval $(0,1)$.

Unlike the approach in (Ciabattoni et al., 2010), our probabilistic formalization is *equisatisfiable* with Φ_{CB} (see Proposition 3) and ensures finding all minimal unsatisfiable sets of rules. In (Ciabattoni et al., 2010) the fragment of compound rules in CADIAG-2 is also considered in addition to the binary fragment (at the expense of a further weakening in the information expressed by the formulas in $G^{\sim}$ representing these rules). As mentioned earlier, we do not consider CADIAG-2's compound rules in this paper. Certainly, we would require additional efforts to ensure (if possible at all) equisatisfiability and completeness of our decomposition procedure (as given by Proposition 4 for Φ_{CB}) if we consider CADIAG-2's compound rules, although the former would not be necessary if we assumed a probabilistic interpretation of the rules from the outset.

MINIMAL UNSATISFIABLE SETS IN Φ_{CB}

We present here results concerning the satisfiability check of Φ_{CB} when considering a slightly relaxed interpretation of Φ_{CB} by replacing each rule of type *symptom-disease* of the form $\langle q \mid p, \eta \rangle \in \Phi_{CB}$, for some $p, q \in L$ and $\eta \in (0,1) \cap \mathbb{Q}$, by $\langle q \mid p, \Omega_{\eta} \rangle$, with $\Omega_{\eta} = [\eta - 0.01, \eta + 0.01] = [\underline{\eta}, \overline{\eta}]$. (The degrees of confirmation of the rules in Φ_{CB} are all of the form $k / 100$, for some $k \in \{0,1,\ldots,100\} \subset \mathbb{Z}$, and thus Ω_{η} is well defined).

We have opted for checking satisfiability of this slightly relaxed interpretation of the rules in Φ_{CB} against a point-valued interpretation (i.e., the standard interpretation with point-valued probabilities) because of time constraints. The implementation of our algorithms for the relaxed interpretation of Φ_{CB} completes the task of finding all minimal unsatisfiable subsets in a reasonable amount of time (around one hour). It is a well known fact in model-diagnosis theory that computing *all* minimal unsatisfiable subsets of a certain knowledge base requires a number of satisfiability tests (in our case, PSAT tests) that is exponential in the number of unsatisfiable subsets. Our relaxed interpretation of Φ_{CB} already contains a high number of minimal unsatisfiable sets (which also happen to be minimal under a point-valued interpretation) and a point-valued interpretation adds up more. Furthermore, some of the unsatisfiable sets that are present in the point-valued interpretation and not in our relaxed one are relatively large (some contain 7 rules) and do not overlap with other unsatisfiable sets. Such facts bring the algorithm's running time closer to its worst case.

An example of a type of minimal unsatisfiable set detected under a precise interpretation of the rules but not under our relaxed version is the one that follows:

$$\langle q_1 \mid p_1, \eta_1 \rangle, \langle q_2 \mid p_1, \eta_2 \rangle, \langle q_1 \mid p_2, \eta_3 \rangle, \langle q_3 \mid p_2, \eta_4 \rangle,$$

$$\langle q_3 \mid q_1, 1 \rangle, \langle q_3 \mid q_2, 1 \rangle, \langle p_2 \mid p_1, 1 \rangle,$$

for $p_1, p_2 \in S$, $q_1, q_2, q_3 \in D$, $\eta_1, \eta_2, \eta_3, \eta_4 \in [0,1]$, with $\eta_3 = \eta_4$ and $\eta_1 < \eta_2$. Notice that the rules $\langle q_1 \mid p_2, \eta_3 \rangle$ and $\langle q_3 \mid p_2, \eta_4 \rangle$ along with $\langle q_3 \mid q_1, 1 \rangle$ intuitively claim that the set of patients with symptom p_2 and disease q_2 coincides with the set of patients with symptom p_2 and disease q_3 when assuming $\eta_3 = \eta_4$. Under such an assumption the rules $\langle q_1 \mid p_1, \eta_1 \rangle$ and $\langle q_2 \mid p_1, \eta_2 \rangle$ along with the remaining classical rules generate an inconsistency whenever $\eta_1 < \eta_2$. Notice also that, for example, for $\eta_3 < \eta_4$ the set would not be unsatisfiable and thus our relaxed interval interpretation would yield this set consistent (assuming $\eta_3, \eta_4 < 1$).

For the sake of simplicity we will adopt the same notation for the rules of type *symptom-disease* of the form $\langle q \mid p, \eta \rangle$, with $\eta \in \{0,1\}$. We will write $\langle q \mid p, \Omega_\eta \rangle$, with $\Omega_\eta = [\eta, \eta] = [\underline{\eta}, \overline{\eta}]$.

We list the different types of minimal unsatisfiable sets encountered in Φ_{CB} under this relaxed interpretation of the rules:

Type 1: Our first type of minimal unsatisfiable set in Φ_{CB} is given by a collection of rules of the form

$$\langle q_1 \mid p, \Omega_\eta \rangle, \langle q_2 \mid p, \Omega_\zeta \rangle, \langle q_2 \mid q_1, 1 \rangle,$$

for $p \in S$, $q_1, q_2 \in D$, $\eta, \zeta \in [0,1]$ and $\overline{\zeta} < \underline{\eta}$.

By $\overline{\zeta} < \underline{\eta}$ we are intuitively assuming that the number of patients that have both symptom p and disease q_1 is greater than the number of patients with both symptom p and disease q_2, which contradicts $\langle q_2 \mid q_1, 1 \rangle$ (i.e., the assumption that all patients that have disease q_1 have also disease q_2).

Type 2: Our second type of minimal unsatisfiable set in Φ_{CB} is given by a set of rules of the form

$$\langle q_1 \mid p, \Omega_\eta \rangle, \langle q_2 \mid p, \Omega_\zeta \rangle, \langle q_2 \mid q_1, 0 \rangle,$$

for $p \in S$, $q_1, q_2 \in D$, $\eta, \zeta \in [0,1]$ and $\underline{\eta} + \underline{\zeta} > 1$.

Notice that the rule $\langle q_2 \mid q_1, 0 \rangle$ assumes *disjointness* between q_1 and q_2 (intuitively, there cannot be a patient with both disease q_1 and q_2), which rules out the possibility of consistency whenever $\underline{\eta} + \underline{\zeta} > 1$.

Type 3: The third type of minimal conflict set in Φ_{CB} is given by a set of the form

$$\langle q \mid p_1, \Omega_\eta \rangle, \langle q \mid p_2, \Omega_1 \rangle, \langle p_2 \mid p_1, 1 \rangle,$$

for $p_1, p_2 \in S$, $q \in D$, $\eta \in [0,1]$ and $\overline{\eta} < 1$.

Intuitively, the rule $\langle p_2 \mid p_1, 1\rangle$ says that all patients with symptom p_1 also have symptom p_2. The rule $\langle q \mid p_2, \Omega_1\rangle$ intuitively says that all patients with symptom p_2 have disease D. These two facts together imply that patients with symptom p_1 should all have disease D (i.e., $\overline{\eta} = 1$).

Type 4: The fourth and last type of minimal unsatisfiable set is given by a collection of rules of the form

$$\langle q_1 \mid p, \Omega_\eta\rangle, \langle q_2 \mid p, \Omega_\zeta\rangle, \langle q_3 \mid p, \Omega_\lambda\rangle, \langle q_3 \mid q_1, 1\rangle, \langle q_3 \mid q_2, 1\rangle, \langle q_2 \mid q_1, 0\rangle,$$

with $p \in S$, $q_1, q_2, q_3 \in D$, $\eta, \zeta, \lambda \in [0,1]$, $\overline{\lambda} < \underline{\eta} + \underline{\zeta} \leq 1$ and $\underline{\zeta}, \underline{\eta} \leq \overline{\lambda}$ (to guarantee minimality).

Intuitively, assuming $\langle q_1 \mid p, \Omega_\eta\rangle$, $\langle q_2 \mid p, \Omega_\zeta\rangle$ and $\langle q_2 \mid q_1, 0\rangle$, the proportion of patients that, having symptom p, have either disease q_1 or q_2 is at least $\underline{\eta} + \underline{\zeta}$. On the other hand, assuming $\langle q_3 \mid q_1, 1\rangle$ and $\langle q_3 \mid q_2, 1\rangle$, we have that all patients with disease either q_1 or q_2 have also disease q_3. Thus, under such assumptions, satisfiability requires that $\overline{\lambda} \geq \underline{\eta} + \underline{\zeta}$.

Table 2 shows the amount of minimal unsatisfiable sets found for each type and the number of rules involved in them.

A thorough analysis of these types of inconsistencies in connection with the whole knowledge base and with possible repair strategies and in relation to other sets of inconsistencies obtained under alternative interpretations of Φ_{CB} (as briefly pointed above, under the standard point-valued interpretation of the rules or when regarding η in $\langle q \mid p, \eta\rangle \in \Phi_{CB}$ as a lower-bound threshold) is an ongoing research challenge.

Table 2. Amount of minimal unsatisfiable sets found for each type and the number of rules involved

Type	Amount	Number of rules involved
1	420	3
2	5	3
3	1	3
4	269	6

EVALUATING INCONSISTENCY IN Φ_{CB}

While we have determined that Φ_{CB} is inconsistent and have found various sets of statements and patterns to account for that inconsistency, it is not entirely clear how to interpret this information. In particular, we may wish to determine *how* inconsistent Φ_{CB} is.

We have just seen that Φ_{CB} contains a large number of minimal inconsistent subsets. That, on a straightforward reading, makes Φ_{CB} *highly* inconsistent as each inconsistent subset is *an inconsistency* and thus Φ_{CB} contains a lot of inconsistencies. Such a reading is the basis of several approaches in the literature to *measuring* the amount of inconsistency of a database (or even of each particular statement in the database (Hunter et al., 2008) based on the number and composition of its minimal inconsistent subsets –see (Hunter et al., 2004) for a review–. Clearly, under some of these approaches Φ_{CB} would certainly be regarded as *highly* inconsistent.

However, while appealing, this is not the only way to measure inconsistency. We consider here an alternative approach to measuring the degree of inconsistency by considering *how far* the knowledge base is from consistency (see Thimm, 2009 for an example of such an approach for probabilistic knowledge bases), with the ultimate goal of giving an alternative evaluation of the amount of inconsistency of Φ_{CB} and providing a tool for determining possible, *minimal* repair strategies for Φ_{CB} and similar knowledge bases.

Distance to Consistency

For what follows let $\Im^c \subset \Im$ denote the set of closed intervals in $\Im$ and define

$$\mathcal{PK}^c = \{(\Delta, v) \in \mathcal{PK} \mid v(\phi \mid \theta) \in \Im^c \text{ for all } \phi \mid \theta \in \Delta\}.$$

We define a *measure of inconsistency* for $(\Delta, v) \in \mathcal{PK}^c$ based on the quantification of the *minimal* adjustment that one needs to make on v in order for (Δ, v) to be satisfiable. We call the measure presented here *distance to consistency*. Our notion of *distance to consistency* is similar in nature to that defined in Thimm (2009). The main difference between our approach and that of Thimm (2009) is the notion of satisfiability for probabilistic conditional statements: null probability for the conditioning event in a probabilistic statement is allowed in (Thimm, 2009) and makes the statement satisfiable by default. Our approach becomes much more complex in comparison to Thimm (2009) due mostly to our definition of satisfiability (see Definition 2), which we believe is much more natural and intuitive than that of Thimm (2009).

Let ϵ be a *non-zero infinitesimal* in the set of hyperreal numbers (i.e., ϵ is such that $0 < \epsilon < 1/n$ for all $n \in \mathbb{N}$). We will be working with the set $\mathcal{A} = \{t, t+\epsilon, 1/\epsilon \mid t \in \mathbb{R}\}$.

The reason why we consider ϵ will be made clear later. We are not interested in infinitesimal precision and thus we do not consider algebraic operations involving infinitesimals.

For what follows let $(\Delta, v) \in \mathcal{PK}^c$ and $\Gamma \subset \Delta$, with $\Delta' = \Delta - \Gamma = \{\phi_1 \mid \theta_1, \ldots, \phi_k \mid \theta_k\}$, for some $k \in \mathbb{N}$, and $v(\phi_i \mid \theta_i) = [\underline{\eta}_i, \overline{\eta}_i]$ for all $i \in \{1, \ldots, k\}$. Γ is intended to represent the set of conditional statements that are *correctly* evaluated by v and thus should (arguably) not be considered when assessing the *distance to consistency* of (Δ, v).

We define (Δ, v_x) to be the set

$$\{v_x(\phi_i \mid \theta_i) = [\underline{\eta}_i - \underline{x}_i, \overline{\eta}_i + \overline{x}_i] \mid i \in \{1, \ldots, k\}\} \cup \{v_x(\phi \mid \theta) = v(\phi \mid \theta) \mid \phi \mid \theta \in \Gamma\},$$

where $\underline{x}_i$, $\overline{x}_i$ are positive real variables satisfying the constraint $0 \le \underline{\eta}_i - \underline{x}_i \le \overline{\eta}_i + \overline{x}_i \le 1$, for all $i \in \{1, \ldots, k\}$.

For the next definitions let $(\Delta, v) \in \mathcal{PK}^c$ and $\Gamma \subset \Delta$ as above.

Definition 6: We define $F_\Gamma(\Delta, v)$ as follows:

$$F_\Gamma(\Delta, v) = \{a \ge 0 \mid \sum_{i=1}^{k} (\underline{x}_i + \overline{x}_i) = a, (\Delta, v_x)$$

is satisfiable}

Notice that *inf*$(F_\Gamma(\Delta, v))$ –the infimum of $F_\Gamma(\Delta, v)$ - needs to exist.

Definition 7: We define the *distance to consistency* of (Δ, v) with respect to Γ-denoted $DC_\Gamma(\Delta, v)$ – as follows:

- If $F_\Gamma(\Delta, v) \neq \varnothing$ and *min*$(F_\Gamma(\Delta, v))$ exists then $DC_\Gamma(\Delta, v) =$*min*$(F_\Gamma(\Delta, v))$.
- If $F_\Gamma(\Delta, v) \neq \varnothing$ and *min*$(F_\Gamma(\Delta, v))$ does not exist then we set $DC_\Gamma(\Delta, v) =$*inf*$(F_\Gamma(\Delta, v)) + \epsilon$.
- If $F_\Gamma(\Delta, v) = \varnothing$ then we set $DC_\Gamma(\Delta, v) = 1/\epsilon$.

That DC_Γ is well defined is clear. If $(\Gamma, v_{|\Gamma})$ is unsatisfiable then $F_\Gamma(\Delta, v) = \varnothing$ and thus we have that $DC_\Gamma(\Delta, v) = 1/\epsilon$. If $(\Gamma, v_{|\Gamma})$ is satisfiable and define Π to be the set of probability distributions on L that satisfy $(\Gamma, v_{|\Gamma})$ we have that each $\omega \in \Pi$ with $\omega(\theta_i) > 0$ for all $i \in \{1, \ldots, k\}$ satisfies (Δ, v_x) for some real values $\underline{x}_1, \overline{x}_1, \ldots, \underline{x}_k, \overline{x}_k$ and thus, if any such probability distribution existed, $F_\Gamma(\Delta, v)$ would not be empty. On the other hand, if there were no such probability distributions then $F_\Gamma(\Delta, v)$ would be empty, in which case we would have $DC_\Gamma(\Delta, v) = 1/\epsilon$.

We will write *DC* instead of $DC_\varnothing$ whenever there is no set $\Gamma \subset \mathcal{K}$ with respect to which we are defining the distance to consistency. We will apply the same convention when referring to the map $F_\varnothing$ on $\mathcal{PK}^c$.

Let $(\Delta, v) \in \mathcal{PK}^c$ and $\Gamma \subset \Delta$. It is not generally true that $DC_\Gamma(\Delta, v) \in \mathbb{R}$. To see this consider the following example:

$$(\Delta, v) = \{v(\phi \mid \theta) = 1, v(\psi \mid \phi) = 1, v(\psi \mid \theta) = 1/2\}.$$

Notice that $DC(\Delta, v) = \epsilon$. (Δ, v) is certainly inconsistent and becomes consistent by replacing $v(\psi \mid \phi) = 1$ and/or $v(\phi \mid \theta) = 1$ by $v(\psi \mid \phi) = \eta$ and/or $v(\psi \mid \theta) = \zeta$ respectively, for any values η, ζ strictly less than 1.

Measuring $DC(\Phi_{CB})$

The computation of *DC* is certainly not a trivial matter for the general case. The main difficulty stems from our definition of satisfiability (i.e., from the fact that conditioning events are required to have a strictly positive probability). Some heuristics can be of much help in this matter. In fact, in order to compute $DC(\Phi_{CB})$, we can take advantage of its *simple* structure, as we will shortly show.

For the next proposition let $(\Delta, v) \in \mathcal{PK}^c$ be as follows:

- $\phi, \theta \in L$ for all $\phi \mid \theta \in \Delta$.
- (Δ, v) is, as a directed graph, acyclic.
- $v(\phi \mid \theta) \in (0,1) \cap \mathbb{Q}$, for all $\phi \mid \theta \in \Delta$.

Proposition 5: (Δ, v) is satisfiable.

Proof: By Proposition 3 the pair (Δ, v) will be satisfiable if and only if it has a classical model. We aim at constructing a classical model of (Δ, v).

Let $C = \{v(\phi \mid \theta) \mid (\phi \mid \theta) \in \Delta\}$. By assumption on (Δ, v), C will be a set of rational values. Let Q be the least common multiple of the denominators of all the values in C.

For the construction of $\mathcal{I}$ we consider first the set of *nodes* in (Δ, v) that have no *parents*, when dealing with (Δ, v) as a graph. Let p be a node in (Δ, v) with no parents. We set a collection of Q elements for p, labeled $D_p = \{a_1^p, \ldots, a_Q^p\}$. At the nth step in the construction of $\mathcal{I}$ we select a node q in (Δ, v), with parents $q_1, \ldots, q_k$ (for some $k \in \mathbb{N}$) and assume, without loss of generality, that the sets $D_{q_1}, \ldots, D_{q_k}$ have been defined at a previous step. We set a collection of $Q(\sum_{i=1}^{k} |D_{q_i}|)$ elements for q, labeled

$$D_q = \{a_1^q, \ldots, a^q_{Q(\sum_{i=1}^{k} |D_{q_i}|)}\}.$$

We impose some restrictions on the sets of the form D_p, for $p \in L$. We construct $\mathcal{I}$ in a way that, for $p, q \in L$, $D_p \cap D_q \neq \varnothing$ if and only if one of *p*|*q*, *q*|*p* is in Δ or there exists $r \in L$ such that $p \mid r, q \mid r \in \Delta$. (In general, we could impose the condition that distinct sets of the form D_p, for $p \in L$, should have as little domain elements in common as possible). That this can be achieved is clear given the restrictions on the cardinality of such sets and the fact that $v(\phi \mid \theta)$ is at most $(Q-1)/Q$ for all $\phi \mid \theta \in \Delta$.

For $p \in L$, with parents $q_1, \ldots, q_k$ (for some $k \in \mathbb{N}$) and sets $D_{q_1}, \ldots, D_{q_k}$ already defined, we will set D_p to have exactly $|D_{q_i}| v(p \mid q_i)$ elements of D_{q_i}, for each $i \in \{1, \ldots, k\}$. The elements of D_{q_i} chosen for D_p could also be elements of D_{q_j}, for $j \in \{1, \ldots, i-1, i+1, \ldots, k\}$, (depending on whether q_i and q_j are related in Δ by a conditional statement or not) but of no other sets thus far defined. That a suitable definition of D_p can be achieved (considering that the sets $D_{q_1},\ldots,D_{q_k}$ might not be pair wise disjoint) is clear given the restrictions on the cardinality of such sets and the fact that $1/Q \le v(\phi \mid \theta) \le (Q-1)/Q$ for all $\phi \mid \theta \in \Delta$.

We define $D^{\mathcal{I}} = \bigcup_{p \in L} D_p$ and $v^{\mathcal{I}}$ on $L \times D^{\mathcal{I}}$ as expected. For $p \in L$ and $a \in D^{\mathcal{I}}$,

$$\nu^{\mathcal{I}}(p,a) = \begin{cases} 1 & \text{if } a \in D_p \\ 0 & \text{otherwise} \end{cases}$$

This completes the proof.

Proposition 6: $DC(\Phi_{CB}) = \epsilon$.

Proof: We know from results in previous sections that Φ_{CB} is inconsistent and thus that $DC(\Phi_{CB}) > 0$ (i.e., at least ϵ). On the other hand Φ_{CB} is, when regarded as a graph, acyclic and with nodes in L. Replacing 0 and 1 by any values in $(0,1) \cap \mathbb{Q}$ as close as desired to 0 and 1 in rules of the form $\langle q \mid p, 0\rangle, \langle q \mid p, 1\rangle \in \Phi_{CB}$ respectively guarantees satisfiability, by Proposition 5. Therefore we can conclude that $DC(\Phi_{CB}) = \epsilon$.

REPAIR STRATEGIES FOR Φ_{CB}

In this section we discuss some tools and methodology aimed at helping the modeler to repair CADIAG-2-like knowledge bases in the presence of inconsistency (in this section, by CADIAG-2-like knowledge bases we mean those that can be represented as elements in $\mathcal{PK}^c$). Our account is certainly not exhaustive. There are a vast number of methods and tools in the literature related to dealing with inconsistency in knowledge bases. We discuss some that we believe are of particular interest for CADIAG-2 and similar systems.

A very natural repair strategy for inconsistent knowledge bases consists of removing at least one statement from each of its minimal unsatisfiable subsets (provided we have them). Knowledge of the information represented by the system (i.e., for CADIAG-2 in particular, medical knowledge in the field of internal medicine) could certainly help in determining which statements should be removed and which should be kept. In the lack of such support, however, some *minimization* criterion (possibly along with other criteria) could be a good alternative, the most straightforward being the cardinality of the set of rules to be removed from the database (i.e., the cardinality of the repair subset). The literature in this direction is numerous (see for example Kalyanpur et al., 2006; Lam et al., 2008; Roussey et al., 2009).

The size of *minimal repair subsets* in Φ_{CB} for its relaxed interval interpretation (defining minimality in terms of just cardinality) is pretty small. That is due to the presence of some conditional statements in many minimal unsatisfiable subsets, which seems to indicate a higher contribution of these statements to the inconsistency of Φ_{CB} (see Hunter et al., 2008).

Graded approaches are also an alternative. We might think that it would be more suitable, since we are working with graded statements (i.e., uncertain statements along with a degree of uncertainty), an adjustment of the degrees of uncertainty in the knowledge base rather than the removal of the statements themselves. A *minimal* adjustment as measured by a function like *DC* would be desirable from that point of view. The computation of *DC* and the obtainment of a minimal adjustment in these terms are, as mentioned in the previous section, not an easy task in the general case.

We can place a strictly positive lower bound δ for the probability of the conditioning events. This way our problem reduces to finding an optimal solution to a (non-linear) constrained optimization problem (see Boyd et al., 2004 for basic concepts and, in general, for more on constrained optimization).

Let us consider $(\Delta, v) \in \mathcal{PK}^c$, with $\Delta' = \Delta - \Gamma, \Gamma \subset \Delta$,

$$(\Gamma, v_{|\Gamma}) = \{v(\psi_1 \mid \chi_1) = [\underline{\lambda}_1, \overline{\lambda}_1], ..., v(\psi_j \mid \chi_j) = [\underline{\lambda}_j, \overline{\lambda}_j]\}$$

and

$$(\Delta', v_{|\Delta'}) = \{v(\phi_1 \mid \theta_1) = [\underline{\eta}_1, \overline{\eta}_1], ..., v(\phi_k \mid \theta_k) = [\underline{\eta}_k, \overline{\eta}_k]\},$$

for some $j \in \{0\} \cup \mathbb{N}$ and $k \in \mathbb{N}$.

Consider the following constrained optimization problem:

Minimize $\sum_{i=1}^{k} (\underline{x}_i + \overline{x}_i)$ given the following constraints: (3)

- $(\underline{\eta}_i - \underline{x}_i)\vec{r}_{\theta_i} \cdot \vec{y} \leq \vec{r}_{\theta_i \wedge \phi_i} \cdot \vec{y} \leq (\overline{\eta}_i + \overline{x}_i)\vec{r}_{\theta_i} \cdot \vec{y}$ for each
- $i \in \{1, ..., k\}$,
- $\underline{\lambda}_i \vec{r}_{\chi_i} \cdot \vec{y} \leq \vec{r}_{\psi_i \wedge \chi_i} \cdot \vec{y} \leq \overline{\lambda}_i \vec{r}_{\chi_i} \cdot \vec{y}$ for each $i \in \{1, ..., j\}$,
- $\sum_{i=1}^{2^l} y_i = 1$,
- $y_i \geq 0$ for each $i \in \{1, ..., 2^l\}$,
- $\vec{r}_\theta \cdot \vec{y} \geq \delta$ for each $\phi \mid \theta \in \Delta$ for fixed $\delta \in (0, 1]$,
- $\underline{x}_i, \overline{x}_i \geq 0$ for each $i \in \{1, ..., k\}$,
- $0 \leq \underline{\eta}_i - \underline{x}_i \leq \overline{\eta}_i + \overline{x}_i \leq 1$ for each $i \in \{1, ..., k\}$.

Notice that for any $(\Delta, v) \in \mathcal{PK}^c$ the optimization problem (3) with variables $\underline{x}_i, \overline{x}_i$ and y_j, for each $i \in \{1, ..., k\}$ and $j \in \{1, ..., 2^l\}$, has an *optimal solution* for any $\delta \in (0, 1/2^l]$ (since its feasible set is compact) provided $\Gamma = \varnothing$ and that there is no conditional of the form $\phi \mid \perp$ in Δ (though in many cases a much bigger upper bound can be determined. For example, for $(\Delta, v) = \Phi_{CB}$, with $\Gamma = \varnothing$, the optimization problem (3) has an optimal solution for any $\delta \in (0, 1]$). A solution to (3) for $\delta > 0$ yields an adjustment to v that, although maybe not minimal, restores consistency in the knowledge base. In general, the closer δ is to 0 the closer to minimality the adjustment to v given by (3).

If $\Gamma \neq \varnothing$ then (3) is not guaranteed to have a solution for some value $\delta > 0$. Knowledge of the information represented by (Δ, v) would be indeed important in order to determine Γ. We have seen in the previous section that $DC(\Phi_{CB}) = \epsilon$ and thus an adjustment of infinitesimal magnitude is sufficient in order to restore consistency in Φ_{CB}. If, however, we take a collection of statements $\Gamma \subset \Delta$ (for $(\Delta, v) = \Phi_{CB}$) as fixed then it may not be case anymore that an adjustment of infinitesimal magnitude be sufficient to restore consistency (i.e., $DC_\Gamma(\Delta, v) \neq \epsilon$ for some $\Gamma \subset \Delta$). Consider for example the following subset of rules of Type 1 in Φ_{CB} where *S0730* is a code for a symptom and *D071, D247* codes for some diagnoses in Φ_{CB}:

$$\langle D071 \mid S0730, 0.5\rangle, \langle D247 \mid S0730, 0.4\rangle, \langle D247 \mid D071, 1\rangle.$$

If we assume $D247 \mid D071 \in \Gamma$ then

$$DC_\Gamma(\{\langle D071 \mid S0730, 0.5\rangle, \langle D247 \mid S0730, 0.4\rangle, \langle D247 \mid D071, 1\rangle\}) = 0.1 > \epsilon$$

and $DC_\Gamma(\Phi_{CD}) \geq 0.1$.

Maybe it is not too adventurous to assume, given the large number of minimal inconsistent subsets in Φ_{CB} and their simple structure, that the intended knowledge to be represented by at least some of these subsets could respond to a different (although in a way similar) representation. That gives rise to another repair strategy that consists of devising alternative representations for the presumably intended knowledge. For example, in CADIAG-2, one might think that the intended knowledge behind a representation of the form

$$\langle q_1 \mid p, \eta\rangle, \langle q_2 \mid p, \eta\rangle, \langle q_2 \mid q_1, 0\rangle,$$

for $p \in S$, $q_1, q_2 \in D$ and $\eta > 1/2$ could be better expressed by

$$\langle q_1 \vee q_2 \mid p, \eta \rangle, \langle q_2 \mid q_1, 0 \rangle.$$

Clearly, the latter is probabilistically satisfiable. Certainly, medical support would help in devising such alternative structures but, in the lack of it, assumptions like the one above (slightly more conservative than the original one) could be suitable.

One last possibility we mention in our brief account is directly related to the inference process of the system and to the possibility of *redundant* information. For example, some minimal inconsistent sets of Type 4 in CADIAG-2 contain rules that are *inferentially redundant* (by this we mean, roughly, that its presence or non-presence does not have a bearing in the outcome of a run of the inference engine on the knowledge base). Consider a minimal inconsistent set of the form

$$\langle q_1 \mid p, \eta \rangle, \langle q_2 \mid p, \zeta \rangle, \langle q_3 \mid p, \lambda \rangle, \langle q_3 \mid q_1, 1 \rangle,$$
$$\langle q_3 \mid q_2, 1 \rangle, \langle q_2 \mid q_1, 0 \rangle,$$

with $p \in S$, $q_1, q_2, q_3 \in D$, $\eta, \zeta, \lambda \in [0,1]$, $\lambda < \eta + \zeta \leq 1$ and $\zeta, \eta \leq \lambda$. If, further, we have that $\lambda = \eta$ or $\lambda = \zeta$ then $\langle q_3 \mid p, \lambda \rangle$ is inferentially redundant in Φ_{CB} (see Ciabattoni et al., 2010; Picado Muiño, 2010) for a brief description of the inference engine in CADIAG-2– and could be removed at no loss for the system.

CONCLUSION

While the knowledge base of CADIAG-2, formalized as a probabilistic logic theory, is highly unsatisfiable it is unclear what action this calls for. Inconsistency in a knowledge base may capture critical information and maintaining it may be critical to the integrity of the represented knowledge (see Gabbay et al., 1991 for a more comprehensive discussion). Furthermore, the inference engine in CADIAG-2 does not explode in the presence of the inconsistencies found. In this paper we have presented an analysis of the inconsistency which abstracts from the particular details of the inference mechanism in CADIAG-2 and serves as a foundation for extracting, understanding and reusing the knowledge embodied in it.

Regardless of one's preferred strategy for resolving the conflicts, it is clear that detecting them is critical to a complete understanding of the knowledge base which is challenging when we reach the size of CADIAG-2. Even with our (fortuitous) decomposition, the extraction of all conflicts under the standard interpretation of the rules in CADIAG-2 is unfeasible for everyday knowledge base development (we estimate that it will take weeks to extract all conflicts. Of course, if the modelers decide that producing and maintaining a satisfiable version is the right course of action then even several weeks would not be unreasonable as a one-time cost). Subsequent satisfiability checks would go much faster, especially as one can check only the relevant fragment a modeler is working on. This is similar to various proposals from the description logic community for modular ontology development (Sattler et al., 2009; Grau et al., 2009a; Grau et al., 2009b). As part of our future work, we intend to integrate more general modular analysis into our reasoner as an optimization. We intend to investigate whether it is necessary to do this decomposition outside of the solver (that is, by decomposing the input knowledge base before even starting to solve PSAT) in the rather crude manner we currently do, or whether modular analysis can be more tightly integrated with the reasoning process. As a related issue, we hope that CADIAG-2, or CADIAG-2-like problems, will be taken up by the PSAT solving community. CADIAG-2 is interestingly different in kind, not only in size, from traditional generated problems while its size sets a new base line for scalable PSAT.

We believe our analysis demonstrates the value of formalization and automated reasoning services. Merely detecting whether the knowledge base is satisfiable is obviously valuable. However, without conflict set extraction, there was no hope of understanding CADIAG-2's inconsistency. Considering alternative inconsistency metrics generated alternative understandings of the scope and nature of the inconsistency. Together, these services help make the knowledge base more transparent to new modelers.

We have, as yet, to attempt probabilistic entailment from CADIAG-2 or any of its fragments. It is not clear yet the extent to which one could generate interesting queries for CADIAG-2's knowledge base (or, more generally, for CADIAG-2-like knowledge bases) once it has been repaired and possibly modified for inferential purposes (see Picado Muiño, 2010).

REFERENCES

Adlassnig, K. (1986). Fuzzy set theory in medical diagnosis. *IEEE Transactions on Systems, Man, and Cybernetics*, *16*(2), 260–265. doi:10.1109/TSMC.1986.4308946

Adlassnig, K., Kolarz, G., Effenberger, W., & Grabner, H. (1985). CADIAG: Approaches to computer-assisted medical diagnosis. *Computers in Biology and Medicine*, *15*, 315–335. doi:10.1016/0010-4825(85)90014-9

Adlassnig, K., Kolarz, G., Scheithauer, W., & Grabner, H. (1986). Approach to a hospital based application of a medical expert system. *Informatics for Health & Social Care*, *11*(3), 205–223. doi:10.3109/14639238609003728

Boyd, S., & Vandenberghe, L. (2004). *Convex Optimization*. Cambridge, UK: Cambridge University Press.

Ciabattoni, A., & Rusnok, P. (2010). On the classical content of monadic G with involutive negation and its application to a fuzzy medical expert system. In F. Lin, U. Sattler, & M. Truszczynski (Eds.), *Proceedings of the Twelfth International Conference on the Principles of Knowledge Representation and Reasoning* (pp. 373-381). AAAI Press.

Ciabattoni, A., & Vetterlein, T. (2009). On the fuzzy (logical) content of CADIAG-2. *Fuzzy Sets and Systems*, *161*(14), 1941–1958.

Gabbay, D. M., & Hunter, A. (1991). Making inconsistency respectable: A logical framework for inconsistency in reasoning. In P. Jorrand & J. Kelemen (Eds.), *Proceedings of the International Workshop on Fundamentals of Artificial Intelligence Research* (LNCS 535, pp. 19-32).

Grau, B. C., Horrocks, I., Kazakov, Y., & Sattler, U. (2009a). Extracting modules from ontologies: A logic-based approach. In H. Stuckenschmidt, C. Parent, & S. Spaccapietra (Eds.), *Modular Ontologies: Concepts, Theories and Techniques for Knowledge Modularization* (LNCS 5445 pp. 159-186).

Grau, B. C., Parsia, B., & Sirin, E. (2009b). Ontology integration using ε-connections. In H. Stuckenschmidt, C. Parent, & S. Spaccapietra (Eds.), *Modular Ontologies: Concepts, Theories and Techniques for Knowledge Modularization* (LNCS 5445, pp. 293-320). Springer.

Hooker, J. (1988). Quantitative approach to logical reasoning. *Decision Support Systems*, *4*, 45–69. doi:10.1016/0167-9236(88)90097-8

Horridge, M., Parsia, B., & Sattler, U. (2008). Laconic and precise justifcations in OWL. In A.P. Sheth, S. Staab, M. Dean, M. Paolucci, D. Maynard, T. Finin, et al. (Eds.), *Proceedings of the Seventh International Semantic Web Conference* (LNCS 5318, pp. 323-338).

Hunter, A., & Konieczny, S. (2005). Approaches to measuring inconsistent information. In *Inconsistency Tolerance* (LNCS 3300, pp. 189-234).

Hunter, A., & Konieczny, S. (2008). Measuring inconsistency through minimal inconsistent sets. In G. Brewka & J. Lang (Eds.), *Proceedings of the Eleventh International Conference on the Principles of Knowledge Representation and Reasoning* (pp. 358-366). AAAI Press.

Kalyanpur, A., Parsia, B., Sirin, E., & Grau, B. C. (2006). Repairing unsatisfiable concepts in OWL ontologies. In Y. Sure & J. Domingue (Eds.), *Proceedings of the Third European Semantic Web Conference. The Semantic Web: Research and Applications* (LNCS 4011, pp. 170-184).

Klinov, P., & Parsia, B. (2010). Pronto: A practical probabilistic description logic reasoner. In T. Lukasiewicz, R. Peñaloza, & A. Turhan (Eds.), *Proceedings of the First International Workshop on Uncertainty in Description Logics,* Edinburgh, UK.

Klir, G., & Folger, T. (1988). *Fuzzy Sets, Uncertainty and Information.* Upper Saddle River, NJ: Prentice-Hall International.

Lam, J. S. C., Sleeman, D. H., Pan, J. Z., & Vasconcelos, W. W. (2008). A fine-grained approach to resolving unsatisfiable ontologies. *Journal of Data Semantics, 10,* 62–95. doi:10.1007/978-3-540-77688-8_3

Leitich, H., Adlassnig, K., & Kolarz, G. (2002). Evaluation of two different models of semiautomatic knowledge acquisition for the medical consultant system CADIAG-2/RHEUMA. *Artificial Intelligence in Medicine, 25,* 215–225. doi:10.1016/S0933-3657(02)00025-8

Lukasiewicz, T. (2008). Expressive probabilistic description logics. *Artificial Intelligence, 172*(6-7), 852–883. doi:10.1016/j.artint.2007.10.017

Moser, W., & Adlassnig, K. (1992). Consistency checking of binary categorical relationships in a medical knowledge base. *Artificial Intelligence in Medicine, 8,* 389–407. doi:10.1016/0933-3657(92)90022-H

Parker, M., & Ryan, J. (1996). Finding the minimum weight IIS cover of an infeasible system of linear inequalities. *Annals of Mathematics and Artificial Intelligence, 17*(1-2), 107–126. doi:10.1007/BF02284626

Picado Muiño, D. (2010). The (probabilistic) logical content of CADIAG-2. In J. Filipe, A. Fred, & B. Sharp (Eds.), *Second International Conference on Agents and Artificial Intelligence: Vol. 1. Artificial Intelligence,* Valencia, Spain (pp. 28-35).

Reiter, R. (1987). A theory of diagnosis from first principles. *Artificial Intelligence, 32,* 57–95. doi:10.1016/0004-3702(87)90062-2

Roussey, C., Corcho, O., & Blázquez, L. M. V. (2009). A catalogue of OWL ontology antipatterns. In *Proceedings of the Fifth International Conference on Knowledge Capture* (pp. 205-206). New York: ACM Press.

Sattler, U., Schneider, T., & Zakharyaschev, M. (2009). Which kind of module should I extract? In B.C. Grau, I. Horrocks, B. Motik, & U. Sattler (Eds.), *Proceedings of the Twenty-second International Workshop on Description Logics* (Vol. 477). CEUR

Thimm, M. (2009). Measuring inconsistency in probabilistic knowledge bases. In *Proceedings of the Twenty-fifth Conference on Uncertainty in Artificial Intelligence* (pp. 530-537). Corvallis, OR: AUAI Press.

Zadeh, L. (1965). Fuzzy sets. *Information and Control, 8,* 338–353. doi:10.1016/S0019-9958(65)90241-X

Zadeh, L. (1975). Fuzzy logic and approximate reasoning. *Synthese*, *30*, 407–428. doi:10.1007/BF00485052

Zimmermann, H. (1991). *Fuzzy Set Theory and its Applications*. Dordrecht, The Netherlands: Kluwer.

This work was previously published in the Journal of Information Technology Research, Volume 4, Issue 1, edited by Mehdi Khosrow-Pour, pp. 1-20, copyright 2011 by IGI Publishing (an imprint of IGI Global).

Chapter 2
Development of a Knowledge Based System for an Intensive Care Environment Using Ontologies

Ana Torres Morgade
University of A Coruña, Spain

Marcos Martínez-Romero
University of A Coruña, Spain

José M. Vázquez-Naya
University of A Coruña, Spain

Miguel Pereira Loureiro
Meixoeiro Hospital of Vigo, Spain

Ángel González Albo
University of A Coruña, Spain

Javier Pereira Loureiro
University of A Coruña, Spain

ABSTRACT

In intensive care units (ICUs), clinicians must monitor patients' vital signs and make decisions regarding the drugs they administer. The patients' lives depend on the quality of these decisions but experts can make mistakes. Recent technological strategies and tools can decrease these errors. In this paper, the authors describe the development of a knowledge based system (KBS) to provide support to clinicians with respect to the drugs they administer to patients with cardiopathies in ICUs to stabilize them. To develop the system, knowledge from medical experts at the Meixoeiro Hospital in Vigo (Spain) has been extracted and formally represented as an ontology. As a result, a validated KBS has been obtained, which can be helpful to experts in ICUs and whose underlying knowledge can be easily shared and reused.

INTRODUCTION

During the past few decades, the development of new technological advances and tools in the field of medicine has helped clinicians to make complex decisions in critical situations. When a patient enters an intensive care unit (ICU), either after surgery or due to a serious clinical condition, his vital signs change continuously, forcing the medical expert to make rapid decisions, which frequently imply modifications on the dosage of drugs being supplied.

DOI: 10.4018/978-1-4666-3625-5.ch002

This kind of care requires the intervention of highly specialized and trained health personnel, and particularly the continuous monitoring of the parameters on the monitors showing the patient's condition, due to the serious situation of the patient and the important repercussions these drugs cause.

According to the values of the patient's vital signs, the kind of drug is selected by the doctor and, on the basis of his evolution, the amount or type of drug may be modified. The decision making process to determine the variation of drug dosage necessary to stabilize the patient's clinical situation is a complex task that requires exhaustively (but rapidly) analyzing the evolution of a large set of parameters within a period of time. An intelligent tool may be useful to support clinicians in this process.

One of the multiple subareas of Artificial Intelligence (AI) is concerned with de development of a special class of computer systems that use expert knowledge to assist humans in performing specific intellectual tasks. This kind of systems, which were born in the 70s, are widely known as knowledge based systems (KBSs) or expert systems. Since KBSs were born, one of their main fields of application has been, and is medicine. Generation of real time alarms and notifications, diagnosis support, detection of errors and inconsistencies treatment plans, or recognition and interpretation of medical images, are some examples of the different roles that KBSs may play in medicine.

KBSs are very effective to analyze large amounts of data, interpret them and provide a recommendation on the basis of these data as soon as possible. However, one of the main problems of these systems is related to knowledge representation. Knowledge they use to make decisions is often represented using traditional strategies, which make it difficult to share with other experts around the world or to be reused by other similar systems.

At late 80s, ontologies started to gain popularity in the field of AI as a good way to share and reuse knowledge. The word *ontology* (from the Greek *ontos*=being and *logos*=science, study, theory) comes from Philosophy, where refers to "the science of what is, of the kinds and structures of objects, properties, events, processes and relations in every area of reality" (Smith, 2003). Ontologies were originally used by ancient Greek philosophers to name and classify the things they saw in the universe and the relationships between them. Besides the philosophical point of view, towards the end of the 20th and the beginning of the 21st centuries, ontologies emerged as an important research field in computer science.

There are several definitions of ontology in AI, which have evolved over the years. However, one the most precise and complete definitions provided up to date is the one given by Studer and colleagues in 1998, who stated that "An ontology is a formal, explicit specification of a shared conceptualization" (Studer, Benjamins, & Fensel, 1998).

At present, ontologies are viewed as a practical way to conceptualize information that is expressed in electronic format, and are being used in a variety of applications, including the Semantic Web, bioinformatics and biomedicine, natural language processing, intelligent information integration or e-Commerce, promoting a better data interoperability and reuse.

The basic idea behind these applications is to use ontologies to reach a common level of understanding or comprehension within a particular domain (Gómez-Pérez, Fernández-López, & Corcho, 2004). In contrast to syntactic standards, understanding is not restricted to a common representation or structure. Ontologies go beyond, providing the support to reach a common understanding of the meaning of terms.

Unification of medical terminology is a well known problem. Nowadays, there are large amounts of medical information stored using different terminologies and formats all around the world, and it constitutes an important barrier to process and reuse it in an integrated manner. Due to this, developing methods and technologies to organize and access these vast amounts of data has become a priority for researchers. Since some years ago, the increasing popularity of ontologies as a tool for representing shared knowledge, has attracted attention of medical experts, who see them as a potential solution to the problem of terminological heterogeneity in medicine. As a result, multiple ontologies have been developed during the last decade, aimed to formalize knowledge in different medical fields.

The Meixoeiro Hospital, located in the city of Vigo, is one of the most important hospitals in the north-west region of Spain. In this hospital there are three ICUs, which jointly receive around 1,600 patients per year. One of these ICUs (Post-operatory Cardiac ICU or PC-ICU) is specifically addressed to treat patients with cardiopathies (in general, patients who enter the ICU after cardiac surgery). When a patient enters the PC-ICU his vital signs are constantly monitored by different monitoring devices. On the basis of these parameters, doctors administer different types of drugs to stabilize the patient, if necessary. These drugs are supplied through a set of infusion pumps located at the foot of each patient's bed. The doctor has to constantly make rapid decisions based on each patient's vital signs, and life of patients depends on the quality of these decisions.

Nevertheless, this method has a series of pitfalls that may be corrected: the human factor leads to errors occurring in the decision making process; sometimes not all of the parameters that may be known are taken into account; stress and the number of cases mean that often there is not enough time to analyze the case in detail; and it is not possible to continuously analyze all of the data generated, particularly when dealing with a large number of patients. In addition, in spite of that there are multiple guidelines related to the treatment of patients affected by cardiopathies in ICUs, it does not exist a shared, synthesized, formal and explicit protocol that serves as a reference for doctors to make the most adequate decision in critical situations. When experts have to make rapid decisions, they do not have the enough time to look for the most accurate information in clinical guidelines, so they often make decisions on the basis of their knowledge and previous experience. Sometimes, this procedure is a source of imprecisions and mistakes.

These problems could be overcome with the help of an intelligent system, able to provide decision support to clinicians in ICUs on the basis of a agreed and formally specified protocol.

This protocol would consist on a set of well-defined, ICU-related concepts and their relationships, as well as a set of semantic rules expressed using the mentioned concepts and relationships, which would guide the decision making process. Representation of the protocol using ontologies would make it easy to share and discuss it with other experts around the world. Also, the resulting ontology could be reused in other KBSs with the same or similar purpose.

This work describes the development of a KBS to provide decision support to personnel in ICUs regarding treatment of patients with cardiopathies, on the basis of a decision making protocol. The terms used and the decisions made by physicians in each case have been formally represented using an ontology. The process of ontology construction is also explained.

RELATED WORK

Apart from the classical KBSs, like the popular MYCIN system (Shortliffe, 1976), for determining the diagnosis and therapy for infectious blood diseases, or INTERNIST (Miller, Pople, & Myers, 1982), aimed to provide diagnostic support in the domain of internal medicine, during the last decades, a variety of systems based on different technologies have been developed to solve problems in ICUs. For example, fuzzy logic has proven to be well suited to a variety of industrial applications, and fuzzy control strategies are, in many cases, more efficient than traditional alternatives.

One of the interesting ironies of medical practice is that its practitioners strive for objectivity and precision while dealing with data that are inherently imprecise. In this field there are systems to control the administration of different fluids, for example, anesthesia (Meier, Nieuwland, Zbinden, & Hacisalihzade, 1992; Martin, 1994) or oxygen (Hanson, Weiss, Frasch, Marshall, & Marshall, 1998), or a system to control mean arterial pressure by means of drug supply (Ying & Sheppard, 1994). Another example is an expert system for electroencephalogram monitoring in the pediatric ICU (Si et al., 1998). Also, case-based reasoning has been demonstrated to be useful to select a group of patients with similar characteristics from a demographic database (Frize et al., 1995), or to determine the most adequate antibiotics for patients suffering a particular disease (Heindl et al., 1997).

On the other hand, the number, size and scope of available ontologies has been increasing, especially in the biomedical domain (known as *bio-ontologies*). A popular example of clinical ontology is SNOMED-CT (Systematized NOmenclature of MEDicine-Clinical Terms), developed by the College of American Pathologists. SNOMED-CT is considered the reference terminology for supporting electronic applications during the entire healthcare process. It is a highly complex ontology containing more than 350,000 unique concepts organized into multiple hierarchies (IHTSDO, n.d.).

As another example, the US National Cancer Institute (NCI) maintains a widely used ontology for the cancer domain, known as the NCI Thesaurus (Golbeck et al., 2003). It provides information (definition, synonyms, etc.) on nearly 10,000 cancers and related diseases, 8,000 single agents and combination therapies, and a wide range of other topics related to cancer and biomedical research.

Another important ontological resource is the Unified Medical Language System (UMLS) Metathesarus (Bodenreider, 2004) by the US National Library of Medicine (NLM), which is a large compilation of names, relationships, and associated information from a variety of biomedical ontologies (including SNOMED-CT and the NCI Thesaurus).

As the number and variety of free publicly available bio-ontologies continues to grow steadily, so does the number of initiatives aimed at indexing and classifying them for researchers. Current largest and most referenced repository of bio-ontologies is the Open Biomedical Ontologies (OBO) resource (Smith et al., 2007), supported by the NIH National Center for Biomedical Ontology (NCBO), and available through the BioPortal Website (National Center for Biomedical Ontology, 2010). At the moment of writing this paper, the OBO repository contains more than 60 well-structured and controlled bio-ontologies. These ontologies are being evolved and extended through the OBO Foundry collaborative endeavor, which establishes a set of principles for ontology development with the goal of creating a suite of reference ontologies in the biomedical domain (Smith et al., 2007).

In spite of all the related work that has been done, to the best of our knowledge, the KBS we present in this paper as well as the ontology that provides the underlying knowledge to the KBS, constitute an innovate contribution in the field of ICUs.

DEVELOPMENT OF A CARDIAC CARE ONTOLOGY

Doctors in ICUs constantly monitor and analyze the evolution of patients' vital signs and, depending on them, they decide the drugs that must be supplied to stabilize the patients.

However, there are several factors that interfere in the complex decision making process carried out by the medical experts (e.g. tiredness, stress, absence of an adequate reference protocol, etc.).

Because of this fact, doctors need a tool to support them in the decision making process, based on a unified and shared decision protocol. Latest technological advances can be very useful to solve this problem.

The development of such tool required the extraction and formal representation of the knowledge used by the experts to treat patients. This knowledge was extracted from the medical experts in the ICUs of the Meixoeiro Hospital (Vigo, Spain). Several meetings with these experts were held, where they explained all the knowledge they use to make decisions to stabilize patients with cardiopathies in real situations.

It is worth highlighting that the knowledge-extraction task was an extremely difficult and time-consuming process, mainly because of that medical experts do not have the enough time to carefully think all their actions in every possible real situation. Also, they use specialized terms that cannot be easily understood by knowledge engineers without experience in ICUs.

As a result of these initial meetings, a set of paper sketches and diagrams were obtained, reflecting the different potential decisions according to patients' status. This knowledge was formalized to allow that the proposed KBS could use it. During subsequent periodic meetings, knowledge was reviewed and improved.

Knowledge was formalized as an ontology, which has been called the Cardiac Care Ontology (CCO). This ontology contains a set of well-defined concepts frequently used by experts in the area of ICUs to treat patients with cardiopathies, a set of relationships among these concepts, and a set of inference rules describing the decision making process. To the best of our knowledge, this is the first time that knowledge to treat patients with cardiopathies in ICUs is formalized as an ontology. Some of the terms we needed were already contained in existing ontologies, and others did not exist yet. That is why we decided to create a new ontology which reuses some existing terms and defines the terms that did not exist in other ontologies..

The ontology building process was guided by Methontology (Fernandez, Gomez-Perez, & Juristo, 1997), a widely known methodology for ontology development. OBO Foundry principles were also followed.

Firstly, the set of concepts (also called *classes*), concept properties and relations that describe the specific domain were defined. An example of concept is *Mean Arterial Pressure*. This concept has a concept property *value*, which stores its particular value in a particular time instant. An example of relation is *is_a*, which would relate a child concept to its parent (or parents, in case of multiple inheritance).

According to the OBO Foundry rules, when creating an ontology it is recommended to reuse existing knowledge from other ontologies. There are three options to do this (Courtot et al., 2009):

- Generate and import several modules, which are subsets of external ontologies.
- Import whole ontologies.
- Create some new own terms and reference other ones, adding annotations to external ontologies.

In this work, we decided to build the ontology according to the third option, that is, import only concepts that are needed. The reason is that, after studying existing ontologies, we observed that the major part of the concepts we needed were already contained in other ontologies, so it just was necessary to create some new terms and reference existing ones, obeying the knowledge reusing principle.

The following stage is ontology conceptualization. It consists on listing and establishing taxonomical relations among ontology concepts. A *bottom-up* approach was followed, that is, start from the most specific classes (directly obtained from the experts) and group them in most general ones, using *is_a* relationships. Figure 1 shows all the classes (concepts) in the CCO ontology, as well as the relations between them. Each class name is

Figure 1. Classes and relationships in the Cardiac Care Ontology (CCO)

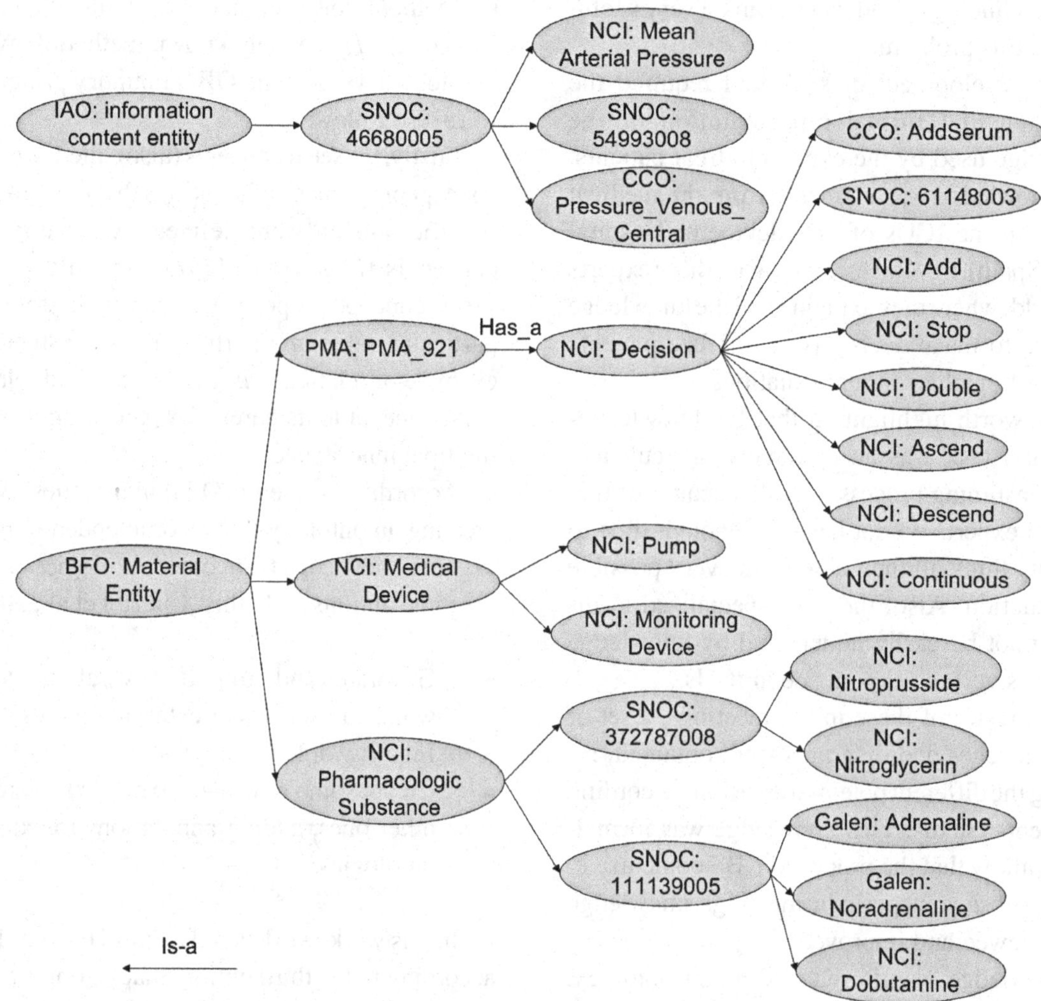

preceded by a prefix that indicates the ontology from which each concept was imported (e.g. the class "NCI: Pump" refers to the class "Pump" in the NCI Thesaurus ontology).

Finally, the ontology has been formally represented using the Ontology Web Language (OWL) (Lacy, 2005) and the Protégé Ontology Editor (Musen, 1989), which is the most popular tool for building ontologies. OWL is the recommended knowledge representation language for building ontologies. It provides computational reasoning capabilities, which can be used to infer new knowledge from existing information.

After defining and representing all the concepts and relationships in the domain, the following step was formalizing the set of inference rules that guide the decision making process, and that are essential to provide the system with the reasoning capabilities necessary to propose decisions in the ICU. As the language to represent the rules, we selected SWRL (Semantic Web Rule Language) (Horrocks, 2004), which is the rule representation language recommended by the Semantic Web community and allows to express rules on the basis of ontology concepts, so that it can be understood by people or systems all around the world.

Decision rules were extracted from the medical experts during the meetings carried out. The set of rules that have been identified is composed by 40 rules and 8 different decisions (or actions that the expert must take). These decisions are: (1) increase the dose that is being supplied by the infusion pump by a normal increase; (2) increase the dose by a double increase; (3) increase the dose by a quadruple increase; (4) decrease the dose; (5) add serums; (6) continue current treatment; (7) stop current treatment; (8) add a new infusion pump.

These rules were expressed on the basis of the concepts already defined in the CCO ontology and were written according the following pattern: *Access to ontology classes + Access to class properties + Check hypothesis → Decision.*

In the following, an example of rule is shown:

```
Mean_Arterial_Pressure(?x),
372787008(?y), 54993008(?z), low-
er_limit_value(?x, ?lowLimitPam),
lower_limit_value(?z, ?lowLimitIc),
upper_limit_value(?x, ?uppLimitPam),
upper_limit_value(?y, ?uppLimitVa-
sod), value(?x, ?valuePam), value(?y,
?valueVasod), value(?z, ?value-
Ic), <http://www.w3.org/2003/11/
swrlb#greaterThan>(?valuePam,
?uppLimitPam), <http://
www.w3.org/2003/11/
swrlb#lessThan>(?valueIc, ?lowLimit-
Ic), <http://www.w3.org/2003/11/
swrlb#lessThan>(?valueVasod, ?uppLim-
itVasod) -> Ascend(?y)
```

In this case, the system would check if the value of the class *Mean_Arterial_Pressure* is higher than its upper limit and if the value of the class *54993008* (Cardiac Index) is lower than its lower limit. In addition, it would check if the infusion pump is supplying a dose lower than its upper limit. If all these conditions are true, the system would suggest the experts to ascend the dose of the infusion pump of type *372787008* (Vasodilator pump) applying a standard increase.

DEVELOPMENT OF A KBS FOR AN INTENSIVE CARE ENVIRONMENT

After extracting all the required knowledge from experts, the following task is the development of a tool able to provide support to them on the basis of such knowledge. In the following, methods followed to develop a KBS to provide decision taking support in ICUs to treat patients with cardiopathies are presented.

The required KBS should fulfill the following requirements:

- The system must be easily integrable with other systems, that is, its input and output should follow interoperability standards.
- The system's decision making time must be reasonable and accepted by the medical experts from the hospital.
- The system must be independent of the inference engine selected to carry out the reasoning process.
- Knowledge used by the system must be implemented in such a way that it can be easily reused by other experts.

Figure 2 shows the main components of the KBS, which are described in the following:

- **Concept Identifier:** The system receives an XML file with all the information about the patient's vital signs and the considered infusion pumps. Then, this module is in charge of identifying all the ontological concepts (from the CCO ontology) contained in the system's input. It also identifies the concepts associated to the decision made by the system and represents it in an XML output file.

- **Core of ICU System:** This element controls the workflow of the KBS. It receives the input data, loads the knowledge and fact bases and provides the inference engine with all the information it need to make a decision. Finally, it transmits the decision to the Concept Identifier, which builds the system's output.
- **Jena API:** Popular Java application programming interface Java (McBride, 2001) that allows to carry out common operations with ontologies in an easy manner. The KBS uses this API to load the CCO ontology and create a set of instances of classes that represent the system's input. It is also used to guide the reasoning process.
- **Knowledge and Fact Bases:** The expert knowledge is stored in two independent structures: the knowledge base and the fact base. The knowledge base contains the ontology that has been developed (CCO ontology) and the inference rules. The fact base contains all the temporal data corresponding to the values monitored from the patient during a particular period of time. It consists on multiple instances of classes, created from the input data. All this knowledge (knowledge base and fact base) is used by the inference engine to make decisions.
- **Ontology Reasoner:** It is the inference engine and can be considered the key element of the KBS. On the basis of the knowledge and fact bases, this component is able to carry out a reasoning process and execute the specific rule that provides a decision as a result. We decided to use the popular Pellet Reasoner (Clark & Parsia, 2004) as the inference engine because it is able to work with knowledge represented using ontologies in OWL format and it is based on *tableau* algorithms (Schmidt-Schau & Smolka, 1991). These types of algorithms structure the rules as a tree and subsequently analyze each branch until reaching the branch that satisfies all the initial hypothesis. This branch is the one that provides the final decision.

Finally, it is important to point out that the *Jena API* and the *Pellet Reasoner* are generic, reusable components that have not been developed in this work. The KBS has been designed in such a way that this elements that could be replaced by other components able to do the same tasks without interfering with the system's functionality.

EVALUATION

When talking about evaluation of KBSs, it is necessary to distinguish between evaluation of the intrinsic properties of a KBS (technical evaluation) from the evaluation of its actual use and utility within a given organization (user's evaluation or assessment). Technical evaluation is divided in two components: verification and validation (Gómez-Pérez, 1994). In the following, we describe how the developed KBS was verified and validated. User's evaluation is suggested as a future work.

Verification refers to building the system correctly, that is, substantiating that the system correctly implements its specifications. This stage was carried out by the development team according to the specifications extracted from the medical experts.

Validation refers to building the right system. It consists on checking that the KBS performs the real-world tasks for which it was created. The system was validated using a set of real scenarios (test cases) defined by a medical expert, checking that the decisions provided by the system matched the decisions expected by the expert.

Preparing a high-quality set of test cases is essential to achieve an accurate and complete validation. This set must offer an adequate coverage of the domain (Churchill, 1979). A good criteria to construct the set of test cases is try that this set

Figure 2. Architecture of the knowledge based system

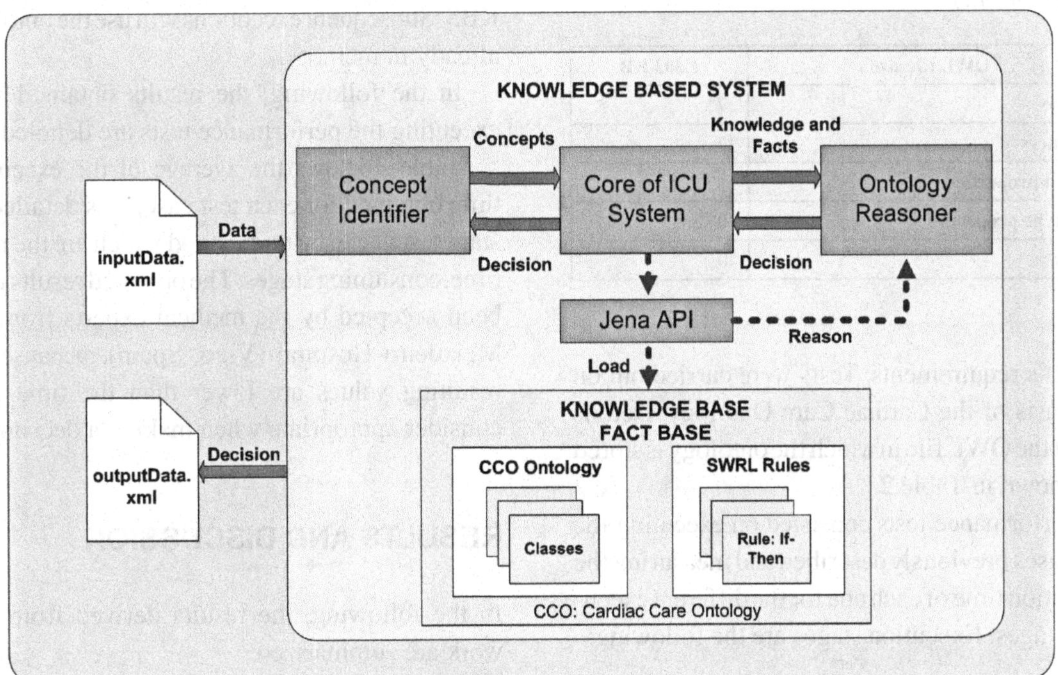

covers all the possible system outputs in a particular moment (García-Crespo, Rodríguez, Mencke, Gómez-Berbís, & Colomo-Palacios, 2009).

Having this into account, a set of test cases has been defined, covering all the possible decisions. As explained before, there are 8 different decisions, but it was necessary to define 11 test cases (because there are 3 decisions: "add pump", "decrease dose" and "increase dose" that can be applied both to vasodilator and inotropic drugs, so each one implies two different test cases). Each test case consists on a set of input parameters (values of patient's vital signs and associated infusion pumps) and an expected output (decision). The test cases were created on the basis of real data, collected at the ICU and inserted into system by means of a software application. An example of one of these test cases is shown in Table 1. It is important to emphasize that all the executed test cases have provided the decision expected by the expert.

Apart from this set of test cases, the validation procedure also included a set of performance tests. The ICU is an environment where it is crucial to make rapid decisions. These tests were addressed to evaluate if the system is fast enough to satisfy

Table 1. Example of test case

		Parameter (measurement unit)	Value	Lower limit	Upper limit
INPUT	Vital signs	Mean Arterial Pressure (mmHg)	20,0	60,0	90,0
		Cardiac Index (l/min/m²)	1,0	2,0	9,0
	Infusion pumps	Dobutamine pump (ml/h)	2,0	0,0	20,0
EXPECTED OUTPUT	Descend vasodilator	-	-	-	-

Table 2. Details about the Cardiac Care Ontology (OWL format)

OWL file size	1,303 KB
Classes	37
Instances	17
Object properties	5
Datatype properties	20
Rules	40

expert's requirements. Tests were carried out on the basis of the Cardiac Care Ontology. Details about the OWL file in which the ontology is stored are shown in Table 2.

Performance tests consisted on executing the test cases previously described and measuring the execution time of each one for the different execution stages. Execution stages are the following:

1. Concepts identification. Identify CCO ontology concepts in the system´s input.
2. Individuals creation. Create instances of CCO concepts.
3. Reasoning. Obtain a decision based on input data.
4. Concepts identification. Identify CCO ontology concepts in the system´s decision.

Before these stages, it is necessary a model preparation, that is, loading the ontology into memory in order to work with it. This stage just will be executed during the first execution of the KBS. Subsequent executions will use the ontology already in memory.

In the following, the results obtained after executing the performance tests are detailed.

Table 3 shows the average of the execution time obtained for each test case. It is detailed by stages, so it can be understood which are the most time-consuming stages. The obtained results have been accepted by the medical experts from the Meixoeiro Hospital (Vigo, Spain), because the resulting values are lower than the time they consider appropriate when making a decision.

RESULTS AND DISCUSSION

In the following, the results derived from this work are summarized:

On the one hand, a knowledge based system for a critical care environment has been developed. This system is able to make decisions to treat patients with cardiopathies in ICUs. It is based on expert knowledge, which has been formalized by using ontologies. It has been designed based on interoperability standards (XML) to make it easy its integration with other systems and it has been technically evaluated (verified and validated) to guarantee its quality. It has been successfully tested that the system is able to imitate the decisions provided by the medical experts. Also, its processing time has been approved by medical ex-

Table 3. Results of performance tests

Stage	Average of execution time for each test case (TC), detailed by stages (ms)											Average of execution time for each stage (ms)
	TC1	TC2	TC3	TC4	TC5	TC6	TC7	TC8	TC9	TC10	TC11	
A	13	7	22	8	12	9	11	18	12	11	5	**12**
B	16	8	16	10	15	10	12	9	8	5	8	**11**
C	861	734	723	735	719	718	687	718	719	734	719	**861**
D	12	16	21	9	14	12	2	4	3	9	18	**11**
Total	**902**	**765**	**782**	**762**	**760**	**749**	**712**	**749**	**742**	**759**	**750**	**895**

perts in the Meixoeiro Hospital, which guarantees that it can be used to support expert's decisions in real situations.

On the other hand, an ontology for the critical care domain has been developed. The name of this ontology is Cardiac Care Ontology (CCO) and it contains thirty seven concepts used by experts in ICUs when treating patients, as well as the relationships between these concepts and the set of inference rules written on SWRL language that guide the decision making process in ICUs. This ontology can be download in OWL format from http://tinyurl.com/2wdvjyv.

CONCLUSION AND FUTURE WORK

From this work, the following conclusions can be extracted:

Experts in critical care environments are very interested in the development of tools that provide them support in their decisions. This kind of systems make their daily work easier and help them to avoid mistakes in patients' treatment.

Ontologies are currently a widely known technology. However, knowledge based systems using ontologies as the proposed in this papers are still in an early stage. Another important conclusion is that, in spite of that ICUs are a critical environment in which patients' life depends directly on quality of doctor's decisions, terminologies and protocols in this field present a high heterogeneity. Due to this, applying ontologies to this area may be useful to overcome heterogeneity, facilitating knowledge understanding and reusing by specialists.

Finally, after discussing the obtained results and presenting the conclusions, some future work is outlined.

The following stage will be to integrate the presented KBS with a system prepared to interoperate with the devices connected to the patient in ICU (i.e. monitor and infusion pumps), so that the whole system can obtain input data in real time and then can be used by experts to improve patients' treatment.

In addition, we will try to publish the Cardiac Care Ontology on Bioportal (NCBO, 2005), which is a public online repository of ontologies and collaborative development environment, developed by the National Center for Biomedical Ontology of US. This will facilitate that the ontology can be freely reused and improved by other experts.

ACKNOWLEDGMENT

We thank funding support from the Carlos III Health Institute (grant FIS-PI061524) and the General Directorate of Scientific and Technologic Promotion of the Galician University System of the Xunta de Galicia (grant 2007/127). The work of Marcos Martínez is supported by a predoctoral grant from the University of A Coruña. We also thank to the Service of Anesthesia, Resuscitation and Intensives Cares of the Meixoeiro Hospital, headed by Gerardo Baños.

REFERENCES

Bodenreider, O. (2004). The Unified Medical Language System (UMLS): integrating biomedical terminology. *Nucleic Acids Research*, *32*, 267–270. doi:10.1093/nar/gkh061

Churchill, G. A. Jr. (1979). A paradigm for developing better measures of marketing constructs. *JMR, Journal of Marketing Research*, *16*(1), 64–73. doi:10.2307/3150876

Clark & Parsia. (2004). *Pellet: The Open Source OWL 2 Reasoner.* Retrieved June 27, 2010, from http://clarkparsia.com/pellet/

Courtot, M., Gibson, F., Lister, A., Malone, J., Schober, D., & Brinkman, R. (2009). *MIREOT: the Minimum Information to Reference an External Ontology Term*. Nature Proceedings.

Fernandez, M., Gomez-Perez, A., & Juristo, N. (1997). *Methontology: from ontological art towards ontological engineering*. Paper presented at the AAAI97 Spring Symposium Series on Ontological Engineering.

Frize, M., Solven, F. G., Stevenson, M., Nickerson, B., Buskard, T., & Taylor, K. (1995). Computer-assisted decision support systems for patient management in an intensive care unit. *Medinfo*, *8*, 1009.

García-Crespo, Á., Rodríguez, A., Mencke, M., Gómez-Berbís, J. M., & Colomo-Palacios, R. (2009). ODDIN: Ontology-driven differential diagnosis based on logical inference and probabilistic refinements. *Expert Systems with Applications*, *37*(3).

Golbeck, J., Fragoso, G., Hartel, F., Hendler, J., Oberthaler, J., & Parsia, B. (2003). The national cancer institute's thesaurus and ontology. *Journal of Web Semantics*, *1*(1), 75–80. doi:10.1016/j.websem.2003.07.007

Gómez-Pérez, A. (1994). *From Knowledge Based Systems to Knowledge Sharing Technology: Evaluation and Assessment*. Stanford, CA: Knowledge Systems Laboratory, Stanford University.

Gómez-Pérez, A., Fernández-López, M., & Corcho, O. (2004). *Ontological Engineering: with examples from the areas of Knowledge Management, e-Commerce and the Semantic Web*. Berlin: Springer Verlag.

Hanson, C. W., Weiss, Y., Frasch, F., Marshall, C., & Marshall, B. (1998). A fuzzy control strategy for postoperative volume resuscitation. *Anesthesiology-Philadelphia then Hagerstown*, *89*, 475-475.

Heindl, B., Schmidt, R., Schmid, G., Haller, M., Pfaller, P., & Gierl, L. (1997). A case-based consiliarius for therapy recommendation (ICONS): computer-based advice for calculated antibiotic therapy in intensive care medicine. *Computer Methods and Programs in Biomedicine*, *52*(2), 117–127. doi:10.1016/S0169-2607(96)01789-0

Horrocks, I., Patel-Schneider, P. F., Boley, H., Tabet, S., Grosof, B., & Dean, M. (2004). *SWRL: A Semantic Web Rule Language Combining OWL and RuleML*. Retrieved June 16, 2010, from http://www.daml.org/2004/04/swrl/rules-all.html

IHTSDO. (n.d.) *SNOMED-CT*. Retrieved April 19, 2010, from http://www.ihtsdo.org/snomed-ct/

Lacy, L. W. (2005). *OWL: Representing information using the web ontology language*. Bloomington, IN: Trafford Publishing.

Martin, J. F. (1994). Fuzzy control in anesthesia. *Journal of Clinical Monitoring and Computing*, *10*(2), 77–80. doi:10.1007/BF02886818

McBride, B. (2001). *Jena – A Semantic Web Framework for Java*. Retrieved June 20, 2010, from http://jena.sourceforge.net

Meier, R., Nieuwland, J., Zbinden, A. M., & Hacisalihzade, S. S. (1992). Fuzzy logic control of blood pressure during anesthesia. *IEEE Control Systems Magazine*, *12*(9), 12–17. doi:10.1109/37.168811

Miller, R. A., Pople, H. E., & Myers, J. D. (1982). Internist-1, an experimental computer-based diagnostic consultant for general internal medicine. *The New England Journal of Medicine*, *307*(8), 468. doi:10.1056/NEJM198208193070803

Musen, M. (1989). *Protégé*. Retrieved June 21, 2010, from http://protege.stanford.edu

National Center for Biomedical Ontology. (2010). *BioPortal Website*. Retrieved February 19, 2010, from http://bioportal.bioontology.org

NCBO. (2005). *NCBO Bioportal*. Retrieved June 16, 2010, from http://bioportal.bioontology.org

Schmidt-Schau, M., & Smolka, G. (1991). Attributive concept descriptions with complements. *Artificial Intelligence*, *48*(1), 1–26. doi:10.1016/0004-3702(91)90078-X

Shortliffe, E. H. (1976). *Computer-based medical consultations, MYCIN*. Amsterdam, The Netherlands: Elsevier.

Si, Y., Gotman, J., Pasupathy, A., Flanagan, D., Rosenblatt, B., & Gottesman, R. (1998). An expert system for EEG monitoring in the pediatric intensive care unit. *Electroencephalography and Clinical Neurophysiology*, *106*(6), 488–500. doi:10.1016/S0013-4694(97)00154-5

Smith, B. (2003). Ontology: philosophical and computational. In Floridi, L. (Ed.), *The blackwell guide to the philosophy of computing and information*. Oxford, UK: Blackwell Publishers.

Smith, B., Ashburner, M., Rosse, C., Bard, J., Bug, W., & Ceusters, W. (2007). The OBO Foundry: coordinated evolution of ontologies to support biomedical data integration. *Nature Biotechnology*, *25*(11), 1251–1255. doi:10.1038/nbt1346

Studer, R., Benjamins, V. R., & Fensel, D. (1998). Knowledge engineering: principles and methods. *Data & Knowledge Engineering*, *25*(1-2), 161–197. doi:10.1016/S0169-023X(97)00056-6

Ying, H., & Sheppard, L. C. (1994). Regulating mean arterial pressure in postsurgical cardiac patients. A fuzzy logic system to control administration of sodium nitroprusside. *IEEE Engineering in Medicine and Biology Magazine*, *13*(5), 671–677. doi:10.1109/51.334628

This work was previously published in the Journal of Information Technology Research, Volume 4, Issue 1, edited by Mehdi Khosrow-Pour, pp. 21-33, copyright 2011 by IGI Publishing (an imprint of IGI Global).

Chapter 3
Breast Cancer Diagnosis Using Optimized Attribute Division in Modular Neural Networks

Rahul Kala
Indian Institute of Information Technology & Management Gwalior, India

Anupam Shukla
Indian Institute of Information Technology & Management Gwalior, India

Ritu Tiwari
Indian Institute of Information Technology & Management Gwalior, India

ABSTRACT

The complexity of problems has led to a shift toward the use of modular neural networks in place of traditional neural networks. The number of inputs to neural networks must be kept within manageable limits to escape from the curse of dimensionality. Attribute division is a novel concept to reduce the problem dimensionality without losing information. In this paper, the authors use Genetic Algorithms to determine the optimal distribution of the parameters to the various modules of the modular neural network. The attribute set is divided into the various modules. Each module computes the output using its own list of attributes. The individual results are then integrated by an integrator. This framework is used for the diagnosis of breast cancer. Experimental results show that optimal distribution strategy exceeds the well-known methods for the diagnosis of the disease.

INTRODUCTION

There has been a vast amount of research in the use of neural networks for problem solving. The neural networks are extensively used for a variety of problems including biometrics, bioinformatics, robotics, and so forth (Shukla, Tiwari, & Kala, 2010a). The ease of modelling and use makes the neural networks good problem solving agents. The neural networks carry the task of machine learning. Here a training database is given to the system. This database is a source of large amount of information regarding patterns, trends, and knowledge about the problem domain. The task of the learning

DOI: 10.4018/978-1-4666-3625-5.ch003

algorithm is to extract this knowledge and use it as per the system knowledge representation. In the neural network this knowledge is in the form of weights between the various neurons and the individual neuron biases. A commonly used architecture of the neural networks is the Multi-Layer Perceptron. Here the various neurons are arranged in a layered manner, the first layer being the input layer and the last being output layer. The input and output layer may be separated by a number of hidden layers. Back Propagation Algorithm is commonly used for training the neural networks. This algorithm works over the gradient descent approach for fixing the various weights and biases. The back propagation algorithm is however likely to get struck at some local minima, considering the very complex nature of the search space over which it operates (Konar, 1999).

The weakness in the various soft computing paradigms has led to the emergence of the field of hybrid soft computing. Here we mix two similar or different paradigms so as to magnify the advantages of each of these and diminish their disadvantages. This coupling of individual systems may result in complementation of the limitations of the systems, for an overall enhanced performance. The evolutionary neural networks are commonly used hybrid systems, where neural modelling fuses with evolutionary computation to result in good problem solving agents.

The architecture of the neural networks is a major criterion that decides the system performance. The traditional neural networks use human expertise to design the optimal architecture, which may then be trained by the training algorithm. This however is a human-intensive task which may hence yield sub-optimal results. The training algorithm in turn may get struck at some local minima, with very poor exploration of the search space. The evolutionary algorithms are very strong optimizing agents that optimize the given problem in an iterative manner, and fix all the values of the parameters so as to optimize the final objective (Mitchell, 1999). Evolutionary neural networks hence use the optimization potential of the evolutionary algorithms for evolving the complete architecture of the neural networks, along with the weights and biases (Nolfi, Parisi, & Elman, 1990; Yao, 1999). Many times the evolutionary process may be assisted by a local search strategy like BPA or simulated annealing to search for local minima in the vicinity of the current location of the evolutionary individual in the search space (Yao, 1993).

Classification is a fundamental problem of study. The classification system is given a set of features as inputs, and is expected to return the class to which the input belongs as the output. The classifier is supposed to build the decision boundaries in the feature space that separates the various classes. Ideally the features must be such that the various instances of the classes have a high inter-class separation and low intra class separation. This makes it very easy for the classifier to construct decision boundaries across the various classes, separating them from each other. Every input attribute in this classifier is a dimension in the feature space. The additional dimensions usually make the task of construction of the decision boundary by the classifier easier. Two classes lying very close to each other may get separated by the addition of some dimension. This however may require more training instances, and would result in immense increase of computation time. The decision boundaries, across various dimensions, may become very complex and difficult to model and train (Shukla, Tiwari, & Kala, 2010b; Kala, Shukla, & Tiwari, 2009). Hence the number of inputs to the classifier needs to be limited in nature.

Modular Neural Network is advancement over the conventional neural networks. Here we try to introduce modularity into the structure and working of the neural network. This leads to the creation of multiple modules that together solve the entire problem. The results generated by the different modules are integrated using an integrator. Each of the modules of the modular neural network is a neural network that aids in the solution building. These networks can hence model very complex problems and give effective decisions in smaller times (Fu et al., 2001; Gruau, 1995; Jenkins & Yuhas, 1993). A related concept is ensemble, where the same problem is solved by a number of experts. Each of them computes the output to the problem which is then integrated using an integration mechanism (Dietterich, 2000; Hansen & Salamon, 2000; Jacobs, et al., 1991).

The immense increase in computation has led to automation in the diagnosis of disease. A considerable effort is being given for the use of computation and engineering principles in the field of medical sciences. This leads to an exciting field of Biomedical Engineering. The automatic diagnosis of disease helps in the early detection of diseases, and hence suitable preventive measures may be taken. These systems may be used to assist the doctors for decision making (Bronzino, 2006; Shukla & Tiwari, 2010a, 2010b). Breast Cancer is an emerging problem which has attracted the interests of a large number of researchers. A number of diagnostic techniques are built for the diagnosis of this disease. These systems take the various attributes observed in the patient and try to predict the presence or absence of disease (Breastcancer.org, 2010; Janghel et al., 2009, 2010; Shukla et al., 2009a, 2009b).

Attribute division is a novel concept where we use multiple neural networks for solving the problem in place of a single neural network. Each of the neural networks is given a part of the complete set of attributes. As a result every neural network or module gets a problem of limited complexity. Each network tries to train itself so as to make the best prediction as per the attributes given. Each network has a limited view of the feature space, comprising of limited dimensions. This is unlike the view of the complete feature space. Each network tries to make the best prediction as per its view. The predictions of all the neural networks are integrated using an integration mechanism, and the final decision is made. Here we try to integrate the views of the various modules, to optimally construct the global view of the complete feature space. As per the working guidelines of ensemble, it is known that the various modules must all give high performance, and must disagree as much as possible (Pedrajas & Fyne, 2008). These contradictory conditions, when held together solve the problem efficiently. The various modules give diverse view to the integrator which makes the final decision. The detail not seen by some module gets compensated by another module.

In this paper we propose a method of deciding the distribution of attributes among the various modules of the modular neural network. A large set of attributes is given as the input, using which a set of modules need to be made. An attribute can be given to any number of modules or to none at all. The ultimate aim is to make network that gives the best performance over the testing database. For this reason we penalize the network structure with large number of attributes which may give a higher training accuracy but a low generality. Diversity in attributes is further encouraged.

RELATED WORK

A considerable amount of work is done into the domain of evolutionary and modular neural networks in the past decade. A review of the various evolutionary approaches, operators, and other concepts behind the evolution of fixed and variable architecture neural networks can be found in the work of Yao (1999). The use of Evolutionary Programming for a behavioural evolution of the neural network is found in (Yao, 1997). Symbiotic Adaptive Neuro-Evolution (SANE) is a major development into the field (Moriarty, 1997; Moriarty & Miikkulainen, 1997). This algorithm uses the concept of co-evolution for carrying the task of optimization of the neural network architecture and parameters (Potter, 1997; Rosen & Belew, 1996; Stanley & Miikkulainen, 2004). Here it is assumed that the neural network consists of a single hidden layer. A hidden layer may be connected to any number of neurons from the input and output layer, which is optimized as the algorithm runs. The evolution takes place at two levels. The first level is the neuron level. Here the genetic individual is a neuron connected to some other neurons with some weights. The next level is the network level. Here the individual is a collection of neurons that makes the complete neural network. Pedrajas (2003) proposed a novel framework of using co-operative evolution or co-evolution for the task of modular neural network evolution. Their solution used two levels of evolution. The first level was the nodule level. Here the individuals corresponded to the individual neural networks. The next level was the network level which tried to figure out the best combination of nodules for an effective overall recognition. The fitness function used in this algorithm encouraged the individuals to possess a good overall fitness, as well as rewarded them for adding unique characteristics to the network. The results showed a better performance of these networks over the conventional approaches.

Fieldsend and Singh (2005) used Multi-objective optimization to evaluate the evolutionary neural network for a set of error functions into a pareto front. The use of multiple error functions enabled strong check against generalization loss or over-fitting. This neural network was further extended to use a validation data set to avoid over-fitting, and booststrapping to make use of a number of small data sets for training and validation. The net decision was made using the training on validation errors in all these sets. Jung and Reggia (2006) present another interesting approach where the users are provided with a language specification they can use to tell the system about the general architecture of the neural network. The architectural parameters to be optimized may be explicitly specified. The system carries the rest of the evolution as per the user set architectural specifications. In this manner the human expertise and evolutionary optimizing potential interact at user front for the generation of optimal neural network. Rivera *et al.* (2007) used co-operative evolution for the task of generation of Radial Basis Function network. Each individual here was a neuron of this network or a radial basis function. The impact of the neuron was measured against its performance, error and overlapping with the other neurons. The final evaluation was done using a Fuzzy Rule Based system. This enabled the neurons to attain diverse roles, which collectively made an effective network. Cho and Shimohara (1998) used Genetic Programming for the generation of Modular Neural Network. Here the chromosome was framed to model the architecture and parameters of the various modules of the modular neural network. Different types of modules were used to performed different functions.

Boosting is another novel concept applied for effective machine learning. Here we assign different weights to the different data instances, which denote their ease of being learned. The more difficult instances have a greater impact on the final network error. These weights are updated as per the system readings of errors (Freund, 1995; Freund & Schapire, 1996). Pedrajas (2009) presents an interesting application to boosting. In his approach multiple classifiers are made. Computation of the boosting weights takes place as the system learns. The projection of input space to the hidden layer space (outputs of the hidden layer) is passed as inputs to next classifier.

Division of the entire input set into multiple input sets for easier and better recognition is a commonly used task. A good use of modular neural network can be found in the work of Melon and Castilo (2005). Here the authors carried out the task of multi-modal biometric fusion. Each biometric modality was handled separately by a modular neural network, which were all integrated using fuzzy integration. Each of the biometric identification system was a modular neural network consisting of one module for each part of the biometric modality. Each modality input was broken into three parts, each part being performed by a different neural network. The parts were also integrated using fuzzy integration. A similar concept was applied by Kala et al. (2010) for bi-modal biometric recognition. Here the entire pool of attribute set from both modalities was distributed into four recognition neural networks. All outputs were integrated using probabilistic sum technique.

METHODOLOGY

The basic motive behind the approach is to devise an optimal distribution of the attributes of the problem, into the classifiers. We assume here that the number of classifiers is already fixed. Let there be *n* classifiers into the system. Let the complete attribute set be given by $<p_1, p_2, p_3, ...p_N>$. Here *N* is the total number of attributes in the problem of consideration. It is assumed that any classifier may have any number of attributes. Further it is assumed that any attribute may be given to any number of classifiers. Once a classifier gets the stated attributes, it trains itself with the training data set. Training algorithm may be specific to the classifier. We propose the use of Genetic Algorithm for carrying out this distribution. The Genetic Algorithm Framework is discussed. The construction and training of the neural network is then presented. The fitness evaluation is also given.

Genetic Algorithm

The first task in the implementation of the genetic algorithm is the individual representation technique. The individual in our case consists of *n* number of vectors $< V_1, V_2, V_3, V_4, ... V_n>$. Each vector V_i contains the set of attributes that are given to classifier *i*. Each set is a collection of integers denoting the attributes it is assigned. It is natural that the number of attributes may vary from 1 to *N*. Further we assume that the various neural networks used would have a single hidden layer. This is a valid assumption considering the fact that most problems give best results when trained and tested with a small number of neurons and a single hidden layer. The number of neurons in the neural network for every module constitutes the structure of the module or neural network. Hence every vector is appended with the number of neurons present in the module. This can be any integer between 1 and neu_{max}. neu_{max} is the maximum allowable number of neurons that is specified by the user. Based on the same mechanism an initial population is designated. Random attribute numbers are assigned to the various vectors. The number of attributes in the vectors is itself determined randomly. The number of neurons of various modules is also assigned randomly.

The next task is the use of genetic operators to aid in the evolutionary process. For this we use a variety of genetic operators. These are (i) crossover, (ii) mutation, (iii) elite, (iv) add attribute, (v) delete attribute, (vi) mutate number of neurons, and (viii) repair.

The crossover operator uses two parents to generate two children. The crossover is carried for each of the *n* attribute sets, the results are then combined to get the final genetic individual. Let the two attribute sets be V^x_j and V^y_j. Here *x* and *y* are the two parents, and *j* is the attribute set. Let n^x_j and n^y_j be the number of attributes in these sets. The major problem in crossover is the difference in the number of attributes in each of the attribute sets. For this we first make a pool of distinct attributes from both these attribute sets V^x_j and V^y_j. The number of attributes in the two children are kept as $ceil((n^x_j \text{ and } n^y_j)/2)$ and $floor((n^x_j \text{ and } n^y_j)/2)$. Where *ceil(.)* is the greatest integer greater than function, and *floor(.)* is the greatest integer less than function. These many attributes are randomly given to the two children using a scattered crossover technique. Every attribute from this attribute set is given to the first parent with a probability of 0.5, and to the other parent with a probability of 0.5. The left spaces in the children are filled with random attributes, provided they are not currently in the possession of the children. The number of neurons for the children per module is changed using the same phenomenon. If neu^x_j and

neu^y_j denote the number of neurons of module j of the parents x and y, the number of neurons in children is given by $ceil((neu^x_j \text{ and } neu^y_j)/2)$ and $floor((neu^x_j \text{ and } neu^y_j)/2)$.

The mutation operator simply replaces an attribute randomly with a new attribute. The replacement is governed by the mutation rate that follows a normal distribution. Elite passes the best individual of a generation directly to the next generation. Add attribute selects an attribute set of the individual randomly. It then adds a new distinct attribute to this attribute set. The delete attribute genetic operator performs in a similar manner. It however deletes an attribute from the available list. The mutate neurons selects a module randomly and changes the number of neurons in it. The change follows a normal distribution.

The repair operator checks the individuals and removes any anomalies in them. One of the constraints in the individuals is that the various vectors cannot contain the same attribute more than once. This is natural since multiple occurrence of an input attribute would not be useful for the neural network training. Hence the repeated attributes are deleted by this operator. Further the various attributes are stored in a sorted order in their attribute sets. The sorting of the attributes is done by this operator. The number of neurons must also be within the designated limits. Every attribute also needs to be within the limited values. The number of attributes must be greater between 1 to N.

Modular Neural Network

The other major task is the formulation of modular neural network using the specifications of the genetic individual. This would enable the computation of the fitness of the genetic individual as per previous discussions. Each of the modules of the modular neural network is a multi-layer perceptron that is trained using back propagation algorithm. Each neural network gets the designated attributes as represented by the genetic individual. The network is supposed to output the diagnosis of the disease.

Each individual of the genetic algorithm is decoded to make the designated number of modules. Each module further has designated number of neurons. Each network is trained using back propagation algorithm. Only the selected attributes are given to the network for training, out of all the available attributes. Figure 1 shows the general evolutionary and neural architecture used in the algorithm. It may be easily seen from figure that the entire algorithm is based on evolutionary principles where Genetic Algorithms carry optimization. Each individual, for fitness computation, is decoded which results in many modules, each being a neural network. All modules are trained by the specific attributes represented by the individual from training database. Trained modules are then used for performance evaluation over training database. Integration of results for various modules is done by the integrator. Figure 2 specifically stresses upon the mechanism of division of attributes and the further processing with the neural network. The entire set of attributes available in the problem is divided into a set of modules. Each attribute may be given to none, one, or more than one module. Each module is a neural network that takes the selected attributes as input and produces a probability set as output. The integrator sums the probabilities recorded by various modules and declares the class with maximum probability as the winning class.

Fitness Evaluation

The last task associated with the use of genetic algorithm is to devise a fitness function. The fitness function is an evaluation of the performance of the individual. Here we try to simultaneously optimize four objectives. These are (i) Diagnostic Performance (DP), (ii) Left Attributes (LA), (iii) Average Module Size (AMS), and (iv) Difference

Figure 1. The general algorithm framework

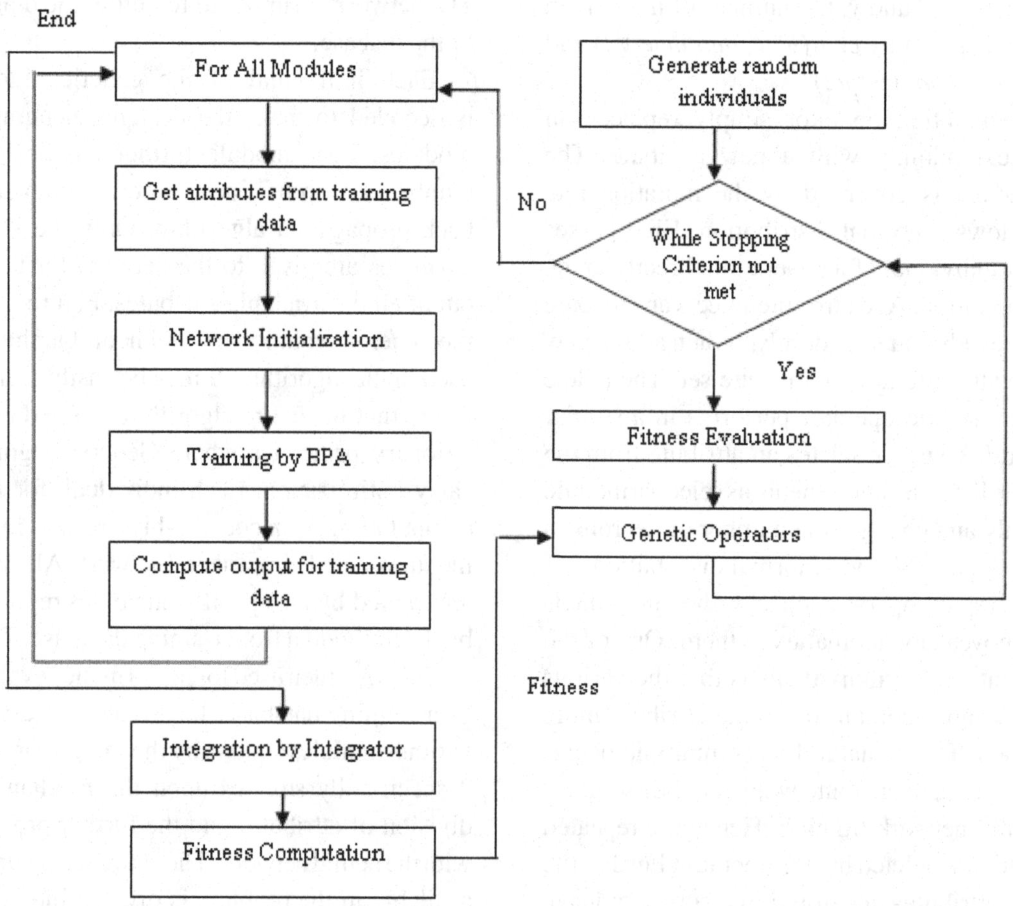

in attributes within modules (DA). Diagnostic performance is a measure of the number of cases correctly diagnosed by the system and is measured as given in Equation (1)

DP = Correctly Diagnosed Cases/Total Number of Cases (1)

This is a number between 0 and 1.

The Left Attributes (LA) measures the total number of attributes that did not go to any of the modules. This means that the resultant system is deprived of these attributes, which may lead to sub-optimal performance. We hence try to make this number as small as possible. LA is normalized to lie between 0 and 1 by dividing by the total number of attributes *N*.

Average Module Size (AMS) is measured as given by Equation (2). This is also normalized to lie between 0 and 1 by division by *N*.

$$AMS = \frac{\sum_{i=1}^{n} n_i}{n} \quad (2)$$

Here n_i is the number of attributes in module *i*. *n* is the total number of modules.

The difference in number of attributes (DA) is an indication of the variance in the size of the various modules. We keep this number as small as possible, so that the different modules are similar

Figure 2. Attribute division in the modules

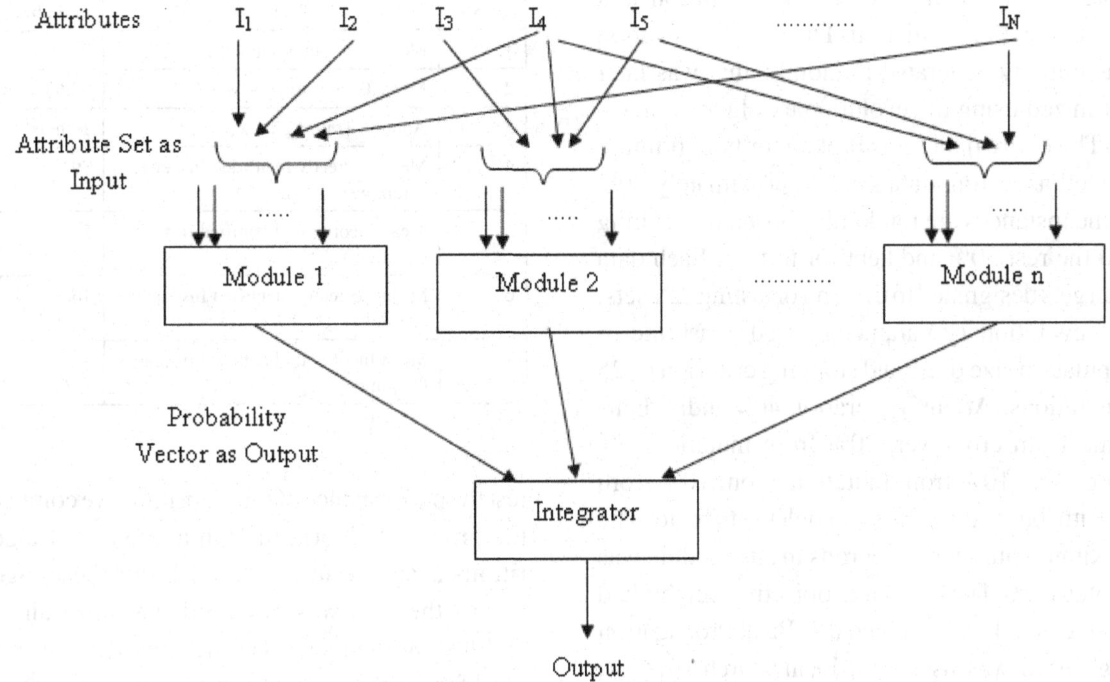

in size and action. DA is measured as given in Equation (3).

$$DA = \sum_{i=1}^{n} \sum_{j=1,j>i}^{n} \left| n_i - n_j \right| \quad (3)$$

The fitness function is a weighted sum of all these objectives given by Equation (4). The signs denote maximization or minimization.

$$Fit = -\alpha_1 DP + \alpha_2 LA + \alpha_3 AMS + \alpha_4 DA \quad (4)$$

Here α_1, α_2, α_3, and α_4 are the multi-objective optimization constants.

RESULTS

The discussed model was applied over the problem of Breast Cancer diagnosis. Here we are given a set of attributes and these needs to be classified into malignant or benign. We take the breast cancer data from the UCI Machine Learning Repository for this purpose (Wolberg, Mangasarian, & Aha, 1992). This database consists of 30 real valued inputs. These correspond to the following features for each cell nucleus: radius (mean of distances from center to points on the perimeter), texture (standard deviation of gray-scale values), perimeter, area, smoothness (local variation in radius lengths), compactness (perimeter^2/area - 1.0), concavity (severity of concave portions of the contour), concave points (number of concave portions of the contour), symmetry, fractal dimension ("coastline approximation" - 1). The entire data set consists of a total of 357 benign and 212 malignant cases, totaling to 569 instances in the database.

JAVA was used as the simulation platform. The evolutionary algorithm used for the same was coded in the same platform. Back Propagation algorithm was taken as a library from (Cole, 2009). The various modules of evolutionary algorithm, individual, fitness evaluation, data manager, and neural networks were made and integrated. The system had three modules that were kept constant throughout the simulation. The initial population was initially generated randomly, that was later optimized using the evolutionary algorithm.

The entire data set is broken for both training as well as testing data sets. Approximately 70% of the instances are randomly chosen for training and the rest 30% and kept for testing. Each data item gets designated to training or testing datasets. The evolutionary parameters used constitute of population size of 25 and stopping criterion of 25 generations. At any generation 40% individuals came from crossover, 20% from mutation, 5% from elite, 10% from mutate neuron, 10% from add attribute, and 10% from delete attribute. The maximum number of neurons in any module was limited to 20. The four multi-objective weights had a value of 0.4, 0.4, 0.1, and 0.1. Back Propagation Algorithm was used as a local search strategy. Learning rate was fixed to 0.1, and momentum was kept as 0.7. The training was carried for 1000 generations. On training and testing the algorithm gave an accuracy of 98.63% for the testing data and 98.10%for the testing data. The algorithm took approximately 10 hours for the evolution. The results of the algorithm are summarized in Table 1.

We further study the convergence of the algorithm by plotting the fitness of the best individual of the population along with time. This is given in Figure 3. The figure clearly shows a large improvement in the performance value in the initial few generations. This improvement however becomes small as the generations increase. Towards the later stages, the algorithm converges to the optimal value. It may be noted that the database taken had limited instances, and hence the training accuracy can only increase by some discrete amounts, corresponding to the increase in accuracy due to a single data instance.

The high accuracies achieved in the use of proposed algorithm encourage a high usage of the algorithm for medical diagnosis. In order to fully

Table 1. Analysis of the results of the algorithm

S. No.	Property	Value
1.	Mean Training Accuracy	98.10%
2.	Mean Testing Accuracy	98.63%
3.	Approx. Training Time	10 hours
4.	Mean Correctly Identified Instances (Training)	391
5.	Mean Incorrectly Identified Instances (Training)	7
6.	Mean Correctly Identified Instances (Testing)	168
7.	Mean Incorrectly Identified Instances (Testing)	3

test the performance of the algorithm, we compare the proposed algorithm with a number of algorithms available in literature. In all these algorithms the data was broken down into training and testing data sets. The training data set was used for network tuning the network parameters. The testing dataset was used for the testing purposes.

The first method applied was the conventional neural network model Multi-Layer Perceptron trained with Back Propagation Algorithm. Here MATLAB was used for the simulation purposes. The network had 1 hidden layer with 18 neurons. Learning rate was fixed to be 0.05. Momentum was fixed to 0.7. The network was trained for 3500 epochs. The resultant network gave a training accuracy of 97.01% and a testing accuracy of 94.61%.

The other model trained was a fixed architecture evolutionary neural network. Here the neural network architecture was the same as discussed in the previous approach. The weights and biases were optimized using genetic algorithm. The genetic algorithm consisted of 10 individuals, each trained in 15 generations. The various weights and biases could vary from -2 to 2. Rank based scaling with stochastic uniform selection was used. Elite count was kept as 2. Crossover rate was 0.8. Gaussian mutation with a spread and scale of 1 each was used. The genetic algorithm used back propaga-

Figure 3. Performance of best networks against generations

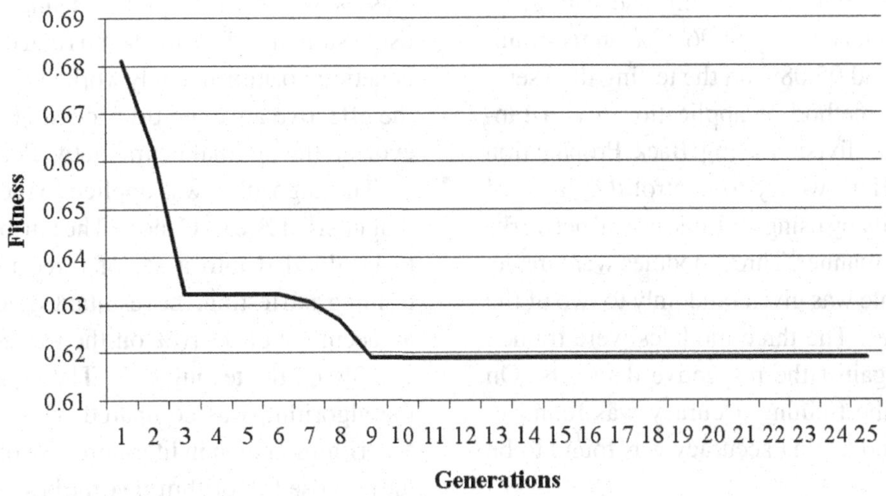

tion algorithm as the local search strategy. The BPA had a learning rate of 0.05, and momentum of 1. Training was carried for 30 epochs. The algorithm had a training accuracy of 93.92% and testing accuracy of 95.40%.

The next algorithm we use to test the accuracy with is the variable architecture Evolutionary Neural Network. Here we follow a connectionist approach. The neural network is assumed to be consisting of one hidden layer. In place of an all-connected architecture, we assume that only some connections are allowed from the input layer to hidden layer and hidden layer to output layer. The information regarding the connections is stored into the genetic individual. The various parameters used in this approach are the same as the ones used in the fixed architecture neural network. Extra connections were penalized by assigning a penalty of 0.01 per connection. The hidden layer could have a maximum of 30 neurons. The accuracy in this case was 97.01% for the training data and 95.21% for testing data.

The next approach tried to test the accuracy of the algorithm was ensemble. Here we made 3 experts, each being a neural network with similar architecture as discussed in the previous approaches. These three neural networks gave their probability vectors corresponding to the various classes as outputs. A probabilistic sum of these vectors was taken, to get the final output vector. The winning class was determined from this vector. On training and testing, the system gave an accuracy of 97.98% on the training data and 95.95% on the testing data.

The other method applied for testing the accuracy of the algorithm was modular neural network, where the complete feature space was partitioned into three modules. Each of these modules was given a separate neural network for training. The

Table 2. Comparisons between various algorithms

S. No.	Algorithm	Training Accuracy	Testing Accuracy
1.	Proposed Algorithm	98.10%	98.63%
2.	MLP with BPA	97.01%	94.61%
3.	Fixed Architecture Evolutionary ANN	93.92%	95.40%
4.	Variable Architecture Evolutionary ANN	97.01%	95.21%
5.	Ensemble	97.98%	95.95%
6.	Feature Space Modular ANN	96.49%	95.08%
7.	Attribute Modular ANN	97.19%	96.03%

architecture of the neural network was the same as discussed earlier. After training and testing, the system gave an accuracy of 96.49% on the training data set and 95.08% on the testing data set.

The next method of application was a random attribute division using Back Propagation Algorithm. Here we try to control the curse of dimensionality by using multiple neural networks in a modular manner. Three modules were made. Every attribute was given randomly to two of the three modules. The three modules were trained and tested against the respective data sets. On simulation, the training accuracy was found to be 97.19% and testing accuracy was found to be 96.03%.

The various algorithm results have been summarized in Table 2.

From Table 2, it is clear that the proposed algorithm gave the best generalization and testing accuracy as compared to all the methods presented. Hence using this approach we have been successful in removing the adverse effects of curse of dimensionality in an effective manner using an evolutionary approach. The high recognition score illustrates an effective diagnostic system.

CONCLUSION

Curse of dimensionality is a major problem that the neural networks face. Modularity is a welcome step to remove the curse of dimensionality problem with the least loss of information. One of the primary ways of implementation of modularity is by attribute division. In this paper we used genetic algorithms for devising an effective division of attributes amongst the various modules of the modular neural network. The system so formed tried to make as effective modules as possible, with limited size and limited number of attributes. The overall modular neural network used these modules for the decision making. Each module was a multi-layer perceptron which was trained using back propagation algorithm. The modules returned the probabilities of the occurrence of the various classes, which was combined using an integrator using sum rule. This made the final decision. The genetic algorithm not only worked for formulating the effective attribute division strategy, but also evolved the optimal neural network architecture.

This algorithm was applied to the problem of diagnosis of Breast Cancer. The attributes needed to be divided into a set of three modules. On training and testing, the resultant system recorded an accuracy of 98.10% on the training data and 98.63% on the testing data. The performance of the algorithm was compared with a number of algorithms known in literature. We observed that the proposed algorithm gave the best performance in terms of both the training and testing data. This shows the high diagnostic capability of the network. Hence we have been able to remove the problem of dimensionality from the conventional neural network to a good extent by working over effective modularity.

The present algorithm is used over a single database from biomedical engineering. The algorithm may be further extended to more databases from diverse applications. This would enable use of the algorithm in different fields. Time complexity is another major problem associated with the algorithm. Effective models may be built to control execution time. This would enable an even better optimization. The approach is primarily used using the genetic algorithm with multi-layer perceptron model. More combinations of neural and genetic models may be tried for better perforce. All this may be done in future.

REFERENCES

Breastcencer.org. (2010). *Understanding the Breast Cancer*. Retrieved February 1, 2010, from http://www.breastcancer.org

Bronzino, J. D. (2006). *Biomedical Engineering Fundamentals*. Boca Raton, FL: CRC Press.

Cho, S. B., & Shimohara, K. (1998). Evolutionary Learning of Modular Neural Networks with Genetic Programming. *Applied Intelligence*, *9*, 191–200. doi:10.1023/A:1008388118869

Cole, G. (2009). *Backprop1*. Retrieved February 1, 2010, from http://sourceforge.net/projects/backprop1

Dietterich, T. (2000). Ensemble methods in machine learning. In J. Kittler & F. Roli (Eds.), *Multiple Classier Systems,* Cagliari, Italy (LNCS 5519, pp. 1-15).

Fieldsend, J. E., & Singh, S. (2005). Pareto Evolutionary Neural Networks. *IEEE Transactions on Neural Networks*, *16*(2), 338–354. doi:10.1109/TNN.2004.841794

Freund, Y. (1995). Boosting a weak learning algorithm by majority. *Information and Computation*, *121*, 256–285. doi:10.1006/inco.1995.1136

Freund, Y., & Schapire, R. E. (1996). Experiments with a New Boosting Algorithm. In *Proceedings of the Thirteenth International Conference on Machine Learning,* Bari, Italy (pp. 148-156). San Francisco: Morgan Kaufmann.

Fu, H. C., Lee, Y. P., Chiang, C. C., & Pao, H. T. (2001). Divide-and-Conquer Learning and Modular Perceptron Networks. *IEEE Transactions on Neural Networks*, *12*(2), 250–263. doi:10.1109/72.914522

Gruau, F. (1995). Automatic definition of modular neural networks. *Adaptive Behavior*, *3*(2), 151–183. doi:10.1177/105971239400300202

Hansen, L. K., & Salamon, P. (2000). Neural network ensembles. *IEEE Transactions on Pattern Analysis and Machine Intelligence*, *12*(10), 993–1001. doi:10.1109/34.58871

Jacobs, R. A., Jordan, M. I., Nowlan, S. J., & Hinton, G. E. (1991). Adaptive mixtures of local experts. *Neural Computation*, *3*, 79–87. doi:10.1162/neco.1991.3.1.79

Janghel, R. R., Shukla, A., & Tiwari, R. (2010). Decision Support system for fetal delivery using Soft Computing Techniques. In *Proceedings of the Fourth International Conference on Computer Sciences and Convergence Information Technology,* Seoul, Korea (pp. 1514-1519). Washington, DC: IEEE.

Janghel, R. R., Shukla, A., Tiwari, R., & Tiwari, P. (2009). Clinical Decision support system for fetal Delivery using Artificial Neural Network. In *Proceedings of the 2009 International Conference on New Trends in Information and Service Science,* Gyeongju, Korea (pp. 1070-1075). Washington, DC: IEEE.

Jenkins, R., & Yuhas, B. (1993). A simplified neural network solution through problem decomposition: The case of the truck backer-upper. *IEEE Transactions on Neural Networks*, *4*(4), 718–722. doi:10.1109/72.238326

Jung, J. Y., & Reggia, J. A. (2006). Evolutionary Design of Neural Network Architectures Using a Descriptive Encoding Language. *IEEE Transactions on Evolutionary Computation*, *10*(6), 676–688. doi:10.1109/TEVC.2006.872346

Kala, R., Shukla, A., & Tiwari, R. (2009). Fuzzy Neuro Systems for Machine Learning for Large Data Sets. In *Proceedings of the IEEE International Advance Computing Conference, IACC '09,* Patiala, India (pp. 541-545). Washington, DC: IEEE.

Kala, R., Shukla, A., & Tiwari, R. (2010a). Clustering Based Hierarchical Genetic Algorithm for Complex Fitness Landscapes. *International Journal of Intelligent Systems Technologies and Applications*, *9*(2), 185–205. doi:10.1504/IJISTA.2010.034320

Kala, R., Shukla, A., & Tiwari, R. (2010b). Handling Large Medical Data Sets for Disease Detection. In Shukla, A., & Tiwari, R. (Eds.), *Biomedical Engineering and Information Systems: Technologies, Tools and Applications*. Hershey, PA: IGI Global.

Kala, R., Vazirani, H., Shukla, A., & Tiwari, R. (2010). Fusion of Speech and Face by Enhanced Modular Neural Network. In *Proceedings of the Springer International Conference on Information Systems, Technology and Management, ICISTM 2010,* Bankok, Thailand (pp. 363-372). Washington, DC: IEEE.

Konar, A. (1999). *Artificial Intelligence and Soft Computing: Behavioral and Cognitive Modeling of the Human Brain*. Boca Raton, FL: CRC Press. doi:10.1201/9781420049138

Melin, P., & Castilo, O. (2005). *Hybrid Intelligent Systems for Pattern Recognition Using Soft Computing*. Berlin: Springer.

Mitchell, M. (1999). *An Introduction to Genetic Algorithms*. Cambridge, MA: MIT Press.

Moriarty, D. E. (1997). *Symbiotic Evolution of NeuralNetworks in SequentialDecision Tasks*. Unpublished doctoral dissertation, Department of Computer Science, University of Texas, Austin, TX.

Moriarty, D. E., & Miikkulainen, R. (1997). Forming neural networks through efficient and adaptive coevolution. *Evolutionary Computation*, *5*(4), 373–399. doi:10.1162/evco.1997.5.4.373

Nolfi, S., Elman, J. L., & Parisi, D. (1990). *Learning and Evolution in Neural Networks* (CRL Tech. Rep. 9019). La Jolla, CA: University of California at San Diego.

Pedrajas, N. G. (2003). COVNET: A Cooperative Coevolutionary Model for Evolving Artificial Neural Networks. *IEEE Transactions on Neural Networks*, *14*(3), 575–596. doi:10.1109/TNN.2003.810618

Pedrajas, N. G. (2009). Supervised projection approach for boosting classifiers. *Pattern Recognition*, *42*, 1742–1760. doi:10.1016/j.patcog.2008.12.023

Pedrajas, N. G., & Fyne, C. (2008). Construction of classifier ensembles by means of artificial immune systems. *Journal ofHeuristics*, *14*, 285–310. doi:10.1007/s10732-007-9036-0

Potter, M. A. (1997). *The design and analysis of a computational model of cooperative coevolution*. Unpublished doctoral dissertation, George Mason University, Fairfax, VA.

Rivera, A. J., Rojas, I., Ortega, J., & del Jesus, M. J. (2007). Anew hybrid methodology for cooperative-coevolutionary optimization of radial basis function networks. *Soft Computing*, *11*, 655–668. doi:10.1007/s00500-006-0128-9

Rosin, C., & Belew, R. (1996). New Methods for Competitive Coevolution. *Evolutionary Computation*, *5*, 1–29. doi:10.1162/evco.1997.5.1.1

Shukla, A., & Tiwari, R. (Eds.). (2010a). *Intelligent Medical technologies and Biomedical Engineering: Tools and Applications*. Hershey, PA: IGI Global Publishers.

Shukla, A., & Tiwari, R. (Eds.). (2010b). *Biomedical Engineering and Information Systems: Technologies, Tools and Applications*. Hershey, PA: IGI Global Publishers.

Shukla, A., Tiwari, R., & Kala, R. (2010a). *Real Life Applications of Soft Computing*. Boca Raton, FL: CRC Press. doi:10.1201/EBK1439822876

Shukla, A., Tiwari, R., & Kala, R. (2010b). *Towards Hybrid and Adaptive Computing: A Perspective*. Berlin: Springer.

Shukla, A., Tiwari, R., & Kaur, P. (2009). Intelligent System for the Diagnosis of Epilepsy. In *Proceedings of the IEEE World Congress on Computer Science and Information Engineering,* Los Angeles, CA (pp. 755-758). Washington, DC: IEEE.

Shukla, A., Tiwari, R., Kaur, P., & Janghel, R. R. (2009). Diagnosis of Thyroid Disorders using Artificial Neural Networks. In *Proceedings of the IEEE International Advanced Computing Conference,* Patiala, India (pp. 1016-1020). Washington, DC: IEEE.

Stanley, K. O., & Miikkulainen, R. (2004). Competitive Coevolution through Evolutionary Complexification. *Journal of Artificial Intelligence Research, 21*, 63–100.

Wolberg, W. H., Mangasarian, O. L., & Aha, D. W. (1992). *UCI Machine Learning Repository.* Retrieved from http://www.ics.uci.edu/~mlearn/MLRepository.html

Yao, X. (1993). A review of evolutionary artificial neural networks. *International Journal of Intelligent Systems, 8*(4), 539–567. doi:10.1002/int.4550080406

Yao, X. (1997). A New Evolutionary System for Evolving Artificial Neural Networks. *IEEE Transactions on Neural Networks, 8*(3), 694–713. doi:10.1109/72.572107

Yao, X. (1999). Evolving Artificial Neural Networks. *Proceedings of the IEEE, 87*(9), 1423–1447. doi:10.1109/5.784219

This work was previously published in the Journal of Information Technology Research, Volume 4, Issue 1, edited by Mehdi Khosrow-Pour, pp. 34-47, copyright 2011 by IGI Publishing (an imprint of IGI Global).

Chapter 4
DISMON:
Using Social Web and Semantic Technologies to Monitor Diseases in Limited Environments

Ángel Lagares-Lemos
Universidad Carlos III de Madrid, Spain

Miguel Lagares-Lemos
Universidad Carlos III de Madrid, Spain

Ricardo Colomo-Palacios
Universidad Carlos III de Madrid, Spain

Ángel García-Crespo
Universidad Carlos III de Madrid, Spain

Juan M. Gómez-Berbís
Universidad Carlos III de Madrid, Spain

ABSTRACT

Information technology and, more precisely, the internet represent challenges and opportunities for medicine. Technology-driven medicine has changed how practitioners perform their roles in and medical information systems have recently gained momentum as a proof-of-concept of the efficiency of new support-oriented technologies. Emerging applications combine sharing information with a social dimension. This paper presents DISMON (Disease Monitor), a system based on Semantic Technologies and Social Web (SW) to improve patient care for medical diagnosis in limited environments, namely, organizations. DISMON combines Web 2.0 capacities and SW to provide semantic descriptions of clinical symptoms, thereby facilitating diagnosis and helping to foresee diseases, giving useful information to the company and its employees to increase efficiency by means of the prevention of injuries and illnesses, resulting in a safety environment for workers.

DOI: 10.4018/978-1-4666-3625-5.ch004

INTRODUCTION

Nonfatal workplace injuries and illnesses among private industry employers in 2008 occurred at a rate of 3.9 cases per 100 equivalent full-time workers (U.S. Bureau of Labor Statistics, 2009). Due to these sick leaves the companies are forced to hire new workers in order to fill the temporary vacancies, often employing the new members of the staff in short time-frames. Thus, it drives the company to carry out a quick selection process which entails a bad performance of this task and finally it can conclude with a no proper decision. In addition in most of the cases the incorporation of the new employees comprises an in-service training period or/and an adaptation period, therefore an efficiency loss. On the other, hand if the company does not hire new workers, it presents a worse scenario. Hence all these issues can imply loss of money by the company; unsatisfied clients; loss of partners; and unhappy stakeholders.

This paper proposes an automatic system for monitoring and helping to foresee the diseases using the social web and semantic technologies, giving useful information to the company and its employees in order to increase the efficiency by means of the prevention of injuries and illnesses, resulting in a safety environment for the workers. The system by means of analyzing the different information exchanged in the social web, will detect the diseases that are suffering the employees of a given company in a particular time. Furthermore the system will inform to the company about the spreading of the different illnesses and the recognized patterns. The aim of DISMON is to prevent massive infections and by means of the recognized patterns inferring which environmental conditions of the working place could have been the cause of a given disease, for instance temperature of the offices, contaminated air or water. In addition the system will report to each employee how probably is for them to be infected, based on the profile of the user, as age, location, previous illnesses or allergies in order to compare them with the characteristics of the previous infected workers, obtaining a percentage of the possibilities of the workers to get an illness.

STATE OF THE ART

Social Web

In latest years, the number of Social Web Sites has increased very quickly; these webs allow the knowledge to be generated just by using the contributions of the users via blogs, wikis, forums, online social networks, and so forth (Kinsella et al., 2009). The Web 2.0 phenomenon made the Web social, initiating an explosion in the number of users of the Web, thus empowering them with a huge autonomy in adding content to web pages, labeling the content, creating folksonomies of tags, and finally, leading to millions of users constructing their own web pages (Breslin & Decker, 2007). Therefore the user participation is the key and the main value of the Social Web. This participation concludes in a "collective intelligence" or "wisdom of crowds" where the opinion taking into account is the one expressed by a group of individuals rather than single or expert opinions answering a question.

The concept of collective intelligence, or "wisdom of the crowds" (Surowiecki, 2004), stands that when working cooperatively and sharing ideas, communities can be significantly more productive than individuals working in isolation. Moreover, the ability of multitudes to generate accurate information from diverse data sets has been well documented elsewhere and is not unique to Web 2.0 (Surowiecki, 2004). That's why social web has demonstrated its success with efforts like the Wikipedia, in which the "wisdom of the crowds" is creating and maintaining world's largest online encyclopedia.

The Social Web can be used by anybody with internet connection, but for the Social Web to work properly, the web developers have to provide websites with the capability of being social. This is becoming easier because the costs of gathering and computing the user's contributions have decreased and today, even the companies with very modest budgets can offer to the users social websites (Gruber, 2007).

With the purpose of summarize, the evolution of the web has brought about the Social Web which is based on dynamic public content that is changing depending on the people's input. The communication inside this web is not just between the machine and the person, but between all the people that is using the web application (Porter, 2008). And it is very important to remark how important has been the mind change into the users, that used to enter into the Internet just to read the webs and at the present time they are involved in the web creation process converting the web in a Social Web.

Semantic Technologies

Semantic Technologies have emerged as a new and highly promising context for knowledge and data engineering (Vossen, Lytras, & Koudas, 2007; Fensel & Munsen, 2001), being pointed to out as the future of the Web (Benjamins et al., 2008) and the next step in the evolution of the World Wide Web (Lukasiewicz & Straccia, 2008). The fields under Semantic Technologies are applied allowing support knowledge comprise a wide range of domains (Lytras & García, 2008), including medicine. Moreover, according to Ding (2010), semantic web is fast moving in a multidisciplinary way. Semantic Technologies, based on ontologies (Fensel, 2002), provide a common framework that enables data integration, sharing and reuse from multiple sources. Durguin and Sherif (2008) portrays the semantic web as the future web where computer software agents can carry out sophisticated tasks for users.

Ontologies (Fensel, 2002) are the technological cornerstones of the Semantic Technologies, because they provide structured vocabularies that describe a formal specification of a shared conceptualization. Ontologies were developed in the field of Artificial Intelligence to facilitate knowledge sharing and reuse (Fensel et al., 2001). An ontology can be defined as "a formal and explicit specification of a shared conceptualization" (Stude, Benjamins, & Fensel, 1998). Ontologies provide a common vocabulary for a domain and define, with different levels of formality, the meaning of the terms and the relations between them. Knowledge in ontologies is mainly formalized using five kinds of components: classes, relations, functions, axioms and instances (Gruber, 1993). Languages such as Resource Description Framework (RDF) and Ontology Web Language (OWL) have been developed; these languages allow for the description of web resources, and for the representation of knowledge that will enable applications to use resources more intelligently (Horrocks, 2008). These languages, and the tools developed to support them, have rapidly become de facto standards for ontology development and deployment; they are increasingly used, not only in research labs, but in large scale IT projects (Horrocks, 2008). The Semantic Web consists of several hierarchical layers, where the Ontology layer, in form of the OWL Web Ontology Language (recommended by the W3C), is currently the highest layer of sufficient maturity (Lukasiewicz & Straccia, 2008).

Due to the increasing maturity of semantic technologies, the adoption of these technologies in industrial and corporate environments is becoming closer (Lytras & García, 2008). There have been numerous applications of the Semantic Web in industrial service environments. Applications have been seen in human resources management (e.g. Gómez-Berbís et al., 2008; Colomo-Palacios et al., 2010a; Colomo-Palacios et al., 2010b), software development (Colomo-Palacios et al., 2008; García-Crespo et al., 2009a), tourism (García-Crespo et al., 2009b), learning (Naeve, Sicilia, & Lytras, 2008; Collazos & García, 2007) to cite some of the most relevant and recent cases.

Using Social Web in Medicine

According to Giustini (2006), Web 2.0 is changing medicine. Several authors have identified tools that highlight the usefulness of the social web as a modifying element for future medical practice and education (McLean et al., 2007). In the education field, many works have been produced that recommend the usage of social web tools for freshmen education (Kamel-Boulos & Wheeler, 2007; Sandars & Schroter, 2007). In the working domain, the utility of Web 2.0 has been demonstrated in professional organization and collaboration (Schleyer et al., 2008; Eysenbach, 2008), volunteer recruitment (Seeman, 2008), patient self care and self-empowerment and research (Seeman, 2008), remote patient monitoring (Czejdo & Baszun, 2010) among other application areas. On the other hand, some researchers have also identified threats regarding the usage of Web 2.0 in the medical environment, such as unwanted behaviors in patients – for example, the avoidance of consultations with physicians (Hughes et al., 2008) or inaccurate online information (Seeman, 2008; Hughes et al., 2008). In relation to the latter case, some initiatives have recently emerged to approve medical web content, using both supervised and automatic methods (Karkaletsis et al., 2008). Moreover, since the internet is crucial for developing nations (Khasawneh, 2009), this can be a way to improve medical services in these nations.

Recently, two new terms have come into use: Medicine 2.0 and Health 2.0. According to Hughes et al. (2008), Medicine 2.0 is the broader concept and umbrella term which includes consumer-directed "medicine" or Health 2.0. Medicine 2.0 is the use of a specific set of Web tools (blogs, podcasts, tagging, wikis, etc) by entities in health care including doctors, patients, and scientists, using principles of open source and generation of content by users, and the power of networks in order to personalize health care, collaborate, and promote health education.

However, Web 2.0 capacities can be extended by the use of SW. Its usefulness has been identified in medical environments from a generic point of view (Giustini, 2007) as well as in its application (Karkaletsis et al., 2008; Falkman et al., 2008).

DISMON, the approach presented in this paper combines Web 2.0 capacities and SW in order to provide semantic descriptions of clinical symptoms, thereby facilitating diagnosis and helping to foresee the diseases, giving useful information to the company and its employees in order to increase the efficiency by means of the prevention of injuries and illnesses, resulting in a safety environment for the workers.

Using Semantic Technologies in Medicine

The evolution of the semantic web and knowledge management technologies in the last years set a new context for the exploitation of patient-centric strategies based on well-defined semantics and knowledge (Lytras, Sakkopoulos, & Ordóñez de Pablos, 2009). According to Fuentes-Lorenzo, Morato, and Gómez-Berbís (2009), semantic technologies can be exploited to reveal machine-readable latent relationships within information in the medical field, where the homogeneity of terminology is particularly problematic. In this way, modern formal ontology facilitates the creation of knowledge-based systems such as those required for managing medical information (Sicilia et al., 2009).

Ontologies are currently being used in the medical domain as an integration of heterogeneous sources (e.g. Deogun & Spaulding, 2010; Dogac et al., 2006; Orgun & Vu, 2006), as a tool to engineer formal knowledge descriptions from existing and diverse medical terminologies (Lee, Supekar, & Geller, 2006) or to enable differential diagnosis (García-Crespo et al., 2010a). A recent review of the use of ontologies in the medical domain can be found in Schulz, Stenzhorn, Boeker, and Smith (2009). In addition, the adaptation of clinical ontologies to real world scenarios is depicted in Stenzhorn, Schulz, Boeker, and Smith (2008).

State of the Art Conclusion

The social web comprises an environment to share information. The users employ the social web to post comments regarding personal information, current status, opinions, links to relevant information, etc. The social web offers a place where the medical knowledge can be shared.

According to Lytras, Sakkopoulos, and Ordóñez de Pablos (2009), semantic web provides an excellent scientific domain capable of developing sound propositions and applications for the health domain. Moreover, the use of semantic technologies in social webs allows the possibility of process the amount data by means of a computer, offering interoperability between the users and the system. This is why the use of medical ontologies in limited environments can be used for detecting injuries and illnesses which are taking place within an organization. This is the case of the intranet of a given company. It can be considered as a corporative social web where the semantic technologies can be applied. Following the path described in García-Crespo et al. (2010a, 2010b), this paper presents DISMON, a tool that combines Web 2.0 capacities and SW in order to provide semantic descriptions of clinical symptoms, thereby facilitating diagnosis in limited environments.

ARCHITECTURE AND INTERNALS

The architecture has been designed to offer the best flexibility and usability for the development and the maintenance of the system, dividing it in three layers with the required elements in each layer to cover all the functionalities (see Figure 1).

The first layer is the closest to the user. It contains the DISMON interface to organizational applications. This component provides to the user the availability of interact with the system using existing applications. This layer also contains the crawler. This component is in charge of exploring the intranet of the company surfing for symptoms. The second layer contains the main part of the system, in this layer all the data is processing using the four subsystems designed to work with the data provided by the crawler of the first level and the data obtained from the third layer. The third layer contains the data correspondent to the diseases and the employees of the company, this data will be processed by the second layer.

Interface Layer

This layer contains two elements, the Enterprise Application Interface and the Crawler. The Company Intranet is located at the same level in the graphic of the architecture but it is not a part of the system. This layer is connected with three external elements, the rest of the applications of the company, the Intranet and it is connected with the second layer too.

The first element is the crawler. A crawler (also called a spider or robot) is a program controlled by a crawl control module that "browses" the Web. It collects documents by recursively fetching links from a set of start pages (Pokorny, 2004). In this case, this element crawls a given set of pages edited by employees in search of relevant information about diseases.

The intranet is the principal resource to look for information related with diseases suffered by the personnel. The relevant parts of the intranet for the DISMON system are the opinions of the employees, where the information about the diseases inside the company will be extracted. This opinions are inserted into the intranet by the employees via blogs, microblogs, forums and suggestion boxes, therefore the system will search for information about diseases in all the public places of the intranet where the users has the ability to publish.

The web crawler of DISMON system scans the intranet to look for the opinions mentioned. Once

Figure 1. DISMON Schema of the architecture

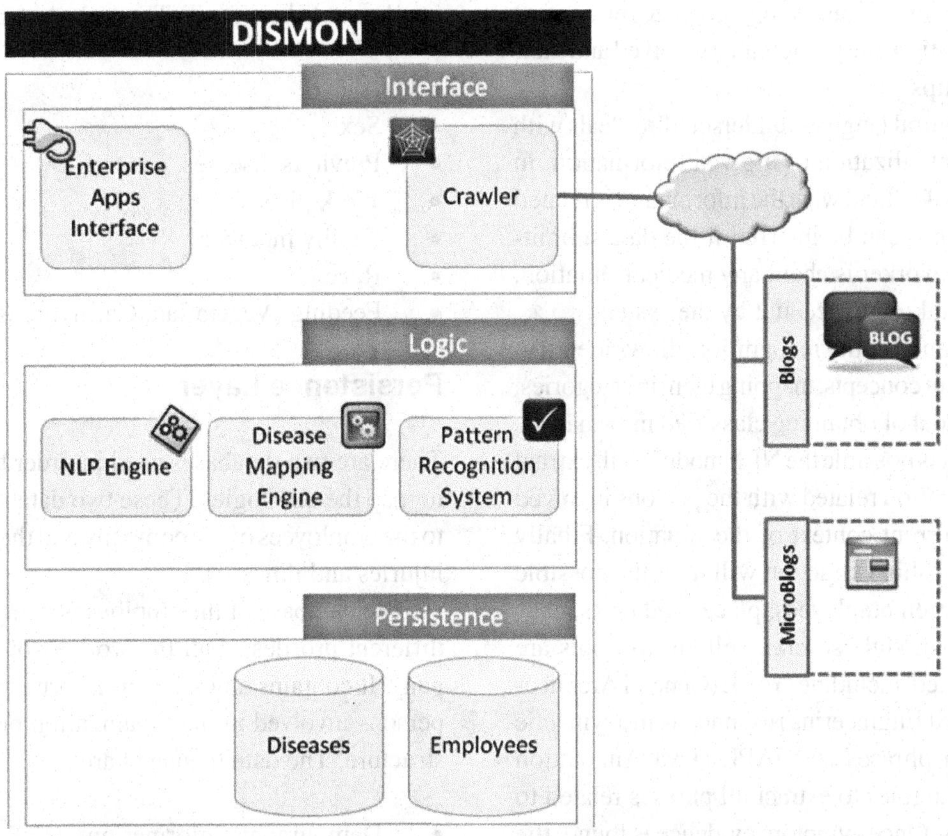

detected, the obtained URLs will be processed in the Logic layer. This component populates an ontology using RDF triples obtained from HTML obtained from the Crawler using wrappers based on predefined patterns.

The second element in this layer is the Enterprise Applications Interface. This component allows the communication with external solutions using a web service.

Logic Layer

This layer is between the other two layers that conform the system and it is the one that contains the main functionality of the software because it is dedicated to process all the information coming in from the other two layers, then this layer will process and analyze the information and finally will return the results to be shown to the user.

The Natural Language Processing Engine module entails a Natural Language Processing (or NLP) that provides with intelligence to the whole system. NLP is in charge of processing all the comments, posts, status and any other text information updated from the employees to the intranet. The objective of processing all this information is to give a computer understanding to all the data shared within the workers of the company. This processing will be carried out making use of medical knowledge by means of medical and regular dictionaries.

For the extraction of comprehensive information, the system uses of several subtasks: natural language understanding, named entity recognition and relationship extraction. The main objective of these subtasks is to identify text related with medical information and to recognize the context of the situation, the participants involved and their relationships.

The natural language understanding deals with the contextualization of a given information, in order to understand what the information is related with. Then it can be inferred if the data submitted by the worker is about any medical situation, therefore taking in account by the system.

The named entity recognition allows identifying different concepts, mapping them in categories, with the goal of obtaining classified information. Whether it is possible the NLP module will extract the information related with the persons involved and the current context of the situation. Finally the relationship extraction will infer the possible links between employees, places and tasks.

In this module several well known tools are implemented, including GATE (General Architecture for Text Engineering) to annotate in a syntactic way noun phrases and JAPE (Java Annotation Patterns Engine) to extract all phrases related to symptoms. Once symptom evidence is found, the Disease Mapping Engine will be responsible of its classification and storage.

The second element in this layer is the Disease Mapping Engine. This engine will match the words found in the URLs returned by the crawler with the diseases in the ontology, therefore this engine provides the system with the capability of recognize if the opinions found in the intranet are related to diseases or they are related to any other topic. It is also responsible of dealing with disease ontology and stores information of symptom evidences in the persistence layer. It hides competence complexity to other components of the system.

The last element in this layer is the Pattern Recognition System. With the information of every employee in the database, the system will match the current disease employee characteristics with the similar characteristics of other employees, concluding a percentage of probability for the similar employees to become ill. These characteristics are:

- Age
- Sex
- Previous diseases
- Work places
- Family members
- Race
- Feeding (Vegetarian, Carnivorous, etc.)

Persistence Layer

There are two databases used in order to be able to map the ontologies. These two databases refer to the employees of the company and the different injuries and illnesses.

The database of the employees comprises the different profiles of all the workers of the company. It contains any relevant information of the persons involved in the organization breakdown structure. The data managed are:

- Demographic information.
- Place of work inside the organization.
- Role within the organization.
- Relationships.

The database of the different injuries and illnesses consists on all the medical terminology employed for each injury or sickness and the any relevant information to take in account when the injury or the illness could be produced by environment conditions or it could entail any infection to other people. Then the data managed are:

- Medical name/s of the injury or illness.
- Common name/s of the injury or illness.
- Possible causes.
- Infectious level.
- At risk group.
- Possible days away from work.

The diseases ontology allows establishing the relations between the diseases. Given these relations implemented, DISMON is able to group diseases. Different diseases in the database can have almost the same symptoms and the same treatment, the ontology adds the intelligence to the database and permits to consider these two diseases together. Both the ontology and some of the intelligence given to the systems inherits directly from García-Crespo et al. (2010a).

USE CASE

To explain the realization of DISMON in a functional environment, as referred to in the previous section, a use case will be included. GreenHR is an organization devoted to human resources consultancy that implements DISMON. The company has an intranet where its 3,000 employees consult and add information, using the company's internal blog, forums and microblogs. The headquarters of the company is placed in Sydney, where a total of 1,500 work. There are several branches of GreenHR in the cities of Paris, London and New York.

The director of human resources and the marketing manager, working in the Sydney headquarter, are planning a trip to the branch of London. The human resources director is 45 years old and is a healthy person; he has no children and is single. The marketing director is 58 years old, has had pneumonia nine months ago and has a wife and two children. At the branch of London two days ago it has been detected an outbreak of flu, according to user's comments about common symptoms of this disease (Fever, Aches, Chills, Tiredness, etc.). This detection is performed by ODDIN, an ontology-driven medical diagnosis system (García-Crespo et al., 2010a). Once the system interacts with scheduling system it detects that HR and Marketing managers are planning to visit London and, given that the latter suffered from pneumonia, this trip is not desirable. In such circumstance, DISMON warns the other system to ask for cancelling the trip to both directors.

With the impending visit of the directors, DISMON assess potential risks, detecting that the director of marketing is among the risk groups and thus advising against his trip. The director of human resources is warned by DISMON that there is an outbreak of flu in London, but he is not considered within the risk groups. Besides all this, DISMON has alerted to all risk groups who work at headquarters in London to take precautions and avoid contact with the departments most affected.

Given this example, DISMON has prevented several aspects:

- The possible infection of the director of marketing, given their background and condition.
- The transportation of the virus from London to Sydney, perhaps preventing the spread of many employees working at the headquarters of Sydney and are easily infected by the influenza virus.
- There will be partially mitigated infections in the London headquarters.

CONCLUSION AND FUTURE WORK

It is a fact that systems that allow foreseeing and preventing contagion in an automated manner improve the quality of life, welfare, and in this particular case, the efficiency and functioning of companies. Moreover, the advent of the information age represents both a challenge and an opportunity for knowledge management and employee relationship management. In this new scenario, counting on with tools to prevent diseases in the scope of the corporation could improve personnel efficiency and this improved efficiency could be a competitive advantage for the company.

DISMON, following the path of some previous works (García-Crespo et al., 2010a), is an innovative system that is based on semantic and social web technologies along with NLP. The combination these technologies allow creating a system that provides the user with a tool that seeks to foresee any medical problems in the workplace. This tool is not only relevant to health workers. Counting on a tool that enables the diagnosis of diseases to improve employee performance could be a competitive advantage for the firm.

Limitations on the system can be found in two main areas. On the one hand, confidentiality issues and other matters relative to the acceptation of both users and organizations. DISMON is based on the analysis of personal blogs, nanoblogs and other Web 2.0 tools. Given the fact that many of these resources are personal, the overall acceptation of the system depends on the capacity of acquiring information from this sources. On the other hand, NLP techniques still suffer from imprecision and dealing with aspects as ironies is not easy as reveled in previous studies (e.g. García-Crespo et al., 2010c).

Future work will focus on the expansion of the system in order to read data from any resource available in the internet. By doing this, DISMON will be able to detect diseases in broader contexts such as cities, regions or countries.

REFERENCES

Benjamins, V. R., Davies, J., Baeza-Yates, R., Mika, P., Zaragoza, H., & Gómez-Pérez, J. M. (2008). Near-Term Prospects for Semantic Technologies. *IEEE Intelligent Systems*, *23*(1), 76–88. doi:10.1109/MIS.2008.10

Breslin, J. G., & Decker, S. (2007). The Future of Social Networks on the Internet: The Need for Semantics. *IEEE Internet Computing*, *11*(6), 86–90. doi:10.1109/MIC.2007.138

Collazos, C. A., & García, R. (2007). Semantics-supported cooperative learning for enhanced awareness. *International Journal of Knowledge and Learning*, *3*(4/5), 421–436. doi:10.1504/IJKL.2007.016703

Colomo Palacios, R., García Crespo, A., Gómez Berbís, J. M., Casado-Lumbreras, C., & Soto-Acosta, P. (2010b). SemCASS: technical competence assessment within software development teams enabled by semantics. *International Journal of Social and Humanistic Computing*, *1*(3), 232–245. doi:10.1504/IJSHC.2010.032685

Colomo-Palacios, R., Gómez-Berbís, J. M., García-Crespo, A., & Puebla-Sánchez, I. (2008). Social Global Repository: using semantics and social web in software projects. *International Journal of Knowledge and Learning*, *4*(5), 452–464. doi:10.1504/IJKL.2008.022063

Colomo-Palacios, R., Ruano-Mayoral, M., Soto-Acosta, P., & García-Crespo, Á. (2010a). The War for Talent: Identifying competences in IT Professionals through semantics. *International Journal of Sociotechnology and Knowledge Development*, *2*(3), 26–36.

Czejdo, B. D., & Baszun, M. (2010). Remote patient monitoring system and a medical social network. *International Journal of Social and Humanistic Computing*, *1*(3), 273–281. doi:10.1504/IJSHC.2010.032688

Deogun, J. S., & Spaulding, W. (2010). Conceptual Development of Mental Health Ontologies. In Ras, Z. W., & Tsay, L.-S. (Eds.), *Advances in Intelligent Information Systems. Studies in Computational Intelligence* (*Vol. 265*, pp. 299–333). Berlin: Springer.

Ding, Y. (2010). Semantic Web: Who is who in the field — a bibliometric analysis. *Journal of Information Science*, *36*(3), 335–356. doi:10.1177/0165551510365295

Dogac, A., Laleci, G. B., Kirbas, S., Kabak, Y., Sinir, S., & Yidiz, A. (2006). Artemis: Deploying semantically enriched Web services in the healthcare domain. *Information Systems*, *31*(4-5), 321–339. doi:10.1016/j.is.2005.02.006

Durguin, J. K., & Sherif, J. S. (2008). The semantic web: a catalyst for future e-business. *Kybernetes*, *37*(1), 49–65. doi:10.1108/03684920810850989

Eysenbach, G. (2008). Medicine 2.0: Social Networking, Collaboration, Participation, Apomediation, and Openness. *Journal of Medical Internet Research*, *10*(3), e22. doi:10.2196/jmir.1030

Falkman, G., Gustafsson, M., Jontell, M., & Torgersson, O. (2008). SOMWeb: A Semantic Web-Based System for Supporting Collaboration of Distributed Medical Communities of Practice. *Journal of Medical Internet Research*, *10*(3), e25. doi:10.2196/jmir.1059

Fensel, D. (2002). *Ontologies: A silver bullet for knowledge management and electronic commerce*. Berlin: Springer.

Fensel, D., & Munsen, M. A. (2001). The Semantic Web: A Brain for Humankind. *IEEE Intelligent Systems*, *16*(2), 24–25. doi:10.1109/MIS.2001.920595

Fensel, D., van Harmelen, F., Horrocks, I., McGuinness, D. L., & Patel-Schneider, P. F. (2001). OIL: An ontology infrastructure for the semantic web. *IEEE Intelligent Systems*, *16*(2), 38–45. doi:10.1109/5254.920598

Fuentes-Lorenzo, D., Morato, J., & Gómez-Berbís, J. M. (2009). Knowledge management in biomedical libraries: A semantic web approach. *Information Systems Frontiers*, *11*(4), 471–480. doi:10.1007/s10796-009-9159-y

García Crespo, A., Chamizo, J., Rivera, I., Mencke, M., Colomo Palacios, R., & Gómez Berbís, J. M. (2009b). SPETA: Social pervasive e-Tourism advisor. *Telematics and Informatics*, *26*(3), 306–315. doi:10.1016/j.tele.2008.11.008

García-Crespo, A., Colomo-Palacios, R., Gómez-Berbís, J. M., Chamizo, J., & Mendoza-Cembranos, M. D. (2010b). S-SoDiA: a semantic enabled social diagnosis advisor. *International Journal of Society Systems Science*, *2*(3), 242–254. doi:10.1504/IJSSS.2010.033492

García-Crespo, A., Colomo-Palacios, R., Gómez-Berbís, J. M., & Mencke, M. (2009a). BMR: Benchmarking Metrics Recommender for Personnel issues in Software Development Projects. *International Journal of Computational Intelligence Systems*, *2*(3), 257–267. doi:10.2991/ijcis.2009.2.3.7

García-Crespo, A., Colomo-Palacios, R., Gómez-Berbís, J. M., & Ruiz-Mezcua, B. (2010c). SEMO: a framework for customer social networks analysis based on semantics. *Journal of Information Technology*, *25*(2), 178–188. doi:10.1057/jit.2010.1

García-Crespo, A., Rodríguez, A., Mencke, M., Gómez-Berbís, J. M., & Colomo-Palacios, R. (2010a). ODDIN: Ontology-driven differential diagnosis based on logical inference and probabilistic refinements. *Expert Systems with Applications*, *37*(3), 2621–2628. doi:10.1016/j.eswa.2009.08.016

Giustini, D. (2006). How Web 2.0 is changing medicine. *British Medical Journal*, *333*, 1283–1284. doi:10.1136/bmj.39062.555405.80

Giustini, D. (2007). Web 3.0 and medicine. Make way for the semantic web. *British Medical Journal*, *335*, 1273–1274. doi:10.1136/bmj.39428.494236.BE

Gómez Berbís, J. M., Colomo Palacios, R., García Crespo, A., & Ruiz Mezcua, B. (2008). ProLink: a semantics-based social network for software projects. *International Journal of Information Technology and Management*, *7*(4), 392–405. doi:10.1504/IJITM.2008.018656

Gruber, T. R. (1993). A translation approach to portable ontology specifications. *Knowledge Acquisition*, *5*(2), 199–220. doi:10.1006/knac.1993.1008

Gruber, T. R. (2007). Collective knowledge systems: Where the Social Web meets the Semantic Web. *Web Semantics: Science. Services and Agents on the World Wide Web*, *6*, 4–13.

Horrocks, I. (2008). Ontologies and the Semantic Web. *Communications of the ACM, 51*(12), 58–67. doi:10.1145/1409360.1409377

Hughes, B., Joshi, I., & Wareham, J. (2008). Health 2.0 and Medicine 2.0: tensions and controversies in the field. *Journal of Medical Internet Research, 10*(3), e23. doi:10.2196/jmir.1056

Kamel-Boulos, M. N., & Wheeler, S. (2007). The emerging Web 2.0 social software: an enabling suite of sociable technologies in health and health care education. *Health Information and Libraries Journal, 24*, 2–23. doi:10.1111/j.1471-1842.2007.00701.x

Karkaletsis, V., Stamatakis, K., Karmapyperis, P., Svátek, V., Mayer, M. A., Leis, A., et al. (2008, July 21-25). Automating Accreditation of Medical Web Content. In *Proceedings of the 18th European Conference on Artificial Intelligence (ECAI 2008), 5th Prestigious Applications of Intelligent Systems (PAIS 2008),* Patras, Greece (pp. 688-692).

Khasawneh, A. (2009). Arabia online: internet diffusion in Jordan. *International Journal of Society Systems Science, 1*(4), 396–401. doi:10.1504/IJSSS.2009.026511

Kinsela, S., Passant, A., Breslin, J. G., Decker, S., & Jaokar, A. (2009). The Future of Social Web Sites: Sharing Data and Trusted Applications with Semantics. *Advances in Computers, 76*(4), 121–175. doi:10.1016/S0065-2458(09)01004-3

Lee, Y., Supekar, K., & Geller, J. (2006). Ontology integration: Experience with medical terminologies. *Computers in Biology and Medicine, 36*(7-8), 893–919. doi:10.1016/j.compbiomed.2005.04.013

Lukasiewicz, T., & Straccia, U. (2008). Managing uncertainty and vagueness in description logics for the Semantic Web. *Web Semantics: Science. Services and Agents on the World Wide Web, 6*(4), 291–308. doi:10.1016/j.websem.2008.04.001

Lytras, M. D., & García, R. (2008). Semantic Web applications: a framework for industry and business exploitation - What is needed for the adoption of the Semantic Web from the market and industry. *International Journal of Knowledge and Learning, 4*(1), 93–108. doi:10.1504/IJKL.2008.019739

Lytras, M. D., Sakkopoulos, E., & Ordóñez-De Pablos, P. (2009). Semantic Web and Knowledge Management for the health domain: state of the art and challenges for the Seventh Framework Programme (FP7) of the European Union (2007-2013). *International Journal of Technology Management, 47*(1-3), 239–249. doi:10.1504/IJTM.2009.024124

McLean, R., Richards, B. H., & Wardman, J. I. (2007). The effect of Web 2.0 on the future of medical practice and education: Darwikinian evolution or folksonomic revolution? *The Medical Journal of Australia, 187*(3), 174–174.

Naeve, A., Sicilia, M. A., & Lytras, M. D. (2008). Learning processes and processing learning: from organizational needs to learning designs. *Journal of Knowledge Management, 12*(6), 5–14. doi:10.1108/13673270810913586

Orgun, B., & Vu, J. (2006). HL7 ontology and mobile agents for interoperability in heterogeneous medical information systems. *Computers in Biology and Medicine, 36*(7-8), 817–836. doi:10.1016/j.compbiomed.2005.04.010

Pokorny, J. (2004). Web searching and information retrieval. *Computing in Science & Engineering, 6*(4), 43–48. doi:10.1109/MCSE.2004.24

Porter, J. (2008). *Designing for the Social Web.* Berkeley, CA: New Riders.

Sandars, J., & Schroter, S. (2007). Web 2.0 technologies for undergraduate and postgraduate medical education: an online survey. *Postgraduate Medical Journal, 83*, 759–762. doi:10.1136/pgmj.2007.063123

Schleyer, T., Spallek, H., Butler, B. S., Subramanian, S., Weiss, D., & Poythress, M. S. (2008). Facebook for Scientists: Requirements and Services for Optimizing How Scientific Collaborations Are Established. *Journal of Medical Internet Research, 10*(3), e24. doi:10.2196/jmir.1047

Schulz, S., Stenzhorn, H., Boeker, M., & Smith, B. (2009). Strengths and limitations of formal ontologies in the biomedical domain. *Electronic Journal of Communication Information & Innovation in Heath, 3*(1), 31–45.

Seeman, N. (2008). Web 2.0 and chronic illness: New Horizons, New Opportunities. *Healthcare Quarterly (Toronto, Ont.), 11*(1), 104–110.

Sicilia, J. J., Sicilia, M. A., Sánchez-Alonso, S., García-Barriocana, E., & Pontikaki, M. (2009). Knowledge Representation Issues in Ontology-based Clinical Knowledge Management Systems. *International Journal of Technology Management, 47*(1-3), 191–206. doi:10.1504/IJTM.2009.024122

Stenzhorn, H., Schulz, S., Boeker, M., & Smith, B. (2008). Adapting Clinical Ontologies in Real-World Environments. *Journal of Universal Computer Science, 14*(22), 3767–3780.

Studer, R., Benjamins, V. R., & Fensel, D. (1998). Knowledge engineering: Principles and methods. *Data & Knowledge Engineering, 25*(1-2), 161–197. doi:10.1016/S0169-023X(97)00056-6

Surowiecki, K. (2004). *The wisdom of crowds*. New York: Doubleday.

U.S. Department of Labor, Bureau of Labor Statics (BLS). (2009). *Nonfatal occupational injuries and illnesses from the Survey of Occupational Injuries and Illnesses*. Retrieved from http://www.bls.gov/iif/

Vossen, G., Lytras, M., & Koudas, N. (2007). Editorial: Revisiting the (Machine) Semantic Web: The Missing Layers for the Human Semantic Web. *IEEE Transactions on Knowledge and Data Engineering, 19*(2), 145–148. doi:10.1109/TKDE.2007.30

This work was previously published in the Journal of Information Technology Research, Volume 4, Issue 1, edited by Mehdi Khosrow-Pour, pp. 48-59, copyright 2011 by IGI Publishing (an imprint of IGI Global).

Chapter 5
Self-Organizing Tree Using Artificial Ants

Hanene Azzag
Université Paris 13, France

Mustapha Lebbah
Université Paris 13, France

ABSTRACT

In this paper, the authors propose a new approach for topological hierarchical tree clustering inspired from the self-assembly behavior of artificial ants. The method, called SoTree (Self-organizing Tree), builds, autonomously and simultaneously, a topological and hierarchical partitioning of data. Each ''cluster'' associated to one cell of a 2D grid is modeled by a tree. The artificial ants similarly build a tree where each ant represents a node/data. The benefit of this approach is the intuitive representation of hierarchical relations in the data. This is especially appealing in explorative data mining applications, allowing the inherent structure of the data to unfold in a highly intuitive fashion.

INTRODUCTION

The quantity of information that is stored in databases is rapidly growing. Additionally, databases are not only composed of numeric or symbolic attributes but may also be enriched, for instance, by sounds, images, videos, texts or Web sites. Finding the relevant hidden information in structured datasets is a difficult task. Clustering and visualization methods are one of the basic techniques which are often applied in analyzing the structured data sets. The main focus of this paper is on helping the domain expert to intuitively analyze such data sets. In our opinion, intuitive analysis of data implies the use of hierarchical clustering and visualization techniques (Jain & Dubes, 1988; Jain & Murty, 1999; Handl, Knowles, & Dorigo, 2003). These methods use both heuristic and mathematics principles.

DOI: 10.4018/978-1-4666-3625-5.ch005

Concerning heuristics methods, the numerous abilities of ants have inspired researchers for more than ten years regarding designing new clustering algorithms (Goss & Deneubourg, 1991; Lumer & Faieta, 1994). The initial and pioneering work in this area is due to Deneubourg and his colleagues (Goss & Deneubourg, 1991). These researchers have been interested in the way real ants sort objects in their nest by carrying them and dropping them in appropriate locations without a centralized control policy (Deneubourg, Goss, Franks, Sendova-Franks, Detrain, & Chretien, 1990). They have proposed the following principles: artificial ants move in a 2D grid where all objects to be sorted are initially scattered. An ant has a local perception of objects around its location and does not communicate directly with other ants. Instead, ants influence themselves using the configurations of objects on the grid. An ant has a variable probability of picking an encountered object. This probability is high when the frequency of encountering an object is low in the recent history of the ant. Similarly, an ant will drop a carried object with a high probability when similar objects have been perceived in ant's neighborhood. Using this simple and distributed principle, ants are able to collectively sort the objects.

The next step toward data clustering has been performed in (Lumer & Faieta, 1994). These researchers have adapted the previous algorithm by assuming that an object is a datum and by tuning the picking/dropping probabilities according to the similarities between data. These ants-based algorithms inherit interesting properties from real ants, such as the local/global optimization of the clustering, the absence of need of a priori information on an initial partitioning or number of classes, or parallelism. Furthermore, the results are presented as visualization: a property which is coherent with an important actual trend in data mining called 'visual data mining' where results are presented in a visual and interactive way to the expert.

Many authors have used and extended this model especially in the case of real and more difficult data with very interesting results, such as in graph partitioning for VSLI (Very-large-scale integration) technology (Kuntz, Layzell, & Snyers, 1997; Kuntz, Snyers, Layzell, & Paul, 1998), in Web usage mining (Abraham & Ramos, 2003) or in document clustering (Handl, Knowles, & Dorigo, 2003). Other models of 'clustering ants' have been developed (Venturini, Labroche, & Guinot, 2004), but the model which has been studied the most is the way ants sort objects in their nest. In this work we introduce a new method named SoTree: Self-Organizing Tree which uses in the same way: a hierarchical and a topological clustering. Data moves autonomously toward a 2D Grid respecting bio-inspired rules, where each cell represents a tree structured data. Thus we will obtain in one pass: a Horizontal topological clustering and a vertical hierarchical clustering (tree in each cell). The topological function of the proposed algorithm is based on Kohonen approach (Kohonen, 2001) and the rules for building tree are based on artificial ants method named AntTree (Azzag, Guinot, Oliver, & Venturini, 2006; Azzag, Guinot, & Venturini, 2006).

The remaining of this paper is organized as follows: in the next section, we present the artificial ants model, followed by the topological model. We layout the main principles of the combined model and propose rules to build tree clustering. We also present the methodology and experimental results. The final section concludes this work and proposes some perspectives.

FROM REAL TO ARTIFICIAL ANTS: ANTTREE ALGORITHM

Biological Inspiration

The self-assembly behavior of individuals can be observed in several insects like bees or ants for instance (see a survey with spectacular photographs in (Anderson, Theraulaz, & Deneubourg, 2002). We are interested here in the complex structures which are built by ants. We have specifically studied how two species were building such structures, namely the Argentina ants *Linepithema humiles* and ants of gender *Oecophylla* that we briefly describe here (Lioni, Sauwens, Theraulaz, & Deneubourg, 2001; Theraulaz, Bonabeau, Sauwens, Deneubourg, Lioni, Libert, Passera, & Sol, 2001). These insects may become fixed to one another to build live structures with different functions. Ants may thus build "chains of ants" in order to fill a gap between two points. These structures disaggregate after a given period of time.

Artificial Ants

The general principles that govern these behaviors are the following: ants start from an initial point (called the support). They begin to connect themselves to this support and then progressively to previously connected ants. When an ant is connected, it becomes a part of the structure and other ants may move over this ant or connect themselves to it. The structure grows over time according to the local actions performed by ants. Moving ants are influenced by the local shape of the structure and by a visual attractor (for instance, the point to reach). Ants which are in the middle of the structure cannot easily disconnect themselves.

From those elements, we define the outlines of AntTree computer model which simulates this behavior for tree building (see Figure 1a). The n ants $N_1,...,N_n$ represent each of the n data $\mathbf{x}_1,...,\mathbf{x}_n$ of the database. These ants are initially placed on the support which is denoted by N_0. Then, we successively simulate one action for each ant. An ant can be in two states: it can be free (i.e. disconnected) and may thus move over the structure in order to find a place where it can connect, or it can be connected to the structure without any possibility of moving apart from to disconnect. In this work, an ant may become connected to only one other ant, which ensures that ants will build a tree.

Ants locally perceive the structure: a moving ant N_i located over a connected ant N_{pos} perceives a neighborhood V_{pos} (see the striped ants in Figure 1b), which is limited (1) to the (mother) ant to which N_{pos} is connected, and (2) to the (daughter) ants which are connected to N_{pos}. N_i can perceive the similarities between the data $\mathbf{x}_i$ it is representing and the data represented by ants of V_{pos}. According to these similarities, N_i may either get connected to N_{pos}, or move to one of the ants in V_{pos}. We also include in this study the use of ''ants disconnections'' in order to change choices made previously in the growth of the structure. Once all ants are connected to the structure, then our algorithms stop (see Figure 2).

The main principles of the deterministic algorithm are the followings: at each step, an ant N_i is randomly selected and connects itself or move according to the similarity (Euclidean measure) with its neighbors. While there is still a moving ant N_i, we simulate an action for N_i according to its position (i.e. on the support or on another ant). In the following, N_{pos} denotes the ant or the support over which the moving ant N_i is located, and N^+ is the ant (daughter) connected to N_{pos} which is the most similar to N_i.

For clarity, we assume that ant N_i is located on an ant N_{pos} and that N_i is similar to N_{pos}. As will be seen in the following, when an ant moves toward another one, this means that it is similar enough to that ant. So N_i will become connected to N_{pos} provided that it is dissimilar enough to ants connected to N_{pos}. N_i will thus form a new sub-category of N_{pos} which is as dissimilar as possible from the other existing sub-categories. For this purpose, let us denote by

Figure 1. (a) General principles of tree building with artificial ants, (b) the computation of an ant's neighborhood

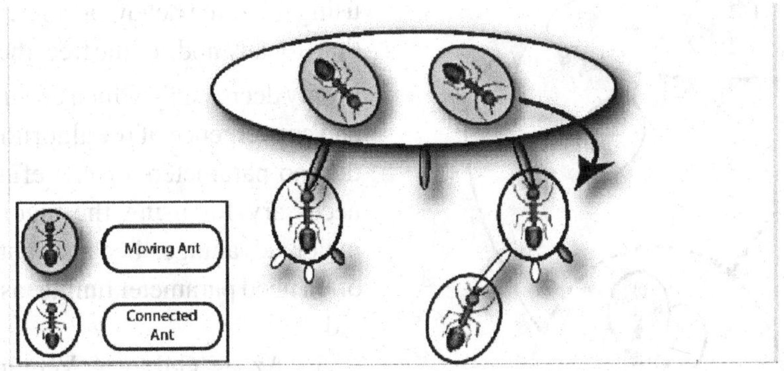

a.

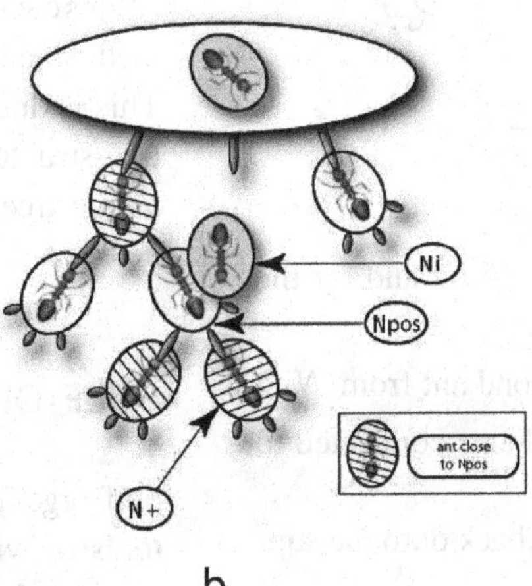

b.

$T_{Dist}(N_{pos})$ the highest distance value which can be observed among the daughters of N_{pos}. N_i is connected to N_{pos} if and only if the connection of N_i increases further this value. The test that we perform consists of comparing N_i to the most similar ant N^+. If these two ants are dissimilar enough $(Dist(N_i, N^+) < MaxT_{Dist}(N_{pos}))$, then N_i is connected to N_{pos}, else it is moved toward N^+.

Since this minimum value $T_{Dist}(N_{pos})$ can only be computed with at least two ants, then the two first ants are automatically connected without any tests. This may result in 'abusive' connections for the second ant. Therefore the second ant is removed and disconnected as soon as third ant is connected (for this latter ant, we are certain that the dissimilarity test has been successful). When this second ant is removed, all ants that were connected to it are also dropped, and all these ants are placed back onto the support (see Figure 2). This algorithm can thus be stated, for a given ant N_i, via the following ordered list of behaviour rules:

- R_1 (no ant or only one ant connected to N_{pos}): N_i connects to N_{pos}

Figure 2. Disconnection of ants

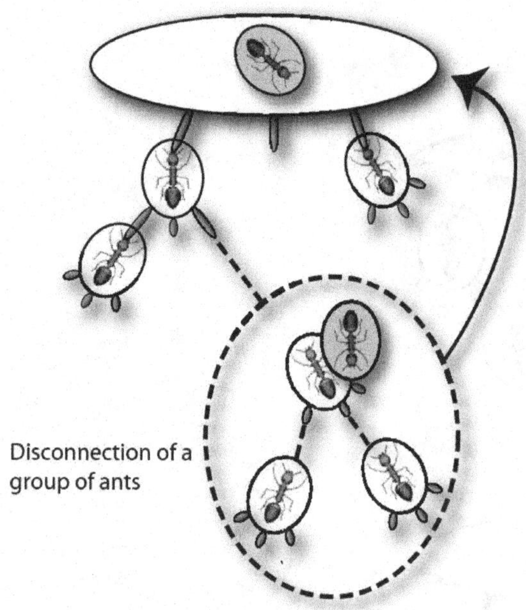

- R'_1 (2 ants connected to N_{pos}, and for the first time):
  a. Disconnect the second ant from N_{pos} (and recursively all ants connected to it)
  b. Place all these ants back onto the support N_0
  c. Connect N_i to N_{pos}
- R_2 (more than 2 ants connected to N_{pos}, or 2 ants connected to N_{pos} but for the second time):
  a. let $T_{Dist}(N_{pos})$ be the highest distance value between daughters of N_{pos} (i.e. $T_{Dist}(N_{pos}) = Max\ Dist(N_j, N_k)$ where N_j and $N_k \in$ {ants connected to N_{pos}}),
  b. If N_i is dissimilar enough to N^+ ($Dist(N_i, N^+) > T_{Dist}(N_{pos})$) Then N_i connects to N_{pos}
  c. Else N_i moves toward N^+

When ants are placed back on the support, they may find another place where to connect using the same behavior rules. It can be observed that, for any node of the tree, the value $T_{Dist}(N_{pos})$ is only decreasing, which ensures the termination and convergence of the algorithm. One can notice that no parameters or predefined thresholds are necessary for using the algorithm: this is one major advantage, because ants based methods often need parameter tuning, as similarity threshold.

In (Azzag, Guinot, & Venturini, 2006) authors have presented a complete studies of AntTree algorithms and have shown that AntTree algorithms clearly outperformed traditional clustering methods and had a low complexity (near $n\ log(n)$). This is due to the fact that AntTree exploits the tree-structure very well and avoids exploring the whole tree (only sub-trees) when connecting a new ant.

SELF-ORGANIZING MAP

Self-organizing maps are increasingly used as tools for visualization, as they allow projection over small areas that are generally two dimensional. The basic model proposed by Kohonen (SOM: Self-Organizing-Map) consists on a discrete set C of cells called map. This map has a discrete topology defined by undirected graph; it is usually a regular grid in 2 dimensions. We denote p as the number of cells. For each pair of cells (c, r) on the map, the distance $\delta(c,r)$ is defined as the length of the shortest chain linking cells r and c on the grid. For each cell c this distance defines a neighbor cell; in order to control the neighborhood area, we introduce a kernel positive function K ($K \geq 0$ and $\lim_{|x|\to\infty} K(x) = 0$). We define the mutual influence of two cells c and r by $K(\delta(c,r))$. In practice, as for traditional topological map we use smooth function to control the size of the neighborhood as

$K(\delta(c,r)) = \exp(\frac{-\delta(c,r)}{T})$. Using this kernel function T becomes a parameter of the model. As in the Kohonen algorithm, we increase T from an initilal value T_{max} to a final value T_{min}. Let $\mathcal{R}^d$ be the euclidean data space and $\mathcal{A} = \{\mathbf{x}_i; i = 1,...,n\}$ a set of observations, where each observation $\mathbf{x}_i = (x_i^1, x_i^2, ..., x_i^d)$ is a continuous vector in $\mathcal{R}^d$. For each cell c of the grid, we associate a referent vector $\mathbf{w}_c = (w_c^1, w_c^2, ..., w_c^j, ..., w_c^d)$ of dimension d. We denote by W the set of the referent vectors. The set of parameter W, has to be estimated from $\mathcal{A}$ iteratively by minimizing a cost function defined as follows:

$$R(\varphi, W) = \sum_{\mathbf{x}_i \in \blacklozenge} \sum_{r \in C} K(\delta(\varphi(\mathbf{x}_i), r)) \, || \, \mathbf{x}_i - \mathbf{w}_r \, ||^2 \quad (1)$$

where φ assign each observation $\mathbf{x}$ to a single cell in the map $\mathcal{C}$. In this expression $|| \, \mathbf{x} - \mathbf{w}_r ||^2$ is a square of the Euclidean distance. At the end of learning, SOM provides a partition of p subsets.

UNIFIED MODEL: SOTREE

A variety of topological maps algorithms are derived from the first original model proposed by Kohonen. All models are different from each other but share the same idea: depict large datasets on a simple geometric relationship projected on a reduced topology (2D). The model that we propose uses the same grid process, combined with a new concept of neighborhood.

Our model SoTree (Self-Organizing Tree) seeks to find an automatic clustering that provides a hierarchical and topological organization of a set of observations $\mathcal{C}$. This model is presented as regular grid in 2D that has a topological order of p cells. Each cell c is the 'root support' of a sub-tree denoted $Tree_c$ and each node $N_{\mathbf{x}_i}$ of the sub-tree represents a data $\mathbf{x}_i$. More precisely the proposed model defines a set of sub-trees projected on a 2D grid called $\mathcal{C}$. Taking into account the proximity between two sub-trees on the map $\blacklozenge$ is useful information, which allows defining a topological neighborhood relation previously used in traditional topological maps. Thus, for each pair of cells c and r on the map, the distance $\delta(c,r)$ is defined as the length of the shortest chain linking cells r and c on the grid associated to sub-trees $Tree_c$ et $Tree_r$. To model the influence of two cell r and c (depending on their proximity), we use a neighborhood function K. Thus, the mutual influence between two sub-trees $tree_c$ and $tree_r$ which are roots of two cells c and r is defined by the function $K^T(\delta(c,r))$ where T represents the temperature function that controls the size of the neighborhood.

We also associate to each sub-tree a representative point denoted $\mathbf{w}_c$ which is a given data denoted $\mathbf{x}_i$ in the sub-tree $tree_c$ ($\mathbf{w}_c = \mathbf{x}_i \in tree_c$). Choosing a representative point allows easily adapting our algorithm to any type of data (categorical, binary, and mixed data etc). We just need to define a new measure of similarity. The quality and the objective function of self-organizing sub-trees is rewritten as follows:

$$R(\phi, W) = \sum_{c \in \mathbf{Cx}_i} \sum_{\in Tree_c} \sum_{r \in C} K(\delta(\phi(\mathbf{x}_i), r)) \left\| \mathbf{x}_i - \mathbf{w}_r \right\|^2 \quad (2)$$

Minimizing the cost function $R(\phi, W)$ is a combinatorial optimization problem. In practice, we seek to find the best (optimal) solution by using batch version. In this work we propose to minimize the cost function in the same way as "batch" version but using statistical characteristics provided by sub-trees (associated to each cell) to accelerate the convergence of the algorithm. Three necessary basic steps for minimizing the cost function are defined as follows.

Step of Building Tree

In this step we seek to find the best position of a given data x_i in the tree $Tree_c$ associated to cell c. We use connections/disconnections rules inspired from AntTree (Azzag, Monmarché, Slimane, Venturini, & Guinot, 2003). The particularity of the obtained tree is that each node N whether it is a leaf or an internal node represents a given data $\mathbf{x}_i$. In this case, $N_{\mathbf{x}_i}$ denotes the node that is connected and associated to the data $\mathbf{x}_i$, $N_{\mathbf{x}_{pos}}$ represents current node of the tree and $N_{\mathbf{x}_{i+}}$ the node connected to $N_{\mathbf{x}_{pos}}$, which is the most similar (closest by distance) to $N_{\mathbf{x}_i}$.

As it was defined previously, $T_{Dist}(N_{\mathbf{x}_{pos}})$ is the highest distance value which can be observed among the local neighborhood V_{pos}. $\mathbf{x}_i$ is connected to $N_{\mathbf{x}_{pos}}$ if and only if the connection of $N_{\mathbf{x}_i}$ further increases this value. Thus, this measure represents the value of the maximum distance observed in the local neighborhood V_{pos}, between each pair of data connected to the current node $N_{\mathbf{x}_{pos}}$:

$$T_{Dist}(N_{\mathbf{x}_{pos}}) = Max_{j,k} \left\| N_{\mathbf{x}_j} - N_{\mathbf{x}_k} \right\|^2 = Max_{j,k} \left\| \mathbf{x}_j - \mathbf{x}_k \right\|^2 \quad (3)$$

In other words, connections rules consist of comparing a node $N_{\mathbf{x}_i}$ to the nearest node $N_{\mathbf{x}_{i+}}$. In the case where both nodes are sufficiently far away $\left\| N_{x_i} - N_{x_{i+}} \right\|^2 > T_{Dist}(N_{x_{pos}})$ then the node $N_{\mathbf{x}_i}$ is connected to its current position $N_{\mathbf{x}_{pos}}$.

Otherwise, the node $N_{\mathbf{x}_i}$ associated to data $\mathbf{x}_i$ is moved toward the nearest node $N_{\mathbf{x}_{i+}}$. Therefore, the value T_{Dist} increases for each node connected to the tree. In fact, each connection of a given data $\mathbf{x}_i$ implies a local minimization of the value of the corresponding T_{Dist}. Therefore a minimization of the cost function (2).

At the end of the tree construction step, each cell c of the map $\mathcal{C}$ will be associated to a sub-tree $tree_c$. Connections rules are based on Nearest Neighbor approach. Each data will be connected to its nearest neighbor.

Assignment Step

Each datum $\mathbf{x}_i$ is connected in the sub-tree $Tree_c$ forming a hierarchical relation noted parent-child. We use $nodeChild(\mathbf{x}_i)$ function which provides all child node of a same node parent $N_{\mathbf{x}_i}$ associated to data $\mathbf{x}_i$. At step $t = 0$, $nodeChild(\mathbf{x}_i) = \mathbf{x}_i$.

Assignment step consists of finding for each given data $\mathbf{x}_i$ a cell called "Winner" using the assignment function named χ. This cell is also designated as winner cell for all k-nearest-neighbors of $\mathbf{x}_i$. In other words, a complete root sub-tree $N_{\mathbf{x}_i}$ is recursively assigned to the winning cell. The assignment function is defined as follows:

$$\chi(\ nodeChild(\mathbf{x}_i)) = \arg\min_r \sum_{c \in C} K^T\left(\delta(r,c)\right) \left\| \mathbf{x}_i - \mathbf{w}_c \right\|^2 \quad (4)$$

Representation Step

Minimizing the cost function $R(\varphi, W)$ with respect to $\mathbf{w}_c$ corresponds to finding the point that minimizes all local distances.

$$\mathbf{w}_c = min_{\mathbf{w}_c \in tree_c} \sum_{\mathbf{x}_i \neq \mathbf{w}_c; \mathbf{x}_i \in tree_c} \left\| \mathbf{x}_i - \mathbf{w}_c \right\|^2, \quad \forall c \in C \quad (5)$$

The temperature parameter T varies according to the iterations from T_{max} to T_{min} in the same way as in traditional topological maps. We present the details of the developed Algorithm 1.

TOPOLOGICAL ORDER IN SOTREE MODEL

The decomposition of the cost function R that depends on the value of T, permit to put its expression as follows:

$$R^T(\phi, W) = \left[\sum_{c \in C} \sum_{r \neq c} \sum_{\mathbf{x}_i \in tree_r} K^T(\delta(c,r)) \left\| \mathbf{x}_i - \mathbf{w}_r \right\|^2 \right]$$

$$+ \left[K^T(\delta(c,r)) \sum_{c \in C} \sum_{\mathbf{x}_i \in tree_r} \left\| \mathbf{x}_i - \mathbf{w}_c \right\|^2 \right]$$

where $\delta(c,c) = 0$

The cost function R^T is decomposed on two terms. In order to maintain the topological order between trees, minimizing the first term will bring trees corresponding to two neighboring cells. Indeed, if $tree_c$ and $tree_r$ are neighbors on the map, the value of $\delta(c,r)$ is lowest and in this case the value of $K^T(\delta(c,r))$ is highest. Thus, minimizing the first term has as effect to reducing the value of the cost function. Minimizing the second term corresponds to the minimization of the inertia of points attached to the $tree_c$ (in the case of Euclidean space). Minimizing this term is considered as applying hierarchical clustering algorithm (AntTree).

For different values of temperature T, each term of the cost function has a relative importance in the minimization process. For large values of the temperature T, first term is dominant and in this case, the priority is to preserve the topology. When value of T is lowest, the second term is considered in the cost function. In this case, the priority is to determine representative compact trees. SoTree algorithm provides a solution to regularized AntTree algorithm: regularization is achieved through the constraint of ordering on the trees.

COMPARATIVE RESULTS

Visual Results

We have tested and compared the proposed algorithm on several datasets that have been generated with Gaussian and Uniform distributions. Others have been extracted from the machine learning repository (Blake & Merz, 1998) and have several difficulties (fuzzy clustering, no relevant feature, etc.). Before comparing our numerical results, we present map visualization with associated treemaps.

Treemap is a visualization technique introduced in (Shneiderman, 1992). An important feature of treemaps is that they make very efficient use of display space. Thus it is possible to display large trees with many hierarchical levels in a minimal amount of space (2D). Treemap can be especially helpful when dealing with large clustered tree. Treemaps lend themselves naturally to showing the information encapsulated in the clustering tree. Viewing a tree at some level of abstraction, the viewer is really looking at nodes belonging to some level in the tree. A treemap can display the whole structure of trees and allow the users to place the current view in context.

In the proposed visualization technique each tree of the cell is represented by a treemap. This aims to obtain an automatic organization of treemaps on a 2D map. Figure 3 shows an example of four tree structures with its corresponding treemaps. The positioning of tree nodes in a treemap is a recursive process. The nodes are represented as rectangles of various shapes. First, the children of the root are placed across the display area horizontally. Then, for each node N already displayed, each of N's children is placed across vertically within N's display area. This process is repeated, alternating between horizontal and vertical placement until all nodes have been displayed. We note that each rectangle is colored according to the real label of its corresponding node/data. This makes easy a visual comparison

Algorithm 1. Details of SoTree algorithm

```
Input: Map C of p cells, learning set A, the number of iteration n_iter
Output: Map C
For c to C
        w_c = x_i  /* random initialization of the map */
        For t = 1 to n_iter
                For x_i ∈ A
                        T = T^max × (T^min / T^max)^(t / (n_iter − 1))
                if first assignment of x_i then
                - Find the best match unit χ(x_i) using assignment function defined in (eq. 4)
                - Associate the data x_i to a node N_{x_i},
- Connect the node N_{x_i} in the sub-tree Tree_{χ(x_i)} using the connections rules to build the tree
                - Update the representative point w_c by using the defined expression (eq. 5)
                else /* t^th assignment of the data x_i */
-Find the winner cell c_new = χ( nodeChild(x_i)) by using function defined in expression (4)
                if c_new ≠ c_old then
                - Assign data x_i and node child nodeChild(x_i) to the new cell c_new
- Connect the node N_{x_i} and nodes child in the sub-tree tree_{c_new} using connections rules.
- Update the two representative points w_{c_old} and w_{c_new} using the defined expression (eq.5)
```

of their relevance and homogeneous clusters (see below visual results discussion).

In Figure 3 each treemap represents a hierarchical organization of data's belonging to cluster "tree". Thus, SoTree approach has several properties that allow obtaining a simultaneous topological hierarchical clustering.

Overall, we have developed SoTree rules that respect the following properties: Each node $N_{\mathbf{x}_i}$ is the most representative of its subtree. We observe in Figure 3 that data placed in $tree_c$ are similar to $N_{\mathbf{x}_i}$ and the child nodes of $N_{\mathbf{x}_i}$ represent recursively subtrees that are dissimilar to their "sister" subtrees.

Concerning visual results, to best analyze the obtained result, we have learned for each dataset 1×1 SoTree in order to build a single treemap. Figures 4, 5, and 6 display some example of 1×1 SoTree and 4×4 SoTree. Observing both maps on each dataset, we find that our algorithm provides

Figure 3. Forest of trees and its treemaps representation: 2×2 *SoTree*

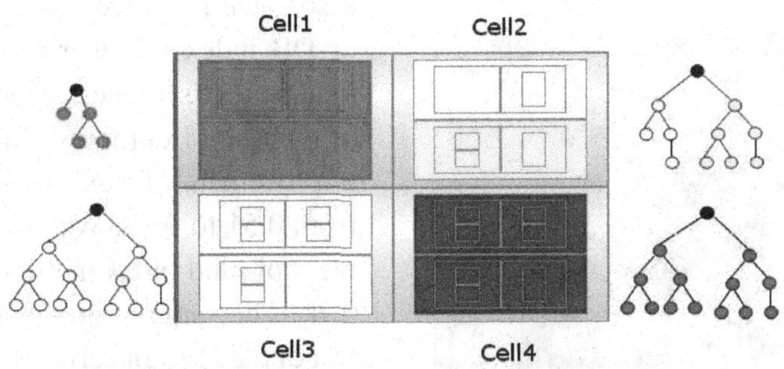

a SoTree which is a multi-division of the main treemap. We can see that topological and hierarchical organization of data is more apparent. In order to visualize the coherence between intra-organization of treemaps and the labeling of points, we assign one color to each label. In each figure, we distinguish two regions on the SoTree that are dedicated to the pure and mixed clusters. In Figure 4b we can observe that diagonal from right to left is dedicated to one class (colored in blue) and the treemap positioned in the bottom right is a mixed cluster. We observe in this treemaps, that yellow point is positioned in a lower level on the tree, this behavior is normal since the yellow classes are situated in the neighborhood. Same remarks concern Lsun and Tetra dataset. In Figure 6 observing the top right treemap (cell) and who which is in the bottom left, we can conclude on the level and the side where cluster will become mixed. Thus, this visual analysis is done using only 2D visualization unlike SOM method where we can not conclude on which level data is positioned.

This visual system allows a domain expert to easily navigate trough the databases. In this way, we hope to be able to browse large databases and to let the user easily interact with data and perceive both detail, global context and shape of the tree.

1. [1×1 Treemap of data set]
2. [4×4 SoTree]

1. [1×1 Treemap of data set]
2. [4×4 SoTree]

1. [1×1 Treemap of data set]
2. [5×5 SoTree]

Numerical Results

We remind here that SoTree model provides more information than traditional hierarchical models, K-means or others. In this work we compare the obtained result with SOM model. In this case we adopt the same parameter: map size, initial neighborhood, and final neighborhood.

Table 1 reports clustering evaluation criterion obtained with SoTree and SOM clustering. To evaluate the quality of map clustering, we adopt the approach of comparing results to a "ground truth". We use two criterions for measuring the clustering results. The first one is Rand index which measures the percentage of observation pairs belonging to the same class and which are assigned to same cluster of the map (Saporta & Youness, 2001). The second index is Davies Bouldin criterion which (Davies & Bouldin, 1979) is used to determine the optimal number K of centroids for K-means. This index suggested by Davies and Bouldin (Davies & Bouldin, 1979) is defined as in the following, in order to combine

Figure 4. Iris dataset

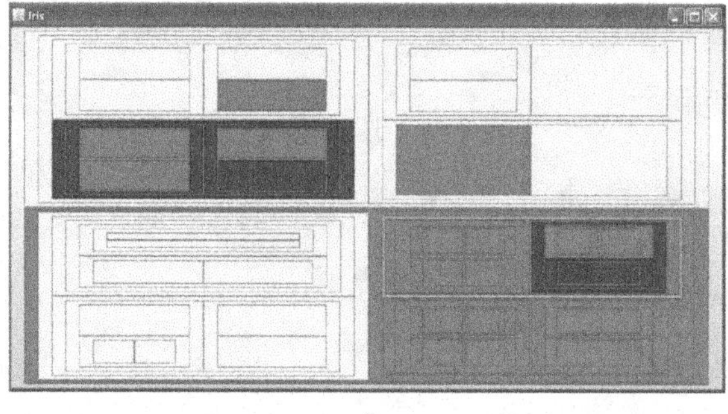

a.

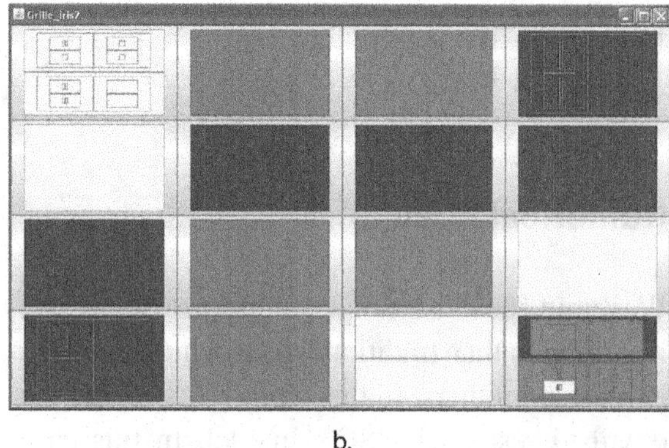

b.

the concepts of cluster separation (denominator) and cluster compactness (numerator):

$$DB = \frac{1}{C}\sum_{i=1}^{C}\frac{s_i + s_j}{\left\|\mathbf{w}_i - \mathbf{w}_j\right\|^2}$$

Being s_i the square root of the average error (within-cluster variance) of cluster i with the centroid c_i. This is a common approach in the general area of data clustering.

Indeed, as shown in the Table 1, we can see that SoTree method provides similar results and quite comparable SOM method on the majority of datasets. Looking to columns (DB and Rand) associated to SoTree, we can observe that value of DB index is lower using our algorithm and rand index is highest near one for the majority of datasets. Looking to Table 1, we observe an improvement of rand index using Atom dataset, from 0.51 to 0.88. We also observe an improvement of rand index in Glass dataset from 0.65 to 0.70. The same improvement is observed in the rest of data set. In certain cases we obtain similar rand rate as in Lsun, Hepta and ART1 datasets

In Table 2, we present a comparative study of our algorithm with two standard and well known methods in clustering field, named AHC and K-means (Jain & Dubes, 1988; Jain & Murty, 1999). AHC is a standard, very well known and competitive method. It also uses hierarchical principles and can be applied to any type of data. The

Figure 5. Lsun dataset

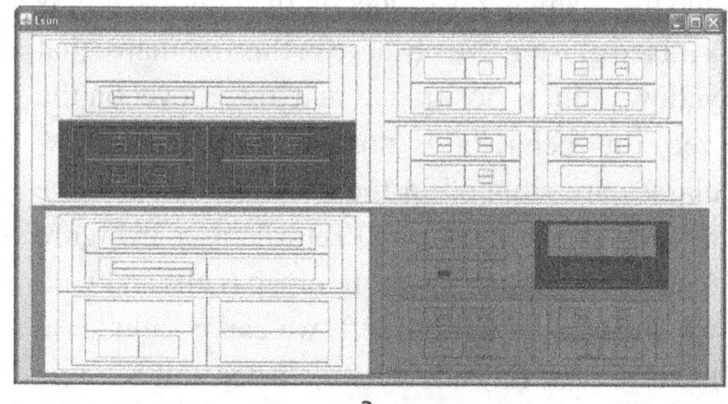

a.

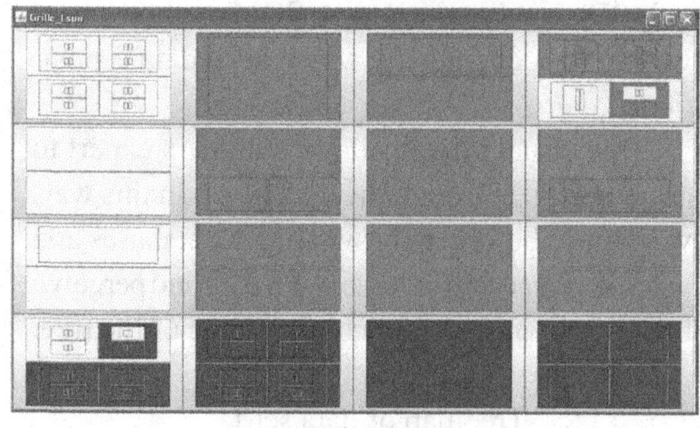

b.

Figure 6. Tetra dataset

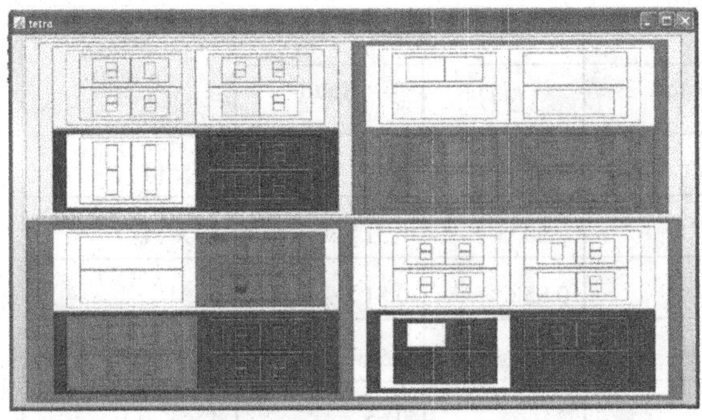

a.

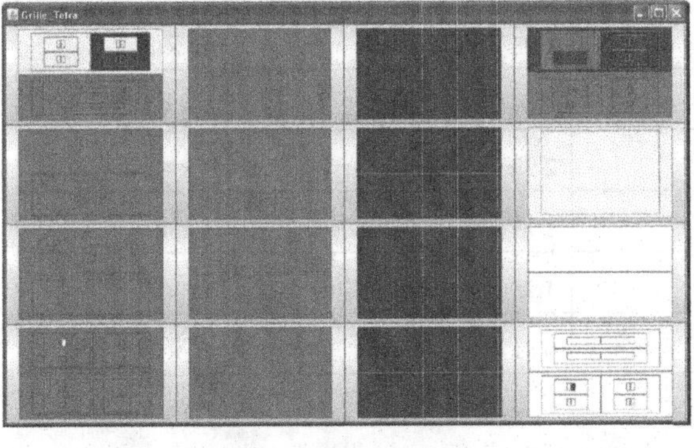

b.

K-means is well adapted to numeric data because it directly makes use of the notion of center of mass. This method is efficient but suffers from an initialization problem.

In both methods, we have use DB index to choose the best partition of K-means and to automatically cut the dendrogram in AHC algorithm. This justifies the best results obtained by K-means and AHC using DB index. Indeed DB is lower for the majority of case but no far away comparing to DB index obtained by SoTree. Concerning Rand index values, SoTree obtains similar results than AHC and K-means for the majority of datsets. In SoTree we don't use DB index to choose the best map. Observing simultaneously Table 1 and Table 2, we may remark closes values of rand rate in SoTree, K-means and AHC algorithm. Our purpose through this comparison is not to assert that our method is the best, but to show that SoTree method can obtains quite same good results as SOM or other well-known clustering algorithms. Unlike SOM method, K-means or AHC, SoTree does not require a posterior processing to analyze the structure of data belonging to clusters (cells). SoTree also provides simultaneously hierarchical and topological clustering which is more interesting for visualization task.

CONCLUSION AND PERSPECTIVE

We have developed a new method of hierarchical clustering that provides a local hierarchical clustering of data allowing better visualization of data organization. It generates both 2D self-organization of the trees and a hierarchical organization provided by the constructed tree. Concerning the results we have seen that our approach obtains competitive results on several datasets. The major benefits of our SoTree approach compared with the standard SOM are the following. First SoTree uncovers the hierarchical structure of the data allowing the user to understand and analyze large amounts of data. Second, with the various emerging trees at each cell being rather small in size, it is much easier for the user to keep an overview of the various clusters.

The obtained results are preliminary and much work will be done. It is obvious that using trees for data clustering greatly speeds up the learning process, we wish to generalize these algorithms to other kind of structures which may not be trees. The same principles seem to be applicable also to graphs. Finally, it will be necessary to focus on the visual aspect of our approach. Indeed, we will develop a 2D/3D view of the different trees that result from the hierarchical clustering in order to allow an interactive exploration of data.

Table 1. Competitive results obtained with SoTree and SOM using same parameter (map size, initial and final parameter T). DB is the Davies-Bouldin index

Datasets	Size	SoTree		SOM		Size of map
		DB	Rand	DB	Rand	
Atom(2)	800	1.4	0.88	1.47	0.51	10×14
Ring (2)	1000	0.80	0.61	0.90	0.51	10×14
ART1(4)	400	0.98	0.81	0.85	0.81	4×4
Circle (2)	600	0.58	0.60	0.67	0.5	10×14
Glass(7)	214	1.56	0.70	2	0.65	4×4
Hepta(7)	212	0.92	0.92	0.85	0.93	3×3
Iris(3)	150	1.06	0.75	1.03	0.75	10×14
Lsun(3)	400	0.97	0.71	1.09	0.72	4×4
Pima(2)	768	1.09	0.5	2.23	0.43	4×4
Target(6)	770	1.4	0.85	1.17	0.58	4×4
Tetra(4)	400	0.82	0.81	1.25	0.76	10×14
TwoDiamonds(2)	800	0.86	0.60	0.81	0.51	10×14

Table 2. Competitive results obtained with K-means and CAH

Datasets	Size	K-means		CAH		SoTree	
		DB	Rand	DB	Rand	DB	Rand
Atom(2)	800	0.82	0.76	0.81	0.77	1.40	0.88
Ring (2)	1000	0.50	0.56	0.50	0.55	0.80	0.61
ART1(4)	400	0.72	0.89	0.79	0.88	0.98	0.81
Circle(2)	600	0.46	0.55	0.48	0.55	0.58	0.60
Glass(7)	214	0.91	0.66	0.65	0.72	1.56	0.70
Hepta(7)	212	0.60	0.94	0.35	1.00	0.92	0.92
Iris(3)	150	0.47	0.77	0.43	0.77	1.06	0.75
Lsun(3)	400	0.56	0.80	0.54	0.85	0.97	0.71
Pima(2)	768	0.73	0.52	0.65	0.56	1.09	0.50
Target(6)	770	0.58	0.58	0.44	0.81	1.40	0.85
Tetra(4)	400	0.69	1.00	0.71	0.99	0.82	0.81
TwoDiamonds(2)	800	0.57	1.00	0.57	1.00	0.86	0.60

REFERENCES

Abraham, A., & Ramos, V. (2003, December 8-12). Web usage mining using artificial ant colony clustering and linear genetic programming. In *Proceedings of the IEEE Conference on Evolutionary Computation*, Canberra, Australia (pp. 1384-1391). Washington, DC: IEEE Computer Society.

Anderson, C., Theraulaz, G., & Deneubourg, J. L. (2002). Self-assemblages in insect societies. *Insectes Sociaux*, *49*, 99–110. doi:10.1007/s00040-002-8286-y

Azzag, H., Guinot, C., Oliver, A., & Venturini, G. (2006). A hierarchical ant based clustering algorithm and its use in three real-world applications. *European Journal of Operational Research*, *179*(3), 906–922. doi:10.1016/j.ejor.2005.03.062

Azzag, H., Guinot, C., & Venturini, G. (2006). Data and text mining with hierarchical clustering ants. In Abraham, A., Grosan, C., & Ramos, V. (Eds.), *Swarm intelligence and data mining* (pp. 153–190). doi:10.1007/978-3-540-34956-3_7

Azzag, H., Monmarché, H., Slimane, M., Venturini, G., & Guinot, C. (2003, December 8-12). Anttree: a new model for clustering with artificial ants. In *Proceedings of the IEEE Conference on Evolutionary Computation*, Canberra, Australia. Washington, DC: IEEE Computer Society.

Blake, C. L., & Merz, C. L. (1998). *Uci repository of machine learning databases*. Irvine, CA: Department of Information and Computer Science, University of California. Retrieved from ftp://ftp.ics.uci.edu/pub/machine-learning-databases

Carey, M., Heesch, D., & Roger, S. (2003) Info navigator: A visualization tool for document searching and browsing. In *Proceedings of the 9th International Conference on Distributed Multimedia Systems (DMS'2003).*

Davies, D. L., & Bouldin, D. W. (1979). A cluster separation measure. *IEEE Transactions on Pattern Recognition and Machine Intelligence*, *1*(2), 224–227. doi:10.1109/TPAMI.1979.4766909

Deneubourg, J.-L., Goss, S., Franks, N. R., Sendova-Franks, A., Detrain, C., & Chretien, L. (1990). The dynamics of collective sorting: robot-like ant and ant-like robots. In *Proceedings of the First International Conference on Simulation of Adaptive Behavior* (pp. 356-365).

Goss, S., & Deneubourg, J.-L. (1991). Harvesting by a group of robots. In F. Varela & P. Bourgine (Eds.), *Proceedings of the First European Conference on Artificial Life*, Paris, France (pp. 195-204). Amsterdam, The Netherlands: Elsevier Publishing.

Handl, J., Knowles, J., & Dorigo, M. (2003). On the performance of ant-based clustering. In *Proceedings of the 3rd International Conference on Hybrid Intelligent Systems* (pp. 204-213).

Jain, A. K., & Dubes, R. C. (1988). *Algorithms for Clustering Data*. Upper Saddle River, NJ: Prentice Hall Advanced Reference Series.

Jain, A. K., Murty, M. N., & Flynn, P. J. (1999). Data clustering: a review. *ACM Computing Surveys*, *31*(3), 264–323. doi:10.1145/331499.331504

Johnson, B., & Shneiderman, B. (1991). Treemaps: A space-filling approach to the visualization of hierarchical information structures. In *Proceedings of the Visualization 1991 Conference,* San Diego, CA (pp. 284-291).

Kohonen, T. (2001). *Self-organizing Maps*. Berlin, Germany: Springer.

Kuntz, P., Layzell, P., & Snyers, D. (1997). A colony of ant-like agents for partitioning in VLSI technology. In P. Husbands & I. Harvey (Eds.), *Proceedings of the Fourth European Conference on Artificial Life* (pp. 417-424).

Kuntz, P., Snyers, D., & Layzell, P. (1998). A stochastic heuristic for visualising graph clusters in a bi-dimensional space prior to partitioning. *Journal of Heuristics*, *5*(3), 327–351. doi:10.1023/A:1009665701840

Lioni, A., Sauwens, C., Theraulaz, G., & Deneubourg, J.-L. (2001). The dynamics of chain formation in oecophylla longinoda. *Journal of Insect Behavior*, *14*, 679–696. doi:10.1023/A:1012283403138

Lumer, E. D., & Faieta, B. (1994). Diversity and adaptation in populations of clustering ants. In D. Cliff, P. Husbands, J. A. Meyer, &n W. Stewart (Eds.), *Proceedings of the Third International Conference on Simulation of Adaptive Behavior* (pp. 501-508). Cambridge, MA: MIT Press.

Robertson, G. G., Mackinlay, J. D., & Card, S. K. (1991). Cone trees: animated 3d visualizations of hierarchical information. In *CHI '91: Proceedings of the SIGCHI Conference on Human factors in computing systems* (pp. 189-194). New York, NY: ACM Press.

Saporta, G., & Youness, G. (2001). Concordance e-ntre deux partitions: quelques propositions et expériences. In *Proceedings of the Actes des 8es rencontres de la SFC*, Pointe-à-Pitre, Guadeloupe.

Shneiderman, B. (1992). Tree visualization with tree-maps: A 2-D space-filling approach. *ACM Transactions on Graphics*, *11*, 92–99. doi:10.1145/102377.115768

Theraulaz, G., Bonabeau, E., Sauwens, C., Deneubourg, J.-L., Lioni, A., & Libert, F. (2001). Model of droplet formation and dynamics in the argentine ant (linepithema humile mayr). *Bulletin of Mathematical Biology*, *63*, 1079–1093. doi:10.1006/bulm.2001.0260

Venturini, G., Labroche, N., & Guinot, C. (2004). Fast unsupervised clustering with artificial ants. In *Proceedings of the Parallel Problem Solving from Nature (PPSN VIII) Conference,* Birmingham, UK (pp. 1143-1152).

Zhang, T., Ramakrishnan, R., & Livny, M. (1996). BIRCH: an efficient data clustering method for very large databases. In *Proceedings of the 1996 ACM SIGMOD International Conference on Management of Data* (pp. 103-114). New York, NY: ACM.

This work was previously published in the Journal of Information Technology Research, Volume 4, Issue 2, edited by Mehdi Khosrow-Pour, pp. 1-16, copyright 2011 by IGI Publishing (an imprint of IGI Global).

Chapter 6
Co-Evolutionary Algorithms Based on Mixed Strategy

Wei Hou
Harbin Engineering University & Northeast Agricultural University, China

HongBin Dong
Harbin Engineering University, China

GuiSheng Yin
Harbin Engineering University, China

ABSTRACT

Inspired by evolutionary game theory, this paper modifies previous mixed strategy framework, adding a new mutation operator and extending to crossover operation, and proposes co-evolutionary algorithms based on mixed crossover and/or mutation strategy. The mixed mutation strategy set consists of Gaussian, Cauchy, Levy, single point and differential mutation operators; the mixed crossover strategy set consists of cuboid, two-points and heuristic crossover operators. The novel algorithms automatically select crossover and/or mutation operators from a given mixed strategy set, and improve the evolutionary performance by dynamically utilizing the most effective operator at different stages of evolution. The proposed algorithms are tested on a set of 21 benchmark problems. The results show that the new mixed strategies perform equally well or better than the best of the previous evolutionary methods for all of the benchmark problems. The proposed MMCGA has shown significant superiority over others.

INTRODUCTION

Several mutation operators have been proposed in evolutionary programming (EP), e.g., Gaussian, Cauchy, Levy, Single Point and Differential mutations. Experiments show that Gaussian mutation has a good performance for some unimodal functions and multimodal functions with only a few local optimal points; Cauchy mutation works well on multimodal functions with many local optimal points; Levy mutation can lead to a large variation and a large number of distinct values in evolutionary search, and is said to be more general and flexible because of its scaling parameter;

DOI: 10.4018/978-1-4666-3625-5.ch006

Single Point mutation is based on the coordinate ordering for each solution, it can converge to global optimum more than other algorithms; DE is arguably one of the most powerful stochastic real-parameter optimization algorithms in current use and it shows strikingly better performance as compared to classical evolutionary algorithms (EAs) on numerical benchmarks.

According to no free lunch theorem, none of mutation operators is efficient in solving all optimization problems, but only in a subset of problems. Overall performance of the EP can be improved by using different mutation operators simultaneously or by integrating several mutation operators into one algorithm or by adaptively controlled usage of mutation operators. An early implementation is a linear combination of Gaussian and Cauchy distributions (Chellapilla, 1998). This combination can be viewed a new mutation operator, whose probability distribution is a convolution of Gaussian and Cauchy's probability distributions. IFEP (Yao, Liu & Lin, 1999) adopts another technique: each individual implements Cauchy and Gaussian mutations simultaneously and generates two individuals; the better one will be chosen in the next generation. Lee (2004) developed the idea of IFEP further into mixing Levy distribution with various scaling parameters. SPMEP is superior to both CEP (Fogel, Owens & Walsh, 1966) and FEP (Yao, Liu & Lin, 1999) for many multimodal and high-dimensional functions. The mixed mutation strategy integrates several mutation strategies into one algorithm within one population in our previous work. An individual can adjust its mixed strategy based on the payoffs of strategies and select a mutation operator with higher probability to adapting different operators to different stages of evolution. An ensemble approach is where each mutation operator has its associated population and every population benefits from every function call (Mallipeddi & Suganthan, 2010).

The crossover is the most significant operator to generate dissimilar individuals which may be possible solutions to the problem under consideration. A mixed strategy evolutionary programming has been proposed in our previous work, achieving good performances on numerical optimization. In this work, we add the differential mutation operator into the mixed mutation strategy in our previous work and extend the mixed strategy to crossover operation. We discuss four variations of evolutionary algorithm based on the mixed crossover or/ and mutation strategy and their performances on numerical optimization.

The work presented in this paper is organized as follows. The next section presents the framework of evolutionary algorithm based on mixed strategy. The modified mixed mutation strategy by adding differential mutation operator into the framework is discussed and a novel mixed crossover strategy is proposed. The automated operator selection techniques based on mixed crossover and mutation strategies is presented, as well as the experimental design and the performance of each algorithm.

THE FRAMEWORK OF EVOLUTIONARY ALGORITHM BASED ON MIXED STRATEGY

In theory mixed strategies (Dutta, 1999; Ficici, Melnik & Pollack, 2000) have some potential advantages over pure strategies (He & Yao, 2005). Individuals are regarded as players in a game. Each individual will choose a crossover or mutation strategy from its strategy set based on a selection probability and generate an offspring by this strategy.

The mixed strategy is described as follows: at each generation, an individual chooses one mutation strategy s from its strategy set based on a selection probability $p(s)$. This probability distribution is called a mixed strategy distribution in the game theory. The key question is to find out a good, if possible an optimal, mixed probability $p(s)$ for every individual. This mixed distribution may be changed over generations.

A mixed strategy for an individual i is defined by a probability distribution $p_i(s)$ over its strategy set. It is used to determine the probability of each strategy being applied in the next iteration. It is dependent on the payoffs of strategies. Denote $p_i(s) = (p_i(1), \cdots, p_i(m))$. m is the number of the pure strategies in a mixed strategy set.

The above mixed strategy also can be applied to crossover operation.

The mixed strategy is used to solve a global optimization problem:

$$\min f(x_1,x_2,\ldots,x_n),$$

$$\text{s.t. } x_i \in [a_i,b_i],\ i=1,2,\ldots,n.$$

where n is the dimension of search space R^n and f is a real-valued continuous function.

The modified framework of evolutionary algorithm based on mixed strategy is as follows, some detailed descriptions are in our previous works:

1. **Initialization:** Generate randomly an initial population consisting of μ individuals real vectors, and for each individual i, assign an initial probability distributions of crossover operators to the vector $q_i(s)$ or/and mutation operators to the vector $p_i(s)$.
2. **Crossover and/or mutation:** For a crossover individual i, another individual j is selected randomly, and a crossover strategy s with a higher probability is chosen from its mixed crossover strategy vector $q_i(s)$ to be executed. For a mutation individual i, a mutation strategy s is selected from its mixed mutation strategy vector $p_i(s)$ to be executed.
3. Fitness evaluation.
4. q-Tournament selection.
5. Update the mixed strategy probabilities of the individual i and j.
6. Repeat step 2-5 until the stopping criterion is satisfied.

THE EVOLUTIONARY ALGORITHM BASED ON MIXED STRATEGY

The Evolutionary Algorithm Based on Mixed Mutation Strategy

In recent past, researchers working in the area of pattern recognition showed some interest into a promising algorithm for numerical optimization, known as the differential evolution (DE) (Storn & Price, 1995). DE is arguably one of the most powerful stochastic real-parameter optimization algorithms in current use and it shows strikingly better performance as compared to classical evolutionary algorithms (EAs) on numerical benchmarks. However, it has been observed that the convergence rate of DE do not meet the expectations in cases of highly multimodal problems. Many of the most recent developments in DE algorithm design (Qin & Suganthan, 2005; Yang, Tang & Yao, 2007; Yang, Tang & Yao, 2008) and applications, such as image classification (Maulik & Saha, 2009; Omran, Engelbrecht & Salman, 2005), multi-objective optimization (Xue, Sanderson & Graves, 2003), multi-objective clustering (Das, Abraham & Konar, 2008; Kaushik, 2009), and so forth can be found. A classical differential mutation strategy is added into the mixed mutation strategy set in this paper.

The crucial idea behind DE is a new scheme of mutation. DE executes its mutation by adding a weighted difference vector between two individuals to a third individual. The mutation operations of classical DE (Storn & Price, 1997) can be summarized as follows:

$$x'_i = x_{i1} + F \cdot (x_{i2} - x_{i3})$$

where $i, i1, i2, i3 \in [1, NP]$, are integers and mutually different, and $F > 0$, is a constant coefficient used to control the differential variation $d_i = x_{i2} - x_{i3}$.

For an individual i, its probability distribution $p_i(s) = (p_i(1), p_i(2), p_i(3), p_i(4), p_i(5))$, $p_i(1)$,

$p_i(2)$, $p_i(3)$, $p_i(4)$ and $p_i(5)$ are the probabilities of Gaussian, Cauchy, Levy, single point, differential mutation operator respectively.

Algorithm 1: An evolutionary programming based on mixed mutation strategy (MSEP) is designed as follows:

1. **Initialization:** Generate randomly an initial population and assign a same initial probability distribution for each individual, $p_i(1)=p_i(2)=p_i(3)=p_i(4)=p_i(5)=1/5$.
2. Mutation.
3. Fitness evaluation.
4. **q-Tournament selection:** According to the payoffs of strategies of total population individuals, select *NP* individuals with the best payoff values to next generation.
5. Update the mixed mutation strategy probabilities of all individuals.
6. Repeat step 2-5 until the stopping criterion is satisfied.

In fact, any available mutation operator can be extended into the mixed mutation strategy set to utilize its advantages to provide higher levels of disruption and exploration.

The Evolutionary Algorithm Based on Mixed Crossover Strategy

Competent crossover operators in GA are able to capture and adapt themselves to the underlying problem structure. Crossover causes a structured, yet randomized exchange of genetic material between solutions, with the possibility that 'good' solutions can generate 'better' ones. Notable crossover techniques include the single-point, two-point, uniform, arithmetic and heuristic types.

In this section, we introduce the mixed crossover strategy set which consists of cuboid crossover operator (CCO), two-point crossover operator (TCO), heuristic crossover operator (HCO) and probability distributions of these operators.

1. Cuboid crossover operator (CCO), namely arithmetic or linear crossover operator (Michalewicz, 1994). Arithmetic crossover technique linearly combines two parent chromosomes to produce two new offspring. As the condition U(0,1) < Cr, two offspring are created as follows:

$$u_k=r_k x_k + (1-r_k)y_k$$

$$v_k=(1-r_k)x_k + r_k y_k$$

where r_k is the weight which governs dominant individual in reproduction and it is a random number between zero and two, $r_k=U_k(0,2)$. U(a,b) is an uniformly distributed random number between a and b, Cr is called cuboid crossover probability, $Cr\in(0,1)$. CCO can generate offspring at random within the space of the supercube including the parents, which increases the diversity of the solutions to improve evolution.

Two-point crossover operator (TCO) (Nomura, 1997), Two crossover parents are randomly selected, genes from the begging of a chromosome to the first crossover point is copied from one parent; Genes between the two crossover points are copied from the second parent; The rest of genes are copied from the first parent. As the condition U(0,1) > Cr, two offspring are created as follows:

$$u=(x_1, x_2,..., x_{l1-1}, y_{l1}, y_{l1+1},..., y_{l2}, x_{l2+1}, x_{l2+2},..., x_n)$$

$$v=(y_1, y_2,..., y_{l1-1}, x_{l1}, x_{l1+1},..., x_{l2}, y_{l2+1}, y_{l2+2},..., y_n)$$

where $1<l_1<n$, $1<l_2<n$, $l_1<l_2$.

2. Two-point crossover operator is able to generate offspring on the vertexes of the supercube formed by the parents, which enhances the space search rate and the precision of the crossover operator.
3. Heurist crossover operator (HCO) (Mühlenbein & Schlierkamp, 1993), it only produces one offspring and uses the values

of the objective function to determine the direction of search. The offspring are created as follows:

$u = y + Radio * (x - y)$

where *Radio* is a random number between 0 and 1.

The heurist crossover operator can improve the convergence speed of real-coded GA by using the heuristic information.

Algorithm 2: An evolutionary algorithm based on mixed crossover strategy (MCEA) is designed as follows:

1. **Initialization:** Generate randomly an initial population and assign a same initial probability distribution for each individual *i*, $q_i(1) = q_i(2) = q_i(3) = 1/3$.
2. Crossover.
3. Fitness evaluation.
4. q-Tournament selection.
5. Update the mixed crossover strategy probabilities of the individuals.
6. Repeat step 2-5 until the stopping criterion is satisfied.

AUTOMATED OPERATOR SELECTION TECHNIQUES BASED ON MIXED STRATEGY

The genetic operators in GA can vary depending on the problem and may be either standard genetic operators or custom built operators that are designed to solve a particular problem more effectively. As the number of problems applied to GAs has increased, the number of custom built crossover and mutation operators has also grown considerably. Consequently, selecting or designing appropriate operators for a specific problem to be solved with a GA has become a significant task requiring much trial and error. In order to overcome much of the difficulty in deciding which crossover and mutation operators to use on a specific problem, an automated operator selection technique based on mixed strategy is presented in this paper. The algorithms can automatically select crossover and/or mutation operators from a given mixed strategy set, and also improve the evolutionary performance by dynamically utilizing the most effective operator at different stages of evolution. There are two mixed strategies to be designed for selecting operators: (1) There is a mixed strategy set consisted of several crossover and mutation operators together. An individual executes crossover or mutation once in every generation; (2) There are two mixed strategy sets consisted of crossover operators and mutation operators respectively. An individual first executes crossover, then mutation in every generation.

The Evolutionary Algorithm Based on Mixed Crossover or Mutation Strategy

The mixed crossover or mutation strategy consists of cuboid, two-point, heuristic crossover operators, Gaussian, Cauchy, Levy, single point and differential mutation operators.

Algorithm 3: An evolutionary algorithm based on mixed crossover or mutation strategy (MCMEP) is designed as follows.

1. **Initialization:** Generate randomly an initial population and assign a same initial probability distribution for each individual *i*, $p_i(1) = p_i(2) = \ldots = p_i(8) = 1/8$, $p_i(1)$ to $p_i(8)$ are the probability of CCO, TCO, HCO, Gaussian, Cauchy, Levy, single point and differential operators respectively.
2. Crossover or mutation.
3. Fitness evaluation.
4. q-Tournament selection.
5. Update the mixed crossover strategy probabilities of the individuals.
6. Repeat step 2-5 until the stopping criterion is satisfied.

The Evolutionary Algorithm Based on Mixed Crossover and Mutation Strategies

The mixed crossover strategy consists of cuboid, two-point, heuristic crossover operators; the mixed mutation strategy consists of Gaussian, Cauchy, Levy, single point, differential mutation operators.

Algorithm 4: An evolutionary algorithm based on mixed crossover and mutation strategy (MMCGA) is designed as follows:

1. **Initialization:** Generate randomly an initial population, assign an initial crossover probability distributions, $q_i(1)= q_i(2)= q_i(3) =1/3$, and an initial mutation probability distributions, $p_i(1)=p_i(2)=\ldots=p_i(5)=1/5$, for each individual i.
2. Crossover.
3. Fitness evaluation.
4. Mutation.
5. Fitness evaluation.
6. q-Tournament selection.
7. Update the mixed crossover and mutation strategy probabilities of the individuals.
8. Repeat step 2-7 until the stopping criterion is satisfied.

EXPERIMENTAL RESULTS AND ANALYSIS

Comparison of MSEP and Traditional EP

To evaluate the performance of the MSEP and compare it to other EP approaches, including our previous proposed MSEP-4. The mixed mutation strategy in MSEP-4 consists of four operators, Gaussian, Cauchy, Levy and single point mutations. 21 test functions of the CEC 2005 benchmark are chosen, including three groups: unimodal, multimodal and expanded functions.

We set MSEP's population size $NP = 50$, the scaling factor of the differential mutation operator $F=N(0.5,0.5)$, $N(0.5,0.5)$ denotes a Gaussian random number with mean 0.5 and standard deviation 0.5 (Yang, Tang & Yao, 2008). Other comparing EP algorithms' population size $NP = 100$. The remaining parameters are the same as in MSEP-4. The stopping criterion of all algorithms is the maximum generations. Each algorithm is run 50 times independently on each problem. The mean and the standard deviation (std) values of the function values are reported in Table 1.

From the results in Table 1, it can be observed that MSEP performs better than other EPs on f_1-f_9. MSEP performs just as well as MSEP-4 on the mean values for f_{12}–f_{21} and attains higher precision on f_1-f_3, f_8-f_9, f_{12}–f_{14}, f_{16}–f_{18}. MSEP does not work very well on f_{10}–f_{11}. In general, the two mixed strategy algorithms, especially MSEP, perform as well as or better than the best of the four pure strategies considered here.

Comparison of Proposed Four EAs Based on Mixed Strategy

This experiment compares the proposed four variations based on mixed strategy in this paper, the MSEP, in where the mixed mutation strategy is used, the MCEA, in where the mixed crossover strategy is executed, the MCMEP, in where the mixed crossover or mutation strategy is carried out, the MMCGA, in where the mixed crossover and mutation strategies are performed. All four methods are tested on the same 21 test functions as the first experiment.

All algorithms set same parameters, population size $NP = 50$, the scaling factor of the differential mutation operator $F=N(0.5,0.5)$, the cuboid crossover rate Cr=0.7. The results for comparing four algorithms are displayed in Table 2. The best

Table 1. Comparison between MSEP and other EP approaches on functions f_1-f_{21}

Func	MSEP		MSEP-4		SPMEP		FEP		CEP	
	Mean	Std	Mean	Std	Mean	Std	Mean	Std	Mean	Std
f_1	1.61 e-8	2.83 e-8	1.0 e-4	1.3 e-5	1.3 e-4	1.0 e-4	5.7 e-4	1.3 e-4	2.2 e-4	5.9 e-4
f_2	2.28 e-6	2.70 e-6	4.1 e-4	2.1 e-4	5.1 e-4	1.5 e-5	8.1 e-3	7.7 e-4	2.6 e-3	1.7 e-4
f_3	9.09 e-18	8.18 e-18	2.7 e-2	1.7 e-2	6.5 e-3	2.0e-3	0.3	0.5	2	1.2
f_4	0	0	0	0	0	0	0	0	577.76	1125.76
f_5	5.53 e-3	3.12 e-3	6.1 e-3	1.7 e-3	1.0 e-2	1.5 e-3	7.6 e-3	2.6 e-3	1.8 e-2	6.4 e-3
f_6	-12569.49	1.19 e-11	-12569.48	3.4 e-4	-12569.48	9.1 e-12	-12554.5	52.6	-7917.1	634.5
f_7	3.00 e-7	1.94 e-7	2.5 e-5	2.1 e-5	2.9 e-7	6.0 e-8	4.6 e-2	1.2 e-2	89	23.1
f_8	3.02 e-4	2.41 e-4	1.7 e-3	4.3 e-4	1.9 e-3	4.4 e-4	1.8 e-2	2.1 e-3	9.2	2.8
f_9	2.25 e-10	3.56 e-10	8.5 e-4	2.3 e-3	5.6 e-3	1.7 e-3	1.6 e-2	2.2 e-2	8.6 e-2	0.12
f_{10}	2.03 e-4	2.24 e-4	7.5 e-7	4.0 e-7	8.5 e-7	9.7 e-9	9.2 e-6	3.6 e-6	1.76	2.4
f_{11}	1.09 e-4	9.49 e-5	1.2 e-5	1.1 e-5	1.4 e-5	9.2 e-6	1.6 e-4	7.3 e-5	1.4	3.7
f_{12}	0.998004	7.85 e-16	0.998004	1.6 e-15	1	1.6 e-15	1.22	0.56	1.66	1.19
f_{13}	3.08 e-4	4.53 e-7	3.08 e-4	1.3 e-6	4.5 e-4	1.5 e-4	5.0 e-4	3.2 e-4	4.7 e-4	3.0 e-4
f_{14}	-1.03163	1.33 e-10	-1.03	2.69 e-8	-1.03	4.3 e-10	-1.03	4.9 e-7	-1.03	4.9 e-7
f_{15}	0.397887	2.75 e-7	0.398	0	0.398	5.7 e-10	0.398	1.5 e-7	0.398	1.5 e-7
f_{16}	3	1.72 e-10	3	2.7 e-6	3	5.6 e-9	3.02	0.11	3	0
f_{17}	-3.86278	4.86 e-8	-3.86	6.6 e-7	-3.86	1.5 e-9	-3.86	1.4 e-5	-3.86	1.4 e-2
f_{18}	-3.32237	9.58 e-7	-3.32	1.7 e-4	-3.25	5.4 e-2	-3.27	5.9 e-2	-3.28	5.8 e-2
f_{19}	-10.1041	7.12 e-5	-10.1	5.0 e-5	-6.63	3.5	-5.52	1.59	-6.86	2.67
f_{20}	-10.4029	6.76 e-6	-10.4	4.7 e-6	-7.4	3	-5.52	2.12	-8.27	2.95
f_{21}	-10.5363	1.41 e-4	-10.54	1.3 e-4	-6.53	4	-6.57	3.14	-9.1	2.92

results among the four approaches are shown in bold.

The results in Table 2 show that the performances of the proposed four EAs are significantly better than that of the traditional EPs in Table 1. Especially, MMCGA outperforms among all methods on the mean value and standard deviation. For f_1-f_3, MCEA works better than MSEP, that is to say, the mixed crossover strategy is better than the mixed mutation strategy on unimodal functions; while for f_6, f_{10}, f_{11}, MSEP performs better than MCEA, the mixed mutation strategy is better than the mixed crossover strategy on multimodal functions; MSEP achieves similar results as MCEA on other functions. As it is seen from Table 2, the mixed strategy simultaneously adopting crossover and mutation performs better than only using crossover or mutation. The algorithms MCMEP and MMCGA can automatically select crossover and/or mutation operators from a given mixed strategy set according to the probability distributions, the two mixed strategies can improve the evolutionary performance by dynamically utilizing the most effective operator at different stages of evolution. Due to coexistence of crossover and mutation operators, a balance between local and global search can be achieved better in MCMEP and MMCGA. The

Table 2. The performance of MSEP, MCEA, MCMEP and MMCGA on 21 benchmark functions

Func.	Gen's	MSEP		MCEA		MCMEP		MMCGA	
		Mean	Std	Mean	Std	Mean	Std	Mean	Std
f_1	1500	1.61 e-8	2.83 e-8	1.68 e-50	4.96 e-50	1.48 e-73	4.45 e-73	2.11 e-106	3.68 e-106
f_2	2000	2.28 e-6	2.70 e-6	1.45 e-48	2.69 e-48	5.10 e-54	9.71 e-54	2.23 e-86	4.46 e-86
f_3	5000	9.09 e-18	8.18 e-18	1.75 e-54	5.44 e-54	5.45 e-59	1.14 e-58	5.62 e-114	8.80 e-114
f_4	1500	0	0	0	0	0	0	0	0
f_5	3000	5.53 e-3	3.12 e-3	8.11 e-4	7.63 e-4	7.50 e-4	6.48 e-4	1.71 e-4	8.66 e-5
f_6	9000	-12569.49	1.19 e-11	-8622.06	7.04 e+2	-12417.13	1.32 e+2	-12569.49	1.84e-12
f_7	5000	3.00 e-7	1.94 e-7	0	0	0	0	0	0
f_8	1500	3.02 e-4	2.41 e-4	4.00 e-15	2.39 e-30	4.00 e-15	2.39 e-30	4.44 e-16	2.99 e-31
f_9	2000	2.25 e-10	3.56 e-10	0	0	0	0	0	0
f_{10}	1500	2.03 e-4	2.24 e-4	2.17 e-3	3.42 e-3	1.03 e-10	1.35 e-10	2.37 e-12	2.78 e-12
f_{11}	1500	1.09 e-4	9.49 e-5	5.90 e-1	1.71 e-1	2.69 e-9	2.93 e-9	1.45 e-10	2.98 e-10
f_{12}	100	0.998004	7.85 e-16	0.998004	7.85 e-16	0.998004	7.85 e-16	0.998004	7.85e-16
f_{13}	4000	3.08 e-4	4.53 e-7	5.01 e-4	1.97 e-4	4.16 e-4	2.88 e-4	3.08 e-4	2.93 e-7
f_{14}	100	-1.03163	1.33 e-10	-1.03162845	0	-1.03162845	0	-1.03162845	0
f_{15}	100	0.39788744	2.75 e-7	0.39788736	1.68 e-16	0.39788736	1.68 e-16	0.39788736	1.68e-16
f_{16}	100	3	1.72 e-10	3	2.24 e-15	3	5.51 e-15	3	1.79 e-15
f_{17}	100	-3.86278	4.86 e-8	-3.86278	5.17 e-15	-3.86278	6.6 e-14	-3.86278	4.68 e-16
f_{18}	200	-3.32237	9.58 e-7	-3.32237	2.38 e-12	-3.32	9.79 e-11	-3.32237	2.69 e-15
f_{19}	100	-10.10414	7.12 e-5	-10.1042	4.82 e-7	-10.1042	1.92 e-6	-10.1042	1.79 e-15
f_{20}	100	-10.40293	6.76 e-6	-10.4029	1.21 e-5	-10.4029	1.39 e-6	-10.4029	8.97 e-15
f_{21}	100	-10.5363	1.41 e-4	-10.5364	4.75 e-5	-10.5364	2.21 e-5	-10.5364	8.97 e-15

statistically superior performance of the MMCGA over MCMEP can be observed.

Comparison of Proposed Four Mixed Strategy EAs on Convergence

The convergence characteristics in terms of best fitness value of the median run for each algorithm of each test function is shown in Figure 1.

Comparing the convergence curves of the four algorithms in Figure 1, the MMCGA exhibits significantly faster convergence than other approaches on functions f_1-f_{12}, f_{18}-f_{21}. The four algorithms attain similar convergent characteristics on functions f_{14}-f_{17}, finding the optimal values in only few of generations. The MCMEP exhibits faster convergence than MCEA on functions f_1-f_2, f_5-f_6, f_9-f_{11}, f_{16}-f_{17}, f_{20}-f_{21}. The MSEP more easily falls into the local minimum, with increasing of the number of generations, the convergence will slow down and even standstill. The MMCGA has a superior solution searching ability when finding optimal solutions compared to other three algorithms.

Comparison of MMCGA and MECA

The M-elite co-evolutionary algorithm (MECA) (Mu, Jiao & Liu, 2009) is proposed on the basis of co-evolutionary algorithm and elitist strategy. The whole population is divided into two subpopulations which are elite population composed of M

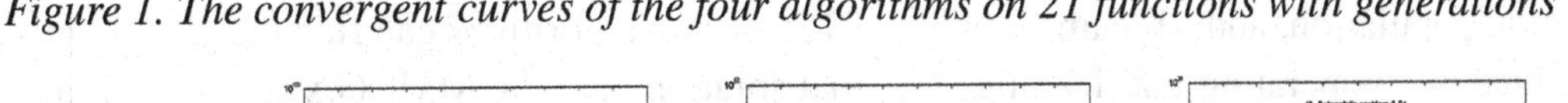

Figure 1. The convergent curves of the four algorithms on 21 functions with generations

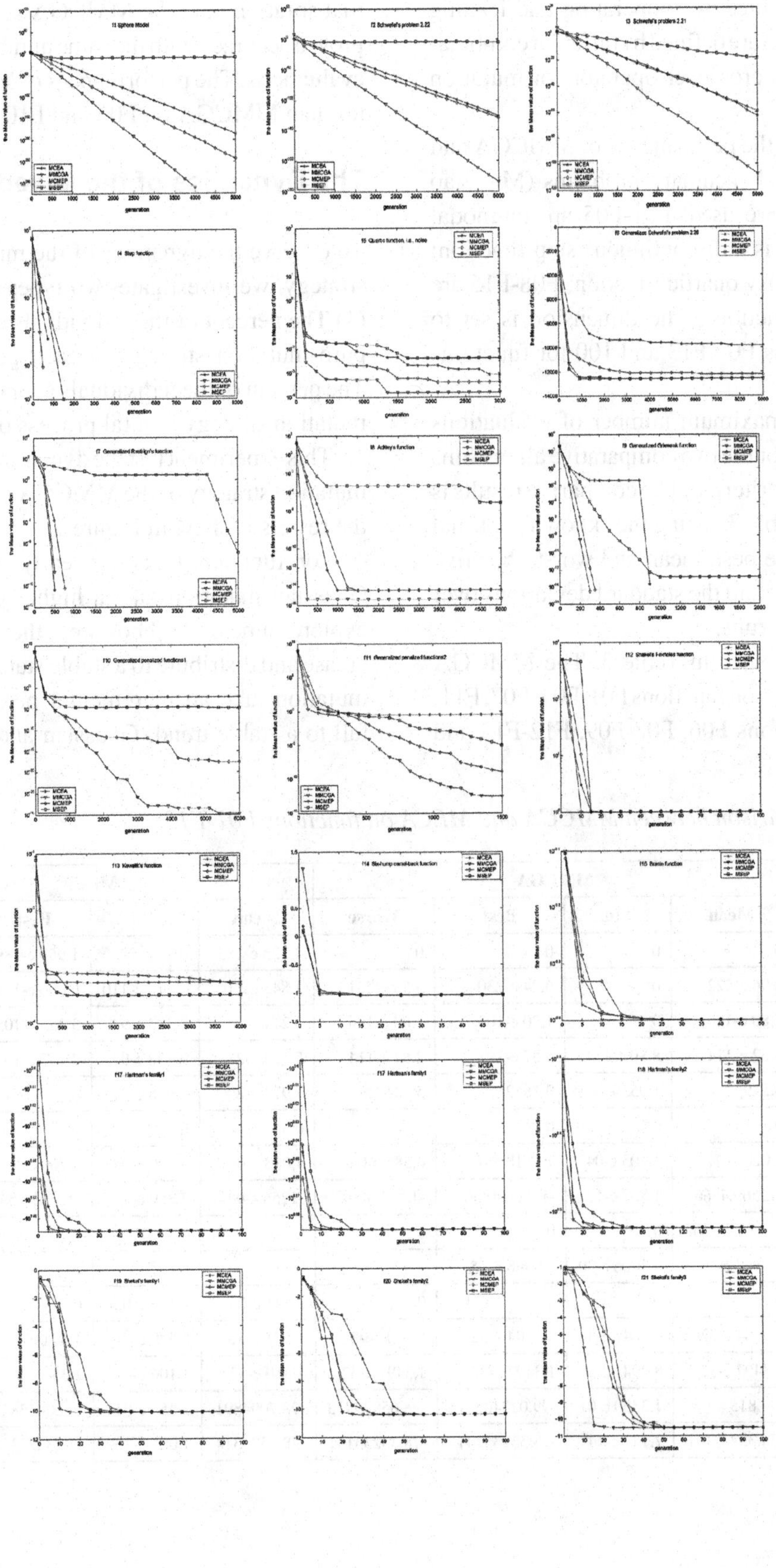

elites and common population, and M teams are formed by M elites by cooperating and leading operation, which are defined by different combinations of several crossover operators or mutation operators.

To evaluate the performance of MMCGA and MECA, the 15 benchmark problems (Mu, Jiao & Liu, 2009) are used. F01-F05 are unimodal functions; F06 is a discontinuous step function; F07 is a is a noisy quartic function; F08-F15 are multimodal functions. The dimension is set to 30 for functions F01-F13 and 100 for functions F14-F15.

The same maximum number of evaluations 300, 000 is set for the two comparative algorithms as the stopping criterion. The comparing results is displayed in Table 3, listing the "known" optimal solution and the best, mean and worst objective function values, and the standard deviations over 50 independent runs.

It can be seen from Table 3, The MMCGA surpasses MECA on functions F01-F04, F07, F11, F14. For functions F06, F08-F09, F12-F13 and F15, the two algorithms can find the global optimal solution, and the MMCGA achieves an improved accuracy with the same number of function evaluations. The performances of MECA are better than MMCGA on F05 and F10.

The Dynamics of the Mixed Strategy

To observe the dynamics of the mixed mutation strategy, we investigate two types of dynamics: (1) The percent of the individuals adopting each pure mutation strategy in each generation; (2) The percent of the individuals adopting each pure mutation strategy in total process of evolution.

This experiment test the dynamics of the mixed mutation strategy of the MMCGA on function f1, the results is show in Figure 2.

For function f_1, at the early search phase, Gaussian mutation take a higher percentage to explore in near neighbor area, then begin to decrease and distribute to a stable state; single point mutation take an incremental percentage, then fall to a stable trend; Gaussian and single point

Table 3. Comparison between MMCGA and MECA on functions F01-F15

F	Fmin	MMCGA				MECA			
		Mean	Std	Best	Worse	Mean	Std	Best	Worse
F01	0	0	0	0	0	4.228 e-183	0	1.959 e-189	1.191 e-181
F02	0	8.96 e-222	0	6.24 e-230	3.58 e-221	1.845 e-110	3.113 e-110	6.866 e-114	1.607 e-109
F03	0	7.80 e-186	0	1.20 e-103	1.00 e-185	3.274 e-95	2.313 e-94	3.253 e-105	1.635 e-93
F04	0	5.62 e-114	8.80 e-114	5.57 e-117	2.84 e-114	5.124 e-2	9.732 e-02	8.167 e-10	5.037 e-01
F05	0	3.219	1.9556	0.1852	5.9652	7.973 e-2	5.638 e-01	0	3.987
F06	0	0	0	0	0	0	0	0	0
F07	0	4.020 e-04	1.405 e-04	7.2518 e-05	6.585 e-04	4.083 e-04	3.800 e-04	3.760 e-06	1.693 e-03
F08	-12569.5	-12569.4866	1.837 e-12	-12569.4866	-12569.4866	-12569.4866	7.350 e-12	-12569.4866	-12569.4866
F09	0	0	0	0	0	0	0	0	0
F10	0	3.9968 e-15	2.3906 e-30	3.9968 e-15	3.9968 e-15	0	0	0	0
F11	0	0	0	0	0	3.844 e-03	7.130 e-03	0	2.464 e-02
F12	0	1.5704 e-32	2.7647 e-48	1.5704 e-32	1.5704 e-32	1.571 e-32	5.529 e-48	1.571 e-32	1.571 e-32
F13	0	1.3497 e-32	8.2941 e-48	1.3497 e-32	1.3497 e-32	1.350 e-32	1.106 e-47	1.350 e-32	1.350 e-32
F14	-99.60	-98.815	1.3360 e-01	-99.02340357	-98.65839973	-98.7094891	1.450 e-01	-99.0043822	-98.2435226
F15	-78.33236	-78.33233141	7.177 e-14	-78.33233141	-78.33233141	-78.3323314	1.005 e-13	-78.3323314	-78.3323314

Figure 2. The dynamics of the mixed mutation strategy of the MMCGA, (a)-(e): The percent of the individuals adopting Gaussian, Cauchy, Levy, Single Point and Differential mutation strategy in each generation respectively, (f): The percent of the individuals adopting each pure mutation strategy in total process of evolution

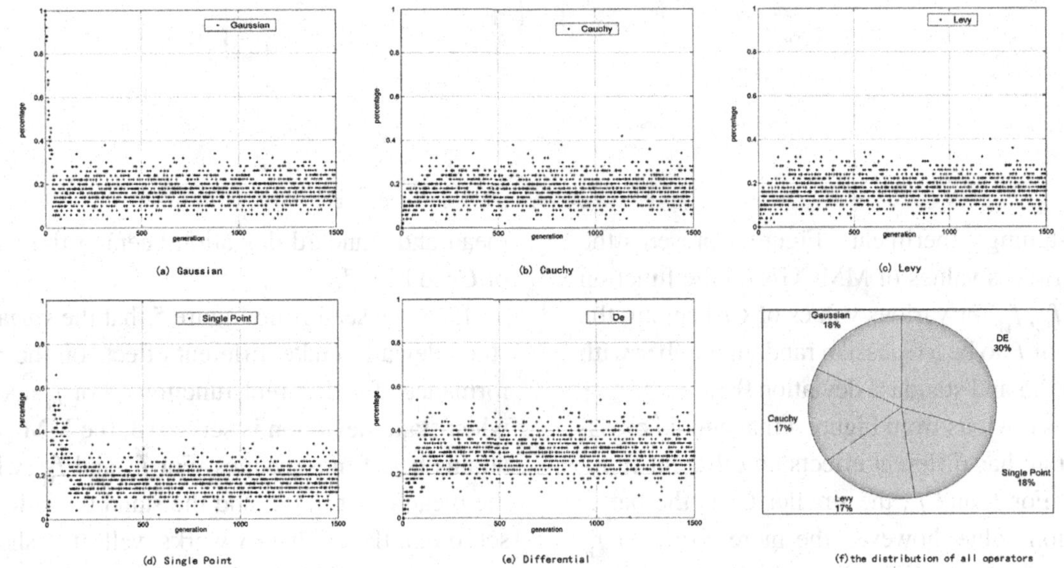

mutation take same percentage in entire explore; Cauchy, Levy and differential mutation take an incremental percentage, then to a stable state; differential mutation holds a higher percentage than other strategies, which indicates its advantages in evolution.

To observe the dynamics of the mixed crossover strategy, we take similar experiment as mixed mutation strategy. The results are shown in Figure 3.

The percentage of individuals selecting CCO strategy is distributed approximately to between 15% to 40%; TCO approximately to between 40% to 65%, holding a dominant position in the process of search; HCO strategy takes a lower percentage, distributing roughly to between 10% to 40%.

Parameters for the Algorithms

Cuboid Crossover Rate (Cr)

In order to investigate the effect of *Cr* on the performance of the MMCGA, we perform a series of

Figure 3. The dynamics of the mixed crossover strategy of the MMCGA: (a)-(c) The percent of the individuals adopting CCO, TCO and HCO strategy in each generation respectively, (d) The percent of the individuals adopting each pure crossover strategy in total process of evolution

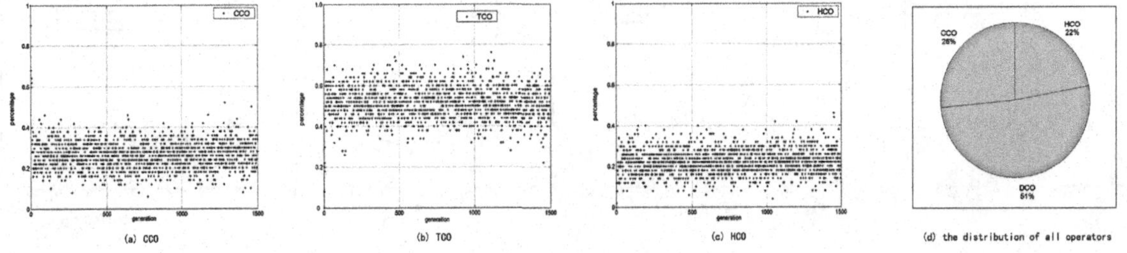

Figure 4. Final fitness values on the function f1, f2, f10, f11 with MMCGA for different settings of cuboid crossover rate Cr

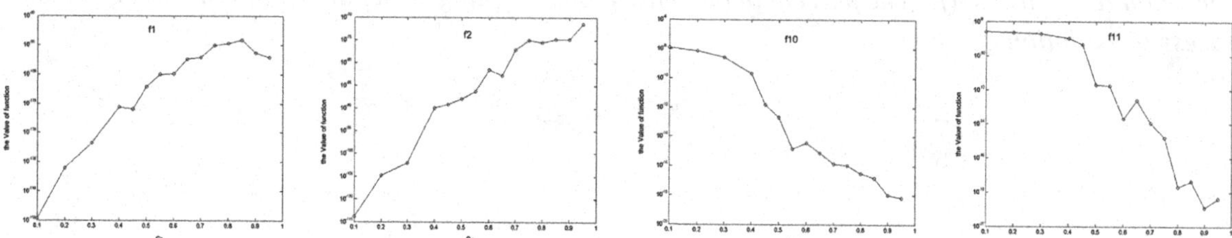

hand-tuning experiments. Figure 4 presents the final fitness values of MMCGA on the function f_1, f_2, f_{10}, f_{11} for various values of *Cr* keeping the value of *F* to be a Gaussian random number with mean 0.5 and standard deviation 0.5.

It is obvious from Figure 4 that cuboid crossover rate has different effects on different functions. For f_1 and f_2, the smaller *Cr* is the better function value, however, the more NFE; for f_{10} and f_{11}, the larger *Cr* is, the better function value. A reasonable selection is made, *Cr*=0.7, considering the performances of both fitness and NFE.

The Scaling Factor of Differential Mutation Operator (F)

In this paper, the scaling factor of differential mutation operator *F* is a Gaussian random number. In order to select appropriate mean and standard deviation of the Gaussian distribution, we perform a series of hand-tuning experiments. Figure 5 presents the final function values of MMCGA on the function f_1, f_2, f_{10}, f_{11} for various values of mean and standard deviation keeping the value of *Cr* to be 0.7.

It can be seen from Figure 5 that the variable stand deviation take different effects on the performances for different functions. For f_1 and f_2, when stand deviation is set to 0.3, the MMCGA attains best fitness values. For f_{10} and f_{11}, when the mean is set to 0.5 and the stand deviation is set to 0.5, the MMCGA works well. It is shown from the figures that the suggested parameter setting (the values of mean and the stand deviation are set to 0.5) gives best performance with the MMCGA.

CONCLUSION

This article compared the performances of four state-of-the-art evolutionary algorithms variants with other methods. The initial mixed strategy framework is added a new mutation operator into and extended to crossover operation. The better performances are attained by utilizing the mixed

Figure 5. Final function values on the function f1, f2, f10, f11 with MMCGA for different settings of mean and standard deviation on Gaussian distribution of F

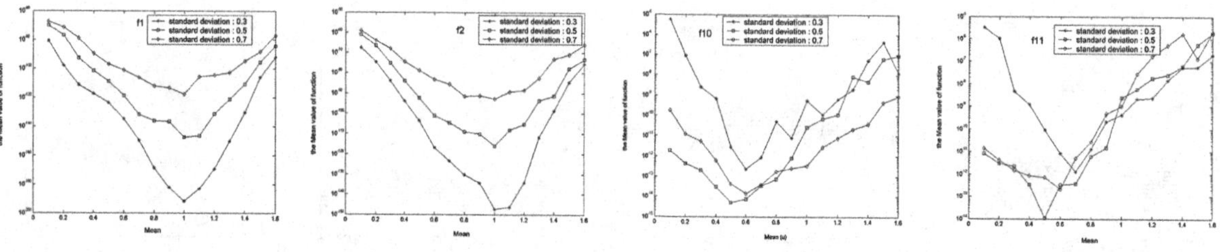

crossover and mutation strategies to select the most effective operator at different stages of evolution. Especially, the proposed MMCGA has indicated a superior solution searching ability over others. The evolutionary framework based on the mixed strategy is simple, easy to implement and extend, it may be utilized for various real life applications.

ACKNOWLEDGMENT

This work is partially supported by the National Natural Science Foundation of China under Grant No.60973075 and No.61075113, and the Natural Science Foundation of Heilongjiang Province of China under Grant No.F200937.

REFERENCES

Chellapilla, K. (1998). Combining mutation operators in evolutionary programming. *IEEE Transactions on Evolutionary Computation*, *2*(3), 91–96. doi:10.1109/4235.735431

Das, S., Abraham, A., & Konar, A. (2008). Automatic clustering using an improved differential evolution algorithm. *IEEE Transactions on Systems, Man, and Cybernetics. Part A, Systems and Humans*, *38*, 1–20. doi:10.1109/TSMCA.2007.909595

Dutta, P. K. (1999). *Strategies and Games*. Cambridge, MA: MIT Press.

Ficici, S. G., Melnik, O., & Pollack, J. B. (2000). A game-theoretic investigation of selection methods used in evolutionary algorithms. In *Proceedings of the 2000 IEEE Conference on Evolutionary Computation* (pp. 880-887).

Fogel, L. J., Owens, A. J., & Walsh, M. J. (1966). *Artificial Intelligence through Simulated Evolution*. New York, NY: Wiley.

He, J., & Yao, X. (2005). A Game-Theoretic Approach for Designing Mixed Mutation Strategies. In *Advances in Natural Computation* (LNCS 3612, pp. 279-288).

Ji, M. J., Tang, H. W., & Guo, J. (2004). A single-point mutation evolutionary programming. *Information Processing Letters*, *90*, 293–299. doi:10.1016/j.ipl.2004.03.002

Lee, C. Y., & Yao, X. (2004). Evolutionary programming using mutations based on the Levy probability distribution. *IEEE Transactions on Evolutionary Computation*, *8*, 1–13. doi:10.1109/TEVC.2003.816583

Mallipeddi, R., Mallipeddi, S., & Suganthan, P. N. (2010). Ensemble strategies with adaptive evolutionary programming. *Information Sciences*, *180*, 1571–1581. doi:10.1016/j.ins.2010.01.007

Maulik, U., & Saha, I. (2009). Modified differential evolution based fuzzy clustering for pixel classification in remote sensing imagery. *Pattern Recognition*, *42*, 2135–2149. doi:10.1016/j.patcog.2009.01.011

Michalewicz, Z. (1994). *Genetic Algorithms + Data Structures = Evolution Programs*. Berlin, Germany: Springer-Verlag.

Mu, C. H., Jiao, L. C., & Liu, Y. (2009). M-Elite Coevolutionary Algorithm for Numerical Optimization. *Chinese Journal of Software*, *20*(11), 2925–2938. doi:10.3724/SP.J.1001.2009.03496

Mühlenbein, H., & Schlierkamp-Voosen, D. (1993). Predictive Models for the Breeder Genetic Algorithm I. Continuous Parameter Optimization. *Evolutionary Computation*, *1*, 25–49. doi:10.1162/evco.1993.1.1.25

Nomura, T. (1997). An Analysis on Crossovers for Real Number Chromosomes in an Infinite Population Size. In *Proceedings of the 1997 International Joint Conference on Artificial Intelligence* (Vol. 2, pp. 936-941).

Omran, M., Engelbrecht, A. P., & Salman, A. (2005). Differential evolution methods for unsupervised image classification. In *Proceedings of the Seventh Conference on Evolutionary Computation (CEC-2005)* (Vol. 2, pp. 966-973).

Qin, A. K., & Suganthan, P. N. (2005). Self-adaptive differential evolution algorithm for numerical optimization. In *Proceedings of the IEEE Conference on Evolutionary Computation, 2*, 1785–1791. doi:10.1109/CEC.2005.1554904

Storn, R., & Price, K. (1995). *Differential Evolution-a simple and efficient adaptive scheme for global optimization over continuous spaces* (Tech. Rep. No. 12). Berkeley, CA: International Computer Science Institute.

Storn, R., & Price, K. (1997). A simple and efficient heuristic for global optimization over continuous spaces. *Journal of Global Optimization, 11*(4), 341–359. doi:10.1023/A:1008202821328

Suresh, K., Kundu, D., Ghosh, S., Das, S., Abraham, A., & Han, S. Y. (2009). Multi-Objective Differential Evolution for Automatic Clustering with Application to Micro-Array Data Analysis. *Sensors (Basel, Switzerland), 9*, 3981–4004. doi:10.3390/s90503981

Weibull, J. W. (1995). *Evolutionary Game Theory*. Cambridge, MA: MIT Press.

Xue, F., Sanderson, A. C., & Graves, R. J. (2003). Pareto-based multi-objective differential evolution. In *Proceedings of the 2003 Conference on Evolutionary Computation (CEC'2003)* (Vol. 2, pp. 862-869).

Yang, Z. Y., He, J., & Yao, X. (2008). Making a difference to differential evolution. In Michalewicz, Z., & Siarry, P. (Eds.), *Advances in Metaheuristics for Hard Optimization* (pp. 397–414). Heidelberg, Berlin: Springer-Verlag. doi:10.1007/978-3-540-72960-0_19

Yang, Z. Y., Tang, K., & Yao, X. (2007). Differential evolution for high-dimensional function optimization. In *Proceedings of the 2007 Conference on Evolutionary Computation* (pp. 3523-3530).

Yang, Z. Y., Tang, K., & Yao, X. (2008). Large scale evolutionary optimization using cooperative coevolution. *Information Sciences, 178*, 2985–2999. doi:10.1016/j.ins.2008.02.017

Yao, X., Liu, Y., & Lin, G. (1999). Evolutionary programming made faster. *IEEE Transactions on Evolutionary Computation, 3*, 82–102. doi:10.1109/4235.771163

This work was previously published in the Journal of Information Technology Research, Volume 4, Issue 2, edited by Mehdi Khosrow-Pour, pp. 17-30, copyright 2011 by IGI Publishing (an imprint of IGI Global).

Chapter 7
A Hyper-Heuristic Using GRASP with Path-Relinking:
A Case Study of the Nurse Rostering Problem

He Jiang
Dalian University of Technology, China

Junying Qiu
Dalian University of Technology, China

Jifeng Xuan
Dalian University of Technology, China

ABSTRACT

The goal of hyper-heuristics is to design and choose heuristics to solve complex problems. The primary motivation behind the hyper-heuristics is to generalize the solving ability of the heuristics. In this paper, the authors propose a Hyper-heuristic using GRASP with Path-Relinking (HyGrasPr). HyGrasPr generates heuristic sequences to produce solutions within an iterative procedure. The procedure of HyGrasPr consists of three phases, namely the construction phase, the local search phase, and the path-relinking phase. To show the performance of the HyGrasPr, the authors use the nurse rostering problem as a case study. The authors use an existing simulated annealing based hyper-heuristic as a baseline. The experimental results indicate that HyGrasPr can achieve better solutions than SAHH within the same running time and the path-relinking phase is effective for the framework of HyGrasPr.

INTRODUCTION

Hyper-heuristics aim to design general solving technologies for various problems by choosing existing heuristics (Burke, Hyde, Kendall, Ochoa, Ozcan, & Woodward, 2010). In contrast to meta-heuristics focused on the domain knowledge, hyper-heuristics tend to produce the High Level Heuristics (HLHs) for guiding the Low Level Heuristics (LLHs) (Burke, Hyde, Kendall, Ochoa, Ozcan, & Qu, 2010). The high level heuristics are referred to the heuristics designed by algorithm experts over the problem domains while the LLHs

DOI: 10.4018/978-1-4666-3625-5.ch007

are referred to the heuristics designed by the problem domain experts. Since the domain knowledge is necessary for a particular problem and is hard to explore by an algorithm designer (Ochaoa, Qu, & Burke, 2009), the primary motivation behind the hyper-heuristics is to help the algorithm designers to jump out of the limit from the problem domain and to produce general approaches. Based on the ability of general problem solving, hyper-heuristics have been applied to many kinds of problems, especially NP-hard problems, such as the timetabling (Burke, McCollum, Meisels, Petrovic, & Qu, 2007; Qu & Burke, 2009), the cutting stock (Terashima-Martin, Moran-Saavedre, & Ross, 2005), the workforce scheduling (Remde, Cowling, Dahal, & Colledge, 2006; Remde, Dahal, Cowling, & Colledge, 2009) and the p-median (Ren, Jiang, Xuan, & Luo, 2010).

In general, the goal of a hyper-heuristic is to design HLH to find an optimal LLH sequence, which can generate optimal solutions to the problems. As one kind of heuristics, most of hyper-heuristics draw on the experiments from the existing meta-heuristics, e.g., a simulated annealing based hyper-heuristic (Dowsland, Soubeiga, & Burke, 2007) and a genetic algorithm based hyper-heuristic (Ross, Martin-Blazquez, Schulenburg, & Hart, 2003). However, the kinds of hyper-heuristics are much fewer than those of meta-heuristics. The insufficiency of hyper-heuristics has limited the development of hyper-heuristics (Burke, Hyde, Kendall, Ochoa, Ozcan, & Woodward, 2010).

Greedy Randomized Adaptive Search Procedure (GRASP) with path-relinking is one of the effective meta-heuristics for problem solving (Resende & Ribeiro, 2003). There is no hyper-heuristic based on GRASP with path-relinking. As a typical meta-heuristic, GRASP with path-relinking is an iterative procedure to find the optimal solution. GRASP with path-relinking consists of three phases, such as the construction phase, the local search phase, and the path-relinking phase.

Motivated by the success of this algorithm in meta-heuristics, we propose a Hyper-heuristic using GRASP with Path-Relinking (HyGrasPr) in this paper. Our algorithm, HyGrasPr, generates LLH sequences to produce solutions in an iterative procedure. In each iteration, HyGrasPr builds an initial LLH sequence and applies a local search operator to find a relatively good LLH sequence. To avoid to be trapped as a local optimal LLH sequence, the path-relinking strategy is applied to obtain potential good solutions. To show the experimental results of HyGrasPr, we take the nurse rostering problem as a case study. On this problem, an existing simulated annealing based hyper-heuristic (SAHH) is employed as an experiment baseline. The results indicate that HyGrasPr can achieve better solutions than SAHH within the same running time.

The rest of this paper is organized as follows. First, we give the background of our work. We then propose the details of our HyGrasPr and present the experiments results with a case study on the nurse rostering problem.

BACKGROUND

Hyper-Heuristics and Meta-Heuristics

Hyper-heuristic technology is able to handle a wide range of problem domains rather than current meta-heuristic technology concentrated on a particular problem or a narrow class of problems (Burke, Kendall, Newall, Hart, Ross, & Schulenburg, 2003). A solution of a meta-heuristic is a structure abstracted from the problem domain; on the other hand, a solution of a hyper-heuristic is a sequence of LLHs. Many hyper-heuristics are based on the mechanism from meta-heuristics, e.g., hyper-heuristics based on tabu search for timetabling and rostering (Burke, Kendall, & Soubeiga, 2003), simulated annealing for determining shipper sizes (Dowsland et al., 2007), for automated planograms (Bai & Kendall, 2005), genetic algorithm (bin-packing) (Ross et al.,

2003), and for 2D-regular cutting stock problems (Terashima-Martin et al., 2005), genetic programming for two dimensional strip packing (Burke, Hyde, Kendall, Ochoa, Ozcan, & Qu, 2010), and ant colony optimization for project presentation scheduling (Burke, Kendall, Silva, O'Brien, & Soubeiga, 2005) and for p-median by Ren et al. (2010). Moreover, Bai, Burke and Kendall (2008) investigate both the meta-heuristics and hyper-heuristics for fresh produce inventory control and shelf space allocation. Considering the similarity between meta-heuristics and hyper-heuristics, many experiments from meta-heuristics can be employed to guide the hyper-heuristic design. Thus in this paper, we introduce another meta-heuristic to serve for hyper-heuristics, i.e., GRASP with path-relinking.

GRASP with Path-Relinking

GRASP is a multi-start meta-heuristic, in which each iteration consists a construction phase and a local search phase while path-relinking is a strategy to provide various solutions by "relinking" existing solutions (Resende & Ribeiro, 2003). For some of the applications, path-relinking is combined with GRASP to conduct a post-optimization or an intensification strategy to each local optimum (Festa, Pardalos, Pitsoulis, & Resende, 2006). Path-relinking is an enhancement strategy to build paths between solutions and to find other relevant solutions in the paths. Since time-consuming in practice, path-relinking is not applied at each GRASP iteration, but only periodically (Resende & Ribeiro, 2003).

HYPER-HEURISTIC USING GRASP WITH PATH-RELINKING

Framework

In this section, we present the details of our HyGrasPr. The solution generated by HyGrasPr is an LLH sequence, which can be applied to the problem instance in order to obtain the final solution to the problem. The LLH sequence is generated by an iterative procedure of GRASP with the path-relinking phase. In HyGrasPr, we first build an LLH sequence with the fixed length in GRASP construction phase. Then, we search the neighborhood of the LLH sequence for obtaining the local optimal LLH sequence (Croes, 1958). If an LLH sequence gets the best solution, we store it as the current best LLH sequence. Next, we use the current best LLH sequence and the local optimal LLH sequence to conduct the path-relinking phase. In each iteration, we apply the local optimal LLH sequence to the current solution to find the optimal LLH sequence for the problem. In our framework, we give three parameters, namely the number of iteration, the length of LLH sequence in each iteration, and the controllable parameter for the greedy or random strategies.

The pseudo-code for HyGrasPr is presented in Table 1. The kernel idea of our algorithm is to find the optimal LLH sequence by combining GRASP with path-relinking. In our implementation, we store the current best LLH sequence, which can be used for guiding problem solving in the path-relinking phase. Specifically, after a particular number of GRASP iterations, the local optimal LLH sequence is compared with the

Table 1. Pseudo-code for HyGrasPr

Procedure GRASP with path-relinking Input: maximum iteration *Iteration*, *Seq* length *N*, parameter used in construction α, call path-relinking frequency *PF* Output: Solution *S*

for $i = 1, \ldots,$ *Iteration* do
Seq = GRASP_Construction(N, α, S_{begin}, S_{next})
Seq_{local} = Local_Search(N, S_{begin}, S_{next}, Seq)
if i % PF= 0 then
Path-Relinking(Seq_{best}, Seq_{local}, S_{begin}, S_{next})
endif
update Seq_{best}
$S_{begin} \leftarrow S_{nextNew}$
endfor

current best LLH sequence found by now. If the two LLH sequences are different with each other, we call the path-relinking phase. At the end of each iteration, the current best LLH sequence is updated for the next iteration. Existing work on the path-relinking for the meta-heuristics shows that the input length for the path-relinking can increase the running time (Resende & Ribeiro, 2003). In this work, the length of LLH sequence is determined according to an empirical result.

Each iteration of our HyGrasPr begins with an initial solution S_{begin} as an input and ends with a new solution S_{next} as an output. The new solution S_{next} is obtained by applying an LLH sequence to the initial solution S_{begin}. The goal of the hyper-heuristics is to find an optimal LLH sequence, which is applied to the original problem. We denote the LLH sequence as *Seq*. The final sequence of HyGrasPr is combined by all the LLH sequence obtained for each iteration.

GRASP

Based on an LLH sequence with the length *N*, the hyper-heuristic may provide various solutions for the original problem. To generate an optimal LLH sequence, the GRASP procedure works with two parameters, namely used to denote the length of the LLH sequence and to conduct the construction of the restricted candidate list.

In general, each iteration of GRASP consists of two phases, namely the construction phase and the local search phase. We describe the construction phase and the local search phase for GRASP in our HyGrasPr. The construction phase of HyGrasPr is different from the typical GRASP construction for the meta-heuristics. The output of the construction phase is an LLH sequence, which is built from an empty sequence. In each iteration of the construction phase, we add an LLH to the current LLH sequence until the LLH sequence length reaches the particular value *N*. The LLH to be added is randomly selected from the Restricted Candidate List (RCL). The RCL is a subset of the set of all candidate LLHs. If an LLH can generate a solution according with the given threshold, the LLH will be added to the RCL. The threshold is defined as $c^{\min} + \alpha(c^{\max} - c^{\min})$, where $c^{\min}$ and $c^{\max}$ are the minimum and maximum of the evaluation function values for a new solution after applying the LLH to the current solution. The parameter α is a controllable parameter and $0 \leq \alpha \leq 1$. If $\alpha = 0$, the construction phase can be viewed as a greedy construction while if $\alpha = 1$, the construction phase can be viewed as a random construction. We present the pseudo-code of the construction phase in Table 2.

After the construction phase of the HyGrasPr, we apply a local search phase to optimize the current LLH sequence. The 2-opt search is em-

Table 2. Pseudo-code for construction of GRASP in HyGrasPr

Procedure construction Input: LLH sequence length *N*, parameter α, the initial problem solution S_{begin} Output: LLH sequence *Seq*, a new problem solution S_{next}

Seq $\leftarrow \Phi$,
best value by LLH sequence of current Iteration *Best* $\leftarrow \infty$
while the length of *Seq* < *N*
for every LLH $H_i \in H$(the set of low level heuristics) do
apply H_i to current solution $S_{current}$ get new solution S_i
C_i = objective value of S_i
endfor
$c^{\max} \leftarrow \max\{ c_i \mid c_i \in C\}$
$c^{\min} \leftarrow \min\{ c_i \mid c_i \in C\}$
the restricted candidate list $RCL \leftarrow \{i \in H \mid c_i \leq c^{\min} + \alpha(c^{\max} - c^{\min}) \}$
randomly select a heuristic num *h* from *RCL*
if $c_h < Best$ then
$Best = c_h$
endif
add *h* to *Seq*
$S_{current} \leftarrow S_h$
endwhile
$S_{next} \leftarrow S_{current}$

ployed in the local search phase. To find the optimal LLH sequence, each LLH in the *Seq* is traversed to search for the opportunity to build the final optimal LLH sequence. In each step, we change the selected LLH with other candidate LLHs, and then apply the new LLH sequence Seq_{temp} to the solution S_{begin}. If the new Seq_{temp} in the neighborhood could obtain a better solution, we replace Seq_{local} with Seq_{temp}. After applying the current best LLH sequence to the solution S_{begin}, the new obtained solution is used as the initial solution in the next iteration. In Table 3, we present the pseudo-code of the local search.

Path-Relinking

In this section, we propose the path-relinking phase for HyGrasPr. Path-relinking can be viewed as an enhancement to the GRASP procedure. The main idea of the path-relinking is to explore the trajectories that connect an initial LLH sequence to a guiding LLH sequence. The initial LLH sequence is the input of the path-relinking while the guiding LLH sequence is the objective to guide the exploration. In HyGrasPr, a move of the path-relinking phase is defined as a change from one LLH to another for reducing the difference between the guiding LLH sequence and the initial LLH sequence. In our experiments, the initial LLH sequence is the best LLH sequence found up till now and the guiding LLH sequence is the local optimal LLH sequence in current iteration. The initial LLH sequence can be defined as Seq_i and the guiding solution can be defined as Seq_g. We present the pseudo-code for this phase in Table 4.

Table 3. Pseudo-code of local search of GRASP in HyGrasPr

Procedure local search
Input: LLH sequence length *N*,
LLH sequence *Seq*,
initial problem solution S_{begin},
best value by LLH sequence of current Iteration *Best*,
S_{next} got from construction phase
Output: local optimal LLH sequence Seq_{local},
problem solution S_{next}

$Seq_{local} \leftarrow Seq$
for $i = 0, ..., N$ do
for $j = 0, ..., H_{num}$ (the number of low level heuristics) do
if the *i*th LLH of $Seq != j$ then
get a new LLH sequence Seq_{temp} by replacing *i*th LLH of *Seq* with *j*
$S_{temp} \leftarrow S_{begin}$
localOptimalFlag = false
for $k = 0, ..., N$ do
apply *k*th LLH of Seq_{temp} to S_{temp}
compute the objective value of S_{temp} *value*
if *value* < *Best* then
Best = *value*
$Seq_{local} = Seq_{temp}$
localOptimalFlag = true
endif
endfor
if *localOptimalFlag* then
$S_{next} \leftarrow S_{temp}$
endif
endif
endfor
endfor

A CASE STUDY OF THE NURSE ROSTERING PROBLEM

The Nurse Rostering Problem

The nurse rostering problem is a typical problem in the family of the personnel scheduling problem (Burke, Causmaecker, Berghe, & Landeghem, 2004). The goal of the nurse rostering problem is to decide the assignment of each nurse working over a specific planning period subject to various constraints (Burke, Li, & Qu, 2010). In this paper, we take the nurse rostering problem as a case study to investigate the performance of our HyGrasPr. The benchmark instances can be obtained from the nurse rostering problem website (http://www.cs.nott.ac.uk/~tec/NRP/). These instances in our experiments are generated from the real-world scenarios. All the constraints in the nurse rostering problem instances are modeled as the weighted objectives (Curtois, Ochoa, Hyde, & Vazquez-Rodriguez, 2010). The mathematical formulation of these objectives is described in (Burke, Curtois, Qu, & Vanden-Berghe, 2008).

Table 4. Pseudo-code of path-relinking in HyGrasPr

Procedure path-relinking Input: initial solution Seq_i, guiding solution Seq_g Output: the best LLH sequence Seq_{best}
1 compute the sum *Number* of different LLHs between Seq_i and Seq_g 2 save the different LLHs in the move set, *M* 2 for $i = 0,\ldots,Number$ do 3 find the *bestmove* in the move set, *M* 4 apply the *bestmove* 5 update the Seq_{best} 6 update the best problem solution 7 delete the selected *bestmove* from *M*. 8 endfor

To show the performance of our HyGrasPr, we use 12 LLHs in this paper. These LLHs are obtained in the hyper-heuristic competition website (http://www.asap.cs.nott.ac.uk/chesc2011/index.html). A detailed description of these heuristic is reproduced here for completeness (Curtois et al., 2010):

- h_1, local search heuristic using "hill climbers" with vertical neighborhood operator (moving shifts vertically between two employees in the roster);
- h_2, local search heuristic using "hill climbers" with horizontal neighborhood operator (moving shifts horizontally in single employee's work pattern in the roster);
- h_3, local search heuristic using "hill climbers" with new neighborhood operator (introducing new shifts or deleting shifts into the roster);
- h_4, local search heuristic, variable depth search using new moves as links in the ejection chain;
- h_5, local search heuristic, variable depth search using new moves as links in the ejection chain and test replacing an entire work pattern for a single employee as a link in the chain;
- h_6, ruin and recreate heuristic, un-assigning $x = Round\ (\beta \times 4) + 2$ schedules (β is the intensity of mutation and *Round*() is the rounding function). The heuristic first randomly selects x employee's schedules and un-assigning all the shifts in them. They are rebuilt by first satisfying objectives related to requests to work certain days or shifts and then by satisfying objectives related to weekends;
- h_7, same as h6 but "$x = Round\ (\beta \times$ Number of employees in roster)";
- h_8, same as h6 but creating a small perturbation in the solution by using $x = 1$;
- h_9, crossover heuristic, choosing the best x assignments in each parent and make these assignments in the offspring;
- h_{10}, crossover heuristic, it creates a new roster by using all the assignments made in the parents. It makes those that are common to both parents first and then alternately selects an assignment from each parent and makes it in the offspring unless the cover objective is already satisfied;
- h_{11}, crossover heuristic, creating the new roster by making assignments which are only common to both parents;
- h_{12}, mutation heuristic, randomly mutating a selected roster.

Results

We show the performance of our HyGrasPr in the experiments. All the experiments are run on a PC with Intel Core Duo 2.53 GHz and 4GB RAM running on a Microsoft Windows 7 Ultimate.

Before showing the experimental results, we give some experiments on the parameter values and performance. We test our algorithm on 4 typical problem instances (ORTEC02, Ikegami-3Shift-DATA1, Ikegami-3Shift-DATA1.1, and Ikegami-3Shift-DATA1.2) with different parameters. The parameter α which is the probability of choosing RCL in GRASP is set to 0.3. The parameter *N*, the length of LLH sequence is set to 5, 10, 15, and 20, respectively. We limit the time bound to 30 minutes. The results are shown in Table 5.

It is showed that when the parameter α is fixed to 0.3, the LLH sequence length with the value 15 gets the best result. In general, for the length from 5 to 15, the objective function of solutions is decreasing when the length increases. That is the length with the value 15 may bring better solutions than others. On the other hand, when the sequence length increases, the running time may increase. Therefore, the experiment with the length of the value 20 can cost more time than the previous three experiments. Since we limit the time bound, the experiment with the length 20 cannot finish the process of searching. Thus, we choose 15 as the sequence length in the following experiments.

We study the parameter α with the values among 0.1, 0.3, 0.5, and 0.7. We also limit the time bound to 30 minutes. The results are showed in Table 6.

In the structure of the construction phase, the parameter α is a trade-off between greedy and random. From the results, we can see that the value 0.3 maybe a good value for the instances in our experiments.

The experiments of adjusting the parameters in our HyGrasPr on the nurse rostering problem above show that $\alpha = 0.3$ and $N = 15$ can make our HyGrasPr perform well. Then we compare our hyper heuristic with an existing algorithm on the instances.

We choose 10 typical problem instances from the nurse rostering problem instances. We make comparison with the Simulated Annealing Hyper-Heuristic (SAHH) (Bai, Blazewicz, Burke, Kendall, & McCollum, 2007) proposed by Bai et al. SAHH is a hyper heuristic which includes a stochastic heuristic selection mechanism, a simulated annealing acceptance criterion, and a short-term memory. SAHH learns priorities of different low level heuristics from their historical performance and starts to select them depending on priorities. Therefore, the heuristics with good performance have higher priorities and are more likely to be chosen. The simulated annealing acceptance criterion is used to determine whether to be applied the selected heuristic. Information about the acceptance decisions by the acceptance criterion is then fed back to the heuristic selection mechanism in order to make good better decisions in the future. In (Bai et al., 2007), it was shown that SAHH is a well performed hyper-heuristic. SAHH can also be used for the nurse rostering problem. The number of iterations of SAHH is set to $K = 12000$ as described in (Bai et al., 2007). On each instance, the running time of our HyGrasPr is limited to the used time of SAHH. In Table 7, we present the results for HyGrasPr, SAHH and HyGrasPr without Path-relinking.

Table 5. Objective functions for HyGrasPr with different sequence length on 4 typical instances

Sequence length	5	10	15	20
ORTEC02	335.0	350.0	310.0	335.0
Ikegami-3Shift-DATA1	18.0	11.0	17.0	22.0
Ikegami-3Shift-DATA1.1	23.0	21.0	13.0	21.0
Ikegami-3Shift-DATA1.2	20.0	23.0	18.0	20.0

Table 6. Objective functions for HyGrasPr with different α on 4 typical instances

Value of α	0.1	0.3	0.5	0.7
ORTEC02	365.0	310.0	330.0	380.0
Ikegami-3Shift-DATA1	22.0	17.0	13.0	15.0
Ikegami-3Shift-DATA1.1	20.0	13.0	15.0	31.0
Ikegami-3Shift-DATA1.2	19.0	18.0	21.0	23.0

Table 7. Results for SAHH, HyGrasPr, and HyGrasPr without path-relinking

Problem instance	Time(s)	SAHH	HyGrasPr	HyGrasPr without path-relinking
BCV-3.46.1	17870	3321.0	3307.0	3322.0
BCV-A.12.2	12012	2210.0	2005.0	2340.0
ORTEC02	4972	395	300.0	440.0
Ikegami-3Shift-DATA1	5981	12.0	11.0	21.0
Ikegami-3Shift-DATA1.1	6315	15.0	13.0	25.0
Ikegami-3Shift-DATA1.2	5990	15.0	14.0	36.0
CHILD-A2	43331	1103.0	1108.0	1240.0
ERRVH-A	20022	2165.0	2156.0	2344.0
ERRVH-B	16948	3167.0	3167.0	4093.0
MER-A	38369	9289.0	8934.0	14964.0

From the result we can conclude that our hyper heuristic can outperform the existing algorithm, SAHH. Among the 10 instances, HyGrasPr can get 8 better solutions out of 10 instances. We also compare HyGrasPr with the hyper heuristic implemented by GRASP without path-relinking. The performance of HyGrasPr is much better than that of HyGrasPr without path-relinking. This result shows that the path-relinking mechanism is very useful in our framework. In the path-relinking

Figure 1. Solving procedures of SAHH and HyGrasPr on the ORTEC02 instance

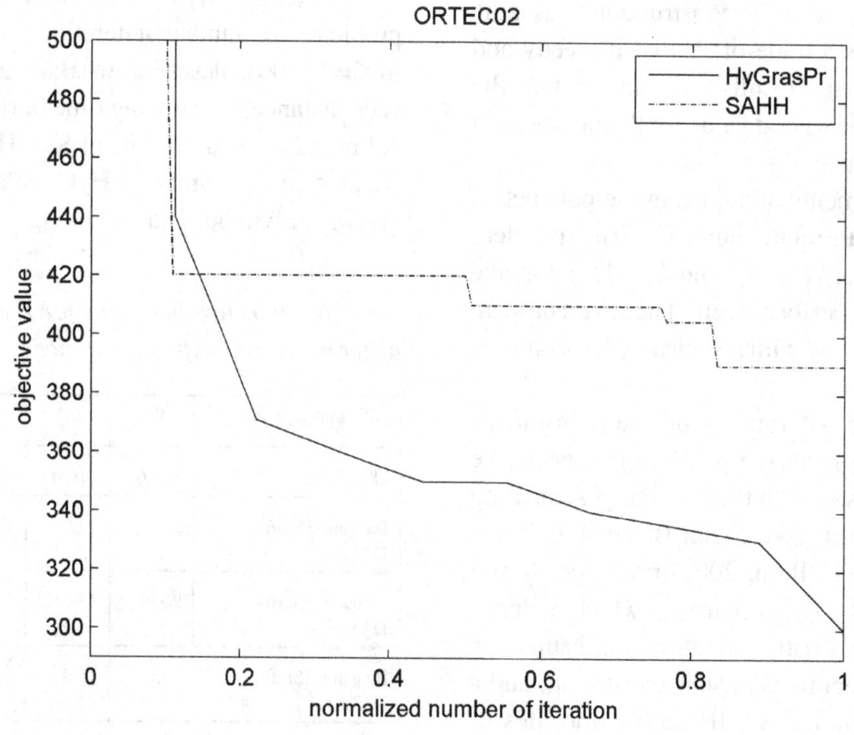

phase, the process the guidance of the LLH sequence from the initial one to the guiding one can provide various LLH sequences as the candidate LLH sequences. The performance of HyGrasPr is also better than that of SAHH.

To show the details of our experiments, we analyze the solving procedure of two algorithms, SAHH and HyGrasPr. Figure 1 presents the details of the processes when solving the instance ORTEC02 using SAHH and HyGrasPr. The results show that our algorithm HyGrasPr can improve solution step by step while SAHH provides a jumping curve. At the same time for both the algorithms, the solutions in SAHH are not as better as those in HyGrasPr. Our HyGrasPr provides a much stronger searching ability.

CONCLUSION AND FUTURE WORK

In this paper, we propose a Hyper-heuristic using GRASP with Path-Relinking (HyGrasPr). The procedure of HyGrasPr consists of three phases, such as the construction phase, the local search phase, and the path-relinking phase. To present the experimental results, we give a case study on the nurse rostering problem. The results show that HyGrasPr can achieve better solutions on 8 out of 10 instances than the existing simulate annealing hyper-heuristic.

In future work, we plan to give an empirical study on the performance of our HyGrasPr. Since the mechanism behind HyGrasPr is a little time-consuming, we want to design some improvement to reduce the running time. Another future work is to apply our HyGrasPr to some other problems. For example, we plan to give a comparison among the family of the nurse rostering problem. This work can show the generalization ability of our work.

ACKNOWLEDGMENT

Our work is partially supported by the Natural Science Foundation of China under Grant No. 60805024, the National Research Foundation for the Doctoral Program of Higher Education of China under Grant No. 20070141020.

REFERENCES

Bai, R., Blazewicz, J., Burke, E. K., Kendall, G., & McCollum, B. (2007). *A simulated annealing hyper-heuristic methodology for flexible decision support* (Tech. Rep. No. NOTTCS-TR-2007-8). Nottingham, UK: University of Nottingham, School of Computer Science and Information Technology.

Bai, R., Burke, E. K., & Kendall, G. (2008). Heuristic, meta-heuristic and hyper-heuristic approaches for fresh produce inventory control and shelf space allocation. *The Journal of the Operational Research Society*, *59*, 1387–1397. doi:.doi:10.1057/palgrave.jors.2602463

Bai, R., & Kendall, G. (2005). An investigation of automated planograms using a simulated annealing based hyper-heuristics. In T. Ibaraki, et al. (Eds.), *Metaheuristics: Progress as a real problem solver* (pp. 87–108). Berlin, Germany: Springer. doi:doi:10.1007/0-387-25383-1_4

Burke, E. K., Causmaecker, P. D., Berghe, G. V., & Landeghem, H. V. (2004). The state of the art of nurse rostering. *Journal of Scheduling*, *7*(6), 441–499. doi:.doi:10.1023/B:JOSH.0000046076.75950.0b

Burke, E. K., Curtois, T., Qu, R., & Vanden-Berghe, G. (2008). *Problem model for nurse rostering benchmark instances.* Retrieved December 14, 2010, from http://www.cs.nott.ac.uk/~tec/NRP/papers/ANROM.pdf

Burke, E. K., Hyde, M., Kendall, G., Ochoa, G., Ozcan, E., & Qu, R. (2010). *Hyper-heuristics: a survey of the state of the art* (Tech. Rep. No. NOTTCS-TR-SUB-0906241418). Nottingham, UK: University of Nottingham, School of Computer Science and Information Technology.

Burke, E. K., Hyde, M., Kendall, G., Ochoa, G., Ozcan, E., & Woodward, J. R. (2010). A classification of hyper-heuristic approaches. In M. Gendreau & J. Potvin (Eds.), *Handbook of metaheuristics* (2nd ed., pp. 449–468). Berlin, Germany: Springer. doi:doi:10.1007/978-1-4419-1665-5_15

Burke, E. K., Kendall, G., Newall, J., Hart, E., Ross, P., & Schulenburg, S. (2003). Hyper-Heuristics: An emerging direction in modern search technology. In Glover, F., & Konchenberger, G. (Eds.), *Handbook of metaheuristics* (pp. 457–474). New York, NY: Kluwer Academic Publishers.

Burke, E. K., Kendall, G., Silva, D. L., O'Brien, R., & Soubeiga, E. (2005). An ant algorithm hyperheuristic for the project presentation scheduling problem. In *Proceedings of the IEEE Conference on Evolutionary Computation* (pp. 2263-2270). Washington, DC: IEEE Computer Society.

Burke, E. K., Kendall, G., & Soubeiga, E. (2003). A tabu-search hyperheuristic for timetabling and rostering. *Journal of Heuristics*, *9*(6), 451–490. doi:.doi:10.1023/B:HEUR.0000012446.94732.b6

Burke, E. K., Li, J., & Qu, R. (2010). A hybrid model of integer programming and variable neighbourhood search for highly-constrained nurse rostering problems. *European Journal of Operational Research*, *203*(2), 484–493. doi:.doi:10.1016/j.ejor.2009.07.036

Burke, E. K., McCollum, B., Meisels, A., Petrovic, S., & Qu, R. (2007). A graph-based hyper-heuristic for educational timetabling problems. *European Journal of Operational Research*, *176*(1), 177–192. doi:.doi:10.1016/j.ejor.2005.08.012

Croes, G. A. (1958). A method for solving traveling salesman problem. *Operations Research*, *6*, 791–812. doi:.doi:10.1287/opre.6.6.791

Curtois, T., Ochoa, M., Hyde, M., & Vazquez-Rodriguez, J. A. (2010). *A HyFlex module for the personnel scheduling problem*. Nottingham, UK: University of Nottingham, School of Computer Science and Information Technology.

Dowsland, K. A., Soubeiga, E., & Burke, E. K. (2007). A simulated annealing based hyperheuristic for determining shipper sizes for storage and transportation. *European Journal of Operational Research*, *179*(3), 759–774. doi:.doi:10.1016/j.ejor.2005.03.058

Festa, P., Pardalos, P. M., Pitsoulis, L. S., & Resende, M. G. C. (2006). GRASP with path relinking for the weighted MAXSAT problem. *Journal of Experimental Algorithmics*, *11*, 1–16.

Ochoa, G., Qu, R., & Burke, E. K. (2009). Analyzing the landscape of a graph based hyper-heuristic for timetabling problems. In F. Rothlauf (Ed.), *Proceedings of the 11th Annual Conference on Genetic and Evolutionary Computation* (pp. 341-348). New York, NY: ACM.

Qu, R., & Burke, E. K. (2009). Hybridizations within a graph-based hyper-heuristic framework for university timetabling problems. *The Journal of the Operational Research Society*, *60*(9), 1273–1285. doi:.doi:10.1057/jors.2008.102

Remde, S., Cowling, P. I., Dahal, K. P., & Colledge, N. (2006). Exact/heuristic hybrids using rVNS and hyperheuristics for workforce scheduling. In C. Cotta et al. (Eds.), *Evolutionary computation in combinatorial optimization* (LNCS 4446, pp. 188-197).

Remde, S., Dahal, K. P., Cowling, P. I., & Colledge, N. (2009). Binary exponential back off for tabu tenure in hyperheuristics. In C. Cotta et al. (Eds.), *Evolutionary computation in combinatorial optimization* (LNCS 5482, pp. 109-120).

Ren, Z., Jiang, H., Xuan, J., & Luo, Z. (2010). Ant based hyper heuristics with space reduction: A case study of the p-Median problem. In R. Schaefer et al. (Eds.), *Proceedings of the Parallel Problem Solving from Nature Conference (PPSN XI)* (LNCS 6238, pp. 546-555).

Resende, M. G. C., & Ribeiro, C. C. (2003). Greedy random adaptive search procedures. In Glover, F., & Konchenberger, G. (Eds.), *Handbook of metaheuristics* (pp. 219–251). New York, NY: Kluwer Academic Publishers.

Ross, P., Marin-Blazquez, J. G., Schulenburg, S., & Hart, E. (2003). Learning a procedure that can solve hard bin-packing problems: A new GA-Based approach to hyper-heuristics. In E. Cantú-Paz et al. (Eds.), *Proceedings of the Genetic and Evolutionary Computation Conference (GECCO 2003)* (LNCS 2724, pp. 1295-1306).

Terashima-Marin, H., Moran-Saavedra, A., & Ross, P. (2005). Forming hyper-heuristics with GAs when solving 2D-regular cutting stock problems. In *Proceedings of the IEEE Conference on Evolutionary Computation* (pp. 1104-1110). Washington, DC: IEEE Computer Society.

This work was previously published in the Journal of Information Technology Research, Volume 4, Issue 2, edited by Mehdi Khosrow-Pour, pp. 31-42, copyright 2011 by IGI Publishing (an imprint of IGI Global).

Chapter 8
Pareto Artificial Life Algorithm for Multi-Objective Optimization

Jin-Dae Song
Hyosung Ebara Engineering Co., Korea

Bo-Suk Yang
Pukyong National University, Korea

ABSTRACT

Most engineering optimization uses multiple objective functions rather than single objective function. To realize an artificial life algorithm based multi-objective optimization, this paper proposes a Pareto artificial life algorithm that is capable of searching Pareto set for multi-objective function solutions. The Pareto set of optimum solutions is found by applying two objective functions for the optimum design of the defined journal bearing. By comparing with the optimum solutions of a single objective function, it is confirmed that the single function optimization result is one of the specific cases of Pareto set of optimum solutions.

INTRODUCTION

Most engineering optimization deals with multiple objective functions rather wthan a single objective function. Basically, there are two kinds of approaches to solve a multi-objective optimization problem (MOP). The first approach is the transformation of a given MOP into a single objective optimization problem (SOP). The motivation of this approach is to establish a single basis of comparing each candidate solution in the course of optimization and finally to derive a single optimum solution (or approximate to the optimum solution). One method which could be used for this approach is to aggregate multiple objective functions into a single overall objective function. Optimization of the objective function is then conducted with one optimal design as a result. This result is greatly dependent on how the objectives are aggregated (Anderson, 2000). The form which is either linear combination or multiplication is usually employed as an aggregated

DOI: 10.4018/978-1-4666-3625-5.ch008

single objective function. Another method is to select only the most interesting object function as a final objective function and to set the other objective functions as constraints.

The second approach is to consider simultaneously the multiple objective functions, which is called Pareto optimization. In order to provide possible solutions for the final decision maker, the downside which is not able to find other possibilities besides a single solution obtained through conversion into a single objective function is supplemented. To avoid this difficulty and to explore various possibilities, the concept of Pareto optimality is employed.

Recently, many researches on Pareto optimization problems have been carried out to enable the application of heuristic global optimization algorithms such as evolutionary algorithm (Schaffer, 1985; David, 1985; Goldberg, 1989; Horn et al., 1994; Srinivas & Deb, 1995) and tabu search method (Shiyou & Ni, 1998; Ho et al., 2002). In the case of function optimization, heuristic optimization methods have the advantages of not being subjected to special restrictions on problem formulations. They are also evaluated as an outstanding search capability in finding a global optimum solution of optimization. As a heuristic global optimization technique, artificial life algorithm (AL) (Yang & Lee, 2000; Yang et al., 2001; Yang & Song, 2002) has been applied to determine optimum design problems of journal bearing (Song et al., 2005) and engine mount (Ahn et al., 2003, 2005). However, the expansion onto Pareto optimization has merely been attempted in real applications.

In order to apply AL to MOP in engineering problems, it is necessary to solve the Pareto optimization problem. Therefore, in this study, AL has been enlarged on enabling the application of Pareto optimization to solve the MOPs.

MULTI-OBJECTIVE OPTIMIZATION PROBLEMS

A MOP is defined as a problem which has two or more objective functions. A general MOP is defined as

$$\text{Minimize } \mathbf{F}(\mathbf{x}) = (f_1(\mathbf{x}), f_2(\mathbf{x}), \ldots, f_k(\mathbf{x}))^T \quad (1)$$

$$\text{subject to } \mathbf{c}(\mathbf{x}) = (c_1(\mathbf{x}), c_2(\mathbf{x}), \ldots, c_m(\mathbf{x}))^T \geq 0 \quad (2)$$

$$\mathbf{x} = (x_1, x_2, \ldots, x_n)^T, \ \mathbf{x} \in S \quad (3)$$

where fi(x) is the set of k objective functions, ci(x) is the set of m constraints, xj is the n optimization parameters, and S ∈ Rn is the solution or parameter space. Obtainable objective vectors {F(x)|x ∈ S} are denoted as Y, where Y ∈ Rk is usually referred to the attribute space.

In MOP, it is important to emphasize that there might be constraints imposed on the objectives. It is normal for the objectives of MOP to be in conflicting with each other (Coello & Zacatenco, 2006). However, most MOPs do not lend themselves to a single solution but have a set of solutions. Such solutions are trade-offs or good compromises among the objectives. In order to generate these trade-off solutions, an old notion of optimality is normally adopted. This notion of optimality was generalized by Pareto (1896) and is called Pareto optimum. The solution for a MOP is Pareto optimal if no other feasible solutions exist that would decrease some objective function values without causing a simultaneous increased in at least one other objective function value.

PARETO OPTIMIZATION

Let's consider a minimization problem which has two or more objective functions. A change in design variables (or design vector) in order to lower the value of an objective function may generally result in the increasing values of other objective functions. Therefore, in the most cases, a set of solutions that simultaneously minimize all the objective functions becomes a null set. This problem leads to a new concept called Pareto set.

The Pareto set consists of solutions that are not dominated by any other solutions. Considering a minimization problem with two solution vectors x and y∈S, where x is said to dominate y, and is denoted by $\mathbf{x} \prec \mathbf{y}$, if:

$$\forall i \in \{1, 2, \ldots, k\} : f_i(\mathbf{x}) \leq f_i(\mathbf{y}) \text{ and } \exists j \in \{1, 2, \ldots, k\} : f_j(\mathbf{x}) < f_j(\mathbf{y}) \quad (4)$$

The space in Rk formed by the objective vectors of Pareto optimal solutions is known as the Pareto optimal front.

Let's consider a minimization problem comprising two objective functions, f1 and f2. For the two design vectors of A and B, the case in which all objective function values of A are the same or smaller than all objective function values of B and also at least one objective function value is smaller than B is described as "B is dominated by A". In case where the first objective function value of A, f1(A), is smaller than f1(B), but the second objective function value, f2(A), is larger than f2(B), A and B are referred to as the "non-dominated solution".

Ultimately, Pareto optimization problem is considered finding the set of all non-dominated solutions and this set of solutions is referred to as Pareto set of solutions. Also, the set of objective function values in the range of Pareto set of solutions are referred to Pareto front. A range holds the same dimension as the number of objective functions. If there are four or more objective functions, it is difficult to express them geometrically. Therefore, this study deals with simple problems which two design variables and two objective functions are employed in order to validate and confirm the proposed method.

PARETO ARTIFICIAL LIFE ALGORITHM

For convenience, artificial life optimization algorithm for a single objective function (Ho et al., 2002) is called AL, and the artificial life optimization algorithm used to find the optimum Pareto solution is called Pareto artificial life algorithm (PAL). For AL, the course of finding solution imitates cluster formation, which is one of the ecological processes of natural phenomena. The basic concept is to promote cluster formation in proximity in order to optimize the solution and carry out an extensive search in the cluster. For PAL, the fitness evaluation method in AL has been improved to befit multi-objective function. Also, by adding the Pareto list, adjustment has been made to enable application to multi-objective function optimization problem.

Fitness Evaluation

In AL, cluster formation by artificial objects has been promoted in areas of outstanding fitness within the space of design variables by evaluating the fitness based on objective function values. In the case of multi-objective function optimization problem, changes in design variables generally result in a reduction of one objective function value and an increase in another objective function value. Therefore, a new method must be found for fitness evaluation.

Horn et al. (1994) attempted to solve the Pareto optimal design problem with evolutionary algorithm by proposing a modified shared fitness evaluation method. This method introduced the niche concept into the shared fitness concept proposed by Goldberg (1989). The Horn's shared fitness was found by dividing the ordinary fitness used in genetic algorithms (GA), with the number of niches. Niche is defined as biological position in biology area. The detailed concept of niche used for GA can be interpreted as a type of density of solutions. Also, once the number of niches was found, the Euclid distance dij of two objects, i and j defined in the space of objective functions was evaluated and reflected. However, the Horn's approach evaluated the density with only the number of solutions within the set proximity. Ho et al. (2002) modified the shared fitness in order that it could be applied the tabu search method for the Pareto optimization problem. The Ho's shared fitness used the concept of the density of solutions. In Ho's algorithm, instead of using the ordinary fitness rules for GA to employ the tabu search method, the reciprocal number of the density of solutions was considered.

In PAL, the shared fitness is improved by using density evaluation method reflected in distances among solutions in the Ho's shared fitness concept. In detail, shared fitness of PAL is defined as of Equation (5).

$$f_{share(i)} = \frac{1/d_i}{\sum_{j=1}^{NAC_i} 1/d_j} \tag{5}$$

$$d_j = \frac{NAC_j}{RC_j} \tag{6}$$

$$RC_j = \begin{cases} = \dfrac{\sum_{k=1}^{NAC_j-1} \left\| \mathbf{F}^{(k)} - \mathbf{F}^{(j)} \right\|}{NAC_j - 1} & \text{if } NAC_j = 1 \\ = RC_0 & \text{else} \end{cases} \tag{7}$$

where, fshare, dj, RC0, RCj and NACj represent the shared fitness, density of solutions of object j (or candidate solution), radius to calculate density dj on the basis of the location of object j, radius of the final proximity used in calculating dj, and number of objects including itself in proximity to the object j defined with RC0, respectively.

In the Ho's shared fitness, RCj is a fixed value regardless of the distribution status of solutions or objects and corresponds with RC0 in this study. However, by introducing RCj for PAL, the density evaluation of solutions could be further improved not only by the number of solutions in the proximity set by user, but also by evaluating the distance between these solutions and the center point.

Pareto Set of Solutions

The concept of Pareto can be interpreted as a type of long-term memory collection of past memory set in PAL such as tabu search method. To find Pareto set of solutions, Pareto archive is renewed by adding and replacing non-dominated solutions among all artificial objects of each generation. It is also renewed in each generation.

Pareto Artificial Life Algorithm (PAL)

The flow diagram of the algorithm to describe the process of the proposed PAL is shown in Figure 1. The overall processes are explained as follows.

Step 1: Initial artificial life objects and resources are distributed randomly in solution space and granted initial internal energy for each organism.

Step 2: All artificial objects conduct search, metabolism, movement and reproduction.

Search: Artificial life object searches the resources to exist within proximity domain of its own to hold the radius as defined by Equation (8),

Figure 1. Flowchart of Pareto artificial life algorithm

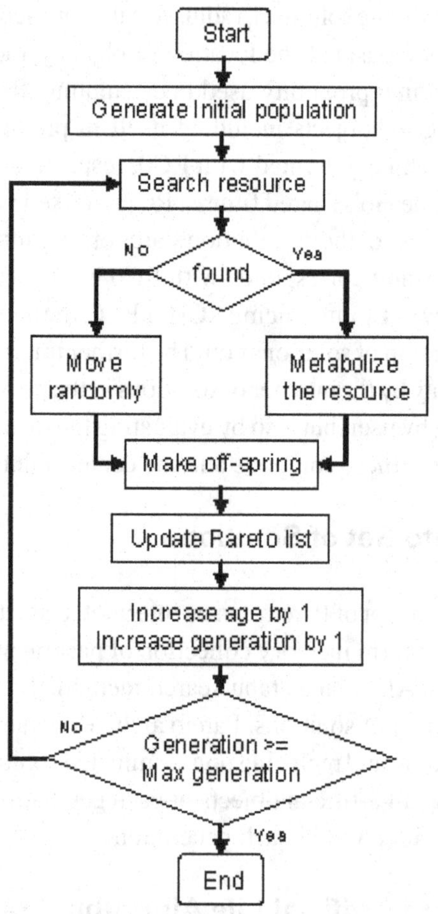

$$D = e^{-\alpha(G/G_{\max})} \tag{8}$$

where, G, Gmax and α respectively represent the number of current generations, the maximum number of generations, and factor to reduce the radius of proximity domain according to generation. In particular, α was reviewed by Yang and Lee (2000) and was set as $\alpha = 3$ in this study.

Metabolism: When the resources are searched, the artificial life object moves to the most closely located resource and metabolizes the closest resource. The metabolized resource is eliminated and the object increases internal energy. It also disposes waste in a random position within the proximity domain.

Movement: In case where the resources are not found in proximity, a random location is selected within the proximity. If the selected location has a higher fitness than the current location, the artificial life object moves to the selected location. If not, the process of randomly selecting new locations is repeated.

Reproduction: For objects of which the internal energy are over the minimum energy to enable reproduction, the closest object among artificial life objects of the same species is selected as itself within the proximity domain. If the same conditions are satisfied, the object carries out reproduction. By reproduction, two new objects are created as offspring. Initial location of each of these objects is decided as random location with higher fitness than the fitness of each of their parent objects within proximity domain for locations of each of the parent objects.

Step 3: Renew Pareto archives with the method described.

Step 4: Increase the number of generation and age of organism by 1.

Step 5: When internal energy is of critical value as internal energy reduced, the artificial life object is considered extinct and is deleted.

Step 6: Return to step 2 in case where the number of generations does not reach the maximum value, and if it reaches the maximum value, end the process.

Examples

The performance verification is carried out by applying PAL to three test functions, of which the optimum solutions were known. The first test function (Fonseca & Fleming, 1995) is defined by Equation (9) in which the number of design variables n is set as 2.

Minimize

$$\mathbf{F}(\mathbf{x}) = (f_1(\mathbf{x}), f_2(\mathbf{x}))^T \tag{9}$$

$$f_1(\mathbf{x}) = 1 - \exp\left(-\sum_{i=1}^{n}\left(x_i - \frac{1}{\sqrt{n}}\right)^2\right), \quad f_2(\mathbf{x}) = 1 - \exp\left(-\sum_{i=1}^{n}\left(x_i + \frac{1}{\sqrt{n}}\right)^2\right)$$

subjected to $-2 \le x_i \le 2$.

There are no constraints with the exception of the upper and lower limits of design variables. Pareto set of solutions and Pareto front are shown in Figure 2 together with the results by PAL. The "dots" represent Pareto set of solutions and "O" marks are the solutions obtained by PAL.

The second test function (Srinivas & Deb, 1995) is defined by Equation (10).

Minimize

$$\mathbf{F}(\mathbf{x}) = (f_1(\mathbf{x}), f_2(\mathbf{x}))^T$$
$$f_1(\mathbf{x}) = 2 + (x_1 - 2)^2 + (x_2 - 1)^2, \quad f_2(\mathbf{x}) = 9x_1 - (x_2 - 1)^2 \tag{10}$$

subjected to

$$c_1(\mathbf{x}) \equiv x_1^2 + x_2^2 - 225 \le 0,$$
$$c_2(\mathbf{x}) \equiv x_1 - 3x_2 + 10 \le 0,$$
$$-20 \le x_1, x_2 \le 20$$

There are two constraints in addition to the upper and lower limits of design variables. Feasible solutions are the intersections at the top of straight line and inside the circle shown in Figure 3(a). In this figure, Pareto set of solutions is expressed with dots. The overlapping "O" marks represent Pareto set of solutions calculated by PAL. Pareto front is shown in Figure 3(b). From the second example, it is confirmed that Pareto set of solutions could be successfully found while satisfying the constraints in cases where there are simple constraints.

The third test function (Tanaka, 1995) is defined by Equation (11).

Minimize

$$\mathbf{F}(\mathbf{x}) = (f_1(\mathbf{x}), f_2(\mathbf{x}))^T$$
$$f_1(\mathbf{x}) = x_1, f_2(\mathbf{x}) = x_2 \tag{11}$$

subjected to

$$c_1(\mathbf{x}) = x_1^2 + x_2^2 - 1 - 0.1\cos\left(16\tan^{-1}\frac{x}{y}\right) \le 0,$$
$$c_2(\mathbf{x}) \equiv (x_1 - 0.5)^2 + (x_2 - 0.5)^2 - 0.5 \le 0,$$
$$0 \le x_1, x_2 \le \pi$$

The small insert at the bottom left-hand corner of Figure 4 shows the Pareto solutions. According to the two constraints, feasible solutions are those which correspond to the part filled with slashes. Here, by c2, Pareto solutions of Figure 4 are shown by thick lines in the small insert and is based on the second constraints c1. Among the feasible solutions marked with slashes, those shown with dotted lines are active constraints and therefore are feasible solutions. However, they cannot be Pareto set of solutions as they are not the non-dominated solutions. In particular, this problem is useful in evaluating the search capabilities in relations to the problems in which active constraints exist. It is also confirmed that PAL has successfully found the set of solutions.

PARETO OPTIMUM DESIGN OF JOURNAL BEARING

Pareto optimization problem of high-speed and short journal bearing shown in Figure 5 is considered with the two objective functions which are temperature increase and supply flow.

Optimum design of journal bearing has been studied by many researchers. Hashimoto (1997), Yang et al. (2001) and Song et al. (2005) studied the optimization by using sequential quadratic programming (SQP), AL and the enhanced AL, respectively. However, these approached only

Figure 2. Pareto set and Pareto front of test function 1, (a) Pareto set (b) Pareto front

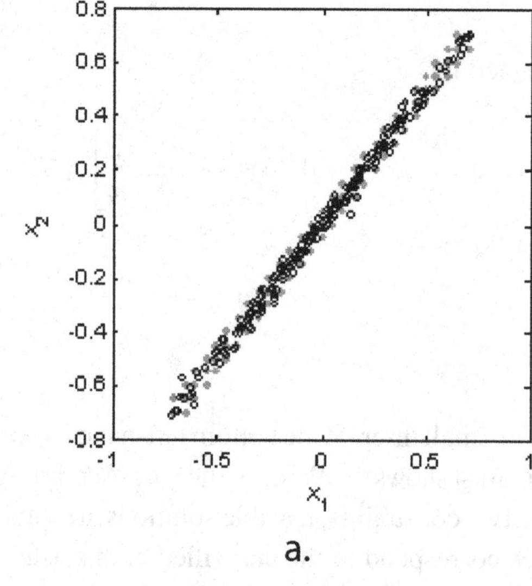

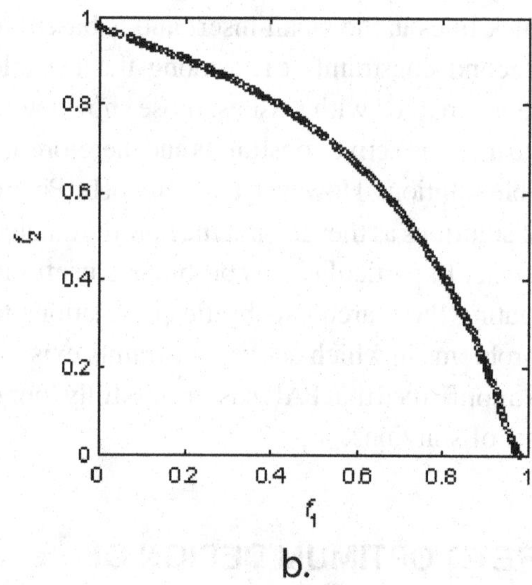

Figure 3. Pareto set and Pareto front of test function 2, (a) Pareto set (b) Pareto front

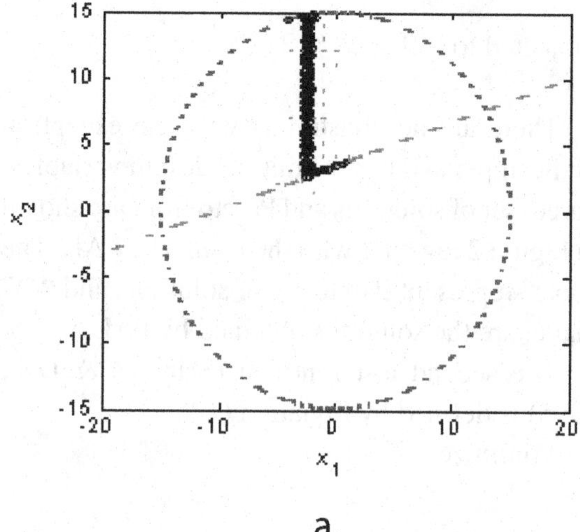

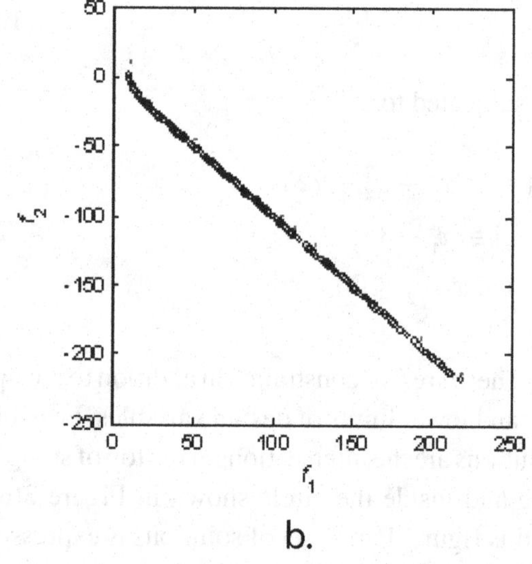

searched the optimization of a single objective function and only used the form of linear combination for two temperature increase and supply flow objective functions. Therefore, this study intends to provide Pareto set of solutions for carrying out Pareto optimization.

Defining State Variables of Journal Bearing

As state variables used in the objective functions or constraints, bearing load W (N), operating speed ns (rps), eccentricity ratio ε0, oil film pressure p (MPa), oil film temperature T (°K), journal surface friction Fj (N), supply flow Q (m3/s) and whirling onset speed ωcr (rad/s) are considered.

Figure 4. Pareto set and Pareto front of test function 3

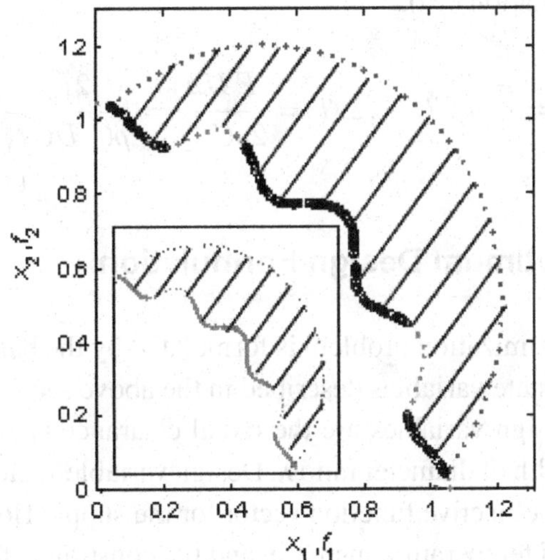

Generally, these state variables are determined by design variables (see Table 1). For design variables, the radial clearance C and bearing width to diameter ratio λ (= L/D) are considered. The state variables defined in Equations (12) through (19) are obtained from Hashimoto (1997).

The average Reynolds number is defined as of $R_e(X) = \rho CU / \mu$, where μ represents the viscosity. The correction coefficients α_m and G_θ^* are defined by the following equations according to Reynolds number.

$$R_e < 510 : \alpha_m = 1,\ G_\theta^* = 1/12$$

$$510 \le R_e \le 1125 : \alpha_m = 5.914 R_e^{-0.285}, G_\theta^* = 2.915 R_e^{-0.57} \quad (12)$$

$$1125 \le R_e \le 13500 : \alpha_m = 0.798,\ G_\theta^* = 2.915 R_e^{-0.57}$$

$$R_e > 13500 : \alpha_m = 0.756,\ G_\theta^* = 14.45 R_e^{-0.57}$$

Figure 5. Geometry of a hydrodynamic journal bearing

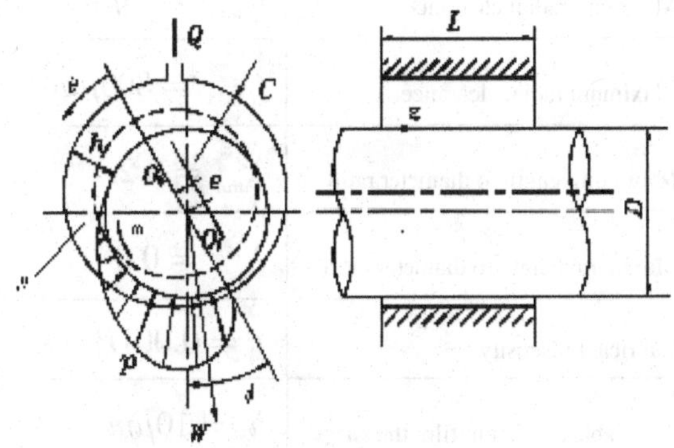

Modified Sommerfeld number S is the most important factor in bearing design, and eccentricity ratio ε0 expressed as the function of S, is obtained from the following equation.

$$S = \frac{n_s \mu D^3 \lambda}{48 G_\theta^* C^2 W}, \text{ and } \varepsilon_0 = \exp(-2.236 \alpha_m \lambda \sqrt{S}) \quad (13)$$

The minimum oil film thickness hmin, whirling start speed ωcr and the maximum oil film pressure pmax under the steady-state condition are respectively obtained from Equations (14), (15) and (16).

$$h_{\min} = C(1 - \varepsilon_0) \quad (14)$$

$$\omega_{cr} = \left[0.0584 \exp(6.99 \varepsilon_0^{2.07}) - 1.318 \varepsilon_0 + 2.87\right] (g / C)^{1/2} \quad (15)$$

$$p_{\max} = \frac{\pi n_s \mu D^2 \alpha_m^2 \lambda^2}{8 G_\theta^* C^2} \frac{\varepsilon_0 \sin \theta_0}{(1 + \varepsilon_0 \cos \theta_0)^3} \quad (16)$$

where g represents acceleration of gravity, θ0 represents the angular location of the maximum oil film pressure occurs and is defined by Equation (17).

Table 1. Input parameters for optimum design

Minimum radial clearance	$C_{\min} = 40\mu m$
Maximum radial clearance	$C_{\max} = 300\mu m$
Minimum length to diameter ratio	$\lambda_{\min} = 0.2$
Maximum length to diameter ratio	$\lambda_{\max} = 0.6$
Lubricant viscosity	$\mu = 0.001 Pa \cdot s$
Allowable minimum film thickness	$h_a = 10\mu m$
Allowable maximum film pressure	$P_a = 10MPa$
Allowable maximum film pressure	$\Delta T_a = 70^{\circ}K$
Density of lubricant	$\rho = 860 kg / m^3$
Specific heat of lubricant	$C_p = 4.19 \times 103 J / kg.^{\circ}K$

$$\theta_0 = \cos^{-1}\left(\frac{1 - \sqrt{1 + 24\varepsilon_0^2}}{4\varepsilon_0}\right) \tag{17}$$

The journal surface friction is approximately given by Equation (18) according to Reynolds number.

$R_e < 1125$:

$$F_j \cong \frac{\pi^2 \mu n_s D^3 \lambda}{48 G_\theta^* C}\left\{\frac{1}{\sqrt{1-\varepsilon_0}} + \frac{1-\varepsilon_0}{(1-\varepsilon_0^2)^{3/2}}\right\}$$

$$1125 \leq R_e \leq 13500 : F_j \cong \frac{\pi^2 \mu n_s D^3 \lambda}{48 G_\theta^* C}(1.109\varepsilon_0^2 - 1.490\varepsilon_0 + 2.748)$$

(18)

$R_e > 13500$:

$$F_j \cong \frac{\pi^2 \mu n_s D^3 \lambda}{48 G_\theta^* C}(1.792\varepsilon_0^3 - 1.523\varepsilon_0^2 - 3.697\varepsilon_0 + 8.734)$$

Lastly, flow of supplied lubricant Q and oil film temperature increase ΔT can be found from Equation (19).

$$Q = \frac{\pi}{4} n_s C D^2 \varepsilon_0, \Delta T = \frac{F_j D \omega}{2\rho C_p Q} = \frac{2F_j}{\rho C_p D C \varepsilon_0} \tag{19}$$

Optimum Design Formulation

Optimization problem is formulated by the basis of state variables described in the above section. Design variables are the radial clearance C and width of diameter ratio λ. Design variable vector, the objective function vector for the supply flow and temperature increase, and the constraints for the design variables are defined as Equations (20), (21), and (22), respectively.

$$\mathrm{x} = (C, \lambda)^T \tag{20}$$

$$\mathrm{F(x)} = (Q(\mathrm{x}), \ \Delta T(\mathrm{x}))^T \tag{21}$$

$$c_i \equiv g_i(\mathrm{x}) \leq 0, \ (i = 1\sim8) \tag{22}$$

$$\begin{aligned}
&g_1 = C_{\min} - C, \quad g_2 = C - C_{\max}, \\
&g_3 = \lambda_{\min} - \lambda, \quad g_4 = \lambda - \lambda_{\max}, \\
&g_5 = h_a - C\{1 - \varepsilon_0(\mathbf{x})\} = h_a - h_{\min}, \\
&g_6 = \Delta T(\mathbf{x}) - \Delta T_a, \quad g_7 = \omega - \omega_{cr}(\mathbf{x}), \\
&g_8 = p_{\max}(\mathbf{x}) - p_a
\end{aligned}$$

From g1 to g4 of Equation (22), the suffixes of min and max, respectively, represent the lower and upper limit values of the design variables. In order to observe the changes in Pareto front and Pareto set of solutions according to major state variables, optimization is carried out by changing the operating speed ns and load W exerted on bearing.

Figure 6. Comparison of Pareto optimal and single optimal $((\alpha_1,\alpha_2)=\{(1.0,0.0),(0.5,0.5)(0.0,1.0)\}$, *W = 10 kN,* n_s *= 100 rps), (a) Pareto set (b) Pareto front*

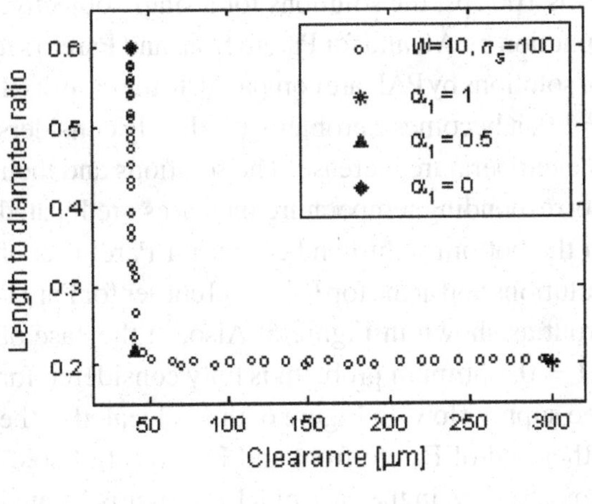

a.

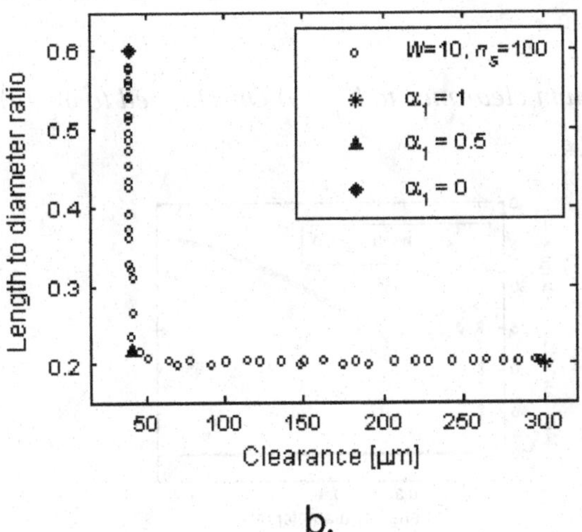

b.

Figure 7. Comparison of Pareto optimal and single optimal $((\alpha_1,\alpha_2)=\{(1.0,0.0),(0.5,0.5)(0.0,1.0)\}$, *W = 10 kN,* n_s *= 200 rps), (a) Pareto set (b) Pareto front*

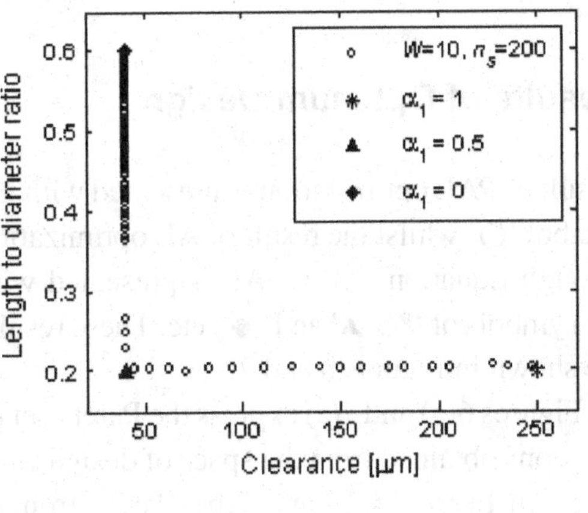

a.

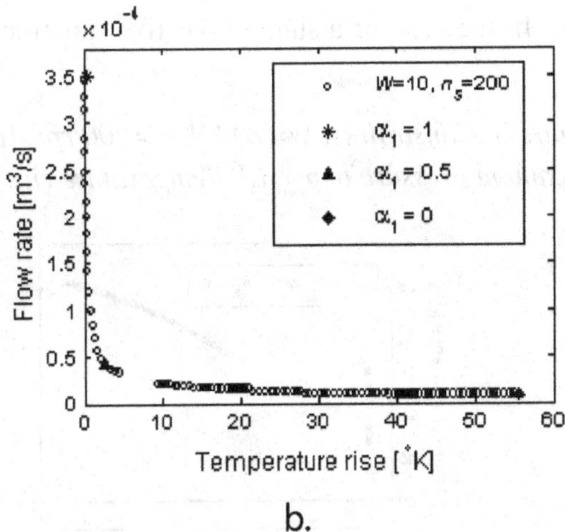

b.

Lastly, to investigate the relevance between Pareto set of solutions and optimum solutions obtained from changing this problem into a single objective function in the form of linear combination, optimization problem with one objective function of Equation (23) was

$$F(x) = \alpha_1\beta_1 Q\,(\mathrm{x}) + \alpha_2\beta_2\Delta T\,(\mathrm{x}), \text{ and } (\alpha_1 + \alpha_2 = 1) \tag{23}$$

where, α_1 and α_2 are weighting factors.

In particular, for comparison with Pareto set of solutions, scale factors were fixed as β1 = 1, β2 = 1/5000 and the weighting factors were considered as the following:

$$(\alpha_1, \alpha_2) = \{(1.0,0.0),(0.8,0.2),(0.6,0.4),(0.5,0.5),(0.4,0.6),(0.2,0.8),(0.0,1.0)\} \quad (24)$$

Then, optimization was carried out for each case.

Results of Optimum Design

Result of PAL optimization is presented with the symbol 'O' whilst the result of AL optimization through Equation (23) by AL is presented with the symbols of '*', '▲' and '◆', etc. These results are shown in Figures 6 and 7.

Figures 6(a) and 7(a) express the Pareto set of solutions obtained from the space of design variables. In Figures 6(b) and 7(b), Pareto front is consisted of objective function vector obtained from Pareto set of solutions in Figures 6(a) and 7(a). In the case of a single objective function, calculation is carried out on 7 cases of weighting factors defined as Equation (24). However, to clarify the expression, only 3 cases are expressed.

When load W is 10 kN and operating speed ns is 100 rps, the solutions for a single objective function by AL and for Pareto front and Pareto set of solutions by PAL are compared. In the case of α1 = 1.0, it becomes a problem which only considers the temperature increase. The solutions and their corresponding temperature increases are located at the bottom right-hand corner for Pareto set of solutions and at the top left-hand corner for Pareto front as shown in Figure 6. Also, in the case of α1 = 0, optimum problem is only considered for the supply flow. In Figure 6, this is located at the other end of Pareto front and Pareto set of solutions. Lastly, in the case of α1 = 0.5, it is located in between the two cases described above for Pareto front and Pareto set of solutions. In other

Figure 8. Constraints: W=10 kN, n_s=200 rps, (a) Minimum clearance to h_{min} (b) Onset speed to ω_{cr} (c) Maximum pressure to p_{max} (d) Temperature rise to ΔT.

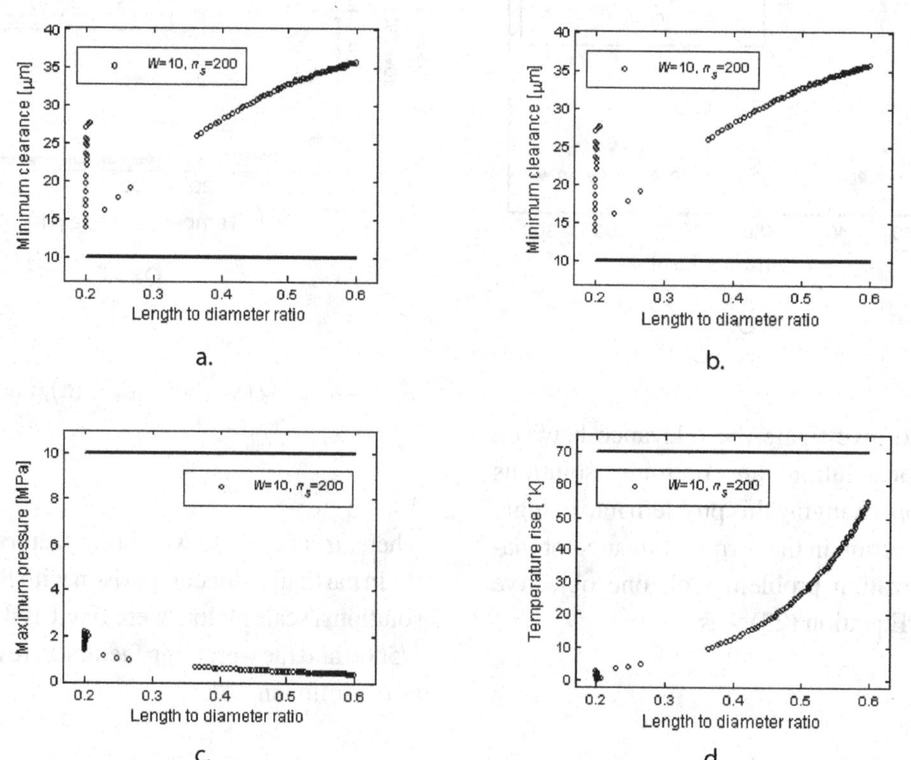

Figure 9. Pareto optimal and Pareto front (W=10 kN, n_s=100, 150, 200 rps) (a) Pareto optimal (b) Pareto front

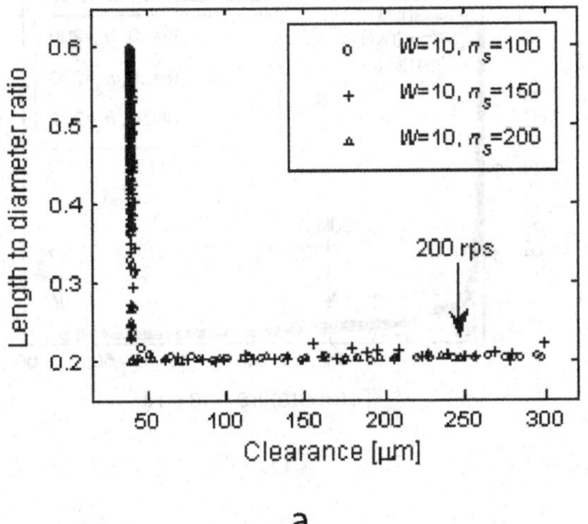

a.

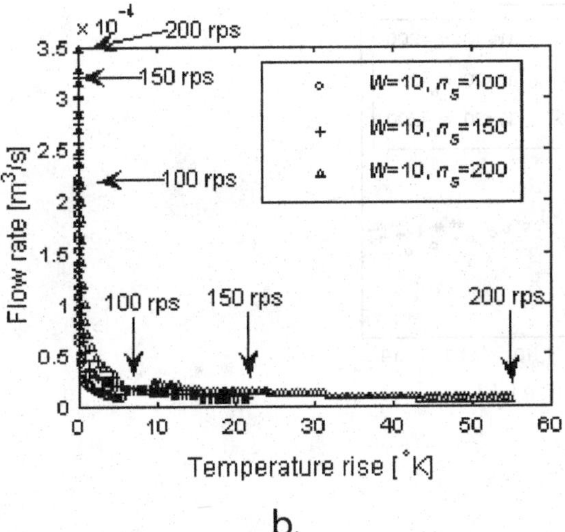

b.

words, it can be confirmed that the problem of optimizing a single objective function in the form of linear combination is a specific solution of the corresponding Pareto optimization problem. From a different perspective, a designer can make selection according to the given situations by utilizing Pareto set of optimum solutions obtained.

Of the results obtained from PAL, value of the far-right solution in Figure 7(a) is given by (λ, C) = (0.200, 247.3). It shows a difference of 52 μm or more in the upper limit of radial clearance of 300 μm. This result is related to temperature increase. When the operating speed ns = 200 rps, load W = 10 kN and width to diameter ratio λ = 0.2, the temperature increase ΔT discontinuously rises for radial clearance exceeds 249.8 μm. As shown by Equations (12) and (18), this is due to the discontinuity of correction coefficients αm, and Gθ* and friction Fj according to Reynolds number.

As a result, in the above conditions, solutions exceeding C = 249.8 μm cannot be non-dominated solutions. Therefore, the domain below is excluded from the final Pareto set of solutions.

$$S_{ex} = \{(\lambda, C) \mid C \geq 249.8\ \mu\text{m}\} \tag{25}$$

In Figures 7(a) and (b), there are blanks in Pareto set of solutions and Pareto front and these are related to the constraints. Figure 8 shows the applicable constraints in the case of W = 10 kN and ns = 200 rps. The solid lines in Figure 8 represent the limit values (ha, ΔTa, ω, pa). Although all other constraints are satisfied, whirling start at lower speed than operating speed as shown in Figure 8(b). Therefore, a domain does not satisfy c7 of Equation (22) for constraints to exist. Also, this domain corresponds to the domain of discontinuity in Pareto set of solutions shown in Figure 7(a). When W = 10 kN, all constraints, with the exception of upper and lower limits of design variables do not influence Pareto set of solutions in case where ns = 100 or 150 rps.

Figure 9 shows Pareto set of solutions and Pareto front when the load is fixed at 10 kN and operating speeds change to 100, 200 and 300 rps. The arrows in Figure 9(a) show the domain of radial clearance being excluded from Pareto set of solutions due to discontinuity of correction coefficient, as described previously. The six arrows in Figure 9(b) point toward both ends of Pareto front. As predicted, it is confirmed that Pareto front moves in the direction of temperature

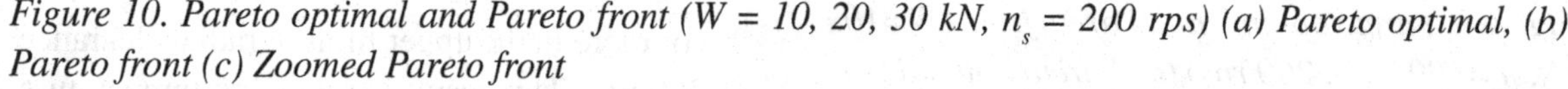

Figure 10. Pareto optimal and Pareto front (W = 10, 20, 30 kN, n_s = 200 rps) (a) Pareto optimal, (b) Pareto front (c) Zoomed Pareto front

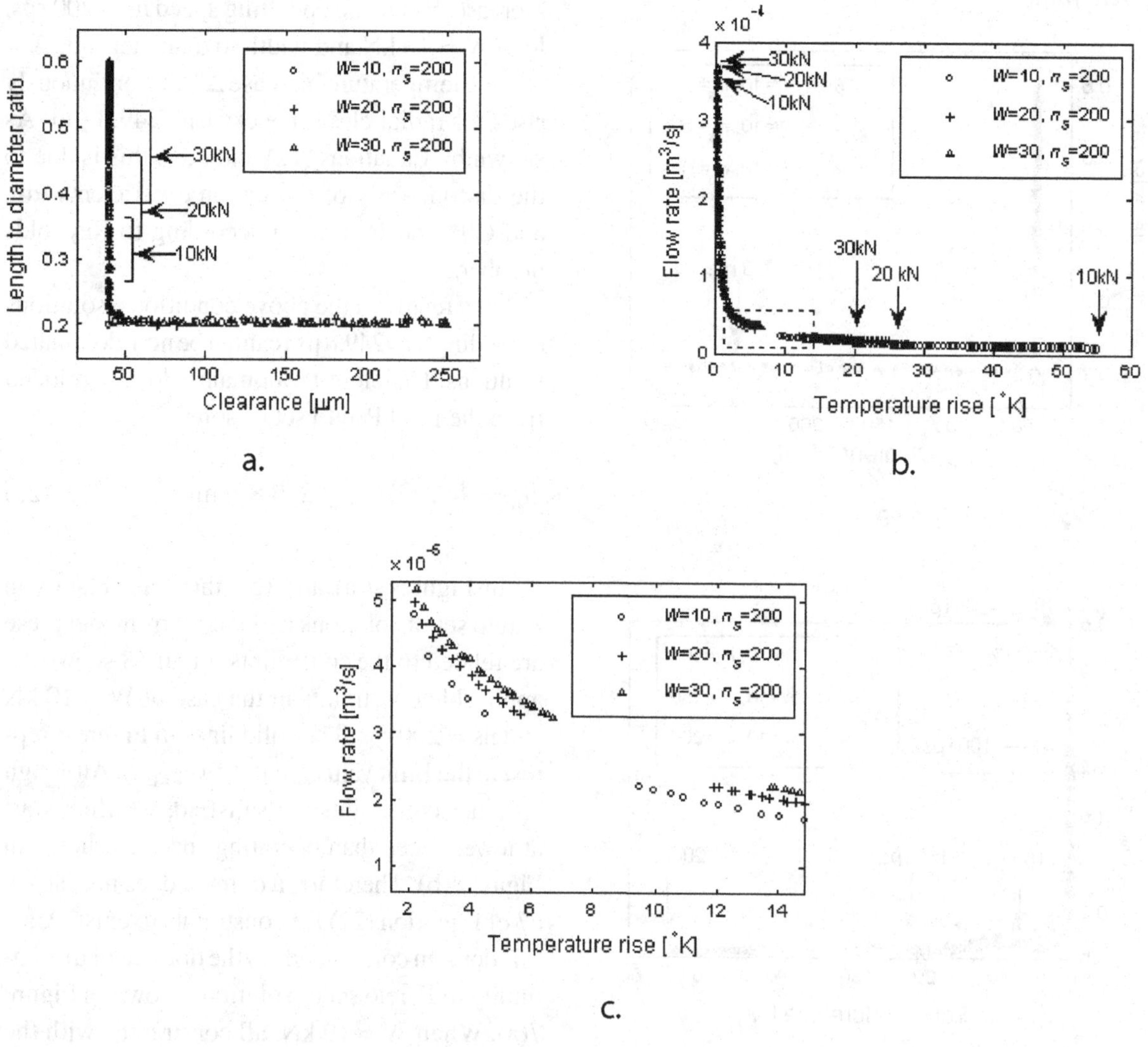

increase as operating speed increases. At the same time, the expansion for Pareto front is also observed.

Figure 10 shows the Pareto set of solutions and Pareto front in the case of the load W is changed to 10, 20 and 30 kN, and operating speed fixes at ns = 200 rps. For each case, the solutions of single objective functions in the form of linear combination are found and the results show no noticeable discrepancy other than the contents of execution administered by changing the operation speed. Therefore, the result of single objective function is not fully explained. The domains marked with three arrows in Figure 10(a) represent the domains excluded from Pareto set of solutions due to constraints under each load condition. The description for the operating condition of W = 10 kN and ns = 200 rps was described previously. As the load increases, the domains excluded from the set of solutions start moving. Domains discontinuously broken by constraints in three sets of solutions from Pareto front as shown in Figure

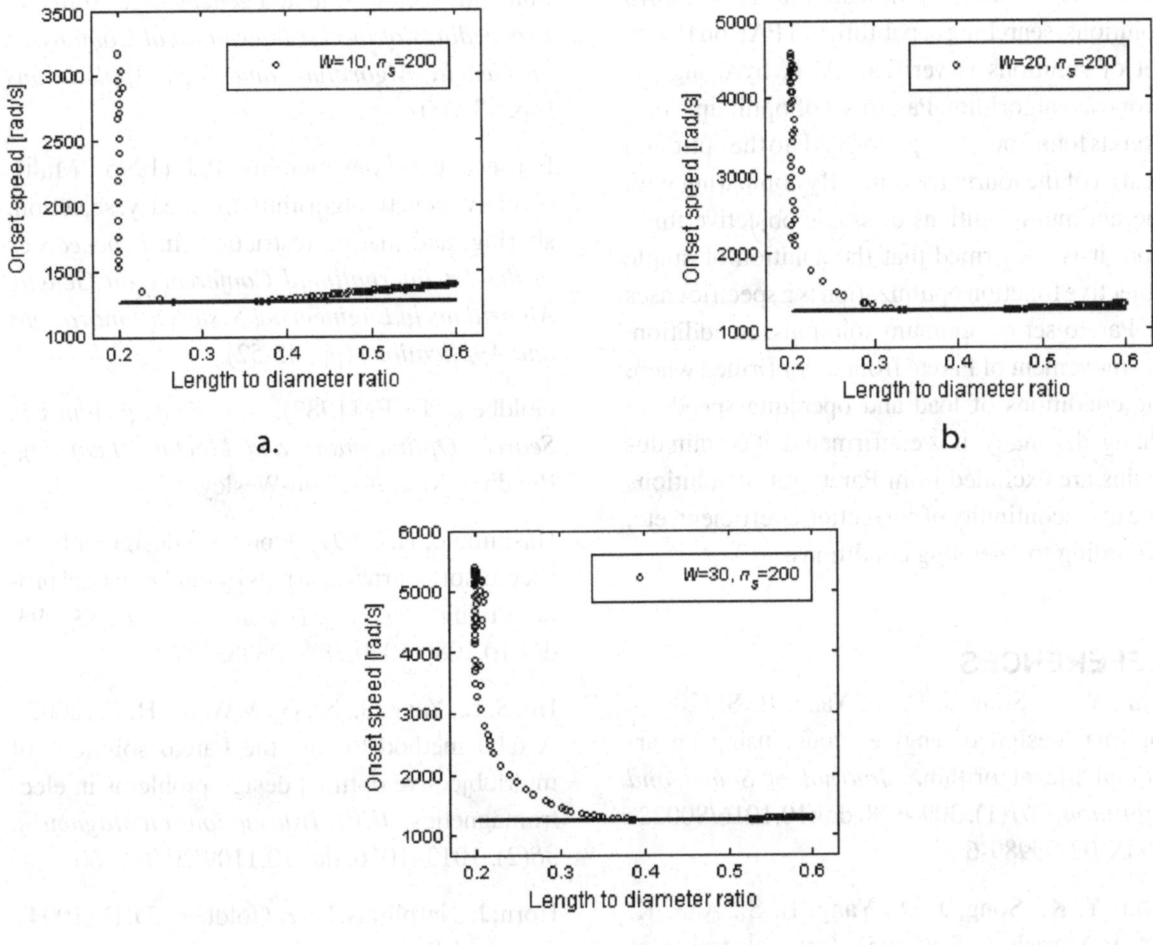

Figure 11. Onset speed to ωcr (ns = 200 rps) (a) W = 10 kN (b) W = 20 kN (c) W = 30 kN

10(b) are expanded and present in Figure 10(c). In Figure 11, the constraints for whirling starting speed are expressed according to each load. Figure 8(b) is repeated in Figure 11(a) for clarity. As shown in Figure 8, design limits (ωcr) are marked with solid lines. The three discontinuous domains in Figure 10(a) correspond to the domains which do not satisfy the constraints as shown in the three inserts of Figure 11.

In all Pareto sets of solutions expressed in Figure 10(a), Sex in Equation (25) is excluded. In other words, the exclusion from Pareto set of solutions due to discontinuity of correction coefficients and others occur in all cases. However, approximating the correction coefficients to eliminate this phenomenon will produce results which are not physically possible in reality. This phenomenon has been reflected with the physically existing discontinuity. Therefore, modification are not required if the equations represent well reality.

CONCLUSION

On the basis of artificial life algorithm, The Pareto artificial life algorithm is proposed, which is capable of searching Pareto set of solutions for multiple objective functions. Through the three problems of Pareto optimization to hold known solutions, searching capabilities of PAL on Pareto set of solutions is verified. Also, by using the proposed algorithm, Pareto set of optimum solutions is found out by applying PAL to the optimum design of the journal bearing. By comparing with the optimum solutions of single objective function, it is confirmed that the solution of single objective function optimization is a specific cases of Pareto set of optimum solutions. In addition, the movement of Pareto front is confirmed where the conditions of load and operating speed are changed. Finally, it is confirmed that certain domains are excluded from Pareto set of solutions due to discontinuity of correction coefficient, etc. according to operating conditions.

REFERENCES

Ahn, Y. K., Song, J. D., & Yang, B. S. (2003). Optimal design of engine mount using an artificial life algorithm. *Journal of Sound and Vibration*, *261*(1), 309–328. doi:10.1016/S0022-460X(02)00989-6

Ahn, Y. K., Song, J. D., Yang, B. S., Ahn, K. K., & Morishita, S. (2005). Optimal design of nonlinear fluid engine mount. *Journal of Mechanical Science and Technology*, *19*(3), 768–777. doi:10.1007/BF02916125

Anderson, J. (2000). *A Survey of Multiobjective Optimization in Engineering Design (Tech. Rep. No. LiTH-IKP-R-1097)*. Linköping, Sweden: Linköping University.

Coello, C. A. C., & Zacatenco, C. S. P. (2006). Twenty years of evolutionary multi-objective optimization: a historical view of the field. *IEEE Computational Intelligence Magazine*, *1*(1), 28–36. doi:10.1109/MCI.2006.1597059

David, S. J. (1985). Multiple objective optimization with vector evaluated genetic algorithms. In *Proceedings of the 1st International Conference on Genetic Algorithms and Their Applications* (pp. 93-100).

Fonseca, C. M., & Fleming, P. J. (1995). Multiobjective genetic algorithms made easy: selection, sharing, and mating restriction. In *Proceedings of the 1st International Conference on Genetic Algorithms in Engineering Systems: Innovations and Applications* (pp. 45-52).

Goldberg, D. E. (1989). *Genetic Algorithms in Search, Optimization, and Machine Learning*. Reading, MA: Addison-Wesley.

Hashimoto, H. (1997). Optimum design of high-speed short journal bearings by mathematical programming. *Tribology Transactions*, *40*, 283–293. doi:10.1080/10402009708983657

Ho, S. L., Yang, S., Ni, G., & Wong, H. C. (2002). A tabu method to find the Pareto solutions of multiobjective optimal design problems in electromagnetics. *IEEE Transactions on Magnetics*, *38*(2), 1013–1016. doi:10.1109/20.996260

Horn, J., Nafpliotis, N., & Goldberg, D. E. (1994). A niched Pareto genetic algorithm for multiobjective optimization. In *Proceedings of the 5th International Conference on Genetic Algorithms* (pp. 82-87).

Pareto, V. (1896). *Cours d'economie politique, Vol. I and II*. Lausanne, Switzerland: F. Rouge.

Schaffer, J. D. (1985). Multiobjective optimization using nondominated sorting in genetic algorithms. In *Proceedings of the 1st International Conference on Genetic Algorithms and Their Applications* (pp. 160-168).

Shiyou, Y., & Ni, G. (1998). An universal tabu search algorithm for global optimization of multimodal functions with continuous variables in electromagnetics. *IEEE Transactions on Magnetics*, *34*, 2901–2904. doi:10.1109/20.717676

Song, J. D., Yang, B. S., Choi, B. K., & Kim, H. J. (2005). Optimum design of short journal bearings by enhanced artificial life optimization algorithm. *Tribology International*, *38*, 403–412. doi:10.1016/j.triboint.2003.10.008

Srinivas, N., & Deb, K. (1995). Multi-objective optimization using nondominated sorting in genetic algorithms. *Evolutionary Computation*, *2*(3), 221–248. doi:10.1162/evco.1994.2.3.221

Tanaka, M. (1995). GA-based decision support system for multi-criteria optimization. In *Proceedings of the International Conference on Systems, Man and Cybernetics* (Vol. 2, pp. 1556-1561).

Yang, B. S., & Lee, Y. H. (2000). Artificial life algorithm for function optimization. In *Proceedings of the 2000 ASME Design Engineering Technical Conference*.

Yang, B. S., Lee, Y. H., Choi, B. K., & Kim, H. J. (2001). Optimum design of short journal bearings by artificial life algorithm. *Tribology International*, *34*(7), 427–435. doi:10.1016/S0301-679X(01)00034-2

Yang, B. S., & Song, J. D. (2002). Development of an enhanced artificial life optimization algorithm and optimum design of short journal bearings. *Transactions of the Korean Society of Noise and Vibration Engineering*, *12*(6), 478–487. doi:10.5050/KSNVN.2002.12.6.478

This work was previously published in the Journal of Information Technology Research, Volume 4, Issue 2, edited by Mehdi Khosrow-Pour, pp. 43-60, copyright 2011 by IGI Publishing (an imprint of IGI Global).

Chapter 9
An Optimization Model for the Identification of Temperature in Intelligent Building

ZhenYa Zhang
Anhui University of Architecture & University of Science & Technology of China, China

HongMei Cheng
Anhui University of Architecture, China

ShuGuang Zhang
University of Science & Technology of China, China

ABSTRACT

Methods for the reconstruction of temperature fields in an intelligent building with temperature data of discrete observation positions is a current topic of research. To reconstruct temperature field with observation data, it is necessary to model the identification of temperature in each observation position. In this paper, models for temperature identification in an intelligent building are formalized as optimization problems based on observation temperature data sequence. To solve the optimization problem, a feed forward neural network is used to formalize the identification structure, and connection matrixes of the neural network are the identification parameters. With the object function for the given optimization problem as the fitness function, the training of the feed forward neural network is driven by a genetic algorithm. The experiment for the precision and stability of the proposed method is designed with real temperature data from an intelligent building.

INTRODUCTION

With the rapid development of modern information technology on computer, communication and automation (Braun, 2007; Luo, Lin, Chen, & Su, 2006; Yang & Peng, 2001; Deo, 2006), intelligent building (Flax, 1991; Ralegaonkar & Gupta, 2010; Chen, Clements-Croome, Hong, Li, & Xu, 2006) is presented to describe the phenomena that more and more new building, especially new large public building are equipped with more and more smart equipments (Krukowski & Arsenijevic, 2010; Seo, Oh, Suh, & Park, 2007; Sazonov, Janoyan,

DOI: 10.4018/978-1-4666-3625-5.ch009

& Jha, 2004; Hagras, 2008; Osterlind, Pramsten, Roberthson, Eriksson, Finne, & Voigt, 2007). Because there are many automated equipment in an intelligent building, the energy consumed in an intelligent building is cared by user and researcher. Because the distributing of temperature and it's variety in intelligent building are related to the energy efficiency and comfort grade of the building closely, many researchers put their attention on temperature filed in intelligent building. If the temperature field in an intelligent building can be forecasted rightly, the process of energy consuming of the building can be interfered for higher energy efficiency while the comfort grade is kept better level on. To reconstruct temperature field with observation data of discrete observation position in intelligent space, more and more researchers are focused on the identification of temperature in intelligent building.

Although the identification of temperature field in a building is researched widely (Carmody & O'Mahony, 2009; Li, Qin, & Yue, 2008; Jiménez & Madsen, 2008; Zhang, 2009; Jiang, Mahadevan, & Adeli, 2007; Malti, Victor, & Oustaloup, 2008) and some valuable models are gained, most of those models are depended strictly on some constrains such as specific architecture structure, specific heat source as incentive environment. It is difficult and costly to gather those parameters related to temperature field in a building because the architecture of the building may be variety and there are many kinds of building equipment as heat source in intelligent building. For most building equipments can be treated as heat source and the architecture of that building may be variety, it is difficult to collect values of those parameters in real time. To value those parameters with time requirement satisfied, temperature of some observation positions in an intelligent building can be sampled in long term time and the temperature field in the building can be constructed according to the analysis result of those observation data (Lu, Miao, & He, 2009; Yu, 2006).

Identification structure and parameter estimating methods are two key factors of temperature identification (Xiao, Bai, & Yu, 2006; Zhong & Song, 2008). Because temperature in an intelligent building is influenced by many complicated parameters (Wang & Xu, 2005; Hassan, Guirguis, Shaalan, & El-Shazly, 2007), it is practical to assume that all of those parameters are stable in recent time. With this assumption, it is right to construct the identification model of temperature field in intelligent building with high frequency observation data of temperature in that building (Yu, Yi, & Zhao, 2008). To forecast the temperature near an observation position in a building, an optimization model for the reconstruction of temperature in an intelligent building and a method for the temperature identification in that building with feed forward neural network as identification structure and genetic algorithm for the parameter optimization of the method are presented in this paper. The rest of this paper is organized as following. The identification structure based on feed forward neural network and the optimization of identification parameters based on genetic algorithm are presented. Experimental results are shown with observation data of temperature in the electronic reading room of south laboratory in Anhui Architecture University.

MODEL FOR TEMPERATURE IDENTIFICATION

The identification model for temperature field inside a building is a function with time, maintenance structure and other thermodynamic parameters as variable. If the maintenance structure of the building and other parameters are not clear, temperature field inside the space can be identified based on temperature context of space. Suppose $<t_1 \ldots t_n>$ be n observation temperature value of an observation position with constant time interval, $t'_n = f(t_1, t_2 \ldots t_{n-1})$ where t'_n is the estimate value of t_n according to $t_1, t_2 \ldots t_{n-1}$ and f is estimating method,

$g(f)=(t'_n - t_n)^2/2$. If $g(f_0)=\min g(f)$, f_0 should be the basic temperature identification model for < $t_1 \ldots t_n$ > and t'_{n+1} can be estimated as $f_0(t_1, t_2 \ldots t_n)$. Although it is reasonable to estimate t'_{n+1} as $t'_{n+1}=f_0(t_1, t_2 \ldots t_n)$, it is inefficient if the value of n is large enough for f_0 is the function with all observation temperature data as variable.

Definition 1: Suppose $<t_1 \ldots t_n>$ be n observation temperature value of one observation position with constant time interval, $t'_m=f(t_{m-k}, t_{m-k+1} \ldots t_{m-1})$, $k<m\leq n$ is the estimate value for t_m and f is estimate method, $g(f)=((t'_{k+1}-t_{k+1})^2+(t'_{k+2}-t_{k+2})^2+\ldots+(t'_{n-1}-t_{n-1})^2)/(2(n-k)$. If $g(f_0)=\min g(f)$, f_0 is the identification model for $<t_1 \ldots t_n>$.

In definition 1, f_0 is the temperature identification model and can be constructed based on temperature sequence $<t_1 \ldots t_n>$ meanwhile the (n+1)*th* observation temperature value can be estimated as $t'_{n+1}=f_0(t_{n-k-1},\ldots,t_n)$. At this case, the temperature identification model in the building is the function with all observation temperature data in least recent observation time fragments.

To compute the temperature of observation position at least recent future with the temperature identification model in definition1, feed forward neural network with single hidden layer can be used as the identification structure and parameters for the identification model are weigh matrixes of the desired neural network. The topology of the desired feed forward neural network is shown at Figure 1. The number of input neurons is $n+1$. The first n input neurons are for n observation temperature data and input signal for the last input neuron is always 1 for bias of hidden neurons. The number of hidden neurons of desired network is $k+1$ and the input signal of the $(k+1)th$ of hidden neurons is always 1 for bias of neurons in output layer. The number of output neurons in the desired network is 1. The transform function of hidden neurons $f_1(x)$ and the transform function of output neurons $f_2(x)$ can be appointed with experience.

Proposition 1: Let $W_i=(w_{i1} \ldots w_{in} w_{i,n+1})^T$,i=1,2 ... k, $W=(W_1, W_2 \ldots W_k)^T$ be the connection matrix between input layer and hidden layer of the desired feed forward neural network for temperature identification and $U=(u_{11},\ldots, u_{1k}, u_{1,k+1})$ be the connection matrix between hidden layer and output layer, $f_1(x)$ be the transform function for non bias neurons in hidden layer and $f_2(x)$ be the transform function for neurons in output layer. If $X=(x_1 \ldots x_n)$

Figure 1. The topology of feed forward neural network for temperature identification

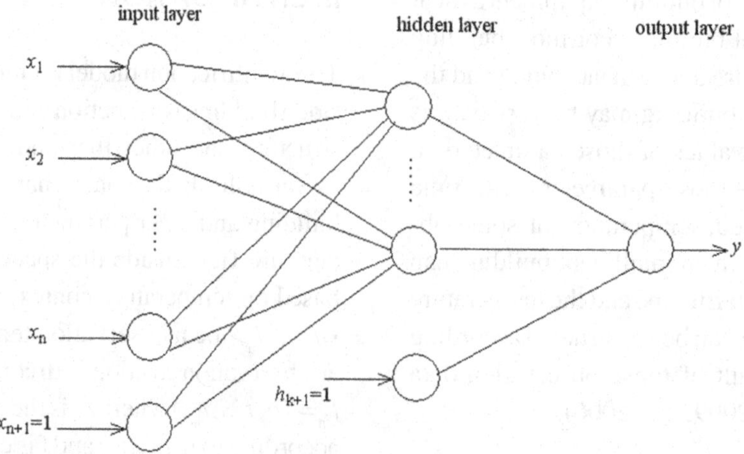

be the input vector for first n input neurons, y be the output of the desired network and $X'=(X, 1)^T$, thus $y=f_2(U^*((f_1(W^*X'))^T, 1)^T)$.

Proof:

- $\because$ W is the connection matrix for input layer and hidden layer of desired neural network.
- $\therefore$ The net input for hidden layer of desired network is W^*X'.
- $\because$ The transform function of first k neurons in hidden layer of desired network is f_1.
- $\therefore$ The output of hidden layer of desired network is $(f_1(W^*X'))^T, 1)^T$.
- $\because$ U is the connection matrix between hidden layer and output layer of desired network.
- $\because$ f_2 is the transform function of neurons in output layer and y is the output of the network.
- $\therefore$ $y=f_2(U^*((f_1(W^*X'))^T, 1)^T)$.

When the feed forward neural network shown in Figure 1 is used as the identification structure for the temperature identification in intelligent building, it is necessary to value W and U where W the connection matrix between input layer and hidden layer and U the connection matrix between input layer and hidden layer. If transform function for each hidden neurons and output neurons are differentiable, the desired feed forward neural network can be trained with back propagation (BP) algorithm. If the transform function for output neuron is linear function, the desired network can be treated as RBF network. If the differentiability of transform function for each hidden neurons and output neurons is uncertain, W and U can be optimized with direct search algorithm such as genetic algorithm. The detail for the optimization progress with genetic algorithm is given as Algorithm 1.

Algorithm 1: The training of feed forward neural network for temperature identification based on genetic algorithm is designed as follows:

1. Generate population according to coding rule randomly. Each individual in the population is corresponding to an assignment for connection matrixes of the feed forward neural network.
2. Calculate the fitness of each individual in population.
3. Repeat step 4-6 until the stopping criterion is satisfied
4. Selection operation
5. Crossover operation
6. Mutation operation
7. Decode the best individual as connection matrixes which is the output of this algorithm

The chromosome for individual in Algorithm 1 is coded according to connection matrixes of the desired neural network. If $W_i=(w_{i1} \ldots w_{in}\ w_{i,n+1})^T$, $i=1,2 \ldots k$, $W=(W_1, W_2 \ldots W_k)^T$ is the connection matrix for input and hidden layer of desired neural network and $U=(u_{11}, \ldots, u_{1k}, u_{1,k+1})$ is the connection matrix for hidden and output layer of that network, the code for chromosome of individual is $(w_{11} \ldots w_{1n}, w_{1,n+1}, w_{21} \ldots w_{2n}, w_{2,n+1} \ldots w_{k1} \ldots w_{kn}, w_{k,n+1}, u_{11}\ u_{12} \ldots u_{1k}\ u_{1,k+1})$.

Let $P=\{X_1, \ldots, X_S\}=\{(x_{11}\ x_{12} \ldots x_{1n})^T \ldots (x_{S1}\ x_{S2} \ldots x_{Sn})^T\}$ be sample set with s sample for the training of desired neural network, $T=\{t_1\ t_2 \ldots t_S\}$ be target signal for each sample in P orderly, the transform function for each non bias hidden neurons be $f_1(x)$, the transform function for output neurons be f_2(x) and $X'_i=(X^T_i, 1)^T$. According to proposition 1, $y_i=f_2(U^*((f_1(W^*X'_i))^T, 1)^T)$, $i=1,2\ldots S$. According to definition 1, the fitness function in Algorithm 1 can be appointed with $E=((t_1-y_1)^2+(t_2-y_2)^2+\ldots+(t_s-y_s)^2)/(2S)$.

EXPERIMENTAL RESULTS

To verify the validity of Algorithm 1, temperature observation data of the electronic reading room of south laboratory at Anhui Architecture University is collected. Temperature value of each observation position is sampled every minute by a wireless sensor network. Observation data of one node (ID=17) in 1354 minutes is used in our experiment following and those data can be described as $<data_1, data_2... data_n>$ with n=1354. Topology for the wireless sensor network and the location of the 17*th* node in the electronic reading room is shown in Figure 2 and it is obvious that 17*th* node is in the center of that room.

The time window for temperature identification model constructing is 30 according to experience. With this assumption, it is possible to predict $data_{k+31}$ by our temperature identification model with $<data_{k+31-LL}, data_{k+32-LL} \dots data_{k+30}>$ and Algorithm 1. To complete the predication task, the sample set, $P=\{<data_{k-LL+1}, data_{k-LL+2} \dots data_k>, <data_{k-LL+2} \dots data_{k+1}> \dots <data_{k-LL+30} \dots data_{k+29}>\}$ for desired neural network training is constructed according to $<data_{k+31-LL}, data_{k+32-LL} \dots data_{k+30}>$ and the target signal for sample set is $T=\{<data_{k+1}>, <data_{k+2}> \dots <data_{k+30}>\}$ where there are LL+1 input neurons in the desired feed forward neural network. Because both BP and RBF network can complete this task, to compare the performance of algorithm to BP network and RBF network expediently, the transform function for non bias hidden neurons of desired neural network is appointed with $f_1(x) = 2/(1+\exp(-x))-1$ and the transform function for output neurons of desired neural network is appointed with $f_2(x) = x$.

Because there are LL+1 input neurons in the desired feed forward neural network, to ascertain the value of LL for the construction of desired network, RBF network is used to compete the same identification task in our experiment and the value of LL is changed form 1 to 20. There are two kind of phenomenon in the experiment. One is that when the value of LL is changed from

Figure 2. Topology for wireless sensor network in the electronic reading room

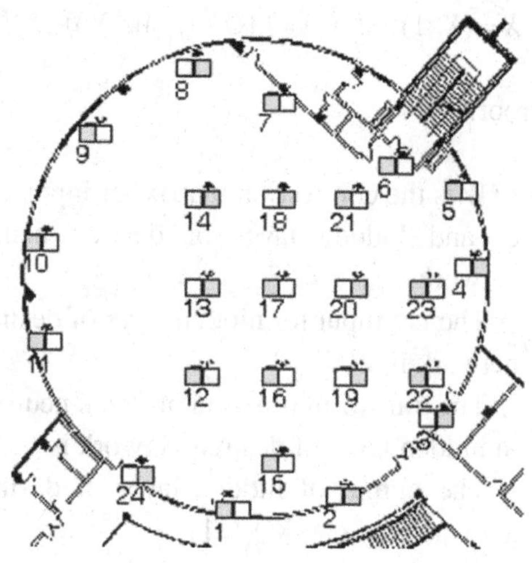

1 to 7, the learning of RBF network may stop with convergence prematurely. The other is that all $LL \geq 10$, mean temperature error curve are closer and stable. Because the value of LL is greater, more computing time is used, the number of non bias input neurons of desired neural network is valued with 10, i.e. LL =10.To ascertain the number of non bias hidden neurons in the desired neural network, a BP neural network with LL=10 input neurons is used to complete the same task with the number of hidden neurons changed form 1 to 30. And mean temperature error is saved with the number of hidden neurons in the BP network. Because the mean temperature error is greater if the number of hidden neurons in BP network is greater in our experiment, the number of non bias hidden neurons in the desired neural network is 1.To verify the reasonability of desired neural network with 10 non bias input neurons and 1 non bias hidden neuron, the mean temperature error with the number of input neurons and the number of hidden neurons in a BP neural network as variable are shown in Figure 3 when the BP neural network is used to complete the same task. In our experiment, when the number of input neurons of the BP network is changed form 1 to 7, the learning of BP network may stop with convergence

Figure 3. Mean error of BP network on temperature identification

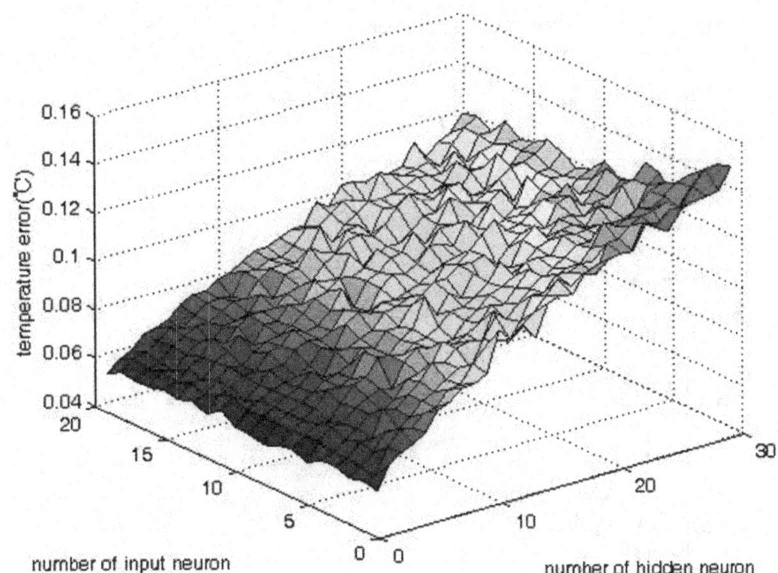

prematurely. And further more, the mean error of temperature prediction is less when the number of input neurons is 10 and the number of hidden neurons is 1.

Once the topology of desired neural network is ascertained, connection matrixes of desired network are optimized by Algorithm 1 with 20 individual in our experiment. The convergence of algorithm 1 for one data prediction is shown at Figure 4. In experiment for Figure 4, the number of iterative is 51 when Algorithm 1 is convergent. The fitness of best individual is 7.6261×10^{-5} and the mean fitness of all individuals is 0.36635.

The comparison result for performance of Algorithm 1, BP network and RBF network on the prediction for temperature in lease future is shown at Table 1. It is obvious that the performance of Algorithm 1 is best on the view of error and stable according to data in Table 1.

In our experiment for the performance of our proposed method, neural network toolbox under Matlab R2007b is used for construction of BP neural network and RBF neural network. Genetic algorithm and direct search toolbox is used for the implementation of genetic algorithm. The constructor for BP network creating is newff and the constructor for RBF network designing is newrb. The constructor of genetic algorithm is ga.

Table 1. Comparison for Performance of Algorithm 1, BP network and RBF network

Method	Absolute Error	Variance of Absolute Error	Relative Error	Variance of Relative Error
Algorithm 1	0.0498	0.0703	0.0028	0.0039
BP network	0.0552	0.0876	0.0032	0.0049
RBF network	0.0578	0.1276	0.0033	0.0071

Figure 4. The convergent curves of Algorithm 1

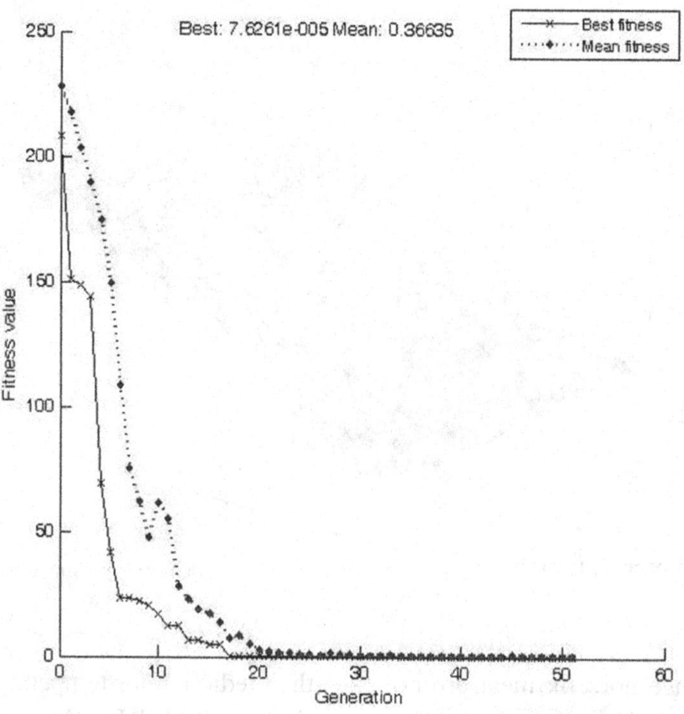

CONCLUSION

Energy saving is focused by research and application on intelligent building. To save energy consumed in an intelligent building dynamically, temperature field of that building in last recent future is needed to be forecasted accurately. That temperature field can be constructed according to temperature of observation location in that building recently. In this paper, model for the identification of temperature in intelligent build is discussed and a feed forward neural network trained with genetic algorithm is proposed. Experimental results show that the precision and stable of the proposed method is good. The mean computing time of our proposed method is 9.0572 seconds in our experiment. The proposed method is best and effective according to its precision on temperature prediction because the time interval for two closest observations in our application is 60 seconds.

Temperature field is one kind of scalar information field in an intelligent building and there are other scalar information fields such as humidity, luminosity which is correlative with energy saving in that building. Identification models and methods for those information fields are one of our research focuses in intelligent building. The application of the proposed method is our ongoing research.

ACKNOWLEDGMENT

This work is partially supported by National Basic Research Program of China (973 Program) under Grant No.2007CB814901, Nature Science Key Fund of Anhui Education Department under Grant No.KJ2009A143, China Postdoctoral Foundation under Grant No. 20100480702 and Anhui Provincial Natural Science Foundation under Grant No.09412069.

REFERENCES

Braun, J. E. (2007). Intelligent Building Systems – Past, Present, and Future. In *Proceedings of the 2007 American Control Conference* (pp. 4374-4381).

Carmody, C. A., & O'Mahony, T. (2009). System identification of a domestic residence using Wireless sensor node data. In *Proceedings of the 17th Mediterranean Conference on Control and Automation* (pp. 987-992).

Chen, Z., Clements-Croome, D., Hong, J., Li, H., & Xu, Q. (2006). A multicriteria lifespan energy efficiency approach to intelligent building assessment. *Energy and Building*, *38*(5), 393–409. doi:10.1016/j.enbuild.2005.08.001

Deo, D. S. (2006). Applications of expert system/neural networks/genetic algorithms in an intelligent building complex. *Journal of the Institution of Engineers: Architectural Engineering Division*, *87*(10), 4–9.

Flax, B. M. (1991). Intelligent Buildings. *IEEE Communications Magazine*, *29*(4), 24–27. doi:10.1109/35.76555

Hagras, H. (2008). Employing computational intelligence to generate more intelligent and energy efficient living spaces. *International Journal of Automation and Computing*, *5*(1), 1–9. doi:10.1007/s11633-008-0001-7

Hassan, M. A., Guirguis, N. M., Shaalan, M. R., & El-Shazly, K. M. (2007). Investigation of effects of window combinations on ventilation characteristics for thermal comfort in buildings. *Desalination*, *209*, 251–260. doi:10.1016/j.desal.2007.04.035

Jiang, X., Mahadevan, S., & Adeli, H. (2007). Bayesian wavelet packet denoising for structural system identification. *Structural Control and Health Monitoring*, *14*(2), 333–356. doi:10.1002/stc.161

Jiménez, M. J., & Madsen, H. (2008). Models for describing the thermal characteristics of building components. *Building and Environment*, *43*(2), 152–162. doi:10.1016/j.buildenv.2006.10.029

Krukowski, A., & Arsenijevic, D. (2010). RFID-based positioning for building management systems. In *Proceedings of the 2010 IEEE International Symposium on Circuits and Systems: Nano-Bio Circuit Fabrics and Systems* (pp. 3569-3572).

Li, J., Qin, L.-L., & Yue, D.-Z. (2008). Experiment Greenhouse Temperature System Modeling and Simulation. *Journal of System Simulation*, *20*(7), 1869–1875.

Lu, Y., Miao, K.-K., & He, W. (2009). Context-aware approach for temperature monitoring and fire alarming. *Journal of Computer Applications*, *29*(2), 583–594. doi:10.3724/SP.J.1087.2009.00583

Luo, R. C., Lin, T. Y., Chen, H. C., & Su, K. L. (2006). Multisensor Based Security Robot System for Intelligent Building. In *Proceedings of the 2006 IEEE International Conference on Multisensor Fusion and Integration for Intelligent Systems* (pp. 408-413).

Malti, R., Victor, S., & Oustaloup, A. (2008). Advances in system identification using fractional models. *Journal of Computational and Nonlinear Dynamics*, *3*(2), 1–7. doi:10.1115/1.2833910

Osterlind, F., Pramsten, E., Roberthson, D., Eriksson, J., Finne, N., & Voigt, T. (2007). Integrating building automation systems and wireless sensor networks. In *Proceedings of the 12th IEEE International Conference on Emerging Technologies and Factory Automation* (pp. 1376-1379).

Ralegaonkar, R., & Gupta, R. (2010). Review of intelligent building construction: A passive solar architecture approach. *Renewable & Sustainable Energy Reviews*, *14*(8), 2238–2242. doi:10.1016/j.rser.2010.04.016

Sazonov, E., Janoyan, K., & Jha, R. (2004). Wireless intelligent sensor network for autonomous structural health monitoring. In *Proceedings of the International Society for Optical Engineering Conference* (pp. 305-314).

Seo, K.-Y., Oh, S.-W., Suh, S.-H., & Park, G.-K. (2007). Intelligent steering control system based on voice instructions. *International Journal of Control. Automation and Systems*, *5*(5), 539–546.

Wang, S., & Xu, X. (2005). Models for describing the Simplified building model for transient thermal performance estimation using GA-based parameter identification. *International Journal of Thermal Sciences*, *45*(4), 419–432. doi:10.1016/j.ijthermalsci.2005.06.009

Xiao, J., Bai, Y.-F., & Yu, L. (2006). Overview of Fuzzy System Structure Identification. *Journal of Southwest Jiao Tong University*, *41*(2), 135–142.

Yang, J., & Peng, H. (2001). Decision support to the application of intelligent building technologies. *Renewable Energy*, *22*(1), 66–67. doi:10.1016/S0960-1481(00)00085-9

Yu, J. (2006). CBR and ANFIS based Emergent Decision Support System of Intelligent Buildings. [Natural Science]. *Journal of Shenyang Jianzhu University*, *22*(2), 315–318.

Yu, Y., Yi, J.-Q., & Zhao, D.-B. (2008). Survey on Smart Spaces Research. *Computer Science*, *35*(8), 1–20.

Zhang, W. (2009). On momentum and learning rate of the generalized ADLINE neural network for time varying system identification. In *Proceedings of the 6th International Symposium on Neural Networks* (pp. 1002-1013).

Zhong, L.-S., & Song, Z.-H. (2008). Hierarchical Optimization Identification of LTI State-space Systems by Projected Gradient Search. *ACTA Automatica Sinica*, *34*(6), 711–715. doi:10.3724/SP.J.1004.2008.00711

This work was previously published in the Journal of Information Technology Research, Volume 4, Issue 2, edited by Mehdi Khosrow-Pour, pp. 61-69, copyright 2011 by IGI Publishing (an imprint of IGI Global).

Chapter 10
Research of Biogeography-Based Multi-Objective Evolutionary Algorithm

Hongwei Mo
Harbin Engineering University, China

Zhidan Xu
Harbin Engineering University, China

ABSTRACT

Biogeography-based optimization algorithm (BBO) is an optimization algorithm inspired by the migration of animals in nature. A new multi-objective evolutionary algorithm is proposed, which is called Biogeography-based multi-objective evolutionary algorithm (BBMOEA). The fitness assignment and the external population elitism of SPEA2 are adapted to ensure even distribution of the solution set. The population evolutionary operators of BBO are applied to the evolution of the external population to ensure the convergence of the solution set. Simulation results on benchmark test problems illustrate the effectiveness and efficiency of the proposed algorithm.

INTRODUCTION

Many real world problems require the simultaneous optimization of many conflicting objectives. The solutions to such problems are known as Pareto optimal set and the corresponding objective values are known as the Pareto front. For solving such problems, traditional mathematical program methods have limitations to the distribution of solutions in objective space. Evolutionary algorithms (EAs) are stochastic global search methods based on population evolution and many Pareto optimal solutions can be found in a single run. So many EAs had been developed for solving multi-objective optimization problems (MOP).

Over the past decade, a number of multi-objective evolutionary algorithms (MOEAs) have been suggested, such as Genetic algorithm for multi-objective optimization (MOGA) (Fonseca & Fleming, 1993), the Non-dominated Sorting

DOI: 10.4018/978-1-4666-3625-5.ch010

Genetic Algorithm (NSGA) (Srinivas & Deb, 1995), the Niched Pareto Genetic Algorithm by Horn, Nafpliotis, and Goldberg (NPGA) (Horn, Nafpliotis & Goldberg, 1994). These MOEAS adopt the selection mechanisms based on Pareto ranking and fitness sharing to maintain diversity of the populations. After the algorithms mentioned above, MOEAS based on the elitism strategy were presented, such as the improved version of NSGA (NSGA-II), which is with a more efficient non-dominated sorting method, elitism and a crowded comparison operator without specifying any additional parameters for maintaining diversity (Deb, Pratap, Agarwal, & Meyarivan, 2002), the improved version of SPEA (SPEA2) (Zitzler, Laumanns, & Thiele, 2001), which is with a revised fitness assignment strategy, a nearest neighbor density estimation technique and an enhanced archive truncation method. All these MOEAs use recombination and mutation operator of GA to evaluate the population. In addition, some hybrid EAs were proposed, such as multi-objective algorithm based on particle swarm optimization (MOPSO) (Coello Coello, Pulido, & Lechuga, 2004), multi-objective algorithm based on ant colony (Zhang & Huang, 2005), multi-objective algorithm based on immune algorithm IDCMA (Jiao, Gong, Shang, et al., 2005) and Multi-objective Immune Algorithm with Non-dominated Neighbor-Based Selection (NNIA) (Gong, Jiao, Du, & Bo, 2008), a differential evolution based on double populations for solving multi-objective constrained optimization problem (Meng, Zhang, & Liu, 2008), and so on. Different evolutionary algorithms have its specific advantages for solving MOP.

In 2008, Biogeography-Based optimization (BBO) was proposed firstly by Dan Simon (Simon, 2008), which is a new stochastic search algorithm based on the principle of animal migration. BBO were compared with seven optimization algorithms and the results demonstrated its better performance for solving single objective optimization problem.

The science of biogeography can be traced to the work of nineteenth century naturalists such as Alfred Wallace (Wallace, 2005) and Charles Darwin (Darwin, 1859). In the early 1960s, Robert MacArthur and Edward Wilson began working together on mathematical models of biogeography. They were interested in mathematical models for the extinction and migration of species. Since their distinct work, biogeography has become a major area of research (Hanski & Gilpin, 1997). Mathematical models of biogeography describe how species migrate from one island to another, how new species arise, and how species become extinct. The term "island" here is used descriptively rather than literally. That is, an island is any habitat that is geographically isolated from other habitats.

In view of this, Simon presented the first paper on biogeography inspired algorithm for engineering (Simon, 2008), which is called biogeography based optimization (BBO). In his creative work, he merged the burgeoning field of biogeography with engineering in order to see how the two disciplines can be of mutual benefit. Although the idea of application of biogeography to engineering is similar to those nature inspired algorithms mentioned above, it has completely different mechanisms and process from those ones. It is again to prove the great power of nature.

In the past two years, Simon and other researchers had published several papers about BBO. In the first paper on BBO, Simon introduced the main idea of how to use biogeography to design an optimization algorithm and gave us the basic definitions, steps of algorithms. He had tested the new algorithm on two kinds of problems, and one is sensor selection for aircraft engine health estimation. The BBO was compared with the other main nature inspired computing (NIC), such as ACO, PSO, GA and so on. The experiments results showed that BBO is indeed effective in solving these problems. And it should be the new member of family of NIC.

Simon simplified the original BBO in order to analyze its theory (Simon, 2009). He presented a simplified version of BBO and then analyzed its population using probability theory. The analysis provided approximate values for the expected number of generations before the population's best solution improves, and the expected amount of improvement. These expected values are functions of the population size. In the past year, many improvement to BBO had been finished by Simon and some other researchers (Simon, Ergezer, & Du, 2009; Ergezer, Simon, & Du, 2009; Du, Simon, & Ergezer, 2009; Rarick, Simon, Villaseca, & Vyakaranam, 2009; Gong, Cai, Ling, & Li, 2010; Ma, 2010). In the respect of applications of BBO, Bhattacharya and Chattopadhyay used BBO to solve the problem of economic load dispatch problem (Bhattacharya & Chattopadhyay, 2010). BBO was also combined with quantum to be a new kind of hybrid algorithm for solving the knapsack problem (Tan & Guo, 2009).

BBO had been successfully applied to solve the Traveling salesman problem (Mo & Xu, 2010). The experiment results showed that the modified BBO (named TSPBMA) is good at solving the TSP and has better performance than most the other classical bio-inspired computing, including Genetic Algorithm, Immune Algorithm, Particle Swarm Optimization and son. But its convergence speed is slower than Ant System and the accuracy is also worse than AS.

In order to explore the feasibility of BBO for MOP, we propose a new algorithm called Biogeography-based Multi-Objective Evolutionary Algorithm (BBMOEA). The evolution operators of BBO are used to the evolution of the external populations. The fitness evaluation and the external population elitism mechanism of SPEA2 are adapted to ensure the distribution of the solutions set. By benchmark test problems, simulation results demonstrate the feasibility and effectiveness of the proposed BBMOEA for solving MOP. It is compared with SPEA2 and NSGA-II.

BASIC CONCEPT OF MOP

The minimization problem of (MOP) can be mathematically described as:

$$\begin{aligned} Miny &= f(x) = [f_1(x), f_2(x), \cdots, f_m(x)] \\ s.t \quad & g_i(x) \le 0, i = 1, 2, \cdots p \\ & h_i(x) = 0, i = 1, 2, \cdots q \end{aligned} \tag{1}$$

where $x = (x_1, x_2, \cdots, x_n) \in D \subset R^n$ is the vector of decision variables, D decision space, $y = (f_1, f_2, \cdots, f_m) \in Y \subset R^m$ the objective vector to be optimized, Y objective space. p and q are the number of inequality constraints and equality constraints respectively.

Definition 1 (Dominance): A vector $u = (u_1, u_2, \cdots u_n)$ dominates another vector $v = (v_1, v_2, \cdots v_n)$ if and only if

$$\begin{aligned} f_i(u) &\le f_i(v), \quad \forall i = 1, 2 \cdots m \\ f_i(u) &< f_i(v), \quad \exists i \in \{1, 2 \cdots m\} \end{aligned} \tag{2}$$

denoted as $u \succ v$.

Definition 2 (Pareto Optimal solution): A vector x^0 is Pareto optimal solution if there is not another vector x such that $x \succ x^0$.

Definition 3 (Pareto Optimal Set): Pareto Optimal Set is the set of all Pareto Optimal solutions

$$P_s = \{x^0 \mid \neg \exists x^1 \succ x^0\} \tag{3}$$

Definition 4 (Pareto optimal front): the corresponding image of the Pareto optimal set under the objective function space

$$P_F = \{f(x) \mid x \in P_s\} \tag{4}$$

BBO

In geography, the habitat that is well suited as residences for biological species has a high habitat suitability index (HIS). Factors that correlate with HIS include such as rainfall, diversity of vegetation, diversity of topographic features and temperature which are called suitability index variables (SIVs). Habitats with a high HIS tend to have much more species so that they are easy to saturate. So some species of the habitats will emigrate to nearby habitats. Then the habitats will have higher emigration rate and lower immigration rate. On the contrary, the habitats with low HIS have lower emigration rate and higher immigration rate. This principle can be adapted to design new algorithm for solving engineering problems. We can image that when a problem is presented, a good solution of the problem is analogous to a habitat with a high HIS and a poor solution to a habitat with a low HSI. High HIS solutions tend to share their features with low HIS solutions. Poor solutions accept a lot of new features to convert to good solutions. Similar to other EAs, BBO is also a population, stochastic global optimizer based on the fitness value which evaluate the superiority of individuals, Good characteristics are shared between the individuals so that the fitness value of individuals are increased. The difference between EAs and BBO is that original solution is displaced by the new solutions generated in EAs, but BBO maintains the set of solution from one iteration to the next iteration.

DESCRIPTION OF BBMOEA

In our method, it uses the fitness assignment and the external population elitism mechanism of SPEA2 to evaluate and truncate the external population and adopts the operators of BBO to the evolution of the external population. The implementation process is as follows:

Fitness Assignment

For fitness assignment, solutions dominated and non-dominated are all taken into account, then each individual of the population and the external populations is given a strength value $S(i)$ which denotes the number of solutions dominated by individual i

$$S(i) = \left|\left\{j \middle| x^j \in P_t \cup A_t, x^i \succ x^j\right\}\right| \tag{5}$$

The original individual fitness value $R(i)$ equals to the strength of all individuals as

$$R(i) = \sum_{x^j \in P_t \cup A_t, x^j \succ x^i} S(j) \tag{6}$$

In order to discriminate individuals with the same fitness value, the density of a solution is defined as the inverse of the distance to k th nearest neighbors in objective space.

Then the density of individual i is

$$D(i) = \frac{1}{\sigma_i^k + 2} \tag{7}$$

where σ_i^k is the distance in objective space between individual i and the k th nearest individual. And $k = \sqrt{N + M}$, M is population size, N the external population size. The final fitness value of individual i is

$$F(i) = R(i) + D(i) \tag{8}$$

Population Evolution

Based on the fitness, the individual is sorted in descending order, and the species number of i th habitat is

$$k = S_{\max} - i \tag{9}$$

$$S_{\max} = M + N - 1 \tag{10}$$

where $S_{\max}$ is the maximum number of species that the habitat can include.

The immigration rate λ_k and the emigration rate μ_k (Simon, 2008) of the ith habitat is

$$\lambda_k = I(1 - \frac{k}{n}) \tag{11}$$

$$\mu_k = \frac{Ek}{n} \tag{12}$$

With the number of species of habitats changing, species count probability is introduced to denote the probability of the habitat just containing S species. Assume that in a relatively short period of time, only a species immigrate or only a species emigrate, or none species immigrate or emigrate, more species is negligible (Simon, 2008), then

$$\dot{P}_s = \begin{cases} -(\lambda_s + \mu_s)P_s + \mu_{s+1}P_{s+1} & S = 0 \\ -(\lambda_s + \mu_s)P_s + \lambda_{s-1}P_{s-1} + \mu_{s+1}P_{s+1} & 1 \le S \le S_{\max} - 1 \\ -(\lambda_s + \mu_s)P_s + \lambda_{s-1}P_{s-1} & S = S_{\max} \end{cases} \tag{13}$$

By using the immigration rate, emigration rate and count probability are gained. The population evolutionary operators are as follows:

Migration: According to the immigration rate λ_k of individuals, they are randomly selected to be modified. If a solution is selected, then its immigration rate is used to decide whether or not to modify each SIV in that solution. If a given SIV is selected to be modified, then a solution will be decided to emigrate a randomly selected SIV to the corresponding position of the above solution to be modified according to the emigration rate of other solutions. During the process, the original individual does not disappear. It only changes some SIVs and shares the good SIVs with other individuals so that individuals can convert to the better ones. So the migration is an adaptive evolutionary operator.

Mutation: According to individuals count probability P_s, individuals are mutated to increase the diversity of the population. The mutation probability is (Simon, 2008):

$$m = P_m(1 - \frac{p_s}{p_{\max}}) \tag{14}$$

where $P_m = 0.5$ is the initial mutation probability. $P_{\max}$ is the maximum value of all count probability. By mutation operator, the more stable the individuals are, the smaller mutation probability they have. The stable individuals' immigration rate and emigration rate are near the intersection of immigration rate and emigration rate of species. However, the farther the individuals are from the intersection, the greater mutation probability they have.

Elitism with External Populations

An external population is used to store non-dominated individuals obtained so far. Consider the distribution of non-dominated individuals, the elitism mechanism of SPEA2 is applied in our algorithm. All non-dominated individuals in the population p_t and the external population A_t are copied to the population A_{t+1}.

If $|A_{t+1}| = M$, then the external population is accepted.

If $|A_{t+1}| < M$, then copy the best $M - |A_{t+1}|$ dominated solutions from p_t and A_t based on their fitness values to A_{t+1}.

If $|A_{t+1}| > M$, then truncate $|A_{t+1}| - M$

Solutions are gained by iteratively removing solutions with the maximum σ_i^k distance till $|A_{t+1}| = M$.

Main Loop of BBMOEA

The main loop of BBMOEA can be described as follows:

Step 1: Initialize of the parameters, the size of the population M, the size of the external population N, initial mutation probability P_m, the maximum immigration rate I, the maximum emigration rate E, the maximum number of generations $g_{\max}$.

Step 2: Randomly generate an initial population P_0 and an external population $A_0 = \phi$. Set $t = 0$.

Step 3: According to (8), all individuals' fitness value of P_t and A_t are calculated.

Step 4: Based on the above fitness value, all individuals are sorted in descending order. Identify non-dominated solutions of p_t and A_t, copy them to A_{t+1}, and then use the above elitism mechanism to truncate A_{t+1}.

Step 5: If $t > g_{\max}$ then return A_{t+1}, otherwise go to Step6.

Step 6: The fitness values of individuals in A_{t+1} are recalculated using Equation (8). The species number of the corresponding individual k, the immigration rate λ_k, emigration rate μ_k and counter probability p_s can be gained by (9), (10), (11), (12) and (13), respectively.

Step 7: The individuals of A_{t+1} are selected randomly based on immigration rate λ_k

Step 8: Perform immigration operator on the individuals selected in A_{t+1} to gain the population B_{t+1}.

Step 9: By (14), perform mutation operator on B_{t+1} to form the population P_{t+1}, then $t = t + 1$, go to Step 3

EXPERIMENT RESULT AND ANALYSIS

Benchmark Optimization Problems

In order to test the feasibility and the effectiveness of BBMOEA for solving MOP, 12 standard benchmark optimization problems are selected. The optimization problem with two objectives is SCH, which is representative of the test functions. ZDT is a series of test functions proposed by Deb. ZDT1 has a convex Pareto front and converge easily, ZDT2 a non-convex Pareto front, ZDT3 a non-continuous Pareto front. All of them have 30 decision variables. ZDT4 has a highly multi-modal Pareto front and a total of 219 local Pareto front. ZDT6 has solutions that are non-uniformly distributed. Both of them have 10 decision variables. The function expression can refer to (Zheng, 2007).

In the experiments, real number coding is adopted. The parameters are set as follows: initial mutation probability $p_m = 0.001$, the population size N=100, the external population size M=100, the maximum number of generations $g_{\max} = 200$, the maximum immigration rate and migration rate E = I = 1. The Pareto front obtained are shown in Figure 1, solid line denote the true Pareto front (Gong, Jiao, Du, & Bo, 2008), '*'denote the Pareto front generated by BBMOEA. From Figure 1, it can be seen that BBMOEA can converge to the true Pareto front for each test functions and the solutions are distributed evenly and broadly.

In order to validate the ability of solving three dimension problems, the test functions with three objectives are selected, including Viennet and Viennet (2) which have two decision variables. The objective space of them is the entire continuous region. In addition, there are four DTLZ problems with which decision variables can be extended to any number. According to Deb's proposition (Deb, Pratap, Agarwal, & Meyarivan, 2002), k and $|X_M|$ are set as follows: DTLZ1, $k = 3, |X_M| = 5$, with 7 decision variables, DTLZ2

Figure 1. Pareto front obtained

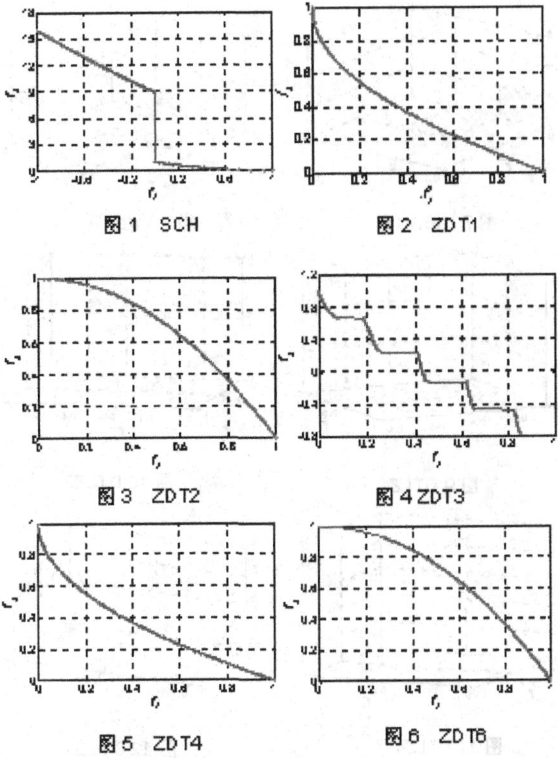

and DTLZ4, $k = 3, |X_M| = 10$, with 12 decision variables, DTLZ6, $k = 3, |X_M| = 20$, with 22 decision variable.

The selected parameters are the same as the above except for the maximum number of generations, $g_{\max} = 500$. By experiments, the Pareto front planes gained by BBMOEA are shown in Figure 2, the true Pareto plane can refer to (Zheng, 2007). From the figure, it can be seen that BBMOEA can converge to the true Pareto front surface for different types of test questions and has better distribution and diversity. The results show the feasibility of BBMOEA for solving MOP.

Performance Metrics

The main goal of MOEA is to generate the solutions of even distribution and keep convergence. In this work, two metrics are selected as:

1. **Generational distance (GD):** GD is a measure of the distance between the true and generated Pareto front. It is a convergence evaluation metric and defined as:

$$GD = \frac{\sqrt{\sum_{i=1}^{n} d_i^2}}{n} \quad (15)$$

where n is the number of non-dominated solutions found so far and d_i is the Euclidean distance between each of non-dominated solutions and the nearest solution of Pareto optimal set. It is clear that a smaller value of GD demonstrates a better convergence to the Pareto front.

2. **Spacing (SP):** The metric measures how evenly is for the distribution of solution set generated and it is given by:

$$SP = \sqrt{\frac{1}{n-1}\sum_{i=1}^{n}(\bar{d} - d_i^2)} \quad (16)$$

Figure 2. Pareto front planes gained by BBMOEA

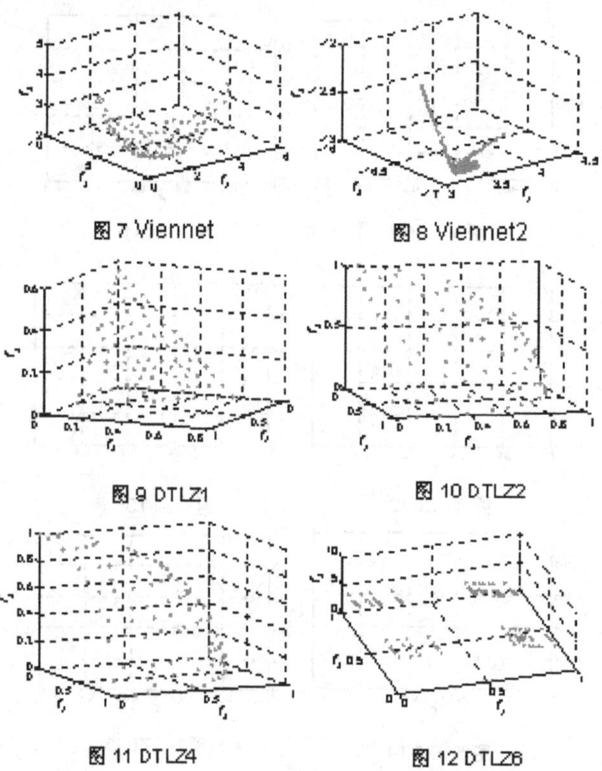

where n is the number of the solutions generated,

$$d_i = \min_j(|f_1^i(x) - f_1^j(x)| + |f_2^i(x) - f_2^j(x)|), i, j = 1, 2, \cdots, n, \quad (17)$$

where $\bar{d}$ is the average of all d_i. A smaller SP implies a more uniform distribution of solutions generated.

COMPARATIVE STUDY

In order to examine the effectiveness of BBMOEA, six test problems are used to compare the performance of BBMOEA against SPEA2 and NSGA-II. In comparison study, the simulated binary crossover operator and polynomial mutation are used in SPEA2 and NSGA-II. Some parameters are the same, crossover probability $p_c = 1$, mutation probability $p_m = 1/n$. For SPEA2, the population size is 100 and equal to the external population size. For NSGA-II, the population size is 100. Twenty independent runs are performed on each of test problem by each algorithm. Figure 3 shows the distributions of the two performance metrics for benchmark problems by different algorithms. In Figure 3, "1" denotes BBMOEA, "2" is SPEA2, "3" is NSGA-II.With respect to the metric of convergence, BBMOEA is clearly the best in most of the test problems. It is particularly evident for ZDT3, ZDT4 and ZDT6. ZDT4 is proved to be the most difficult problem for all algorithms. But BBMOEA shows better performance than the other two algorithms. In addition, BBMOEA is particularly outstanding in the metric of spacing in test problems of ZDT1, ZDT4 and ZDT6. Compared with the other two algorithms, BBMOEA produces better performance in two metrics for ZDT2, ZDT4 and ZDT6. Simulation results illustrate the good performance of BBMOEA that the Pareto optimal solutions gained by BBMOEA convergence to the true Pareto optimal solutions and distribute evenly.

CONCLUSION

In this paper, the principle of geography based optimization is applied to solve MOP. A new MOP algorithm called BBMOEA is proposed. Through various types of test functions, simulation results demonstrate the feasibility and effectiveness of BBMOEA for solving MOP. At the same time, the

Figure 3. Simulation results for ZD1, ZDT2, ZDT3, ZDT4, ZDT6

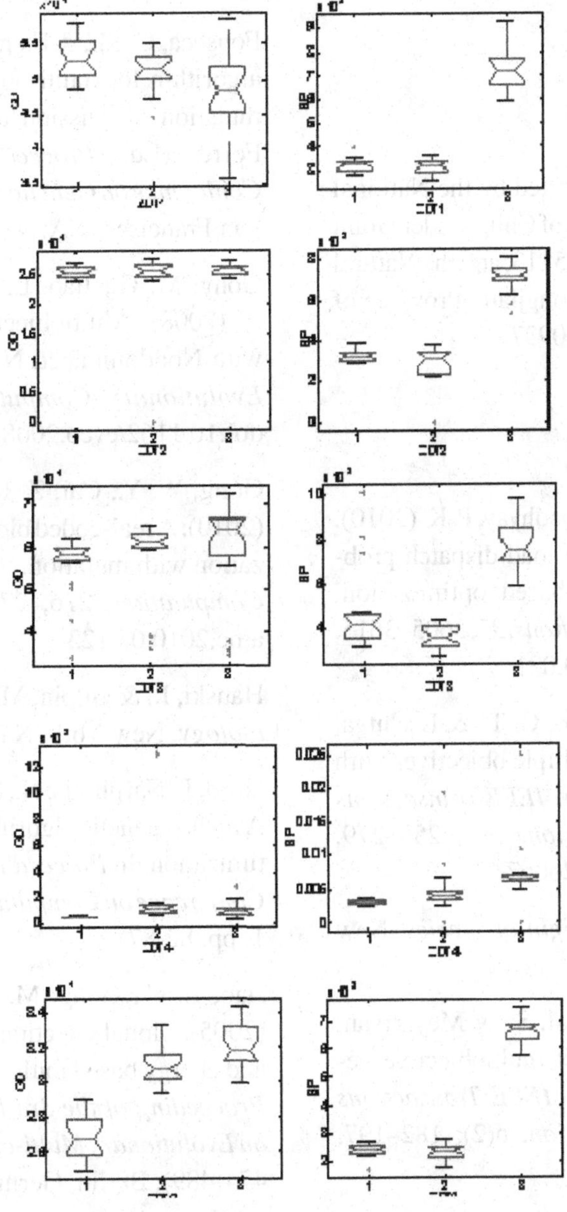

algorithm is compared with SPEA2 and NSGA-II of MOEA. The experiment results show that the metrics performance of the proposed algorithm is better than that of the other two MOEAs in most of test problems. It demonstrates that the solutions set generated by BBMOEA have good convergence and even distribution. It also proves that the principle of biogeography can be used to solve MOP. In future, we will analyze the proposed algorithm in theory and apply it in some real problems. We will also use it to solve dynamic and constrained MOP.

ACKNOWLEDGMENT

This work is partially supported by the National Natural Science Foundation of China under Grant No. 60973075 and No. 61075113, and the Natural Science Foundation of Heilongjiang Province of China under Grant No. F200937.

REFERENCES

Bhattacharya, A., & Chattopadhyay, P. K. (2010). Solving complex economic load dispatch problems using biogeography-based optimization. *Expert Systems with Applications*, *37*, 3605–3615. doi:10.1016/j.eswa.2009.10.031

Coello Coello, C. A., Pulido, G. T., & Lechuga, M. S. (2004). Handling multiple objectives with particle swarm optimization. *IEEE Transactions on Evolutionary Computation*, *8*(3), 256–279. doi:10.1109/TEVC.2004.826067

Darwin, C. (1859). *The origin of species*. New York, NY: Gramercy.

Deb, K., Pratap, A., Agarwal, S., & Meyarivan, T. (2002). A fast and elitist multiobjective genetic algorithm: NSGA-II. *IEEE Transactions on Evolutionary Computation*, *6*(2), 182–197. doi:10.1109/4235.996017

Du, D. W., Simon, D., & Ergezer, M. (2009). Biogeography-based optimization combined with evolutionary strategy and immigration refusal. In *Proceedings of the 2009 IEEE International Conference on Systems, Man, and Cybernetics*, San Antonio, TX (pp. 1023-1028).

Ergezer, M., Simon, D., & Du, D. W. (2009). Oppositional biogeography-based optimization. In *Proceedings of the 2009 IEEE International Conference on Systems, Man, and Cybernetics*, San Antonio, TX (pp. 1035-1040).

Fonseca, C. M., & Fleming, P. J. (1993). Genetic algorithm for multi-objective optimization: formulation, discussion and generalization. In S. Forrest (Ed.), *Proceedings of 5th International Conference on Genetic Algorithms* (pp. 416-423). San Francisco, CA: Morgan Kauffman.

Gong, M. G., Jiao, L. C., Du, H. F., & Bo, L. F. (2008). Multiobjective Immune Algorithm with Nondominated Neighbor-Based Selection. *Evolutionary Computation*, *16*(2), 225–255. doi:10.1162/evco.2008.16.2.225

Gong, W. Y., Cai, Z. H., Ling, C. X., & Li, H. (2010). A real-coded biogeography-based optimization with mutation. *Applied Mathematics and Computation*, *216*, 2749–2758. doi:10.1016/j.amc.2010.03.123

Hanski, I., & Gilpin, M. (1997). *Metapopulation biology*. New York, NY: Academic.

Horn, J., Nafpliotis, N., & Goldberg, D. E. (1994). A niched genetic algorithm for multiobjective optimization. In *Proceedings of the 1st IEEE World Conference on Computational Computation* (Vol. 1, pp. 82-87).

Jiao, L. C., Gong, M. G., Shang, R. H., et al. (2005). Clonal selection with immune dominance and energy based multiobjective optimization. In *Proceeding of the 3rd International Conference on Evolutionary Multi-criterion Optimization* (pp. 474-489). Berlin, Germany: Springer.

Ma, H. P. (2010). An analysis of the equilibrium of migration models for biogeography-based optimization. *Information Science*, *180*, 3444–3464. doi:10.1016/j.ins.2010.05.035

Meng, H. Y., Zhang, X. H., & Liu, S. Y. (2008). A Differential Evolution Based on Double Populations for Constrained Multi-Objective Optimization Problem. *Chinese Journal of Computers*, *31*(2), 228–235. doi:10.3724/SP.J.1016.2008.00228

Mo, H. W., & Xu, L. F. (2010). Biogeography Migration Algorithm for Traveling Salesman Problem. In . *Proceedings of the International Conference on Swarm Intelligence*, *1*, 405–414.

Rarick, R., Simon, D., Villaseca, F. E., & Vyakaranam, B. (2009). Biogeography-based optimization and the solution of the power flow problem. In *Proceedings of the IEEE Conference on Systems, Man, and Cybernetics,* San Antonio, TX (pp. 1029-1034).

Simon, D. (2008). Biogeography-Based optimization. *IEEE Transactions on Evolutionary Computation*, *12*(6), 702–713. doi:10.1109/TEVC.2008.919004

Simon, D. (2008). *The Matlab code of biogeography-based optimization*. Retrieved from http://academic.csuohio.edu/simond/bbo/

Simon, D. (2009). A Probabilistic analysis of a simplified biogeography-based optimization algorithm. *Evolutionary Computation*, 1–22.

Simon, D., Ergezer, M., & Du, D. W. (2009). Population distributions in biogeography-based optimization algorithms with elitism. In *Proceedings of the IEEE Conference on Systems, Man, and Cybernetics,* San Antonio, TX (pp. 1017-1022).

Srinivas, N., & Deb, K. (1995). Multiobjective optimization using nondominated sorting in genetic algorithms. *Evolutionary Computation*, *2*(3), 221–248. doi:10.1162/evco.1994.2.3.221

Tan, L. X., & Guo, L. (2009). Quantum and biogeography based optimization for a class of combinatorial optimization. In *Proceedings of the 2009 World Summit on Genetic and Evolutionary Computation* (pp. 969-972).

Wallace, A. (2005). *The Geographical distribution of animals*. Boston, MA: Adamant Media Corporation.

Zhang, Y. D., & Huang, S. B. (2005). On ant colony algorithm for solving multiobjective optimization problems. *Control and Decision*, *20*(2), 170–173.

Zheng, J. H. (2007). *Multi-Objective Evolutionary Algorithms and Their Applications*. Beijing, China: Science Press.

Zitzler, E., Laumanns, M., & Thiele, L. (2001). *SPEA2: Improving the Strength Pareto Evolutionary Algorithm* (Tech. Rep. No. 103). Zurich, Switzerland: Swiss Federal Institute of Technology.

This work was previously published in the Journal of Information Technology Research, Volume 4, Issue 2, edited by Mehdi Khosrow-Pour, pp. 70-80, copyright 2011 by IGI Publishing (an imprint of IGI Global).

Chapter 11
The Effects of Investments in Information Technology on Firm Performance:
An Investor Perspective

Jeffrey Wong
University of Nevada, Reno, USA

Kevin E. Dow
University of Alaska, Anchorage, USA

ABSTRACT

Analyzing the beneficial effects of investments in information technology (IT) is an area of research that interests investors and academics. A number of studies have examined whether investments in IT have a positive effect on some measure of earnings or other form of financial return. Results from these studies have been mixed. This paper extends the literature by adopting an investor's perspective on firm performance when IT investments are made, using the preservation of capital as a performance measure. The authors examine companies that made public announcements of their investments in technology to see if they were able to mitigate losses to investors by reducing their downside risk to investors. This study further discusses whether different types of IT investments have different impacts on firm risk from an investor's viewpoint. Findings suggest that IT investments impact a firm's downside risk, and the authors offer an alternative perspective on the benefits of IT investments, particularly where no positive incremental financial results are evident.

INTRODUCTION AND BACKGROUND

Comprehensive evidence of the impact that investments in information technology (IT) have on firm performance continues to elude researchers and investors (Mittal & Nault, 2009). Labeled the "productivity paradox" by Nobel Laureate Robert Solow, this phenomenon has been blamed on a number of factors, including the mismanagement of IT resources and the use of the wrong performance measures. Carr (2003) has even suggested that investments in IT have become so common-

DOI: 10.4018/978-1-4666-3625-5.ch011

place that they are now similar to other ordinary business investments that offer no distinguishable competitive advantage.

A majority of the studies that have examined the relationship between IT investments and firm performance have used traditional measures of firm performance (i.e., productivity and profitability) that best meet the needs of management (Kohli & Davaraj, 2003). However, results of these studies have been mixed. For example, Brynjolfsson and Hitt (1993), Bharadwaj, Bharadwaj, and Konsynski (1999), and Stratopoulis and Dehning (2000), among others found a positive association between investments in IT and firm performance. On the other hand, researchers such as Loveman (1994) and Roach (1987) found a significantly negative association between investments in IT and resulting firm performance.

We contribute to the literature by examining the relationship between investments in IT and a firm's risk profile using a non-traditional measure of firm performance that is not captured in either productivity gains or increased profitability. Although IT investments may allow firms to achieve superior profits relative to their competitors, we believe that IT investments also serve to reduce a firm's financial risk profile, or its downside risk. Downside risk has been proposed by economists as the perspective that characterizes investor sentiment towards making investments (Nawrocki, 1999). Economists have posited that the disutility incurred by a loss outweighs the utility of a gain of the same amount. Our research should be of interest to both researchers and investors (Heine, Grover, & Malhotra, 2003; Melville, Kraemer, & Gurbaxani, 2004).

Our study provides evidence that there is an association between reductions in downside risk following the announcement of IT investments. We also find evidence that suggests the type of IT investment affects the degree of downside risk following the announcement of the investment, as well as whether the firm is a leader in defining IT strategies for their industry.

In the following section, we briefly discuss literature related to IT investments relevant to this study. The next section develops our hypotheses relating firms' investments in IT to downside risk and discusses the model we use to test these hypotheses. We then focus on methodological issues and discuss the results of our study. We conclude and summarize the paper, comment on limitations of our study, and discuss and directions for future research in the final section.

LITERATURE RELATED TO IT INVESTMENTS AND FIRM PERFORMANCE

Prior literature relating investments in IT to the effect on firms has focused primarily on positive outcomes such as productivity gains or financial returns. Kohli and Davaraj (2003) and Melville et al. (2004) have noted that the results of studies focusing on the specific organizational performance and productivity improvements have been mixed. Given the mixed results of past studies, our use of the investor's perspective provides an alternative explanation about how IT investments may have a positive effect on firm performance. We will briefly discuss some of the key studies related to measuring the impact of IT investments on firm performance and then explain why using downside risk as an alternative measure makes sense.

Research has documented a positive performance associated with the announcements of certain types of IT investments. Dos Santos, Peffers, and Mauer (1993) investigated the effect of IT investments on the market value of firms. Two particular attributes, industry type and IT investment type, were examined to see if either had an effect on the cumulative abnormal returns (CARs) near the dates of the announcements. Evidence indicates that only announcements of innovative IT investments were (positively) associated with CARs. Im, Dow, and Grover (2001) extended the literature by investigating whether industry size and time lag had an effect on firm market value using a larger sample of IT investment announcements over a longer time period. Small firm size and announcements made from 1991 and after (time lag) were found to be positively associated with market value effects. Additionally, Im et al. (2001) found that IT investment announcements firms in the financial industry were positively associated with market value, but only for announcements made after 1991.

Dehning, Richardson, and Zmud (2003) built upon this stream of literature by examining the relationship between the industry strategic role of IT investments and firm value. Using the IT strategic role construct conceptualized by Schein (1992), IT investment announcements were classified as those that automate, informate, or transform an organization. Dehning et al. (2003) tested the associations between market value and the classification of IT investment announcement by firms. Findings from this study provide evidence that the industry strategic role of IT investments does influence the market value of a firm. Specifically, firms that announce transformational IT investments, and firms announcing IT investments in industries in which transformational investments dominate the industry experience positive market value reactions from those announcements. Additionally, Dehning et al. (2003) found firms that announce IT investments, and are leaders in their industry, experience positive market value reactions.

Recent studies have sought to further refine the circumstances under which firms experience positive returns on IT investments. Stone, Good, and Baker-Eveleth (2007) found that in certain situations, IT can have a positive effect on a firm's marketing performance, which can in turn, enhance revenue generation. Mittal and Nault (2009) find evidence that IT affects certain firms in different ways. The effects of IT tend to be indirect on IT intensive firms, while direct effects are associated with non-IT intensive firms. Chari, Devaraj, and Parthiban (2008) posit that investments in IT pay off when firms own and operate businesses in multiple industries because IT facilitates control and coordination.

While studies prior to ours have focused on measuring the positive impact of IT on performance, our paper extends the literature by employing a measure that captures a different aspect of performance than preceding studies (e.g., Stone et al., 2007; Mittal & Nault, 2009; Chari et al., 2008; Dos Santos et al., 1993; Im et al., 2001; Dehning et al., 2003). The downside risk performance measure focuses on mitigating losses instead of focusing on positive returns, thereby complementing the studies previously discussed. Our study provides a deeper understanding about the influence that IT investments ultimately have on what is important to investors.

The concept of risk as a measure of performance is absent from much of prior research. One long-standing method to measure business risk is the volatility of returns. Two of the methods used to operationalize the volatility of returns are the mean variance and downside risk. The mean variance considers both positive and negative fluctuations of returns relative to some target level, whereas downside risk focuses on the negative fluctuations. It has been argued that the mean variance has deficiencies as a measure of risk because it is based upon utility functions that are unlikely to reflect the true attitudes of investors, that is risk neutrality (Grootveld & Hallerbach, 1999).

Downside risk is considered by some to be the most consistent with investors' perceptions of risk. As discussed in Nawrocki (1999), an investor has to make a trade-off between risk and return. Roy (1952) felt that investors will prefer safety of principal first, and then desire some minimum level of return that will preserve the principal amount. Roy's concepts would prove fundamental to the ultimate development of the downside risk measures that allow investors to minimize the probability of the portfolio falling below some target rate of return. Tversky and Kahneman (1992) find that the disutility of losses are weighted about twice that of the utility of gains. Veld and Veld-Merkoulova (2008) found in their experimental study that the most common risk measure used by investors was downside risk. Therefore, we chose the investor's perspective of risk, downside risk, as a measure to evaluate one of the effects that IT investments may have on firm performance. Details on how we operationalized the downside risk metric are discussed in a later section.

Hypotheses Development and Model Specification

The beneficial effects of investments in IT that allow a business to maintain current or forecasted levels of profitability will not necessarily be manifested in incremental profitability. Instead, the risk to decreases in a company's future stream of earnings may have been mitigated. One measurement that can capture this risk mitigation is downside risk, the risk that actual financial performance is less than a target level. Behavioral decision theory (Lant, 1992; Lant & Montgomery, 1987), finance research (Harlow & Rao, 1989; Sortino & Price, 1994), and management studies on risk (Miller & Leiblein, 1996; Reuer & Leiblein, 2000) have employed downside risk measurement. We test the following hypothesis to see if there is a relationship between downside risk and investments in IT:

H1: A firm's investment in IT will be inversely related to its downside risk.

It is feasible that the impact on downside risk will depend on the type of IT investment made. Recent research has examined the impact of different kinds of investments in technology on financial returns to the companies making these investments. Dehning, Dow, and Stratopoulis (2003) examined the association between cumulative abnormal stock returns and investments in technology that fell into three broad categories. The categories indicated the intent of the investments to "automate", "informate", or "transform" a company's operations. Automate refers to automating business processes that may have been executed in part or wholly by human labor. As discussed in Dehning et al. (2003), it may be difficult for companies to maintain competitive advantages merely by automating processes, especially if this is a trend in the industry that a company belongs to. Investments in technology that automate processes may, in some instances, be a necessity to for a particular company to remain in business at best. If these investments require significant sums of money, it is possible that there is a net negative impact on earnings. Accordingly, we predict that there will be no effect on downside risk made by IT investments intended to automate company processes.

Informate refers to enriching the flow of information through the company either horizontally or vertically. Enhancing the ability of decision makers to communicate with each other in a timely manner, and to better cross-utilize information for decision support may have positive effects on how a business utilizes its intellectual assets and knowledge base. Therefore, we predict that there will be a negative association between investments in IT to informate and downside risk. This notion is consistent with Chari et al. (2008) who posit that IT facilitates coordination and control of diversified entities.

Transform refers to a major shift in the way a business conducts its internal processes or relationships with customers or other business entities. Investments in IT to transform may be part of a broader re-engineering or strategy shift. We suspect that these investments are not made independent of deploying significant amounts of other resources in the transformational effort. It is possible that the transformational efforts of a company will create competitive advantages that may be sustained for some time, or create barriers to entry for competitors. Accordingly, we predict that there will be a negative association between investments in IT to transform. We test the following hypothesis to see if different investment types have a differential effect on downside risk:

H2: The strategic role of investment in IT affects downside risk in different ways.

Moreover, we predict that the leadership role firms play within their respective industries in terms of making IT investments will be related to downside risk. We classify the role of firms based on whether they lead, follow, or lag behind their industry in the announcement of their IT investments. We posit that firms that lead their industry in announcing IT investments will exhibit a significant reduction in downside risk relative to firms that either follow or lag behind industry leaders. We classify the strategic role of firms into three categories: those who lead, are the same as, or lag their industry in the timing of making strategic IT investments. The industry context is likely to be important to how investors perceive IT events for any particular firm, since factors which can positively (negatively) impact one company may have similar effects on other participants of the industry. We acknowledge that leadership in IT investments may not pose long lasting barriers to entry or technological advantages, but may provide windows of opportunity for capturing market share and enhancing profitability. Additionally, they may be perceived as corroborating evidence of the innovative nature of a business that fosters success. Therefore, we assert that firms which lead their industry in making strategic IT investments will be associated with decreased downside risk, relative to their peers who make strategic investments at the same time as or behind the industry. We test this assertion with the following hypothesis:

H3: Firms that lead their industry will experience more of a decrease in downside risk than firms that either lag or are the same as their industry when investments in IT are announced.

We analyze the effect of IT investment announcements on downside risk by examining downside risk when IT investment announcements are made, relative to before the announcements have been made. Our model employs various controls to better isolate the incremental change in downside risk attributable to the IT investment announcements, and takes the following form:

$$\text{Downside risk}_{post} = \beta_0 + \beta_1\text{Downside\_risk}_{pre} + \beta_2\text{Investment\_type} + \beta_3\text{Lead} + \beta_4\text{Leverage}_{post} + \beta_5\text{Growth\_Potential}_{post} + \beta_6\text{Size}_{post} + \beta_7\text{Time\_Period} + \beta_8\text{Industry} + \beta_9\text{Organizational\_Slack}_{post} + \varepsilon$$

where:

- Downside risk_{post} = post-investment measure calculated based on Equation 1.
- Downside risk_{pre} = pre-investment measure calculated based on Equation 1.
- Investment type = categorical variable for the type of IT investment (automate, informate, or transform).
- Lead = categorical variable for the IT strategic role of the firm within its industry (leads, follows, or lags).
- Industry = industry affiliation (see the Appendix).
- Time period = categorical variable indicating whether the IT announcement occurred during or after the productivity paradox period.
- Leverage_{post} = categorical variable indicating whether the company could be subject to financial distress at the end of the reporting year in which the announcement was made.
- $\text{Growth\_Potential}_{post}$ = book value of equity/market value of equity.
- Size_{post} = natural log of the market value of shareholder equity.

- $Organizational\_slack_{post}$ = AR/Sales, INV/Sales, and SGA/Sales at the end of the reporting year in which the announcement was made.

The control variables in the model were included in an attempt to isolate the incremental effect of IT investment announcements on downside risk. The controls were based on previous studies mentioned in our literature review that examined the effect of IT investments on firm performance (e.g., Dos Santos et al., 1993; Im et al., 2001; Dehning et al., 2003). Publicly available data at the end of the year in which the IT investment announcement was made was used to calculate the control variables.

All event studies must employ a time window on or about the time that the event occurs, in this case the announcement of an IT investment. Our study used a window of two contiguous 40-day periods (-50 to -10 days and 10 to 50 days) was used to calculate the downside risk metric and its determinants. This window allows us to obtain sufficient time series data to construct the downside measure. We excluded a 10 day window surrounding the announcement date to provide a reasonable assurance that any downside risk captured by our calculations would not be contaminated by the announcement effect. This exclusion also provides some assurance that any volatility associated with the short term announcement is not included in our measure of downside risk. The next section provides more specific detail about the measures used in the model and the sample employed in this study.

SAMPLE AND MEASURES

Downside risk is defined as a firm's daily stock price relative to its industry's mean stock price (Barth, Beaver, Hand, & Landsman, 1999). To calculate downside risk, our study uses stock returns derived from stock prices. Since stock prices are believed to impound all available information affecting future cash flows, stock prices should reflect market expectations of IT investment impact on future cash flows of an entity.

Downside risk is operationalized as a probability weighted function of below-target performance outcomes. This differs from measures of volatility because only below-target performance is measured as opposed to any deflection from the target performance. Specifically, we measure downside risk as a firm's daily stock price return relative to a target level that changed over time. Target level is specified as the mean stock price return for a firm's industry (Barth et al., 1999). Downside risk is measured as a second-order root lower partial moment, and can be expressed as:

$$Downside\ Risk = \sqrt{\frac{1}{n}\sum_{1}^{n} Max(0, t - R_t)^2}$$

where,

R_t *is the firm return during the time period*

t is the tar get return (industry mean return during the period)

n is the number of observations in the period

(1)

To classify the investments in IT into a particular category, we follow the method used in Dehning et al. (2003). Accordingly, IT investments in our sample are coded as those made to informate, automate, or transform a company's operations. Dehning et al. (2003) relied upon a panel of experts to categorize IT investments, taking into consideration the timing and particular industry making those investments. Responses from the experts independently queried had a high degree of agreement.

Factors in addition to investments in IT may affect a firm's downside risk. To isolate the incremental effect that IT investments may have on downside risk, our model contains covariates (control) variables to represent the firm size, industry affiliation, time period, organizational slack, growth potential, leverage, and liquidity of the firm.

The timing of an IT investment announcement captures whether the investment was made before or after the productivity paradox time period. During this period researchers were unable to find a consistent pattern of associations between investments in IT and firm performance. Two variables that proxy for firm size are total assets and total liabilities, each scaled by total sales. We include both variables because assets alone may under-represent size if outsourcing is a material part of operations.

Leverage influences the financial the risk of an entity. The debt-to-equity ratio is used as a measure of financial leverage (Chen & Lee, 1993). The inability of a firm to meet their obligations to debt holders results ultimately in insolvency, bankruptcy, and the eventual demise of the entity. We employ a categorical variable to indicate whether the company was experienced relatively high levels of total debt to the total market value of equity. A debt-to-equity level equal to or greater than 4:1 was chosen as the benchmark to indicates a high level of leverage. Firms with debt-to-equity ratios greater than 4 were classified as having a high level of leverage and firms with debt-to-equity ratios of less than 4 were classified as not having a high level of leverage.

Organizational slack represents the cushion of excess resources available to be used in a discretionary manner. These resources allow firms to buffer themselves from adverse effects when their performance is below targeted levels. It is represented by resources that are accumulated during periods where firms perform above their targeted levels. Miller and Leiblein (1996) posit that slack will mitigate subsequent downside risk.

Our analysis includes a variable to control for the affect growth potential may have on stock price. Book-to-market ratio measures the relationship between the accounting value of a company and the value of its stock. This measure is considered as a proxy for the future growth potential. Since the market value of a company's stocks impounds expectations for future cash flows, the book-to-market ratio represents the expectations for growth.

The particular industry a firm belongs to may affect the downside risk of the firm. To control for this, we include a variable representing the class of industry. Our study classifies firms into twelve different categories ranging from companies manufacturing goods to service sector and financial companies. Refer to the Appendix for more detail on the industry classifications used in this study.

The ability of a company to meet the financial obligations of current liabilities from resources generated by operations is captured by liquidity. Low levels of liquidity may indicate financial distress, and greater risk levels for a firm. This study employs the current ratio (current assets/current liabilities) as a measure of a firm's liquidity.

This study employs a sample consisting of organizations that announced significant investments in IT from the period 1981-1997 (Hunter, 2003; Im et al., 2001). The sample time frame was chosen to maximize the amount of data prior to the build-up and subsequent burst of the "tech bubble". Speculative inflation of stock prices appears to have occurred from early 1998 through February 2000 (Ofek & Richardson, 2003). Though the tech bubble phenomenon is attributed to stocks of internet companies, the effects were pervasive to other industry sectors (Anderson, Brooks, & Katsaris, 2005). Because of the potential distortions in calculating downside risk during this tech bubble period, our sample date stops at 1997. Anecdotally, examining a graph of the S&P 500 over time reveals that prices of the index do not return to pre-bubble levels until after 2001. The events of September 11, 2001, and subsequent recession in 2002 and 2003 hold the potential to distort or mask findings in our study. Therefore, our sample time frame terminates at the end of 1997.

To screen our sample, we began with the 238 IT announcements found in Im et al. (2001) and the 150 IT announcements found in Hunter, resulting in 388 possible IT announcements. 137 announcements were dropped because of inconsistent or incomplete data obtained from CRSP for the individual firms or problems in constructing the industry returns. Additionally, the inability to determine the investment type because the announcement was missing or the announcement did not provide enough information about the nature of the IT investment prevented some firms from being included in our sample. We estimated the downside risk measures using the remaining 251 IT investment announcements (see Table 1).

Descriptive statistics for the total sample can be seen in Table 2. The average firm had sales of $20 billion with an average net income of $785 million. Firms' total assets averaged $31 billion and ranged from $49 million to $272 million. Table 3 presents correlations for the continuous variables examined in this study.

RESULTS

We used analysis of covariance (ANCOVA) to compare the change in downside risk before and after the IT announcements. In this ANCOVA formulation, the dependent variable is the downside risk of the firm following the IT investment announcement. Investment type and IT strategic role were random factors in the model. Our model explained nearly 60 percent of the variance in the downside risk of the sample firms.

Hypothesis 1 predicted that investment in IT will result in a reduction in organizational downside risk. Although we predicted firms that made significant investments in IT would experience less downside risk after the announcement date, downside risk increased significantly for all firms. At first it appears that H1 is not be supported. However, further examination of the data reveals the result that IT investment announcements prior to 1991 resulted in increased downside risk whereas later announcements resulted in a decrease in downside risk thereby suggesting that there might be a temporal nature to the events

Table 1. IT investment announcements

	Announcements
IT Announcements found in Im et al., 2001	238
IT Announcements found in Hunter, 2003	150
Total possible IT Investment Announcements	388
Less: Firms with incomplete CRSP data	117
Less: Firms unable to be coded	20
Usable IT Investment Announcements	251

Table 2. Descriptive statistics for study variables

Variable	Mean	Std Dev	Minimum	Maximum
Downside $risk_{pre}$	0.0324	0.0901	0	0.8299
Downside $risk_{post}$	0.0301	0.0766	0	0.6862
$Assets_{post}$ (in $000,000's)	31,285	43,858	49.481	272,402
$Sales_{post}$ (in $000,000's)	20,151	27,335	81.664	165,370
Net $Income_{post}$ (in $000,000's)	785.07	1,163	-1985	7,280
Total $Debt_{post}$ (in $000,000's)	9,914	19,431	0	162,406
$Leverage_{post}$	2.438	8.513	0	151.43
Growth $Potential_{post}$	5.679	8.862	0.0020	105.186
Market Value of $Equity_{post}$	32,540	86,845	3.541	1,036,061
Organizational $Slack_{post}$	1.743	2.376	0	9.796

Table 3. Correlation Matrix for variables in downside risk ANCOVA model

	1	2	3	4	5	6
1. Downside $Risk_{pre}$	1					
2. Downside $Risk_{post}$	0.690**	1				
3. Leverage	0.139**	0.190**	1			
4. Growth Potential	0.107*	0.122*	0.028	1		
5. Size	-0.417**	-0.365**	-0.059	0.371**	1	
6. Liquidity	0.197**	0.123*	0.103	-0.138*	-0.286**	1
7. Organizational Slack	-0.151**	-0.153**	-0.027	-0.182**	-0.055	-0.122*

** p<0.01
* p<0.05

that were used in this study. Therefore, we cannot fully reject the first hypothesis. The fact that downside risk decreased significantly after the productivity paradox period suggests that the growing evidence at that time about the positive impact of IT investments on firm productivity led to a shift in investor perceptions (Brynjolfsson, 1993; Im et al., 2001).

Hypothesis 2 predicted a differential effect of investment type on downside risk. The hypothesis appears to be supported because the ANCOVA coefficient for this variable was statistically significant. Further investigation using linear contrasts (the Tukey test for multiple comparisons) indicated that transformational IT investments do have a differential effect on downside risk resulting in higher levels of downside risk for those investments relative to IT investments that are either automate or informate. There was no statistical difference between automate and informate IT investment announcements. Thus, there appears to be empirical evidence that suggests the type of IT investment does have an impact on a firm's level of downside risk. Specifically transformational IT investments appear to have a more beneficial impact on downside risk than either automate or informate IT investments.

Hypothesis 3 predicted that leaders of IT investments will experience more beneficial effects of downside risk than will their counterparts. The results of the ANCOVA analysis (shown in Table 4) indicate that there is a significant difference in the change in downside risk after implementing IT. As can be seen in Table 4, the change is partially determined by the IT strategic role of the investment and whether the IT investment leads the IT Strategic Role of the industry. Therefore, the results of the ANCOVA analysis appear to support hypothesis H3.

Investigation using linear contrasts (the Tukey test for multiple comparisons) indicated that firms that lead their industry IT strategic role have a differential effect on downside risk than those firms that either lag or are the same as their industry IT strategic role. Specifically, firms that lead their industry IT strategic role enjoy lower levels of downside risk relative to the other firms. There was no significant difference in firms that lag their industry IT strategic role and firms that are investing in the same type of technology as their industry IT strategic role. Therefore, H3 is only partially supported.

Analysis of the covariates reveals that five covariates were also significantly related to changes in downside risk. They are: (1) leverage; (2) growth potential; (3) size; (4) liquidity; and (5) the time period in which the investment takes place (in the productivity paradox period or not). Firms that announced IT investments prior to 1991 showed significant increases in downside risk whereas

Table 4. The Results of the ANCOVA analysis

Source	DF	Type III SS	Mean Square	F-Value	Significance
Downside $Risk_{pre}$	1	0.0033	0.00328	102.25	<.0001
Automate, Inform, Transform	2	0.00017	0.000083	2.58	0.0783
Lead, Follow, Lag	2	0.00017	0.000083	2.58	0.0783
Leverage	1	0.00016	0.00016	4.93	0.0274
Growth Potential	1	0.00025	0.00025	7.65	0.0061
Size	1	0.00030	0.00030	9.43	0.0032
Time Period	1	0.00014	0.00014	4.31	0.0390
Industry Affiliation	10	0.00025	0.000024	0.76	0.6634
Organizational Slack	1	0.000096	0.000096	3.00	0.0848
Error	226	0.00514	0.00003		
Total	246	0.01506			
R^2=0.587					

firms that announced IT investments after 1991 showed significant decreases in downside risk. The remaining control variables were not statistically significant in the downside risk model.

DISCUSSION, LIMITATIONS, AND DIRECTIONS FOR FUTURE RESEARCH

Academic researchers and investors remain keenly interested in determining how investments in technology affect firm performance. We contribute to the literature by taking the investor perspective and using downside risk as an alternative measure the value made by IT investments. The prior work in this area has focused on measuring abnormal returns or some earnings-based metric in the days surrounding the announcement. However, research on perceptions of risk indicates that investors generally conceptualize risk in terms of failure to achieve performance targets. They value the preservation of capital. The findings of this study provide a compelling argument to consider downside risk as a complement to traditional performance metrics when conducting research on how investments in IT ultimately affect firm performance.

Our results suggest that a number of variables influence the level of downside risk associated with IT investment announcements. For example, firms that were the first in their industry to make announcements of significant IT investments experienced significantly less downside risk than those firms that followed or lagged behind them. We acknowledge that industry leadership in IT investments does not insure continued technological supremacy but may provide windows of opportunity for capturing market share and enhancing profitability. As noted by Dos Santos et al. (1993), firms that exploit new IT capabilities perform significantly better than firms that only explore their current IT capabilities.

We found that firms making IT investments facilitating major shifts in their internal processes and/or external customer/competitor relationships experienced significantly less downside risk than those that automated business processes or invested in IT that improved decision support systems. Transformational investments in IT are likely to be part of a broader re-engineering or strategic shift requiring the deployment of significant amounts of other resources as part of the transformational effort. As a result, transformational investments in IT may create sustainable or prolonged competitive advantages over competitors.

One of the more interesting findings of our study was the relationship between the time frame associated with the productivity paradox and the level of downside risk associated with a firm's stock price. As noted above, this time frame moderated the relationship between IT investment announcements and the level of downside risk. Our findings are consistent with the literature on the value of IT. The literature provides evidence that prior to the early 1990s investors penalized firms that announced significant investments in IT. Subsequent evidence supported the notion that investments in IT favorably impacted the efficiency of internal business processes, and investors updated their investment protocols. It is possible that this is an example of a market that is ultimately efficient.

The event study methodology proved to be a viable way to examine the relationship between important firm-related decisions and downside risk. However, the methodology has its limitations. For example, event studies may be prone to over or underestimate an outcome unless the event window is well calibrated. Nonetheless, event studies are an excellent method for examining the outcomes associated with corporate policy decisions such as the decision to make significant investments in IT.

Future research could examine how different types of IT investments might have a stronger impact on downside risk, as opposed to the different categories of IT investments (automate, informate, and transform) used in this study. For example, the impact of ERP investments on downside risk could be examined. This might be a fertile research area because several of the selling points of ERP system implementations were the efficiency and productivity gains that might be realized from the investment, particularly when associated with process reengineering.

Another idea for future research might involve a multi-dimensional approach to measure benefits firms reap from IT investments. A single productivity or risk measure may not fully capture the benefits of IT investments, and a more holistic approach might be more fruitful. Future studies might examine multiple performance measures. One idea might involve jointly examining the impact of IT investments on both the cumulative abnormal returns and the downside risk of the stock returns.

REFERENCES

Anderson, K., Brooks, C., & Katsaris, A. (2005). *Speculative bubbles in the S&P 500: Was the tech bubble confined to the tech sector?* Reading, UK: ICMA Centre.

Barth, M. E., Beaver, B., Hand, J., & Landsman, W. (1999). Accruals, cash flows, and equity values. *Review of Accounting Studies*, *3*, 205–229. doi:10.1023/A:1009630100586

Bharadwaj, A., Bharadwaj, S., & Konsynski, B. (1999). Information technology effects on firm performance as measured by Tobin's q. *Management Science*, *45*(6), 1008–1024. doi:10.1287/mnsc.45.7.1008

Brynjolfsson, E. (1993). The productivity paradox of information technology. *Communications of the ACM*, *40*(12), 1645–1662.

Brynjolfsson, E., & Hitt, L. E. (1993). Is information systems spending productive? New evidence and new results. In *Proceedings of the 14th International Conference on Information Systems* (pp. 47-64).

Carr, N. G. (2003). IT doesn't matter. *Harvard Business Review*, *81*(5), 41–49.

Chari, M. D., Devaraj, S., & Parthiban, D. (2008). The Impact of Information Technology Investments and Diversification Strategies on Firm Performance. *Management Science*, *54*(1), 224–234. doi:10.1287/mnsc.1070.0743

Chen, K. C., & Lee, C. J. (1993). Financial ratios and corporate endurance: A case of the oil and gas industry. *Contemporary Accounting Research*, *9*(2), 667–694. doi:10.1111/j.1911-3846.1993.tb00903.x

Dehning, B., Richardson, V., & Zmud, B. (2003). The value relevance of announcements of transformational information technology investments. *Management Information Systems Quarterly*, *27*(4), 637–656.

Dos Santos, B., Peffers, K., & Mauer, D. (1993). The impact of information technology investment announcements on the market value of the firm. *Information Systems Research*, *4*(1), 1–23. doi:10.1287/isre.4.1.1

Grootveld, H., & Hallerbach, W. (1999). Variance vs. downside risk: Is there really that much difference? *European Journal of Operational Research*, *114*(2), 304–319. doi:10.1016/S0377-2217(98)00258-6

Harlow, W. V., & Rao, R. K. S. (1989). Asset pricing in a generalized mean-lower partial moment framework. *Journal of Financial and Quantitative Analysis*, *24*, 285–311. doi:10.2307/2330813

Heine, M. L., Grover, V., & Malhotra, M. K. (2003). The relationship between technology and performance: A meta-analysis of technology models. *Omega: An International Journal of Management Science*, *31*(3), 189–204. doi:10.1016/S0305-0483(03)00026-4

Hunter, S. D. (2003). Information technology, organizational learning, and the market value of the firm. *Journal of Information Technology Theory and Applications*, *5*(1), 1–28.

Im, K. S., Dow, K. E., & Grover, V. (2001). A reexamination of IT investment and the market value of the firm—an event study methodology. *Information Systems Research*, *12*(1), 103–117. doi:10.1287/isre.12.1.103.9718

Kohli, R., & Davaraj, S. (2003). Measuring information technology payoff: A meta-analysis of structural variables in firm-level empirical research. *Information Systems Research*, *14*(2), 127–145. doi:10.1287/isre.14.2.127.16019

Lant, T. K. (1992). Aspiration level adaptation: An empirical exploration. *Management Science*, *38*, 623–644. doi:10.1287/mnsc.38.5.623

Lant, T. K., & Montgomery, D. B. (1987). Learning from strategic success and failure. *Journal of Business Research*, *15*, 503–517. doi:10.1016/0148-2963(87)90035-X

Loveman, G. W. (1994). An assessment of the productivity impact of information technologies. In Allen, T. J., & Scott Morton, M. S. (Eds.), *Information Technology and the Corporation of the 1990s: Research Studies* (pp. 84–110). Cambridge, MA: MIT Press.

Melville, N., Kraemer, K., & Gurbaxani, V. (2004). Information Technology and Organizational Performance: An Integrative Model of IT Business Value. *Management Information Systems Quarterly*, *28*(2), 283–322.

Miller, K. D., & Leiblein, M. J. (1996). Corporate risk-return relations: Returns variability versus downside risk. *Academy of Management Journal*, *39*(1), 91–122. doi:10.2307/256632

Mittal, N., & Nault, B. R. (2009). Investments in Information Technology: Indirect Effects and Information Technology Intensity. *Information Systems Research*, *20*(1), 140–154. doi:10.1287/isre.1080.0186

Nawrocki, D. N. (1999). A brief history of downside risk measures. *Journal of Investing*, *8*(3), 9–26. doi:10.3905/joi.1999.319365

Ofek, E., & Richardson, M. (2003). DotCom mania: The rise and fall of internet stock prices. *The Journal of Finance*, *58*(3), 1113–1137. doi:10.1111/1540-6261.00560

Reuer, J., & Leiblein, M. J. (2000). Downside risk implications of multinationality and international joint ventures. *Academy of Management Journal*, *43*(22), 203–214. doi:10.2307/1556377

Roach, S. S. (1987). *America's technology dilemma: A profile of the information economy*. San Mateo, CA: Morgan Stanley.

Roy, A. D. (1952). Safety first and the holding of assets. *Econometrica: Journal of the Econometric Society*, *20*(3), 431–449. doi:10.2307/1907413

Schein, E. H. (1992). *Organizational culture and leadership*. San Francisco, CA: Jossey-Bass.

Sortino, F. A., & Price, L. N. (1994). Performance measurement in a downside risk framework. *Journal of Investing*, *3*(3), 59–64. doi:10.3905/joi.3.3.59

Stone, R. W., Good, D. J., & Baker-Eveleth, L. (2007). The impact of information technology on individual and firm marketing performance. *Behaviour & Information Technology*, *26*(6), 465–482. doi:10.1080/01449290600571610

Stratopoulis, T., & Dehning, B. (2000). Does successful investment in information technology solve the productivity paradox? *Information & Management*, *38*(2), 103–117. doi:10.1016/S0378-7206(00)00058-6

Tversky, A., & Kahneman, D. (1992). Advances in prospect theory: Cumulative representation of uncertainty. *Journal of Risk and Uncertainty*, *5*, 297–323. doi:10.1007/BF00122574

Veld, C., & Veld-Merkoulova, Y. V. (2008). The risk perceptions of individual investors. *Journal of Economic Psychology*, *29*(2), 226–252. doi:10.1016/j.joep.2007.07.001

APPENDIX

Industry Classifications for Firms in Study

Table 1A. Industry definitions (adapted from Barth et al., 1999)

Industry	Industry Name	SIC Codes
A	Food	2000-2111
B	Textiles & Printing/Publishing	2200-2780
C	Chemicals	2800-2824, 2840-2899
D	Pharmaceuticals	2830-2836
E	Extractive	1300-1399, 2900-2999
F	Durable Manufacturing	3000-3569, 3580-3669, 3680-3999
G	Computers	3570-3579, 3670-3679, 7370-7379
H	Transportation	4000-4899
I	Utilities	4900-4999
J	Retail	5000-5999
K	Financial Institutions	6000-6999
L	Services	7000-7369, 7380-8999

*Note: The industries for Agriculture and for Mining and Construction have been removed from this classification because there were no announcing firms in these industries.

This work was previously published in the Journal of Information Technology Research, Volume 4, Issue 3, edited by Mehdi Khosrow-Pour, pp. 1-13, copyright 2011 by IGI Publishing (an imprint of IGI Global).

Chapter 12
Design of an Integrated Project Management Information System for Large Scale Public Projects:
Iranian Case Study

Mona Taghavi
University Kebangsaan Malaysia, Malaysia

Ahmed Patel
University Kebangsaan Malaysia, Malaysia, & Kingston University, UK

Hamed Taghavi
Iranian Strategic Information Solutions Company (ISISCO), Iran

ABSTRACT

Due to the unprecedented growth of outsourcing ICT projects by the Iranian government, a critical need exists for the proper execution and monitoring of these projects. In this paper, the authors propose a web-based project management system to improve the efficiency and effectiveness of the management processes and accelerate decision making. Based on the requirements and information flow between various units involved in the complete life-cycle of ICT project management, a functional model and system architecture with various underlying structures has been designed. The functional model contains two sub-systems: process management and information service. The proposed system structure is based on a four-layer client-server computing model. As a part of a publically available ICT system, it must be secure against cybercrime activities. This system can bring efficiency in managing the projects, improve decision making, and increase the overall management process with total accounting and management transparency. The proposed system overcomes the problems associated with a central system and traditional management processes, as is currently the case in Iran.

DOI: 10.4018/978-1-4666-3625-5.ch012

INTRODUCTION

In recent decades, it has become increasingly obvious that ICT projects tend to be more large-scale and complex (He, Jiang, Li, & Le, 2010), thus creating new challenges, especially for developing countries. Furthermore, the existing commercially available project management software tools have many limitations and drawbacks which are particularly unsuitable for handling large and complex projects (White & Fortune, 2002; He et al., 2010). Hence, these commercial software tools are proven to be unsatisfactory in terms of the functional coverage scope, flow process adaptation and collaboration arrangements to meet the complicated management demands of large-scale ICT outsourced projects (Tseng, 2006; Buddhakulsomsiri, 2006). This is particularly true in the case of Iran, since at present, there are no matured techniques both domestically and abroad to be borrowed for practice in respect of the business and capital flows descriptions, public and private collaboration towards multi-purpose decision-making based on multi-source data flows for effective and efficient management of large-scale ICT projects (Simon, 2006; Crawford, Pollack, & England, 2006).

Two studies (Zhang, Li, & Tam, 2006; Olsson, 2006) indicate that any project participant can only hold less than 65 percent of the project information at the closure phase because of the multiple player and asymmetrical timelines. These problems pose serious constraints to the development of large-scale information-based management of ICT projects. Crawford et al. (2006) have found variation in project management knowledge and practices between industries, countries and application areas as well as the amount of attention with focus on construction industry. Due to this variation in understanding and application of project management, it is useful to investigate its application in developing countries which are trying to close the digital divide by performing more large and complex ICT projects through government and private sector partnerships.

Iran is a classic example of this partnership. It is at the threshold of closing the digital divide by making ICT official government policy to achieve a knowledge-based economy and society in a relatively short time. The Web-based project management of ICT projects outsourced by the government to external contractors one such example. It is also geared to overcome inefficiencies in managing large-scale projects.

Background-Problem Statement

Like any other developing country, Iranian ICT public projects are growing rapidly in all forms in government businesses ranging from financial services to social and public services (Jahangard, 2004). The government usually experiences huge problems trying to manage outsourcing of large ICT projects. Traditional outsourced project management methods are inadequate and fragmented. Project management systems are already ineffective for public projects that are causing numerous work bottlenecks, overloading workers, and inefficiencies from human-centered management systems and processes (Karami, 2003). The huge variety and quantities of paper and document handling make management persons very confused, which degrades over time to the point where good personal are not readily available, resulting in over-stretched management teams and the overall smooth functioning of the institution (Ahamdi, Ghazanfari, Aliahmadi, & Mohebi, 2003). These practices showed that the traditional management theories and methods for a simple and single project are not adequate or appropriate any more, when applied to large complex projects. In this day and age, one would expect a web-based project management utility that is simple and offering tools to managing teams and institutions to provide optimum project management and with transparency.

Furthermore, Iran's General Policies affirm constitutional and twenty year principles which refer to developing modern technologies, creating an effective IT system, using advanced technologies in education and research, and emphasizing private sector development. The Iran Strategic document on Information and Communications Technology affirms the need for balanced development in all dimensions of the Information Society with emphasis on ICT's function in facilitating, enabling and improving (Supreme Council of Information and Communication Technology, 2008). Therefore, certain prominent issues arose when the Iranian government chose to procure ICT services and systems from private sector providers based on their new regulatory reforms and policies regardless of boundaries. Control and supervising of the projects outsourced to third parties is a big challenge due to slow information flow and decision making process between the different units which serve as a knowledge network to the various units. Also, the exchange of information between major players such as project managers, professionals, contractors, and administrators occur very frequently in the forms of letters, change orders, and drawings to name but a few. Moreover, the lack of correct communication and exchange between the user and the supplier channels, varied and confusing forms of applying managerial methods, which are incompatible with traditional forms, experience other major problems. These are low quality, increased cost, delay in achieving correct deliverables and to avoid incompatible delivery to meet customer requirements. From the Iranian experience, corruption and failing of many serious public projects not only resulted in loss of national resources and investment, but also generated negative social influence and verbal abuse of the government and its policies (Taghavi, Patel, & Taghavi, 2011).

In addition, the government confronted incidents of cybercrime activities which resulted in modification of sensitive information, and loss of management control affecting public utilities such as telecommunications and transport. Therefore, security and trust are major issues in the developing and deploying of a Web-based Project Management System (WPMS), since some clients would be completely trustworthy whilst others would need to be checked and authenticated all the time during access. There is definitely a priority to ensure that the public users are assured and encouraged to use this system and to support technology as a benefit rather than a threat.

This paper proposes a framework which applies management methods and processes based on integrated governmental project management information systems and information flows between various parties and departments. This study is to analyze and design the construction of a web based project management system aligned with Iran's Policies and "Twenty Year Principles" to overcome all the problems mentioned before regarding development of ICT projects outsourced by the government agencies. Furthermore, it illustrates the system structure and supporting mechanisms.

PROJECT ORGANIZATION AND INFORMATION FLOW

From the management point of view, three levels are involved in managing and executing a project: strategic level, tactical level and operational level (Scott, Kwan, & Cheong, 2003). Major units which are involved in a public project according to their levels of responsibilities are shown in Figure 1.

Government Administrative and Procurement (GAP) departments have a key role in constructing and directing the execution of ICT projects. This department is the sponsor of public projects; therefore they directly supervise all kinds of projects. Moreover, monitoring work in progress at regular times, assigning funds and assessing quality of work already performed are part of their responsibility with checks and balances. It is a complete project management life-cycle.

Figure 1. Public project stakeholders

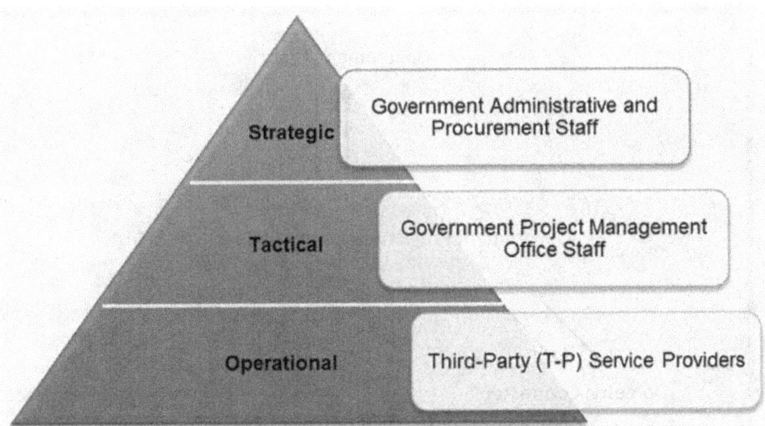

The Iranian Government Project Management Office (GPMO) represents a government administrative department which performs tactical responsibilities like bidding, contract management, evaluating project progress, funds, consistency and quality management. This unit is in charge of integrating management and supervising the accomplishments. According to the defined levels, Third-Party (T-P) performs the project processes. Most of the time private companies are the third parties. They are in command of conformation on quality and project progress, provide deliverables, and report work progress to the GPMO. Vendors for designing, supervising and constructing are identified in bidding. After selecting the vendors and negotiating the contract, the contractors are supposed to accomplish their tasks and receive payment according to their legally signed contractual agreement and schedule of work.

US Project Management Association (PMI) defines PMO as a kind of organizational element responsible for controlling and supervising the entire management system which improves organizational capacity to implement projects comprehensively and systematically and to obtain the greatest outcome aligned with organization strategy (Kanamanapalli, 2010). Since it provides more effective functioning of the environment for project portfolio management and workgroup management, it integrates and allocates the resources, assists in decision making of the corporate management, and has very frequent and interrelated interaction with the project stakeholders.

Figure 2 shows the key information flows concerning public projects. The difficulties existing in public projects are due to the great volume of information and high interrelation between information services. Information provided by services should be supplied to various people with different needs across the geographically diverse groups, ranging from government administration to public domain as well as national and international contractors. The information flows become very complex when it involves one or more subcontractors with other government departments.

REQUIREMENTS

In considering the Web-based Project Management System (WPMS), the general unit of the system's functions and operations are described as:

- **Input:** *Who* is responsible to input *What* into the system, *When* and *How*;
- **Process:** Data to go through a series of processes in the system;

Figure 2. Public project information flows

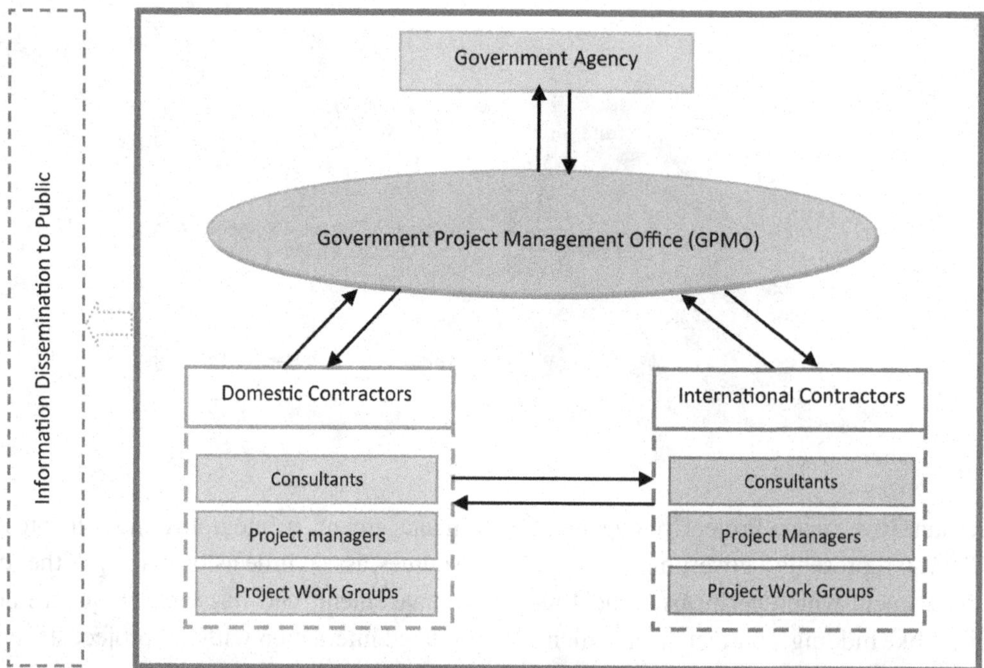

- **Output:** Through a series of processes, system outputs, *What* to *Whom*, *When* and *How*.

Management of the project entails:

- **Who:** WPMS stakeholders;
- **When:** Project management lifecycle phases according to *PMBOK* (Project Management Body Of Knowledge) (PMI, 2008);
- **What:** Data or information;
- **How:** User interface and mode of access.

Primarily, WPMS requirements are composed of such elements and the links between them (Liu, Zhao, Sun, & Yin, 2008; Mustafa, 2010). The WPMS functional requirements are as follows:

1. Infrastructure services indicate the basic services which are known as business processes of the framework and system. It is the standard functional requirements of designing a framework and system.
2. Data system is supposed to be consisted of the data warehouse of the current public projects. These include the data warehouse of all public projects, the data mart that provides management information from different aspects, project data warehouse which memorizes all the information concerning the current projects, such as bidding invitation, process, closure, evaluation, identification, project design, construction, funds distribution, compensation claims and accomplishments. According to the projects' concerning topics, project data warehouse stores all the information of the public projects, including projects' constructing information with different granularity. Data Mart should be built according to the relative elements' decision-making requirement and information needs.

3. Technical support for both design and implementation which covers the necessary software and hardware for the project management system development for users. It also includes the middleware and the Application Program Interfaces (API) which separates the application from the underlying services and resources.

PROPOSED SOLUTION OF WPMS

Functional Model

The only way to overcome traditional non-computer or web-based project management is to specify and make one that is integrated as a whole inter-locking system of subsystems which execute various critical aspects of the project management functions (Gałęzowski, Zabierowski, & Napieralski, 2009). In general, the aim of an Integrated Management (IM) is the understanding and effective direction of every aspect of an organization.

This concept can be applied and expanded to many management areas which include the concept of integrated cost management, and integrated quality management.

Based on this definition, public project management uses project resources properly, improves management ability and by directing, satisfies all the various interacting groups. Viewing from the government's aspect, public project management communication and coordination have a significant role in the success of the project. At this point, the government is challenged with two problems:

1. The first problem is co-operation and control of integration management in the different project process, such as bidding and working process management.
2. The second problem is to realize these process tasks, project information should be collected and distributed. The proposed system consists of two sub-systems to meet the mentioned requirements: process management sub-system and information service sub-system.

Our proposed functional model is shown in Figure 3.

Process Management Sub-System

The process management sub-system, as depicted in Figure 3, is of concern to all of the activities related to managerial project processes like contract management. It is primarily concerned with three areas: Information management, management standard and process control.

Project departments, the GPMO unit and the work groups need a multitasking information system from the beginning until the end of the project. It has four components which include Document Management (DM), Workflow Management (WM), Team Communication (TC) and Task Assignment (TA). Figure 4 is about a multitasking information system which enables easy information management with standardized and monitored processes. Document Management System can be viewed as three main layers: input layer, document process layer, and storage layer.

The main function of the input layer is to upload files. In uploading files, metadata of the file which is saved in XML format, such as author, date and description are required (Chan & Leung, 2004; W3C, 2002). Core document management functionality is performed in the document process layer. Two main functions of this layer are to search files and topics. In the case of file searching, the system has the capability of offering various search results based on the user's search criteria, such as the category of the file or by text in the description of the metadata of the file that results in improving search quality. Topic search is an integrated information search and display facility which shows results as per user request at near instant response. It allows users to extract

Figure 3. WPMS functional model

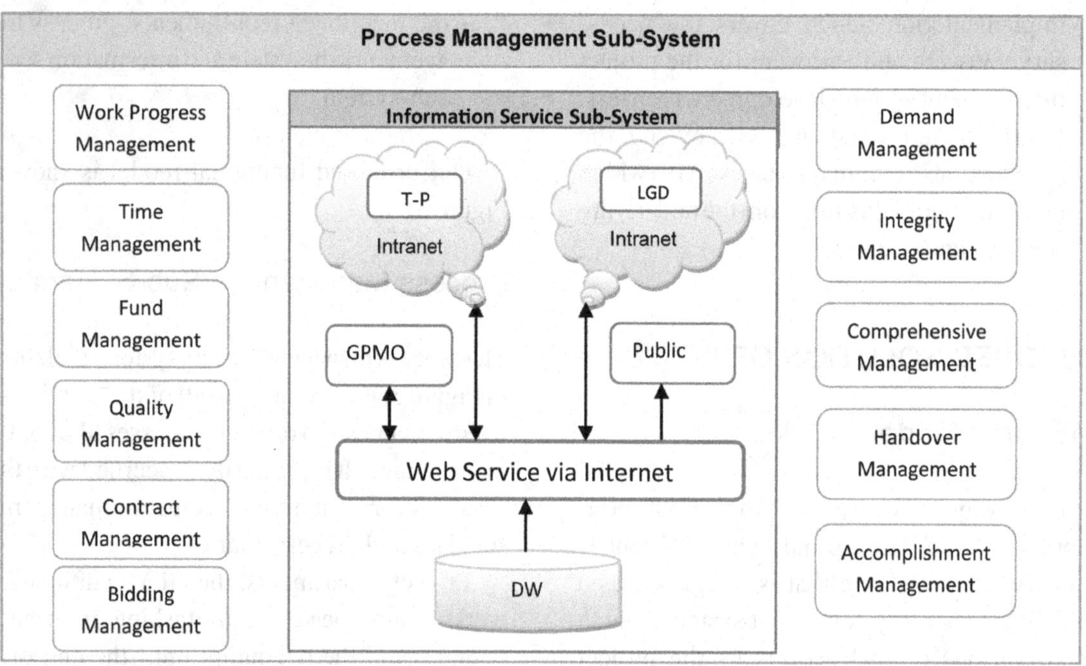

Figure 4. Process management sub-system framework

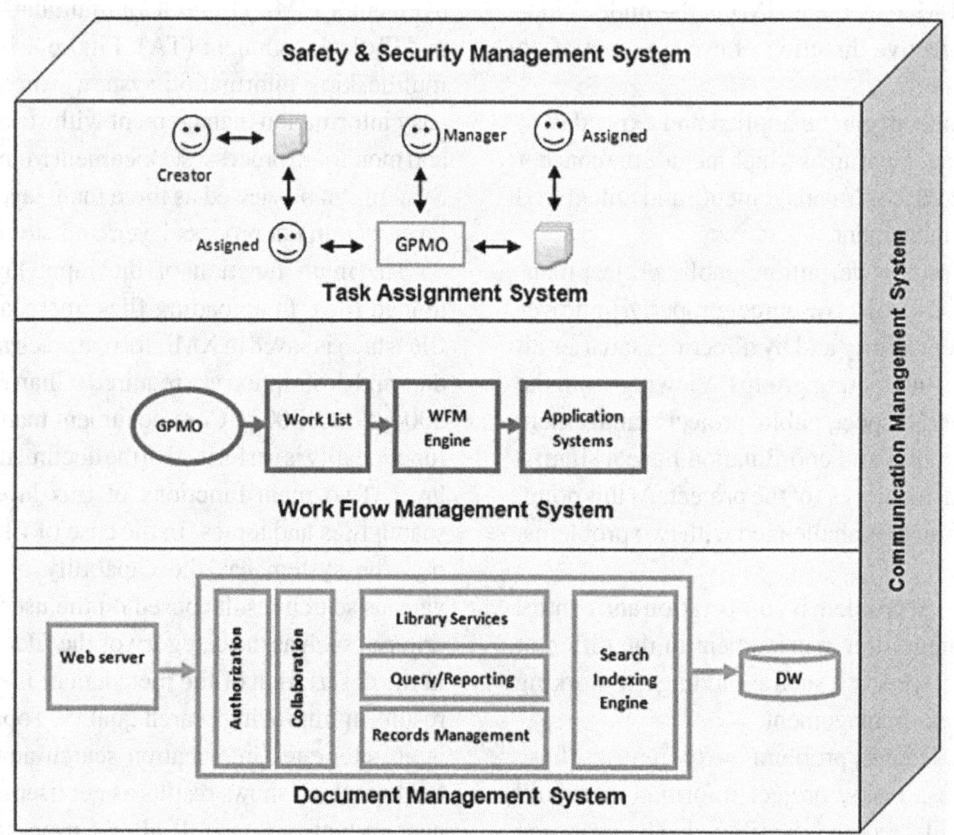

useful information from all sources in the project for analysis and decision-making by researching related information in the project website, and integrating the search result (Mehrdad, Mokhtari, & Aski, 2005). In the third layer, Data Warehouse (DW) stores all the information of the public projects according to their concerning topics to feed information needs to the various clients.

In the Workflow Management System, by adopting standardized workflow management method through information templates and automatic execution of business rules, they speed up the communication and confirmation of decisions. A workflow consists of several tasks, which are assigned to different project roles. GPMO defines the main tasks of "Process definition" and "Workflow administration".

After a task is finished, the system projects and schedules the next task to be done. Team communication is a form of less formal discussion through instant messaging as chat or buzz, online conferencing, emailing, and project calendar. It facilitates and simplifies workflow management. Task Assignment System is a personalized tool. Each user can assign a task and view his own tasks, alarms and status relevant to his job. This enables the users' environment to focus on relevant information. After the task creation is authorized, members should update their task information.

The proposed multitasking information system can intelligently search for relevant information, extract useful data, share updated information on progress, retrieve historical data for new applications, and control the sequence relation of project management steps through these four components. Advanced tools in intelligent information flow and workflow handling are essential for smart decision making.

In the meantime, a safety and security management system is developed to support the collaboration activities. This subsystem is able to carry out multi-tiered safety authorizations starting from the network platform going through the system platform and the database management system and ending with the application data and visit control.

Each public project applies different standards like obeying contractual procedures and schedules or evaluation criteria. For example, evaluation criteria for selecting a project have a different rate in each unit. So the system should be able to allow users to define different factors, weights and scoring methods by revising predefined factors. Project management involves a series of steps and processes that have complex relation to each other. It means that the output from one activity is an input to another activity. This subsystem is applied to ensure the steps sequence and relation among them.

Information Service Sub-System

This sub-system (refer to Figure 3) provides information services to satisfy a client's demand for information. Therefore, it enables permitted users to access a broad range of information resources by designing a data warehouse and proposing inquiry services to promote transparency of management processes.

The Third-Parties (T-P) and Local Government Departments (LGD) interwork via the intranet to jointly organize themselves respectively, and use the Web Services via the Internet to interact with other stakeholders. The data warehouse is the repository of all data from which information is derived that is meaningful in the context of its use. It is capable of comprehensively serving information for various client groups. For example, it offers to government administrative departments development project progress, information inquiry services, actual and budget cost, schedule information services, and payment accounts services to facilitate both technical and financial auditing of projects in real-time.

In our model, the public is informed about project news such as work-in-progress of projects through the inquiry services on different project items and the relevant information in a layman understandable manner.

The information service sub-system can adopt various methods for providing the platform to produce information from project data which is meaningful and expressed in a readily understood manner to offer direct and dramatic information services for both the client and the project contractor (W3C, 2004). For example, it can show work progress by Gantt chart or make comparisons by using the histograms, pie charts and graphs besides the statistics (Forsberg, Mooz, & Cotterman, 2005).

Web-Based Public Project Management System Structure

The proposed system is constructed based on four-layers of a typical Client/Server presentation data processing and calculating model that is shown in Figure 5. It has:

1. Computer interface is the first layer. Clients of this system are from various levels with different applications that should be considered in the user interface at the design stage. Clients in the government administrative departments focus on a project progress and assess whether the project process is compatible with other contractual obligations or not. Thus, their interface style can be of a variety of charts (like Gantt/PERT charts), figures and tables showing the reports of the project progression, the quality evaluation results, and funds' ratio and providing a feedback and comments. The Application Integration module exists as an integrator *"mashup"* function between the user interface (the client HCI) and Web Services to manage context-related events within the host application and to process and display data returned from the information layer. This is technically the middleware layer with a plethora of services, ranging from database access, cross mapping of data and it transformation to a common format, as well other object management services.

Figure 5. WPMS structure

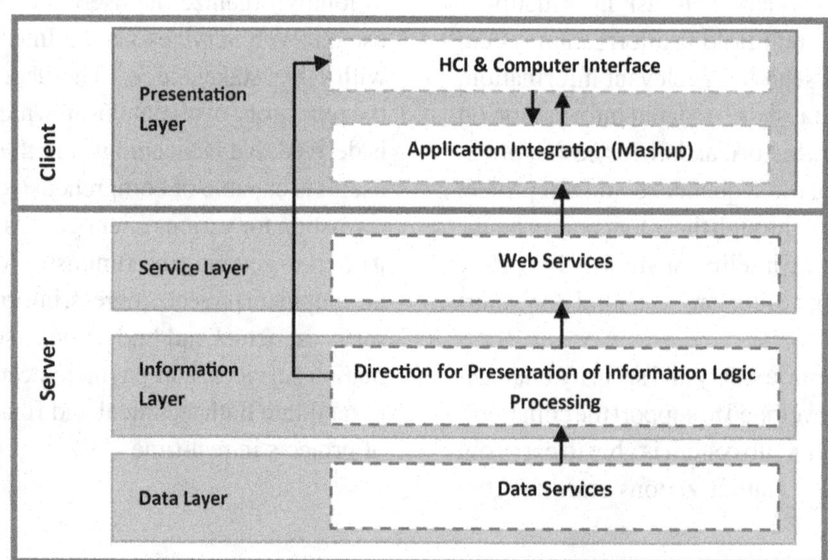

2. Web service is the second layer. It provides information services as well as a standard means of interoperating between different clients and applications. It means that the web services share business logic, data and processes through the appropriate interfaces of the composite system. For example, when a unit needs to report a project status, a function would be chosen from the third layer, logic processing, to process the data for data-recoding and then would be processed in the computer interface layer. Once the work of the logic processing layer is complete, feedback information reaches the web service layer, which chooses a method or function to deliver the information with the proper computer interface.
3. Direction for information logic processing is the third layer, which deals with specific logic affairs, including data maintenance for budget and quality information, contracts, bid documents, and work progress. It also analyzes the data of funds comparison, work progress comparison, and quality records. In conclusion, it responds to a client information query.
4. The forth layer is a data service which scans the data by reading, writing and sorting. Relational data warehouse is adopted as a storage media for structured data such as for funds, and quality in contrast to unstructured content where the photo or video data file is adopted. Also, a web server should be provided to deliver and support the public Internet services in a safe manner with appropriate security, privacy, trust, audit and digital forensic functions and processes to give the overall system a very high level of confidence (Patel, 2010).

The adoption of a distributed data warehouse repository hosted in a distributed system computing environment with high-speed data accesses is essential to cover the whole country especially where the government departments are located in different towns and cities. This requires a very high standard of security and operational safety in order to avoid inconvenience to the client by having to visit the central data warehouse directly and also to deter the hackers from penetrating the system to cause damage. The four-layered proposed model ensures integrating and extending the capabilities of the system as well as reducing the degree of coupling in the system's modules to achieve connectivity, efficiency and openness in a safe and secure computing environment. It includes safety measures comprising of security, privacy, identity management, trust, audit and digital forensics. This is necessary to ensure high levels of confidence, connectivity and reliability of the overall system.

It is largely self-managing system based on autonomic principles. An autonomic system primarily has four basic self-managing characteristics: self-configuring, self-optimizing, self-healing, and self-protecting functions. Hence, the essence of autonomic computing systems is self-management, the intent of which is to free system administrators and technical support from the details of system operation and maintenance, and to provide computing services which run at optimum performance 24 hours per day, 7 days a week. Their availability is paramount for ICT-based workflow operations.

The WPMS sub-system's structure and their functions are designed by selecting the latest open system technology to ensure ease of use, deployment and compliance to meet all essential requirements. It is also based on the Client-Server model but the server side is more than just a data service operator. It is heavily supported by the underlying self-management autonomic functions.

PROTECTION AND SAFETY ISSUES

It is inconceivable to imagine all the countless ways in which today's ICT affects us daily. Our social, business and political behavior as an Information Society is based on the rapid growth, deployment and uptake of ICT. This fact alone necessitates a very high *dependency* on ICT in all walks of life. It provokes a fundamental thought and requirement that these strongly interrelated technological infrastructures, as well as the information systems that underpin them with their networking technologies, become highly critical if their disruption would lead to a serious economical, material and, sometimes, human loss. As a consequence, the protection and safety of these critical information infrastructures is a major goal for the Iranian government, companies and various other interacting organizations.

As is shown in Figure 4, our proposed Web-Based Project Management System is architected to ensure that as part of the critical information infrastructures, it covers both the data security of information content through the use of cryptographic methods and access through open networks in cyber space through a set of safety measures in the form security solutions by means of protection, control and evaluation mechanisms (Patel, 2010). These solutions are increasingly using wireless networks as one of the main technological platforms because it facilitates distributed control and allows the different components of the system and network to remain functional and operative, even in extremely high alert or disruptive situations.

In order to guarantee the faultless interoperability of the protection, control and evaluation mechanisms, creation of new security services are essential. These services are integrated into a service-oriented architecture of the Web Based Project Management System with the aid of a trust management model designed for this specific purpose.

The functionality of the architecture can be verified in different ways. The management and maintenance systems embedded into the architecture, such as an early warning, dynamic reconfiguration and auditing systems based on some autonomic computing schemes should be tested for operability. On the other hand, the infrastructure tools for decision, support, risk analysis and management should be exercised periodically to ensure compliance against cyber security rules and regulations.

Moreover, these trends are expected to intensify because ICT and its applications are becoming more and more pervasive to society, leading to new types of and larger scale vulnerabilities and risks. Economic and societal interests go beyond technical security, as they relate to:

- **Business opportunities and growth:** New business models, virtual enterprising, delocalized workforces, tailored services, digital asset management and economic value of knowledge.
- **Individual:** Privacy, confidentiality, intimacy, cyber-crime, protection of minors and ethics.
- **Society:** New dependencies on volatile technologies, long lasting preservation of knowledge, culture and digital divide.
- **Government's recognition, power-base and control:** Interdependencies of critical and sensitive departments, critical interworking ICT infrastructures, national defense, social order and international cooperation and governance.

Security issues are not new. They have been around for a very long time, but however, as the Internet and other information-communication networks become an ever-increasing part of our daily lives, so does our dependency upon their underlying infrastructure. Unfortunately, as our dependency has grown, so have the hostile attacks on the infrastructures. Newly discovered forms of attacks, the availability and wide distribution of attack tools, as well as the flaws in common desktop computing software have resulted in networks becoming increasingly vulnerable. Simple viruses, malware and denial of service attacks are argued to have cost billions, if not trillions of dollars worldwide in lost productivity. More recently it has become known that sophisticated distributed denial of service attacks on the Internet are on the rise, causing severe damage, loss of revenue and functioning of basic information applications and infrastructures. It is expected that more serious threats are still to come in the future (El Sheikh & Khadra, 2009).

As many factors are causing ICT, from the lowest to the highest levels, to migrate from centralized systems and components into more autonomously distributed structures, such as:

- Large scale systems of casually networked and evolving real-time embedded devices, like wireless sensors.
- Mobile codes in heterogeneous and mobile environments.
- Volatility of networks and service infrastructures, and end-user applications.

Safety and security are serious concerns. Therefore, security issues and their accompanying trust functions in the digital environment are becoming everyday features. In addition, geographical, trans-border and jurisdictional boundaries are fast disappearing and the ultimate basis for *trust* and the recognition of *powers* in the digital environments are changing, uncontrolled and giving unlimited access with resulting increase in potentially harmful side-effects of technologies and services. This can cause a high scale of potential disruptions of ICT services worldwide with the high dependencies on the Internet.

Recently we have seen a rapid growth in the number of attacks on identity, since acquiring such information allows miscreants to commit fraud that is hard to detect. Breaking the weakest link in the network is a cause for serious concern to individuals and businesses alike, because they depend on it for survival. A trusted authority on the Internet could be a fraudulent authority. It reminds us of the danger of security and identity failures. The fact that even the basic technology of security is sometimes flawed is also interesting. They have an impact on our privacy as well. Much work on the future Internet and Web requires monitoring of research, but at the same time ensure that the real user's privacy is not compromised. It is difficult to reconcile these two conflicting aspects/goals. Indeed, in gathering data about network use there are legal requirements relating to intercept laws and user privacy that must be met.

However, regardless of the tools provided to protect personal privacy on the Internet, currently privacy aware network monitoring is required in order to promulgate new legislations, standards of behavior, design protocols and most importantly offer near absolute trust to the end users. Similarly, new tools are required to pro-actively protect systems under illegitimate attacks while laying bate to prosecute the culprit, and also to invoke processes to trace the culprit in order to prosecute after post-event has taken place. Systems are never perfect, and this is never more true than for security and privacy because we can never prove that a system is secure and guarantees privacy, but only discover (eventually) when it no longer is.

Under the bane of safety measures incorporating *security, privacy, identity management, trust, audit* and *digital forensics,* our proposed architecture of Web Based Project Management System takes all of this into consideration.

DISCUSSION

With application of the above-mentioned theories and methods and in accordance with the actual conditions of current infrastructure, Iran can benefit from a fully web information system in order to lead ICT projects. The proposed WPMS can contribute to increased collaboration and cooperation among various roles executed either by persons or by automated processes playing the role of persons in the project management processes.

The proposed system is compatible with not only the traditional manual systems but other ICT or web-based systems which are much more reliable and easily support on an ongoing basis.

The proposed web-based project management system can bring efficiency in managing projects effectively and has a key role in enabling,, facilitating, and improving functions aligned with Iranian ICT policy statement. Over time, it will simplify and improve data collection which is currently fragmented in various units and departments that do not even communicate with each other properly. This will speed up decision making in various managerial levels regardless of the exchange of official letters. In the long term, it will decrease cost and make information available in real-time for administration and other departments to improve public projects. This will allow skilled personnel more time to concentrate and deal with other more urgent and important matters. At the same time they will be able to monitor the work in-progress, quality management, funds control, technical and financial audit much more effectively which will improve the overall project management efficiency and level of trust in the system.

However, for strengthening of the government's supervision, a perfect system of internal and external control is needed to prevent individual and tissue fraud. In order to facilitate the public and private co-operation, an easy and feasible system is needed for the contractor's entry and interaction. This proposed system needs to be investigated in terms of available infrastructure such as the Internet access to be validated to apply across the entire country level.

CONCLUSION

This paper proposed a web based project management system for the Iranian government to manage all its projects more constructively, regardless whether they were ICT based or not. The important issue was to use ICT and web technology to construct such a system. This paper described a functional model and system structure which has enormous capability to achieve robustness and transparency of the management process and to improve decision making in an open distributed computing environment. This is currently lacking in the Iranian government's administrative departments and project management units. It overcame all the problems associated with a central system and traditional management processes, as is currently the case in Iran. It overcomes all the problems associated with a central system and traditional management processes, as is currently the case in Iran.

Now, what is required is a detailed study against very good terms of reference to determine all the requirements for the proposed system and then present it to the Iranian government for their consideration. The detailed study is an absolute requirement as it concerns Iran as a whole, taking into account the concerns of access to the Internet, level of security and user acceptance. It will also help close the gap in the digital divide. ICT is perceived to be the only enabler, which can meet the demands of a modern, forward looking Iran heading in the direction of a fully developed country or nation in the fraternity of nations of the world. This paper is a provocative action in that direction.

REFERENCES

Ahamdi, A., GhazanfarI, M., Aliahmadi, A., & Mohebi, A. (2003). Strategic Planning for Implementing E-Government in Iran: Formulating the strategies. *Farda Management Journal, 2*.

Chan, S. L., & Leung, N. N. (2004). Prototype Web-Based Construction Project Management System. *Journal of Construction Engineering and Management*, *130*(6), 935–943. doi:10.1061/(ASCE)0733-9364(2004)130:6(935)

Crawford, L., Pollack, J., & England, D. (2006). Uncovering the trends in project management: Journal emphases over the last 10 years. *International Journal of Project Management, 24*(2), 175–184. doi:10.1016/j.ijproman.2005.10.005

El Sheikh, A., & Khadra, H. A. (2009). Governing Information Technology (IT) and Security Vulnerabilities: Empirical Study Applied on the Jordanian Industrial Companies. *Journal of Information Technology Research, 2*(1), 70–85. doi:10.4018/jitr.2009010105

Forsberg, K., Mooz, H., & Cotterman, H. M. (2005). *Visualizing project management: models and frameworks for mastering complex systems* (3rd ed.). Hoboken, NJ: John Wiley & Sons.

Gałęzowski, G., Zabierowski, W., & Napieralski, A. (2009, February 24-28). Web-based Project Management System. In *Proceedings of the 10th International Conference on the Experience of Designing and Application of CAD Systems in Microelectronics (CADSM'2009),* Polyana-Svalyava, Ukraine (pp. 407-410).

Ge, N., Li, H., Gao, L., Zang, Z., Li, Y., Li, J., et al. (2010). A web-based Project Management System for Agricultural Scientific Research. In *Proceedings of the 2010 International Conference on Management and Service Science (MASS 2010)* (pp. 1-2).

He, Q., Jiang, W., Li, Y., & Le, Y. (2010). The Study on Paradigm Shift of Project Management Based on Complexity Science – Project Management Innovations in Shanghai 2010 EXPO Construction Program. In *Proceedings of the 2009 IEEE International Conference on Industrial Engineering and Engineering Management* (pp. 603-607).

Jahangard, N. (2004). Iran's Road to Knowledge-based Development. In *Proceedings of the Meeting and Workshop on Development of a National IT Strategy Focusing on Indigenous Content Development.* Tehran, Iran: Ministry of Science, Research & Technology, Iranian Information and Documentation Center. Retrieved from http://unpan1.un.org/intradoc/groups/public/documents/APCITY/UNPAN021357.pdf

Kanamanapalli, V. B. (2010). *The Setting Up of Project Management Offices (PMOs) for Large Project Initiative*. Retrieved from http://www.pmi.org/en/Knowledge-Center/Knowledge-Shelf/Project-Management-Offices.aspx

Karami, R. (2003). *IT Project Pathology*. Retrieved from http://www.golsoft.com/links/ITP-projects-problems.0.pdf

Liu, W., Zhao, S., Sun, Y., & Yin, M. (2008). An Approach to Project Management Information System Requirements Analysis. In *Proceedings of the International Conference on Intelligent Computation Technology and Automation* (pp. 957-961).

Mehrdad, J., Mokhtari, A., & Aski, H. R. (2005). Designing the conceptual model of an electronic document management system for the institute of technical and vocational higher education. *Iranian Journal of Information Science and Technology, 3*(2), 57–70.

Mustafa, B. A. (2010). Comparing the Effect of Use Case Format on End User Understanding of System Requirements. *Journal of Information Technology Research, 3*(4), 1–20. doi:10.4018/jitr.2010100101

Olsson, N. O. E. (2006). Management of flexibility in projects. *International Journal of Project Management, 24*(1), 66–74. doi:10.1016/j.ijproman.2005.06.010

Patel, A. (2010). Concept of Mobile Agent-based Electronic Marketplace – Safety Measures. In Lee, I. (Ed.), *Encyclopedia of E-Business Development and Management in the Digital Economy* (pp. 252–264). Hershey, PA: Business Science Reference.

Patel, A., Qi, W., & Wills, C. (2010). A Review and Future Research Directions of Secure and Trustworthy Mobile Agent-based E-marketplace Systems. *Journal of Information Management and Computer Security*, *18*(3), 144–161. doi:10.1108/09685221011064681

Project Management Institute (PMI). (2008). *A Guide to the Project Management Body of Knowledge (PMBOK® Guide)* (4th ed.). Retrieved from http://www.pmi.org/PMBOK-Guide-and-Standards/Standards-Library-of-PMI-Global-Standards.aspx

Scott, D., Kwan, M., & Cheong, W. (2003). Web-based construction information management systems. *The Australian Journal of Construction Economics and Building*, *3*(1), 43–52.

Simon, L. (2006). Managing creative projects: An empirical synthesis of activities. *International Journal of Project Management*, *24*(2), 116–126. doi:10.1016/j.ijproman.2005.09.002

Supreme Council of Information and Communication Technology. (2008). *Policy Intelligence Source Book*. Tehran, Iran: Iranian Information and Documentation Center.

Taghavi, M., Patel, A., & Taghavi, H. (2011). Web Based Project Management System for Development of ICT Project Outsourced by Iranian Government. In *Proceedings of the 2011 IEEE International Conference on Open Systems (ICOS2011)*, Langkawi, Malaysia (pp. 273-278).

W3C. (2002). *Extensible Markup Language*. Retrieved June 5, 2011, from http://www.w3c.org/XML/

W3C. (2004). *Web Services Architecture*. Retrieved June 5, 2011, from http://www.w3.org/TR/2004/NOTE-ws-arch-20040211/

White, D., & Fortune, J. (2002). Current practice in project management – an empirical study. *International Journal of Project Management*, *20*(1), 1–11. doi:10.1016/S0263-7863(00)00029-6

Zhang, H., Li, H., & Tam, C. M. (2006). Particle swarm optimization for resource-constrained project scheduling. *International Journal of Project Management*, *24*, 83–92. doi:10.1016/j.ijproman.2005.06.006

This work was previously published in the Journal of Information Technology Research, Volume 4, Issue 3, edited by Mehdi Khosrow-Pour, pp. 14-28, copyright 2011 by IGI Publishing (an imprint of IGI Global).

Chapter 13
An Aspect Oriented Component Based Archetype Driven Development

Rachit Mohan Garg
Jaypee University of Information Technology, India

Deepak Dahiya
Jaypee University of Information Technology, India

ABSTRACT

This paper incorporates the concepts of aspects and software reuse in archetype driven architecture. The proposed work develops the software by partitioning the whole system into different independent components and aspects to facilitate component reuse. The authors illustrate the ease of modeling the components separately and emphasize concerns that the OOP paradigm has failed to address. This paper places emphasis on designing and modeling the software rather than coding. Identification of reusable components is carried out using the hybrid methodology and aspects are identified by domain experts. Along with the components, the PIM and aspects developed are stored in separate repositories to be used in development of other software of similar requirements and basic structure.

INTRODUCTION

To survive the cut throat world of competition organizations have started spending most of their time in coding thereby resulting in a software that becomes less reliable, less adaptable since the actual and the hidden needs of the customer are not addressed completely. Moreover organizations are trying to develop the software in a cost effective way so they are using more of the available reusable components. The work presented in this paper describes a design methodology which will help in creating highly reliable, adaptable software products in a timely fashion.

DOI: 10.4018/978-1-4666-3625-5.ch013

A brief overview of the proposed methodology is as follows. It uses the concept of model driven architecture (IEEE-SA Standards Board, 2000; Jacobson, Christerson, Jonsson, & Övergaard, 1992; OMG, 2011), components (Pour, 1998; Cai, Lyu, Wong, & Ko, 2000; Wu & Offutt, 2003), aspects (Zhang, Chen, Li, & Liu, 2009; Laddad, 2009; Simmonds, Solberg, Reddy, France, & Ghosh, 2005). Firstly the whole software is investigated or analyzed so as to reveal all the details. This includes the hidden or the inferred details along with the concerns corresponding to the software. Then the modeling of PIM and aspects is done separately using UML models. The aspects are modeled as separate entity so as to avoid tangling with the business logic. After the modeling, the PIM generated is stored in the repository for reuse in other projects. Then the reusable components are identified from this optimized platform independent model (PIM) using a hybrid identification approach. After the identification of the components, a repository of the components is maintained for future use. The aspects that are modeled separately are also stored in an aspect repository for future usage. The code for the aspects and software is generated in code generation and artifact generation phase respectively. They are weaved together to provide a complete application. Figure 1 represents the whole methodology with the help of a block diagram.

In this paper, the next section provides the literature review corresponding to integration of aspect oriented development, component based development and MDA. The following section describes the research methodology being proposed. The implementation of the methodology and the results and significance of the methodology are then presented.

RELATED WORK

UML Profiles

In MDA, UML profile plays a very important role in expressing the PIM models, the PSM models, and the transformation rules. This profile can also be used as a semantic profile which enables archetype to express specific information. It can also be used for tagging purpose so as to supply more information during archetype transformation and code generation (Jin, 2006; Fuentes-Fernández & Vallecillo-Moreno, 2004).

Figure 1. Brief overview of the methodology

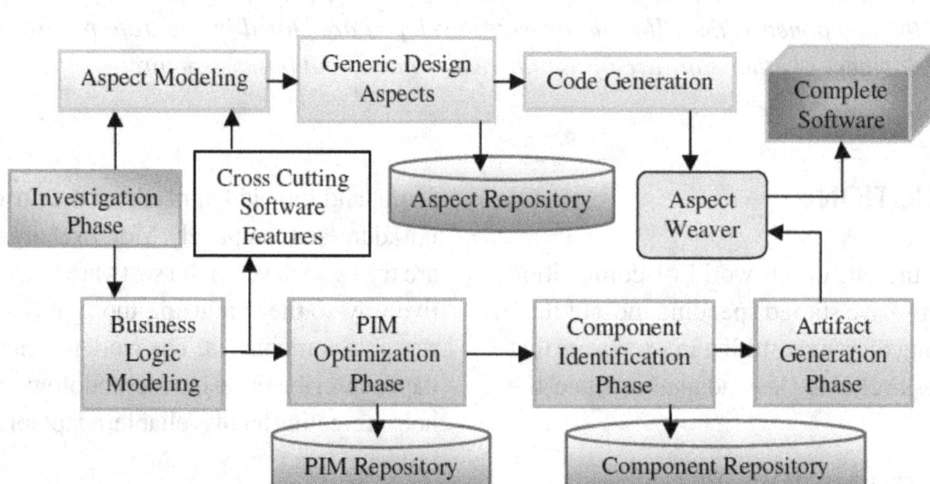

A UML profile is a combination of stereotype, tagged value and constraints. It uses stereotypes to assign special meaning to designated model elements, i.e., how an existing meta-class may be extended. Whenever a stereotype is applied to a model element, this is shown by either an icon or the stereotype name between guillemets, i.e., <<>>. Figure 2 shows an example of stereotype.

When a stereotype is applied to a model element, the values of the properties may be referred to as tagged values. The profile constraints are used to specify the domain restrictions.

Component Identification and Integration Techniques

Identification of reusable components in software is one the most important task of the component based software development. Many approaches for component identification are proposed but in the end it's the work of the experts to separate out the components manually as these approaches only provide the knowledge of the component without actually separating them out.

Slicing Technique

The slicing technique for identification of components is a family of techniques for isolating parts of a program according to the specified slicing criterion. It makes use of the control flow graphs (CFG) and program dependence graphs (PDG). By using both of these graphs the program is sliced into subprograms basically performing a specific function related to the overall software. Slicing techniques have been generally applied to the full-fledged software and not during the modeling phase as in the case of Rodrigues and Barbosa (2005). So an implementation of slicing technique or a variant of this methodology can be used during the modeling phase so as to figure out the desired components.

Fuzzy Clustering Method

This method is basically used when there exist ambiguous boundaries among the clusters and objects belong to many clusters with a certain degree of membership (Höppner, Klawonn, & Kruse, 1999). This allows the experts to discover new, undiscovered relations between the object and the corresponding clusters. FCM, one of the popular fuzzy clustering algorithm find a parti-

Figure 2. UML profile

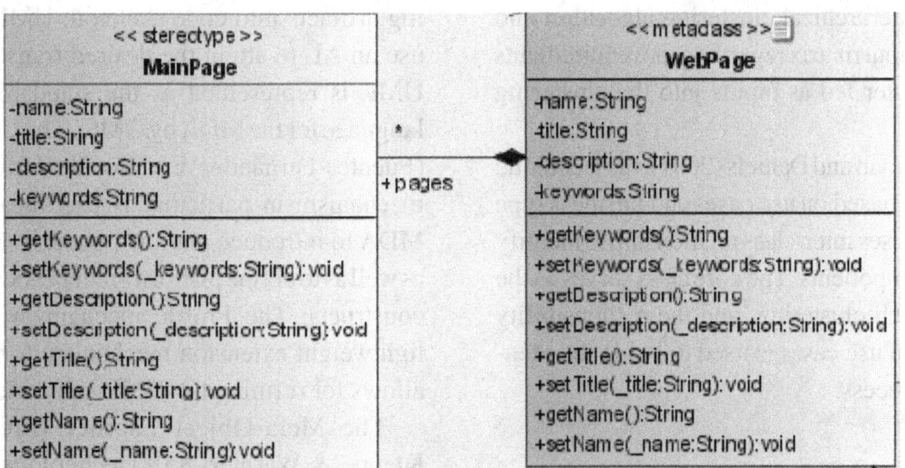

tion/clusters for a set of data points $x_j \in R^d$, j=1 to N while minimizing the cost function. FCM suffers from the problem of not able to identify the initial partitions.

Clustering Techniques

The proposed technique in Meng, Zhan, and Xu (2005) makes use of the concept that class relationships can be weighed according to their types. To identify business object component, the concept of resemblance degree between these objects is used. Resemblance degree depends on the relationship among the objects. The static relationships between business objects can be classified as general, compound, aggregation and association, and have different weights. The technique is composed of two steps: 1) The object-activity relation matrix is used to calculate the dynamic resemblance degree, and 2) To identify business object components, the technique uses a hierarchical clustering technique based on business object relation graph according to the edge strength metric. The strength of edge considers both cohesion and coupling between business objects. Problem lies in the applicability of this technique to medium/big systems since it relies on the number of possible pairs of business objects.

The conversion of requirements into corresponding components is presented in Lung, Zaman, and Nandi (2004). This method makes use of the hierarchical clustering algorithm and defines an input matrix regarding the requirements which are later fed as inputs into the clustering technique.

In Cheesman and Daniels (2001), the technique described is based on use cases and business type models that uses inter-class relationship to identify business components. The core class serves as the center of each clustering, and the responsibility derived from use cases is used to guide the identification process.

Component Based Archetype Driven Development

Model-Driven Development (MDD) is an approach in which the problem is modeled at a high level of abstraction and the implementation is derived from these high level models. In Model Driven Architecture (MDA) (IEEE-SA Standards Board, 2000) given by OMG, business processes and applications are specified using platform-independent models (PIM's) or the analysis model (Jacobson et al., 1992) that define the required features at a level of abstraction above the details of possible implementation platforms. Standardized mapping techniques transform the PIM's into platform-specific models (PSM's) and ultimately into implementations. The three primary goals of MDA are portability, interoperability and reusability through architectural separation of concerns which are in lieu with the MDA viewpoints (IEEE-SA Standards Board, 2000; OMG, 2011) of the system.

The key functionality that is required in a modeling language so as to make it suitable for designing artifacts for MDA development is the ability of the language to transform the design models into the code artifacts. Although translation tools are used to attain this transformation, yet, the importance of the modeling language cannot be neglected. Modeling languages use Action Language (AL) that has the ability of transforming artifacts into code skeleton. UML explicitly use an AL to attain the desired transformations. UML is represented as the standard modeling language for the MDA by OMG. The UML Profile (Fuentes-Fernández & Vallecillo-Moreno, 2004) mechanism in particular is used heavily in the MDA to introduce platform-specific annotations as well as to define platform-independent language constructs. The Profile mechanism provides a lightweight extension mechanism for UML that allows for refining the UML semantics.

The Meta-Object Facility (MOF) (Bast, Kleppe, & Warmer, 2004) technology provides a archetype repository that can be used to specify and manipulate models, thus encouraging consistency in manipulating models in all phases of MDA. Figure 3 illustrates the connection of both of these to MDA.

In Aßmann (2007), a general discussion of applicability of CBSD in MDA is given but any approach to that is not depicted or showed. It just provides a possibility of the collaboration.

Not much research has been done on collaboration of CBSD with MDA. Most of the literature studied only provides the background of CBSD and MDA and whether they can be combined or not for effective software development.

Integration of Aspects with Archetype Driven Development

The separation of concerns from the core business logic is a standard practice that helps in the development of better software that is free from the problem of scattering and tangling

Concerns

The term *concerns* (Fuentes-Fernández & Vallecillo-Moreno, 2004) doesn't reflect the issues related to the program, they represent the priorities and the requirements related to the software product. Concerns are basically divided into two broad categories:

- **Core Concerns:** These comprise of the program elements that constitute towards the business logic. For instance, in the *address book* example the core concern is adding, removing and updating the entries.
- **Secondary Concerns:** These comprise of the program element related to requirements other than that of the business logic. It includes functional, organizational, policy, etc. Concerns addressing the authentication, logging, persistence concerns.

Figure 4 gives a pictorial representation of the concerns discussed.

Some of the secondary concerns especially the functional one's depends on many parts of the system and not only the single one, i.e., their implementation cuts across many program elements of the software product. These are known as *cross-cutting* concerns (Fuentes-Fernández & Vallecillo-Moreno, 2004; Bast et al., 2004) due to their relation with many elements. Since these concerns relate to many elements they cause the problem of *code scattering and tangling* (Fuentes-Fernández & Vallecillo-Moreno, 2004; Bast et al., 2004).

- **Tangling:** It refers to the interdependencies between different elements within a program, i.e., when two or more concerns are implemented in the same module, it becomes more difficult to understand it.

Figure 3. Interrelation of UML and MDA

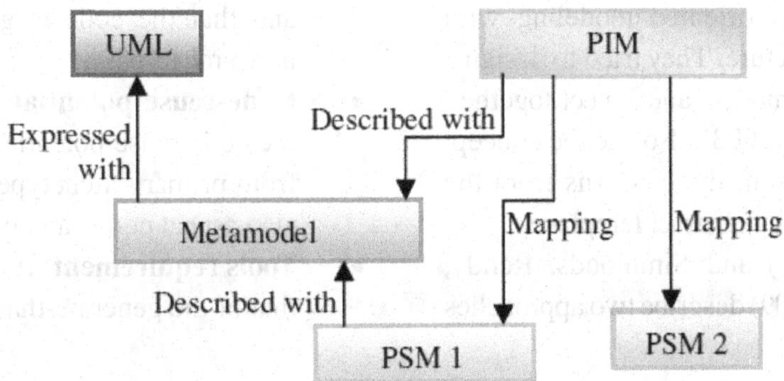

Figure 4. Various types of concerns

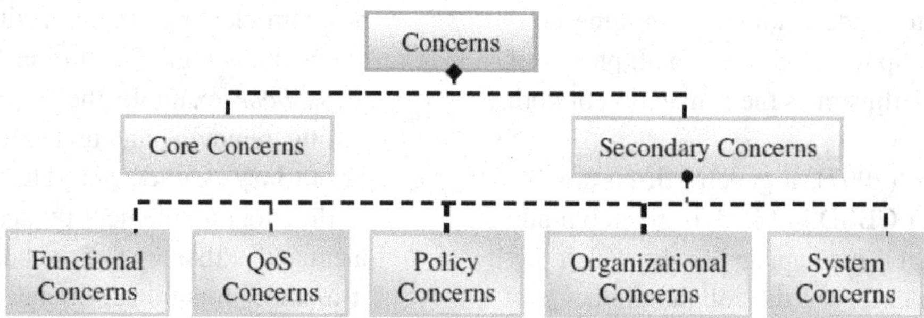

Changes to implementation of any concern may cause unintended changes to other tangled concerns.

- **Scattering:** It refers to distribution of similar code throughout many program modules. It creates problem if functionality of that code is to be changed. Changes to the implementation may require finding and editing all affected code.

Jacobson (2003) describes how the design aspects can be developed using use cases. It uses the concept of composition techniques that maps the work directly into the program level aspects. The proposed work does not provide details about models transformations, composition rules, structural relations, etc.

Reina, Toress, and Toro (2004) proposed an application of meta-models and UML profiles to separate out the concerns. The main problem addressed in the proposed methodology was that different meta-models were required for each of the concerns.

Kulkarni and Reddy (2003) proposed the integration of aspect oriented modeling with model driven architecture. They tried to design a framework to bring models and aspect together. Kulkarni and Reddy (2003) also use the concept of MDA to separate out the concerns from the business logic by using abstract templates.

Simmonds (2008) and Simmonds, Reddy, Song, and Grant, (2009) describe two approaches for integration of the aspects with the model driven development. The first approach Weave-then-Generate creates an integrated design model and from that model the code artifacts are generated. The second approach Generate-then-Weave creates a complete software application by the aspect code and the business logic code generated separately from the aspect model and primary model respectively.

The former approach lacks behind the latter one due to the following reasons:

- **Presence of large semantic gap:** Due to presence of potentially large semantic gap between individual design models and code.
- **Scattering and Tangling:** These are not eliminated completely as aspects are weaved in models which may lead to the occurrence of these problems.
- **Traceability:** It is difficult as design archetype is complex.
- **Error correction:** It is difficult as aspect archetype is to be modified, than weaved and that the code is generated using the new archetype.
- **Code-reuse potential:** It lacks behind in the code reuse potential as code generated from primary archetype can be reused and also aspect code can be reused.
- **Tools requirement:** It is much higher than that of the generate-than-weave approach.

Optimization of UML Models

The process of changing the internal structure of the product by applying some modifications so as to improve the overall readability and design and preserving its overall behavior is known as software refactoring. Mens, Van Eetvelde, Demeyer, and Janssens (2005) pointed out some key features like extensibility, capability of defining complex and parameterized transformations, and support of constraint analysis in models being transformed that must be present in a model optimizer.

GReAT or Graph Rewriting and Transformation language described in Balasubramanian, Narayanan, van Buskirk, and Karsai (2006) consists of a collection of sublanguages for specifying patterns, transformation rules and control flow for advanced transformation.

Transformation of Models

The process of transformation is categorized into three major types (Jilani, Usman, & Halim, 2010).

Direct Manipulation

In this category the internal model representation is made available to the user. The user can manipulate the model using Application Programming Interface (API) like Java, VB.Net, etc. Due to use of the API the process of direct manipulation lacks high level of abstraction as API have limited abilities thereby restricting some kinds of transformations.

Intermediate Representation

In this category the model is converted into XML or XMI standards. This representation is difficult when the changes in the model are very frequent. This happens as there is no cross model synchronization.

Language Support

In this approach the language specific transformations are used since the language provides all the necessary constituents like properties rules, constructs for expressing, composing and applying transformation. One advantage gained in this approach is that the language chosen can be declarative, procedural or a combination of both.

Techniques and Approaches for Model Transformations

This section provides an overview of the techniques and approaches used in the transformations applied at various stages of the development.

Model to Model Transformation

This includes transformation from PIM to PSM.

- **Graph Transformation (GT):** Graph Transformation is the most widely used technique for conducting transformation. It consists of L.H.S and R.H.S rule which is to be mapped on source and target model. A L.H.S consists of subgraph and condition which is searched in source model and replaced by the graph in R.H.S. It is a non deterministic technique for rule selection and for applying the rule.
- **Relational Approach (RA):** It is a declarative approach, which mainly focuses on mathematical relations and on source and target model relationship (Akehurst & Kent, 2002). Relationships are composed of complex mathematics. Predicates and constraints are used to define mathematical relationships. Due to mathematical foundation Relational approach is bidirectional and also supports backtracking. It does not allow in-place transformation.
- **Structural Approach (SA) (Jilani et al., 2010):** This approach assumes that the

structures of the source and target model are similar. By assuming this it generate target element for each source element, it creates a hierarchal structure for target model, sets attribute and references in the target model. User has to provide rule and schedule for transformation.

Model to Code Transformation

This includes generation of the code artifacts from the PSM generated. An overview of the main techniques for code transformation is provided.

- **Visitor Based Approach (VA) (Jin, 2006):** In this approach source model is traversed and code is generated for each model element. Meta-Concept defines the traversing order of the model elements.
- **Template Based Approach (TA):** Template based approach uses template to generate code. A template consists of rules which are mapped on source model. As compare to visitor base code generation, template is more specific for code generation. The structure of template resembles more closely to the generated code results in more accurate and precise code generation.

Analysis of the Model Transformations

The transformation techniques and approaches (model-model and model-code) are analyzed on the basis of some parameters (Jilani et al., 2010).

- **Stateless:** This parameter checks that whether the state of the model is preserved or not, i.e., whether the original model is modified or a copy of the original model is used.
- **Understandability:** Checks whether the transformation syntax is easily understandable or not.
- **Bidirectional:** Checks whether the PIM can be transformed to PSM and PSM back to the PIM.
- **Change Tracking:** Transformation track changes or not, i.e., the transformation technique took care of changes and change can be track.
- **Validity of the Model:** Checks whether the model produced is in compliance with the OMG standards.

On the basis of these parameters a comparison of the techniques is provided in Table 1.

PROPOSED METHODOLOGY

Currently, most of the organizations are using the UML diagrams only to fulfill the designing phase requirements and understand the flow of data. After that these are thrown away as if they were of no use. This was due to the fact that these models were only depicting the flow of data and control and had no relation with the coding.

The underlying proposed methodology incorporates the concept of aspects and component based development in model driven development. It also provides a repository based architecture in which the modeled PIM is stored so that it can be used in future project with the similar type of requirements and specifications along with the basic structure. Component Identification uses the process of *Forward Identification* (Wang, Xu, & Zhan, 2005) in which designers make use of the requirement models to identify business components (BC) and implement these BCs as Software Components (SC), then use these SCs to construct objective software systems. The generalized version of component identification process is depicted in Figure 5.

Table 1. Comparison table

S.No.	Technique Name	Analysis Parameter			
		Stateless	Understandability	Bidirectional	Change Tracking
1	GT	Y	N	N	Y
2	RA	N	N	Y	Y
3	SA	N	N	N	N
4	VB	N/A	Y	N	N
5	TB	N/A	Y	N	N

Components are identified using a hybrid approach that uses the concept of both clustering and slicing. In a general term it is slicing followed by clustering so as to get the appropriate clusters that can be reused in other software products.

As opposed to the traditional approaches of software development this methodology along with the facility of the reuse of the developed PIM and the identified components, also provide support to the developers in coding by generating artifacts of the software for different platforms from the PIM created during design phase.

The proposed methodology is divided into different phases that perform specific tasks related to the design and development of the software. A description of these phases is provided as follows.

Investigation Phase

This is the first and one of the most important phases of the methodology. As depicted from the name, this phase deals with the analysis of software under consideration. In this phase the software is analyzed so as to bring out each of its details. Many approaches are used to bring out these hidden features like questionnaire, meetings, holding interviews, holding focus groups, etc. The compilation of the results of these different approaches helps in revealing all the features intended by the customer in software. Use case diagrams are one of the important tools used for showing the result of the proper analysis of the software's functionality in a graphical manner. It brings out many important details such as the intended users, their functionalities, interdependence of the functionalities of different users, etc. Figure 6 represents the investigation process in a graphical way.

Modeling Phase

This is the second phase of the proposed methodology that deals with the modeling of PIM. From the information collected in the investigation phase, the information regarding the aspects is separated from the core business requirements. Both the aspects and the core functionality are modeled in parallel. In this phase the corresponding UML diagrams viz. class diagram, state machine diagram, sequence diagram, etc., for the software are modeled. The modeling is done in such a way that the diagrams don't include any information related to a specific platform or a language. The class diagram depicts different classes, interfaces, enumerations related to the software. Classes compose of the attributes and the related functionality for that particular class. Sequence diagram, State machine diagrams are used to depict the flow of control in a scenario or for a particular system or for a whole system as a whole. After the modeling of PIM information regarding the cross cutting software features revealed is provided to the aspect modeling so as to generate effective aspects. The modeled aspects are stored in an aspect repository so that the archetype of the aspects can be used in future. The whole process of modeling phase is illustrated graphically in Figure 7.

Optimization Phase

This is the third phase of the methodology that deals with the optimization of the independent archetype created in previous step. The approach used for optimization of the archetype extracts the additional information required to perform the archetype transformation from the constraints that are embedded in the archetype (Karaulov & Strabykin, 2009).

This phase consists of two parts viz. analyzer and transformer. Analyzer provides useful additional information that is provided to the optimizer. The analyzer propagates the constraints iteratively over the archetype so as to associate with each action a set of associated constraints. For example, if parameter of any operation is defined as m: Integer with a constraint on the range of m, i.e., m ϵ [0,k] than if any action declares a variable x as twice of m than the associated constraint with the variable x is that x ϵ [0,2k].

The transformer operates on the input provided by the analyzer using a set of transformation descriptions. The description consists of two parts; patterns and constraints. Patterns are the entities that are matched against the user archetype and defined on a meta-level making them independent of the matched archetype. Constraints are defined over the patterns. For a successful pattern match the constraints related to the pattern must be satisfied. Matching process tries to find out a part of the archetype that is an instantiation of the meta-model pattern. If all the constraints are satisfied then the transformation operation is added to list of possible operations.

Figure 8 presents an internal view of the optimization phase. The PIM is passed as input to the analyzer that for categorization of the actions with constraints. Transformer takes as input the solution set or the categorization created by the analyzer along with the transformation descriptions and the PIM to give the optimized PIM.

Figure 5. Component identification process

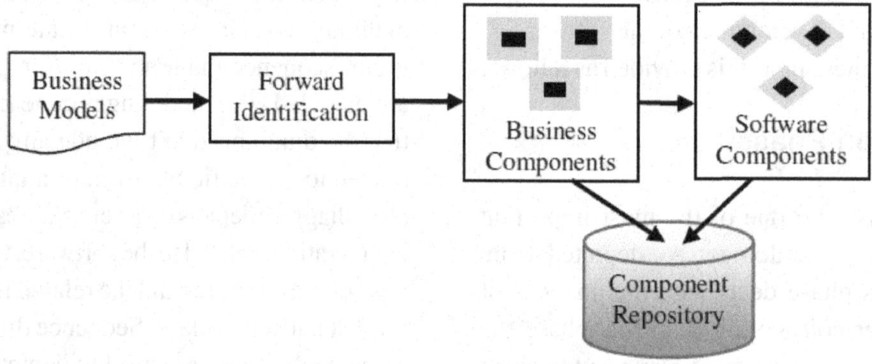

Figure 6. Investigation phase

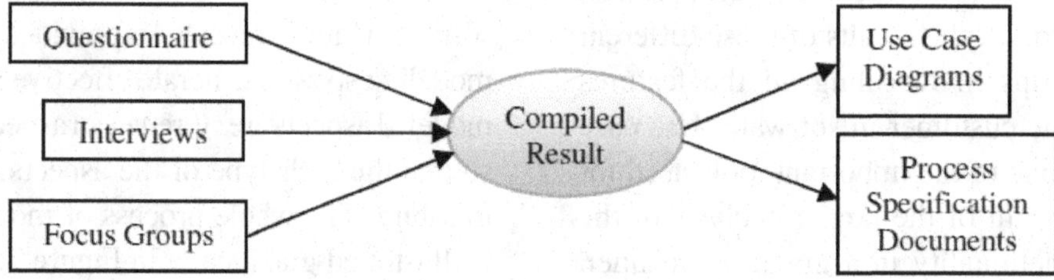

Figure 7. Modeling phase

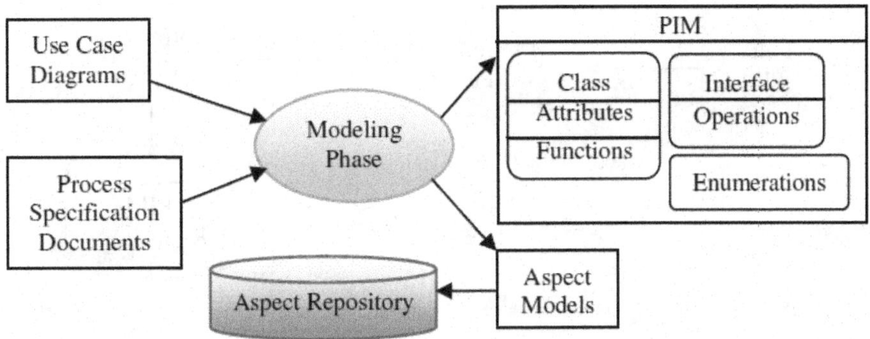

After the optimization, the PIM is stored in the PIM repository to facilitate the primary concept of MDA which is 'One Model Different Implementations'. Figure 9 represents the overall process of the optimization phase.

Component Identification Phase

This is the fourth phase of the methodology that deals with the identification of the reusable components in the software. The proposed identification technique makes use of the advantages of slicing and clustering techniques so as to identify components more clearly without any ambiguity. Slicing has been applied to full-fledged software till now but here it is applied on the models. This is followed by clustering of the slices into clusters.

In this approach after the designing of the PIM, the functional dependency graph (FDG) for the whole system is drawn. The graph can be drawn with ease as the entire model providing the entities and the interaction information of the whole system have already been modeled. A component that implements a specific service in the system is isolated from the whole system. The process starts from the top and continues to go downward, looking for the top level components that characterize the desired service. Once these functions are found, forward dependency slicing is applied taking the corresponding FDG node as the starting point. This produces slices of the archetype that are a part of a component and thereby have to be merged. Since a single forward dependency slice consists of all the program entities that are

Figure 8. Internal view of the optimization phase

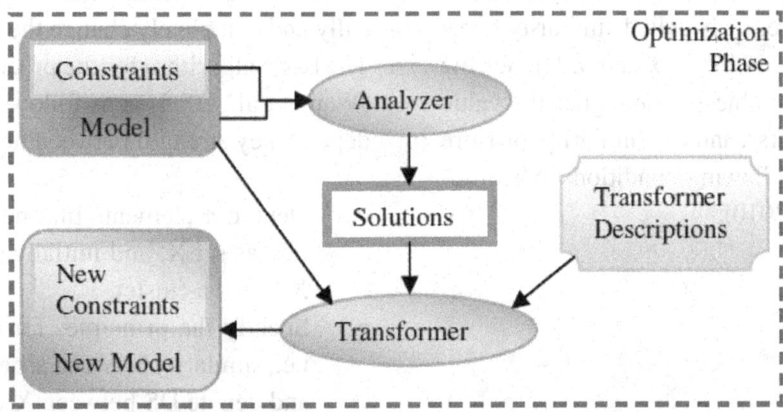

Figure 9. Optimization phase

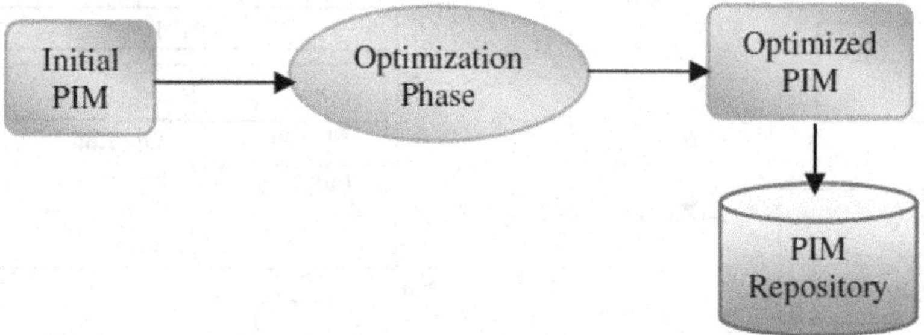

required for the proper operation of the service so by merging all the forward dependency slices corresponding to a particular service a component can be created. This process leads to the identification of a new component which, besides being reusable in other contexts, will typically be part of the (modular) reconstruction of the original legacy system.

But we only use the slicing technique to perform forward slices. The combination of these slices into clusters is performed using clustering technique which is as follows. Slicing technique produced the slices of the whole software which would be joined by the clustering algorithm based on the similarity between the objects. This makes use of a quantitative measure among vectors that is arranged in a matrix called proximity matrix. Two types of quantitative measures (Shahmohammadia, Jalilia, & Hasheminejada, 2010) are Similarity Measures, and Dissimilarity Measures. The quantitative measure used here is similarity measures. These are used to find similar pairs of objects in software. s_{xy} is called similarity coefficient between two objects x and y. Higher the similarity between objects, the higher the value of s_{xy}. For all objects x and y, a similarity measure must satisfy the following conditions (Shahmohammadia et al., 2010):

- $0 \leq s_{xy} \leq 1$
- $s_{xx} = 1$
- $s_{xy} = s_{yx}$

Slices are organized in a hierarchical structure according to the proximity matrix which in this case is similarity measure. In the hierarchical structure root represent the whole system and the leaf node represents objects. Non-leaf nodes represent the extent to which these objects are similar to each other. To combine the similar objects into a cluster merge operations are performed in a bottom-up fashion. Bottom-up methodology treats each module as a singleton cluster at the outset and then successively merge (or agglomerate) pairs of clusters until all clusters have been merged into a single cluster that represents the software as a whole. In this the concept of complete-link clustering or complete-linkage clustering is used. This states that the similarity of two clusters is the similarity of their most dissimilar members. Since the complete-link merge criterion is non-local, the entire structure of the clustering can influence the merge decisions. A single member of the module far from the center can increase diameters of candidate merge clusters dramatically and completely change the final clustering. The basic algorithm for the process of clustering (Wang et al., 2005) is as follows. DS represents dependency strength between nodes

- Denote *n* elements that need to be classified as set X, and initially each element in X forms a cluster.
- Specify the principles for calculating DS, i.e., similarity between arbitrary two nodes, and denote DS between X_i and X_j as R_{ij}.

- Calculate DS between arbitrary two nodes in X and obtain the DS matrix D of n elements.
- Choose a sound "Minimum DS" R_{min} as the judgment principle for merge two elements into one cluster.
- According to each R_{ij} in D, execute the following clustering process:
    - (Valve value) If $R_ij \geq R_{min}$, then set X_i and X_j into one cluster.
    - (Transitivity) If X_i and X_j, X_i and X_k belong to the same cluster respectively, then merge X_i, X_j, X_k into one cluster.
- Map elements in each cluster together into a business component.

Figure 10 represents the hybrid process of component identification. After the successful identification of components and their clustering the components are stored in the reusable components repository that can be used within the organization in other projects or can be sold off to other organizations for the development of the projects.

Artifact Generation Phase

This is the fifth phase of the methodology. In this phase the code artifacts are generated for the specific platforms by transforming the independent archetype developed in the modeling phase into platform specific models one for each of the desired language. These platform/language specific models are then further transformed to produce the code artifacts for the specific languages. The translation of PIM to PSM is carried out by a model translator that either makes use of the OMG's predefined mapping rules or the user defined mapping rules.

The basic condition of writing the transformation rules is that elements in the source should be related to elements in the target. So we have to define for each and every element of PIM an element in PSM. The transformation rules for performing this are written as underlying (Ruscio, Cicchetti, & Salle, 2007).

- For each class named <class Name> in the PIM there is a class named <class Name> in the PSM.
- For each public attribute named <attribute Name>: <Type> of class <class Name> in the PIM there is a public attribute with the same name: <attribute Name>: <Type> in the PSM.

Since the computers won't understand this these rules are represented with the help of XML. Every transformation rule should mandatorily include some of the rules. These are listed in Table 2 (Bhatti & Malik, 2009).

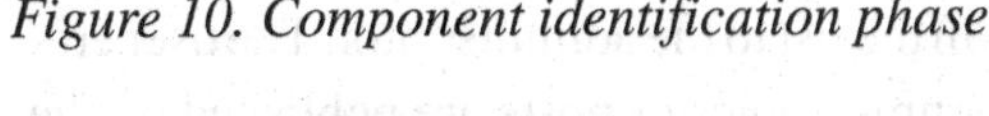

Figure 10. Component identification phase

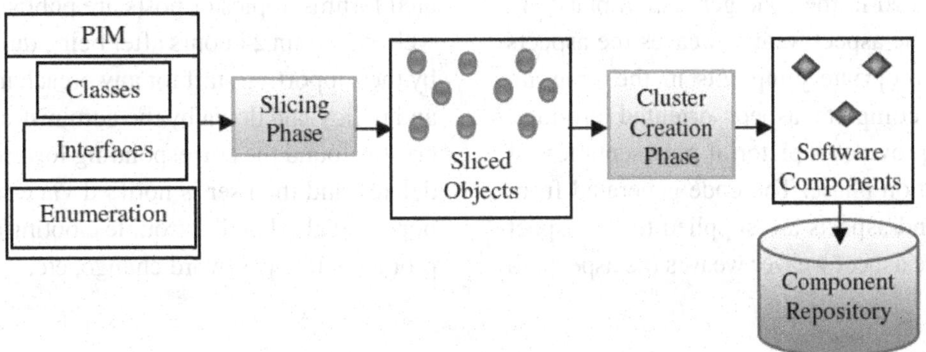

Table 2. Mandatory transformation rules

Rules	Description
Source Language	<Source Language> UML </Source Language>
Target Language	<Target Language> SQL </Target Language>
Parameters	<Params><SetterPrefix>Set</SetterPrefix> <GetterPrefix>Get</GetterPrefix></Params>
NamedSource Language Elements	<Source><class>Class</class> <attribute>Attribute</attribute> </Source>
NamedTarget Language Elements	<Target><table>Table</table> <column>Column</column> <fkey>ForeignKey</fkey></Target>
SourceLanguage Condition	Conditions that must prevail in the source model for the application of these transformation rule
TargetLanguage Condition	Conditions that must hold in the target model for this transformation rule to apply.
Mapping Rules	<Mapping> <c>t</c> <a>c</a> </Mapping>

In PSM the platform specific information is incorporated. From this PSM the code artifacts are generated by the code generator that makes use of the template based approach to generate the code artifacts. It takes as input the PSM along with the OMG's predefined templates for the generation of the artifacts. The aspect code generator module generated the code for the aspect from the aspect models.

Figure 11 shows the diagrammatic representation of the code generation process for some of the aspects, e.g., transaction aspect and security aspect. Figure 12 shows the diagrammatic representation of the artifact generation phase from the PSM.

Integration Phase

This is the last phase of the methodology. The code generated in the code generation phase. In this phase the aspect weaver weaves the aspects to their appropriate joinpoints in the program to give a complete aspect oriented product. Figure 13 provides a pictorial representation of the integration phase. The code generated from the PSM and aspects are supplied to the aspect weaver. The aspect weaver weaves the aspects to their corresponding joinpoints. The information about the location of weaving is interpreted from the pointcuts defined in each of the aspect. The output is the final integrated product.

CASE STUDY EFFECTUATION: ONLINE FORUMS

The significance of the proposed work is shown by effectuation of an online forum website case study.

Case Study Overview

In this scenario the website allows its users to create forums, topics, posts, etc., related to the different specified domains by the administrator. User can give suggestions of other domains that they want to add in the list to the administrator. The user created forums, topics or posts are published on the website within 24 hours after being duly checked by the supporting staff for any breach in the rules and policy laid down by the administrator. If any error is found the corresponding forum or post is deleted and the user is notified via e-mail. Support Staff also handles troubleshooting of various problems like password change, etc.

Figure 11. Aspect code generation process

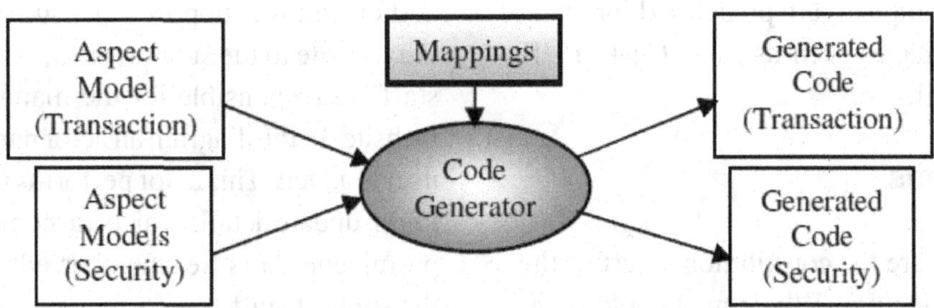

Figure 12. Artifact generation phase

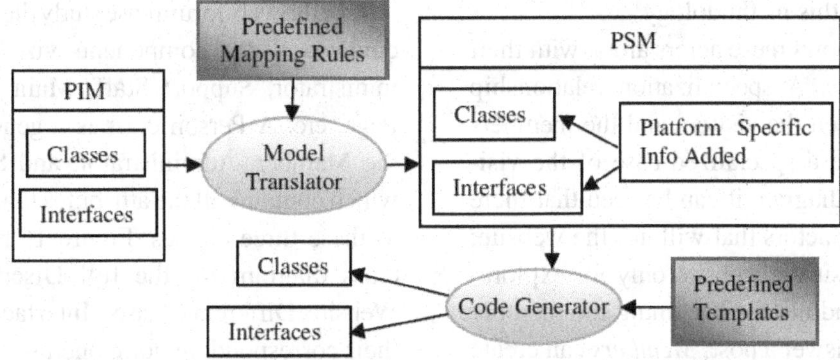

Figure 13. Artifact generation phase

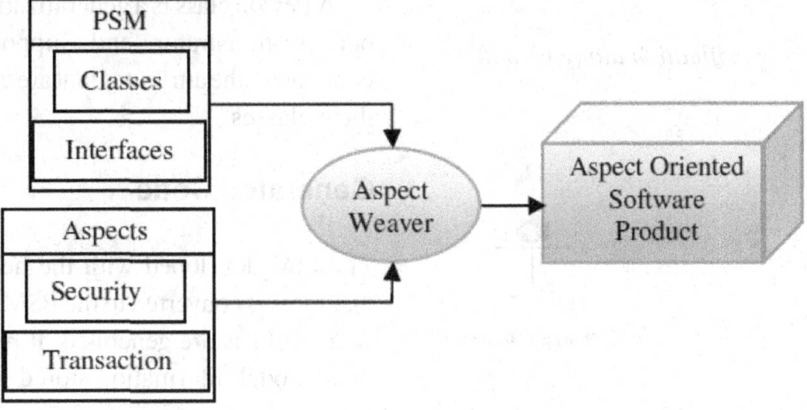

Tool Overview

For the development of the UML diagrams of the case study described above *Poseidon for UML professional edition 6.0* is used as the base tool. One of the most valuable features of Poseidon for UML and the basis for using it in the case study is its code skeleton generation technology (Boger, Graham, & Köster, 2011). This feature makes use of the predefined templates. The syntax of the resultant model depends on the corresponding template. The templates are predefined for many high level languages such as Java, C++, PHP, XML and HTML.

UML Diagrams

UML diagrams are the constitutional part of the proposed methodology. Whole methodology revolves around these UML diagrams as the final code artifacts are generated from these diagrams. Use-cases and the class diagrams are the main components of this methodology.

Figure 14 shows these actors along with their prescribed roles. A specialization relationship is shown between the visitors and the members as members are a specialized case of the visitors. From the diagram it can be seen that there are mainly four actors that will use the website: *Visitors* that visit the website only for exploration purpose and not for becoming the member or publish or answer a post; *Members* can create new forums/topics/posts, delete forums/topics/posts, give feedback, etc.; *Administrators* define the policy and rules that are to be followed, accept or reject any visitors membership request, add or remove support staff, suggest changes in the website to the support staff, etc.; and *Support* staff are responsible for the maintenance of the website. In the diagram an actor named as generic user is added. This actor performs the actions viz. login, update details which are common for all the prominent actors, i.e., member, administrator, and the support staff.

Figure 14. Actors' specification along with their roles

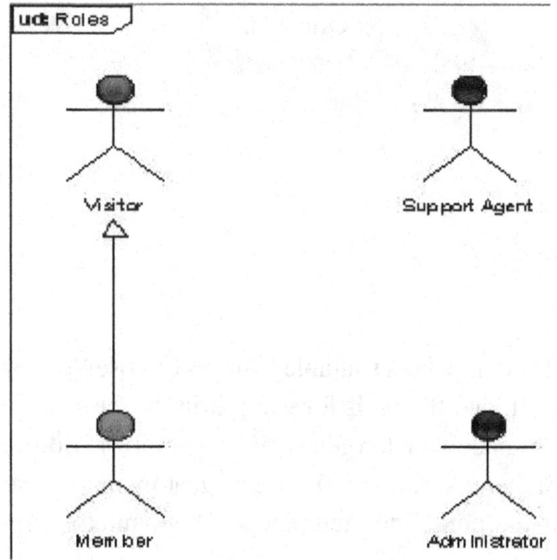

The use-case diagram depicting the functions that can be performed by the various actors is shown in Figure 15.

For the web-forum case study the class diagram contains all the components viz. Member, Administrator, Support Staff, Main Page, Forum Page, etc. A Person class is a generalization of the Member, Administrator, and Support Staff which contains all the attributes that are common to these three classes. Figure 16 represents the class diagram for the full Discussion-Forum Website. Different Classes, Interfaces are put into their corresponding components. These components are then assembled together with the help of associations, dependencies to give a full-fledged representation of the Website.

A Person class is a generalization of the Member, Administrator, and Support Staff which contains all the attributes that are common to these three classes.

Generated Code

The PIM developed with the help of the UML diagrams is converted to the PSM from which the code artifacts are generated. It makes use of the meta-model information stored in the XMI file. Since our case study is an online application thus the code artifact presented here is in Java and PHP as both of these languages are widely used for developing websites like the one considered in this paper. Figures 17 and 18 show the code generated from the models in Java and PHP respectively for the administrator class.

Figure 15. Use-case for the online web-forum website

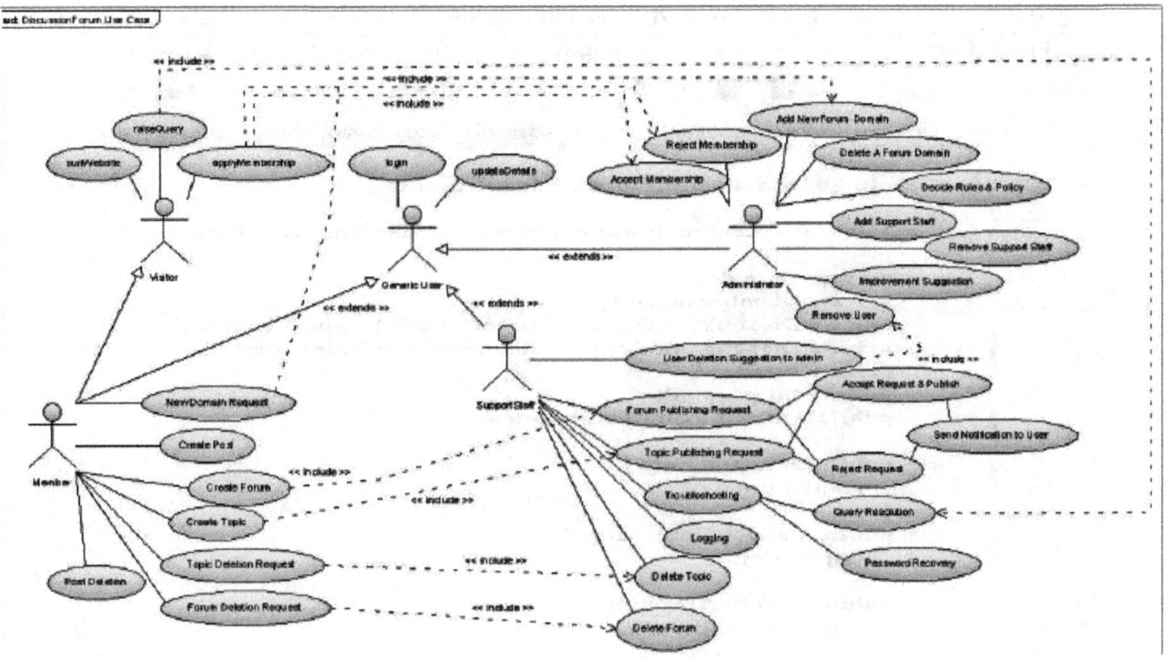

Figure 16. Class diagram for the online web-forum website

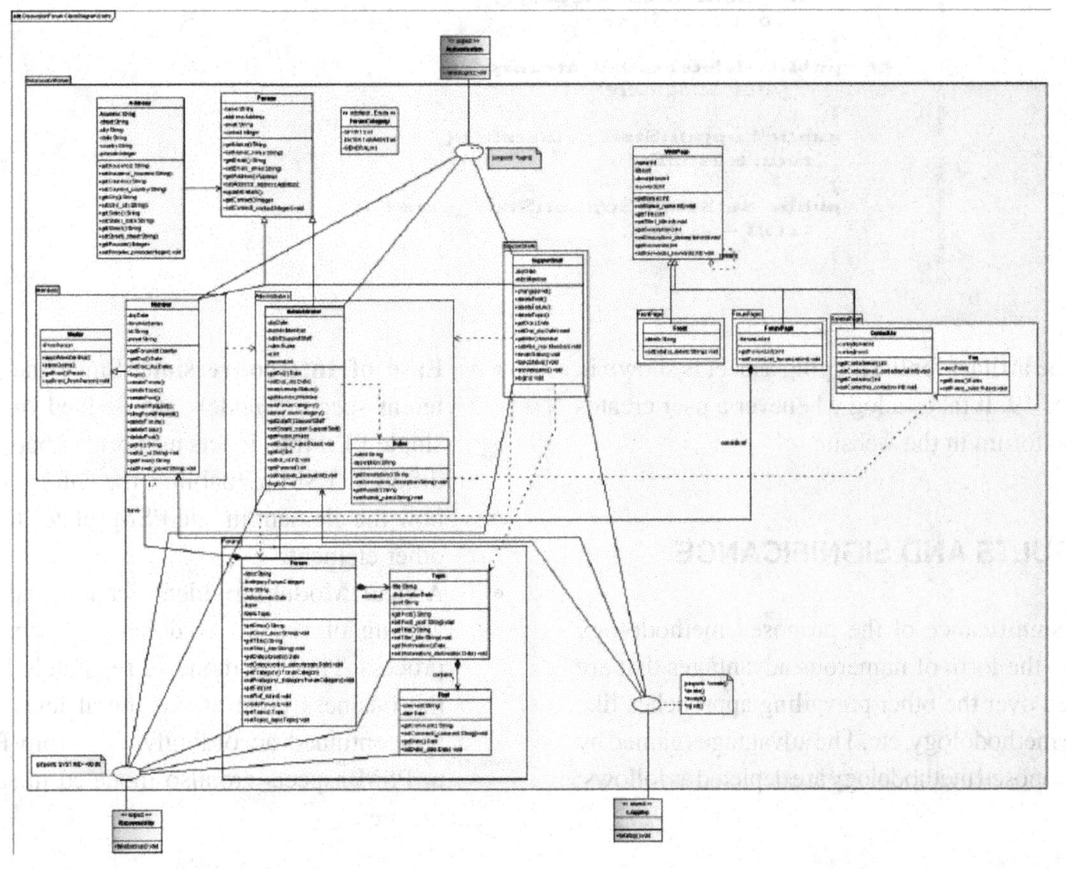

Figure 17. Code artifact for the administrator class in Java

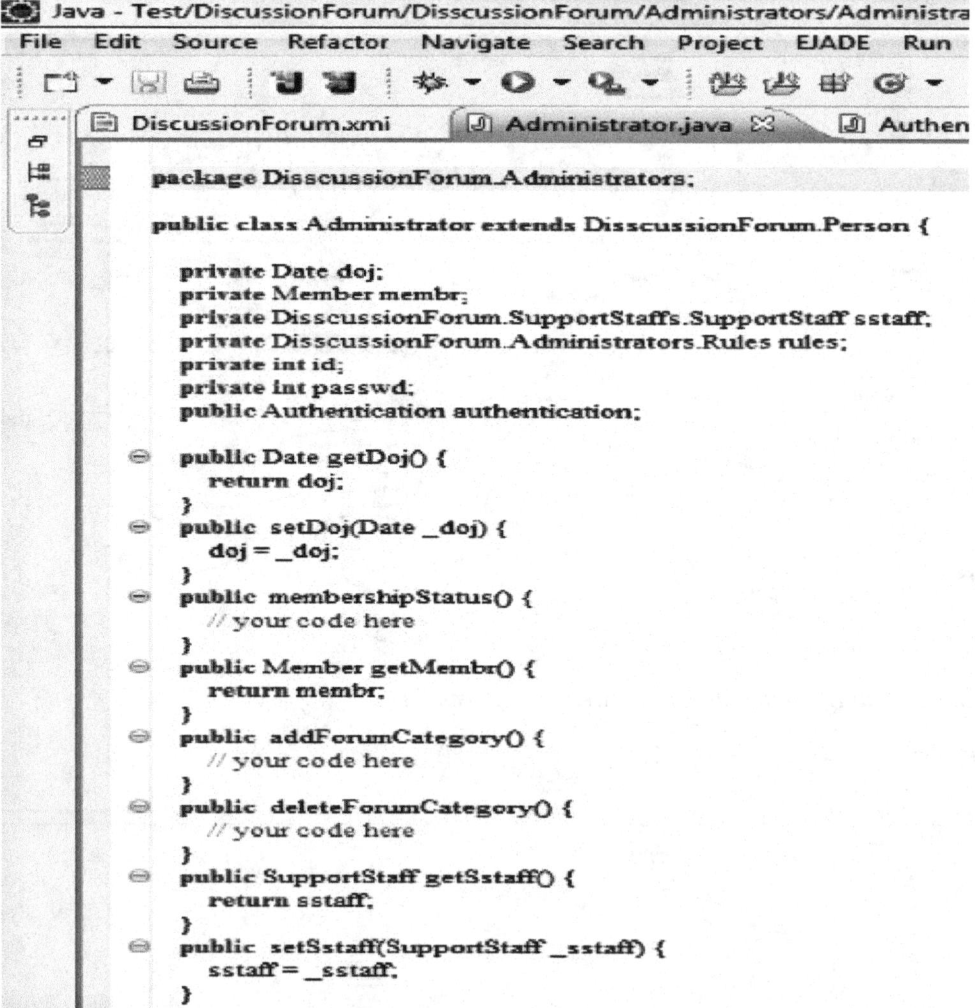


```
package DisscussionForum.Administrators;

public class Administrator extends DisscussionForum.Person {

   private Date doj;
   private Member membr;
   private DisscussionForum.SupportStaffs.SupportStaff sstaff;
   private DisscussionForum.Administrators.Rules rules;
   private int id;
   private int passwd;
   public Authentication authentication;

   public Date getDoj() {
      return doj;
   }
   public setDoj(Date _doj) {
      doj = _doj;
   }
   public membershipStatus() {
      // your code here
   }
   public Member getMembr() {
      return membr;
   }
   public addForumCategory() {
      // your code here
   }
   public deleteForumCategory() {
      // your code here
   }
   public SupportStaff getSstaff() {
      return sstaff;
   }
   public setSstaff(SupportStaff _sstaff) {
      sstaff = _sstaff;
   }
```

The artifact for the logging aspect is shown in Figure 19. It takes a log whenever a user creates a new forum in the website.

RESULTS AND SIGNIFICANCE

The significance of the proposed methodology lies in the form of numerous advantages that are gained over the other prevailing approaches like agile methodology, etc. The advantages gained by the proposed methodology are depicted as follows:

- **Ease of Interconversion:** Since the different specific models are derived from a single PIM thus it acts as a bridge between different PSM's enabling the information how the element in one PSM relates to the other element.
- **Aspect Modeling:** Identification and designing of aspects is done as a separate process. They are modeled separately from the business code at the initial level and are continued accordingly, i.e., from PIM to PSM aspects are also modeled in same manner.

Figure 18. Code artifact for the administrator class in PHP

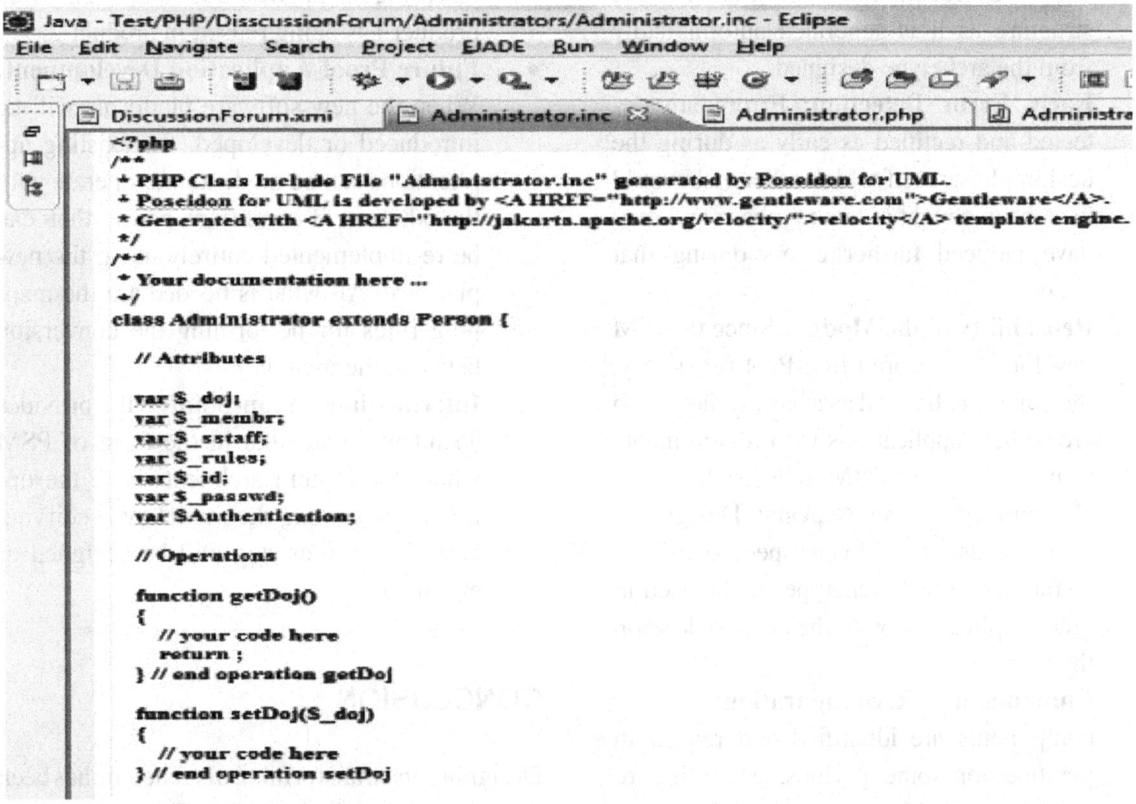

```
Java - Test/PHP/DisscussionForum/Administrators/Administrator.inc - Eclipse
File Edit Navigate Search Project EJADE Run Window Help
DiscussionForum.xmi   Administrator.inc   Administrator.php   Administra

<?php
/**
 * PHP Class Include File "Administrator.inc" generated by Poseidon for UML.
 * Poseidon for UML is developed by <A HREF="http://www.gentleware.com">Gentleware</A>.
 * Generated with <A HREF="http://jakarta.apache.org/velocity/">velocity</A> template engine.
 */
/**
 * Your documentation here ...
 */
class Administrator extends Person {

  // Attributes

  var $_doj;
  var $_membr;
  var $_sstaff;
  var $_rules;
  var $_id;
  var $_passwd;
  var $Authentication;

  // Operations

  function getDoj()
  {
    // your code here
    return ;
  } // end operation getDoj

  function setDoj($_doj)
  {
    // your code here
  } // end operation setDoj
```

Figure 19. Logging aspect

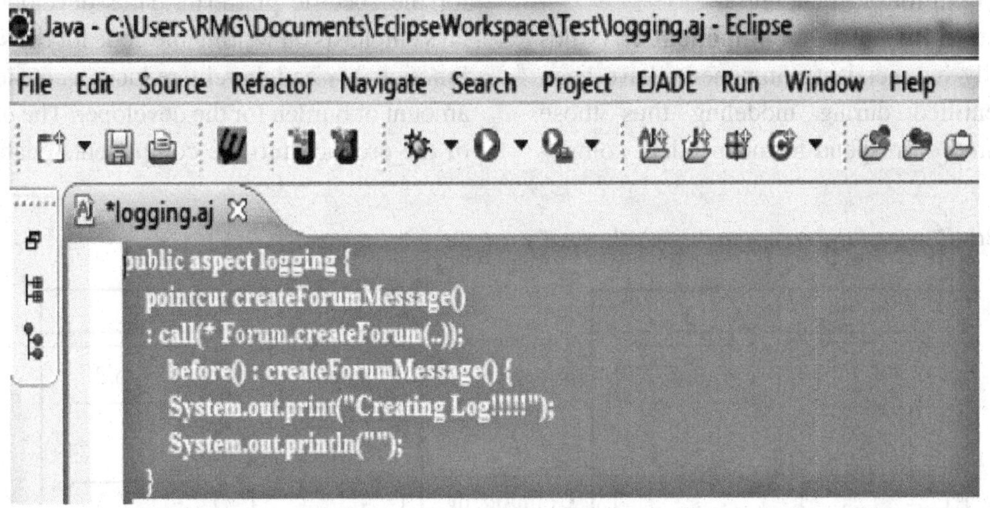
Java - C:\Users\RMG\Documents\EclipseWorkspace\Test\logging.aj - Eclipse
File Edit Source Refactor Navigate Search Project EJADE Run Window Help
*logging.aj
public aspect logging {
pointcut createForumMessage()
: call(* Forum.createForum(..));
before() : createForumMessage() {
System.out.print("Creating Log!!!!!");
System.out.println("");
}

- **Developer Overhead Reduction:** Developers have to emphasize on the coding of the functionality and not he basic structure as it is generated automatically from the archetype designed.
- **Early Error Detection:** Errors are detected and rectified as early as during the design phase itself which otherwise would have been caught at testing phase and may have induced further errors during that coarse.
- **Reusability of the Models:** Since the PIM developed are stored in a PIM repository, thus they can be used as a base archetype to create new applications with requirements same as that of the PIM to be used.
- **Reusability of the Aspects:** Design aspects are also stored in an aspect repository so that the aspect archetype can be used in other applications with the need to develop them.
- **Component Reconfiguration:** After components are identified and reused in practice for some periods, according to the accumulated reuse data, deficiencies in component design are analyzed, then the structure and the semantics of these components are re-designed to make them more fit for practical reuse.
- **Reusability of the Components:** As initially independent components have been identified during modeling thus those would correspond to independent components in coding that can be reused in other products of similar type. This is represented in Figure 20 where a component from product 1 is being reused in product 2.
- **Future Proof Application Development:** When the new software platforms will be introduced or developed, the existing applications can be made to interoperate with the others or if conditions permit than can be re-implemented entirely using the new platform. All what is needed are the mapping rules for performing the conversion between the models.
- **Intermediate Stop-point:** It provides an intermediate step in the form of PSM where the system architects have the option of enhancing the model by specifying how a particular step will be designed or executed.

CONCLUSION

Designing and transforming of archetype has been the core functionality of MDA. The methodology proposed integrates the concept of aspects and software reuse in MDA. Models are developed and later transformed to generate the code artifacts for the specific platform. Thus developer only lays emphasis on writing the code for the specific functionality and thereby reduces a considerable amount of burden for the developer. The division of the product into the components enables the

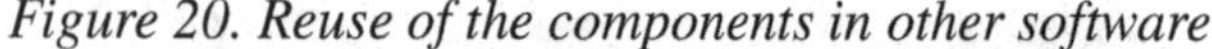
Figure 20. Reuse of the components in other software

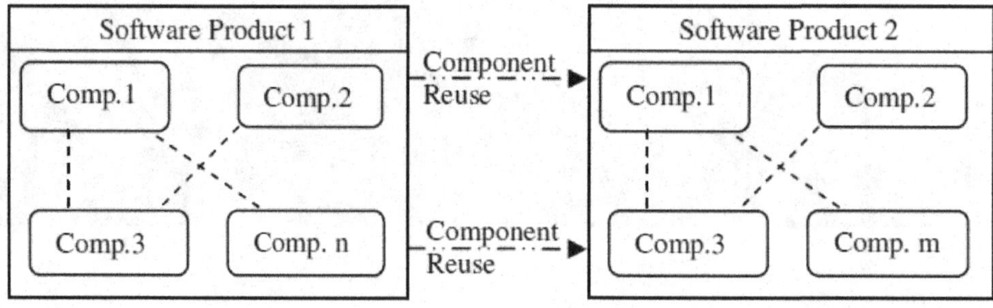

concept of software reuse. Along with reuse of the components the PIM developed can be reused in other products of same specification and structure. Aspects are modeled separately from the business logic thereby eliminating the problem of scattering and tangling. Thus the major concepts in software development viz. reusability and aspects get incorporated into the MDA approach to make it more robust in nature.

REFERENCES

Akehurst, D. H., & Kent, S. (2002). A Relational Approach to Defining Transformations in a Metamodel. In *Proceedings of the Unified Modeling Language 5th International Conference (UML-02)*, Dresden, Germany (LNCS 2460, pp. 243-258).

Aßmann, U. (2007, February 7). Model Driven Architecture (MDA) and Component-Based Software Development (CBSD). *Xootic Magazine*, pp. 5-7.

Balasubramanian, D., Narayanan, A., van Buskirk, C., & Karsai, G. (2006). The Graph Rewriting and Transformation Language: GReAT. *Electronic Communications of the EASST*, *1*, 1–8.

Bast, W., Kleppe, A., & Warmer, J. (2004). *MDA Explained: The Model Driven Architecture: Practice and Promise*. Reading, MA: Addison-Wesley.

Bhatti, S. N., & Malik, A. M. (2009). An XML-Based Framework for Bidirectional Transformation in Model-Driven Architecture (MDA). *SIGSOFT Software Engineering Notes, 34*(3).

Boger, M., Graham, E., & Köster, M. (2011). *Poseidon for UML*. Retrieved October 9, 2011, from http://www.gentleware.com/fileadmin/media/pdfs/userguides/PoseidonUsersGuide.pdf

Cai, X., Lyu, M. R., Wong, K.-F., & Ko, R. (2000). Component-Based Software Engineering: Technologies, Development Frameworks, and Quality Assurance Schemes. In *Proceedings of the 7th IEEE Asia-Pacific Software Engineering Conference* (pp. 372-379).

Cheesman, J., & Daniels, J. (2001). *UML Components. A Simple Process for Specifying Component-Based Software*. Reading, MA: Addison-Wesley.

Fuentes-Fernández, L., & Vallecillo-Moreno, A. (2004). An Introduction to UML Profiles. *Journal of Informatics Professional*, *5*(2), 6–13.

Höppner, F., Klawonn, F., & Kruse, R. (1999). *Fuzzy Cluster Analysis: Methods for Classification, Data Analysis, and Image Recognition*. New York, NY: Wiley.

IEEE-SA Standards Board. (2000). *IEEE Recommended Practice for Architectural Description of Software-Intensive Systems (IEEE 1471-2000)*. Washington, DC: IEEE Computer Society.

Jacobson, I. (2003). *Case for Aspects - Part I & II* (pp. 32–37). Software Development Magazine.

Jacobson, I., Christerson, M., Jonsson, P., & Övergaard, G. (1992). *Object-Oriented Engineering*. Reading, MA: Addison-Wesley.

Jilani, A. A. A., Usman, M., & Halim, Z. (2010). Model Transformations in Model Driven Architecture. *Universal Journal of Computer Science and Engineering Technology*, *1*(1), 50–54.

Jin, X. (2006). *Applying Model Driven approach to Model Role Based Access Control System*. Unpublished master's thesis, University of Ottawa, Ottawa, ON, Canada.

Karaulov, A., & Strabykin, A. (2009). Constraint-based Optimizations of Executable UML Models. In *Proceedings of the 3rd Spring/Summer Young Researchers' Colloquium on Software Engineering*.

Kulkarni, V., & Reddy, S. (2003). Separation of Concerns in Model driven Development. *IEEE Software*, *20*, 64–69. doi:10.1109/MS.2003.1231154

Laddad, R. (2009). *AspectJ in Action* (2nd ed.). Shelter Island, NY: Manning Publications.

Lung, C. H., Zaman, M., & Nandi, A. (2004). Applications of Clustering Techniques to Software Partitioning, Recovery and Restructuring. *Journal of Systems and Software*, *73*, 227–244. doi:10.1016/S0164-1212(03)00234-6

Meng, F.-C., Zhan, D.-C., & Xu, X. (2005). Business Component Identification of Enterprise Information System: A hierarchical clustering method. In *Proceedings of the 2005 IEEE International Conference on e-Business Engineering* (pp. 473-480).

Mens, T., Van Eetvelde, N., Demeyer, S., & Janssens, D. (2005). Formalizing refactoring with graph transformations. *International Journal on Software Tools for Technology Transfer*, *17*, 247–276.

Object Management Group (OMG). (2011). *MDA Guide Version 1.0.1*. Retrieved October 9, 2011, from http://www.omg.org/mda/

Pour, G. (1998). Moving toward Component-Based Software Development Approach. In *Proceedings of the IEEE Conference on Technology of Object-Oriented Languages and Systems* (pp. 296-300).

Reina, A. M., Toress, J., & Toro, M. (2004). Towards developing generic solutions with aspects. In *Proceedings of the Workshop in Aspect Oriented Modeling in Conjunction with the UML 2004 Conference.*

Rodrigues, N. F., & Barbosa, L. S. (2005). Component Identification through Program Slicing. In *Proceedings of the Formal Aspects of Component Software Conference (FACS 2005)* (pp. 291-304).

Ruscio, D., Cicchetti, A., & Salle, A. (2007). Software customization in model driven development of web applications. In *Proceedings of the ACM Symposium on Applied Computing* (pp. 1025-1030).

Shahmohammadia, G. R., Jalilia, S., & Hasheminejada, S. M. H. (2010). Identification of System Software Components Using Clustering Approach. *Journal of Object Technology*, *9*(6), 77–98. doi:10.5381/jot.2010.9.6.a4

Simmonds, D. M. (2008). Aspect-oriented Approaches to Model Driven Engineering. In *Proceedings of the International Conference on Software Research and Practice*, Las Vegas, NV.

Simmonds, D. M., Reddy, Y. R., Song, E., & Grant, E. (2009). A Comparison of Aspect-Oriented Approaches to Model Driven Engineering. In *Proceedings of the Conference on Software Engineering Research and Practice* (pp. 327-333).

Simmonds, D. M., Solberg, A., Reddy, R., France, R., & Ghosh, S. (2005). An Aspect Oriented Model Driven Framework. In *Proceedings of the 9th IEEE International EDOC Enterprise Computing Conference* (pp. 119-130)

Wang, Z., Xu, X., & Zhan, D. (2005). A Survey of Business Component Identification Methods and Related Techniques. *International Journal of Information Technology*, *2*, 229–238.

Wu, Y., & Offutt, J. (2003). Maintaining Evolving Component-Based Software with UML. In *Proceedings of the 7th IEEE European Conference on Software Maintenance and Reengineering* (pp. 133-142).

Xu, W., Yin, B. L., & Li, Z. Y. (2003). Research on the business component design of enterprise information system. *Journal of Software*, *14*(7), 1213–1220.

Zhang, J., Chen, Y., Li, H., & Liu, G. (2009). Research on Aspect-Oriented Modeling in the Framework of MDA. In *Proceedings of the 2nd IEEE International Conference on Computer Science and Information Technology* (pp. 108-111).

This work was previously published in the Journal of Information Technology Research, Volume 4, Issue 3, edited by Mehdi Khosrow-Pour, pp. 29-49, copyright 2011 by IGI Publishing (an imprint of IGI Global).

Chapter 14
Software Developers in India and Norway:
Professional or National Cultures?

Gheorghita Ghinea
Brunel University, UK, & Norwegian School of Information Technology, Norway

Bendik Bygstad
Norwegian School of Information Technology, Norway

Manoranjan Satpathy
Abo Akademi University, Finland

ABSTRACT

In this paper, the authors investigate the professional practices of software developers from two different cultures—Norway and India. The authors examine if systematic differences exist between Norwegian and Indian software developers in their professional practice. Using Hofstede's cultural dimensions, the authors expected to find cultural differences between the two groups of professionals. Building on a survey among software developers in the two countries, the authors have the following conclusions. Firstly, the main finding is that there are surprisingly few differences between the two groups, giving support to the view of a common professional culture. Secondly, the few differences that are observed cannot easily be explained by Hofstede's cultural dimensions.

INTRODUCTION

The discipline of software development is now over 40 years old, and practitioners (and researchers) are working in almost every country in the world. An interesting question is whether a common professional culture has emerged among software practitioners, or whether national cultures are still dominant. This issue has mainly been investigated in the context of distributed software E development projects, with participants from several countries (Olson & Olson, 2003; Gibbs, 2009). Usually, building on Hofstede's (2001) dimensions, the

DOI: 10.4018/978-1-4666-3625-5.ch014

findings have emphasized the need to understand and address national cultural differences (Dafoulas & Macaulay, 2001; Walsham, 2001).

However, some researchers also suggest that professional culture tends to override national differences in many respects (Castells, 1996; Friedman, 2005). Professional culture rests on a common education, a shared skill and problem solving repository, and often also a shared value system. Thus, belonging to a profession does not only provide the individual with tools and techniques, but it also constitutes a significant part of the person's identity, as most clients of doctors and lawyers may testify.

Does the same apply to software professionals? Constantine (1995) proposed that software professionals belong to a global computer subculture that is stronger than other professional cultures. In some ways, this view is contradicted by the many studies that emphasize the national culture aspect. For example, in a large study of Norwegian and Japanese computer professionals, it was found that the cultural differences between the two groups were significant, both in their general cultural orientations and their professional attitudes (Andersen, 2002). It is probably hard to produce conclusive evidence on this issue, but in the context of an increasingly global IT industry it is important to shed some more light on this question, which is the objective of this paper.

Our approach differs from most other studies, in that we do not investigate attitudes, but practices. We do this by comparing the practices of software professionals in two very different national cultures, namely India and Norway. Our research question is:

- Are there systematic differences between Norwegian and Indian software developers in their professional practice?

The two aspects of professional practice that we have chosen to investigate are system development methods and usability, and the relationship between them. They were selected because they are key issues for software developers, and they are also issues where cultural differences are potentially very influential.

We proceed by reviewing relevant literature on culture and software development practices. In the following section, we present our method, which was a web based survey. We then present our findings, and discuss them, before we offer conclusions and point to further research in the last section.

REVIEW

With the advent of globalization, software development is being undertaken by teams hailing from different contexts, in terms of both geography and culture. It therefore comes as no surprise that there is an increasing amount of research exploring the impact of these two contextual dimensions on Software Development Methods (SDMs). The need for cross-cultural sensitivity, good communication strategies, semantic loss, coordination, differences in work-style and power distribution, are all issues that have been highlighted in these respects (Barthelmess, 2003; Kersten, Kersten, & Rakowski, 2002; Layman, Williams, Damian, & Bures, 2006; MacGregor, Hsieh, & Kruchten, 2005; Mishra & Mishra, 2011; Niazi, Babar, & Verner, 2010; Taxen, 2006; Walsham, 2001).

Culture is a multi-dimensional construct, which is hard to measure. Although Hofstede's categories have been criticized, they remain the most accepted dimensions of national culture. The five dimensions are (Hofstede, 2001):

- **Low vs. high power distance:** This dimension measures how much the less powerful members of institutions and organizations expect and accept that power is distributed unequally.
- **Individualism vs. collectivism:** This dimension measures how much members of

the culture define themselves apart from their group memberships

- **Masculinity vs. femininity:** This dimension measures the value placed on traditionally male or female values (as understood in most Western cultures).
- **Low vs. high uncertainty avoidance:** This dimension measures how much members of a society attempt to cope with anxiety by minimizing uncertainty.
- **Long vs. short term orientation:** This dimension describes a society's "time horizon," or the importance attached to the future versus the past and present.mpt to cope with anxiety by minimizing uncertainty.

In work related to ours, Borchers (2003) analyses two global development projects spread across Japan, India and the United States. He reports that whilst Indian team members were likely to fix each other's software bugs, U.S.-based teams only did so if the bug was specifically assigned to them; he then posits that an explanation might lie in the fact that Indian culture is more collectivist, whilst U.S. culture is more individualistic. Anecdotal evidence from another study also suggests that Japanese software developers are more likely to report bugs late to team colleagues in other countries – this, as they first tend to try and de-bug the problem locally and, if this is not possible, then review any communication to be transmitted to external partners so that it does not sound abrupt or rude (MacGregor et al., 2005). In related work, Kankanhalli, Tan, Wei, and Holmes (2004) explore the impact of cross-cultural differences on information systems (IS) developer values in Singapore and the U.S. Based on a total of 211 responses (115 from Singapore and 96 from the U.S.). Results showed that individualism-collectivism and masculinity-femininity had statistically significant impact on the values of IS developers.

In an interesting study in 2005 Phongpaibul and Boehm investigated why modern software process improvement initiatives did not succeed in Thailand (Phongpaibul & Boehm, 2005). Their results showed clearly that the reason was cultural differences. For example, the low adoption rate in Thailand of the CMM framework was explained this way: CMM is a methodology which is characterized by the individual/masculine/short-term U.S. culture. It is resisted by the more collective/feminine/long-term Thai culture.

Recently, traditional SDMs are progressively being replaced by so-called *agile* SDMs, with Extreme Programming (XP) probably being the most popular (Beck, 2000). Consequently, there is a growing body of research which has examined the impact of global software development on agile SDMs, in general, and XP, in particular. Of these, we mention Hazzan and Dubinsky's (2005) study which explored connections between national culture and the culture inspired by SDMs. Focusing on the success of XP in the context of the Israeli hi-tech software industry, they propose a model to show if an SDM is suited to a national culture. This model, centred around the concept of 'tightness' – the degree to which a national culture or an SDM inspires strict and ordered habits – has five axes: project plan, procedures and standards, responsibility and accountability, time estimation, and need satisfaction.

Interesting related work was also done by Livermore (2008), whose research explored factors which impact the implementation of agile SDMs. 112 responses were received to an online survey sent to software developers worldwide. Although the distribution of the respondents' countries/cultures is not given in the paper, he identifies four management oriented factors which impact the implementation of an agile SDM (methodology training, active management involvement and support, access to external resources, company size). Indeed, the identification of success factors in the adoption of agile SDMs seems to be a theme of recent research (Bosch & Bosch-Sijtsema, 2010; Misra, Kumar, & Kumar, 2009).

Indeed, agile software engineering frameworks, such as XP (Beck, 2000) and Scrum

(Schwaber, 2004) claim to have a strong focus on usability. Both XP and Scrum recommend very close interaction between users and developers, and also include continuous usability testing as a core practice. In work related to the one reported in this paper, Jokela and Abrahamsson (2004) explored, in the confines of a software project, the degree to which XP facilitates the development of usable software, with findings revealing that XP does a rather poor job in this respect; however, this is not an exclusive characteristic of XP, as the tension between usability and SDM in practice is well noted (Boivie, Aborg, Persson, & Lofberg, 2003; Boivie, Gulliksen, & Goransson, 2006; Bygstad, Ghinea, & Brevik, 2008; Iivari, 2006). National culture, was not a dimension considered here; however, neither was it in Salo and Abrahamsson's (2008) work which surveyed the use (and success) of XP and Scrum methods in 35 projects from 13 software organisations of different sizes hailing from a eight European countries (Belgium, Bulgaria, Finland, France, Italy, Netherlands, Slovenia, Spain). Whilst one might argue that all respondents came from European countries and therefore share the same cultural values, a West-East dimension could certainly have been explored.

The impact of organizational culture on user involvement/representation in software development was investigated by Iivari (2006). In related work, Iivari and Husman (2007) explored, in an excellent article, the enabling organizational culture factors behind the deployment of SDMs - in a single country (South Africa). Based on survey responses from IT managers (73 organizations) and software developers (234 developers from 71 organisations) the broad conclusion of the study was that the hierarchical culture seems to be the most benign environment for SDM deployment; at the other extreme lies the rational culture, whilst developmental culture and group culture are neutral.

The study reported in this paper builds on previous work of ours (Bygstad et al., 2008) in which we have examined the relationship between usability and SDMs within the context of one national culture (Norway). Using the same survey instrument and questions as the current study, we generally found a positive bias towards usability among software developers, but – somewhat surprisingly – that the importance of usability testing was perceived as less important than usability in requirements. We now chose to conduct our study in two countries with very different national cultures, as illustrated in Table 1.

RESEARCH DESIGN AND METHOD

A survey instrument was used to gather data from software developers in Norway and India. A questionnaire was designed, with 5 questions on SDMs and 8 questions on usability. We also asked how many persons were engaged in systems development in the company. The respondents were also invited to comment on each of the topics of the survey.

The survey was implemented electronically by using the QuestBack system (http://www.questback.com). This system is based on e-mail distribution of a link to the actual survey and replies via a web browser on the Internet. The

Table 1. India and Norway: national cultures according to Hofstede's taxonomy

	Power Distance	Uncertainty avoidance	Individualism	Masculinity	Long term
India	High	High	Low	High	High
Norway	Low	Low	Medium	Low	Medium

QuestBack system has an automatic reminder, which was scheduled once to those who had not responded after the request to participate in the survey was sent out. The survey was run over a four week period.

Sampling was done the following way. In Norway the survey was distributed to 250 software developers, working in well known companies. These were contacts of the Norwegian School of IT, and selected because we knew that they were SOFTWARE development companies. For the Indian sample, we used contacts in the software industry to identify 90 possible respondents were selected U.S. and European multinationals, as well as Indian software firms. In the Norwegian sample 78 (33%) respondents replied; in the Indian sample we received 49 replies (54%).

RESULTS AND DISCUSSION

This section presents the results and discussion, and is divided into three parts: (1) Adoption of SDM, (2) Usability in requirements and testing, and (3) The relationship between SDMs and usability. The first two sections are descriptive, while we examine our research questions in part 3.

Chi-squared analysis and Analysis of Variance (ANOVA), suitable to analyse the difference in responses between two cohorts with regard to categorical, respectively, ordinal dependent variables were used. A significance level of $p<0.05$ was employed in our study.

Adoption of SDM

Table 2 shows the responses of the two cohorts in respect of usage of a formal SDM. As can be seen, the responses of the two cohorts are quite different (especially when it comes to the first two types of responses possible) and chi-squared analysis confirms that this pattern is statistically significant ($\chi^2 = 5.64$; $p<0.05$).

As regards specific usage of SDMs, as can be seen from Table 3, although the percentage of survey respondents who use own (or 'other') methods is very similar, not the same can be said in respect of the usage of other SDMs. Again, chi-squared analysis confirms that, overall, the differences in response patterns are statistically significant ($\chi^2 = 11.69$; $p<0.001$) – the greatest contributors to this being the usage of XP/Agile methods (43% of developers in India professing to use it, with only 18% of Norwegian developers saying they use it) and as regards the Microsoft Solutions Framework (here, the pattern is reversed, with only 12% of Indian developers employing it as opposed to 29% in Norway).

Adoption of Usability Techniques

The first question in the part of the survey addressing usability sought to establish the respondents' position vis a vis the importance of usability in the development projects they undertook. The results are shown in Table 4 and show an almost identical breakdown of responses (chi-squared

Table 2. Formal SDM use

Answer	N (India)	Percent (India)	N (Norway)	Percent (Norway)
Yes	27	55%	27	35%
We do not use a formal SDM, but we use a number of techniques and tools	18	37%	45	57%
No	4	8%	6	8%
Total	**49**	**100%**	**78**	**100%**

Table 3. Formal SDM usage (multiple answers possible)

Method	India	Norway
Own method	67%	68%
Rational Unified Process	20%	29%
XP/Agile methods	43%	18%
Microsoft Solutions Framework	12%	29%
Other methods	19%	19%

analysis confirms there are no significant differences). Accordingly, the vast majority of respondents (78%- India, 77% - Norway) declared that usability is an important element of the projects they develop, with 22% of respondents in both cohorts admitting that usability is only sometimes an important part of the projects, depending on the particular project in question.

Designing for usability typically involves establishing user requirements for a new system, iterative design and testing with representative users (Gould & Lewis, 1985). Thus, in order to examine the interplay between usability and system development methods, in our survey we specifically sought to explore to which degree usability was included in the system requirements and the degree of usability testing. Usability in requirements was measured by two questions, the first being "When will you include usability in requirements?" The result is shown in Table 5.

Chi-squared analysis reveals that the differences in responses was statistically significant between the two cohorts ($\chi^2 = 5.16$; $p<0.05$). Closer inspection of the data reveals that these differences were mainly due to the fact that whilst 72% of the Norwegian sample stated that they always include usability requirements this number drops to 55% in case of the Indian sample; on the other hand, whilst 25% of the Indian cohort admitted that they would only include usability requirements if problems emerge during the project, this proportion goes down to 10% in the case of Norwegian respondents.

Table 4. Answers to the question: "Is usability (of the developed product) an important element in your development projects?" (Q6)

Answer	N (India)	Percent (India)	N (Norway)	Percent (Norway)
Yes, normally	38	78%	61	77%
Sometimes, depends on the project	11	22%	17	22%
No	0	0%	1	1%
Total	**49**	**100%**	**79**	**100%**

Table 5. Answers to the question: "When will you include usability in requirements?"(Q8)

Answer	N (India)	Percent (India)	N (Norway)	Percent (Norway)
Always	27	55%	55	72%
Only if usability problems emerge during the project	12	25%	8	10%
Only if the customer demands it	9	18%	12	15%
Only if we have an internal usability specialist available	1	2%	2	3%
Total	**49**	**100%**	**77**	**100%**

The second question on the topic of requirements in usability was on how these were collected. Results are shown in Table 6.

Here, however, the pattern of responses is similar across the two cohorts and chi-squared analysis confirms that there are no statistically significant differences. From the responses obtained, it appears that developers both in Norway and India, trust experience gained as part of earlier work and, in almost equal measure, rely on interviewing users.

Respondents were also asked two questions on usability testing. The first was "How many users are typically engaged in usability testing?" Results are given in Table 7.

The pattern of responses (expressed in percentages) is strikingly similar here across the two samples and again chi-squared analysis confirms there any differences are not statistically significant. In both cases, two-thirds of usability testing is performed with small cohorts of less than 10 users.

The next question targeted how users were selected for usability testing. For each such category selected, we also show, in Tables 8 and 9, how important respondents considered usability testing to be.

Firstly, chi-squared analysis confirms that the difference in patterns of user selection in the two cohorts are statistically significant ($\chi^2 = 22.14$; $p<0.001$). Thus, whilst almost half (43%) of Indian developers say the companies they work for use their own employees for usability testing, this number drops down to 9% in the case of Norwegian developers; conversely, 40% of Norwegian software developers state that they use a representative sample of users, with the corresponding figure being 25% in the case of their Indian counterparts.

It is however reassuring that those 16% of Indian respondents who claimed that they use customer's employees for testing, rated the importance of usability testing highest (an average of 5.4 out of 6). In Norway, the highest mean score awarded to the importance of usability testing (4.6) was for

Table 6. Answers to the question: "How do you collect requirements for usability?"(multiple answers possible)

Answer	N (India)	Percent (India)	N (Norway)	Percent (Norway)
Interviewing users	30	61%	52	67%
Best practice from earlier projects	36	73%	54	71%
Books, Internet resources	14	29%	15	19%
Other	7	14%	9	12%

Table 7. Number of users in usability testing (Q11)

Answer	N (India)	Percent (India)	N (Norway)	Percent (Norway)
1-10 users	33	67%	52	67%
11-50 users	9	19%	17	21%
More than 50 users	1	2%	2	3%
We do not test usability	6	12%	7	9%
Total	**49**	**100%**	**78**	**100%**

Table 8. India: Selection criteria for users in usability testing vs. importance of usability testing (Q12 & Q13)

Answer	N (India)	Percent (India)	How important is usability testing? (scale 1 to 6)
Arbitrary sample of users	1	2%	4.0
Representative sample of users	12	25%	4.7
Own employees	21	43%	4.9
Customer's employees	8	16%	5.4
Other	1	2%	4.0
Do not test usability	6	12%	-
Total	**49**	**100%**	-

those respondents who stated that they use a representative sample of users in testing (and constituted the largest such category in respect of user selection criteria). These differences are confirmed by the fact that an ANOVA done on responses given to the importance of usability testing highlights that they are statistically significant between the two cohorts ($F=7.232$, $p<0.05$), with the Indian cohort holding usability testing in higher regard (mean = 4.59) than their Norwegian counterparts (mean = 4.05). Given the Scandinavian tradition in participatory and user-centered design, this is a somewhat surprising result.

The latter part of the survey questionnaire targeted the importance that usability requirements and usability testing in the software development process as well as the overall degree of integration of usability in SDMs. The breakdown of results is given in Tables 10 and 11. An inspection of these reveals that the Mean Opinion Score (MOS) for the importance of usability requirements is exactly the same as for usability testing in the case of the Indian Cohort. Moreover, the MOS for importance of Usability Requirements is less in India than

Norway; however, the differences are not statistically significant. Usability requirements are considered more important than usability testing in Norway. In both cohorts, the MOS drops down (to 3.9791, respectively, 4) when the degree of integration of usability in SDM is asked for. The MOS is almost identical; again there are no statistically significant differences between the two cohorts.

Table 9. Norway: Selection criteria for users in usability testing vs. importance of usability testing (Q12 & Q13)

Answer	N (Norway)	Percent (Norway)	How important is usability testing? (scale 1 to 6)
Arbitrary sample of users	4	5%	3.2
Representative sample of users	31	40%	4.6
Own employees	7	9%	4.0
Customer's employees	18	23%	3.7
Other	11	14%	4.0
Do not test usability	7	9%	-
Total	**78**	**100%**	-

Table 10. India: Usability requirements, usability testing - and project success; degree of integration of usability in SDM

Possible Answers(Q10 and Q13)	Usability Requirements(Q10)	Usability Testing (Q13)	Integration of usability in SDM (Q14)	Possible Answers (Q14)
6- Very important	31%	33%	16%	
	6- To a large degree			
5	22%	24.5%	14%	5
4	35%	24.5%	38%	4
3	4%	12%	18%	3
2	6%	2%	6%	2
1 – Quite unimportant	0%	2%	6%	1
0 No answer	2%	2%	2%	0
Total	**100%**	**100%**	**100%**	**Total**
Mean Score	**4.59**	**4.59**	**3.98**	**Mean Score**

Table 11. Norway: Usability requirements, usability testing - and project success; degree of integration of usability in SDM

Possible Answers (Q10 and Q13)	Usability Requirements(Q10)	Usability Testing (Q13)	Integration of usability in SDM (Q14)	Possible Answers (Q14)
6- Very important	33%	14%	14%	6- To a large degree
5	38%	23%	23%	5
4	21%	31%	26%	4
3	6%	19%	18%	3
2	1%	6%	13%	2
1 – Quite unimportant	1%	5%	3%	1
0 No answer	-	-	3%	0
Total	**100%**	**100%**	**100%**	**Total**
Mean Score	**4.91**	**4.05**	**4**	**Mean Score**

DISCUSSION

In this section we first summarize the findings described in the last section. Then, returning to the research question, we discuss the results. Our research question was: *Are there systematic differences between Norwegian and Indian software developers in their professional practice?*

As Table 12 illustrates, the overall answer is no. On 8 of the 12 criteria there are no significant differences, and on the other four there are relatively small differences. Considering the great cultural differences (as documented by Hofstede), we think that it is somewhat surprising that the Norwegian and the Indian developers behave so similar in their software development practices. We take the result as an indication of the existence of a shared professional culture. It gives strength to this argument that the practices that we measured (software development methods and usability) are both central to SW development and sensitive to cultural differences.

Table 12. India vs. Norway: differences and similarities

Survey Issues	Table(s)	Similar	Different
Formal SDM use	2		X
Use of 'own' or 'other' SDMs	3 .	X	
Use of RUP, XP/Agile methods, MSF	3		X
Importance of usability in development projects	4	X	
Inclusion of usability in requirements	5		X
Requirements collection for usability	6	X	
Number of users engaged in usability testing	7	X	
Selection criteria for users in usability testing	8,9		X
Importance of usability requirements	10,11	X	
Importance of usability testing	10,11	X	
Integration of usability in SDM	10,11	X	
MOS Importance of usability requirements >=			
MOS Importance of usability testing >=			
MOS Integration of usability in SDM	10,11	X	

Regarding the four criteria where there are significant differences between the two groups, we will briefly discuss each of them.

Formal SDM Use

As shown in Table 12 the Indian developers report a higher rate of adoption of formal development methods than the Norwegians. This might be consistent with Hofstede's dimension of power distance and uncertainty avoidance, namely that the more hierarchical and uncertainty avoiding Indian culture would adopt more formal approaches.

Use of RUP, XP/Agile Methods, MSF

Comparing the adoption of different systems development methods (see Table 3), the results are amazingly similar, with 67/68% using their own (internal) method. There is one significant difference; the Indian cohort is more likely to use agile methods. Compared with the previous point discussed (formal SDM use) it is hard to explain this finding with Hofstede's categories. Using the same reasoning one might expect the Indians to prefer more planned oriented methods (such as RUP and MSF), but this is not the case.

Inclusion of Usability in Requirements

Table 5 shows that there are significant differences regarding the practices of including usability in requirements. The Norwegians tend to always include usability in requirements (75%) while only 50% the Indians do so. 25% of Indian software developers will include usability in requirements only if usability problems arise later in the project. It is hard to see that Hofstede's cultural categories can explain this finding; it is more easily explained by differences in national IT traditions, i.e., that Norwegians belong to the strong Scandinavian participatory design tradition.

Number of Users Engaged in Usability Testing

This assumption is supported by the findings documented in Tables 8 and 9, which shows that the Norwegians are more likely to use a representative sample of users to test usability (40% versus 25%). Also, the Indians tend to use own employees to a much larger extent than the Norwegians (43% versus 9%) in usability testing activities.

One Professional Culture?

Indian software industry, initially and even now, has a U.S. bias, i.e., primarily, software firms are either subsidiaries of U.S. multinationals like Texas Instruments, Accenture, IBM, etc., or they are Indian firms having international presence. US firms are in India for strategic reasons like (a) cheap labour cost, (b) a large pool of English-speaking skilled work force, and (c) the twelve-hour lead time difference (Arora, 2008). Important Indian software firms primarily develop software for their US clients. Of course, in the recent past, there are a number of European firms in India, and Indian firms have also European clients (D'Mello & Eriksen, 2010). Arora (2008) points out that a number of successful software entrepreneurs in India had substantial overseas experience. Moreover, according to Athreye (2005), out of the 20 leading software exporters identified by NASSCOM, the National Association of Software and Services Companies, 5 were started by Indians living in America, 4 were multinationals and for the remaining, the founders either were educated or worked abroad.

Arora (2008) writes: "In bidding for large scale projects, the established Indian firms will run up against established incumbents such as the global services division of IBM, ACCENTURE and EDS." Since both have relative advantages and disadvantages – in an Indian context – it is likely that one segment has a lot to learn from the other.

Software developers working in the metropolis like Bangalore, Bombay, New Delhi and Chenai come from all corners of India, and so they are from diverse cultural backgrounds. From the above, one can easily infer that, such software developers would have been adequately trained by their employers in the western style of management and software development. This means the professional culture would be western at macro level though there would be Indian elements at the micro level.

Summing-up: The similarities between the two groups are much more prevalent than the differences, indicating a shared professional culture. The differences are relatively minor, and they are hard to explain by differences in national cultures, as described by Hofstede. Rather, the observed differences are explained by *national professional cultures*, i.e., the stronger Scandinavian emphasis on usability. This finding, however, is not strong, and is somewhat contradicted by the fact that the Indian group has a higher score in assessing the importance of usability testing (see Tables 10 and 11).

Limitations

We make no claims about our sample being either random or representative. As such, care should be taken when interpreting the conclusions of our study. More work should be done to explore their generalizability and applicability to other cultures.

Although chi-squared analysis is routinely used for analyzing the differences in Likert-scale responses between two groups, we recognize that the results might have been influenced by the categories being responded to.

We also acknowledge a methodological weakness in our argument: the fact that we do not find statistically significant differences between the two cohorts (in Hofstede's dimensions) does not necessarily mean that there are none. We believe that this does not invalidate our findings, but future work should address this issue.

Last but not least, we also accept that the similarities in software culture between Norwegian and Indian developers cannot be uncritically generalized to imply a global software culture. Certainly, only more empirical research can confirm our proposition. However, in choosing two extremely different national cultures (in Hoftede's scheme) and finding no differences, we believe that we present reasonable evidence for the claim that a non-national software culture does exist.

CONCLUSION

In this paper we have investigated the professional practices of software developers from two different cultures, namely from Norway and India. We asked, are there systematic differences between Norwegian and Indian software developers in their professional practice? Using Hofstede's cultural dimensions, our expectations were that there would be cultural differences between the two groups of professionals.

While previous research has surveyed perceptions of SDMs in various contexts and found some support for cultural differences, our work has focused on practices. Building on a survey among software developers in the two countries, we offer the following conclusions. Firstly, the main finding is that there are surprisingly few differences between the two groups giving support to the view of a common professional culture. Secondly, the few differences that we are observing cannot be explained by the Hofstede cultural dimensions.

Overall, we argue that Larry Constantine's (1995) suggestion of the emergence of a global software developer subculture is strengthened with our investigation. Further research is needed to investigate this hypothesis.

REFERENCES

Andersen, E. (2002). "Never the twain shall meet": exploring the differences between Japanese and Norwegian IS professionals. In *Proceedings of the 2002 ACM SIGCPR Conference on Computer Personnel Research* (pp. 65-71).

Arora, A. (2008). Indian Software Industry and its Prospects. In Bhagwati, J. N., & Calomiris, C. W. (Eds.), *Sustaining India's Growth Miracle*. New York, NY: Columbia University Press.

Athreye, S. (2005). The Indian Software Industry. In Arora, A., & Gambardella, A. (Eds.), *From Underdogs to Tigers: The rise and growth of the Software Industry in Brazil, China, India, Ireland, and Israel*. Oxford, UK: Oxford University Press.

Barthelmess, P. (2003). Collaboration and coordination in process-centered software development environments: a review of the literature. *Information and Software Technology*, *45*(13), 911–928. doi:10.1016/S0950-5849(03)00091-0

Beck, K. (2000). *Extreme Programming Explained: Embrace Change*. Reading, MA: Addison-Wesley.

Boivie, I., Aborg, C., Persson, J., & Lofberg, M. (2003). Why usability gets lost or usability in in-house software development. *Interacting with Computers*, *15*, 623–639. doi:10.1016/S0953-5438(03)00055-9

Boivie, I., Gulliksen, J., & Goransson, B. (2006). The lonesome cowboy: A study of the usability designer role in systems development. *Interacting with Computers*, *18*, 601–634. doi:10.1016/j.intcom.2005.10.003

Borchers, G. (2003). The Software Engineering Impacts of Cultural Factors on Multi-cultural Software Development Teams. In *Proceedings of the 5th International Conference on Software Engineering* (pp. 540-545).

Bosch, J., & Bosch-Sijtsema, P. (2010). From integration to composition: On the impact of software oriduct lines, global development and ecosystems. *Journal of Systems and Software*, *83*, 67–76. doi:10.1016/j.jss.2009.06.051

Bygstad, B., Ghinea, G., & Brevik, E. (2008). Software development methods and usability: Perspectives from a survey in the software industry in Norway. *Interacting with Computers*, *20*(3), 375–385. doi:10.1016/j.intcom.2007.12.001

Castells, M. (1996). *The Rise of the Network Society, The Information Age: Economy, Society and Culture* (*Vol. I*). Cambridge, MA: Blackwell.

Constantine, L. (1995). *Constantine on Peopleware*. Englewood Cliffs, NJ: Yourdon Press.

D'Mello, M., & Eriksen, T. M. (2010). Software, sports day and sheera: Culture and identity processes within a global software organization in India. *Information and Organization*, *20*(2), 81–110. doi:10.1016/j.infoandorg.2010.03.001

Dafoulas, G., & Macaulay, L. (2001). Investigating Cultural Differences in Virtual Software Teams. *The Electronic Journal of Information Systems in Developing Countries*, *7*(4), 1–14.

Friedman, T. L. (2005). *The World Is Flat: A Brief History of the Twenty-first Century*. New York, NY: Farrar, Strauss and Giroux.

Gibbs, J. L. (2009). Culture as kaleidoscope: navigating cultural tensions in global collaboration. In *Proceedings of the 2009 International Workshop on Intercultural Collaboration*.

Gould, J. D., & Lewis, C. (1985). Designing for usability: key principles and what designers think. *Communications of the ACM*, *28*(3), 300–311. doi:10.1145/3166.3170

Hazzan, O., & Dubinsky, Y. (2005). Clashes between Culture and Software Development Methods: The Case of the Israeli Hi-Tech Industry and Extreme Programming. In *Proceedings of the AGILE 2005 Conference* (pp. 59-69).

Hofstede, G. (2001). *Culture's Consequences: comparing values, behaviors, institutions, and organizations across nations*. Thousand Oaks, CA: Sage.

Iivari, J., & Huisman, M. (2007). The Relationship between Organizational Culture and the Deployment of Systems Development Methodologies. *Management Information Systems Quarterly*, *31*(1), 35–58.

Iivari, N. (2006). 'Representing the User' in software development - a cultural analysis of usability work in the product development context. *Interacting with Computers*, *18*, 635–664. doi:10.1016/j.intcom.2005.10.002

Jokela, T., & Abrahamsson, P. (2004). Usability assessment of an Extreme Programming Project: Close Co-Operation with the Customer Does Not Equal to Good Usability. In *Product Focused Software Process Improvement* (LNCS 3009, pp. 339-407).

Kankanhalli, A., Tan, B. C. Y., Wei, K.-K., & Holmes, M. C. (2004). Cross-cultural differences and information systems developer values. *Decision Support Systems*, *38*(2), 183–195. doi:10.1016/S0167-9236(03)00101-5

Kersten, G. E., Kersten, M. A., & Rakowski, W. H. (2002). Software and Culture: Beyond the Internationalization of the Interface. *Journal of Global Information Management*, *10*(4), 86–101. doi:10.4018/jgim.2002100105

Layman, L., Williams, L., Damian, D., & Bures, H. (2006). Essential communication practices for Extreme Programming in a global software development team. *Information and Software Technology*, *48*(9), 781–794. doi:10.1016/j.infsof.2006.01.004

Livermore, J. (2008). Factors that Significantly Impact the Implementation of an Agile Software Development Methodology. *Journal of Software*, *3*(4), 31–36. doi:10.4304/jsw.3.4.31-36

MacGregor, E., Hsieh, Y., & Kruchten, P. (2005). The Impact of Intercultural Factors on Global Software Development. In *Proceedings of the IEEE Canadian Conference on Electrical and Computer Engineering* (pp. 920-926).

Mishra, D., & Mishra, A. (2011). A review of non-technical issues in global software development. *International Journal of Computer Applications in Technology*, *40*(3), 216–224. doi:10.1504/IJCAT.2011.039142

Misra, S. C., Kumar, V., & Kumar, U. (2009). Identifying some important success factors in adopting agile software development practices. *Journal of Systems and Software*, *82*, 1869–1890. doi:10.1016/j.jss.2009.05.052

Niazi, M., Babar, M. A., & Verner, J. M. (2010). Software Process Improvement barriers: A cross-cultural comparison. *Information and Software Technology*, *52*(11), 1204–1216. doi:10.1016/j.infsof.2010.06.005

Olson, J. S., & Olson, G. M. (2003). Culture Surprises in Remote Software Development Teams. *Queue*, *1*(9), 51–59. doi:10.1145/966789.966804

Phongpaibul, M., & Boehm, B. (2005). Improving Quality through Software Process Improvement in Thailand: Initial Analysis. In *Proceedings of the ICSE 2005 Workshop on Software Quality* (pp. 23-28).

Salo, O., & Abrahamsson, P. (2008). Agile methods in European embedded software development organisations: a survey on the actual use and usefulness of Extreme Programming and Scrum. *IET Software*, *2*(1), 58–64. doi:10.1049/iet-sen:20070038

Schwaber, K. (2004). *Agile Project Management with Scrum*. Microsoft Press.

Taxen, L. (2006). An integration centric approach for the coordination of distributed software development projects. *Information and Software Technology*, *48*(9), 767–780. doi:10.1016/j.infsof.2006.01.007

Walsham, G. (2001). *Globalization and ICTs: Working across cultures*. Cambridge, UK: University of Cambridge.

This work was previously published in the Journal of Information Technology Research, Volume 4, Issue 3, edited by Mehdi Khosrow-Pour, pp. 50-63, copyright 2011 by IGI Publishing (an imprint of IGI Global).

Chapter 15
Secure Electronic Healthcare Records Management in Wireless Environments

Petros Belsis
Technological Education Institute, Greece

Christos Skourlas
Technological Education Institute, Greece

Stefanos Gritzalis
University of the Aegean, Greece

ABSTRACT

Wireless technologies have lately been integrated in many types of environments; their development is able to provide innovative services minimizing costs and the time necessary to identify the necessary information. However medical information is very sensitive since it contains critical personal data. Security and privacy preservation are very critical parameters. Lately, innovative technologies such as software agents' technology have been utilized to support distributed environments. Presented is an architecture that allows secure medical related information management using software agents; this work expands previous research (Belsis, Skourlas, & Gritzalis, 2011). The authors present a security oriented solution and also provide experimental evidence about the capability of the platform to operate in wireless environments with large number of users.

INTRODUCTION

During the last years handheld devices have been through a major technology shift. Their memory and processor capabilities have substantially improved providing new features and capabilities to their users; this has led to their integration in a large number of environments. Medical environments have gained a lot from the utilization of wireless devices. Doctors are able to retrieve the necessary information using handheld devices, while being next to the patient. Usually within the range of a clinic a wireless network is easy to deploy, provid-

DOI: 10.4018/978-1-4666-3625-5.ch015

ing thus the doctors with the necessary information independently of the exact location (Belsis, Vassis, Skourlas, & Pantziou, 2008).

From this point of view, access to information becomes ubiquitous since there is no need to approach a steady point to access the necessary information. In the past this was not so easy to achieve, since it was necessary to access a specific stable point for this purpose; on the other side with today's technologies a lot of the necessary functionalities are provided by mobile devices.

For instance, a doctor may acquire valuable information about a patient's condition while approaching a patient using a mobile device which collects data from a sensor attached to the patient; accordingly the doctor using the same device may collect more information by querying a database for details stored regarding the health condition of this patient. This treatment model becomes beneficial in case of emergency situations, or alternatively in emergency camps and in any other case characterized by lack of fixed, wired infrastructures.

The integration of wireless devices to support medical environments enables us to lower the costs, to improve the quality of healthcare services and to provide innovative services. However, there are several things that need to be considered, related mainly to the security and privacy of medical information. Medical information is sensitive, in a matter that allows determination of a person's physical condition. Legislation also imposes very strict rules regarding the storage and processing of medical information.

These issues need to be taken under consideration and must result in the incorporation of appropriate characteristics in the developed architectures, as well as with the embodying of appropriate security solutions that guarantee the security properties of medical information. Among the main design and implementation challenges we can distinguish (Vassis, Belsis, Skourlas, & Pantziou, 2008):

- The capability to provide information to doctors independently of their exact location;
- Achievement of information integration using interoperable standards for medical information storage and exchange;
- The ability to ensure that no sensitive medical information will be disclosed to unauthorized parties.

Mobile environments integrate a variety of heterogeneous applications, and demand flexible management of resources, available to wirelessly interconnected users and devices. Policy based management has supported efficiently the secure management of target resources which often span the borders of an organizational domain. Static oriented security management solutions fail, since there is no central administration available and due to several factors such as the large number of participant users, the mobility of users and devices, there is a necessity for flexible, context related applicability of access control decisions.

- The volatility of these environments makes developers forced to deal with contradictory requirements:
- The necessity to provide access from anywhere to anyone authorised to use medical related information,
- Ensuring at the same time non-disclosure of treatment-related information to non-authorised persons.

These restrictions direct our choices towards the creation of an appropriate architecture and towards the selection of appropriate security technologies that comply with the strict privacy and security restrictions related with medical wireless infrastructures.

The structure of the paper is as follows: after a brief introduction, the authors present related work in context and a brief comparison with our approach, and discuss the security requirements and describe the security models applied; the policy based model is also described and the role of the different software modules is analyzed. We then present the agent based platform that allows automated transparent to the user dissemination of medical information; it also describes issues and solutions in respect to the interoperability features. We describe a use case scenario and also discuss in brief some parameters measured from experimental details. The last section presents a brief discussion and also concludes the paper.

Related Work

There is a lot of ongoing work that focuses on the provision of improved e-health services. Research efforts from both the academia and the industrial sector are focusing towards the provision of high quality services that minimize the needs for binding health professionals to patients, but do not lower on the other side the quality of health related services. Special focus is needed in order to ensure the security properties of medical information processed through the system's modules.

Early clinical trials conducted in the mid-nineties by the National Institute of has indicated that the transmission of critical patient data during emergencies can make significant difference in patient outcomes. This result has led to a proliferation of health-care projects, including CodeBlue (Malan, Fulford-Jones, Welsh, & Moulton, 2004), PPMIM (Jea & Srivastava, 2006), CustoMed (Jafari, Dabiri, Brisk, & Sarrafzadeh, 2006), LiveNet (Sung, Marci, & Pentland, 2005), UbiMon (Ng et al., 2004), AMON (Anliker et al., 2004) and PadNET (Junker, Stager, Tröster, Blttler, & Salama, 2004). Various types of wearable health monitoring sensor devices have been developed and integrated into patients' clothing (Park & Jayaraman, 2003; Paradiso, 2003; Jovanov, Milenkovic, Otto, & de Groen, 2004; Van Laerhoven et al., 2004)

LiveNet, a system developed at the MIT Media Laboratory that measures 3-D acceleration, ECG, EMG, and galvanic skin conductance; LiveNet is a flexible distributed mobile system that can be deployed for a variety of proactive healthcare applications. The LiveNet system allows people to receive real-time feedback from their continuously monitored and analyzed health state, as well as communicate health information with care-givers and other members of an individual's social network for support and interaction. This system supports monitoring of patients with Parkinson or other neurological diseases (Sung et al., 2005).

AMON (Anliker et al., 2006) is a project that uses wearable devices to monitor vital patient parameters and transmits them using GSM/UMTS cellular infrastructure. As a target group the project uses patients with chronic cardiac and respiratory illnesses. The Monitor device, which is a basic component of the AMON project, utilizes sensors to gather information and analyses it using an expert system to provide fast treatment in cases of emergency. It focuses on the acquisition of several patient indications which are sent to authorized medical personnel. The main focus of this research project is to perform the necessary research, development and validation for an advanced wearable, personal health system.

The MobiCare project (Chakravorty et al., 2006) is a system for both in-house and open areas patient monitoring that allows remote monitoring of patients vital parameters using wearable devices and transmits the data using GPRS technology. It enables continuous monitoring for chronically ill patients. It also utilizes a programmable architecture that enables introduction, configuration and customization of diverse medical sensors to a patient sensor network. Client devices can update with new medical features, applications and services that are tailored to meet the requirements of patients and the health providers. Its platform allows also easy configuration of services, thus allowing to effectively address the requirements of the patient's medical monitoring needs – the most significant challenge in mobile healthcare.

Wireless mediCenter (2006) is a system for management of electronic medical records and delivery through secure LANs or high-speed wireless connections. It provides different portals for doctors and patients in order to achieve classification of access permissions. The restriction though to connect through the portal is a serious burden to the user.

The m-Care project (Brazier, 2007) aims at providing secure access through a WAP based architecture. Users and access rights related information is kept in an MS-SQL Server database. In our approach we have enabled a policy based approach which facilitates interoperation with other systems while it also provides a highly distributed nature to our system. PatientService (Choudri et al., 2003) is a trust-based security architecture that enables medical records management in pervasive environments. In this approach access to medical information is provided to a set of users which hold a PDA that keeps the policy in a smart card. In our approach we issue the request form the PDA while the policy evaluation is not performed by the PDA itself. Moreover we attempt to evaluate our approach by performing simulation experiments.

Most of the existing mobile patient monitoring projects employ cellular networks (e.g., GSM, GPRS, or UMTS) to transmit vital signs from BSN to health centers. For instance, in PPMIM project, a remote medical monitoring three-tier architecture with a GSM/GPRS peer to-peer channel is presented, and the concept of multi-resolution is introduced to identify useful information and to reduce communication costs. In MobiCare, a body sensor network (or MobiCare client) and health-care servers employ short-range Bluetooth between BSN and BSN Manager, and GPRS/UMTS cellular networks between BSN Manager and health-care providers. The UbiMon (UbiquitousMonitoring Environment for Wearable and Implantable Sensors) Project aims to provide a continuous and unobtrusive monitoring system for patients in order to capture transient but life threatening events (Ng et al., 2004). CodeBlue (Malan et al., 2004), is one of the projects that employ wireless sensor networks in emergency medical care, hospitals, and disaster areas as an emergency message delivery system. With MICA motes, CodeBlue uses pulse oximetry and electrocardiogram (ECG) sensors to monitor and record blood oxygen and cardiac information from a large number of patients. However, most of the existing systems lack two key features: (1) wireless communication technology that conforms to standards, (2) integration with wireless sensor network platforms such as smart home systems, and (3) secure transmission capability that addresses the resource constraints optimally.

Dağtaş, Pekhteryev, Şahinoğlu, Çam, and Challa (2008) present a ZigBee-based architecture that aims to provide secure wireless communications combined with the widespread infrastructure provided by applications such as smart homes as a key to the effective use of future medical monitoring systems. This is due to the fact that practicality of the sensing, transmission, and processing steps is often the major obstacle against common use of such devices.

Our proposed architecture introduces a hybrid approach that utilizes different wireless interfaces for the transmission of medical data that uses Wi-Fi and GSM interfaces to send patient data to the hospital. We introduce also robust encryption approaches that minimize also the consumption of resources, which is essential when the network uses portable devices with limited resources. For interoperability issues, we have selected interoperable protocols to codify the medical record's parameters is achieved using interoperable protocols and appropriate encoding and encryption standards; Specific attention has been paid to the high security and privacy requirements regarding the transmission of sensitive information, in accordance with the imposed EU legislation.

Requirements Analysis

The development of large scale and high speed Information Systems (IS) as well as the emergence of high performance networked systems did not come without drawbacks. One of the most important challenges is to handle the security challenges and to confront the attacks caused by outside intruders as well as insiders. Managing the resources of a framework is a big challenge that requires a lot of effort on both the design as well as the implementation of countermeasures. Security policies are adopted to a high extent towards this direction. A policy can be considered to consist of a set of authoritative statements that determine the set of acceptable options in future selection processes (Kokolakis & Kiountouzis, 2000). Relative to security, a policy can determine the set of acceptable actions, prohibitions and rights that are defined within the borders of an organization. A part of a security policy is determining the access control rights for each individual. Several challenges arise on this field, due to the very large number of subjects (resources) that need to be administered and due to the very large number of users. The Role Based Access Control (RBAC) (Ahn & Sandhu, 2000; Sandhu, Ferraiolo, & Kuhn, 2000) model seems to be dominant and widely accepted in most of the commercial environments ad software platforms. The main principle of RBAC is related with the fact that usually users with similar roles, need to be accredited for the same actions, and need to have the same access rights. By classifying users to roles and accordingly by relating individuals with a role, the security management is simplified dramatically. For example, each time somebody enters the organization, we simply classify her to one of the predefined roles. Accordingly, when somebody leaves the organization, we do not need to manually withdraw all the access rights for every resource she was assigned to have access rights.

Things can become more complicated in mobile environments since new users enter and leave constantly. In addition, devices are characterized by low computing resources and power. Medical information on the other hand is highly sensitive; thus, we have to design our system so as to demand as less processing and network bandwidth resources, without though decreasing our strict privacy requirements. Among the main requirements for our architecture we can distinguish:

- **Privacy preservation:** Unauthorized disclosure of medical information may lead to disastrous results. EU and US legislation force towards privacy preservation of medical data. Except from protecting appropriately medical databases, transmission of medical information should also be performed in a reliable and secure manner. We have thus employed efficient encryption techniques based on both symmetric and public key cryptography methods, so as to achieve data protection without demanding excessive processing power. In order to transmit data wirelessly we first exchange a shared key using strong encryption based on singing the messages with the private keys of the two parties, and then continue using shared key encryption so as to achieve a lightweight implementation.
- **Network topology instability:** Node mobility and node failure are problems that we have to deal with in ; In order to enable constant connectivity for as long as possible, we have decentralized many of our processing and communication tasks avoiding thus the existence of points of failure. Towards this direction we have adopted the DLS (distributed lookup server approach) (Malatras, Pavlou, Belsis, Gritzalis, Skourlas, & Chalaris, 2005a, 2005b) according to which a number of nodes act collectively as a centralized node. When a node is about to stop transmitting, it passes all of its information to its neighbors.

- **Interoperability:** In order to enable interoperation of our system with other medical systems and architectures we have adopted the HL7 standard for information encoding and exchange. For secure transmission and in compliance with the guidelines of the HL7 that instruct the use of secure protocols, one of the IP Security protocol (IPSec), Secure File Transfer Protocol (SFTP) or Secure Socket Layer Protocol (SSL) can be used for encrypting medical records.
- **Access control management:** In order to apply access control, we have adopted the Role Based Access Control Model (RBAC), due to its simplicity and wide acceptance as a security standard. Access Control is performed in the medical database using a policy based approach (Vassis, Belsis, Skourlas, & Gritzalis, 2009). A policy approach allows determination of privileges according to business roles, accordingly these privileges may be encoded in a suitable policy language and each request is directed towards special purpose modules, which reason over a specific request and either authorize or reject the request. Security policies, provide a flexible means to automate the security management procedures as well as to enable the enforcement of access control decisions on distributed systems. Security policies can be codified in several special purpose languages, some of which provide codification in XML format, which makes them preferable, as they provide support for various platforms, and also makes them highly interoperable. The use of policies can simplify the management of distributed systems, which contain a large number of objects which often span across organizational boundaries. A more challenging option arises when it comes to adapting to this framework resources from different domains which cooperate on the grounds of a common basis.

Mobile e-health environments pose a number of significant challenges from a security perspective. In order to retain fundamental security properties such as availability, confidentiality and integrity, several implementation oriented choices were made in our approach:

- In order to enable a scalable authorization and authentication solution, the RBAC (Sandhu et al., 2000) model was chosen as the most appropriate. This choice was made for several reasons: it is standardized, b) it is supported by most commercial applications, c) it reflects organizational hierarchy and enables easy mapping of privileges to organizational roles and therefore codification of security parameters and classification of roles to security privileges becomes a simpler task.
- Security policies were chosen in order to automate security management of infrastructures. Security policy languages enable determination of access control rules in a suitable format, both machine and human interpretable. Therefore, by configuration of appropriate files, security management becomes an automated process which eliminates the security administrator burden.
- For confidentiality purposes and non-repudiation, Public Key Infrastructure techniques were deployed. Therefore for our framework, a policy server storing the security credentials and the associated with him/her access rights for each role was set up for each domain.

In our case due to the specific features in respect to mobility the RBAC needs to be extended, by incorporating in the role specification scheme domain specific attributes such as the domain's ip range, or it has to be extended so that time-enabled periodicity can be defined for roles (see Table 1).

In our approach we utilize the Extensible Access Control Markup Language (XACML) (OASIS, 2007). XACML is a policy language that supports prohibitions, obligations, and resolution of conflicts. Its expressiveness and XML (Extensible Markup Language) codification support allow its integration on a variety of environments, such as web-service based environments, distributed autonomous systems, and with some modifications to be applied also to pervasive environments. Among XACML's strong points, are:

- It is standardized and it is open, allowing extensions that enable interoperation between various platforms.
- It is codified in (XML) which tends to dominate as codification standard and is operating system independent.
- It allows extensions as to support the needs for a variety of environments.
- It allows context based authorization, which is a big advantage.

A XACML policy management system consists of several modules, with different roles each (see Figure 1). In a mobile environment, the basic XACML module would demand adjustment to the topology-specific characteristics, as well as to the limited resource and processing power capability of the participating devices.

An overview of the XACML operational model is provided in the following: we can distinguish the Policy Enforcement Point (PEP) and the Policy Decision Point (PDP). These two modules are responsible for reasoning about authorization requests as well as for policy enforcement. In the absence of a centralized authorization infrastructure, the policy based module is responsible for distributed security management. The implemented security module is based on the standardized IETF model. A more detailed description of the functionalities as well as of the tasks performed by each one of the modules is given in the following. More specifically, the different modules are:

- The authorization module, which identifies the user's id using X.509 certificates, and issues next SAML (Hughes & Maler, 2007) assertions that can be used further to assist the doctor's interaction with the system, providing thus single sign-on functionality to the system.
- The Policy Enforcement Point (PEP), which enforces the decision, after examining the XACML reply messages sent by the PDP.
- The Policy Decision Point (PDP), which loads the policy and reasons over the request, expressed by means of an XACML message sent to the PDP by the PEP.
- The context handler which facilitates policy decisions in respect to specific context related variables, for example the domain name that a user belongs to.

Table 1. Enabling time – periodicity within pre-specified time intervals

<Rule RuleId="EveryoneDuringWorkingHours" Effect="Allow">
<Condition FunctionId=" Function#time-in-range"> <Apply FunctionId="function:time-one-and-only"> <EnvironmentAttributeDesignator DataType=http://www.w3.org/2001/XMLSchema#time AttributeId=" environment:current-time"/></Apply>
<AttributeValue DataType=" http://www.w3.org/2001/XMLSchema#time"> 08.00</AttributeValue>
<AttributeValue DataType=" http://www.w3.org/2001/XMLSchema#time">17:00:00 </AttributeValue>
</Condition></Rule>

Figure 1. The policy based module

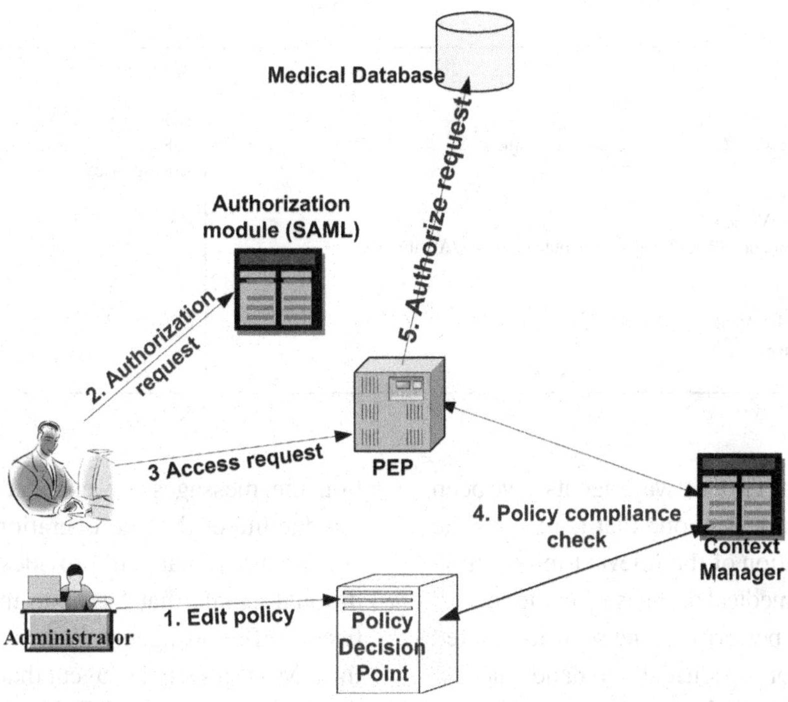

A given use case scenario that is based on the XACML model is the following (see Figure 1): First the administrator edits the policy in XML format and makes it available at the PDP. Considering a user wants to request a resource, the first thing necessary is to obtain an authentication SAML compliant assertion. This is obtained through the authentication module. Then the user's request for a resource is directed from the user's device to the Policy enforcement point. This issues a request and directs it to the context handler which constructs an XACML request message which is further directed to the PDP for evaluation (for example see Table 2 for the structure of the message). The PDP checks the user's permissions and the request and issues a decision. This decision is further directed to the PEP which enforces the decision from the PDP.

Table 2A indicates excerpts from the XACML messages, which describe the requester and object, while Table 2B describes an XACML response. The attributes of the requester are highlighted in Table 2A (left) as well as the resource requested.

SYSTEM ARCHITECTURE

The security module as described above facilitates security management; still, it is essential for not expert users to be able to interact and retrieve the necessary information in a transparent manner to the user. For this purpose, the use of software agents gives an ideal solution (Zafeiris, Doulkeridis, Belsis, & Chalaris, 2005). Software agents are applications that may act as delegate to the user's actions. For example the authentication and authorization process can be simplified if a software agent retrieves the user's credentials and interacts with the system at the user's behalf. Therefore, in order facilitate for medical personnel the identification and retrieval of medical information in a secure manner with low response times and transparently to the user, we have created an agent

Table 2. A (left): an Excerpt from XACML request. The requester's attribute is highlighted, as well as the requested resource. B (right): XACML response message.

A	B
<Request> <Subject> <Attribute > <AttributeValue>secretary@aegean.gr </AttributeValue> </Attribute> </Subject><Resource> <Attribute><AttributeValue> file://record/StudentlRecords/PeterKenn </AttributeValue></Attribute> </Resource> <Action><Attribute> <AttributeValue>read</AttributeValue> </Attribute></Action> </Request>	<Response> <Result> <Decision>NotApplicable </Decision> </Result> </Response>

based application. Two software agents have been installed on each device; one that is responsible for the identification of the relevant information by querying the medical database and the second is responsible to perform all the security related operations, or more specifically to handle access control decisions as a delegate of the device owner (the doctor or medical personnel).

When a doctor requests a medical record, the agent handles the query by looking for the requested information in different locations within the distributed environment. For every database there are different agents that are ready to communicate and interoperate with the user's agent. Next, the security agent is invoked which handles the security related tasks between the device and the policy management system which handles the security related tasks. For the software agents development we have used the JADE (Bellifemine, Caire, & Greenwood, 2007) software agent management software and especially the LEAP module targeted specific for mobile devices. We will briefly discuss the underlying architecture of the JADE platform (see Figure 2): The JADE platform allows the creation of a distributed agent architecture. Therefore, each agent communicates with other agents in this distributed environment and they communicate exchanging messages in the standardized Agent Communication (ACL) language. In order to facilitate the communication the messages are encoded in an ontology that facilitates the interoperation between them.

The agent platform provides also several additional agents that facilitate interoperation between different agents from different domains: the AMS is a software agent that controls and the directory facilitator (DF) that provides yellow services to the other agents. In order to lower the resource demands so that our platform operates well in devices with limited resources, we have used the LEAP component of the Jade platform that is suitable for resource constrained devices.

Exploiting Medical Codification Standards for Interoperability

Many efforts during the last years have dealt with the development of medical standards for the codification of medical information; lately as a widely accepted standard the HL7 has been adopted. In order to achieve interoperation of our approach with other standardized systems, we have selected the HL7 standard to encode and exchange medical information. Table 3 displays an example of a patient admission HL7 message, resulting from a request from a doctor's wireless device (PDA). This message may be easily transformed in XML which facilitates interoperation with most types of applications nowadays. Most of the medical applications nowadays support creation,

Figure 2. Overview of the agent based architecture. Interoperation between different distributed locations is performed b means of different agent based applications

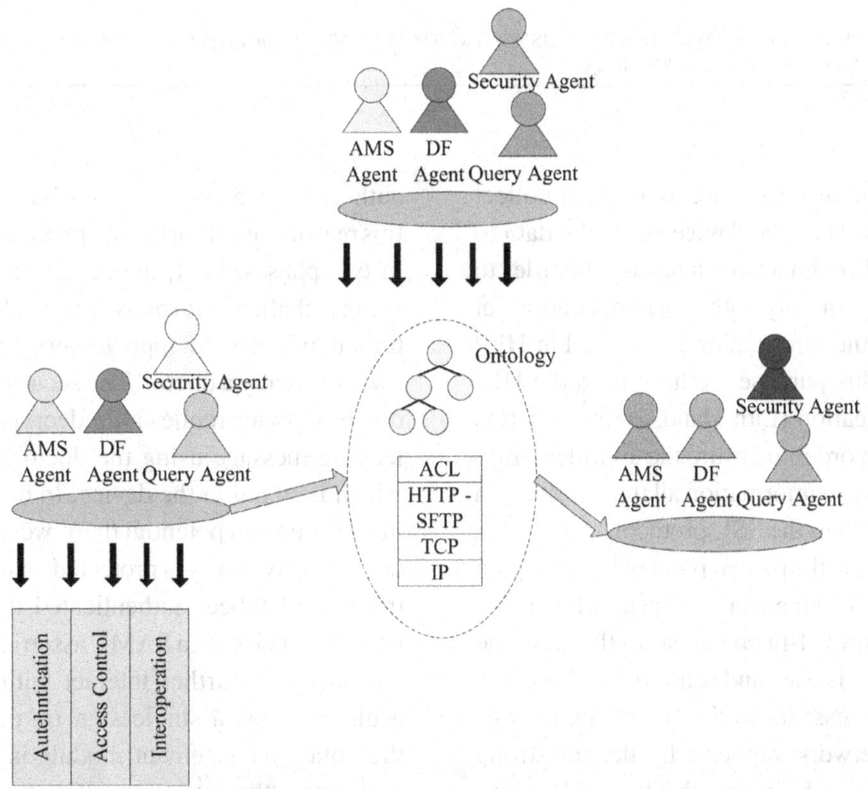

codification and retrieval of HL7 messages. Thus, except from the security parameters in our research we have attempted to measure the effects of the information overhead caused by a combination of the following factors: i) the use of the HL7 standard to encode the medical information, ii) cryptography to align with the privacy requirements and the use of the agent based applications on the user's device. In the following paragraphs we further analyze the technical details related with the development of our framework and we perform simulations measurements that encounter all the aforementioned parameters to ensure the effective operation of our platform.

Example Use Case Scenario

Our architecture enables remote monitoring of patients while they are at home, where through a wireless interface and a DSL connection the data can be sent to the hospital or through a GSM device when the patient is outside from his/her home. This enables to continuously monitor the condition of a patient without to be necessary to hospitalize him/her.

Now imagine the following use case scenario: A patient has attached on his/her body a number of sensors that measure several vital parameters. Using a mobile device, these parameters are collected every few minutes. A device attached to the patient's body equipped with several different wireless interfaces is responsible to collect them. For example while the patient is in home

Table 3. An example of an HL7 message

```
MSH|^~\&|Sys|Hosp|HL7Connect|Hosp|20050313173613||ADT^A01^ADT_A01|0000000403|P|2.3.1EVN|A01|20050313173614149||
|a017
PID|||8665^^^PH||NGO^ELENA^^^Ms||19750514|F|||42SYG STREET^^ATH^VIC^3000PV1||I|2D^13^1^^^^^^Ward 3 Wouth||||TESTD
R^TEST^PETER^^DR|||ORT|||||||||14201|COM|
```

an 802.11 wireless interface is used to collect all the values. Then the device sends the data to the hospital through a DSL interface. In order to ensure interoperability with other applications at the hospital, the information is encoded in HL7 format. For this purpose we have used the HL-7comm application (Litherland, 2009) which is Java based. In order to ensure the confidentiality of the transmitted information all the information is encrypted using the SSL protocol.

Now imagine the patient is out of home. Again the devices collect the vital parameters, but in this case there is no WI-Fi coverage. In this case the GSM interface is used and sends through a GSM provider the messages to the Hospital Gateway. The GSM network supports by default strong encryption methods. In case that the vital parameters of a patient exceed some threshold an alert is produced that notifies the medical personnel to take some kind of action. If the situation demands, an ambulance is sent at the patient's location to transfer him/her to the hospital. In other case the hospital personnel may call the patient at home or at his/her mobile.

We will now explain the architecture of the system at the hospital's side. The doctors carry each a PDA device that is able to collect messages and inform them about events that require their attention. In order to receive these messages through an automated process that does not require their involvement, this process is performed through the software agents developed for this reason. Therefore when a doctor needs to be informed about a patient's condition the agent is retrieving the medical files associated with the specific patient; prior though to bringing the files, the authorization process needs to be completed. For this reason the authorization process is performed in two phases. First, the authentication module using a challenge response protocol and the doctor's public key attempts to verify of the device owner is really a doctor. The security agent at the doctor's device replies after decrypting the challenging message using the doctor's private key which is stored in the device. In order to protect the device from potential theft, we insure that the doctor's private key is protected using a pin. After the doctor has been authenticated, the authentication module issues a SAML assertion that allows the doctor to further interact with the system, achieving thus a single sign on process. Next, the policy management module is invoked that performs authorization specific processes. All the requests to access a specific file are forwarded to the Policy Decision Point. This checks the request according to the existing policies and in case that the requester should be allowed to view the files, it sends a XACML message to the PEP which allows the request. In order further to ensure that all the messages are exchanged in a secure manner we employ a hybrid encryption approach. First, a shared key is exchanged using asymmetric key encryption. This is done to ensure that the shared key will by no means be intercepted. Then since asymmetric encryption would demand a lot of network and device resources, we use the shared key to handle all communications. Therefore we ensure the robustness of our architecture and we ensure that all communications are safe while we also ensure that the system will respond fast and without excessive consumption of device resources.

NETWORK PERFORMANCE PARAMETERS

Using a network that builds upon wireless devices demands more advanced ways to handle network management issues than these that a fixed network demands. Within the hospital range, we consider different types of wireless nodes that participate in the network. First, we consider the central nodes (CN's) that store the medical data and are responsible for authentication and access control enforcement and two types of mobile nodes with different processing and access control capabilities: the Manager Nodes (MN's) which are assigned with more advanced tasks and Terminal Nodes (TN's) which lack in respect to MN's in resources and are assigned secondary tasks. The CN's are responsible for the operation of the policy management module and are responsible to maintain the medical database; they are characterized by adequate processing as well as network bandwidth capabilities. They have also installed the different policy management modules: the Policy Decision Point (PDP) and the Policy Enforcement Point. Authentication is performed through an LDAP server which evaluates the medical personnel's credentials (encoded as X.509 certificates) and issues a SAML assertion which can be further used for identification in every future transaction with the access control enforcement module, providing thus a Single Sign-On (SSO) mechanism. In respect to mobile nodes, we distinguish two organizational roles which characterize also the operation of each node: a) Manager Nodes (MN) are devices with more processing capabilities and RAM memory and are held by doctors; b) Terminal Nodes (TN) are devices with less processing power capabilities and are supplied with a lightweight implementation that allows simple operations, like informing a medical assistant about a patient's medication and when it should be scheduled.

The software installed on MN's includes a local PDP and PEP module which allow enforcement of local (as recorded in the device) policies, enabling thus access to other doctor's to the device's local repository. On the contrary, TN's perform only simple operations, such as informing nursing personnel about an emergency or providing details about a patient's pharmaceutical prescription and the time that this medication is scheduled; a TN is never allowed to access sensitive medical data.

Both TN and MN nodes are able to identify whether they reside within the clinic or in an unknown environment, with the aid of a beacon (see Figure 3) which sends signed messages identifiable by each device when compared to a number of stored signed (within the smart card) messages. Thus, we prevent unauthorized transmission or reception from the device when it resides outside pre-settled space boundaries.

PERFORMANCE EVALUATION

In order to prove the validity of our approach we performed simulation experiments using the Pamvotis simulator (Vassis, 2008). Each simulation scenario considered 30 transmitting devices with a constant packet size distribution and a constant packet generation rate distribution with a rate mean of 8 packets/sec. The duration of the each simulation scenario was set to 100 seconds. Figure 4 displays the delays that a message experiences when traveling to its destination within the wireless network.

Each message needs average 2.99 seconds to reach its final destination from the moment that is born until the moment that is recorded to the database. These delays observed in the message transmission, are very small compared to the time needed for the doctor to see the message and proceed to the appropriate action (this can take more than 2-3 minutes, according to the person). These results are satisfactory in order to provide treatment to a number of patients, if we consider that we do not need to hospitalize them if they don't face some immediate danger for their health

Figure 3. Overall system architecture. The beacon transmits signed messages that are domain specific.

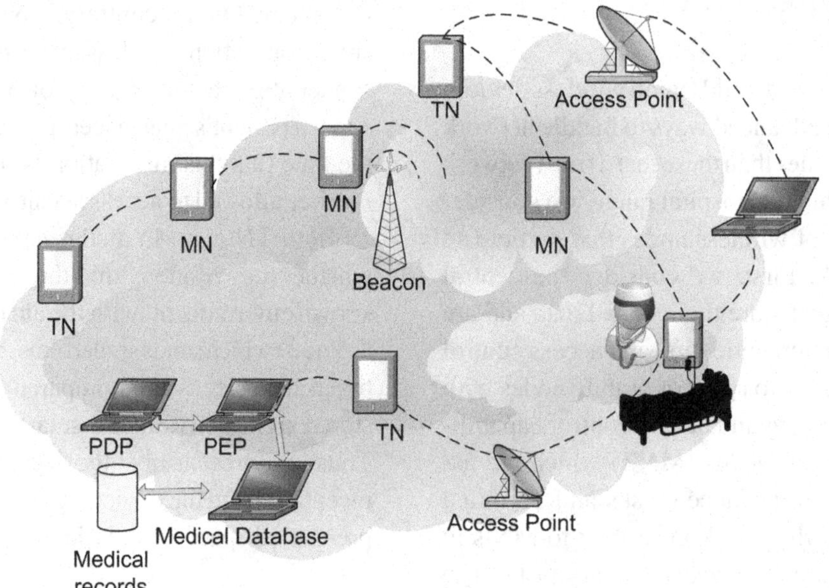

and still whenever necessary we can be notified and take action in short time intervals.

Figure 5 displays the average throughput of the network for the aforementioned scenario. This means that in general the network bandwidth is sufficient and that our application is not susceptible to congestion issues. In general our application performs adequately and through our experiments we have proved the validity of our approach to a number of realistic scenarios.

CONCLUSION

In this paper we presented a wireless architecture that enables transparent identification and secure dissemination of medical information. Several issues and challenges have been described and diverse solutions have been provided; the most notable of these challenges are:

- Security management, using an automated policy-based framework.
- Use of appropriate techniques that ensure confidentiality while they do not consume excessive resources in the network which comprises from mobile low resource devices.
- Enabling transparent to the user identification of medical records.
- Integration of transparent authorization and authentication processes.

In order to achieve the first task, we implemented a policy based management module which uses the XACML framework to enforce access control decisions within the distributed environment. We have selected a Java based framework to develop software agents that act as delegates of the user to identify the relevant medical information as well as to enforce the policy decisions. In order to manage the strict security requirements we have implemented a hybrid encryption approach that uses asymmetric encryption to exchange the shared key and then uses this key to encrypt all further communications. Thus, we allow secure information exchange within our framework

Figure 4. Average delay for our simulation scenario

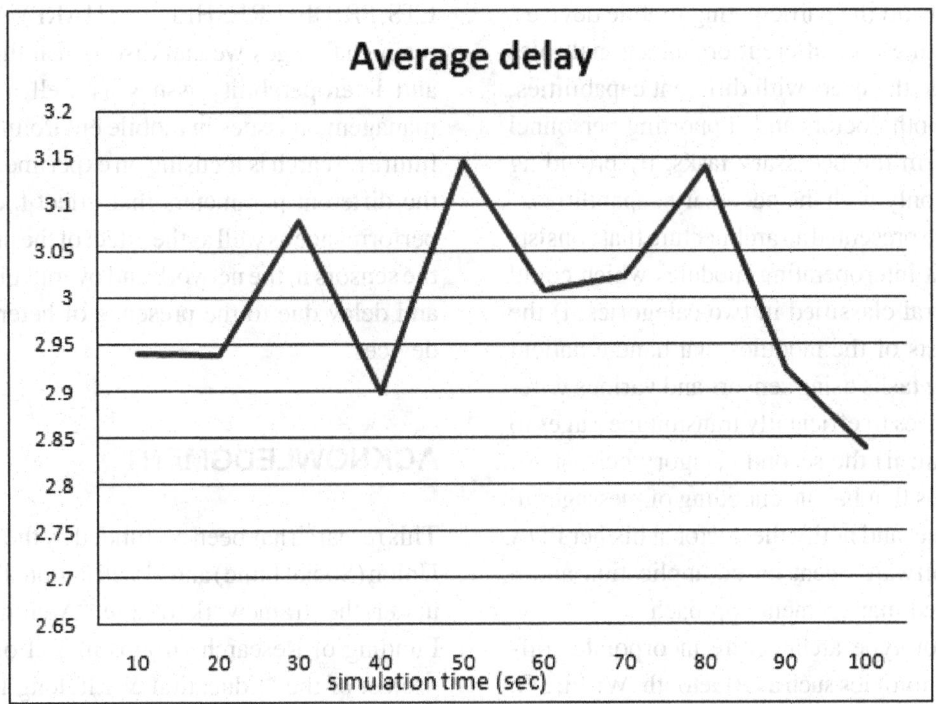

Figure 5. Throughput performance for a set of 30 transmitting nodes

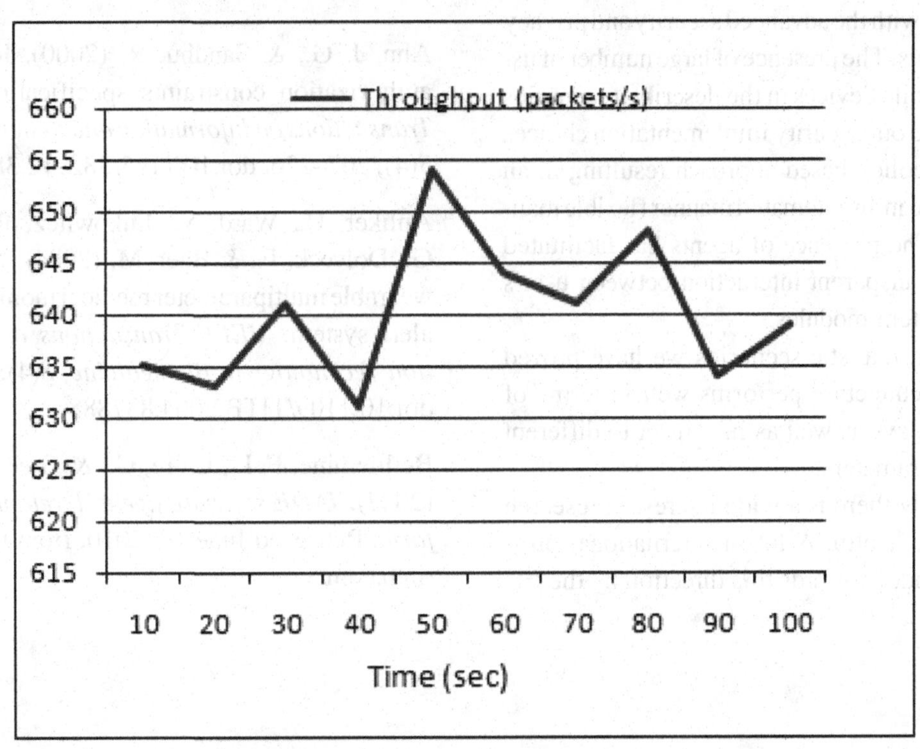

without excessive consumption of the limited resources from the participating mobile devices.

We distinguish different organizational roles and provide the users with different capabilities; therefore both doctors and supporting personnel may perform the necessary tasks, by providing them also only with the necessary capabilities.

We have presented an architecture that consists of different interoperating modules which could be in general classified in two categories: i) the first consists of the modules that handle patient monitoring tasks using sensors and various wireless interfaces to efficiently transmit messages to the hospital; ii) the second category consists of the modules that handle encoding of messages to the database, and notify the doctor at his/her PDA using a software agent based application and a policy based management approach.

The prototype architecture incorporates different technologies such as Bluetooth, Wi-Fi, 3G. In order to ensure that our platform interoperates with other medical applications we have selected the HL7 standard to encode medical information. We have described our implementation choices that handle with the advanced security and privacy requirements. The presence of large number of users and mobile devices in the described scenarios has directed our security implementation choices towards a policy based approach resulting in an efficient and in an automated manner flexible management. The presence of agents has facilitated further a transparent interaction between user's and the system modules.

Through realistic scenarios we have proved that our architecture performs well in terms of the total delays as well as in respect to different network parameters.

Currently there is a wide interest in research related to e-health. A lot of international projects are funded towards this direction by the EU (ISHTAR, TrustHealth, MEDSEC, EUROMEDETS, PRIDEH, RESHEN, and HARP). Among the main challenges we can distinguish the security and interoperability issues as well as network management issues in mobile environments. Our future research is focusing on experimenting with the different parameters that affect the network performance as well as the effect of the presence of the sensors in the network and overall preciseness and delay due to the presence of heterogeneous devices.

ACKNOWLEDGMENT

This research has been co-funded by the European Union (Social Fund) and Greek national resources under the framework of the "Archimedes III: Funding of Research Groups in TEI of Athens" project of the "Education & Lifelong Learning" Operational Programme.

REFERENCES

Ahn, J. G., & Sandhu, R. (2000). Role-based authorization constraints specification. *ACM Transactions on Information and System Security*, *3*(4), 207–226. doi:10.1145/382912.382913

Anliker, U., Ward, V., Lukowitcz, P., Tröster, G., Dolveck, F., & Baer, M. (2004). AMON: A wearable multiparameter medical monitoring and alert system. *IEEE Transactions on Information Technology in Biomedicine*, *8*(4), 415–427. doi:10.1109/TITB.2004.837888

Bellifemine, F. L., Caire, G., & Greenwood, D. (2007). *JADE software agent development platform*. Retrieved June 10, 2010, from http://jade.tilab.com/

Belsis, P., Skourlas, C., & Gritzalis, S. (2011). Secure electronic healthcare records distribution in wireless environments using low resource devices. In Malatras, A. (Ed.), *Pervasive computing and communications design and deployment: Technologies, trends, and applications* (pp. 247–262). Hershey, PA: IGI Global. doi:10.4018/978-1-60960-611-4.ch011

Belsis, P., Vassis, D., Skourlas, C., & Pantziou, G. (2008). Secure dissemination of electronic healthcare records in distributed wireless environments. In *Proceedings of the 21st International Congress of the European Federation for Medical Informatics* (pp. 661-666).

Brazier, D. (2006). *The m-care project*. Scotland, UK: Alpha Bravo Charlie Ltd. Retrieved June 10, 2010, from http://www.m-care.co.uk/tech.html

Chakravorty, R. (2006, March). A programmable service architecture for mobile medical care. In *Proceedings of the 4th Annual IEEE International Conference on Pervasive Computing and Communications Workshops*, Pisa, Italy (pp. 532-536).

Choudhri, A., Kagal, A., Joshi, A., Finin, T., & Yesha, Y. (2003). *PatientService: Electronic patient record redaction and delivery in pervasive environments*. Paper presented at the Fifth International Workshop on Enterprise Networking and Computing in Healthcare Industry (Healthcom), Santa Monica, CA.

Dağtaş, S., Pekhteryev, G., Şahinoğlu, Z., Çam, H., & Challa, N. (2008). Real-time and secure wireless health monitoring. *International Journal of Telemedicine and Applications, 2008*, article 1.

Foundation for Intelligent Physical Agents (FIPA). (2005). *FIPA specifications*. Retrieved June 10, 2010, from http://www.fipa.org/specifications/index.html

Hughes, J., & Maler, E. (2004). *Technical overview of the OASIS security assertion markup language* (SAML) V2.0. Retrieved June 10, 2010, from http://xml.coverpages.org/SAML-TechOverviewV20-Draft7874.pdf

ISHTAR Consortium (Ed.). (2001). *Implementing secure healthcare telematics applications in Europe – ISHTAR*. Amsterdam, The Netherlands: IOS Press.

ISTAG. (2002, June). *Trust, dependability, security and privacy for IST in FP6*. Brussels, Belgium: Office for Official Publications of the European Communities.

Jafari, R., Dabiri, F., Brisk, P., & Sarrafzadeh, M. (2005, April). CustoMed: A power optimized customizable and mobile medical monitoring and analysis system. In *Proceedings of the ACM HCI Challenges in Health Assessment Workshop in Conjunction with Proceedings of the Conference on Human Factors in Computing Systems*, Portland, OR.

Jea, D., & Srivastava, M. B. (2006, June). A remote medical monitoring and interaction system. In *Proceedings of the 4th International Conference on Mobile Systems, Applications, and Service*, Uppsala, Sweden.

Jovanov, E., Milenkovic, A., Otto, C., & de Groen, P. C. (2005). A wireless body area network of intelligent motion sensors for computer assisted physical rehabilitation. *Journal of Neuroengineering and Rehabilitation, 2*, 1–10. doi:10.1186/1743-0003-2-6

Junker, H., Stager, M., Tröster, G., Bltler, D., & Salama, O. (2004, June). Wireless networks in context aware wearable systems. In *Proceedings of the 1st European Workshop on Wireless Sensor Networks* (pp. 37-40).

Kokolakis, S., & Kiountouzis, E. (2000). Achieving interoperability in a multi-security-policies environment. *Computers & Security, 19*(3), 267–281. doi:10.1016/S0167-4048(00)88615-0

L' Hereux, B., McHugh, M., Privett, B., Kinicki, R. E., & Agu, E. (2006). A campus-wide mobile EMS information management system. In *Proceedings of the Fourth Annual International Conference on Pervasive Computing and Communications* (pp. 522-526).

Malan, D., Fulford-Jones, T., Welsh, M., & Moulton, S. (2004, April). Codeblue: Sn ad-hoc sensor network infrastructure for emergency medical care. In *Proceedings of the 1st International Workshop on Wearable and Implantable Body Sensor Networks*, London UK.

Malatras, A., Pavlou, G., Belsis, P., Gritzalis, S., Skourlas, C., & Chalaris, I. (2005a). Deploying pervasive secure knowledge management infrastructures. *International Journal of Pervasive Computing and Communications Troubador Publishing*, *1*(4), 265–276. doi:10.1108/17427370580000130

Malatras, A., Pavlou, G., Belsis, P., Gritzalis, S., Skourlas, C., & Chalaris, I. (2005b). Secure and distributed knowledge management in pervasive environments. In *Proceedings of the IEEE International Conference on Pervasive Services*, Santorini, Greece (pp. 79-87).

Ng, J. W. P., Lo, B. P. L., Wells, O., Sloman, M., Peters, N., & Darzi, A. ... Yang, G. (2004, September). Ubiquitous monitoring environment for wearable and implantable sensors (UbiMon). In *Proceedings of the 6th International Conference on Ubiquitous Computing*, Nottingham, UK (pp. 3-4).

Paradiso, R. (2003, April). Wearable health care system for vital signs monitoring. In *Proceedings of the 4th IEEE International Conference on Information Technology Applications in Biomedicine*, Birmingham, UK (pp. 283-286).

Park, S., & Jayaraman, S. (2003). Enhancing the quality of life through wearable technology. *IEEE Engineering in Medicine and Biology Magazine*, 22(3), 41–48. doi:10.1109/MEMB.2003.1213625

Sandhu, R., Ferraiolo, D., & Kuhn, R. (2000). The NIST model for role-based access control: Towards a unified standard. In *Proceedings of the Fifth ACM Workshop on Role-Based Access Control* (pp. 47-63).

Sung, M., Marci, C., & Pentland, A. (2005). Wearable feedback systems for rehabilitation. *Journal of Neuroengineering and Rehabilitation*, *2*, 17. doi:10.1186/1743-0003-2-17

Telemedicine Project. (1998). *Mobile telemedicine testbed for national information infrastructure.*

Van Laerhoven, K., Lo, B. P. L., Ng, J. W. P., Thiemjarus, S., King, R., & Kwan, S. ... Yang, G. (2004, September). Medical healthcare monitoring with wearable and implantable sensors. In *Proceedings of the 3rd International Workshop on Ubiquitous Computing for Pervasive Healthcare Applications*, Nottingham, UK.

Vassis, D. (2008). *The Pamvotis simulator*. Retrieved from http://www.pamvotis.org

Vassis, D., Belsis, P., Skourlas, C., & Gritzalis, S. (2009). End to end secure communication in ad-hoc assistive medical environments using secure paths. In *Proceedings of the 1st Workshop on Privacy and Security in Pervasive e-Health and Assistive Environments, in conjunction with the 2nd International Conference on Pervasive Technologies related to Assistive Environments* (article 70).

Vassis, D., Belsis, P., Skourlas, C., & Pantziou, G. (2008). A pervasive architectural framework for providing remote medical treatment. In *Proceedings of the 1st International Conference on Pervasive Technologies Related to Assistive Environments* (Vol. 282, article 23).

Wireless Medicenter. (2006). Retrieved from http://www.wirelessmedicenter.com/mc/glance.cfm

XACML. (2007). *XACML extensible access control markup language specification 2.0*. Organization for the Advancement of Structured Information Standards (OASIS). Retrieved June 10, 2010, from http://www.oasis-open.org

Zafeiris, V., Doulkeridis, C., Belsis, P., & Chalaris, I. (2005). *Agent-mediated knowledge management in multiple autonomous domains*. Paper presented at the Workshop on Agent Mediated Knowledge Management, Utrecht, The Netherlands.

This work was previously published in the Journal of Information Technology Research, Volume 4, Issue 4, edited by Mehdi Khosrow-Pour, pp. 1-17, copyright 2011 by IGI Publishing (an imprint of IGI Global).

Chapter 16
Enhancing the Disaster Recovery Plan through Virtualization

Dennis C. Guster
St. Cloud State University, USA

Olivia F. Lee
Northwest University, USA

ABSTRACT

Currently, organizations are increasingly aware of the need to protect their computer infrastructure to maintain continuity of operations. This process involves a number of different concerns including: managing natural disasters, equipment failure, and security breaches, poor data management, inadequate design, and complex/impractical design. The purpose of this article is to delineate how virtualization of hosts and cloud computing can be used to address the concerns resulting in improved computer infrastructure that can easily be restored following a natural disaster and which features fault tolerant hosts/components, isolates applications security attacks, is simpler in design, and is easier to manage. Further, because this technology has been out for a number of years and its capabilities have matured an attempt has been made to describe those capabilities as well as document successful applications.

INTRODUCTION

Numerous types of disasters, both natural and manmade, can be catastrophic to businesses. Without a well thought out disaster recover (DR) plan, such events can seriously disrupt routine business operations. Often times, it is difficult to comprehend the devastation of an unknown future event, let alone create a comprehensive approach to meet and survive it. The most critical challenges are related to understanding the scope and complexity of DR requirements and the risk of inadequate deployment of recovery efforts. Too often in the past companies have

DOI: 10.4018/978-1-4666-3625-5.ch016

relied on specific vendors and the architecture they provide. However, with virtualization the architecture tends to be more open and it is critical that business adopt a structure independent approach (Zheng & Fang, 2009). This lack of understanding is especially applicable to small or medium size businesses (Hill, 2008) due to the limited IT resources they have available. Larger firms are able to apply economy of scale to develop an information technology (IT) department that equips them with the basic infrastructure to support the addition of DR mechanisms. Small and medium sized businesses, on the other hand, often do not have adequate infrastructure and since, they operate on smaller profit margins, devising and supporting a DR plan can be a huge burden. While outsourcing has been an option for some time for small companies, there are options that build on the advantages of a virtual cloud environment. Wood, Cecchet, Ramakrishnan, Shenoy, van der Merwe, and Venkataramani (2010) report the technical advantages of this architecture as well as its cost effectiveness for small business. No matter the model used a business must realize that they need to invest in DR. Recently, Search Security.com reported that disaster recovery often accounts for as much as 25% of the IT budget. Hence, sound disaster recovery planning is a very important undertaking not only due to what might be lost, but also from a budget perspective. Hence, devising a strong DR infrastructure is further justified by the "information intensity" structure of many companies in the 21st century.

Specifically, for many companies in the 21st century, information resources are their livelihood. The loss or unexpected long term disruption of information or data could have a detrimental effect on business operations. Phillippi (2008) reports that 92% of small businesses that experience significant data loss due to a major disaster go out of business within five years. Indeed, due to the high level of internet connectivity required by most operation functions today, the risks are high and warrant a well thought-out plan with appropriate risk assessment (e.g., Hiles, 1992; Jones & Keyes, 2001; Stephens, 2003). There are success stories in regard to the successful application of virtualization to business applications. A great example is reported by Maitra, Shanker, and Mudholker (2011) in which they describe how virtualization was applied to the banking industry and how secure connectivity was achieved.

Although security risks of the internet increase the need for an effective disaster recovery mechanism, the internet connectivity is nevertheless advantageous as it can be effectively used in the data replication process. If the data is not available it could have far reaching effects particularly in mission critical application such as health care. Therefore, it is crucial that the design focus on the concept of high availability (Adeshiyan et al., 2009). Given this need to ensure high availability, an efficient and cost-effective disaster recovery strategy is to utilize the geographic distribution of the critical components model (Adam, 2002). The connectivity can be inexpensively provided by the internet provided secure transmission methods, such as virtual private networks or VPNs (a way of isolating and double encrypting data sent across the internet), are used, and using the internet can minimize the huge cost of leasing dedicated lines (such as T1 a non-switched digital phone line). The data replicas should be at least 150 miles from the data center headquarters (Phillippi, 2008).

Information resource or data recovery can take many forms. In the past, pools of computers, on which a few members worked together and shared resources, could be used to house backup systems. While this approach still has merit and fits reasonably within a service oriented architecture approach (SOA), for small businesses with remote sites and existing corporate partners, there are major trust issues to resolve in regard to the partners that make up the pool. An alternative is the use of virtualization which can potentially minimize costs and server density (Safigan, 2008). This approach has been refined and the work of Calzolari, Arezzini, Ciampa, Mazzoni, Domenici, and Vaglini (2010) provides a blue print on how to achieve high availability while distributing the application across a small number of servers. However, the intent remains the same and organizations can logically partition one high-end computer and place each of its production servers on it in separate zones, thereby reducing management overhead. Another concept to consider is automation as it may significantly reduce the recovery time during an unexpected disaster. Whatever the chosen method, it is important to consider the expensive and on-going personnel costs which could be significantly higher than the additional hardware required.

Another data recovery aspect organizations must consider is the effect of distributed processing in disaster recovery. The advent of distributed processing and cluster computing vastly altered the manner in which data is stored and how access is granted to resources in an enterprise computing environment. No longer are projects simply done on a stand-alone computer. In fact, any given project may share and retrieve resources from several computers. While such processes often improve performance and lead to some degree of fault tolerance, organizations are required to have a resource profile on each required host. As a result, data spread out among hosts, in separate login accounts, can rapidly become an end-user's nightmare. However, by using a global file (such as NFS) and authentication system (such as LDAP) that allows single sign-in capability, as well as a file system that is attached to that sign-in no matter which host is being accessed, the problems can be rectified.

Global systems often reside on one large enterprise level server. Notwithstanding the aforementioned ease of end-user management, and system or network administrative advantages, global systems place a vast majority of the installation resources in "one basket." Such an approach, if properly replicated, not only can enable network administrators to retain the ease of management, but also provide better performance and reliability through the use of replicas. If there are multiple replicas and they are geographically spread out, they can provide the core infrastructure for a disaster recovery plan. In other words, multiple data centers can act as disaster-recovery sites. Recognizing that developing a recovery plan is imperative in distributed business networks, this article, presents a disaster recovery plan based on computer virtualization that is designed to maintain performance and security while at the same time reducing cost. Specifically, eight topics related to virtualization will be discussed in the Topics in Virtualization section:

1. Managing Infrastructure Complexity
2. The Virtualization Model
3. Understanding Fault Tolerance
4. Virtualization and Security Issues
5. Green Virtualization
6. Cost Effectiveness Via a Virtualized Disaster Recovery Plan
7. WAN Connectivity and Optimization
8. Secured Infrastructure Practices and Policy

Background

DR Considerations

Information resource management is a key success and survival factor in today's heavily connected business landscape. An interruption of normal business operations' information can occur as a result of many unforeseen events. Record and information management (RIM) professionals have long argued the importance of developing appropriate administrative programs to protect vital information during disasters (e.g., Dearstyne, 2006; Jones & Keyes, 2001; Wellheiser & Scott, 2002). Any interruption must be prevented or detected early; damage assessment and recovery must be promptly carried out. For smaller organizations, the ability to successfully respond to disasters cannot be viewed as an optional management initiative but is an essential component of survival (Stephen, 2003). Indeed, top executives generally agreed that developing disaster recovery infrastructure is paramount to business survival (Pervan, 1998). Although advocates of disaster planning agree that preparedness makes all the difference, disaster preparedness *per se* is not limited to planning. Rather, it involves assessing and reducing risks, identifying critical business functions, re-evaluating back-up needs, testing the feasibility of recovery plans, and developing relationships with business partners whom can be counted on during emergencies (Dearstyne, 2006). A successful disaster recovery plan is a continuous loop of planning, implementing, reevaluating, and refining to optimize the plan through each cycle. Such a process results in a structured protocol that covers possible scenarios along with a carefully thought-out recovery plan designed to address disasters and mitigate risk in a methodical and organized manner (Tura et al., 2004). However, one needs to understand that the new technology by itself in not a panacea for a failed security strategy. Rather virtualization is just another tool that can help effectively facilitate the implementation of a well thought out security strategy in a complex global environment. This is pointed out by Tolnai (2010) who suggests that one carefully consider compliance and best practices guidelines when devising policy and then use that policy to ensure that the virtualized solution is designed in adherence to those policies.

Paramount in disaster infrastructure design is recovery time. Recovery time is addressed by Guo (2006) who determined that there was a level of tolerance in regard to recovery time. Guo's study pointed out that recovery time in today's complex world of internetworking is somewhat unpredictable due to the concept of primary/secondary paths and the effects of variable workload on any given network segment.

Obviously the supporting infrastructure needs to be designed to minimize this time interval at a cost the company can justify.

The future of disaster recovery will certainly involve increasing virtualization. Safigan (2008) discusses virtualization as an important option because of its speed. Balaouras (2007) compiled results of an online survey concerning disaster recovery and its costs depending on business size. His work is a useful report which includes statistics on how much organizations are spending on disaster preparedness, their disaster testing methodologies, current recovery objectives, and company confidence in the recovery practices they employ. His results verified that there is a relationship between firm size and what expenses can be justified.

Traditional backup plans simply provide a copy of the data. In the event of a disaster, this backup can be used to restore the system, on new hardware, to its original state when the backup was made. The problem with this approach is that the media is set to a daily backup. As a result, a failure of 12 hours into the next cycle would result in 12 hours of data loss because it was assumed that the 12 hours would be backed up on a redundant array of inexpensive disks (RAID) within the host. Natural disasters, such as earthquakes or floods, could cause severe damage to the host and RAID causing both of them to become completely unusable. In these instances, off-site storage of backups cannot be overlooked. Therefore, a good disaster recovery plan should go beyond off-site storage to restoring a system to its prior state which leads to the concept of host replication. By storing the entire system on one enterprise level host (with or without virtualization of multiple hosts) where global authentication and global file systems are used, it is possible, through the use of WAN's, to have many "baskets" geographically scattered either locally or globally. In the event of a disaster at headquarters, it is possible to switch operations to a replica located well away from the site of the disaster. To accomplish this goal, there are plans of varying degrees of sophistication. For example, using a transparent high performance plan based on commercial software is a costly solution. For small and medium size businesses, it is more sensible to sacrifice a little to performance and vendor support for a cost effective solution.

Virtualization Models

The concept of a virtualized operating system is not new in PC (personal computer) architecture; in fact it goes back at least 20 years (Borden, Hennessy, & Rymarczyk, 1989). However, widespread usage of this concept has only occurred in the last five years or so. This willingness to embrace the concept can probably be traced to a commonly available design that made the transition from best effort provisioning to stable platforms but did not compromise secure operations and was still able to provide adequate performance and functionality (Barham et al., 2003). In other words, the technology of today provides the necessary performance, isolation, ease of use and reliability to make virtualization both practical and effective.

In effect, virtualization allows any given computer to be "multiplexed" or shared among multiple applications. The traditional one computer one application model typically results in much idle time per computer and a much more complex environment to manage. There are several structural models that can be employed when adopting virtualization within a data center (Rosenblum, 2009). One of the most common is server consolidation. This model simply transfers the functionality of a single computer to a logical zone on a host computer. For example, a business might be running three applications such as accounts receivable, accounts payable and general ledger with each housed on a separate physical computer. Server consolidation would allow each application to be housed in a single host computer with each application being logically separated into virtual zones. This solution would still provide the desired isolation for security reason, but would result in less CPU idle time and be easier to manage.

A more sophisticated model that builds on the server consolidation idea is the addition of distributed resource management. In this model the number of virtual hosts per physical host could be varied so that the environment can adapt dynamically to workload. This model tends to optimize computing power better than the basic server consolidation model in which the virtual zones are defined statically. This model then can be said to employ on demand computing (Nellitheertha, 2006) which, in effect, is the reallocation of unused resources to other applications.

The most sophisticated structural model employs the dynamic logic not just to a few physical virtual hosts but to all hosts in the data center resulting in a data center wide virtualization layer which means that all the hardware then can be treated as a hardware pool of resources. This creates a highly flexible environment that can be easily adapted to any usage profile resulting in a highly optimized solution. Once again this would be a variant of on demand computing but more efficient than the previous model because the resource pool is much larger.

To this point, the models have all focused on optimizing processing resources. However, the same basic logic can be applied to storage as well (Nellitheertha, 2006). The primary idea behind this model is to link together a number of heterogeneous storage devices of varying size and model so that they appear as a single virtual resource (Massiglia & Bunn, 2003). Once again this model is highly flexible and allows for better access times, high availability, high data capacity, and reduces the operation cost per megabyte of storage. Further, when one share resources there is a concern that those resources will not be allocated in a timely manner and one large application may eat up the resources and slow response time for other applications. The technology related to virtualization has advanced so that this is only a minor problem. The manner in which this "allocation fairness" can be achieved is reported by Stillwell (2010). His methodology called Dynamic

Fractional Resource Scheduling (DFRS), allows the sharing of homogeneous cluster computing platforms among competing jobs. DFRS leverages virtual machine technology to share node resources in a precise and controlled manner. A key feature of this approach is that it defines and optimizes a user-centric metric of performance and fairness.

The concept of virtualization has been extended and optimized within a cloud environment. This architecture allows sharing of unused CPU cycles not only within a multi-cored host, but across hosts themselves. One of the latest architectures in this realm is described by Hwang, Dongarra, and Fox (2011) which they term virtual clustering. Not only does this mode increase efficiency and reliability, but by using this mode, VMs (virtual machines) can communicate with one another freely through the virtual NIC (network interface card) and configure the communication links automatically. This automation also saves on personnel time which in today's IT environment can be quite expensive.

Green Computing and Virtualization

Another important reason to increase use of OS virtualization deals with the concept of sustainability and "green" IT solutions. Data centers experienced rapid growth over the past 10 years to accommodate distributed systems that now have world-wide reach due to the Internet and the access it provides to support a global economy. Prior research on virtual operating systems contribution to a data center's infrastructure has shown that it is certainly possible to reduce the number of physical computers required to perform the same functions. This new architecture draws less power, generates less heat, and takes up less physical space (Armitage & Harrop, 2005). Further, because fewer computers are required in the data center, additional advantages are also gained in regard to less physical maintenance and simplicity of design (Lowell, Saito, & Samberg, 2004). Further, the advantages include the need for fewer employees and given the highest cost within the IT budget is typically personnel, this would be a most welcome reduction.

Besides the readily apparent advantages such as sustainability that green computing through virtualization provides, other advantages may result that are related to fault tolerance and performance. In the physical model, if a host failed only the application actually running on that host would fail. In the virtual model, if the physical host fails all the virtual zones and their respective applications fail as well. So one could view the virtual model structure like as putting all of your "eggs" (running applications) in one basket. This is a troubling scenario, so for this model to be effective multiple baskets are needed (Guster, McCann, Krzenski, & Lee, 2008). There are success stories in regard to using virtualization to promote green computing. A representative example can be seen in the work of King (2011) at Empire State College which was able to realize 70% saving on computing energy related costs.

Replication and Fault Tolerance in Virtualized Models

It would be a good idea to make sure the main production virtualized host would be backed up at least twice. More specifically, two exact copies (or as close as the updating delay would permit) should be kept, one on site and one off-site providing two degrees of fault tolerance. In the event the main site failed then the first replica would become the new production site. In addition to offering fault tolerance capability the replicas can also be used to improve performance by being configured for load balancing. More specifically not all of the data inquiries would be sent to the main production server; rather, they would be equally distributed among the main production host and the available replicas. Some research has shown that the load balancing technique can in fact help improve performance (Lin, Neo, Zhang, Huang, & Gay, 2007). This load balancing technique can extend performance which is important given that the virtualized model in its basic form reduces an application's access to computer resources.

While "greening" the data center, reducing complexity, and enhancing fault tolerance provide strong support for the concept of host virtualization, it is still important to address the security concept of isolating applications. Many worry that the logical isolation it provides is adequate when compared with the physical isolation model. However, given the dire security consequences of being connected to the Internet perhaps it is virtualization's flexible high profile isolation services that are its best attributes. A look at the work of Laureano, Maziero, and Jamhour (2007) provides a good example. They describe the importance of intrusion detection applications to help safeguard against outside attacks and point out the application's vulnerability to external tampering or disabling when run in a straight unviruralized physical host. As one might expect, intrusion detection is the cornerstone of any security strategy and should be protected to the utmost. Further, they were able to use virtualization to successfully isolate the intrusion detection application in their data center, thereby making it invisible and inaccessible to intruders.

Based on the review above, clearly numerous advantages can be gained from integrating virtualization into the computing infrastructure. The main focus of this article will be to delineate specifics within the eight topics presented in the Introduction section.

TOPICS IN VIRTUALIZATION

Managing Infrastructure Complexity

As a basis for understanding infrastructure complexity, we will use the scale-free degree distribution formula.

Complexity does not necessarily translate into sounder infrastructure. In fact, complexity can lead to infrastructure that is both challenging to use and expensive to manage. One factor in assessing complexity is the number of physical hosts housed in the computer system infrastructure. Many autonomous systems have experienced rapid uncontrolled growth in the number of physical hosts often utilized under the guise of application separation or improved performance. Each added host and its network connection (s) add to infrastructure complexity. A curve linear relationship occurs when one realizes that each host must communicate with every other host in an autonomous system. To provide an understanding of this situation, a series of infrastructure examples will be analyzed using the scale-free distribution formulae to assess the number of failure points (i.e., a host or a host connection). Further, several examples will be presented that will delineate how virtualized hosts can reduce complexity while maintaining acceptable security and performance.

Currently, there are three commonly available data backup site categories: cold, warm or hot sites. Through virtualization we will also introduce the modified hot site. A cold site is typically the most inexpensive back-up option to operate and involves minimal set up costs. A cold site has no functioning backup copies of the data at the primary data center, and often no additional hardware is required if the tape backup systems are already available. The recovery methodology is essentially restoration from tape to hardware at a remote site with daily updates.

A warm site is an alternate location where data could be retrieved after disruption. It is equipped with hardware similar to the primary site but does not store exact copies of the data. Often the updates take place hourly. A warm site is moderately expensive to operate and the cost largely depends on the desired speed of recovery.

A hot site is the most expensive DR option with full technological capacity that enables a seemingly fool-proof recovery processes. Due to its sophisticated information technology (IT) infrastructure, hot sites allow real time synchronization between the primary and alternate back-up site, allowing a complete mirroring of the original data using wide area network links (in our case two independent leased links) and advanced software. Following a disruption to the primary location, the data processing can be quickly relocated to the hot site with minimal loss to routine operations.

A modified hot site is a recovery option that provides partial benefits of a hot site with a lower DR investment. We propose this option based on our success in leveraging the benefits of host virtualization via creating multiple logical computers (partitioning the resources of one physical computer into six virtualized resource sets) in one single physical computer. Because all production hosts are virtualized into one physical host, this option generates a smaller complexity index and, as a result, has fewer failure points.

Figure 1 is a graphical representation of the various available options in regard to recovery expenses (investment) versus recovery time. Infrastructure complexity and investment cost are the two major considerations in choosing an appropriate DR model. For small and medium-sized businesses, the availability of technologies and size of the DR budget dictate reasonable recovery spending. However, even with resource limitations well thought out models can still yield effective benefits. Therefore, decisions related to allocating these resources are important in ensuring organizational sustainability. Bryson et al. (2002) advocate using mathematical modeling in analyzing and designing DR models. Past research indicated that the more physical components (hosts) in the DR infrastructure, the greater the probability of a hardware failure. Certainly, additional hardware can provide additional fault tolerance, but it will also increase the DR expenses, particularly from a personnel perspective.

To illustrate the concepts of complexity within this article we employ the scale-free degree distribution theory to determine network growth by applying the formula N*(N-1)/2 to assess the complexity of the communication path within each DR model (Baccaletti, Latora, Morento, Chavez, & Hwang, 2006). Our assumption rests on the premise that a complex model will result in more possible failure points and be more difficult to support from a personnel perspective. The formula allows us to discover the complexity of communication paths and possible failure points based on the total number of computers in

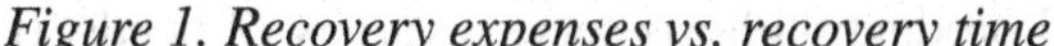

Figure 1. Recovery expenses vs. recovery time

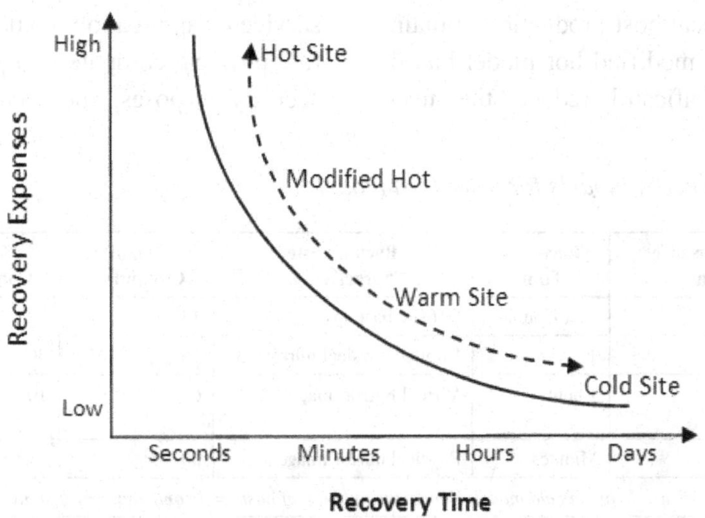

production and the configuration of the replication process. In a simple client/server model that typically consists of a client computer, a server computer, and a network (LAN) connecting them, the complexity index would be one and result in three total model failure points. In this example, a network complexity of one reflects a very simple model. The number of individual possible failure points is three, which is arrived at by adding the number of computers (N) to the network complexity (C). Because this backup scenario is applied to only one host (one instance), the model's total number of failure points is still three.

For the rest of the computations presented in this section of the article, we based our assumptions on a six-host production model because such a quantity is regarded as a representative model for many small and medium sized businesses. Furthermore, that is the number of production hosts in our computing domain and we had experience working with that number. However, any number of hosts (computers) might occur. It is common for organizations to have separate hosts for various applications such as accounting and inventory to manage security and performance indicators. Further, additional hosts are often required to support networking activities such as World Wide Web (WWW), domain name service (DNS) and remote file systems. Table 1 presents a summary of the characteristics of each of the basic models in which a six physical host production domain was replicated. The modified hot model based on virtualization significantly reduced the number of physical computers required, and offered performance that was superior to every model except the hot model which is significantly more complex and vastly more expensive. For a detailed explanation of these models and calculations used to derive the model complexities (Lee, Guster, Schmidt, & McCann, 2009).

Virtualization Model

This topic will describe how to use virtualized hosts to build an entire production network in a single box.

The number of physical hosts required to support the networking and application functions of an autonomous system can often be housed in a single "virtualized" physical box. This method reduces complexity and results in a network that is easier to manage. To illustrate this concept, an example from the authors' autonomous system in which nine physical production hosts were reduced to nine virtual zones in a single physical computer will be described in detail.

The computing domain used in this case study is designed to mirror the functionality of a manufacturing company that sells its own products and maintains its own IT infrastructure. In an environment such as this, numerous physical production hosts serve a variety of needs. If the traditional physical model is followed each service or application would be housed in separate physical computers to provide isolation for security purposes. The assumption in the design

Table 1. Disaster recovery models for a six-host model

Model	Synchronize Time	Recovery Time	Back-up Site Characteristics	No. of Computers	Model Complexity	Tolerance Support
Cold	Days	>24 Hours	Off site backups	12	18	Limited
Warm	Hours	1-24 hours	Limited physical mirroring	18	40	Moderate
Modified Hot	Minutes	1 hour	Virtual mirror image	6	10	High
Hot	Seconds	Minutes	Physical mirror image	30	251	Very high
Note: There is no remote backup site in the cold model. Hence, the total no. of hosts = 2 computers per instance.						

delineated here is that in all cases performance in the separate physical host model was acceptable from a performance perspective and that unused CPU cycles were observed for all hosts. Therefore, one could expect that the core production hosts could be effectively converted to a virtualized host design. The security related assumption then is that the virtual partitions would provide the required isolation needed for security purposes while the performance requirements would still be reasonable. In other words, since all the original physical hosts were using only a fraction of their available computing resources they should function at an acceptable level in a shared virtual host (Lee, Guster, Schmidt, & McCann, 2009). In this case study, nine physical hosts are restructured into virtual zones in a single physical host. In theory, this should mean that each is limited to about 1/9 of the available computing resources. However, the LINUX operating system can be configured to utilize dynamic resource allocation, meaning that the total available resources can be viewed as a pool and any unused resources can be allocated to any virtual partition. The dynamic allocation methodology works well as long as there are several fairly idle virtual machines. If an intense workload is distributed across all nine virtual partitions performance would fall very rapidly and a priority scheme would be needed to control resource allocation. The purpose of each of the nine original physical hosts providing IT infrastructure for a typical medium size business that engages in Ecommerce is described in Table 2. Each partition corresponds to a separate physical host.

The first row in Table 2 describes the characteristics of the physical host for the nine partitions (zones) to follow. This host contains the network time server (NFS) that is used to synchronize all hosts (both virtual and physical) within the domain. It is critical for client/server and database applications that all hosts in the domain be synchronized for data integrity and security purposes. This physical host is configured with the Linux operating system.

Partition number 1 contains the main client access server used to allow people within the company and customers to access IT resources in a secure manner. Because this domain is connected to the internet to support E-commerce activity and financially related applications are run in the domain, it is crucial to monitor client traffic. Therefore, both incoming and outgoing traffic to this partition are tightly filtered at the firewall level and terminal access is only available

Table 2. Virtual host partitions (zones)

Partition No.	Description
Host	**Time Server, Virtual Machine host (Running LINUX)**
1	Main client access server, secure access server (Firewall will forward all port22 traffic to this partition)
2	Secondary client access server, backup secure access server (Firewall will forward alternate port to this partition, port22)
3	Global authentication server (OpenLDAP/Kerberos5-MIT)
4	Network address resolution server (DNS/DHCP/LDAP)
5	E-Mail server (LINUX Mail Server installed)
6	Web server (Apache Tomcat)
7	Global file system server for home folders (NFS Mounted)
8	Financial applications server (accounting, sales, payroll and etc.)
9	Production server to support application services (inventory, product development, advertising and etc.)

through secure shell (ssh) which uses a sophisticated encryption stream.

Partition 2 provides a secondary version of virtual zone 1 (described previously). This zone provides a backup to partition 1 so that clients have an alternate way to connect to the domain in the event partition 1 becomes corrupted. Because the domain uses a global authentication system (active directory), single sign-on can be provided to users so that they are granted access to both partitions one and two, with the same login information.

The global authentication described above is hosted in virtual partition number 3. This global authentication is provided by lightweight directory access protocol which IT managers often select due to its robustness and scalability (Guster, Hall, Herath, Jansen, & Mikluch, 2008). In an effort to provide heightened security to this critical component in the IT security structure, Kerberos (developed by MIT) is used which increases the robustness of the encryption and uses a mechanism so that the password does not have to be sent remotely across the network by the client.

Partition 4 provides the network address resolution services. Specifically, domain name service (DNS) and the dynamic host configuration protocol (DHCP) are hosted in this zone. These services allow resolution of network layers and client work stations to be allocated to a temporary network (IP) address. Domain service would be provided to all domains in the company's enterprise because a given company might support more than one domain name (such as chevy.com and chevrolet.com).

Email services are provided in virtual zone 5. This virtual partition hosts a mail system which provides standard mail services and a browser based email interface that is linked to a standard apache tomcat web server (hosted in partition 6). Both secure and unsecured mail services are supported. Standard web services are supported in partition 6 and, as mentioned earlier, apache tomcat is the web server software of choice. This web service also hosts domain related home pages, web interfaces for company employees, and E-commerce activities.

The global file system is hosted in partition 7 and uses the network file system protocol. This file system can be described as the central depository of company data and allows all user/company data to be stored in a central location for ease of access and management. Further, this global orientation allows a user's home directory (or directory maps) to follow that user no matter which host (virtual or physical) he/she is logged into. The user always has the same default directory no matter which host (virtual or otherwise) he/she is referencing. The concept of centralizing all data at a single location provides management advantages; however, it involves risk in that all the "eggs" (data) are in one basket (location). Therefore, it is critical to have the data reside at multiple locations to provide the multiple "basket" logic. Virtualization makes it easy to accomplish this since the functionality of the entire domain can be hosted in a single physical computer. Placing several computers, all configured with the same file synchronization logic, at various locations world-wide can provide excellent fault tolerance and backup.

Virtual partition 8 is designed to support financial related applications. The software required to run all financial operations is hosted in this zone. This includes applications such as payroll, accounting and sales. Direct access to this zone would not be allowed, so a user would have to authenticate through partition 1 (or 2) and access the application via SSH or some form of tunneled web browser.

The last partition contains the virtual zone that contains the product related application server. This partition would support applications such as inventory, product development and advertising. Once again because security is paramount, direct access to this zone would not be allowed. A user would have to authenticate through partition 1 or 2 and access the application via SSH or some form of tunneled web browser.

Understanding Fault Tolerance

In this section we will describe how to use multiple "virtualized" boxes to provide fault tolerance, load balancing and archiving.

If the functionality of nine computers is placed into one and it fails, the results could be catastrophic; it is synonymous with placing all of your "eggs" (hosts) in one basket. For this strategy to be effective the autonomous system must have multiple baskets (i.e., replicas of the virtualized host). To illustrate how multiple replicas can provide effective fault tolerance, load balancing and data archiving an example will be described from the authors' autonomous system that features three replicas and two archival hosts.

Virtualization makes it easy to provide fault tolerance by simplification of IT infrastructure and easy deployment of replicas housed in a single physical computer. In topic 2 we explained that a whole production domain consisting of nine hosts could be virtualized into one physical computer. So to replicate that whole domain only one physical computer virtualized into the nine zones would be required. Figure 2 illustrates how this scenario might be used to provide three levels of replication while only using four computers.

Figure 2 production virtualized host and, in addition to providing fault tolerance, could be used for load balancing. The design features two other replicas one in a different building, but in the same town and one in a different town at least 300 miles away. Therefore, different levels of disasters are considered, from a building specific disaster such as a localized flood to a disaster that might affect the whole town such as a tornado, in which case operations could be switched to the town 300 miles away.

Further, the same virtualized replicas that provide a multi-level fault tolerance plan can also be used to improve system performance. Inquiry workload can be distributed among the various replicas by using a "load balancing" technique. This technique means that any given replica in the enterprise will be less busy which translates to less service time (wait time) for any given transaction. Distributing the replicas at key geographic locations within a company's global market can also

Figure 2. Fault tolerance through virtualized replicas

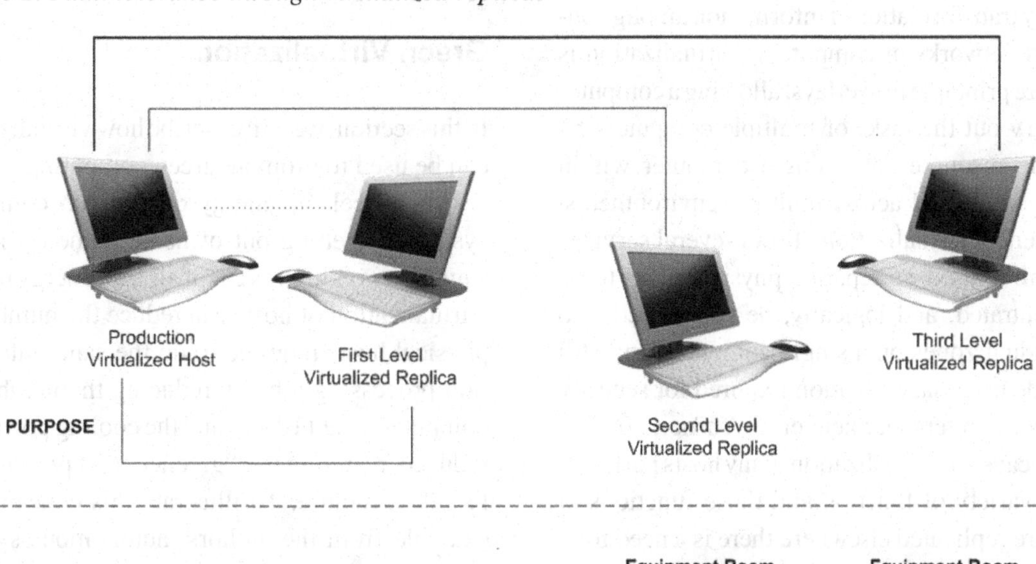

enhance performance by reducing the distance any client needs to travel across the network (internet). For example, a company based in New York may do business in Paris. In a centralized model a customer in Belgium would need to connect to the main server in New York. With the decentralized virtual model that same customer could connect to the replica server in Paris, thereby reducing network travel and response time delay.

Virtualization and Security Issues

This section will describe how virtualization can be used to isolate applications for security reasons.

One of the primary reasons that multiple hosts are housed in different autonomous systems is the need to isolate applications for the sake of security. The logic behind this concept is that if any one host is compromised only the application running on that host will be effected. However, it is also possible to achieve the same isolation via software rather than physical borders and that is what host virtualization does. Thus, in a virtualized host, if one virtual zone is compromised all other zones are not affected. More specifically virtualization, as its name implies, is used in virtual memory and virtual machines. A proven technology, it allows speedy transformation of information among connected networks of computers. Virtualization is the core principle in overlays, allowing a computer to carry out the tasks of multiple computers by sharing resources of a single computer within the network and across multiple environments. In essence, virtualization allows several services that are housed on separate physical hosts to be concentrated, and logically, be partitioned into individual zones on a single computer, and still provide necessary isolation required for security purposes (Peterson, Shenker, & Yurner, 2005).

Because in virtualization many hosts performing a variety of function and those functions in turn are replicated elsewhere there is a need for a well-designed access control strategy. If we were protecting a college campus made up of a group of building we would assess who we would trust to have access to the various rooms within those buildings. The same type of logic can be applied to a virtualized computing environment, in other word a "trust model." An excellent example of such a model is presented by Gebhardt (2011). Specifically, he was able to devise a design that enhances the concept of an instant-on virtual system while maintaining secure, trustworthy and policy enforced compartments.

In the example delineated earlier in Topic 2, nine physical computers were reduced to nine zones in a single physical computer to provide application isolation. Each zone is completely protected from traffic entering another zone within that physical computer. In fact even the network interface is multiplexed, and each logic interface is linked only to the appropriate zone in the virtual hosts. Figure 3 illustrates this concept using the previous nine zone model. Once again, each zone is independent and isolated and has its own unique network node address even though only one network interface card is installed. This configuration does however require each zone be placed on the same network, which in this case would be the internet protocol network style dotted decimal address is 192.1.1.0.

Green Virtualization

In this section, we will describe how virtualization can be used to promote green computing.

Many feel the energy cost to run computer systems is getting out of hand; some estimates suggest it is as high as 2% of all U.S. energy usage. Virtualization of hosts can reduce the number of physical hosts required to do the same information processing job. By reducing the number of computers, the 110 volt and the cooling power are reduced, resulting in a "greener" foot print for the IT infrastructure. To illustrate this concept, the example from the authors' autonomous system described earlier in which nine computers were virtualized into one will serve as a case study to

Figure 3. Security isolation in a virtual host model

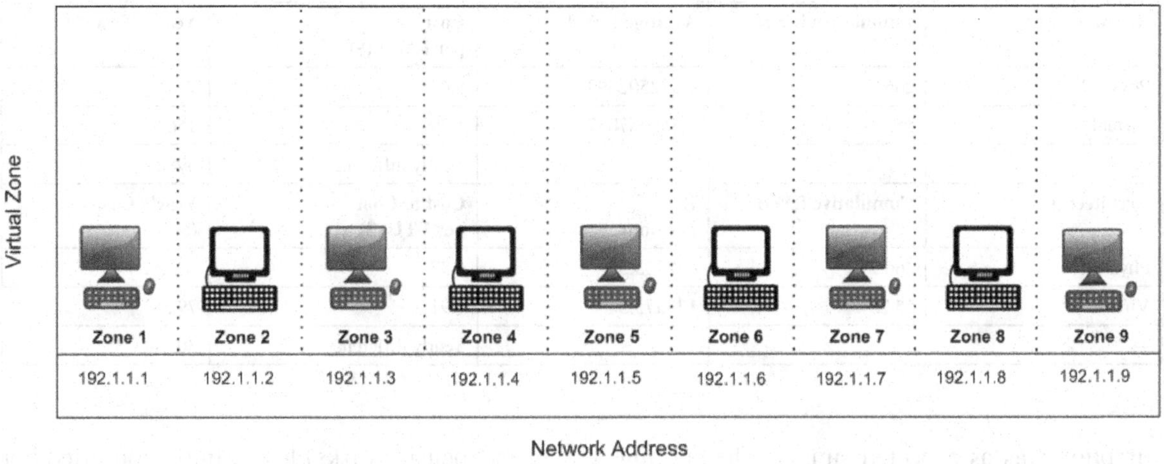

Virtual Zone	Zone 1	Zone 2	Zone 3	Zone 4	Zone 5	Zone 6	Zone 7	Zone 8	Zone 9
Network Address	192.1.1.1	192.1.1.2	192.1.1.3	192.1.1.4	192.1.1.5	192.1.1.6	192.1.1.7	192.1.1.8	192.1.1.9

illustrate how virtualization can result in a $900 a year savings in power consumption.

In the computing domain serving this case study, numerous physical production hosts serve a variety of needs. They were originally placed in separate physical computers to provide isolation for security purposes. In all cases, performance in the separate physical host model was generally excellent and unused CPU cycles were observed in all cases. Therefore, these core production hosts offered an excellent test case for virtualized hosts. The assumption was the virtual partitions would provide the isolation needed for security purposes, and the performance requirements for any one host could be met in a shared resource environment. Specifically, since all hosts were using only a fraction of their available computing resources on their physical host, they would function at an acceptable level in a shared virtual host (Lee, Guster, Schmidt, & McCann, 2009). As stated earlier in the article, our case study nine physical hosts are restructured as virtual machines in a single physical host. In theory that would mean that they would each be limited to 1/9 of the available computing resources. However, in the operating system utilized, the resource allocation is dynamic meaning that the resources are viewed as a pool and any unused resources can be allocated to any virtual machine. This methodology works well as long as there are several fairly idle virtual machines. In the unlikely scenario of intense workload across all nine virtual machines performance would decay exponentially and a priority scheme would need to be used to control the resource allocation. As you will recall the purpose of each of the nine original physical hosts described in partition numbers 1-9 is in Table 2 (Virtual Hosts Zones) was also provided earlier in this article.

To ascertain the effectiveness of the virtual model, a nine day period was selected and power consumption data (using a standard meter) was collected for both the old physical configuration and the new virtual configuration. The result of this comparison is depicted in Table 3. As expected, the virtual model improved upon the physical model. In fact, the cost per KWH for the virtual model was only about 20% of the physical model. This translated into a yearly cost difference (assuming a price of $.07 per KWH) of almost $600.

Table 3 provides information about the cooling requirements for each architecture. The methodology applied is adapted from Larabie (2003). Again, as expected, the virtual model consumed significantly fewer resources than did the physical model. Further, it appears that the ratio of con-

Table 3. Power consumption physical vs. virtual architecture

Architecture	Cumulative KWH	Average KWH	Cost per KWH ($)	Yearly Cost ($)
Physical	266.24	1.232592593	8.63	755.83
Virtual	55.25	0.255787037	1.79	156.85
			Yearly difference	598.98
Architecture	**Cumulative KWH**	**BTU per hour**	**Cost to Cool per BTU ($)**	**Yearly Cost ($)**
Physical	266.24	642703.36	4.37	382.51
Virtual	55.25	133373.5	0.91	79.38
			Yearly difference	303.14

sumption was as expected similar. The cooling cost difference was about $300 higher for the physical model and that coupled with the approximate $600 figure on power consumption, reveals that the physical model would cost almost $900 more a year to run than the virtual model.

Cost Effectiveness via a Virtualized Disaster Recovery Plan

A description of how virtualized hosts can serve as the cornerstone of a disaster recovery plan from a cost effectiveness perspective will be presented in this section. Too often companies tend to skimp on the plan because if they selected a hot model (a complete replication of their entire IT infrastructure) it in effect doubles their infrastructure budget. Virtualization of hosts can provide much of the functionality of a hot model at a fraction of the cost. Once again this will be illustrated using the nine zone virtualized model presented in Table 2, and the characteristics of virtualized models such as cost, reliability, recovery time, complexity and ease of management will be compared to the three common disaster recovery models.

Overview of Replica Strategies

To gain some understanding of the complexity, it may be useful to examine a common fault tolerance concept, the RAID (redundant array of inexpensive disks) logic. In the modified hot site option, the array concept can be expanded to the host level, and the RAIH (redundant array of inexpensive hosts (computers)) concept might be more appropriate because we are mirroring hosts instead of just disks. In a six-host model, all six computers of the production site are equipped with computing power for an instructional domain. These six hosts perform the following functions: host DNS (domain name service), maintain a global file system, enable website service, allow email communication, serve as a firewall, and provide instructional support. The capability of RAIH allows the data to support all functions to be replicated across all hosts, and, therefore, the data is available for any given function when needed to support its primary purpose. In a six-host model, each local disk will have to be logically divided into six separate partitions. Although this model offers excellent fault tolerance, it is inherently complex, and sophisticated personnel are required for system support. In a LAN environment, the additional complexity and inter-processor communication might be practical because there is adequate bandwidth to support them. However, in a WAN environment, the additional communication overhead may negate the model due to the network's inability to complete the needed updates timely and cost effectively due to the slower speeds and the additional number of bytes that a RAIH would generate.

Software Costs

In regard to software, the costs vary based on the complexity of the model and whether shareware or commercial software is used. For the cold site, a commercial tape backup package with nine licenses was selected. In the case of the warm model, a commercial backup/replica package with nine licenses was chosen. Since the modified warm model was devised from scratch using the Unix operating system the openness allowed the use of shareware software at no cost. The complexity and high reliability needs of the hot model necessitated an enterprise level backup replica package with unlimited server licenses.

Hardware Costs

As would be expected, the variance in complexity led to variation in the hardware needs. In all cases we are assuming the production side hardware was in place, as well as the networking infrastructure minus the WAN bandwidth costs. For the cold model, nine low end PCs with tape drives at $1,000 each (this allows for simultaneous backup of all six hosts) were required. In the warm model, nine mid range server level hosts (at $1,000 each) were needed. For the modified hot virtualization model the hardware needs were reduced to three mid range server level hosts at $1,000 each. Lastly, as expected, the hot model required the most hardware, 18 high range enterprise server level hosts at $10,000 each.

Bandwidth Costs

In regard to band width, the tape backup equipment would reside on site so there are no WAN bandwidth requirements for the cold site. A traditional warm site would rely on leased lines for the sake of security. In this case, a leased line (point to point) at 300 miles at 16mbs was selected to meet the bandwidth requirements. The modified hot site developed to save money risks using the internet to provide connectivity (a VPN is used to enhance security) and an internet cable connection at 12mbs has been selected based on the data observed in Guster, Safonov, Hall, and Sundheim (2003). To provide the massive bandwidth and reliability required by the hot site, dual 40 Mbs leased lines at 300 miles were the configuration chosen.

Personnel Cost

Lastly, the personnel costs also varied greatly from model to model. In the cold model the primary operational costs were tape backup operations and the personnel cost is estimated at 10 hours a week at the rate of $20 an hour. In the warm model, we estimated that 10 hours a week, at $50 an hour, for system/network engineering personnel would be required. The lower complexity of the modified hot model reduces the personnel needs down to five hours a week (due to reduced hardware) at $50 an hour for system/network engineering personnel. The hot site had the greatest personnel needs estimated at 20 hours a week (due to added hardware) at $50 an hour for system/network engineering personnel (Krojnewski & Nager, 2006). Table 4 provides a summary of estimated costs incurred for each of the four models that might be used to provide DR for the nine host model described in Table 2.

WAN Connectivity and Optimization

In this section we will describe how virtualized hosts can be integrated into an archiving methodology that relies on WAN connectivity.

One of the concerns with any disaster recovery plan is to have the data spread out over an acceptable geographic distance in the event the whole region might be affected. A basic rule of thumb is that data should be spread out at least 300 miles. However, designing an archival network with replication at remote sites requires a cost effective and secure means of data transfer.

Table 4. Disaster recovery investment and annual maintenance costs (S) based on nine instances

Recovery Sites	Software: Server Site	Hardware: Remote Site	Bandwidth Cost (WAN)	Personnel Cost	Total Cost
Cold	3,225	9,000	0	10,400	22,625
Warm	6,650	9,000	6,384	26,000	48,034
Modified Hot	0	3,000	1,596	13,000	17,596
Hot	66,500	180,000	120,000	52,000	418,500

Leasing private lines to support connectivity can be costly and WANs in general have significantly less bandwidth than LANs. Therefore, the only affordable alternative is to use the internet to transfer the archival information from the main host to the archival replica. Data collected on the authors' autonomous system will be used to illustrate how security can be employed to protect the archival data and how an Internet WAN link can be optimized to support this data intensive transfer. To ascertain if the encryption overhead on this link would not jeopardize performance, a series of experiments were undertaken. Figure 4 depicts the difference in inter-arrival times between the encrypted and non-encrypted traffic. It is clear that the unencrypted traffic arrives much more quickly and would result in a quicker completion of the replica update process.

Then the encrypted backup software was run several times with the fairly intense backup scenario, first without and then with the two types of encryption (tunneled and secure shell, SSH). Since one of the replicas was connected remotely via a WAN, different line speeds were tested to ascertain available bandwidths' influence on performance.

The findings of this experiment provided some interesting results, particularly for the WAN links. On the LAN link, it was clear that the overhead generated by the encryption process contributed to longer transmission times, but only about 10% longer. With the WAN links, line speed makes a major difference in regard to efficiency and if backup scenarios of this magnitude are expected, investing in additional line speed becomes important. In our example, at 1.5Mbs it takes approximately 500 minutes to complete the intense back up scenario tested (about 50 GB), while at 6Mbs it only takes about 100 minutes. It is also worthwhile to note that the influence of encryption overhead is lessened at slower speeds. Indeed, it takes longer for non-encrypted data than with encrypted data. One plausible explanation is the large dependence on buffering the data. Since the data can leave the PC easily at 100Mbs, there is little bandwidth restriction when entering the LAN. In the case of the WANs, the data sits in a buffer for long time periods and as long as the application can keep the buffer full, there is less time loss in actual network transmission. Further, the CPU usage levels provide a similar pattern for the un-encrypted traffic. It took 225 seconds (un-encrypted) on the LAN level versus 250 seconds for the encrypted tunneled traffic. In summary, these results show it is possible to conduct the replica backup/update securely across an internet link if adequate bandwidth is provided (about 10 Mbs in our example).

Secured Infrastructure Practices and Policy Considerations

In this section we will provide some sample policy statements related to the integration of virtualized hosts in an IT infrastructure. Any change in infrastructure needs a framework to follow. Security concerns such as partition design, archival updating across the internet, and firewall settings

Figure 4. Packet inter-arrival times encrypted vs. unencrypted sessions (Wan 1.5 MBS)

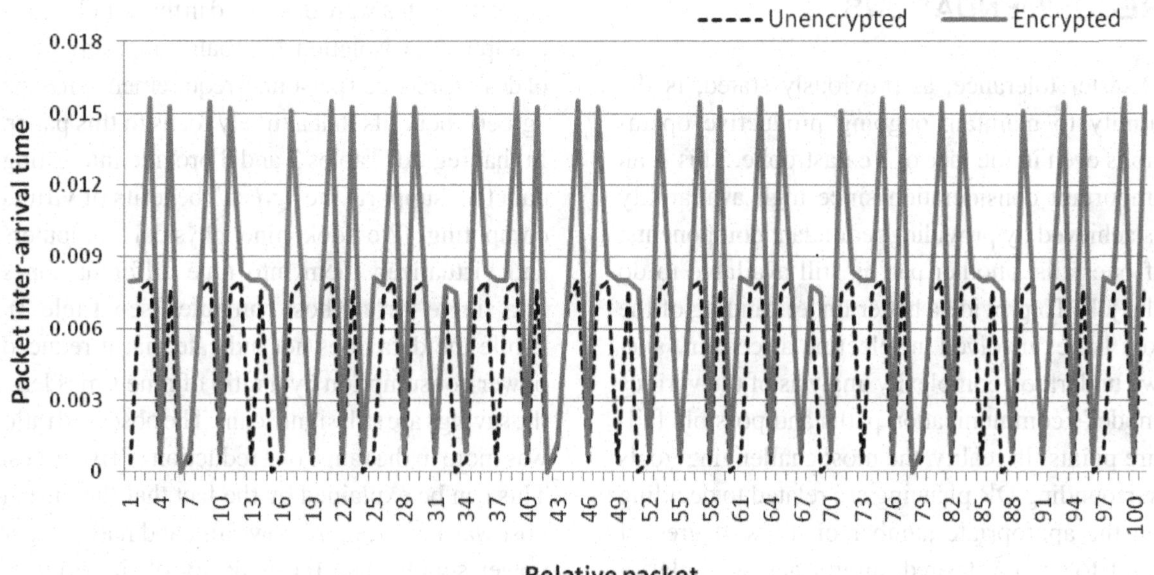

involving inter-host communications which would not be a concern under the old physical model will be discussed. A series of policy statements derived from the authors' virtualized network will be presented below and discussed.

The first policy area to be discussed will involve disaster recovery. Instead of two computers with the same physical image, all logical zones on a virtualized host must be backed up in their entirety to a separate physical machine from that of the virtualization server machine. In other words, it does not make sense to backup to a second logical zone in the same virtual machine. Further, because in a sense you are putting all of "eggs" (data) in one basket there is a need for multiple baskets. Therefore, with virtualization a policy in regard to replication might be: there must be a minimum of the production system, and three duplicate replica backups of that production virtualized host. One backup must be onsite of with the production system, and the second must be housed in a separate building located at least 500 meters from the production system and the third must be housed at least 300 miles away.

A second area of virtualization policy might be related to general operations which might warrant a policy as follows. Because the virtual zones are logical and truly transparent all logical zone installations must be documented in the organization network diagram schematics and on all system hosts files. No logical zone may be created or used for any purpose for which the chief information officer has not authorized in writing.

The last area of discussion will be related to system maintenance. Because the hard drive(s) on a virtual host are supporting data from multiple applications performance and management are paramount. So a policy related to disk defragmentation might look as follows: virtualization servers housing logical zones must have the hard disks defragmented at least once per month. Further, the logical implementations themselves must have their disk partitions defragmented at least once every three months.

SOLUTIONS AND RECOMMENDATIONS

Disaster tolerance, as previously stated, is the ability to maintain ongoing productive operations even in the face of a catastrophe. This is an important consideration since high availability is achieved by providing redundant components; if one fails, another part is still available to do the job. To provide a better understanding of the key issues involved in selecting a recovery site, we undertook complexity analysis of the various model's communication paths and possible failure points. In reality, the most challenging goals surrounding DR planning are related to deciding on the appropriate number of hosts, degree of fault tolerance desired, appropriate granularity and attainment of all of those goals within the available budget. Our analysis indicated that there were some real benefits in adapting the virtual model. Of course, the key advantage for the proposed modified hot site is cost effectiveness. By deploying virtualization to reduce the number of physical hosts and using shareware software, firms can develop a structured and actionable DR plan that has many of the basic benefits of a hot site model. The application of virtualization is a formal approach to DR planning which enables effective DR solutions that are less complex, more cost effective, and close to the performance level of the hot model. We suspect that the proposed virtual option is an optimal solution for small and medium sized businesses due to its capabilities to enable firms to simplistically map out the dependencies between critical business processes, people, IT assets, and other resources. It can also perform simultaneous functions such as hosting DNS, maintaining a global file system, enabling website service, allowing email communication, serving as a firewall, and providing application support, all in a single physical host, while still maintaining the separation of those services for performance and security purposes.

In addition to the numerous benefits of virtual computing that were described in this article (such as application isolation, load balancing, simplicity of design, reduced personnel requirements) it is the "green" benefits that a timely focus to this paper. In that regard, Tables 2 and 3 provide interesting data that supports the "green" benefits of virtual computing. We took nine physical computers and virtualized them into nine different zones in a single virtual host computer (see Table 2). While the data does not indicate that it reduced power consumption by a ratio of nine times less, the savings are still significant. The observed ratio was more in the range of a reduction of five times. This can be explained by the fact that the virtual host was newer, more powerful, and had a larger power supply than the majority of the original physical hosts. Further, because it was housing nine applications, the new virtual host tended to be loaded at a higher level which led to more power consumption. Cost savings on power were about $600 a year and on cooling about $300 a year. This yields an annual combined savings of about $900 a year. If a data center was larger and was a candidate for virtualization and the saving ratio observed is transferrable then reduction of cooling and power costs by a factor of five would be a most welcome development. Further, if that reduction is realized, the added benefit of reducing the physical space to store the equipment could be attained as well. In summary, virtualization offers many benefits and may be applied to classes of problems in which isolation is the primary rationale for running an application in a separate physical computer. It is not designed for situations in which increasing performance is the primary motivation for multiple physical computers (such as a cluster). The data herein certainly indicate that there are sustainability benefits to be gained from virtualization of physical hosts.

Further, the data collected show some interesting results in regard to model sophistication and cost. Often the basic perception of outsourcing is that it is superior to devising an in-house model.

In our case had we not devised a hybrid virtualized model that built upon our existing in-house technical expertise and the adaptation of virtualization/internet access, our solution would have probably been the out-sourced model. While the cold model was relatively inexpensive, it simply was not sophisticated enough. The warm model probably would have been adequate with some tuning on the granularity level, but it was too expensive, while the hot model was a luxury way beyond our budget. It was also interesting that the virtualized model and the outsourcing price tag in our case were very similar. While the design and preparation time for devising and implementing the virtualized model were substantial, we suspect that it was not significantly greater than what would be required to define and convey our backup needs and strategies to an outsourcing company. As one would suspect, effective communication with the outsourcing company is crucial.

Our success in part was related to our staff's sound foundation in technical areas such as virtualization and network encryption techniques. We were able to use existing personnel to accomplish our goal and justify some of the costs by piggybacking the concept of performance improvement through load balancing via replication within the project. Companies without in house expert perhaps should carefully consider the advantages of outsourcing due to the high cost of personnel. While we did not greatly consider the ethics of trusting an outsourcing company with our sensitive data, we suspect it could be an important issue for some companies (especially if they do not already have internal IT personnel resources).

Last, the preliminary results obtained herein are encouraging. First, the hardware and infrastructure required for this plan are inexpensive and would fit into any small business' budget. Second, we were able to inexpensively use shareware software to provide the functionality, ease of use, and performance necessary to create and update the required replicas. Third, the internet WAN connection was viable because the overhead generated by the encryption process was minimal, and it can be effectively employed to protect the transmission of the backup data.

FUTURE RESEARCH DIRECTIONS

Additional research is needed that would replicate the model design effectiveness. Of particular interest would be how well virtualization would scale in larger computing domains. Also, the question of how to best provide inter-connectivity among replicas connected by a WAN needs additional examination, but with backup scenarios that require a much larger volume of data.

Also, the current research did not address in detail the effect that line speed would have upon this process. Because these experiments were conducted on a LAN with line speeds of 100 Mbs, the success obtained herein might not transfer to a WAN situation in which the line speed would probably not exceed 10Mbs at best.

One positive finding from the experiment is related to the majority of the extra overhead related to CPU time. It is easy and relatively inexpensive to obtain and deploy additional CPU resources. From a management perspective, dealing with CPU bottlenecks is much easier than network bottlenecks, especially in regard to high priced WANs. The fact that the total number of bytes increased by only 2% on the encrypted data stream suggests that the network overhead might scale at an acceptable rate as workload intensity increases.

Also, the value and overhead of implementing a more active security strategy needs to be considered. While virtualization makes more CPU cycles available and in a sense reduces the impact of traditional denial of service attacks (certainly DDoS are still an issue) the very nature of virtualization in which multiple applications are leveraged across a common hardware layer presents new vulnerabilities. So if something does go wrong it could impact the entire enterprise not just a single application. Therefore, the work of Hoopes, 2008 in which proactive security mechanisms such as sandboxing are presented needs to be considered as a means to harden the virtual infrastructure and research regarding their effectiveness is needed.

Lastly, the question of how effective virtualization is in fostering personnel savings; personnel should receive further review, again with larger computing domains. This is an especially important question because personnel is the largest portion of the IT budget.

CONCLUSION

The importance of a disaster recovery strategy cannot be underestimated. If a recovery strategy is well thought-out, effectively managed, and cost effective, it is easier to deploy within organizations (Toigo, 1996, 2002). This article presented recovery plans for small and medium sized businesses and determined that there were many advantages to adopting a virtualized model.

In conclusion it appears that the physical traditional models while providing a sound foundation does not provide the flexibility needed in today's internet oriented virtualized world. In fact, the recent work of Ardagna, Tanelli, Lovera, and Zhang (2010) confirms the ability of virtualized servers to provide excellent performance in supporting web delivered applications. Based on our observations, for in-house solutions to be competitive with outsourcing, hybrid models that incorporate parts of the traditional models and expand on recent technology such as virtualization offer the best and most flexible solution in regard to balancing cost versus reliability/low granularity which brings up the question of transferability of the models presented herein to other sites. While there is not direct transferability of the models to other to data centers the basic ideas certainly are. For example, our virtualization model as depicted in Table 2 featured nine virtual zones. The same basic server consolidation model could be accomplished using a different number of zones and of course the number of zones required would be a function of the applications needed. Of course on demand virtual solutions add a degree of complexity, but result in even more flexibility and efficiency. The authors are just beginning to adapt to on demand models. First, by replicating the existing server consolidation models so that if a primary virtualized host fails a second replica of that host automatically takes over. Second, experimentation with "cloud" computing software is being undertaken which in effect takes the resources of the entire autonomous system and allocates them dynamically. As described previously, cloud computing is the operational deployment of the data center wide on demand computing model where its complexity requires a well thought out transition strategy. Based on the author's experience, it makes sense to begin with simple server consolidation (perhaps on a department level), then migrate to some form of on demand computing with that basic consolidation and then after gaining significant experience careful begin the transition to a data center wide plan (perhaps using existing "cloud" computing software).

REFERENCES

Adams, K. (2002). Geographically distributed system for catastrophic recovery. In *Proceedings of the 16th USENIX Conference on System Administration* (pp. 47-64).

Adeshiyan, T., Attanasio, C., Farr, E. M., Harper, R. E., Pelleg, D., & Schulz, C. (2009). Using virtualization for high availability and disaster recovery. *IBM Journal of Research and Development*, *53*(4), 587–597. doi:10.1147/JRD.2009.5429062

Ardagna, D., Tanelli, M., Lovera, M., & Zhang, L. (2010). Black-box performance models for virtualized web service applications. In *Proceeding of the First Joint WOSP/SIPEW International Conference on Performance Engineering* (pp. 153-164).

Armitage, G., & Harrop, W. (2005). Teaching IP networking fundamentals in resource constrained educational environments. *Australasian Journal of Educational Technology*, *21*(2), 263–283.

Baccaletti, S., Latora, V., Morento, Y., Chavez, M., & Hwang, D. U. (2006). Complex networks: Structure and dynamics. *Physics Reports*, *424*, 175–308. doi:10.1016/j.physrep.2005.10.009

Balaouras, S. (2007). The state of DR preparedness. *Forester/Disaster Recovery Journal.* Retrieved July 7, 2010, from http://www.drj.com/index.php?option=com_content&task=view&id=794&Itemid=159&ed=10

Barham, P., Dragovic, B., Fraser, K., Hand, S., Harris, T., & Ho, A. … Warfield, A. (2003, October). Xen and the art of virtualization. In *Proceedings of the 19th Symposium on Operating Systems Principles*, Bolton Landin, NY (pp. 164-177).

Borden, T. L., Hennessy, J. P., & Rymarczyk, J. W. (1989). Multiple operating systems on one processor complex. *IBM Systems Journal*, *28*(1), 104–123. doi:10.1147/sj.281.0104

Calzolari, F., Arezzini, S., Ciampa, A., Mazzoni, E., Domenici, A., & Vaglini, G. (2010). High availability using virtualization. In *Proceeding of the 17th International Conference on Computing in High Energy and Nuclear Physics* (pp. 1-10).

De Tura, N., Reilly, S. M., Narasimhan, S., & Yin, Z. J. (2004). Disaster recovery preparedness through continuous process optimization. *Bell Labs Technical Journal*, *9*(2), 147–162. doi:10.1002/bltj.20031

Dearstyne, B. W. (2006). Taking charge: Disaster fallout reinforces RIM's importance. *The Information Management Journal*, *40*(4), 37–43.

Gebhardt, C. (2010). *Toward trustworthy virtualization: Improving the trusted virtual infrastructure* (Unpublished doctoral dissertation). Royal Holloway, University of London, Surrey, UK.

Guo, L. (2006). Recovery time guaranteed heuristic routing for improving computation complexity in survivable WDM networks. *Computer Communications*, *30*, 1331–1336. doi:10.1016/j.comcom.2006.12.014

Guster, D. C., Hall, C., Herath, S., Jansen, B., & Mikluch, L. (2008). A comparison of popular global authentication systems. In *Proceeding of the Third International Conference on Information Warfare and Security*, Omaha, NE.

Guster, D. C., McCann, B. P., Kizenski, K., & Lee, O. F. (2008). Cost effective, safe and simple method to provide disaster recovery for small and medium sized businesses. *Review of Business Research*, *8*(4), 63–71.

Guster, D. C., Safonov, P., Hall, C., & Sundheim, R. (2003). Using simulation to predict performance characteristics of mirrored WWW hosts. *Issues in Information Systems*, *4*(2), 479–485.

Hiles, A. (1992). Surviving a computer disaster. *Engineering Management Journal*, 2(6), 271–274. doi:10.1049/em:19920071

Hiles, A. (2007). *The definitive handbook of business continuity management.* New York, NY: John Wiley & Sons.

Hoopes, J. (2008). *Virtualization for security: Including sandboxing, disaster recovery, high availability, forensic analysis and honeypotting.* Waltham, MA: Syngress.

Hwang, K., Dongarra, J., & Fox, G. (2011). *Distributed and cloud computing: From parallel processing to the internet of things*. San Francisco, CA: Morgan Kaufmann.

Jones, V. A., & Keyes, K. (2001). *Emergency management for records and information management programs*. Lenexa, KS: Conservation Information Network, ARMA International.

King, C. (2011). *How SUNY - Empire State College solved it's disaster recovery, business continuity, growth, and pandemic planning problems through virtualization and turned green in the process!* Paper presented at the Special Interest Group on University and College Computing Services Conference, San Diego, CA.

Krojnewski, R., & Nager, B. (2006, November 13). Disaster recovery: It's not just an IT problem. *Forrester Report*.

Laureano, M., Maziero, C., & Jamhour, E. (2007). Protecting host-based intrusion detectors through virtual machines, computer networks. *International Journal of Computer and Telecommunications Networking*, *51*(5), 1275–1283.

Lee, O. F., Guster, D. C., Schmidt, M. B., & McCann, B. (2009). Applying the scale-free degree distribution algorithm to assess communication complexity and failure points in disaster recovery model. *Journal of Information Technology Management*, *20*(2), 35–45.

Lin, Q., Neo, H., Zhang, L., Huang, G., & Gay, R. (2007). Grid-based large-scale web3D collaborative virtual environment. In *Proceedings of the 12th International Conference on 3D Web Technology* (pp. 123-132).

Maitra, S., Shanker, M., & Mudholkar, P. K. (2011). Disaster recovery planning with virtualization technologies in the banking industry. In *Proceedings of the International Conference & Workshop on Emerging Trends in Technology* (pp. 298-299).

Massiglia, P., & Bunn, F. (2003). *Virtual storage redefined: Technologies and applications for storage virtualization*. Dublin, Ireland: Veritas.

Nellitheertha, H. (2006). *Virtualization technologies*. Infosys White Paper.

Pervan, G. (1998). How chief executive officers in large organizations view the management of their information systems. *Journal of Information Technology*, *13*(2), 95–109. doi:10.1080/026839698344882

Phillippi, M. (2008). An effective SME disaster recovery strategy for branch offices. *Computer Technology Review*. Retrieved February 15, 2010, from http://www.thefreelibrary.com/An+effective+SME+disaster+recovery+strategy+for+branch+offices.-a0168214596

Rosenblum, M. (2009). *The impact of virtualization on modern computing environments*. Virginia Technological University Distinguished Lecture Series. Retrieved from http://www.cs.vt.edu/DistinguishedLectures/MendelRosenblum

Safigan, C. (2008). Disaster recovery for the masses – The role of OS-level server virtualization in disaster recovery. *Computer Technology Review*. Retrieved July 7, 2010, from http://www.wwpi.com/index.php?option=com_content&task=view&id=1151&Itemid=64

Stephens, D. (2003). Protecting records in the face of chaos, calamity, and cataclysm. *The Information Management Journal*, 33-40.

Stillwell, M. (2010). Dynamic fractional resource scheduling for cluster platforms. In *Proceedings of the IEEE International Symposium on Parallel and Distributed Processing* (pp. 1-4).

Toigo, J. W. (1996). *Disaster recovery planning: For computers and communication resources*. New York, NY: John Wiley & Sons.

Toigo, J. W. (2002). *Disaster recovery planning: Preparing for the unthinkable* (3rd ed.). Upper Saddle River, NJ: Prentice Hall.

Tolnai, A. (2010). A virtualized environment security (VES) model for a secure virtualized environment. In *Proceedings of the International Conference for Internet Technology and Secured Transactions* (pp. 1-6).

Wellheiser, J., & Scott, J. (2002). *An ounce of prevention: Integrated disaster planning for archives, libraries, and record centers* (2nd ed.). Lenexa, KS: Scarecrow Press.

Wood, T., Cecchet, E., Ramakrishnan, K. K., Shenoy, P., van der Merwe, J., & Venkataramani, A. (2010). Disaster recovery as a cloud service: Economic benefits and deployment challenges. In *Proceedings of the 2nd USENIX Conference on Hot Topics in Cloud Computing* (p. 8).

Zheng, W., & Fang, B. (2009). Structure-independent disaster recovery: Concept, architecture and implmentations. *Science in China Series F: Information Sciences*, *52*(5), 813–823. doi:10.1007/s11432-009-0095-8

This work was previously published in the Journal of Information Technology Research, Volume 4, Issue 4, edited by Mehdi Khosrow-Pour, pp. 18-40, copyright 2011 by IGI Publishing (an imprint of IGI Global).

Chapter 17
The Value of Government Mandated Location-Based Services in Emergencies in Australia

Anas Aloudat
The University of Jordan, Jordan

Katina Michael
University of Wollongong, Australia

Roba Abbas
University of Wollongong, Australia

Mutaz Al-Debei
The University of Jordan, Jordan

ABSTRACT

The adoption of mobile technologies for emergency management has the capacity to save lives. In Australia in February 2009, the Victorian Bushfires claimed 173 lives, the worst peace-time disaster in the nation's history. The Australian government responded swiftly to the tragedy by going to tender for mobile applications that could be used during emergencies, such as mobile alerts and location services. These applications have the ability to deliver personalized information direct to the citizen during crises, complementing traditional broadcasting mediums like television and radio. Indeed governments have a responsibility to their citizens to safeguard them against both natural and human-made hazards and today national security has grown to encapsulate such societal and economic securitization. However, some citizens and lobby groups have emphasized that such breakthrough technologies need to be deployed with caution as they are fraught with ethical considerations, including the potential for breaches in privacy, security and trust. The other problem is that real world implementations of national emergency alerts have not always worked reliably and their value has come into question as a result. This paper provides a big picture view of the value of government-mandated location-based services during emergencies, and the challenges ensuing from their use.

DOI: 10.4018/978-1-4666-3625-5.ch017

INTRODUCTION

The aim of this article is to present a case study on how modern technologies, namely mobile applications, are changing the landscape of emergency management in Australia. The article begins by providing a general overview of emergency management and location-based services and then specifically places the reader in an Australian context by describing recent trends in emergency response, especially post the Victorian Bushfires of February 2009. The introduction of new warning and alerting methods and techniques will be a critical element in securing the nation against diverse natural hazards such as bushfires and floods. In today's modern age of technological innovation, it is difficult to comprehend how 173 persons perished and 414 persons were injured during the Black Saturday crisis, partly as a result of accessibility to timely and relevant information on how to respond to the emergency.

The recently deployed national emergency warning system (NEWS), as well as future "location-enabled" components, will be discussed before socio-ethical considerations are explored. It is anticipated that NEWS will force amendments to the *Telecommunications Act 1997*; an issue that was first tabled by the Australian Federal Government. With the pending introduction of such advanced technologies, it was also deemed that the regulations governing the use of the Integrated Public Number Database (IPND) also be reviewed. The IPND grants some government agencies access to Australia-wide consumer telecommunications details during emergencies and is maintained by one commercial mobile operator but may need to be accessed by more than one commercial entity during an emergency.

There are thus a number of socio-ethical considerations which need to be taken into account when reviewing both regulation and legislation in this domain. Despite the potential for breaches in privacy, mobile technologies and specifically location-based services offer a state-of-the art solution to the age old problem of personalized information dissemination based on context. Where a new technology can act as a life-sustaining tool, privacy issues are generally considered less important and wholly overshadowed by issues related to trust. Very few people would opt not to disclose their real-time physical location in the name of privacy, if it meant that they could survive a natural disaster. What is of greater concern to the success of an emergency service offering however, is that users can trust the technology, can trust the supplier of the service, and can trust that the accuracy, reliability and timeliness of the communicated message during a crisis. The findings of the study demonstrate that location-based services are a plausible solution to emergency management problems in Australia and that the benefits to citizens of using such innovations during natural disasters are clear. This does not mean however that government mandated services to citizens are not without their specific risks. Location based mobile alerts for emergencies, for example, are still experiencing significant teething problems in implementation which has brought their value into question. Citizens would rather have no information at all, rather than delayed or inaccurate information about an emergency which is purported to be near their real-time location.

EMERGENCY MANAGEMENT IN AUSTRALIA

Defining Natural and Human-Made Hazards

Managing emergencies with regard to their socially-constructed context is one of the reasons that has led Australia to adopt the all-hazards approach in responding to risks associated with physical phenomena (Templeman & Bergin, 2008). A hazard is any source of potential harm or a situation with a potential to cause loss (Emergency Management Australia, 2004b). Emergency

Management Australia (EMA) defines many types of hazards, which are broadly classified. Most of the known hazards are considered natural because they have their origins in the surrounding natural environment. Examples include bushfires, floods, cyclones, tsunamis, landslides, windstorms and earthquakes. Several other hazards are identified as technological, which are the result of failures in human-made systems and services, or are the outcome of human actions. For example, these include urban structure fires, explosions, and transportation incidents. Some hazards are classified as chemical, biological or radiological due to their specific origin. Some examples of these are toxic material releases, human epidemics and pandemics, exotic animal diseases, and insect and vermin plagues. Remaining hazards can be classified as social in origin, which include civil unrests and acts of violence such as riots, sieges, shooting massacres, hijackings, sabotage and terrorism (Emergency Management Australia, 2008). Table 1 summarizes the different types of hazards.

Throughout history, communities have battled hazards and responded to emergencies with the commensurate technology available to them. Organized attempts to counter emergencies, however, did not occur until much later in modern times (Haddow, Bullock, & Coppola, 2006). These attempts have evolved from simple precautions and scattered actions into systematized and sophisticated policies, programs and applications that include preparedness, response, mitigation, recovery and protection strategies (Canton, 2007). Modern emergency management (EM) could be defined as the discipline dealing with risk and risk avoidance and primarily concerned with developing and improving arrangements and programs that contribute to the goal of a safer, more sustainable community (Haddow, Bullock, & Coppola, 2006).

Emergencies in Australia

The Commonwealth of Australia covers a land mass of approximately 7,692 million square kilometers with a population of about 22 million. Around 85% of the population live in cities within 50 kilometers of the coast, where much of the country's commercial and industrial activity takes place (Australia.gov.au Website, 2010). Australia is divided into six States and two Territories. Each State or Territory has its own government, legislature and constitution. The legislature of Australia comprises a bicameral federal parliament, with a Prime Minister and Cabinet (PM&C).

As a physically large country with a diverse climate and geographic landscape, Australia experiences many types of hazards on a regular basis (Boughton, 1998). In addition, communities across Australia continue to settle into hazard-prone areas, particularly in coastal and river valley regions, exposing themselves to risks from a variety of sources including cyclones, floods and bushfires (The Victorian Bushfires Royal Commission, 2009). Even in regional areas, and as a result of inadequate risk assessments and mitiga-

Table 1. Hazard types

Hazard Classification	Types
Natural hazard	Bushfires, Cyclones, Earthquakes, Floods, Hurricanes, Land gales, Landslides, Mudslides, Storm surges, Tidal waves, Torrential rain, Tsunamis
Technological hazards	Blackouts or main power failures, Explosions, Mining or industry incidents, Pollution, Smog, Transportation incidents, Urban structure fires
Chemical, biological and radiological hazards	Chemical emissions, Epidemics/Pandemics, Exotic animal diseases, Insect or vermin plagues, Toxic spills
Social in origin hazards	Civil unrests, Hijackings, Riots, Sabotage, Shooting Massacres, Sieges, Terrorism

tion actions, transport infrastructure, such as road and rail links, are usually flooded annually, which cause disruption to the carriage of commodities for communities and business, and the supply of materials for industry (The Australian Government: Department of Transport and Regional Services, 2004).

Reliable information on the frequency of emergencies and disasters in Australia extends only from 1967; nonetheless, the number of events has shown an upward trend in frequency over the last 20 years (The Victorian Bushfires Royal Commission, 2009). The same trend is noted worldwide both in the developed and developing countries, caused by several factors including an increase in human activities in hazard-prone areas, military conflicts and climate change (Coyle & Meier, 2009; United Nations News Centre, 2010). Despite that the frequency of emergencies and the numbers of people who live or work in risk-prone areas have increased in Australia, deaths per 100,000 population have continued to fall due to better emergency management policies, arrangements and applications (The Australian Government: Department of Transport and Regional Services, 2004).

Emergency Management Arrangements in Australia

Under Australia's constitutional arrangements, the country takes a Federal approach to emergency management in which the local, state and territory governments have responsibility within their own jurisdiction and have the laws, funding mechanisms and organizational arrangements in place to deal with emergencies. Each sphere of government has a different set of roles and responsibilities for emergency planning, preparedness and mitigation in relation to land, property and the environment, assets and infrastructures, agencies and programmes (Emergency Management Australia, 2009a).

Given that individual States and Territories are highly autonomous, the approach to emergency planning and alerting in Australia is not standardized (The Australian Government: Department of Transport and Regional Services, 2004). Nonetheless, there are similarities in approach that have emerged between states. For example, should a state of emergency be declared, a state-level emergency/disaster response and coordination committee/executive acts as the interface responsible for coordinating the state resources, seeking Commonwealth support if needed, and providing up-to-date reports to the media (Victorian State Parliamentary Offices, 2003). When activated, the committee is mainly responsible for:

1. Information collection, analysis and dissemination of intelligence to emergency response agencies;
2. Coordination of the provision of resources required by divisional emergency response coordinators;
3. Allocation of resources on a priority basis;
4. Requesting Commonwealth physical resources;
5. Briefing the Coordinator in Chief; and
6. Dissemination of information to the media and general public (The Victorian Bushfires Royal Commission, 2009).

The level of emergency response coordination depends on the scope of the emergency. In the first instance, the response to an emergency takes place at the municipal level. If the emergency calls for resources beyond those available at the municipal level, the emergency response coordination is stepped up to the divisional level. An emergency that extends beyond the division will be progressed to the State level (The Victorian Bushfires Royal Commission, 2009).

Although the prime responsibility for the protection of life, property and the environment rests with the states and territories, the Commonwealth Government is strongly committed to supporting local and state governments in developing their capacity for dealing with emergencies and disasters, providing physical assistance and mobilizing resources to States or Territories when they cannot reasonably cope during large-scale events (Emergency Management Australia, 2009a). On the national level, the basis for managing major emergencies and combating disasters is a partnership between the Federal, State and Territory, Local Governments, the community, and the private sector. Accordingly, this national framework for emergency management requires a high level of collaboration and coordination across all spheres of government, and with other non-government stakeholders as well (Emergency Management Australia, 2009a).

Emergency Management Committees and Organizations in Australia

Emergency and disaster management committees and organizations exist at National and State/Territory levels in Australia with specific responsibilities for local governments within their jurisdiction. The main emergency management bodies in Australia include:

1. **The Commonwealth Counter Disaster Task Force:** A senior interdepartmental committee, chaired by the Department of the Prime Minister and Cabinet. It is the peak Commonwealth body with emergency management responsibilities composed of representatives of Commonwealth Government departments and agencies with a significant role to play in the provision of disaster relief or rehabilitation assistance. On the advice of the Director General of the Emergency Management Australia (EMA) agency, the Chair may activate the committee during the response and recovery phase of a disaster in support of EMA's activities (Emergency Management Australia, 2004a).
2. **The Australian Emergency Management Committee:** Australia's principal consultative emergency management forum. It is chaired by the Director General of EMA, and comprises chairpersons and executive officers of State and Territory emergency management committees. The Committee meets bi-annually to provide advice and direction on the coordination and advancement of Commonwealth and State interests related to emergency management issues. As required, it establishes working parties to examine particular issues (Emergency Management Australia, 2004a).
3. **The State and Territory Emergency/Disaster Management Organizations:** Each State and Territory has established a committee of senior members of appropriate departments and agencies to consider emergency management matters. The names and functions of these organizations differ from State to State, but they are responsible for ensuring that proper plans and arrangements are made at State or Territory and local government level, to alert the public to and deal with emergencies and disasters (Emergency Management Australia, 1996).
4. **Emergency Management Australia (EMA):** The Federal agency through which the Attorney-General exercises the responsibility of providing national leadership in the development of emergency management measures to reduce the impact of emergencies on the Australian community (Emergency Management Australia, 2004b). EMA is mainly responsible for shaping and advancing emergency management strategies and policies throughout Australia, advocating emergency management education, and assisting state and territory local emergency management agencies. EMA also plays a key role in coordinating interstate and international assistance at times of major emergencies and disasters (Emergency

Management Australia, 2004b). EMA has an established collaborative relationship with other Commonwealth agencies such as the Department of Finance and Administration, Geoscience Australia and the Bureau of Meteorology. In doing so, EMA seeks to encourage an all hazards, all agencies approach to the prevention or mitigation of emergencies, preparedness for their impact, response to that impact and recovery from the consequences (Emergency Management Australia, 2009b).

5. **Other committees and organizations exist at the State level in Australia:** The names and functions of these organizations and committees differ from State to State but there are similar patterns that have been developed between them in regard to their roles and functions that include the identification of various threats and hazards, the coordination of volunteers and community resources during significant emergency events, hazard management guidelines, declaration of state of emergency, emergency management training and education, and the arranging of warnings in emergencies to the public (The Australian Government: Department of Transport and Regional Services, 2004).

An All-Hazards Approach to National Security in Australia

The Changing Face of Emergency Management

Until recently emergencies were quantified in terms of the loss of life, extent of damage, or based on an event's physical attributes (Emergency Management Australia, 2004b). Emergencies have been traditionally associated to the notion of a "disaster" when the number of casualties and the allocated resources to a given event have been high (Canton, 2007). More contemporary viewpoints, especially from the social sciences have begun to question the validity of traditional classification schemes that have long defined emergencies and disasters or distinguished them according to their origin or scale. Social studies started to perceive these events as social constructions, defined by the nature and the volume of their impact on social systems (Perry, 2007; Quarantelli, 1986; Rosenthal, 1998).

The focus in understanding emergencies has now shifted toward the actual situation created by such phenomena, rather than simply considering the physical attributes that caused them (Emergency Management Australia, 2004b). This shift has come as a result of a growing realization that although there are many different types of emergency events, whether natural- or human-caused, they all have comparable capacity to bring social, economic, environmental and political consequences on the communities they impact (Buzan, Woever, & Wilde, 1998; Rosenthal, 1998). Thus an emergency impacts the organization of human communities and can be thought of only within a larger framework involving the society as a whole (Gilbert, 1998). It is what has caused a redefinition of national security to incorporate large-scale emergencies, and not just things to do with the military. How a government responds to a large scale emergency today has as much to do with national security as traditional security-centric actions like border control. Yet while the government aims to protect the well-being of its citizenry through blanket coverage technologies such as location-based services, they still need to maintain an individual-level of consent. For example, the government's adoption of sophisticated unmanned aerial vehicles (UAVs) to keep out illegal immigrants is very different to the government communicating with citizens via their personal mobile phones, especially when an entity's real-time location can be determined.

The Comprehensive and Integrated Approaches

Australia has adopted both a comprehensive and integrated all-hazards approach to the development of its arrangements and programs. The approach can be summarized as follows.

Under the comprehensive approach there is a general acknowledgment that a potential threat could originate from various types of hazards which have a comparable capacity to impact severely on communities and infrastructure. The all hazards approach to emergency management involves a recognition that most emergency event types cause similar problems and that many of the measures required to deal with them are generic (The Victorian Bushfires Royal Commission, 2009). Australia's comprehensive approach to emergency management identifies four strategies that contribute to the reduction or elimination of hazards, and an increase in community and environmental resilience. EMA (2004b) defines these strategies as follows:

1. **Prevention/mitigation:** Seek to eliminate or reduce the impact of hazards and/or to increase the resilience of the community subject to the impact of those hazards.
2. **Preparedness:** Concerned with establishing arrangements and plans and with providing education and information so as to prepare the community to deal with emergencies and disasters as they may arise.
3. **Response:** Covers the methods that are used to properly activate the preparedness arrangements and plans so as to deal with emergencies and disasters if and when they occur.
4. **Recovery:** Defines the set of arrangements practiced to assist a community affected by an emergency or disaster in reconstruction of the physical infrastructure and restoration of emotional, social, economic and physical well-being.

These emergency management strategies, although tightly related, could be developed independently of each other (Haddow, Bullock, & Coppola, 2006). Nonetheless, under the comprehensive approach to emergency management there is an emphasis that all of the activities, under these strategies, should effectively function as one seamless emergency management framework (Emergency Management Australia, 2004b; Haddow, Bullock, & Coppola, 2006).

The integrated approach emphasizes the need to coordinate different emergency management programs and strategies with the support of other government agencies, and with the community and the private sector (Emergency Management Australia, 2004b). For the comprehensive approach to emergency management to be workable there should be effective arrangements for the coordination of the activities of governments and of the large number of organizations that need to be involved in emergency management activities. These arrangements need to be set within a legislative and public policy framework (Emergency Management Australia, 2004b). It therefore follows that technological solutions deployed to protect citizens also need to be set within a legislative and public policy framework. The problem however with "emergencies," whether they are natural or human-made is that they strike with little warning, if any, and therefore the deployment of specific technologies during a given emergency (e.g., with the requirement for access of citizenry personal data) undergoes limited discussion.

THE EMERGENCE OF LOCATION-BASED SERVICES SOLUTIONS

What are Location-Based Services?

Location-based services (LBS) are also known as location-dependent services, location-related services, location-enabled services, location-sensitive services and location services. See for example the definitions given by Hjelm (2002), Jensen (2002), Holma, Kristensson, Salonen, and Toskala (2004), Lopez (2004), Spiekermann (2004), Bernardos, Casar, and Tarrio (2007), and Uhlirz (2007). Küpper (2005) has previously noted this and argued that one possible reason for terms being used interchangeably is that the character and appearance of LBS have been specified and implemented by different communities and industries, especially in the telecommunications sector and the ubiquitous computing area for a variety of applications. In the context of LBS, *location* always refers to a spatial geographical location that is associated with a physical point or region relative to the surface of the Earth (Dawson, Winterbottom, & Thomson, 2007). Accordingly, LBS are classified as a subset of a larger set called context-aware services, which are electronic services that automatically adapt their behavior (e.g., filtering or presenting information) to one or more parameters (time, location, identity or activity) so as to reflect the context (personal, technical, spatial, social, or physical) of a target (person, animal or object) (Küpper, 2005).

LBS as a concept denotes applications that utilize the available geographic location information of a target device, being fixed, handheld, wearable or implantable, in order to add value to the provided service (Perusco & Michael, 2007; 3rd Generation Partnership Project, 2009). Astroth (2003) defines a LBS as "any application that offers information, communication, or a transaction that satisfies the specific needs of a user in a particular place." Harvey (2008) simply defined LBS as "technologies that add geographical functions to other technologies." Gruber and Winter (2002) argued that a LBS is "any value-added service that takes into account a mobile agent's actual location." Shiode, Li, Batty, Longley, and Maguire (2002) delineate LBS as "services that provide geographically-orientated data and information services to users across mobile telecommunication networks."

Samsioe and Samsioe (2002) assert however that an electronic service that has location capabilities, should be able to fulfill the following three separate activities to be accurately defined as a LBS:

1. Estimate the location of the device;
2. Produce a service based on the estimated location; and
3. Deliver the location-enhanced service to that device.

Based on Samsioe and Samsioe (2002), this strict definition excludes several services that employ location technologies in mobile telecommunications networks such as the cell broadcasting service, since these services cannot change their content when the physical location of a mobile handset changes. However, in the emergency management context, it should be understood that any service that provides information pertinent to the current location of the active mobile handset at a specific period of time can be viewed as a location-based service, regardless of the underlying delivery technology used to convey its information. Although this interpretation may extend to other types of services as well, it is nonetheless, an understanding that harmonizes several different forms of LBS such as those depicted by Holma et al. (2004), Grothe et al. (2005), Guan, Zhou, Zhou, and Zhu (2007), Oh and Haas (2007), Stojanović, Djordjevic-Kajan, Papadopoulos, and Nanopoulos (2007), and Aitenbichler (2008).

The text-based message is the most realized form of LBS, but there are several other possible forms where the service could be received as a bitmap image, voice message, multimedia message (with rich content such as animated image formats), interactive maps or video. However, the final form of the delivered LBS depends on several factors that include existing and dedicated network resources, underlying technologies and protocols, market trends and handset capabilities/limitations (Spiekermann, 2004).

Operational and Non-Operational Stakeholders

Effective deployment of location-based services requires the coordinated effort of multiple stakeholders in the services value chain, each of which provide specific components of the total solution (Astroth, 2003). A stakeholder represents an autonomous entity like a person, a company or an organization, each maintaining or performing one or several roles that characterize either the interests or functions it fulfils from a technical perspective, or the impact it exercises on LBS from an economic or regulatory position (Küpper, 2005).

Roles of LBS stakeholders can be classified as operational and non-operational. The operational roles define the players that cooperate during the operation of the service, which requires each stakeholder to maintain technical infrastructure, ranging from users' mobile handsets to service providers' farm servers to carrier's telecommunications networks, so as to facilitate the request and the provision of sub-services during LBS execution (Küpper, 2005). During an LBS operation, the interaction between these actors takes place through reference points that are defined by a set of protocols and connectivity services offered by various networks, and often determined by Service Level Agreements (SLAs). SLAs are agreed upon and adopted between the participating parties, prior to the provisioning of the services, for fixing quality of service and accounting conditions (Küpper, 2005). With so many stakeholders involved in a single LBS offering, upkeeping locational privacy is not easy. This is where industry level guidelines, contractual agreements between stakeholders, or even company level codes of conduct can play a pivotal role in protecting citizen rights.

A non-operational stakeholder is the one that does not directly engage in the technical operation of LBS but has an indirect impact on the services, either by dictating economic or regulatory circumstances of LBS operation or through the influence it exercises on the adoption of technical service standards (Küpper, 2005). An example from the Australian context could be Australian Communications and Media Authority (ACMA) which exercises a direct influence in regulating (by law) the utilization of location data to protect the privacy of individuals and for other purposes such as lawful interception (The Australian Communications and Media Authority, 2004).

Evolution of Global Positioning Techniques for Location-Based Services

The first location system in use was the satellite-based Global Positioning System (GPS) created, funded and controlled by the U.S. Department of Defense. The system was built and conceived primarily to serve military purposes but since the late 1990s the system was upgraded with new civilian signals making it freely available to the public and commercial use (Kaplan & Hegarty, 2006). The result of this free availability of satellite positioning capabilities led to a real revolution in a wide range of applications that include air, sea and land traffic control, navigation solutions, freight management, and emergency services (Spiekermann, 2004). Other comparable GNSSs are currently also in use or scheduled to operate in the very near future. One such system is the European Union satellite system of Galileo, a GNSS with meter-range accuracies appropriate for applications such as safety and navigation (European Space Agency, 2011).

According to the European Commission (2011), advantages can particularly be attained through the combination of Galileo and GPS capabilities. The Galileo project is presently in the operational stages of development, given the launch of the initial two satellites in 2011 and with two more scheduled for 2012 (European Space Agency, 2011). The development and operation of Galileo is expected to provide enhancements to existing positioning techniques, providing higher levels of accuracy, connectivity and real-time location data, which will have implications for applications areas such as emergency management.

Location-Based Emergency Services in Mobile Networks

Emergency services represent one of the most obvious application areas where the deployment of location technology makes sense (Küpper, 2005). Still, location-based emergency services are in their infancy in several countries around the world including Australia (Küpper, 2005). One reason for this, beyond the socio-ethical issues are technical problems, including location determination mechanisms and accuracy standards, and also issues related to identifying different requirements for emergency systems which have yet to be fully resolved (The European Telecommunications Standards Institute, 2010; Togt, Beinat, Zlatanova, & Scholten, 2005).

In general, there are two types of location-based emergency service applications in mobile telecommunications networks (The European Telecommunications Standards Institute, 2006a). The first is initiated by a person in the form of a phone call or a distress Short Message Service (SMS) in a life-threatening or time-critical situation. The second type is initiated usually by the government in collaboration with telecommunications carriers, in which safety alerts and early warning messages are disseminated (pushed) to all active mobile handsets located in designated threatened area(s) before, during or after a large-scale event. The fundamental idea behind the first type of location-based emergency service application is for an emergency service organization (ESO) (i.e., police force, fire brigade or ambulance service) to reach the caller (or the message sender) with some precision, based on the location information provided by the caller's mobile service provider. In many cases the person will be unable to communicate his or her current location or simply does not know it, so the ESO relies on handset data (Küpper, 2005). The premise behind the second type of emergency service application is to utilize the mobile handset as an additional information channel that is capable of reaching people wherever they are but within the threatened area.

EMERGENCY WARNING AND ALERTING METHODS IN AUSTRALIA

Traditional Warning and Alert Systems

Under emergency management arrangements in Australia, one of the main responsibilities of the government is to communicate and disseminate warnings and safety information to the general public in case of a large-scale emergency (The Australian Government: Department of Transport and Regional Services, 2004). In principle, any means of ensuring that a warning is quickly disseminated to those actually or potentially affected should be used. However, conventional broadcasting systems consisting primarily of local community radio stations and television networks are still the main channels that are currently used for disseminating alerts and warnings to the Australian public (Betts, 2003).

Australians also rely on several other sources of information, including relevant government websites and hotlines, to stay updated with the latest news about events as they unfold. In addition, traditional warning methods are used across the country including banners, door-to-door knocking and signage. Australia also still relies on what are known as triggers, such as the standard emergency warning signal (SEWS) and associated sirens, which are merely techniques prompting the audience to listen carefully for a warning and/or to search for more information (The Victorian Bushfires Royal Commission, 2009).

Modern Warning and Alert Systems: The Short Message Service and Beyond

Other means and methods such as emails, landline and mobile phone calls, and short message service (SMS) have also been considered or used. For example, Telstra (the incumbent telecommunications operator) partnered with the state of Victoria in 2005, to trial the Community Information Warning System (CIWS) that was able to simultaneously telephone every household in a designated area. More than 660 calls were made, on an opt-in basis, to the residents of one specific area who had volunteered to participate in the trial (The Minister for Police and Emergency Services, 2005).

In 2007, SMS and email alerts were considered by the Victorian State Government for the purpose of geographically targeting people in specified areas with information about terror attacks or natural disasters (Dunn & Collier, 2007). In the same year, the New South Wales Premier proposed a warning system for metropolitan Sydney whereby residents could opt-in to real time Government SMS and email air pollution health alerts. The proposal came in response to key recommendations from a Parliamentary air quality inquiry in 2006, which warned that 1600 people were dying every year from air pollution related illness in New South Wales. This project was under the Department of Environment authority (Benson, 2007). The New South Wales Government also proposed an electronic warning system that, in principle, should have allowed ESOs, such as Police, Fire and Ambulance services, to send SMS alerts to all mobile handsets in terrorism or emergency target zones across the State. The design concept identified the system's need to be operable across all telecommunications carrier networks operating in Australia, and was to provide evacuation information, safety advice and alternate routes to avoid the emergency area ("Premier promises mobile phone," 2007).

A similar system is now active in Sydney, New South Wales. The SydneyAlert system is a free, opt-in service that is meant to alert the general public in the event of an emergency in the Sydney and North Sydney Central Business Districts (CBDs). The system provides building managers, emergency wardens and security staff with safety information and instructions to help them manage and assist occupants, staff and others in their buildings during a serious incident. The system uses existing commercial communications networks to disseminate warnings, specifically SMS and e-mail. The State Emergency Operations Centre Controller, a senior NSW Police Officer, is the authority that determines if the system should be activated. This officer also determines who on the subscription list is contacted and what message is sent. The message is sent to the contact details supplied by those who have subscribed to SydneyAlert. The message is simple, giving clear guidance on what needs to be done. Example messages include: "Evacuate to a safety site," "Stay indoors and close windows," or "all clear message and situation is back to normal" (New South Wales Government, 2007).

Despite the SMS technology being available before the Victorian Bushfires, it was not until after the fires in 2009 that it was used to alert Victorians about severe weather conditions and other threatening bushfires (Dobbin, 2009; Ife, 2009). With fire risk and high wind predicted across the state, Telstra, Optus and 3 Hutchison- the three main mobile service providers in Australia- sent SMSs on the third of March 2009, on behalf of the Victorian Government and Victorian Police to more than 3 million mobile subscribers, advising recipients to listen to the Australian Broadcasting Corporation (ABC) radio for emergency updates (Dobbin, 2009; Ife, 2009). The messages were sent using commercial services (i.e., as part of a community service obligation), and not part of any State or National emergency warning system ("Bushfire SMS to assist in," 2009). Some citizens reported receiving the SMS late, while others reported being frightened or made nervous by the message content which was later considered to be over-the-top. In this particular trial, citizens were not warned about the impending message which meant that when they received it, hundreds of anxious citizens called triple zero concerned about the pending adverse weather conditions. While this is a typical response to interpreting instant messages during emergencies by a small portion of the population, more research needs to be done into effective and clear communications via mobile phones (Michael, Stroh, Berry, Muhlhauber, & Nicholls, 2006).

Queensland, in particular, faces the risks of cyclones, bushfires, storm surges and floods on an annual basis. In 2009, the Council of Townsville City started to provide an early warning service to its residents on an opt-in basis. The Early Warning Network (EWN) sends alerts 30 minutes ahead of severe weather conditions via a variety of electronic channels including email, SMS and landline phone call (Chudleigh, 2009). The cost of each message sent is borne by the Council. This system is believed to be the "the world's only location based early warning system for severe weather events" with the ability to pinpoint the area that information is needed "with accuracy to within 10m" according to EWN managing director Mr. Kerry Plowright (The Australian Early Warning Network, 2009).

The National Emergency Warning System of Australia

Not until recently was the standardization of a national emergency planning and alerting approach to public warning across Australia considered for actual implementation. A national emergency warning system has been the subject of discussion between the Commonwealth, States and Territories since 2004. In 2005, there was a prevailing view of the need to introduce a warning system on a national level but it was not subject to agreement by all States and Territories (The Victorian Bushfires Royal Commission, 2009). However, by July 2008, the Council of Australian Governments (COAG) finally reached an agreement to establish a national telephone-based emergency warning system in Australia (The Australian Government: Attorney General's Department, 2009). But according to the Prime Minister of Australia, privacy and data security restrictions in the *Telecommunications Act 1997* combined with interstate disagreements over funding schemes, delayed the system's introduction till after the Victorian bushfires in February 2009 (Bita & Sainsbury, 2009).

New innovations are often subject to a multitude of social-ethical issues such as privacy and security concerns in their incubation period. In this instance, the changes needed to the Telecommunications Act were not made in a timely fashion thus stifling the roll out of the telephone based warning system. This is an example of where the law lags behind new technologies or services. Despite that this system was to merely send a message to a telephone, the appropriate legislative process had not taken place. Laws or amendments to current laws do not usually happen overnight. However, following the worst bushfire season in Australia's history in 2009, the Federal Australian Government, COAG and the State and Territory Governments identified the compelling need for the immediate deployment of the national warning system which would enable them to deliver warnings to landline and mobile telephones based on the billing address of the subscriber (The Australian Government: Department of Broadband Communications and the Digital Economy, 2009). It should be stressed here that after the Victorian Bushfires it only took several days for Honorable Senator John Faulkner, a Cabinet Secretary and Special Minister of the State, to sign the Emergency Bushfires Declaration No.1 on behalf of the Victorian Government. The declaration was made under Section 80J of the *Privacy Act 1988*. Section 80J is primarily concerned with the declaration of an emergency or an event of national significance and only the Prime Minister of Australia or the Minister of relevance may make such a declaration.

The National Emergency Warning System (NEWS) was operational in October 2009 in all States and Territories except Western Australia (WA) which delivered its emergency warning messages through the use of its own WA StateAlert system (The Victorian Department of Treasury and Finance, 2009). Under the COAG agreement, States and Territories retained autonomy of the warning systems they choose to implement (The Australian Government: Attorney General's Department, 2009). NEWS is meant to supplement, and not to replace, the range of traditional measures currently used to warn the public of emergencies, including television and radio, public address systems, door knocking, sirens, signage and the internet (Gibbons, 2009).

Granting NEWS Stakeholders Access to the Integrated Public Number Database

The second stage of NEWS is presently under deliberation, in particular the ability for Australian telecommunications carriers to meet the long term requirements of a national emergency alerting and warning system utilizing location-based technologies to identify active mobile handsets of all carriers within a defined emergency area (The Victorian Department of Treasury and Finance, 2009). For the first stage of NEWS to operate, access to the IPND was required in order to obtain the number and address upon which the warning is disseminated (The Australian Government: Department of Broadband Communications and the Digital Economy, 2009). IPND is an industry-wide, commonwealth-owned database that contains all the residential and business telephone numbers, both listed and unlisted, and other subscriber information such as name, address, and the type of service delivered by each number (i.e., landline, fax, mobile, pager, etc.) (The Australian Communications and Media Authority, 2009). IPND was established and is maintained by Telstra, as a condition of its carrier license. All telecommunications carriers and service providers are required to provide Telstra with subscriber information in order to populate and maintain the database (The Australian Government: Department of Broadband Communications and the Digital Economy, 2009). Maintaining accurate IPND data is extremely important to ESOs as these organizations rely on the IPND to respond to emergency calls from the public in a timely manner (The Australian Communications and Media Authority, 2009).

In accordance with the States and Territories agreement to establish NEWS, the Federal Government immediately commenced drafting legislation to authorize access to the IPND. This was not without some controversy, despite the obvious benefits of the new warning system, even the potential to save lives. Given the sensitive nature of the information contained in the IPND, the *Telecommunications Act 1997*, Sections 276 and 277, restricts access and prohibits disclosure or use of information from the database save for a few exceptions. These exceptions are explicitly specified in the legislation which allow for the release of personal information for a number of reasons including emergency calls, law enforcement and national security purposes (The Australian Communications and Media Authority, 2009).

In 2009, the Federal Government introduced into Parliament *the Telecommunications Amendment Integrated Public Number Database 2009 Bill* that proposed amendments to the *Telecommunications Act 1997* in order to enable access to the IPND for NEWS purposes, in connection with the provision of telephony-based emergency warnings and for the supply of location-based emergency services (The Australian Government: Department of Broadband Communications and the Digital Economy, 2009).

In light of the Victorian Bushfires, the government sought advice from the Solicitor-General on an interim measure to allow immediate access to the IPND by any State or Territory that wished to implement a more limited system, as soon as possible. This interim access was not a substitute for the amendments to the Telecommunications Act contained in the Bill and the planned future access arrangements for the IPND (Gibbons, 2009), but some citizens and civil liberties groups did voice concern over the potential for breaches in information privacy. The amendments to the Telecommunications Act contain a number of privacy protection provisions, which are intended to ensure that subscriber data obtained from the IPND is not used or disclosed for any other purpose than to provide telephone-based emergency warnings. Specifically, emergency agencies will only be permitted to access the data in the event of an actual emergency, in the event of a likely emergency or for testing purposes (i.e., to test whether in the event of an emergency the alert would have reached the people that it needed to) (Gibbons, 2009).

The amendments provide the Attorney-General, as the Minister with portfolio responsibility for emergency management issues, with powers to specify, by legislative instrument, who can use IPND information in the event of an emergency or disaster (The Australian Government: Attorney General's Department, 2009). The amendments also contain accountability measures including a reporting requirement for any government agency that activates a telephony-based emergency warning using IPND data. The agency will be required to report each usage of IPND information to the Attorney-General and to the ACMA, as soon as practicable after each incident occurs (The Australian Government: Department of Broadband Communications and the Digital Economy, 2009). Agencies will be required to report on the nature and location of the emergency or disaster, the number of telephone numbers disclosed, the number of persons to whom the numbers were disclosed and why. Agencies will also be required to report annually to ACMA and to the Office of the Privacy Commissioner (OPC) on each disclosure (The Australian Government: Department of Broadband Communications and the Digital Economy, 2009).

With regard to the location-based emergency services phase of NEWS, the bill clarifies the Telecommunications Act by explicitly allowing carriers and service providers supplying LBS to access listed public number information in the IPND, since the current Telecommunications Act does not contain express authority for use of information in the IPND for the purpose of providing LBS on a large scale (Gibbons, 2009). The Bill seeks to explicitly permit access to IPND data for the purpose of providing location-based emergency services and only limited to that information necessary to provide such services. The amendments also extend the existing secondary usage provisions of the Telecommunications Act to prohibit the use or disclosure of IPND data obtained for the purpose of providing the services, except for the purposes permitted under the Act. The prohibition against secondary usage applies to either the carrier or service provider, which initially requested the data and to any other party who may receive the information (The Australian Government: Department of Broadband Communications and the Digital Economy, 2009).

Location-Based Emergency Services in Australia

Unlike in the United States, technical feasibility in the context of location accuracy standards for emergency purposes does not yet exist in Australia. In addition, the commitments for telecommunications carriers are less restrictive since Australian regulators, primarily the ACMA, do not enforce accuracy levels on carriers (The Australian Communications and Media Authority, 2004). At present, a call from a mobile handset to an emergency call service is accompanied by very broad mobile location information (MoLI) relating to what is known as a standardized mobile service area

(SMSA). These SMSAs can range in size from 2,000 to 500,000 square kilometers, according to the cell's size from where the emergency call is originated, and are thus too broad to assist ESOs to find someone in an emergency. Rather, the SMSAs are used by the emergency call person to identify the requested ESO answering point that is closest to his or her location, a process known as jurisdiction determination (The Australian Communications and Media Authority, 2004). Many aspects of these services are regulated and monitored by ACMA under the primary legislation, namely the *Telecommunications (Consumer Protection and Service Standards) Act 1999* and *Telecommunications Act 1997*, and through two subordinate legislative instruments: (i) *Telecommunications (Emergency Call Service) Determination 2002*; and (ii) *Telecommunications (Emergency Call Persons) Determination 1999* (The Australian Communications and Media Authority, 2004).

High accuracy location techniques to provide accurate MoLI in emergency situations are yet to be implemented in Australia but one future aim is to reach accuracy levels within 50 to 500 meters (The Australian Communications and Media Authority, 2004). Currently, location methods that can identify the mobile base station being used to carry an emergency handset call, thus providing MoLI generally within 500 meters to 30 kilometers of accuracy, are available and ready to be used in Australia but prior to 2009 were not extensively deployed by the country's telecommunications carriers (The Australian Communications and Media Authority, 2004). However, this is expected to change as the feasibility of high accuracy location methods are currently under investigation after the Federal Australian Government, Council of Australian Governments (COAG) and the States and Territories identified the compelling need for this technology in Australia, following the tragic 2009 bushfires (The Victorian Bushfires Royal Commission, 2009).

Accordingly, in regard to the second type of location-based emergency service application, which is initiated by government agencies to people in the event of an emergency, the Victorian Government released a tender in August 2009 on behalf of COAG. The tender sought responses for the purpose of determining the capacity and capability of the Australian telecommunications carriers in meeting the long term future requirements for a national emergency alerting and warning system utilizing location-based technologies to identify the active mobile handsets of all carriers, within a defined emergency area (The Victorian Department of Treasury and Finance, 2009). The tender document envisaged the underlying technology to be capable of the following:

1. The technology will have the ability to receive notifications about any new mobile device entering a previously specified emergency area to alert the user that, for example, an emergency services vehicle has arrived at a location, or a civilian has entered the area and may be unaware of the emergency.
2. The technology will include the ability to receive notifications for any mobile device exiting the defined emergency area. This could facilitate the creation of an evacuation list of people who are still remaining in the emergency area.
3. The technology will be able to locate specific mobile devices in both 2G and 3G networks, and overlay their position onto a map.
4. The technology will have the ability to provide sufficient privacy and authentication checking mechanisms to ensure mobile location security (The Victorian Department of Treasury and Finance, 2009).

SOCIO-ETHICAL CONSIDERATIONS

The location-based emergency warning system should allow the government to determine the almost exact geographic coordinates of all active mobile handsets in a defined emergency area(s) or locate mobile handsets in real time within specific threatened zone(s), and then to disseminate, and be able to re-disseminate when necessary, a warning message to these mobile handsets. Determining and/or locating the mobile handset whereabouts does not necessarily require an explicit consent from its user as pertinent government departments and law enforcement agencies have the power, under the *Privacy Act 1988*, to temporarily waive the person's right to privacy in emergencies based on the assumption that the consent is already implied in such situations.

It is quite true that emergencies do represent unique contexts where privacy is most likely to be one of our least concerns. In theory, the location/determination processes cannot trigger concerns being employed specifically for emergency management, but the perception of the uninterrupted availability of these technologies in the hands of governments during normal daily life situations has the potential to raise concerns about the possibility of utilizing them for other purposes, specially under a one-year long emergency declaration. In addition, the implications of waiving away the consent, even temporarily, has the power to impact adversely on the individual's trust in the government and its mandated LBS solutions. These concerns have the potential to add impetus to the ongoing debate of how much individuals are truly willing to relinquish their right to privacy in exchange for a sense of continuous security. This is especially now true in the current political climate of the so-called "war on terror" where governments have started to bestow additional powers on themselves to monitor, track and gather personal information in a way that never could have been previously justified (Perusco & Michael, 2007). In the name of national security, such measures have become justified albeit in exceptional situations. Despite being beyond the established rule of law these exceptions are now considered an absolute necessity to maintain the security of society and its interdependent critical infrastructures (Cavelty, 2007).

When location-based services are employed by governments the individual may never know the true extent of the location/determination on his or her handset's whereabouts or the breadth of location information being collected. Location information is a particularly sensitive kind of personal information that can have intrusive consequences on individual lives if misused (The Australian Communications and Media Authority, 2004). This kind of information can be collected, stored, aggregated and when correlated with other personal information a broad view of behavioral patterns or detailed portraits of individual habits can be created (Clarke & Wigan, 2008; Parenti, 2003). One need only ponder on what personal data is available on social networking sites. Nicola Green posited that location-based technologies might be used one day to hold individuals institutionally accountable for their day-to-day activities (2001). In his work about location-based profiling, Ronald Leenes provides two cases of where location data was used in criminal investigations (2008). Indeed, this profiling of individuals is what makes people uneasy about LBS being in the hands of governments, because of concerns about privacy in general as well as fears of being incorrectly profiled (Holtzman, 2006). Consider the sensitivity of location information pertaining to minors or the elderly who are vulnerable in different ways, or those persons suffering from mental illness.

In this age of "permanent emergency" (Parenti, 2003), perhaps now more than ever, LBS do emerge as promising technologies that can add significant value to the all-hazards approach governments are advocating in national security. Nonetheless, a transparent society where privacy is completely abolished by governments in the name of security is neither feasible nor acceptable. This is because of the inherent value of privacy for both the individual and society (Schneier, 2008). Privacy is indispensable in a community that recognizes social freedom as good and where many people dislike exposure of their private actions not because they have acted irregularly but because their psychological nature requires privacy (Ben-Ze'ev, 2003). Accordingly, governments have to incur an ethical obligation of defining clear limits on privacy intrusions if these intrusions are to be framed in the name of security. Harkin (2003) raised this issue when he stated that "unless there are clear limits on how government can employ the information that it gleans from our mobile communications – and in the current climate of international terrorism, few governments are keen to impose limits on their own meddling – there may well be a backlash that will impede the development of the technology itself".

Requirements for Location-Based Emergency Systems: Equity and Access

Location-based emergency systems are part of all-hazard alert and warning systems that include other emergency notification mechanisms (The Federal Communications Commission, 2005). Several national authorities, international standards organizations, and a number of specialist researchers have undertaken extensive studies to identify and document different requirements for different public emergency warning systems that should in principle allow support for all current and future emergency event types. In these studies, many aspects were given attention, including legislative, regulatory, administrative, operational, technical, organizational and ethical requirements. Some of these contributions have been by Mileti and Sorensen (1990), the Cellular Emergency Alert Systems Association (2002), ETSI (2003), The European Telecommunications Standards Institute (2006a, 2006b, 2010), Tsalgatidou, Veijalainen, Markkula, Katasonov, and Hadjiefthymiades (2003), FCC (2005), McGinley, Turk, and Bennett (2006), International Telecommunications Union (2007), 3rd Generation Partnership Project (2008, 2009), Fernandes (2008), The Victorian Bushfires Royal Commission (2009), The Victorian Department of Treasury and Finance (2009), and Jagtman (2009), Sanders (2009), and Setten and Sanders (2009) under the European Commission's CHORIST Project (2009).

In general, defining requirements serves several objectives such as establishing a standardized way of developing and implementing a system, prioritizing the system's future functionality while providing guidance on the system's expected performance levels, preventing duplicative reporting for the system's stakeholders (The United States Department of Homeland Security, 2008), and ensuring that people who want access to LBS services during emergencies can have them in addition to other mechanisms they have traditionally enjoyed. With regard to location-based emergency systems, no explicit requirements, specifically legal and administrative requirements, currently exist anywhere in the world (Togt, Beinat, Zlatanova, & Scholten, 2005). Nonetheless, based on the concepts and principles outlined in the above-mentioned works, the following specific requirements have been drawn from the literature for location-based emergency warning and alerting systems. These requirements include, but are not limited to:

1. Ability to be integrated or used along with other alerting and warning systems.
2. Be fully accessible to the right authorities.
3. Be only accessible by the right authorities.
4. Be flexible to allow support for all current and future types or categories of emergency events and not to be designed to support specific type(s) of emergencies or events requiring notification.
5. Ability to operate independently of a specific telecommunications carrier network.
6. The underlying technology should be supported by all telecommunications carriers in the country.
7. Be able to accommodate newer technologies to enable futuristic enhanced transfer modes (e.g., messages with large data content such

as video within the warning notification in order to send, for example, a map of safe area or emergency facilities).

8. Have the ability to provide sufficient privacy and authentication checking mechanisms to ensure mobile location security.
9. Support both pre-planned and dynamic notification events.
10. Reach an unrestricted number of people, ranging from hundreds in rural areas to millions in urban and metropolitan cities.
11. Deliver messages simultaneously to a large number of recipients.
12. Deliver the message in near real-time or within a planned specified time.
13. Reach the appropriate recipients, as efficiently as possible, through the ability of the underlying technology to segment the message recipients by geographic locations.
14. Allow the opportunity to send different messages to different groups of people (e.g., recommend different safety areas for different groups or messages can be targeted at people in the immediate vicinity of an emergency to do one thing, and people traveling to an affected area to do another).
15. Reach all kinds of existing mobile handsets including legacy devices that are largely still in use.
16. Support delivery of messages to those with special needs and unique devices, such as handsets for hearing and vision impaired persons.
17. Reach the residents of remote areas, and people roaming from other mobile telecommunications networks, including visitors from other countries.
18. Support the transmission in languages in addition to English to the extent where it is practical and feasible.
19. Be able to deliver the message under network-congested conditions.
20. Have a message redelivery mechanism when the initial message delivery fails.
21. Have a message reiteration mechanism for as long as the message is valid.

In addition to the base requirements for the location-based emergency system, the requirements for the service/message itself should consider, but are not limited to, the following:

1. Message creation is driven by the country's specific characteristics and its own list of emergencies.
2. Message template is consistent across different warning sources from different emergency authorities.
3. Message is based on standardized digital format for expressing and disseminating a consistent warning message simultaneously over different informative and media channels.
4. Specifically recognizable as being an emergency message that cannot be mistaken for an ordinary message.
5. Credible, secure and authentic.
6. Location-specific, to minimize social anxiety.
7. Relevant, to ensure that recipients realize that the warning relates to their personal situation.
8. Timely, to prevent wrong actions and to provide those at risk with enough time to take protective action.
9. Accurate, to indicate the degree severity, or the predicted severity, of the event.
10. Complete, to offer sufficient details about the situation.
11. Concise, to avoid lengthy messages.
12. Provide adequate instructions to recipients regarding what should and should not be done to protect them.
13. Fully clear and comprehensible to all people including young and senior recipients.
14. Positive, rather than negative to advocate people on what to do.

One of the greatest threats to such service implementation comes from the potential for instant message hoaxes during times of crisis (i.e., disinformation) from unscrupulous citizens to other unsuspecting citizens, as was reported in the fight against SARs (Severe Acute Respiratory Syndrome) in Hong Kong in 2003 (Jardin, 2003). These are not only disruptive to emergency services but can also be life-threatening to individuals who are misinformed. There is unfortunately little authorities can do to guard against such communications.

OVERCOMING EMERGENCY ALERT SHORTCOMINGS

During an emergency, traditional standard emergency warning signal (SEWS) techniques are reliable and dependable because they are easily recognized and trusted by members of the public (Ministry for Police and Emergency Services, 2011). For example, in Australia, the Australian Broadcasting Corporation (ABC) has aired radio and television campaigns for decades that have noted that it is the local "emergency services broadcaster" that citizens need to pay attention to and act accordingly in response. These SEWS services are considered authentic because they reach a mass target audience at exactly the same time, and are coming from a source feed that is difficult to corrupt. With newer emergency warning systems being introduced relying on personal devices like a mobile telephone SMS or fixed line voicemail, human factors and system design issues can become significant problems (Jean, 2011, 2012). Citizens who receive a text message from authorities such as the police, about an impending emergency which does not eventuate are likely to take subsequent messages to their phone less seriously. This is analogous to Aesop's fable, "The Boy Who Cried Wolf." The other problem till now with regards to mobile alerts has been the over-reliance on someone's billing address details to receive a message about an emergency (Hilvert, 2011). This has led to some strange happenings where people who are overseas receive a text message about an emergency that is occurring in their home town many thousands of kilometers away.

Consider the case where an emergency alert is sent out to citizens and riddled with spelling errors. One such example occurred in the chemical fire emergency in the Australian Capital Territory (ACT) in the suburb of Mitchell (Humphries, 2011; Ludwig, 2011). Citizens received a text message on September 16, 2011 in the early hours of the morning, which read: "Emergency. Emergency. The ACT Fire Brigade is responding to a Chemical insadent in Mitchell. Resadents are advised to evacuate the suburb immediately." Such experiences decrease citizen confidence in critical emerging systems deployed by the government. This is despite the fact that the error did not come down to someone who could not spell or who rushed through the system an unchecked message. But rather an officer who reused a phonetically-spelled text destined for a text-to-speech recognition system to also reach out to citizens via SMS. It is still unclear whether the Mitchell incident was a systems design error, or human error based on poor training, or poor implementation of the guidelines for sending out such mobile alerts. Emergency Services Agency Commissioner Mark Crosweller went on record openly declaring his agency had made some mistakes during the Mitchell incident. He said: "[w] e've assessed the way that we used the system, we've improved our procedures, we've improved our training and we've made recommendations back to the system's operator about improving the user interface" (Jean, 2011).

Several other problems plagued the emergency alert system during the Mitchell fire in the ACT which used the fifteen million dollar system instituted on December 1, 2009. Primarily, insufficient time was allocated to allow the system to dial all of the numbers in the target area. In an inquiry following the fire, Attorney-General Robert Mc-

Clelland stated that the emergency alert system had simply not been used correctly. For instance, authorities made 30,530 calls to 86,801 landlines within the first 30 minutes of the fire and of those only 13,784 were answered. In essence, only about a third of the landline numbers could be dialed within thirty minutes. Authorities also sent text messages to more than 52,700 mobile phones, of a total pool of 83,774 mobiles. Despite the emergency alert system used in the Mitchell fire had previously been deployed successfully in Canberra in 2003, and had been previously used 329 times to send 7.12 million messages, this time it failed in its execution (Jean, 2011; Hilvert, 2011). What the Mitchell fire did demonstrate however was the need to steer away from the use of the IPND billing address to a location-based mobile telephone emergency warning system (Environment and Sustainable Development Directorate, 2011). During the fire, the data source for Emergency Alert, the Location Based Number Store (LBNS) came directly from the IPND. The Emergency Alert system was designed to send 1,000 voice messages and 30,000 SMS per minute.

In two other notable incidences where an older emergency alert system was brought into question included the March 30, 2009, Sydney City power failure which affected over 100,000 people. SMS text messages were sent to building managers and site coordinators in the city using the SydneyAlert system, over an hour after the power went down (Robinson, 2012). Employees in 34 tall buildings walked down evacuation stairwells in near darkness without any knowledge of what had occurred. Some suspected a terrorist attack, and were none the wiser as they exited onto the main city streets, only to find 137 intersections with traffic lights that were blank. To add to the confusion, 98 loudspeakers that had been installed to a value of two million dollars were not working, and there was no backup battery generator, so that at least people knew what they had to do. It was up to the Fire Brigade to keep people moving and make their way home.

Prior to this incident on March 2, 2009, Victorian police also used SMS to reach about 5 million mobile phone customers with a message that read: "Extreme weather in VIC expected Mon night and Tues. High wind & fire risk. Listen to Local ABC Radio for emergency updates. Do not reply to this msg" (Schulz, 2009). It is important to note that some members received their SMS several days after it was meant to reach them. In addition, so concerned were some citizens by the directness of the communications, that some anxiously called triple-zero seeking further information. What transpired was not an emergency at all, and so some citizens felt misled by the SMS authorized by the Police.

Enter the possibility of utilizing the Internet for emergency alerting (e.g., Twitter and other microblogging and social networking engines), and one can see how quickly a paradigm shift will be required to enable the new location-based techniques that have been promised in Australia since the Victorian Bushfires. At the beginning of January 2012, the Victorian Government (acting on behalf of all the States and Territories in Australia), entered into a contract with Telstra to provide location-based real-time alerts during emergencies. This means that in future emergency alerts, only people who are in an affected area will be notified of an emergency, and not just those whose billing details are designated in the affected area. Initially only mobile phone users subscribed to Telstra will receive these messages, but the Victorian Government has stepped up its efforts to form contractual agreements with the other two major mobile service providers, Optus and Vodafone (Lee, 2012).

Time and time again, emergency ministers have emphasized that the new technologies should be used in concert with traditional SEWS techniques. We might be getting more sophisticated in how we target citizens for emergency alerting through location-based services, but we still need to emphasize the importance of following due process for government agencies and emergency service organizations (eGov, 2012).

CONCLUSION

Large scale emergencies, that have the potential to disrupt the orderly manner of civil society, are now considered a type of national security challenge. While there is a growing trend by governments to deploy more socially constructed security measures to counter the threatening consequences of extreme events, the public reception has not always been favorable. In Australia, some citizens and lobby groups see the introduction of laws mandating access to certain types of personal information to aid in the gradual relinquishing of individual privacy rights. Beyond unauthorized access and disclosure of citizen personal details is the public perception that authorities will be able to perform continuous tracking after legitimately deploying a one year long emergency declaration. With a limited effort from the government to raise public awareness about the deployed system, most of the concerns, although they may merely be misconceptions, have the power to impact negatively on the practiced emergency response measures while devaluing the purpose of the alert and warning system in the eyes of the public. The time to intervene is now as governments, like Australia, move to introduce basic systems moving to more sophisticated and fully-fledged location based services into the future. It is important for governments, telecommunications carriers and relevant stakeholders to discuss the possible socio-ethical implications of advanced technologies like location based services before they are rolled out in a ubiquitous manner. In trying to respond to the challenge of national security, governments will ironically need to invest even more money into such areas as database security to ensure that private citizen details are not disclosed to unauthorized parties.

REFERENCES

3rd Generation Partnership Project. (2008). *Technical specification group services and system aspects: Study for requirements for a public Warning System (PWS) Service (Release 8)*. Retrieved April 13, 2009, from http://www.3gpp.org/ftp/tsg_sa/WG1_Serv/TSGS1_37_Orlando/Docs/S1-070824.doc

3rd Generation Partnership Project. (2009). *Technical specification group services and system aspects; functional stage 2 description of Location Services (LCS) (Release 9)*. Retrieved January 16, 2010, from http://www.3gpp.org/ftp/Specs/archive/23_series/23.271/

Aitenbichler, E. (2008). A focus on location context. In Mühlhäuser, M., & Gurevych, I. (Eds.), *Handbook of research on ubiquitous computing technology for real time enterprises* (pp. 257–281). Hershey, PA: IGI Global. doi:10.4018/978-1-59904-832-1.ch012

Aloudat, A., Michael, K., & Jun, Y. (2007). Location-based services in emergency management- from government to citizens: Global case studies. In Mendis, P., Lai, J., Dawson, E., & Abbass, H. (Eds.), *Recent advances in security technology* (pp. 190–201). Melbourne, Australia: Australian Homeland Security Research Centre.

Astroth, J. (2003). Location-based services: Criteria for adoption and solution deployment. In Mennecke, B. E., & Strader, T. J. (Eds.), *Mobile commerce: Technology, theory, and applications* (pp. 229–236). Hershey, PA: Idea Group. doi:10.4018/978-1-59140-044-8.ch015

Australia.gov.au Website. (2010). *The Australian continent*. Retrieved March 10, 2010, from http://australia.gov.au/about-australia/our-country/the-australian-continent

Ben-Ze'ev, A. (2003). Privacy, emotional closeness, and openness in cyberspace. *Computers in Human Behavior*, *19*(4), 451–467. doi:10.1016/S0747-5632(02)00078-X

Benson, S. (2007). *SMS smog alerts for Sydney*. Retrieved from http://www.news.com.au/top-stories/sydney-on-smog-alert/story-e6frfkp9-1111113614955

Bernardos, A. M., Casar, J. R., & Tarrio, P. (2007). Building a framework to characterize location-based services. In *Proceedings of the International Conference on Next Generation Mobile Applications, Services and Technologies* (pp. 110-118).

Betts, R. (2003). The missing links in community warning systems: Findings from two Victorian community warning system projects. *The Australian Journal of Emergency Management*, *18*(3), 35–45.

Bita, N., & Sainsbury, M. (2009). *Bungling silenced Victoria bushfires warning*. The Australian.

Boughton, G. (1998). The community: Central to emergency risk management. *Australian Journal of Emergency Management*, 2-5.

Brin, D. (1998). *The transparent society: Will technology force us to choose between privacy and freedom?* (1st ed.). Boulder, CO: Perseus Press.

Bushfire SMS to assist in warning system development. (2009, March 4). *The Australian Broadcasting Corporation*.

Buzan, B., Woever, O., & Wilde, J. D. (1998). *Security: A new framework for analysis* (1st ed.). London, UK: Lynne Rienner.

Canton, L. G. (2007). *Emergency management: Concepts and strategies for effective programs* (1st ed.). Hoboken, NJ: John Wiley & Sons.

Cantwell, B. (2002). *Why technical breakthroughs fail: A history of public concern with emerging technologies*. Cambridge, MA: MIT Press.

Carter, L., & Bélanger, F. (2005). The utilization of e-government services: Citizen trust, innovation and acceptance factors. *Information Systems Journal*, *15*(1), 5–25. doi:10.1111/j.1365-2575.2005.00183.x

Cavelty, M. D. (2007). Cyber-terror–Looming threat or phantom menace? The framing of the US cyber-threat debate. *Journal of Information Technology & Politics*, *4*(1).

Chudleigh, J. (2009, November 10). Earlier alert system for severe weather. *The Courier-Mail*.

Clarke, R., & Wigan, M. (2008). You are where you have been. In Michael, K., & Michael, M. G. (Eds.), *Australia and the new technologies: Evidence based policy in public administration* (pp. 100–114). Canberra, Australia: University of Wollongong.

Code of Practice of Passive Location Services in the UK. (2006). *Industry code of practice for the use of mobile phone technology to provide passive location services in the UK*. Retrieved August 23, 2007, from http://www.mobilebroadbandgroup.com/documents/UKCoP_location_servs_210706v_pub_clean.pdf

Coyle, D., & Meier, P. (2009). *New technologies in emergencies and conflicts: The role of information and social networks*. New York, NY: United Nations.

Dawson, M., Winterbottom, J., & Thomson, M. (2007). *IP location* (1st ed.). New York, NY: McGraw-Hill.

Dobbin, M. (2009, March 3). Victorians receive fire text warning. *The Age*.

Dunn, M., & Collier, K. (2007, February 27). Plan to use SMS for SOS. *Herald Sun*.

eGovernment Resource Centre (eGov). (2012). *Emergency alerts and warnings - Australia*. Retrieved June 15, 2012, from http://www.egov.vic.gov.au/focus-on-countries/australia/government-initiatives-australia/emergencies-and-safety-australia/emergency-alerts-and-warnings-australia.html

Emergency Management Australia. (1996). *Australian counter disaster handbook* (5th ed., *Vol. 2*). Canberra, Australia.

Emergency Management Australia. (2004a). *Disaster recovery: Safer sustainable communities*. Retrieved November 27, 2007, from http://www.ema.gov.au/www/emaweb/rwpattach.nsf/VAP/(3273BD3F76A7A5DEDAE36942A54D7D90)~Manual10-Recovery.pdf/$file/Manual10-Recovery.pdf

Emergency Management Australia. (2004b). *Emergency management in Australia: Concepts and principles*. Retrieved November 27, 2007, from http://www.ema.gov.au/www/emaweb/rwpattach.nsf/VAP/(3273BD3F76A7A5DEDAE36942A54D7D90)~Manual01-Emergency-ManagementinAustralia-ConceptsandPrinciples.pdf/$file/Manual01-EmergencyManagementin-Australia-ConceptsandPrinciples.pdf

Emergency Management Australia. (2008). *Disasters database*. Retrieved January 4, 2008, from http://www.ema.gov.au/www/emaweb/emaweb.nsf/Page/Resources_DisastersDatabase_DisastersDatabase

Emergency Management Australia. (2009a). *Australian emergency management arrangements*. Retrieved from http://www.ema.gov.au/www/emaweb/rwpattach.nsf/VAP/(3A6790B96C927794AF1031D9395C5C20)~Australian+Emergency+Management+Arrangements.pdf/$file/Australian+Emergency+Management+Arrangements.pdf

Emergency Management Australia. (2009b). *Emergency management*. Retrieved December 8, 2008, from http://www.ema.gov.au/www/emaweb/emaweb.nsf/Page/Emergency_Management

Environment and Sustainable Development Directorate. (2011). *Ministerial statement- Mitchell Fire*. Retrieved September 20, 2011, from http://www.environment.act.gov.au/__data/assets/pdf_file/0009/232299/Ministerial_Statement_on_Mitchell_fire,_20_September_2011.pdf

European Commission. (2011). *Satellite navigation: Why Galileo?* Retrieved January 11, 2012, from http://ec.europa.eu/enterprise/policies/satnav/galileo/why/index_en.htm

European Space Agency. (2011). *What is Galileo?* Retrieved January 11, 2012, from http://www.esa.int/esaNA/galileo.html

Fernandes, J. P. (2008). Emergency warnings with short message service. In Coskun, H. G., Cigizoglu, H. K., & Maktav, M. D. (Eds.), *Integration of information for environmental security* (1st ed., pp. 205–210). Dordrecht, The Netherlands: Springer-Verlag. doi:10.1007/978-1-4020-6575-0_14

Gibbons, S. (2009). *Telecommunications amendment (Integrated Public Number Database) Bill 2009: Second Reading*. Retrieved August 6, 2009, from http://parlinfo.aph.gov.au/parlInfo/genpdf/chamber/hansardr/2009-02-26/0032/hansard_frag.pdf;fileType=application%2Fpdf

Gilbert, C. (1998). Studying disaster: Changes in the main conceptual tools. In Quarantelli, E. L. (Ed.), *What is a disaster? A dozen perspectives on the question* (1st ed., pp. 3–12). New York, NY: Routledge.

Gow, G. A. (2005). Pinpointing consent: Location privacy and mobile phones. In Nyíri, K. (Ed.), *A sense of place: The global and the local in mobile communication* (pp. 139–150). Vienna, Austria: Passagen Verlag.

Green, N. (2001). Who's watching whom? Monitoring and accountability in mobile relations. In Brown, B., Green, N., & Harper, R. (Eds.), *Wireless world: Social and interactional aspects of the mobile age* (1st ed., pp. 32–45). New York, NY: Springer. doi:10.1007/978-1-4471-0665-4_3

Grothe, M. J. M., Landa, H. C., & Steenbruggen, J. G. M. (2005). The value of Gi4DM for transport & water management. In P. v. Oosterom, S. Zlatanova, & E. M. Fendel (Eds.), *Geo-information for disaster management* (1st ed., pp. 129-154). Dordrecht, The Netherlands: Springer-Verlag.

Gruber, B., & Winter, S. (2002). *Location based services using a database federation.* Paper presented at the 5th AGILE Conference on Geographic Information Science, Palma, Spain.

Guan, J., Zhou, S., Zhou, J., & Zhu, F. (2007). Providing location-based services under web services framework. In Taniar, D. (Ed.), *Encyclopedia of mobile computing and commerce* (1st ed., pp. 789–795). London, UK: Information Science Reference. doi:10.4018/978-1-59904-002-8.ch134

Haddow, G. D., Bullock, J. A., & Coppola, D. P. (2006). *Introduction to emergency management* (2nd ed.). Burlington, MA: Elsevier Butterworth–Heinemann.

Harkin, J. (2003). *Mobilisation: The growing public interest in mobile technology* (1st ed.). London, UK: Demos.

Harvey, F. (2008). *A primer of GIS: Fundamental geographic and cartographic* (1st ed.). New York, NY: The Guilford Press.

Hilvert, J. (2011). Dodgy text tarnishes SMS emergency service system. *ITNews*. Retrieved September 23, 2011, from http://www.itnews.com.au/promos/interstitial/interstitial_dfp.html?l=10;KnvJuy7QTzEfzPKF8zesJyG8le2WW6,qtlJDF2ITieqTGRqifR;http%3A%2F%2Fwww.itnews.com.au%2FNews%2F272863%2Cdodgy%2Dtext%2Dtarnishes%2Dsms%2Demergency%2Dservice%2Dsystem.aspx

Hjelm, J. (2002). *Creating location services for the wireless Web* (1st ed.). New York, NY: John Wiley & Sons.

Holma, H., Kristensson, M., Salonen, J., & Toskala, A. (2004). UMTS services and applications. In Holma, H., & Toskala, A. (Eds.), *WCDMA for UMTS: Radio access for third generation mobile communications* (3rd ed., pp. 11–46). Chichester, UK: John Wiley & Sons. doi:10.1002/0470870982.ch2

Holtzman, D. H. (2006). *Privacy lost: How technology is endangering your privacy* (1st ed.). San Francisco, CA: Jossey-Bass.

Humphries, G. (2011). Attorney-General: Emergency alert (Question No. 1434). *Senate Debates*. Retrieved November 22, 2011, from http://www.openaustralia.org/senate/?id=2011-11-22.155.1

Ife, H. (2009, March 2). Texts alert victorians of fire danger. *Herald Sun*.

Jagtman, E. (2009). *Reaching citizens with CHORIST: Everything but technology*. Retrieved October 18, 2009, from http://www.chorist.eu/index.php?page=1&sel=1

Jardin, X. (2003). Text messaging feeds SARS rumors. *Wired*. Retrieved October 17, 2009, from http://www.wired.com/medtech/health/news/2003/04/58506

Jean, P. (2011). *Govt rebuked over Mitchell fire response*. Retrieved November 23, 2011, from http://www.canberratimes.com.au/act-news/govt-rebuked-over-mitchell-fire-response-20111123-1v2u0.html

Jean, P. (2012). SMS alert system is short on delivery. *The Age*. Retrieved February 29, 2012, from http://m.theage.com.au/act-news/sms-alert-system-is-short-on-delivery-20120228-1u187.html

Jensen, C. S. (2002, January 8-11). Research challenges in location-enabled m-services. In *Proceedings of the Third IEEE International Conference on Mobile Data Management*, Singapore (pp. 3-7).

Kaplan, E. D., & Hegarty, C. J. (2006). *Understanding GPS: Principles and applications* (2nd ed.). Norwood, MA: Artech House.

Kiefer, J. J., Mancini, J. A., Morrow, B. H., Gladwin, H., & Stewart, T. A. (2008). *Providing access to resilience-enhancing technologies for disadvantaged communities and vulnerable populations*. Retrieved from http://www.orau.org/university-partnerships/files/The-PARET-Report.pdf

Kim, D. J., Braynov, S. B., Rao, H. R., & Song, Y. I. (2001, August 2-5). A B-to-C trust model for online exchange. In *Proceedings of the Seventh Americas Conference on Information Systems*, Boston, MA (pp. 784-787).

Kini, A., & Choobineh, J. (1998). Trust in electronic commerce: Definition and theoretical considerations. In *Proceedings of the Thirty-First Annual Hawaii International Conference on System Sciences* (pp. 51-61).

Krishnamurthy, N. (2002). Using SMS to deliver location-based services. In *Proceedings of the IEEE International Conference on Personal Wireless Communications* (pp. 177-181).

Küpper, A. (2005). *Location-based services: Fundamentals and operation* (1st ed.). Chichester, UK: John Wiley & Sons. doi:10.1002/0470092335

Lee, M. (2012). Telstra adds location to emergency alerts. *ZDNet.* Retrieved January 13, 2012, from http://www.zdnet.com.au/telstra-adds-location-to-emergency-alerts-339329657.htm

Leenes, R. (2008). Reply: Mind my step? In Hildebrandt, M., & Gutwirth, S. (Eds.), *Profiling the European citizen: Cross-disciplinary perspectives* (1st ed., pp. 160–168). Dordrecht, The Netherlands: Springer-Verlag.

Lopez, X. R. (2004). Location-based services. In Karimi, H. A., & Hammand, A. (Eds.), *Telegeoinformatics: Location-based computing and services* (1st ed., pp. 144–159). Boca Raton, FL: CRC Press.

Ludwig, J. (2011). Attorney-General: Emergency alert (Question No. 1434). *Senate Debates.* Retrieved November 22, 2011, from http://www.openaustralia.org/senate/?id=2011-11-22.155.1

Marx, G. T. (1999). What's in a name? Some reflections on the sociology of anonymity. *The Information Society, 15*(2), 99–112. doi:10.1080/019722499128565

McAdams, J. (2006). *SMS does SOS: Short message service earns valued role as a link of last resort for crisis communications.* Retrieved February 2, 2007, from http://fcw.com/articles/2006/04/03/sms-does-sos.aspx?sc_lang=en

McClelland, R. (2011). *Australia's emergency alert system working well.* Retrieved September 1, 2011, from http://www.alp.org.au/federal-government/news/australia-s-emergency-alert-system-working-well/

McGinley, M., Turk, A., & Bennett, D. (2006). Design criteria for public emergency warning systems. In *Proceedings of the 3rd International Conference on Information Systems for Crisis Response and Management*, Newark, NJ.

McKnight, D. H., & Chervany, N. L. (2001). What trust means in e-commerce customer relationships: An interdisciplinary conceptual typology. *International Journal of Electronic Commerce, 6*(2), 35–59.

Michael, K., Stroh, B., Berry, O., Muhlhauber, A., & Nicholls, T. (2006, September 19-21). The AVIAN flu tracker - A location service proof of concept, recent advances in security technology. In *Proceedings of the RNSA Security Technology Conference*, Canberra, Australia (pp. 244-258).

Mileti, D. S., & Sorensen, J. H. (1990). *Communication of emergency public warnings: A social science perspective and state-of-the-art assessment*. Retrieved August 8, 2007, from http://emc.ornl.gov/EMCWeb/EMC/PDF/CommunicationFinal.pdf

Ministry for Police and Emergency Services. (2011). *Standard Emergency Warning Signal (SEWS)*. Retrieved January 21, 2011, from http://www.emergency.nsw.gov.au/sews

New South Wales Government. (2007). *About SydneyALERT*. Retrieved April 17, 2008, from http://www.sydneyalert.nsw.gov.au/content.php/36.html

Oh, J., & Haas, Z. J. (2007). A scheme for location-based internet broadcasting and its applications. *IEEE Communications Magazine*, *45*(11), 136–141. doi:10.1109/MCOM.2007.4378333

Parenti, C. (2003). *The soft cage: Surveillance in America from slavery to the war on terror* (1st ed.). New York, NY: Basic Books.

Perry, R. W. (2007). What is a disaster? In H. A. Rodrıguez, E. L. Quarantelli, & R. Dynes (Eds.), *Handbook of disaster research* (1st ed., pp. 1-16). New York, NY: Springer Science+Business Media.

Perusco, L., & Michael, K. (2007). Control, trust, privacy, and security: Evaluating location-based services. *IEEE Technology and Society Magazine*, *26*, 4–16. doi:10.1109/MTAS.2007.335564

Perusco, L., Michael, K., & Michael, M. G. (2006, October 11-13). *Location-based services and the privacy-security dichotomy*. Paper presented at the Third International Conference on Mobile Computing and Ubiquitous Networking, London, UK.

Premier promises mobile phone terrorism alert. (2007, February 26). *The Australian*.

Pura, M. (2005). Linking perceived value and loyalty in location-based mobile services. *Managing Service Quality*, *15*(6), 509–538. doi:10.1108/09604520510634005

Quarantelli, E. L. (1986). What should we study? Questions and suggestions for researchers about the concept of disasters. *International Journal of Mass Emergencies and Disasters*, *5*(1), 7–32.

Robinson, G. (2009). *Warning: Doubts over Sydney's alarm system*. Retrieved March 31, 2009, from http://www.smh.com.au/national/warning-doubts-over-sydneys-alarm-system-20090331-9hmg.html

Rosenthal, U. (1998). Future disasters, future definitions. In Quarantelli, E. L. (Ed.), *What is a disaster? A dozen perspectives on the question* (1st ed., pp. 147–160). New York, NY: Routledge.

Samsioe, J., & Samsioe, A. (2002). Introduction to location based services: Markets and technologies. In Reichwald, R. (Ed.), *Mobile Kommunikation: Wertschöpfung, Technologien, neue Dienste* (pp. 417–438). Wiesbaden, Germany: Gabler. doi:10.1007/978-3-322-90695-3_25

Sanders, P. (2009). *The CB way forward*. Retrieved October 18, 2009, from http://www.chorist.eu/index.php?page=1&sel=1

Schneier, B. (2008). The myth of the 'transparent society'. *Wired Magazine*. Retrieved from http://www.wired.com/politics/security/commentary/securitymatters/2008/03/securitymatters_0306

Schulz, M. (2009). Emergency services admit SMS bushfire alerts not foolproof. *Herald Sun*. Retrieved March 3, 2009, from http://www.heraldsun.com.au/news/more-news/emergency-services-admit-sms-bushfire-alerts-not-foolproof/story-e6frf7kx-1111119016715

Setten, W. v., & Sanders, P. (2009). *Citizen alert with cell broadcasting: The technology, the standards and the way forward*. Retrieved October 18, 2009, from http://www.chorist.eu/index.php?page=1&sel=1

Shiode, N., Li, C., Batty, M., Longley, P., & Maguire, D. (2002). *The impact and penetration of location-based services* (pp. 1–16). London, UK: Centre for Advanced Spatial Analysis, University College London.

Spiekermann, S. (2004). General aspects of location-based services. In J. Schiller & A. Voisard (Eds.), *Location-based services* (1 ed., pp. 9-26). San Francisco, CA: Elsevier.

Stojanović, D., Djordjevic-Kajan, S., Papadopoulos, A. N., & Nanopoulos, A. (2007). Monitoring and tracking moving objects in mobile environments. In Taniar, D. (Ed.), *Encyclopedia of mobile computing and commerce* (1st ed., pp. 660–665). London, UK: Information Science Reference. doi:10.4018/978-1-59904-002-8.ch110

Tan, Y.-H., & Thoen, W. (2001). Toward a generic model of trust for electronic commerce. *International Journal of Electronic Commerce*, *5*(2), 61–74.

Templeman, D., & Bergin, A. (2008). *Taking a punch: Building a more resilient Australia*. Retrieved February 2, 2009, from http://www.aspi.org.au/publications/publication_details.aspx?ContentID=165

The Australian Communications and Media Authority. (2004). *Location location location: The future use of location information to enhance the handling of emergency mobile phone calls*. Retrieved October 21, 2007, from http://acma.gov.au/webwr/consumer_info/location.pdf

The Australian Communications and Media Authority. (2009). *Australia's emergency call service in a changing environment*. Retrieved September 25, 2009, from http://www.acma.gov.au/webwr/_assets/main/lib311250/future_of_emergency_call_svces.pdf

The Australian Early Warning Network. (2009). *Townsville city council signs up to the early warning network*. Retrieved December 7, 2009, from http://www.ewn.com.au/media/townsville_city_council.aspx

The Australian Government: Attorney General's Department. (2008). *Privacy Act 1988: Act No.119 of 1988 as amended*. Retrieved August 2, 2008, from http://www.comlaw.gov.au/ComLaw/Legislation/ActCompilation1.nsf/0/63C00ADD09B982ECCA257490002B9D57/$file/Privacy1988_WD02HYP.pdf

The Australian Government: Attorney General's Department. (2009). *Rudd Government Implements COAG agreement on telephone-based emergency warning systems (Joint Media Release)*. Retrieved August 2, 2009, from http://www.ag.gov.au/www/ministers/mcclelland.nsf/Page/MediaReleases_2009_FirstQuarter_23February2009-RuddGovernmentImplementsCOAGAgreementonTelephone-BasedEmergencyWarningSystems

The Australian Government: Department of Broadband Communications and the Digital Economy. (2009). *Telecommunications amendment (Integrated Public Number Database) Bill 2009: Explanatory memorandum*. Retrieved August 6, 2009, from http://parlinfo.aph.gov.au/parlInfo/download/legislation/ems/r4062_ems_d2937505-3da9-4059-b9cb-e382e891dd23/upload_word/TelAm(IPND)_EM.doc;fileType=application%2Fmsword

The Australian Government: Department of Transport and Regional Services. (2004). *Natural disasters in Australia: Reforming mitigation, relief and recovery arrangements*. Retrieved February 18, 2009, from http://www.ema.gov.au/www/emaweb/rwpattach.nsf/VAP/(99292794923AE8E7CBABC6FB71541EE1)~Natural+Disasters+in+Australia+-+Review.pdf/$file/Natural+Disasters+in+Australia+-+Review.pdf

The Cellular Emergency Alert Systems Association. (2002). *Handset requirements specification: Reaching millions in a matter of seconds*. Retrieved April 2, 2007, from http://www.ceasa-int.org/library/Handset_Requirements_Specification.pdf

The European Commission. (2009). *The CHORIST Project: Integrating communications for enhanced environmental risk management and citizens safety*. Retrieved November 7, 2009, from http://www.chorist.eu/index.php?page=1&sel=1

The European Telecommunications Standards Institute. (2003). *Requirements for communication of citizens with authorities/organizations in case of distress (Emergency call handling)*. Retrieved May 20, 2007, from http://etsi.org/WebSite/homepage.aspx

The European Telecommunications Standards Institute. (2006a). *Analysis of the short message service and cell broadcast service for emergency messaging applications; emergency messaging; SMS and CBS*. Retrieved May 10, 2007, from http://etsi.org/WebSite/homepage.aspx

The European Telecommunications Standards Institute. (2006b). *Emergency communications (EMTEL): Requirements for communications from authorities/organizations to individuals, groups or the general public during emergencies*. Retrieved May 20, 2007, from http://etsi.org/WebSite/homepage.aspx

The European Telecommunications Standards Institute. (2010). *Study for requirements for a Public Warning System (PWS) service*. Retrieved February 10, 2010, from http://webstats.3gpp.org/ftp/Specs/html-info/22968.htm

The Federal Communications Commission. (2005). *Review of the emergency alert system*. Retrieved April 13, 2008, from http://www.fcc.gov/eb/Orders/2005/FCC-05-191A1.html

The International Telecommunications Union. (2007). *Compendium of ITU'S work on emergency telecommunications*. Geneva, Switzerland: The United Nations Agency for Information and Communication Technologies.

The Minister for Police and Emergency Services. (2005). *First calls made as part of early warning trial*. Retrieved June 4, 2007, from http://www.legislation.vic.gov.au/domino/Web_Notes/newmedia.nsf/35504bc71d3adebcca256cfc0082c2b8/4ae0fe91bdeb3e8aca25704d000729b0!OpenDocument

The United States Department of Homeland Security. (2008). *National emergency communications plan*. Retrieved October 6, 2009, from http://www.dhs.gov/xlibrary/assets/national_emergency_communications_plan.pdf

The Victorian Bushfires Royal Commission. (2009). *Interim report*. Victoria, Australia: Author.

The Victorian Department of Treasury and Finance. (2009). *Request for Information (RFI) for: Location based identification of active mobile handsets for emergency notification purposes* (RFI Number: SS-06-2009). Retrieved November 19, 2009, from https://www.tenders.vic.gov.au/tenders/tender/display/tender-details.do?id=87&action=display-tender-details&returnUrl=%2Ftender%2Fsearch%2Ftender-search.do%3Faction%3Dadvanced-tender-search-closed-tender

Togt, R., Beinat, E., Zlatanova, S., & Scholten, H. (2005). Location interoperability services for medical emergency operations during disasters. In P. v. Oosterom, S. Zlatanova, & E. M. Fendel (Eds.), *Geo-information for disaster management* (pp. 1127-1141). Berlin, Germany: Springer-Verlag.

Tsalgatidou, A., Veijalainen, J., Markkula, J., Katasonov, A., & Hadjiefthymiades, S. (2003). *Mobile e-commerce and location-based services: Technology and requirements*. Paper presented at the 9th Scandinavian Research Conference on Geographical Information Sciences, Espoo, Finland.

Uhlirz, M. (2007). A market and user view on LBS. In Gartner, G., Cartwright, W., & Peterson, M. P. (Eds.), *Location based services and telecartography* (1st ed., pp. 47–58). Berlin, Germany: Springer-Verlag. doi:10.1007/978-3-540-36728-4_4

United Nations News Centre. (2010). *Earthquakes the deadliest of all disasters during past decade*. Retrieved January 29, 2010, from http://www.un.org/apps/news/printnews.asp?nid=33613

Victorian State Parliamentary Offices. (2003). *Watching brief on the war on terrorism: Submission by the State of Victoria to the Joint Standing Committee on Foreign Affairs, Defence and Trade Hearing on Australia's Counter Terrorism Capabilities*. Retrieved January 18, 2009, from http://www.aph.gov.au/House/committee/jfadt/terrorism/subs/sub13.pdf

Weiss, D., Kramer, I., Treu, G., & Kupper, A. (2006). Zone services - An approach for location-based data collection. In *Proceedings of the 8th IEEE International Conference on E-Commerce Technology and the 3rd IEEE International Conference on Enterprise Computing, E-Commerce, and E-Services* (p. 79).

KEY TERMS AND DEFINITIONS

Emergency Management: Typically has four stages including prevention/mitigation, preparedness, response and recovery. Emergency management is integral to a nation's national security from the perspective of societal securitization.

Hazards: These can be natural or technological. Natural hazards are those that have their origin in the natural environment such as bushfires. Technological hazards are a result of failures in human-made systems, such as oil spills. Hazards can also be categorized as chemical, biological or radiological.

Information Privacy: The interest an individual has in controlling the handling of data about themselves.

Information Risk: Personal data being accessed or modified by unauthorized persons.

Integrated Public Number Database (IPND): An industry-wide, commonwealth-owned database that contains all the residential and business telephone numbers (listed and unlisted) of Australia. The IPND also stores subscriber information such as name, address, and the type of service delivered by each number (e.g., landline or mobile).

Location-Based Services: Services that use the location of the target for adding value to the service, where the target is the "entity" to be located. Typical LBS consumer applications include roadside assistance and who is nearest, and typical LBS business applications include fleet management and field service personnel management.

Mandate: A command or an authorization given by a political electorate to its representative often supported by laws and regulations.

Mobile Alerts: A message disseminated during an emergency to mobile devices, typically sent from an authorized government agency.

Security: Freedom from risk or danger; safety. Freedom from doubt, anxiety, or fear.

Short Message Service: SMS is a well-known and accepted asynchronous protocol of communication. It is capable of transmitting a limited size of binary or text messages to one or more recipients. SMS offers virtual guarantee for message delivery to its destination.

This work was previously published in the Journal of Information Technology Research, Volume 4, Issue 4, edited by Mehdi Khosrow-Pour, pp. 41-68, copyright 2011 by IGI Publishing (an imprint of IGI Global).

Compilation of References

3rd Generation Partnership Project. (2008). *Technical specification group services and system aspects: Study for requirements for a public Warning System (PWS) Service (Release 8)*. Retrieved April 13, 2009, from http://www.3gpp.org/ftp/tsg_sa/WG1_Serv/TSGS1_37_Orlando/Docs/S1-070824.doc

3rd Generation Partnership Project. (2009). *Technical specification group services and system aspects; functional stage 2 description of Location Services (LCS) (Release 9)*. Retrieved January 16, 2010, from http://www.3gpp.org/ftp/Specs/archive/23_series/23.271/

Abraham, A., & Ramos, V. (2003, December 8-12). Web usage mining using artificial ant colony clustering and linear genetic programming. In *Proceedings of the IEEE Conference on Evolutionary Computation*, Canberra, Australia (pp. 1384-1391). Washington, DC: IEEE Computer Society.

Adams, K. (2002). Geographically distributed system for catastrophic recovery. In *Proceedings of the 16th USENIX Conference on System Administration* (pp. 47-64).

Adeshiyan, T., Attanasio, C., Farr, E. M., Harper, R. E., Pelleg, D., & Schulz, C. (2009). Using virtualization for high availability and disaster recovery. *IBM Journal of Research and Development*, *53*(4), 587–597. doi:10.1147/JRD.2009.5429062

Adlassnig, K. (1986). Fuzzy set theory in medical diagnosis. *IEEE Transactions on Systems, Man, and Cybernetics*, *16*(2), 260–265. doi:10.1109/TSMC.1986.4308946

Adlassnig, K., Kolarz, G., Effenberger, W., & Grabner, H. (1985). CADIAG: Approaches to computer-assisted medical diagnosis. *Computers in Biology and Medicine*, *15*, 315–335. doi:10.1016/0010-4825(85)90014-9

Adlassnig, K., Kolarz, G., Scheithauer, W., & Grabner, H. (1986). Approach to a hospital based application of a medical expert system. *Informatics for Health & Social Care*, *11*(3), 205–223. doi:10.3109/14639238609003728

Ahamdi, A., GhazanfarI, M., Aliahmadi, A., & Mohebi, A. (2003). Strategic Planning for Implementing E-Government in Iran: Formulating the strategies. *Farda Management Journal, 2*.

Ahn, J. G., & Sandhu, R. (2000). Role-based authorization constraints specification. *ACM Transactions on Information and System Security*, *3*(4), 207–226. doi:10.1145/382912.382913

Ahn, Y. K., Song, J. D., & Yang, B. S. (2003). Optimal design of engine mount using an artificial life algorithm. *Journal of Sound and Vibration*, *261*(1), 309–328. doi:10.1016/S0022-460X(02)00989-6

Ahn, Y. K., Song, J. D., Yang, B. S., Ahn, K. K., & Morishita, S. (2005). Optimal design of nonlinear fluid engine mount. *Journal of Mechanical Science and Technology*, *19*(3), 768–777. doi:10.1007/BF02916125

Aitenbichler, E. (2008). A focus on location context. In Mühlhäuser, M., & Gurevych, I. (Eds.), *Handbook of research on ubiquitous computing technology for real time enterprises* (pp. 257–281). Hershey, PA: IGI Global. doi:10.4018/978-1-59904-832-1.ch012

Akehurst, D. H., & Kent, S. (2002). A Relational Approach to Defining Transformations in a Metamodel. In *Proceedings of the Unified Modeling Language 5th International Conference (UML-02)*, Dresden, Germany (LNCS 2460, pp. 243-258).

Aloudat, A., Michael, K., & Jun, Y. (2007). Location-based services in emergency management- from government to citizens: Global case studies. In Mendis, P., Lai, J., Dawson, E., & Abbass, H. (Eds.), *Recent advances in security technology* (pp. 190–201). Melbourne, Australia: Australian Homeland Security Research Centre.

Andersen, E. (2002). "Never the twain shall meet": exploring the differences between Japanese and Norwegian IS professionals. In *Proceedings of the 2002 ACM SIGCPR Conference on Computer Personnel Research* (pp. 65-71).

Anderson, C., Theraulaz, G., & Deneubourg, J. L. (2002). Self-assemblages in insect societies. *Insectes Sociaux*, *49*, 99–110. doi:10.1007/s00040-002-8286-y

Anderson, J. (2000). *A Survey of Multiobjective Optimization in Engineering Design (Tech. Rep. No. LiTH-IKP-R-1097)*. Linköping, Sweden: Linköping University.

Anderson, K., Brooks, C., & Katsaris, A. (2005). *Speculative bubbles in the S&P 500: Was the tech bubble confined to the tech sector?* Reading, UK: ICMA Centre.

Anliker, U., Ward, V., Lukowitcz, P., Tröster, G., Dolveck, F., & Baer, M. (2004). AMON: A wearable multiparameter medical monitoring and alert system. *IEEE Transactions on Information Technology in Biomedicine*, *8*(4), 415–427. doi:10.1109/TITB.2004.837888

Ardagna, D., Tanelli, M., Lovera, M., & Zhang, L. (2010). Black-box performance models for virtualized web service applications. In *Proceeding of the First Joint WOSP/SIPEW International Conference on Performance Engineering* (pp. 153-164).

Armitage, G., & Harrop, W. (2005). Teaching IP networking fundamentals in resource constrained educational environments. *Australasian Journal of Educational Technology*, *21*(2), 263–283.

Arora, A. (2008). Indian Software Industry and its Prospects. In Bhagwati, J. N., & Calomiris, C. W. (Eds.), *Sustaining India's Growth Miracle*. New York, NY: Columbia University Press.

Aßmann, U. (2007, February 7). Model Driven Architecture (MDA) and Component-Based Software Development (CBSD). *Xootic Magazine*, pp. 5-7.

Astroth, J. (2003). Location-based services: Criteria for adoption and solution deployment. In Mennecke, B. E., & Strader, T. J. (Eds.), *Mobile commerce: Technology, theory, and applications* (pp. 229–236). Hershey, PA: Idea Group. doi:10.4018/978-1-59140-044-8.ch015

Athreye, S. (2005). The Indian Software Industry. In Arora, A., & Gambardella, A. (Eds.), *From Underdogs to Tigers: The rise and growth of the Software Industry in Brazil, China, India, Ireland, and Israel*. Oxford, UK: Oxford University Press.

Australia.gov.au Website. (2010). *The Australian continent*. Retrieved March 10, 2010, from http://australia.gov.au/about-australia/our-country/the-australian-continent

Azzag, H., Guinot, C., Oliver, A., & Venturini, G. (2006). A hierarchical ant based clustering algorithm and its use in three real-world applications. *European Journal of Operational Research*, *179*(3), 906–922. doi:10.1016/j.ejor.2005.03.062

Azzag, H., Guinot, C., & Venturini, G. (2006). Data and text mining with hierarchical clustering ants. In Abraham, A., Grosan, C., & Ramos, V. (Eds.), *Swarm intelligence and data mining* (pp. 153–190). doi:10.1007/978-3-540-34956-3_7

Azzag, H., Monmarché, H., Slimane, M., Venturini, G., & Guinot, C. (2003, December 8-12). Anttree: a new model for clustering with artificial ants. In *Proceedings of the IEEE Conference on Evolutionary Computation*, Canberra, Australia. Washington, DC: IEEE Computer Society.

Baccaletti, S., Latora, V., Morento, Y., Chavez, M., & Hwang, D. U. (2006). Complex networks: Structure and dynamics. *Physics Reports*, *424*, 175–308. doi:10.1016/j.physrep.2005.10.009

Bai, R., Blazewicz, J., Burke, E. K., Kendall, G., & McCollum, B. (2007). *A simulated annealing hyper-heuristic methodology for flexible decision support* (Tech. Rep. No. NOTTCS-TR-2007-8). Nottingham, UK: University of Nottingham, School of Computer Science and Information Technology.

Bai, R., Burke, E. K., & Kendall, G. (2008). Heuristic, meta-heuristic and hyper-heuristic approaches for fresh produce inventory control and shelf space allocation. *The Journal of the Operational Research Society*, *59*, 1387–1397. doi:.doi:10.1057/palgrave.jors.2602463

Bai, R., & Kendall, G. (2005). An investigation of automated planograms using a simulated annealing based hyper-heuristics. In T. Ibaraki, et al. (Eds.), *Metaheuristics: Progress as a real problem solver* (pp. 87–108). Berlin, Germany: Springer. doi:doi:10.1007/0-387-25383-1_4

Balaouras, S. (2007). The state of DR preparedness. *Forester/Disaster Recovery Journal.* Retrieved July 7, 2010, from http://www.drj.com/index.php?option=com_content&task=view&id=794&Itemid=159&ed=10

Balasubramanian, D., Narayanan, A., van Buskirk, C., & Karsai, G. (2006). The Graph Rewriting and Transformation Language: GReAT. *Electronic Communications of the EASST, 1*, 1–8.

Barham, P., Dragovic, B., Fraser, K., Hand, S., Harris, T., & Ho, A. ... Warfield, A. (2003, October). Xen and the art of virtualization. In *Proceedings of the 19th Symposium on Operating Systems Principles*, Bolton Landin, NY (pp. 164-177).

Barth, M. E., Beaver, B., Hand, J., & Landsman, W. (1999). Accruals, cash flows, and equity values. *Review of Accounting Studies, 3*, 205–229. doi:10.1023/A:1009630100586

Barthelmess, P. (2003). Collaboration and coordination in process-centered software development environments: a review of the literature. *Information and Software Technology, 45*(13), 911–928. doi:10.1016/S0950-5849(03)00091-0

Bast, W., Kleppe, A., & Warmer, J. (2004). *MDA Explained: The Model Driven Architecture: Practice and Promise*. Reading, MA: Addison-Wesley.

Beck, K. (2000). *Extreme Programming Explained: Embrace Change*. Reading, MA: Addison-Wesley.

Bellifemine, F. L., Caire, G., & Greenwood, D. (2007). *JADE software agent development platform.* Retrieved June 10, 2010, from http://jade.tilab.com/

Belsis, P., Skourlas, C., & Gritzalis, S. (2011). Secure electronic healthcare records distribution in wireless environments using low resource devices. In Malatras, A. (Ed.), *Pervasive computing and communications design and deployment: Technologies, trends, and applications* (pp. 247–262). Hershey, PA: IGI Global. doi:10.4018/978-1-60960-611-4.ch011

Belsis, P., Vassis, D., Skourlas, C., & Pantziou, G. (2008). Secure dissemination of electronic healthcare records in distributed wireless environments. In *Proceedings of the 21st International Congress of the European Federation for Medical Informatics* (pp. 661-666).

Benjamins, V. R., Davies, J., Baeza-Yates, R., Mika, P., Zaragoza, H., & Gómez-Pérez, J. M. (2008). Near-Term Prospects for Semantic Technologies. *IEEE Intelligent Systems, 23*(1), 76–88. doi:10.1109/MIS.2008.10

Benson, S. (2007). *SMS smog alerts for Sydney.* Retrieved from http://www.news.com.au/top-stories/sydney-on-smog-alert/story-e6frfkp9-1111113614955

Ben-Ze'ev, A. (2003). Privacy, emotional closeness, and openness in cyberspace. *Computers in Human Behavior, 19*(4), 451–467. doi:10.1016/S0747-5632(02)00078-X

Bernardos, A. M., Casar, J. R., & Tarrio, P. (2007). Building a framework to characterize location-based services. In *Proceedings of the International Conference on Next Generation Mobile Applications, Services and Technologies* (pp. 110-118).

Betts, R. (2003). The missing links in community warning systems: Findings from two Victorian community warning system projects. *The Australian Journal of Emergency Management, 18*(3), 35–45.

Bharadwaj, A., Bharadwaj, S., & Konsynski, B. (1999). Information technology effects on firm performance as measured by Tobin's q. *Management Science, 45*(6), 1008–1024. doi:10.1287/mnsc.45.7.1008

Bhattacharya, A., & Chattopadhyay, P. K. (2010). Solving complex economic load dispatch problems using biogeography-based optimization. *Expert Systems with Applications, 37*, 3605–3615. doi:10.1016/j.eswa.2009.10.031

Bhatti, S. N., & Malik, A. M. (2009). An XML-Based Framework for Bidirectional Transformation in Model-Driven Architecture (MDA). *SIGSOFT Software Engineering Notes, 34*(3).

Bita, N., & Sainsbury, M. (2009). *Bungling silenced Victoria bushfires warning*. The Australian.

Blake, C. L., & Merz, C. L. (1998). *Uci repository of machine learning databases.* Irvine, CA: Department of Information and Computer Science, University of California. Retrieved from ftp://ftp.ics.uci.edu/pub/machine-learning-databases

Bodenreider, O. (2004). The Unified Medical Language System (UMLS): integrating biomedical terminology. *Nucleic Acids Research*, *32*, 267–270. doi:10.1093/nar/gkh061

Boger, M., Graham, E., & Köster, M. (2011). *Poseidon for UML*. Retrieved October 9, 2011, from http://www.gentleware.com/fileadmin/media/pdfs/userguides/PoseidonUsersGuide.pdf

Boivie, I., Aborg, C., Persson, J., & Lofberg, M. (2003). Why usability gets lost or usability in in-house software development. *Interacting with Computers*, *15*, 623–639. doi:10.1016/S0953-5438(03)00055-9

Boivie, I., Gulliksen, J., & Goransson, B. (2006). The lonesome cowboy: A study of the usability designer role in systems development. *Interacting with Computers*, *18*, 601–634. doi:10.1016/j.intcom.2005.10.003

Borchers, G. (2003). The Software Engineering Impacts of Cultural Factors on Multi-cultural Software Development Teams. In *Proceedings of the 5th International Conference on Software Engineering* (pp. 540-545).

Borden, T. L., Hennessy, J. P., & Rymarczyk, J. W. (1989). Multiple operating systems on one processor complex. *IBM Systems Journal*, *28*(1), 104–123. doi:10.1147/sj.281.0104

Bosch, J., & Bosch-Sijtsema, P. (2010). From integration to composition: On the impact of software oriduct lines, global development and ecosystems. *Journal of Systems and Software*, *83*, 67–76. doi:10.1016/j.jss.2009.06.051

Boughton, G. (1998). The community: Central to emergency risk management. *Australian Journal of Emergency Management*, 2-5.

Boyd, S., & Vandenberghe, L. (2004). *Convex Optimization*. Cambridge, UK: Cambridge University Press.

Braun, J. E. (2007). Intelligent Building Systems – Past, Present, and Future. In *Proceedings of the 2007 American Control Conference* (pp. 4374-4381).

Brazier, D. (2006). *The m-care project*. Scotland, UK: Alpha Bravo Charlie Ltd. Retrieved June 10, 2010, from http://www.m-care.co.uk/tech.html

Breastcencer.org. (2010). *Understanding the Breast Cancer*. Retrieved February 1, 2010, from http://www.breastcancer.org

Breslin, J. G., & Decker, S. (2007). The Future of Social Networks on the Internet: The Need for Semantics. *IEEE Internet Computing*, *11*(6), 86–90. doi:10.1109/MIC.2007.138

Brin, D. (1998). *The transparent society: Will technology force us to choose between privacy and freedom?* (1st ed.). Boulder, CO: Perseus Press.

Bronzino, J. D. (2006). *Biomedical Engineering Fundamentals*. Boca Raton, FL: CRC Press.

Brynjolfsson, E. (1993). The productivity paradox of information technology. *Communications of the ACM*, *40*(12), 1645–1662.

Brynjolfsson, E., & Hitt, L. E. (1993). Is information systems spending productive? New evidence and new results. In *Proceedings of the 14th International Conference on Information Systems* (pp. 47-64).

Burke, E. K., Causmaecker, P. D., Berghe, G. V., & Landeghem, H. V. (2004). The state of the art of nurse rostering. *Journal of Scheduling*, *7*(6), 441–499. doi:. doi:10.1023/B:JOSH.0000046076.75950.0b

Burke, E. K., Curtois, T., Qu, R., & Vanden-Berghe, G. (2008). *Problem model for nurse rostering benchmark instances*. Retrieved December 14, 2010, from http://www.cs.nott.ac.uk/~tec/NRP/papers/ANROM.pdf

Burke, E. K., Hyde, M., Kendall, G., Ochoa, G., Ozcan, E., & Qu, R. (2010). *Hyper-heuristics: a survey of the state of the art* (Tech. Rep. No. NOTTCS-TR-SUB-0906241418). Nottingham, UK: University of Nottingham, School of Computer Science and Information Technology.

Burke, E. K., Hyde, M., Kendall, G., Ochoa, G., Ozcan, E., & Woodward, J. R. (2010). A classification of hyper-heuristic approaches. In M. Gendreau & J. Potvin (Eds.), *Handbook of metaheuristics* (2nd ed., pp. 449–468). Berlin, Germany: Springer. doi:doi:10.1007/978-1-4419-1665-5_15

Burke, E. K., Kendall, G., Newall, J., Hart, E., Ross, P., & Schulenburg, S. (2003). Hyper-Heuristics: An emerging direction in modern search technology. In Glover, F., & Konchenberger, G. (Eds.), *Handbook of metaheuristics* (pp. 457–474). New York, NY: Kluwer Academic Publishers.

Burke, E. K., Kendall, G., Silva, D. L., O'Brien, R., & Soubeiga, E. (2005). An ant algorithm hyperheuristic for the project presentation scheduling problem. In *Proceedings of the IEEE Conference on Evolutionary Computation* (pp. 2263-2270). Washington, DC: IEEE Computer Society.

Burke, E. K., Kendall, G., & Soubeiga, E. (2003). A tabu-search hyperheuristic for timetabling and rostering. *Journal of Heuristics*, *9*(6), 451–490. doi:.doi:10.1023/B:HEUR.0000012446.94732.b6

Burke, E. K., Li, J., & Qu, R. (2010). A hybrid model of integer programming and variable neighbourhood search for highly-constrained nurse rostering problems. *European Journal of Operational Research*, *203*(2), 484–493. doi:.doi:10.1016/j.ejor.2009.07.036

Burke, E. K., McCollum, B., Meisels, A., Petrovic, S., & Qu, R. (2007). A graph-based hyper-heuristic for educational timetabling problems. *European Journal of Operational Research*, *176*(1), 177–192. doi:.doi:10.1016/j.ejor.2005.08.012

Bushfire SMS to assist in warning system development. (2009, March 4). *The Australian Broadcasting Corporation*.

Buzan, B., Woever, O., & Wilde, J. D. (1998). *Security: A new framework for analysis* (1st ed.). London, UK: Lynne Rienner.

Bygstad, B., Ghinea, G., & Brevik, E. (2008). Software development methods and usability: Perspectives from a survey in the software industry in Norway. *Interacting with Computers*, *20*(3), 375–385. doi:10.1016/j.intcom.2007.12.001

Cai, X., Lyu, M. R., Wong, K.-F., & Ko, R. (2000). Component-Based Software Engineering: Technologies, Development Frameworks, and Quality Assurance Schemes. In *Proceedings of the 7th IEEE Asia-Pacific Software Engineering Conference* (pp. 372-379).

Calzolari, F., Arezzini, S., Ciampa, A., Mazzoni, E., Domenici, A., & Vaglini, G. (2010). High availability using virtualization. In *Proceeding of the 17th International Conference on Computing in High Energy and Nuclear Physics* (pp. 1-10).

Canton, L. G. (2007). *Emergency management: Concepts and strategies for effective programs* (1st ed.). Hoboken, NJ: John Wiley & Sons.

Cantwell, B. (2002). *Why technical breakthroughs fail: A history of public concern with emerging technologies*. Cambridge, MA: MIT Press.

Carey, M., Heesch, D., & Roger, S. (2003) Info navigator: A visualization tool for document searching and browsing. In *Proceedings of the 9th International Conference on Distributed Multimedia Systems (DMS'2003)*.

Carmody, C. A., & O'Mahony, T. (2009). System identification of a domestic residence using Wireless sensor node data. In *Proceedings of the 17th Mediterranean Conference on Control and Automation* (pp. 987-992).

Carr, N. G. (2003). IT doesn't matter. *Harvard Business Review*, *81*(5), 41–49.

Carter, L., & Bélanger, F. (2005). The utilization of e-government services: Citizen trust, innovation and acceptance factors. *Information Systems Journal*, *15*(1), 5–25. doi:10.1111/j.1365-2575.2005.00183.x

Castells, M. (1996). *The Rise of the Network Society, The Information Age: Economy, Society and Culture (Vol. I)*. Cambridge, MA: Blackwell.

Cavelty, M. D. (2007). Cyber-terror–Looming threat or phantom menace? The framing of the US cyber-threat debate. *Journal of Information Technology & Politics*, *4*(1).

Chakravorty, R. (2006, March). A programmable service architecture for mobile medical care. In *Proceedings of the 4th Annual IEEE International Conference on Pervasive Computing and Communications Workshops*, Pisa, Italy (pp. 532-536).

Chan, S. L., & Leung, N. N. (2004). Prototype Web-Based Construction Project Management System. *Journal of Construction Engineering and Management*, *130*(6), 935–943. doi:10.1061/(ASCE)0733-9364(2004)130:6(935)

Chari, M. D., Devaraj, S., & Parthiban, D. (2008). The Impact of Information Technology Investments and Diversification Strategies on Firm Performance. *Management Science*, *54*(1), 224–234. doi:10.1287/mnsc.1070.0743

Cheesman, J., & Daniels, J. (2001). *UML Components. A Simple Process for Specifying Component-Based Software*. Reading, MA: Addison-Wesley.

Chellapilla, K. (1998). Combining mutation operators in evolutionary programming. *IEEE Transactions on Evolutionary Computation*, *2*(3), 91–96. doi:10.1109/4235.735431

Chen, K. C., & Lee, C. J. (1993). Financial ratios and corporate endurance: A case of the oil and gas industry. *Contemporary Accounting Research*, *9*(2), 667–694. doi:10.1111/j.1911-3846.1993.tb00903.x

Chen, Z., Clements-Croome, D., Hong, J., Li, H., & Xu, Q. (2006). A multicriteria lifespan energy efficiency approach to intelligent building assessment. *Energy and Building*, *38*(5), 393–409. doi:10.1016/j.enbuild.2005.08.001

Cho, S. B., & Shimohara, K. (1998). Evolutionary Learning of Modular Neural Networks with Genetic Programming. *Applied Intelligence*, *9*, 191–200. doi:10.1023/A:1008388118869

Choudhri, A., Kagal, A., Joshi, A., Finin, T., & Yesha, Y. (2003). *PatientService: Electronic patient record redaction and delivery in pervasive environments.* Paper presented at the Fifth International Workshop on Enterprise Networking and Computing in Healthcare Industry (Healthcom), Santa Monica, CA.

Chudleigh, J. (2009, November 10). Earlier alert system for severe weather. *The Courier-Mail.*

Churchill, G. A. Jr. (1979). A paradigm for developing better measures of marketing constructs. *JMR, Journal of Marketing Research*, *16*(1), 64–73. doi:10.2307/3150876

Ciabattoni, A., & Rusnok, P. (2010). On the classical content of monadic G with involutive negation and its application to a fuzzy medical expert system. In F. Lin, U. Sattler, & M. Truszczynski (Eds.), *Proceedings of the Twelfth International Conference on the Principles of Knowledge Representation and Reasoning* (pp. 373-381). AAAI Press.

Ciabattoni, A., & Vetterlein, T. (2009). On the fuzzy (logical) content of CADIAG-2. *Fuzzy Sets and Systems*, *161*(14), 1941–1958.

Clark & Parsia. (2004). *Pellet: The Open Source OWL 2 Reasoner.* Retrieved June 27, 2010, from http://clarkparsia.com/pellet/

Clarke, R., & Wigan, M. (2008). You are where you have been. In Michael, K., & Michael, M. G. (Eds.), *Australia and the new technologies: Evidence based policy in public administration* (pp. 100–114). Canberra, Australia: University of Wollongong.

Code of Practice of Passive Location Services in the UK. (2006). *Industry code of practice for the use of mobile phone technology to provide passive location services in the UK.* Retrieved August 23, 2007, from http://www.mobilebroadbandgroup.com/documents/UKCoP_location_servs_210706v_pub_clean.pdf

Coello, C. A., Pulido, G. T., & Lechuga, M. S. (2004). Handling multiple objectives with particle swarm optimization. *IEEE Transactions on Evolutionary Computation*, *8*(3), 256–279. doi:10.1109/TEVC.2004.826067

Coello, C. A. C., & Zacatenco, C. S. P. (2006). Twenty years of evolutionary multi-objective optimization: a historical view of the field. *IEEE Computational Intelligence Magazine*, *1*(1), 28–36. doi:10.1109/MCI.2006.1597059

Cole, G. (2009). *Backprop1.* Retrieved February 1, 2010, from http://sourceforge.net/projects/backprop1

Collazos, C. A., & García, R. (2007). Semantics-supported cooperative learning for enhanced awareness. *International Journal of Knowledge and Learning*, *3*(4/5), 421–436. doi:10.1504/IJKL.2007.016703

Colomo Palacios, R., García Crespo, A., Gómez Berbís, J. M., Casado-Lumbreras, C., & Soto-Acosta, P. (2010). SemCASS: technical competence assessment within software development teams enabled by semantics. *International Journal of Social and Humanistic Computing*, *1*(3), 232–245. doi:10.1504/IJSHC.2010.032685

Colomo-Palacios, R., Gómez-Berbís, J. M., García-Crespo, A., & Puebla-Sánchez, I. (2008). Social Global Repository: using semantics and social web in software projects. *International Journal of Knowledge and Learning*, *4*(5), 452–464. doi:10.1504/IJKL.2008.022063

Colomo-Palacios, R., Ruano-Mayoral, M., Soto-Acosta, P., & García-Crespo, Á. (2010). The War for Talent: Identifying competences in IT Professionals through semantics. *International Journal of Sociotechnology and Knowledge Development*, *2*(3), 26–36.

Constantine, L. (1995). *Constantine on Peopleware.* Englewood Cliffs, NJ: Yourdon Press.

Courtot, M., Gibson, F., Lister, A., Malone, J., Schober, D., & Brinkman, R. (2009). *MIREOT: the Minimum Information to Reference an External Ontology Term*. Nature Proceedings.

Coyle, D., & Meier, P. (2009). *New technologies in emergencies and conflicts: The role of information and social networks*. New York, NY: United Nations.

Crawford, L., Pollack, J., & England, D. (2006). Uncovering the trends in project management: Journal emphases over the last 10 years. *International Journal of Project Management*, *24*(2), 175–184. doi:10.1016/j.ijproman.2005.10.005

Croes, G. A. (1958). A method for solving traveling salesman problem. *Operations Research*, *6*, 791–812. doi:.doi:10.1287/opre.6.6.791

Curtois, T., Ochoa, M., Hyde, M., & Vazquez-Rodriguez, J. A. (2010). *A HyFlex module for the personnel scheduling problem*. Nottingham, UK: University of Nottingham, School of Computer Science and Information Technology.

Czejdo, B. D., & Baszun, M. (2010). Remote patient monitoring system and a medical social network. *International Journal of Social and Humanistic Computing*, *1*(3), 273–281. doi:10.1504/IJSHC.2010.032688

Dafoulas, G., & Macaulay, L. (2001). Investigating Cultural Differences in Virtual Software Teams. *The Electronic Journal of Information Systems in Developing Countries*, *7*(4), 1–14.

Dağtaş, S., Pekhteryev, G., Şahinoğlu, Z., Çam, H., & Challa, N. (2008). Real-time and secure wireless health monitoring. *International Journal of Telemedicine and Applications, 2008*, article 1.

Darwin, C. (1859). *The origin of species*. New York, NY: Gramercy.

Das, S., Abraham, A., & Konar, A. (2008). Automatic clustering using an improved differential evolution algorithm. *IEEE Transactions on Systems, Man, and Cybernetics. Part A, Systems and Humans*, *38*, 1–20. doi:10.1109/TSMCA.2007.909595

David, S. J. (1985). Multiple objective optimization with vector evaluated genetic algorithms. In *Proceedings of the 1st International Conference on Genetic Algorithms and Their Applications* (pp. 93-100).

Davies, D. L., & Bouldin, D. W. (1979). A cluster separation measure. *IEEE Transactions on Pattern Recognition and Machine Intelligence*, *1*(2), 224–227. doi:10.1109/TPAMI.1979.4766909

Dawson, M., Winterbottom, J., & Thomson, M. (2007). *IP location* (1st ed.). New York, NY: McGraw-Hill.

De Tura, N., Reilly, S. M., Narasimhan, S., & Yin, Z. J. (2004). Disaster recovery preparedness through continuous process optimization. *Bell Labs Technical Journal*, *9*(2), 147–162. doi:10.1002/bltj.20031

Dearstyne, B. W. (2006). Taking charge: Disaster fallout reinforces RIM's importance. *The Information Management Journal*, *40*(4), 37–43.

Deb, K., Pratap, A., Agarwal, S., & Meyarivan, T. (2002). A fast and elitist multiobjective genetic algorithm: NSGA-II. *IEEE Transactions on Evolutionary Computation*, *6*(2), 182–197. doi:10.1109/4235.996017

Dehning, B., Richardson, V., & Zmud, B. (2003). The value relevance of announcements of transformational information technology investments. *Management Information Systems Quarterly*, *27*(4), 637–656.

Deneubourg, J.-L., Goss, S., Franks, N. R., Sendova-Franks, A., Detrain, C., & Chretien, L. (1990). The dynamics of collective sorting: robot-like ant and ant-like robots. In *Proceedings of the First International Conference on Simulation of Adaptive Behavior* (pp. 356-365).

Deo, D. S. (2006). Applications of expert system/neural networks/genetic algorithms in an intelligent building complex. *Journal of the Institution of Engineers: Architectural Engineering Division*, *87*(10), 4–9.

Deogun, J. S., & Spaulding, W. (2010). Conceptual Development of Mental Health Ontologies. In Ras, Z. W., & Tsay, L.-S. (Eds.), *Advances in Intelligent Information Systems. Studies in Computational Intelligence* (*Vol. 265*, pp. 299–333). Berlin: Springer.

Dietterich, T. (2000). Ensemble methods in machine learning. In J. Kittler & F. Roli (Eds.), *Multiple Classier Systems,* Cagliari, Italy (LNCS 5519, pp. 1-15).

Ding, Y. (2010). Semantic Web: Who is who in the field — a bibliometric analysis. *Journal of Information Science*, *36*(3), 335–356. doi:10.1177/0165551510365295

D'Mello, M., & Eriksen, T. M. (2010). Software, sports day and sheera: Culture and identity processes within a global software organization in India. *Information and Organization*, *20*(2), 81–110. doi:10.1016/j.infoandorg.2010.03.001

Dobbin, M. (2009, March 3). Victorians receive fire text warning. *The Age*.

Dogac, A., Laleci, G. B., Kirbas, S., Kabak, Y., Sinir, S., & Yidiz, A. (2006). Artemis: Deploying semantically enriched Web services in the healthcare domain. *Information Systems*, *31*(4-5), 321–339. doi:10.1016/j.is.2005.02.006

Dos Santos, B., Peffers, K., & Mauer, D. (1993). The impact of information technology investment announcements on the market value of the firm. *Information Systems Research*, *4*(1), 1–23. doi:10.1287/isre.4.1.1

Dowsland, K. A., Soubeiga, E., & Burke, E. K. (2007). A simulated annealing based hyperheuristic for determining shipper sizes for storage and transportation. *European Journal of Operational Research*, *179*(3), 759–774. doi:. doi:10.1016/j.ejor.2005.03.058

Du, D. W., Simon, D., & Ergezer, M. (2009). Biogeography-based optimization combined with evolutionary strategy and immigration refusal. In *Proceedings of the 2009 IEEE International Conference on Systems, Man, and Cybernetics,* San Antonio, TX (pp. 1023-1028).

Dunn, M., & Collier, K. (2007, February 27). Plan to use SMS for SOS. *Herald Sun*.

Durguin, J. K., & Sherif, J. S. (2008). The semantic web: a catalyst for future e-business. *Kybernetes*, *37*(1), 49–65. doi:10.1108/03684920810850989

Dutta, P. K. (1999). *Strategies and Games*. Cambridge, MA: MIT Press.

eGovernment Resource Centre (eGov). (2012). *Emergency alerts and warnings - Australia*. Retrieved June 15, 2012, from http://www.egov.vic.gov.au/focus-on-countries/australia/government-initiatives-australia/emergencies-and-safety-australia/emergency-alerts-and-warnings-australia.html

El Sheikh, A., & Khadra, H. A. (2009). Governing Information Technology (IT) and Security Vulnerabilities: Empirical Study Applied on the Jordanian Industrial Companies. *Journal of Information Technology Research*, *2*(1), 70–85. doi:10.4018/jitr.2009010105

Emergency Management Australia. (1996). *Australian counter disaster handbook* (5th ed., *Vol. 2*). Canberra, Australia.

Emergency Management Australia. (2004). *Disaster recovery: Safer sustainable communities*. Retrieved November 27, 2007, from http://www.ema.gov.au/www/emaweb/rwpattach.nsf/VAP/(3273BD3F76A7A5DEDAE36942A54D7D90)~Manual10-Recovery.pdf/$file/Manual10-Recovery.pdf

Emergency Management Australia. (2004). *Emergency management in Australia: Concepts and principles*. Retrieved November 27, 2007, from http://www.ema.gov.au/www/emaweb/rwpattach.nsf/VAP/(3273BD3F76A7A5DEDAE36942A54D7D90)~Manual01-EmergencyManagementinAustralia-ConceptsandPrinciples.pdf/$file/Manual01-EmergencyManagementinAustralia-ConceptsandPrinciples.pdf

Emergency Management Australia. (2008). *Disasters database*. Retrieved January 4, 2008, from http://www.ema.gov.au/www/emaweb/emaweb.nsf/Page/Resources_DisastersDatabase_DisastersDatabase

Emergency Management Australia. (2009). *Australian emergency management arrangements*. Retrieved from http://www.ema.gov.au/www/emaweb/rwpattach.nsf/VAP/(3A6790B96C927794AF1031D9395C5C20)~Australian+Emergency+Management+Arrangements.pdf/$file/Australian+Emergency+Management+Arrangements.pdf

Emergency Management Australia. (2009). *Emergency management*. Retrieved December 8, 2008, from http://www.ema.gov.au/www/emaweb/emaweb.nsf/Page/Emergency_Management

Environment and Sustainable Development Directorate. (2011). *Ministerial statement- Mitchell Fire*. Retrieved September 20, 2011, from http://www.environment.act.gov.au/__data/assets/pdf_file/0009/232299/Ministerial_Statement_on_Mitchell_fire,_20_September_2011.pdf

Ergezer, M., Simon, D., & Du, D. W. (2009). Oppositional biogeography-based optimization. In *Proceedings of the 2009 IEEE International Conference on Systems, Man, and Cybernetics,* San Antonio, TX (pp. 1035-1040).

European Commission. (2011). *Satellite navigation: Why Galileo?* Retrieved January 11, 2012, from http://ec.europa.eu/enterprise/policies/satnav/galileo/why/index_en.htm

European Space Agency. (2011). *What is Galileo?* Retrieved January 11, 2012, from http://www.esa.int/esaNA/galileo.html

Eysenbach, G. (2008). Medicine 2.0: Social Networking, Collaboration, Participation, Apomediation, and Openness. *Journal of Medical Internet Research, 10*(3), e22. doi:10.2196/jmir.1030

Falkman, G., Gustafsson, M., Jontell, M., & Torgersson, O. (2008). SOMWeb: A Semantic Web-Based System for Supporting Collaboration of Distributed Medical Communities of Practice. *Journal of Medical Internet Research, 10*(3), e25. doi:10.2196/jmir.1059

Fensel, D. (2002). *Ontologies: A silver bullet for knowledge management and electronic commerce*. Berlin: Springer.

Fensel, D., & Munsen, M. A. (2001). The Semantic Web: A Brain for Humankind. *IEEE Intelligent Systems, 16*(2), 24–25. doi:10.1109/MIS.2001.920595

Fensel, D., van Harmelen, F., Horrocks, I., McGuinness, D. L., & Patel-Schneider, P. F. (2001). OIL: An ontology infrastructure for the semantic web. *IEEE Intelligent Systems, 16*(2), 38–45. doi:10.1109/5254.920598

Fernandes, J. P. (2008). Emergency warnings with short message service. In Coskun, H. G., Cigizoglu, H. K., & Maktav, M. D. (Eds.), *Integration of information for environmental security* (1st ed., pp. 205–210). Dordrecht, The Netherlands: Springer-Verlag. doi:10.1007/978-1-4020-6575-0_14

Fernandez, M., Gomez-Perez, A., & Juristo, N. (1997). *Methontology: from ontological art towards ontological engineering*. Paper presented at the AAAI97 Spring Symposium Series on Ontological Engineering.

Festa, P., Pardalos, P. M., Pitsoulis, L. S., & Resende, M. G. C. (2006). GRASP with path relinking for the weighted MAXSAT problem. *Journal of Experimental Algorithmics, 11*, 1–16.

Ficici, S. G., Melnik, O., & Pollack, J. B. (2000). A game-theoretic investigation of selection methods used in evolutionary algorithms. In *Proceedings of the 2000 IEEE Conference on Evolutionary Computation* (pp. 880-887).

Fieldsend, J. E., & Singh, S. (2005). Pareto Evolutionary Neural Networks. *IEEE Transactions on Neural Networks, 16*(2), 338–354. doi:10.1109/TNN.2004.841794

Flax, B. M. (1991). Intelligent Buildings. *IEEE Communications Magazine, 29*(4), 24–27. doi:10.1109/35.76555

Fogel, L. J., Owens, A. J., & Walsh, M. J. (1966). *Artificial Intelligence through Simulated Evolution*. New York, NY: Wiley.

Fonseca, C. M., & Fleming, P. J. (1993). Genetic algorithm for multi-objective optimization: formulation, discussion and generalization. In S. Forrest (Ed.), *Proceedings of 5th International Conference on Genetic Algorithms* (pp. 416-423). San Francisco, CA: Morgan Kauffman.

Fonseca, C. M., & Fleming, P. J. (1995). Multi-objective genetic algorithms made easy: selection, sharing, and mating restriction. In *Proceedings of the 1st International Conference on Genetic Algorithms in Engineering Systems: Innovations and Applications* (pp. 45-52).

Forsberg, K., Mooz, H., & Cotterman, H. M. (2005). *Visualizing project management: models and frameworks for mastering complex systems* (3rd ed.). Hoboken, NJ: John Wiley & Sons.

Foundation for Intelligent Physical Agents (FIPA). (2005). *FIPA specifications*. Retrieved June 10, 2010, from http://www.fipa.org/specifications/index.html

Freund, Y. (1995). Boosting a weak learning algorithm by majority. *Information and Computation, 121*, 256–285. doi:10.1006/inco.1995.1136

Freund, Y., & Schapire, R. E. (1996). Experiments with a New Boosting Algorithm. In *Proceedings of the Thirteenth International Conference on Machine Learning*, Bari, Italy (pp. 148-156). San Francisco: Morgan Kaufmann.

Friedman, T. L. (2005). *The World Is Flat: A Brief History of the Twenty-first Century*. New York, NY: Farrar, Strauss and Giroux.

Frize, M., Solven, F. G., Stevenson, M., Nickerson, B., Buskard, T., & Taylor, K. (1995). Computer-assisted decision support systems for patient management in an intensive care unit. *Medinfo, 8*, 1009.

Fu, H. C., Lee, Y. P., Chiang, C. C., & Pao, H. T. (2001). Divide-and-Conquer Learning and Modular Perceptron Networks. *IEEE Transactions on Neural Networks*, *12*(2), 250–263. doi:10.1109/72.914522

Fuentes-Fernández, L., & Vallecillo-Moreno, A. (2004). An Introduction to UML Profiles. *Journal of Informatics Professional*, *5*(2), 6–13.

Fuentes-Lorenzo, D., Morato, J., & Gómez-Berbís, J. M. (2009). Knowledge management in biomedical libraries: A semantic web approach. *Information Systems Frontiers*, *11*(4), 471–480. doi:10.1007/s10796-009-9159-y

Gabbay, D. M., & Hunter, A. (1991). Making inconsistency respectable: A logical framework for inconsistency in reasoning. In P. Jorrand & J. Kelemen (Eds.), *Proceedings of the International Workshop on Fundamentals of Artificial Intelligence Research* (LNCS 535, pp. 19-32).

Gałęzowski, G., Zabierowski, W., & Napieralski, A. (2009, February 24-28). Web-based Project Management System. In *Proceedings of the 10th International Conference on the Experience of Designing and Application of CAD Systems in Microelectronics (CADSM'2009),* Polyana-Svalyava, Ukraine (pp. 407-410).

García Crespo, A., Chamizo, J., Rivera, I., Mencke, M., Colomo Palacios, R., & Gómez Berbís, J. M. (2009). SPETA: Social pervasive e-Tourism advisor. *Telematics and Informatics*, *26*(3), 306–315. doi:10.1016/j.tele.2008.11.008

García-Crespo, A., Colomo-Palacios, R., Gómez-Berbís, J. M., Chamizo, J., & Mendoza-Cembranos, M. D. (2010). S-SoDiA: a semantic enabled social diagnosis advisor. *International Journal of Society Systems Science*, *2*(3), 242–254. doi:10.1504/IJSSS.2010.033492

García-Crespo, A., Colomo-Palacios, R., Gómez-Berbís, J. M., & Mencke, M. (2009). BMR: Benchmarking Metrics Recommender for Personnel issues in Software Development Projects. *International Journal of Computational Intelligence Systems*, *2*(3), 257–267. doi:10.2991/ijcis.2009.2.3.7

García-Crespo, A., Colomo-Palacios, R., Gómez-Berbís, J. M., & Ruiz-Mezcua, B. (2010). SEMO: a framework for customer social networks analysis based on semantics. *Journal of Information Technology*, *25*(2), 178–188. doi:10.1057/jit.2010.1

García-Crespo, Á., Rodríguez, A., Mencke, M., Gómez-Berbís, J. M., & Colomo-Palacios, R. (2009). ODDIN: Ontology-driven differential diagnosis based on logical inference and probabilistic refinements. *Expert Systems with Applications*, *37*(3).

Ge, N., Li, H., Gao, L., Zang, Z., Li, Y., Li, J., et al. (2010). A web-based Project Management System for Agricultural Scientific Research. In *Proceedings of the 2010 International Conference on Management and Service Science (MASS 2010)* (pp. 1-2).

Gebhardt, C. (2010). *Toward trustworthy virtualization: Improving the trusted virtual infrastructure* (Unpublished doctoral dissertation). Royal Holloway, University of London, Surrey, UK.

Gibbons, S. (2009). *Telecommunications amendment (Integrated Public Number Database) Bill 2009: Second Reading*. Retrieved August 6, 2009, from http://parlinfo.aph.gov.au/parlInfo/genpdf/chamber/hansardr/2009-02-26/0032/hansard_frag.pdf;fileType=application%2Fpdf

Gibbs, J. L. (2009). Culture as kaleidoscope: navigating cultural tensions in global collaboration. In *Proceedings of the 2009 International Workshop on Intercultural Collaboration.*

Gilbert, C. (1998). Studying disaster: Changes in the main conceptual tools. In Quarantelli, E. L. (Ed.), *What is a disaster? A dozen perspectives on the question* (1st ed., pp. 3–12). New York, NY: Routledge.

Giustini, D. (2006). How Web 2.0 is changing medicine. *British Medical Journal*, *333*, 1283–1284. doi:10.1136/bmj.39062.555405.80

Giustini, D. (2007). Web 3.0 and medicine. Make way for the semantic web. *British Medical Journal*, *335*, 1273–1274. doi:10.1136/bmj.39428.494236.BE

Golbeck, J., Fragoso, G., Hartel, F., Hendler, J., Oberthaler, J., & Parsia, B. (2003). The national cancer institute's thesaurus and ontology. *Journal of Web Semantics*, *1*(1), 75–80. doi:10.1016/j.websem.2003.07.007

Goldberg, D. E. (1989). *Genetic Algorithms in Search, Optimization, and Machine Learning*. Reading, MA: Addison-Wesley.

Gómez Berbís, J. M., Colomo Palacios, R., García Crespo, A., & Ruiz Mezcua, B. (2008). ProLink: a semantics-based social network for software projects. *International Journal of Information Technology and Management*, *7*(4), 392–405. doi:10.1504/IJITM.2008.018656

Gómez-Pérez, A. (1994). *From Knowledge Based Systems to Knowledge Sharing Technology: Evaluation and Assessment*. Stanford, CA: Knowledge Systems Laboratory, Stanford University.

Gómez-Pérez, A., Fernández-López, M., & Corcho, O. (2004). *Ontological Engineering: with examples from the areas of Knowledge Management, e-Commerce and the Semantic Web*. Berlin: Springer Verlag.

Gong, M. G., Jiao, L. C., Du, H. F., & Bo, L. F. (2008). Multiobjective Immune Algorithm with Nondominated Neighbor-Based Selection. *Evolutionary Computation*, *16*(2), 225–255. doi:10.1162/evco.2008.16.2.225

Gong, W. Y., Cai, Z. H., Ling, C. X., & Li, H. (2010). A real-coded biogeography-based optimization with mutation. *Applied Mathematics and Computation*, *216*, 2749–2758. doi:10.1016/j.amc.2010.03.123

Goss, S., & Deneubourg, J.-L. (1991). Harvesting by a group of robots. In F. Varela & P. Bourgine (Eds.), *Proceedings of the First European Conference on Artificial Life*, Paris, France (pp. 195-204). Amsterdam, The Netherlands: Elsevier Publishing.

Gould, J. D., & Lewis, C. (1985). Designing for usability: key principles and what designers think. *Communications of the ACM*, *28*(3), 300–311. doi:10.1145/3166.3170

Gow, G. A. (2005). Pinpointing consent: Location privacy and mobile phones. In Nyíri, K. (Ed.), *A sense of place: The global and the local in mobile communication* (pp. 139–150). Vienna, Austria: Passagen Verlag.

Grau, B. C., Horrocks, I., Kazakov, Y., & Sattler, U. (2009). Extracting modules from ontologies: A logic-based approach. In H. Stuckenschmidt, C. Parent, & S. Spaccapietra (Eds.), *Modular Ontologies: Concepts, Theories and Techniques for Knowledge Modularization* (LNCS 5445 pp. 159-186).

Grau, B. C., Parsia, B., & Sirin, E. (2009). Ontology integration using ε-connections. In H. Stuckenschmidt, C. Parent, & S. Spaccapietra (Eds.), *Modular Ontologies: Concepts, Theories and Techniques for Knowledge Modularization* (LNCS 5445, pp. 293-320). Springer.

Green, N. (2001). Who's watching whom? Monitoring and accountability in mobile relations. In Brown, B., Green, N., & Harper, R. (Eds.), *Wireless world: Social and interactional aspects of the mobile age* (1st ed., pp. 32–45). New York, NY: Springer. doi:10.1007/978-1-4471-0665-4_3

Grootveld, H., & Hallerbach, W. (1999). Variance vs. downside risk: Is there really that much difference? *European Journal of Operational Research*, *114*(2), 304–319. doi:10.1016/S0377-2217(98)00258-6

Grothe, M. J. M., Landa, H. C., & Steenbruggen, J. G. M. (2005). The value of Gi4DM for transport & water management. In P. v. Oosterom, S. Zlatanova, & E. M. Fendel (Eds.), *Geo-information for disaster management* (1st ed., pp. 129-154). Dordrecht, The Netherlands: Springer-Verlag.

Gruau, F. (1995). Automatic definition of modular neural networks. *Adaptive Behavior*, *3*(2), 151–183. doi:10.1177/105971239400300202

Gruber, B., & Winter, S. (2002). *Location based services using a database federation*. Paper presented at the 5th AGILE Conference on Geographic Information Science, Palma, Spain.

Gruber, T. R. (1993). A translation approach to portable ontology specifications. *Knowledge Acquisition*, *5*(2), 199–220. doi:10.1006/knac.1993.1008

Gruber, T. R. (2007). Collective knowledge systems: Where the Social Web meets the Semantic Web. *Web Semantics: Science. Services and Agents on the World Wide Web*, *6*, 4–13.

Guan, J., Zhou, S., Zhou, J., & Zhu, F. (2007). Providing location-based services under web services framework. In Taniar, D. (Ed.), *Encyclopedia of mobile computing and commerce* (1st ed., pp. 789–795). London, UK: Information Science Reference. doi:10.4018/978-1-59904-002-8.ch134

Guo, L. (2006). Recovery time guaranteed heuristic routing for improving computation complexity in survivable WDM networks. *Computer Communications, 30*, 1331–1336. doi:10.1016/j.comcom.2006.12.014

Guster, D. C., Hall, C., Herath, S., Jansen, B., & Mikluch, L. (2008). A comparison of popular global authentication systems. In *Proceeding of the Third International Conference on Information Warfare and Security*, Omaha, NE.

Guster, D. C., McCann, B. P., Kizenski, K., & Lee, O. F. (2008). Cost effective, safe and simple method to provide disaster recovery for small and medium sized businesses. *Review of Business Research, 8*(4), 63–71.

Guster, D. C., Safonov, P., Hall, C., & Sundheim, R. (2003). Using simulation to predict performance characteristics of mirrored WWW hosts. *Issues in Information Systems, 4*(2), 479–485.

Haddow, G. D., Bullock, J. A., & Coppola, D. P. (2006). *Introduction to emergency management* (2nd ed.). Burlington, MA: Elsevier Butterworth–Heinemann.

Hagras, H. (2008). Employing computational intelligence to generate more intelligent and energy efficient living spaces. *International Journal of Automation and Computing, 5*(1), 1–9. doi:10.1007/s11633-008-0001-7

Handl, J., Knowles, J., & Dorigo, M. (2003). On the performance of ant-based clustering. In *Proceedings of the 3rd International Conference on Hybrid Intelligent Systems* (pp. 204-213).

Hansen, L. K., & Salamon, P. (2000). Neural network ensembles. *IEEE Transactions on Pattern Analysis and Machine Intelligence, 12*(10), 993–1001. doi:10.1109/34.58871

Hanski, I., & Gilpin, M. (1997). *Metapopulation biology*. New York, NY: Academic.

Hanson, C. W., Weiss, Y., Frasch, F., Marshall, C., & Marshall, B. (1998). A fuzzy control strategy for postoperative volume resuscitation. *Anesthesiology-Philadelphia then Hagerstown, 89*, 475-475.

Harkin, J. (2003). *Mobilisation: The growing public interest in mobile technology* (1st ed.). London, UK: Demos.

Harlow, W. V., & Rao, R. K. S. (1989). Asset pricing in a generalized mean-lower partial moment framework. *Journal of Financial and Quantitative Analysis, 24*, 285–311. doi:10.2307/2330813

Harvey, F. (2008). *A primer of GIS: Fundamental geographic and cartographic* (1st ed.). New York, NY: The Guilford Press.

Hashimoto, H. (1997). Optimum design of high-speed short journal bearings by mathematical programming. *Tribology Transactions, 40*, 283–293. doi:10.1080/10402009708983657

Hassan, M. A., Guirguis, N. M., Shaalan, M. R., & El-Shazly, K. M. (2007). Investigation of effects of window combinations on ventilation characteristics for thermal comfort in buildings. *Desalination, 209*, 251–260. doi:10.1016/j.desal.2007.04.035

Hazzan, O., & Dubinsky, Y. (2005). Clashes between Culture and Software Development Methods: The Case of the Israeli Hi-Tech Industry and Extreme Programming. In *Proceedings of the AGILE 2005 Conference* (pp. 59-69).

He, J., & Yao, X. (2005). A Game-Theoretic Approach for Designing Mixed Mutation Strategies. In *Advances in Natural Computation* (LNCS 3612, pp. 279-288).

He, Q., Jiang, W., Li, Y., & Le, Y. (2010). The Study on Paradigm Shift of Project Management Based on Complexity Science – Project Management Innovations in Shanghai 2010 EXPO Construction Program. In *Proceedings of the 2009 IEEE International Conference on Industrial Engineering and Engineering Management* (pp. 603-607).

Heindl, B., Schmidt, R., Schmid, G., Haller, M., Pfaller, P., & Gierl, L. (1997). A case-based consiliarius for therapy recommendation (ICONS): computer-based advice for calculated antibiotic therapy in intensive care medicine. *Computer Methods and Programs in Biomedicine, 52*(2), 117–127. doi:10.1016/S0169-2607(96)01789-0

Heine, M. L., Grover, V., & Malhotra, M. K. (2003). The relationship between technology and performance: A meta-analysis of technology models. *Omega: An International Journal of Management Science, 31*(3), 189–204. doi:10.1016/S0305-0483(03)00026-4

Hiles, A. (1992). Surviving a computer disaster. *Engineering Management Journal*, *2*(6), 271–274. doi:10.1049/em:19920071

Hiles, A. (2007). *The definitive handbook of business continuity management*. New York, NY: John Wiley & Sons.

Hilvert, J. (2011). Dodgy text tarnishes SMS emergency service system. *ITNews*. Retrieved September 23, 2011, from http://www.itnews.com.au/promos/interstitial/interstitial_dfp.html?l=10;KnvJuy7QTzEfzPKF8zesJyG8le2WW6,qtlJDF2ITieqTGRqifR;http%3A%2F%2Fwww.itnews.com.au%2FNews%2F272863%2Cdodgy%2Dtext%2Dtarnishes%2Dsms%2Demergency%2Dservice%2Dsystem.aspx

Hjelm, J. (2002). *Creating location services for the wireless Web* (1st ed.). New York, NY: John Wiley & Sons.

Ho, S. L., Yang, S., Ni, G., & Wong, H. C. (2002). A tabu method to find the Pareto solutions of multiobjective optimal design problems in electromagnetics. *IEEE Transactions on Magnetics*, *38*(2), 1013–1016. doi:10.1109/20.996260

Hofstede, G. (2001). *Culture's Consequences: comparing values, behaviors, institutions, and organizations across nations*. Thousand Oaks, CA: Sage.

Holma, H., Kristensson, M., Salonen, J., & Toskala, A. (2004). UMTS services and applications. In Holma, H., & Toskala, A. (Eds.), *WCDMA for UMTS: Radio access for third generation mobile communications* (3rd ed., pp. 11–46). Chichester, UK: John Wiley & Sons. doi:10.1002/0470870982.ch2

Holtzman, D. H. (2006). *Privacy lost: How technology is endangering your privacy* (1st ed.). San Francisco, CA: Jossey-Bass.

Hooker, J. (1988). Quantitative approach to logical reasoning. *Decision Support Systems*, *4*, 45–69. doi:10.1016/0167-9236(88)90097-8

Hoopes, J. (2008). *Virtualization for security: Including sandboxing, disaster recovery, high availability, forensic analysis and honeypotting*. Waltham, MA: Syngress.

Höppner, F., Klawonn, F., & Kruse, R. (1999). *Fuzzy Cluster Analysis: Methods for Classification, Data Analysis, and Image Recognition*. New York, NY: Wiley.

Horn, J., Nafpliotis, N., & Goldberg, D. E. (1994). A niched Pareto genetic algorithm for multiobjective optimization. In *Proceedings of the 5th International Conference on Genetic Algorithms* (pp. 82-87).

Horridge, M., Parsia, B., & Sattler, U. (2008). Laconic and precise justifcations in OWL. In A.P. Sheth, S. Staab, M. Dean, M. Paolucci, D. Maynard, T. Finin, et al. (Eds.), *Proceedings of the Seventh International Semantic Web Conference* (LNCS 5318, pp. 323-338).

Horrocks, I. (2008). Ontologies and the Semantic Web. *Communications of the ACM*, *51*(12), 58–67. doi:10.1145/1409360.1409377

Horrocks, I., Patel-Schneider, P. F., Boley, H., Tabet, S., Grosof, B., & Dean, M. (2004). *SWRL: A Semantic Web Rule Language Combining OWL and RuleML*. Retrieved June 16, 2010, from http://www.daml.org/2004/04/swrl/rules-all.html

Hughes, B., Joshi, I., & Wareham, J. (2008). Health 2.0 and Medicine 2.0: tensions and controversies in the field. *Journal of Medical Internet Research*, *10*(3), e23. doi:10.2196/jmir.1056

Hughes, J., & Maler, E. (2004). *Technical overview of the OASIS security assertion markup language* (SAML) V2.0. Retrieved June 10, 2010, from http://xml.coverpages.org/SAML-TechOverviewV20-Draft7874.pdf

Humphries, G. (2011). Attorney-General: Emergency alert (Question No. 1434). *Senate Debates*. Retrieved November 22, 2011, from http://www.openaustralia.org/senate/?id=2011-11-22.155.1

Hunter, A., & Konieczny, S. (2005). Approaches to measuring inconsistent information. In *Inconsistency Tolerance* (LNCS 3300, pp. 189-234).

Hunter, A., & Konieczny, S. (2008). Measuring inconsistency through minimal inconsistent sets. In G. Brewka & J. Lang (Eds.), *Proceedings of the Eleventh International Conference on the Principles of Knowledge Representation and Reasoning* (pp. 358-366). AAAI Press.

Hunter, S. D. (2003). Information technology, organizational learning, and the market value of the firm. *Journal of Information Technology Theory and Applications*, *5*(1), 1–28.

Hwang, K., Dongarra, J., & Fox, G. (2011). *Distributed and cloud computing: From parallel processing to the internet of things*. San Francisco, CA: Morgan Kaufmann.

IEEE-SA Standards Board. (2000). *IEEE Recommended Practice for Architectural Description of Software-Intensive Systems (IEEE 1471-2000)*. Washington, DC: IEEE Computer Society.

Ife, H. (2009, March 2). Texts alert victorians of fire danger. *Herald Sun*.

IHTSDO. (n.d.) *SNOMED-CT*. Retrieved April 19, 2010, from http://www.ihtsdo.org/snomed-ct/

Iivari, J., & Huisman, M. (2007). The Relationship between Organizational Culture and the Deployment of Systems Development Methodologies. *Management Information Systems Quarterly*, *31*(1), 35–58.

Iivari, N. (2006). 'Representing the User' in software development - a cultural analysis of usability work in the product development context. *Interacting with Computers*, *18*, 635–664. doi:10.1016/j.intcom.2005.10.002

Im, K. S., Dow, K. E., & Grover, V. (2001). A reexamination of IT investment and the market value of the firm—an event study methodology. *Information Systems Research*, *12*(1), 103–117. doi:10.1287/isre.12.1.103.9718

ISHTAR Consortium (Ed.). (2001). *Implementing secure healthcare telematics applications in Europe – ISHTAR*. Amsterdam, The Netherlands: IOS Press.

ISTAG. (2002, June). *Trust, dependability, security and privacy for IST in FP6*. Brussels, Belgium: Office for Official Publications of the European Communities.

Jacobs, R. A., Jordan, M. I., Nowlan, S. J., & Hinton, G. E. (1991). Adaptive mixtures of local experts. *Neural Computation*, *3*, 79–87. doi:10.1162/neco.1991.3.1.79

Jacobson, I. (2003). *Case for Aspects - Part I & II* (pp. 32–37). Software Development Magazine.

Jacobson, I., Christerson, M., Jonsson, P., & Övergaard, G. (1992). *Object-Oriented Engineering*. Reading, MA: Addison-Wesley.

Jafari, R., Dabiri, F., Brisk, P., & Sarrafzadeh, M. (2005, April). CustoMed: A power optimized customizable and mobile medical monitoring and analysis system. In *Proceedings of the ACM HCI Challenges in Health Assessment Workshop in Conjunction with Proceedings of the Conference on Human Factors in Computing Systems*, Portland, OR.

Jagtman, E. (2009). *Reaching citizens with CHORIST: Everything but technology*. Retrieved October 18, 2009, from http://www.chorist.eu/index.php?page=1&sel=1

Jahangard, N. (2004). Iran's Road to Knowledge-based Development. In *Proceedings of the Meeting and Workshop on Development of a National IT Strategy Focusing on Indigenous Content Development*. Tehran, Iran: Ministry of Science, Research & Technology, Iranian Information and Documentation Center. Retrieved from http://unpan1.un.org/intradoc/groups/public/documents/APCITY/UNPAN021357.pdf

Jain, A. K., & Dubes, R. C. (1988). *Algorithms for Clustering Data*. Upper Saddle River, NJ: Prentice Hall Advanced Reference Series.

Jain, A. K., Murty, M. N., & Flynn, P. J. (1999). Data clustering: a review. *ACM Computing Surveys*, *31*(3), 264–323. doi:10.1145/331499.331504

Janghel, R. R., Shukla, A., & Tiwari, R. (2010). Decision Support system for fetal delivery using Soft Computing Techniques. In *Proceedings of the Fourth International Conference on Computer Sciences and Convergence Information Technology,* Seoul, Korea (pp. 1514-1519). Washington, DC: IEEE.

Janghel, R. R., Shukla, A., Tiwari, R., & Tiwari, P. (2009). Clinical Decision support system for fetal Delivery using Artificial Neural Network. In *Proceedings of the 2009 International Conference on New Trends in Information and Service Science,* Gyeongju, Korea (pp. 1070-1075). Washington, DC: IEEE.

Jardin, X. (2003). Text messaging feeds SARS rumors. *Wired*. Retrieved October 17, 2009, from http://www.wired.com/medtech/health/news/2003/04/58506

Jea, D., & Srivastava, M. B. (2006, June). A remote medical monitoring and interaction system. In *Proceedings of the 4th International Conference on Mobile Systems, Applications, and Service*, Uppsala, Sweden.

Jean, P. (2011). *Govt rebuked over Mitchell fire response*. Retrieved November 23, 2011, from http://www.canberratimes.com.au/act-news/govt-rebuked-over-mitchell-fire-response-20111123-1v2u0.html

Jean, P. (2012). SMS alert system is short on delivery. *The Age*. Retrieved February 29, 2012, from http://m.theage.com.au/act-news/sms-alert-system-is-short-on-delivery-20120228-1u187.html

Jenkins, R., & Yuhas, B. (1993). A simplified neural network solution through problem decomposition: The case of the truck backer-upper. *IEEE Transactions on Neural Networks*, *4*(4), 718–722. doi:10.1109/72.238326

Jensen, C. S. (2002, January 8-11). Research challenges in location-enabled m-services. In *Proceedings of the Third IEEE International Conference on Mobile Data Management*, Singapore (pp. 3-7).

Ji, M. J., Tang, H. W., & Guo, J. (2004). A single-point mutation evolutionary programming. *Information Processing Letters*, *90*, 293–299. doi:10.1016/j.ipl.2004.03.002

Jiang, X., Mahadevan, S., & Adeli, H. (2007). Bayesian wavelet packet denoising for structural system identification. *Structural Control and Health Monitoring*, *14*(2), 333–356. doi:10.1002/stc.161

Jiao, L. C., Gong, M. G., Shang, R. H., et al. (2005). Clonal selection with immune dominance and energy based multiobjective optimization. In *Proceeding of the 3rd International Conference on Evolutionary Multi-criterion Optimization* (pp. 474-489). Berlin, Germany: Springer.

Jilani, A. A. A., Usman, M., & Halim, Z. (2010). Model Transformations in Model Driven Architecture. *Universal Journal of Computer Science and Engineering Technology*, *1*(1), 50–54.

Jiménez, M. J., & Madsen, H. (2008). Models for describing the thermal characteristics of building components. *Building and Environment*, *43*(2), 152–162. doi:10.1016/j.buildenv.2006.10.029

Jin, X. (2006). *Applying Model Driven approach to Model Role Based Access Control System*. Unpublished master's thesis, University of Ottawa, Ottawa, ON, Canada.

Johnson, B., & Shneiderman, B. (1991). Tree-maps: A space-filling approach to the visualization of hierarchical information structures. In *Proceedings of the Visualization 1991 Conference*, San Diego, CA (pp. 284-291).

Jokela, T., & Abrahamsson, P. (2004). Usability assessment of an Extreme Programming Project: Close Co-Operation with the Customer Does Not Equal to Good Usability. In *Product Focused Software Process Improvement* (LNCS 3009, pp. 339-407).

Jones, V. A., & Keyes, K. (2001). *Emergency management for records and information management programs*. Lenexa, KS: Conservation Information Network, ARMA International.

Jovanov, E., Milenkovic, A., Otto, C., & de Groen, P. C. (2005). A wireless body area network of intelligent motion sensors for computer assisted physical rehabilitation. *Journal of Neuroengineering and Rehabilitation*, *2*, 1–10. doi:10.1186/1743-0003-2-6

Jung, J. Y., & Reggia, J. A. (2006). Evolutionary Design of Neural Network Architectures Using a Descriptive Encoding Language. *IEEE Transactions on Evolutionary Computation*, *10*(6), 676–688. doi:10.1109/TEVC.2006.872346

Junker, H., Stager, M., Tröster, G., Blttler, D., & Salama, O. (2004, June). Wireless networks in context aware wearable systems. In *Proceedings of the 1st European Workshop on Wireless Sensor Networks* (pp. 37-40).

Kala, R., Shukla, A., & Tiwari, R. (2009). Fuzzy Neuro Systems for Machine Learning for Large Data Sets. In *Proceedings of the IEEE International Advance Computing Conference, IACC '09*, Patiala, India (pp. 541-545). Washington, DC: IEEE.

Kala, R., Shukla, A., & Tiwari, R. (2010). Clustering Based Hierarchical Genetic Algorithm for Complex Fitness Landscapes. *International Journal of Intelligent Systems Technologies and Applications*, *9*(2), 185–205. doi:10.1504/IJISTA.2010.034320

Kala, R., Shukla, A., & Tiwari, R. (2010). Handling Large Medical Data Sets for Disease Detection. In Shukla, A., & Tiwari, R. (Eds.), *Biomedical Engineering and Information Systems: Technologies, Tools and Applications*. Hershey, PA: IGI Global.

Kala, R., Vazirani, H., Shukla, A., & Tiwari, R. (2010). Fusion of Speech and Face by Enhanced Modular Neural Network. In *Proceedings of the Springer International Conference on Information Systems, Technology and Management, ICISTM 2010,* Bankok, Thailand (pp. 363-372). Washington, DC: IEEE.

Kalyanpur, A., Parsia, B., Sirin, E., & Grau, B. C. (2006). Repairing unsatisfiable concepts in OWL ontologies. In Y. Sure & J. Domingue (Eds.), *Proceedings of the Third European Semantic Web Conference. The Semantic Web: Research and Applications* (LNCS 4011, pp. 170-184).

Kamel-Boulos, M. N., & Wheeler, S. (2007). The emerging Web 2.0 social software: an enabling suite of sociable technologies in health and health care education. *Health Information and Libraries Journal, 24,* 2–23. doi:10.1111/j.1471-1842.2007.00701.x

Kanamanapalli, V. B. (2010). *The Setting Up of Project Management Offices (PMOs) for Large Project Initiative.* Retrieved from http://www.pmi.org/en/Knowledge-Center/Knowledge-Shelf/Project-Management-Offices.aspx

Kankanhalli, A., Tan, B. C. Y., Wei, K.-K., & Holmes, M. C. (2004). Cross-cultural differences and information systems developer values. *Decision Support Systems, 38*(2), 183–195. doi:10.1016/S0167-9236(03)00101-5

Kaplan, E. D., & Hegarty, C. J. (2006). *Understanding GPS: Principles and applications* (2nd ed.). Norwood, MA: Artech House.

Karami, R. (2003). *IT Project Pathology.* Retrieved from http://www.golsoft.com/links/ITP-projects-problems.0.pdf

Karaulov, A., & Strabykin, A. (2009). Constraint-based Optimizations of Executable UML Models. In *Proceedings of the 3rd Spring/Summer Young Researchers' Colloquium on Software Engineering.*

Karkaletsis, V., Stamatakis, K., Karmapyperis, P., Svátek, V., Mayer, M. A., Leis, A., et al. (2008, July 21-25). Automating Accreditation of Medical Web Content. In *Proceedings of the 18th European Conference on Artificial Intelligence (ECAI 2008), 5th Prestigious Applications of Intelligent Systems (PAIS 2008),* Patras, Greece (pp. 688-692).

Kersten, G. E., Kersten, M. A., & Rakowski, W. H. (2002). Software and Culture: Beyond the Internationalization of the Interface. *Journal of Global Information Management, 10*(4), 86–101. doi:10.4018/jgim.2002100105

Khasawneh, A. (2009). Arabia online: internet diffusion in Jordan. *International Journal of Society Systems Science, 1*(4), 396–401. doi:10.1504/IJSSS.2009.026511

Kiefer, J. J., Mancini, J. A., Morrow, B. H., Gladwin, H., & Stewart, T. A. (2008). *Providing access to resilience-enhancing technologies for disadvantaged communities and vulnerable populations.* Retrieved from http://www.orau.org/university-partnerships/files/The-PARET-Report.pdf

Kim, D. J., Braynov, S. B., Rao, H. R., & Song, Y. I. (2001, August 2-5). A B-to-C trust model for online exchange. In *Proceedings of the Seventh Americas Conference on Information Systems,* Boston, MA (pp. 784-787).

King, C. (2011). *How SUNY - Empire State College solved it's disaster recovery, business continuity, growth, and pandemic planning problems through virtualization and turned green in the process!* Paper presented at the Special Interest Group on University and College Computing Services Conference, San Diego, CA.

Kini, A., & Choobineh, J. (1998). Trust in electronic commerce: Definition and theoretical considerations. In *Proceedings of the Thirty-First Annual Hawaii International Conference on System Sciences* (pp. 51-61).

Kinsela, S., Passant, A., Breslin, J. G., Decker, S., & Jaokar, A. (2009). The Future of Social Web Sites: Sharing Data and Trusted Applications with Semantics. *Advances in Computers, 76*(4), 121–175. doi:10.1016/S0065-2458(09)01004-3

Klinov, P., & Parsia, B. (2010). Pronto: A practical probabilistic description logic reasoner. In T. Lukasiewicz, R. Peñaloza, & A. Turhan (Eds.), *Proceedings of the First International Workshop on Uncertainty in Description Logics,* Edinburgh, UK.

Klir, G., & Folger, T. (1988). *Fuzzy Sets, Uncertainty and Information.* Upper Saddle River, NJ: Prentice-Hall International.

Kohli, R., & Davaraj, S. (2003). Measuring information technology payoff: A meta-analysis of structural variables in firm-level empirical research. *Information Systems Research, 14*(2), 127–145. doi:10.1287/isre.14.2.127.16019

Kohonen, T. (2001). *Self-organizing Maps*. Berlin, Germany: Springer.

Kokolakis, S., & Kiountouzis, E. (2000). Achieving interoperability in a multi-security-policies environment. *Computers & Security*, *19*(3), 267–281. doi:10.1016/S0167-4048(00)88615-0

Konar, A. (1999). *Artificial Intelligence and Soft Computing: Behavioral and Cognitive Modeling of the Human Brain*. Boca Raton, FL: CRC Press. doi:10.1201/9781420049138

Krishnamurthy, N. (2002). Using SMS to deliver location-based services. In *Proceedings of the IEEE International Conference on Personal Wireless Communications* (pp. 177-181).

Krojnewski, R., & Nager, B. (2006, November 13). Disaster recovery: It's not just an IT problem. *Forrester Report*.

Krukowski, A., & Arsenijevic, D. (2010). RFID-based positioning for building management systems. In *Proceedings of the 2010 IEEE International Symposium on Circuits and Systems: Nano-Bio Circuit Fabrics and Systems* (pp. 3569-3572).

Kulkarni, V., & Reddy, S. (2003). Separation of Concerns in Model driven Development. *IEEE Software*, *20*, 64–69. doi:10.1109/MS.2003.1231154

Kuntz, P., Layzell, P., & Snyers, D. (1997). A colony of ant-like agents for partitioning in VLSI technology. In P. Husbands & I. Harvey (Eds.), *Proceedings of the Fourth European Conference on Artificial Life* (pp. 417-424).

Kuntz, P., Snyers, D., & Layzell, P. (1998). A stochastic heuristic for visualising graph clusters in a bi-dimensional space prior to partitioning. *Journal of Heuristics*, *5*(3), 327–351. doi:10.1023/A:1009665701840

Küpper, A. (2005). *Location-based services: Fundamentals and operation* (1st ed.). Chichester, UK: John Wiley & Sons. doi:10.1002/0470092335

L' Hereux, B., McHugh, M., Privett, B., Kinicki, R. E., & Agu, E. (2006). A campus-wide mobile EMS information management system. In *Proceedings of the Fourth Annual International Conference on Pervasive Computing and Communications* (pp. 522-526).

Lacy, L. W. (2005). *OWL: Representing information using the web ontology language*. Bloomington, IN: Trafford Publishing.

Laddad, R. (2009). *AspectJ in Action* (2nd ed.). Shelter Island, NY: Manning Publications.

Lam, J. S. C., Sleeman, D. H., Pan, J. Z., & Vasconcelos, W. W. (2008). A fine-grained approach to resolving unsatisfiable ontologies. *Journal of Data Semantics*, *10*, 62–95. doi:10.1007/978-3-540-77688-8_3

Lant, T. K. (1992). Aspiration level adaptation: An empirical exploration. *Management Science*, *38*, 623–644. doi:10.1287/mnsc.38.5.623

Lant, T. K., & Montgomery, D. B. (1987). Learning from strategic success and failure. *Journal of Business Research*, *15*, 503–517. doi:10.1016/0148-2963(87)90035-X

Laureano, M., Maziero, C., & Jamhour, E. (2007). Protecting host-based intrusion detectors through virtual machines, computer networks. *International Journal of Computer and Telecommunications Networking*, *51*(5), 1275–1283.

Layman, L., Williams, L., Damian, D., & Bures, H. (2006). Essential communication practices for Extreme Programming in a global software development team. *Information and Software Technology*, *48*(9), 781–794. doi:10.1016/j.infsof.2006.01.004

Lee, C. Y., & Yao, X. (2004). Evolutionary programming using mutations based on the Levy probability distribution. *IEEE Transactions on Evolutionary Computation*, *8*, 1–13. doi:10.1109/TEVC.2003.816583

Lee, M. (2012). Telstra adds location to emergency alerts. *ZDNet*. Retrieved January 13, 2012, from http://www.zdnet.com.au/telstra-adds-location-to-emergency-alerts-339329657.htm

Lee, O. F., Guster, D. C., Schmidt, M. B., & McCann, B. (2009). Applying the scale-free degree distribution algorithm to assess communication complexity and failure points in disaster recovery model. *Journal of Information Technology Management*, *20*(2), 35–45.

Lee, Y., Supekar, K., & Geller, J. (2006). Ontology integration: Experience with medical terminologies. *Computers in Biology and Medicine*, *36*(7-8), 893–919. doi:10.1016/j.compbiomed.2005.04.013

Leenes, R. (2008). Reply: Mind my step? In Hildebrandt, M., & Gutwirth, S. (Eds.), *Profiling the European citizen: Cross-disciplinary perspectives* (1st ed., pp. 160–168). Dordrecht, The Netherlands: Springer-Verlag.

Leitich, H., Adlassnig, K., & Kolarz, G. (2002). Evaluation of two different models of semiautomatic knowledge acquisition for the medical consultant system CADIAG-2/RHEUMA. *Artificial Intelligence in Medicine*, *25*, 215–225. doi:10.1016/S0933-3657(02)00025-8

Li, J., Qin, L.-L., & Yue, D.-Z. (2008). Experiment Greenhouse Temperature System Modeling and Simulation. *Journal of System Simulation*, *20*(7), 1869–1875.

Lin, Q., Neo, H., Zhang, L., Huang, G., & Gay, R. (2007). Grid-based large-scale web3D collaborative virtual environment. In *Proceedings of the 12th International Conference on 3D Web Technology* (pp. 123-132).

Lioni, A., Sauwens, C., Theraulaz, G., & Deneubourg, J.-L. (2001). The dynamics of chain formation in oecophylla longinoda. *Journal of Insect Behavior*, *14*, 679–696. doi:10.1023/A:1012283403138

Liu, W., Zhao, S., Sun, Y., & Yin, M. (2008). An Approach to Project Management Information System Requirements Analysis. In *Proceedings of the International Conference on Intelligent Computation Technology and Automation* (pp. 957-961).

Livermore, J. (2008). Factors that Significantly Impact the Implementation of an Agile Software Development Methodology. *Journal of Software*, *3*(4), 31–36. doi:10.4304/jsw.3.4.31-36

Lopez, X. R. (2004). Location-based services. In Karimi, H. A., & Hammand, A. (Eds.), *Telegeoinformatics: Location-based computing and services* (1st ed., pp. 144–159). Boca Raton, FL: CRC Press.

Loveman, G. W. (1994). An assessment of the productivity impact of information technologies. In Allen, T. J., & Scott Morton, M. S. (Eds.), *Information Technology and the Corporation of the 1990s: Research Studies* (pp. 84–110). Cambridge, MA: MIT Press.

Lu, Y., Miao, K.-K., & He, W. (2009). Context-aware approach for temperature monitoring and fire alarming. *Journal of Computer Applications*, *29*(2), 583–594. doi:10.3724/SP.J.1087.2009.00583

Ludwig, J. (2011). Attorney-General: Emergency alert (Question No. 1434). *Senate Debates*. Retrieved November 22, 2011, from http://www.openaustralia.org/senate/?id=2011-11-22.155.1

Lukasiewicz, T. (2008). Expressive probabilistic description logics. *Artificial Intelligence*, *172*(6-7), 852–883. doi:10.1016/j.artint.2007.10.017

Lukasiewicz, T., & Straccia, U. (2008). Managing uncertainty and vagueness in description logics for the Semantic Web. *Web Semantics: Science. Services and Agents on the World Wide Web*, *6*(4), 291–308. doi:10.1016/j.websem.2008.04.001

Lumer, E. D., & Faieta, B. (1994). Diversity and adaptation in populations of clustering ants. In D. Cliff, P. Husbands, J. A. Meyer, &n W. Stewart (Eds.), *Proceedings of the Third International Conference on Simulation of Adaptive Behavior* (pp. 501-508). Cambridge, MA: MIT Press.

Lung, C. H., Zaman, M., & Nandi, A. (2004). Applications of Clustering Techniques to Software Partitioning, Recovery and Restructuring. *Journal of Systems and Software*, *73*, 227–244. doi:10.1016/S0164-1212(03)00234-6

Luo, R. C., Lin, T. Y., Chen, H. C., & Su, K. L. (2006). Multisensor Based Security Robot System for Intelligent Building. In *Proceedings of the 2006 IEEE International Conference on Multisensor Fusion and Integration for Intelligent Systems* (pp. 408-413).

Lytras, M. D., & García, R. (2008). Semantic Web applications: a framework for industry and business exploitation - What is needed for the adoption of the Semantic Web from the market and industry. *International Journal of Knowledge and Learning*, *4*(1), 93–108. doi:10.1504/IJKL.2008.019739

Lytras, M. D., Sakkopoulos, E., & Ordóñez-De Pablos, P. (2009). Semantic Web and Knowledge Management for the health domain: state of the art and challenges for the Seventh Framework Programme (FP7) of the European Union (2007-2013). *International Journal of Technology Management*, *47*(1-3), 239–249. doi:10.1504/IJTM.2009.024124

Ma, H. P. (2010). An analysis of the equilibrium of migration models for biogeography-based optimization. *Information Science*, *180*, 3444–3464. doi:10.1016/j.ins.2010.05.035

MacGregor, E., Hsieh, Y., & Kruchten, P. (2005). The Impact of Intercultural Factors on Global Software Development. In *Proceedings of the IEEE Canadian Conference on Electrical and Computer Engineering* (pp. 920-926).

Maitra, S., Shanker, M., & Mudholkar, P. K. (2011). Disaster recovery planning with virtualization technologies in the banking industry. In *Proceedings of the International Conference & Workshop on Emerging Trends in Technology* (pp. 298-299).

Malan, D., Fulford-Jones, T., Welsh, M., & Moulton, S. (2004, April). Codeblue: Sn ad-hoc sensor network infrastructure for emergency medical care. In *Proceedings of the 1st International Workshop on Wearable and Implantable Body Sensor Networks*, London UK.

Malatras, A., Pavlou, G., Belsis, P., Gritzalis, S., Skourlas, C., & Chalaris, I. (2005). Deploying pervasive secure knowledge management infrastructures. *International Journal of Pervasive Computing and Communications Troubador Publishing*, *1*(4), 265–276. doi:10.1108/17427370580000130

Malatras, A., Pavlou, G., Belsis, P., Gritzalis, S., Skourlas, C., & Chalaris, I. (2005). Secure and distributed knowledge management in pervasive environments. In *Proceedings of the IEEE International Conference on Pervasive Services*, Santorini, Greece (pp. 79-87).

Mallipeddi, R., Mallipeddi, S., & Suganthan, P. N. (2010). Ensemble strategies with adaptive evolutionary programming. *Information Sciences*, *180*, 1571–1581. doi:10.1016/j.ins.2010.01.007

Malti, R., Victor, S., & Oustaloup, A. (2008). Advances in system identification using fractional models. *Journal of Computational and Nonlinear Dynamics*, *3*(2), 1–7. doi:10.1115/1.2833910

Martin, J. F. (1994). Fuzzy control in anesthesia. *Journal of Clinical Monitoring and Computing*, *10*(2), 77–80. doi:10.1007/BF02886818

Marx, G. T. (1999). What's in a name? Some reflections on the sociology of anonymity. *The Information Society*, *15*(2), 99–112. doi:10.1080/019722499128565

Massiglia, P., & Bunn, F. (2003). *Virtual storage redefined: Technologies and applications for storage virtualization*. Dublin, Ireland: Veritas.

Maulik, U., & Saha, I. (2009). Modified differential evolution based fuzzy clustering for pixel classification in remote sensing imagery. *Pattern Recognition*, *42*, 2135–2149. doi:10.1016/j.patcog.2009.01.011

McAdams, J. (2006). *SMS does SOS: Short message service earns valued role as a link of last resort for crisis communications*. Retrieved February 2, 2007, from http://fcw.com/articles/2006/04/03/sms-does-sos.aspx?sc_lang=en

McBride, B. (2001). *Jena – A Semantic Web Framework for Java*. Retrieved June 20, 2010, from http://jena.sourceforge.net

McClelland, R. (2011). *Australia's emergency alert system working well*. Retrieved September 1, 2011, from http://www.alp.org.au/federal-government/news/australia-s-emergency-alert-system-working-well/

McGinley, M., Turk, A., & Bennett, D. (2006). Design criteria for public emergency warning systems. In *Proceedings of the 3rd International Conference on Information Systems for Crisis Response and Management*, Newark, NJ.

McKnight, D. H., & Chervany, N. L. (2001). What trust means in e-commerce customer relationships: An interdisciplinary conceptual typology. *International Journal of Electronic Commerce*, *6*(2), 35–59.

McLean, R., Richards, B. H., & Wardman, J. I. (2007). The effect of Web 2.0 on the future of medical practice and education: Darwikinian evolution or folksonomic revolution? *The Medical Journal of Australia*, *187*(3), 174–174.

Mehrdad, J., Mokhtari, A., & Aski, H. R. (2005). Designing the conceptual model of an electronic document management system for the institute of technical and vocational higher education. *Iranian Journal of Information Science and Technology*, *3*(2), 57–70.

Meier, R., Nieuwland, J., Zbinden, A. M., & Hacisalihzade, S. S. (1992). Fuzzy logic control of blood pressure during anesthesia. *IEEE Control Systems Magazine*, *12*(9), 12–17. doi:10.1109/37.168811

Melin, P., & Castilo, O. (2005). *Hybrid Intelligent Systems for Pattern Recognition Using Soft Computing*. Berlin: Springer.

Melville, N., Kraemer, K., & Gurbaxani, V. (2004). Information Technology and Organizational Performance: An Integrative Model of IT Business Value. *Management Information Systems Quarterly*, *28*(2), 283–322.

Meng, F.-C., Zhan, D.-C., & Xu, X. (2005). Business Component Identification of Enterprise Information System: A hierarchical clustering method. In *Proceedings of the 2005 IEEE International Conference on e-Business Engineering* (pp. 473-480).

Meng, H. Y., Zhang, X. H., & Liu, S. Y. (2008). A Differential Evolution Based on Double Populations for Constrained Multi-Objective Optimization Problem. *Chinese Journal of Computers*, *31*(2), 228–235. doi:10.3724/SP.J.1016.2008.00228

Mens, T., Van Eetvelde, N., Demeyer, S., & Janssens, D. (2005). Formalizing refactoring with graph transformations. *International Journal on Software Tools for Technology Transfer*, *17*, 247–276.

Michael, K., Stroh, B., Berry, O., Muhlhauber, A., & Nicholls, T. (2006, September 19-21). The AVIAN flu tracker - A location service proof of concept, recent advances in security technology. In *Proceedings of the RNSA Security Technology Conference*, Canberra, Australia (pp. 244-258).

Michalewicz, Z. (1994). *Genetic Algorithms + Data Structures = Evolution Programs*. Berlin, Germany: Springer-Verlag.

Mileti, D. S., & Sorensen, J. H. (1990). *Communication of emergency public warnings: A social science perspective and state-of-the-art assessment*. Retrieved August 8, 2007, from http://emc.ornl.gov/EMCWeb/EMC/PDF/CommunicationFinal.pdf

Miller, K. D., & Leiblein, M. J. (1996). Corporate risk-return relations: Returns variability versus downside risk. *Academy of Management Journal*, *39*(1), 91–122. doi:10.2307/256632

Miller, R. A., Pople, H. E., & Myers, J. D. (1982). Internist-1, an experimental computer-based diagnostic consultant for general internal medicine. *The New England Journal of Medicine*, *307*(8), 468. doi:10.1056/NEJM198208193070803

Ministry for Police and Emergency Services. (2011). *Standard Emergency Warning Signal (SEWS)*. Retrieved January 21, 2011, from http://www.emergency.nsw.gov.au/sews

Mishra, D., & Mishra, A. (2011). A review of non-technical issues in global software development. *International Journal of Computer Applications in Technology*, *40*(3), 216–224. doi:10.1504/IJCAT.2011.039142

Misra, S. C., Kumar, V., & Kumar, U. (2009). Identifying some important success factors in adopting agile software development practices. *Journal of Systems and Software*, *82*, 1869–1890. doi:10.1016/j.jss.2009.05.052

Mitchell, M. (1999). *An Introduction to Genetic Algorithms*. Cambridge, MA: MIT Press.

Mittal, N., & Nault, B. R. (2009). Investments in Information Technology: Indirect Effects and Information Technology Intensity. *Information Systems Research*, *20*(1), 140–154. doi:10.1287/isre.1080.0186

Mo, H. W., & Xu, L. F. (2010). Biogeography Migration Algorithm for Traveling Salesman Problem. In *Proceedings of the International Conference on Swarm Intelligence*, *1*, 405–414.

Moriarty, D. E. (1997). *Symbiotic Evolution of Neural-Networks in SequentialDecision Tasks*. Unpublished doctoral dissertation, Department of Computer Science, University of Texas, Austin, TX.

Moriarty, D. E., & Miikkulainen, R. (1997). Forming neural networks through efficient and adaptive coevolution. *Evolutionary Computation*, *5*(4), 373–399. doi:10.1162/evco.1997.5.4.373

Moser, W., & Adlassnig, K. (1992). Consistency checking of binary categorical relationships in a medical knowledge base. *Artificial Intelligence in Medicine*, *8*, 389–407. doi:10.1016/0933-3657(92)90022-H

Mu, C. H., Jiao, L. C., & Liu, Y. (2009). M-Elite Coevolutionary Algorithm for Numerical Optimization. *Chinese Journal of Software*, *20*(11), 2925–2938. doi:10.3724/SP.J.1001.2009.03496

Mühlenbein, H., & Schlierkamp-Voosen, D. (1993). Predictive Models for the Breeder Genetic Algorithm I. Continuous Parameter Optimization. *Evolutionary Computation*, *1*, 25–49. doi:10.1162/evco.1993.1.1.25

Musen, M. (1989). *Protégé*. Retrieved June 21, 2010, from http://protege.stanford.edu

Mustafa, B. A. (2010). Comparing the Effect of Use Case Format on End User Understanding of System Requirements. *Journal of Information Technology Research*, *3*(4), 1–20. doi:10.4018/jitr.2010100101

Naeve, A., Sicilia, M. A., & Lytras, M. D. (2008). Learning processes and processing learning: from organizational needs to learning designs. *Journal of Knowledge Management*, *12*(6), 5–14. doi:10.1108/13673270810913586

National Center for Biomedical Ontology. (2010). *BioPortal Website*. Retrieved February 19, 2010, from http://bioportal.bioontology.org

Nawrocki, D. N. (1999). A brief history of downside risk measures. *Journal of Investing*, *8*(3), 9–26. doi:10.3905/joi.1999.319365

NCBO. (2005). *NCBO Bioportal*. Retrieved June 16, 2010, from http://bioportal.bioontology.org

Nellitheertha, H. (2006). *Virtualization technologies*. Infosys White Paper.

New South Wales Government. (2007). *About SydneyALERT*. Retrieved April 17, 2008, from http://www.sydneyalert.nsw.gov.au/content.php/36.html

Ng, J. W. P., Lo, B. P. L., Wells, O., Sloman, M., Peters, N., & Darzi, A. … Yang, G. (2004, September). Ubiquitous monitoring environment for wearable and implantable sensors (UbiMon). In *Proceedings of the 6th International Conference on Ubiquitous Computing*, Nottingham, UK (pp. 3-4).

Niazi, M., Babar, M. A., & Verner, J. M. (2010). Software Process Improvement barriers: A cross-cultural comparison. *Information and Software Technology*, *52*(11), 1204–1216. doi:10.1016/j.infsof.2010.06.005

Nolfi, S., Elman, J. L., & Parisi, D. (1990). *Learning and Evolution in Neural Networks* (CRL Tech. Rep. 9019). La Jolla, CA: University of California at San Diego.

Nomura, T. (1997). An Analysis on Crossovers for Real Number Chromosomes in an Infinite Population Size. In *Proceedings of the 1997 International Joint Conference on Artificial Intelligence* (Vol. 2, pp. 936-941).

Object Management Group (OMG). (2011). *MDA Guide Version 1.0.1*. Retrieved October 9, 2011, from http://www.omg.org/mda/

Ochoa, G., Qu, R., & Burke, E. K. (2009). Analyzing the landscape of a graph based hyper-heuristic for timetabling problems. In F. Rothlauf (Ed.), *Proceedings of the 11th Annual Conference on Genetic and Evolutionary Computation* (pp. 341-348). New York, NY: ACM.

Ofek, E., & Richardson, M. (2003). DotCom mania: The rise and fall of internet stock prices. *The Journal of Finance*, *58*(3), 1113–1137. doi:10.1111/1540-6261.00560

Oh, J., & Haas, Z. J. (2007). A scheme for location-based internet broadcasting and its applications. *IEEE Communications Magazine*, *45*(11), 136–141. doi:10.1109/MCOM.2007.4378333

Olson, J. S., & Olson, G. M. (2003). Culture Surprises in Remote Software Development Teams. *Queue*, *1*(9), 51–59. doi:10.1145/966789.966804

Olsson, N. O. E. (2006). Management of flexibility in projects. *International Journal of Project Management*, *24*(1), 66–74. doi:10.1016/j.ijproman.2005.06.010

Omran, M., Engelbrecht, A. P., & Salman, A. (2005). Differential evolution methods for unsupervised image classification. In *Proceedings of the Seventh Conference on Evolutionary Computation (CEC-2005)* (Vol. 2, pp. 966-973).

Orgun, B., & Vu, J. (2006). HL7 ontology and mobile agents for interoperability in heterogeneous medical information systems. *Computers in Biology and Medicine*, *36*(7-8), 817–836. doi:10.1016/j.compbiomed.2005.04.010

Osterlind, F., Pramsten, E., Roberthson, D., Eriksson, J., Finne, N., & Voigt, T. (2007). Integrating building automation systems and wireless sensor networks. In *Proceedings of the 12th IEEE International Conference on Emerging Technologies and Factory Automation* (pp. 1376-1379).

Paradiso, R. (2003, April). Wearable health care system for vital signs monitoring. In *Proceedings of the 4th IEEE International Conference on Information Technology Applications in Biomedicine*, Birmingham, UK (pp. 283-286).

Parenti, C. (2003). *The soft cage: Surveillance in America from slavery to the war on terror* (1st ed.). New York, NY: Basic Books.

Pareto, V. (1896). *Cours d'economie politique, Vol. I and II.* Lausanne, Switzerland: F. Rouge.

Park, S., & Jayaraman, S. (2003). Enhancing the quality of life through wearable technology. *IEEE Engineering in Medicine and Biology Magazine, 22*(3), 41–48. doi:10.1109/MEMB.2003.1213625

Parker, M., & Ryan, J. (1996). Finding the minimum weight IIS cover of an infeasible system of linear inequalities. *Annals of Mathematics and Artificial Intelligence, 17*(1-2), 107–126. doi:10.1007/BF02284626

Patel, A. (2010). Concept of Mobile Agent-based Electronic Marketplace – Safety Measures. In Lee, I. (Ed.), *Encyclopedia of E-Business Development and Management in the Digital Economy* (pp. 252–264). Hershey, PA: Business Science Reference.

Patel, A., Qi, W., & Wills, C. (2010). A Review and Future Research Directions of Secure and Trustworthy Mobile Agent-based E-marketplace Systems. *Journal of Information Management and Computer Security, 18*(3), 144–161. doi:10.1108/09685221011064681

Pedrajas, N. G. (2003). COVNET: A Cooperative Coevolutionary Model for Evolving Artificial Neural Networks. *IEEE Transactions on Neural Networks, 14*(3), 575–596. doi:10.1109/TNN.2003.810618

Pedrajas, N. G. (2009). Supervised projection approach for boosting classifiers. *Pattern Recognition, 42*, 1742–1760. doi:10.1016/j.patcog.2008.12.023

Pedrajas, N. G., & Fyne, C. (2008). Construction of classifier ensembles by means of artificial immune systems. *Journal of Heuristics, 14*, 285–310. doi:10.1007/s10732-007-9036-0

Perry, R. W. (2007). What is a disaster? In H. A. Rodrıguez, E. L. Quarantelli, & R. Dynes (Eds.), *Handbook of disaster research* (1st ed., pp. 1-16). New York, NY: Springer Science+Business Media.

Perusco, L., & Michael, K. (2007). Control, trust, privacy, and security: Evaluating location-based services. *IEEE Technology and Society Magazine, 26*, 4–16. doi:10.1109/MTAS.2007.335564

Perusco, L., Michael, K., & Michael, M. G. (2006, October 11-13). *Location-based services and the privacy-security dichotomy.* Paper presented at the Third International Conference on Mobile Computing and Ubiquitous Networking, London, UK.

Pervan, G. (1998). How chief executive officers in large organizations view the management of their information systems. *Journal of Information Technology, 13*(2), 95–109. doi:10.1080/026839698344882

Phillippi, M. (2008). An effective SME disaster recovery strategy for branch offices. *Computer Technology Review*. Retrieved February 15, 2010, from http://www.thefreelibrary.com/An+effective+SME+disaster+recovery+strategy+for+branch+offices.-a0168214596

Phongpaibul, M., & Boehm, B. (2005). Improving Quality through Software Process Improvement in Thailand: Initial Analysis. In *Proceedings of the ICSE 2005 Workshop on Software Quality* (pp. 23-28).

Picado Muiño, D. (2010). The (probabilistic) logical content of CADIAG-2. In J. Filipe, A. Fred, & B. Sharp (Eds.), *Second International Conference on Agents and Artificial Intelligence: Vol. 1. Artificial Intelligence,* Valencia, Spain (pp. 28-35).

Pokorny, J. (2004). Web searching and information retrieval. *Computing in Science & Engineering, 6*(4), 43–48. doi:10.1109/MCSE.2004.24

Porter, J. (2008). *Designing for the Social Web.* Berkeley, CA: New Riders.

Potter, M. A. (1997). *The design and analysis of a computational model of cooperative coevolution.* Unpublished doctoral dissertation, George Mason University, Fairfax, VA.

Pour, G. (1998). Moving toward Component-Based Software Development Approach. In *Proceedings of the IEEE Conference on Technology of Object-Oriented Languages and Systems* (pp. 296-300).

Premier promises mobile phone terrorism alert. (2007, February 26). *The Australian.*

Project Management Institute (PMI). (2008). *A Guide to the Project Management Body of Knowledge (PMBOK® Guide)* (4th ed.). Retrieved from http://www.pmi.org/PMBOK-Guide-and-Standards/Standards-Library-of-PMI-Global-Standards.aspx

Pura, M. (2005). Linking perceived value and loyalty in location-based mobile services. *Managing Service Quality, 15*(6), 509–538. doi:10.1108/09604520510634005

Qin, A. K., & Suganthan, P. N. (2005). Self-adaptive differential evolution algorithm for numerical optimization. In *Proceedings of the IEEE Conference on Evolutionary Computation, 2,* 1785–1791. doi:10.1109/CEC.2005.1554904

Qu, R., & Burke, E. K. (2009). Hybridizations within a graph-based hyper-heuristic framework for university timetabling problems. *The Journal of the Operational Research Society, 60*(9), 1273–1285. doi:.doi:10.1057/jors.2008.102

Quarantelli, E. L. (1986). What should we study? Questions and suggestions for researchers about the concept of disasters. *International Journal of Mass Emergencies and Disasters, 5*(1), 7–32.

Ralegaonkar, R., & Gupta, R. (2010). Review of intelligent building construction: A passive solar architecture approach. *Renewable & Sustainable Energy Reviews, 14*(8), 2238–2242. doi:10.1016/j.rser.2010.04.016

Rarick, R., Simon, D., Villaseca, F. E., & Vyakaranam, B. (2009). Biogeography-based optimization and the solution of the power flow problem. In *Proceedings of the IEEE Conference on Systems, Man, and Cybernetics,* San Antonio, TX (pp. 1029-1034).

Reina, A. M., Toress, J., & Toro, M. (2004). Towards developing generic solutions with aspects. In *Proceedings of the Workshop in Aspect Oriented Modeling in Conjunction with the UML 2004 Conference.*

Reiter, R. (1987). A theory of diagnosis from first principles. *Artificial Intelligence, 32,* 57–95. doi:10.1016/0004-3702(87)90062-2

Remde, S., Cowling, P. I., Dahal, K. P., & Colledge, N. (2006). Exact/heuristic hybrids using rVNS and hyperheuristics for workforce scheduling. In C. Cotta et al. (Eds.), *Evolutionary computation in combinatorial optimization* (LNCS 4446, pp. 188-197).

Remde, S., Dahal, K. P., Cowling, P. I., & Colledge, N. (2009). Binary exponential back off for tabu tenure in hyperheuristics. In C. Cotta et al. (Eds.), *Evolutionary computation in combinatorial optimization* (LNCS 5482, pp. 109-120).

Ren, Z., Jiang, H., Xuan, J., & Luo, Z. (2010). Ant based hyper heuristics with space reduction: A case study of the p-Median problem. In R. Schaefer et al. (Eds.), *Proceedings of the Parallel Problem Solving from Nature Conference (PPSN XI)* (LNCS 6238, pp. 546-555).

Resende, M. G. C., & Ribeiro, C. C. (2003). Greedy random adaptive search procedures. In Glover, F., & Konchenberger, G. (Eds.), *Handbook of metaheuristics* (pp. 219–251). New York, NY: Kluwer Academic Publishers.

Reuer, J., & Leiblein, M. J. (2000). Downside risk implications of multinationality and international joint ventures. *Academy of Management Journal, 43*(22), 203–214. doi:10.2307/1556377

Rivera, A. J., Rojas, I., Ortega, J., & del Jesus, M. J. (2007). A new hybrid methodology for cooperative-coevolutionary optimization of radial basis function networks. *Soft Computing, 11,* 655–668. doi:10.1007/s00500-006-0128-9

Roach, S. S. (1987). *America's technology dilemma: A profile of the information economy.* San Mateo, CA: Morgan Stanley.

Robertson, G. G., Mackinlay, J. D., & Card, S. K. (1991). Cone trees: animated 3d visualizations of hierarchical information. In *CHI '91: Proceedings of the SIGCHI Conference on Human factors in computing systems* (pp. 189-194). New York, NY: ACM Press.

Robinson, G. (2009). *Warning: Doubts over Sydney's alarm system.* Retrieved March 31, 2009, from http://www.smh.com.au/national/warning-doubts-over-sydneys-alarm-system-20090331-9hmg.html

Rodrigues, N. F., & Barbosa, L. S. (2005). Component Identification through Program Slicing. In *Proceedings of the Formal Aspects of Component Software Conference (FACS 2005)* (pp. 291-304).

Rosenblum, M. (2009). *The impact of virtualization on modern computing environments.* Virginia Technological University Distinguished Lecture Series. Retrieved from http://www.cs.vt.edu/DistinguishedLectures/MendelRosenblum

Rosenthal, U. (1998). Future disasters, future definitions. In Quarantelli, E. L. (Ed.), *What is a disaster? A dozen perspectives on the question* (1st ed., pp. 147–160). New York, NY: Routledge.

Rosin, C., & Belew, R. (1996). New Methods for Competitive Coevolution. *Evolutionary Computation*, *5*, 1–29. doi:10.1162/evco.1997.5.1.1

Ross, P., Marin-Blazquez, J. G., Schulenburg, S., & Hart, E. (2003). Learning a procedure that can solve hard bin-packing problems: A new GA-Based approach to hyper-heuristics. In E. Cantú-Paz et al. (Eds.), *Proceedings of the Genetic and Evolutionary Computation Conference (GECCO 2003)* (LNCS 2724, pp. 1295-1306).

Roussey, C., Corcho, O., & Blázquez, L. M. V. (2009). A catalogue of OWL ontology antipatterns. In *Proceedings of the Fifth International Conference on Knowledge Capture* (pp. 205-206). New York: ACM Press.

Roy, A. D. (1952). Safety first and the holding of assets. *Econometrica: Journal of the Econometric Society*, *20*(3), 431–449. doi:10.2307/1907413

Ruscio, D., Cicchetti, A., & Salle, A. (2007). Software customization in model driven development of web applications. In *Proceedings of the ACM Symposium on Applied Computing* (pp. 1025-1030).

Safigan, C. (2008). Disaster recovery for the masses – The role of OS-level server virtualization in disaster recovery. *Computer Technology Review*. Retrieved July 7, 2010, from http://www.wwpi.com/index.php?option=com_content&task=view&id=1151&Itemid=64

Salo, O., & Abrahamsson, P. (2008). Agile methods in European embedded software development organisations: a survey on the actual use and usefulness of Extreme Programming and Scrum. *IET Software*, *2*(1), 58–64. doi:10.1049/iet-sen:20070038

Samsioe, J., & Samsioe, A. (2002). Introduction to location based services: Markets and technologies. In Reichwald, R. (Ed.), *Mobile Kommunikation: Wertschöpfung, Technologien, neue Dienste* (pp. 417–438). Wiesbaden, Germany: Gabler. doi:10.1007/978-3-322-90695-3_25

Sandars, J., & Schroter, S. (2007). Web 2.0 technologies for undergraduate and postgraduate medical education: an online survey. *Postgraduate Medical Journal*, *83*, 759–762. doi:10.1136/pgmj.2007.063123

Sanders, P. (2009). *The CB way forward*. Retrieved October 18, 2009, from http://www.chorist.eu/index.php?page=1&sel=1

Sandhu, R., Ferraiolo, D., & Kuhn, R. (2000). The NIST model for role-based access control: Towards a unified standard. In *Proceedings of the Fifth ACM Workshop on Role-Based Access Control* (pp. 47-63).

Saporta, G., & Youness, G. (2001). Concordance e-ntre deux partitions: quelques propositions et expériences. In *Proceedings of the Actes des 8es rencontres de la SFC*, Pointe-à-Pitre, Guadeloupe.

Sattler, U., Schneider, T., & Zakharyaschev, M. (2009). Which kind of module should I extract? In B.C. Grau, I. Horrocks, B. Motik, & U. Sattler (Eds.), *Proceedings of the Twenty-second International Workshop on Description Logics* (Vol. 477). CEUR

Sazonov, E., Janoyan, K., & Jha, R. (2004). Wireless intelligent sensor network for autonomous structural health monitoring. In *Proceedings of the International Society for Optical Engineering Conference* (pp. 305-314).

Schaffer, J. D. (1985). Multiobjective optimization using nondominated sorting in genetic algorithms. In *Proceedings of the 1st International Conference on Genetic Algorithms and Their Applications* (pp. 160-168).

Schein, E. H. (1992). *Organizational culture and leadership*. San Francisco, CA: Jossey-Bass.

Schleyer, T., Spallek, H., Butler, B. S., Subramanian, S., Weiss, D., & Poythress, M. S. (2008). Facebook for Scientists: Requirements and Services for Optimizing How Scientific Collaborations Are Established. *Journal of Medical Internet Research*, *10*(3), e24. doi:10.2196/jmir.1047

Schmidt-Schau, M., & Smolka, G. (1991). Attributive concept descriptions with complements. *Artificial Intelligence*, *48*(1), 1–26. doi:10.1016/0004-3702(91)90078-X

Schneier, B. (2008). The myth of the 'transparent society'. *Wired Magazine*. Retrieved from http://www.wired.com/politics/security/commentary/securitymatters/2008/03/securitymatters_0306

Schulz, M. (2009). Emergency services admit SMS bushfire alerts not foolproof. *Herald Sun*. Retrieved March 3, 2009, from http://www.heraldsun.com.au/news/more-news/emergency-services-admit-sms-bushfire-alerts-not-foolproof/story-e6frf7kx-1111119016715

Schulz, S., Stenzhorn, H., Boeker, M., & Smith, B. (2009). Strengths and limitations of formal ontologies in the biomedical domain. *Electronic Journal of Communication Information & Innovation in Heath, 3*(1), 31–45.

Schwaber, K. (2004). *Agile Project Management with Scrum*. Microsoft Press.

Scott, D., Kwan, M., & Cheong, W. (2003). Web-based construction information management systems. *The Australian Journal of Construction Economics and Building, 3*(1), 43–52.

Seeman, N. (2008). Web 2.0 and chronic illness: New Horizons, New Opportunities. *Healthcare Quarterly (Toronto, Ont.), 11*(1), 104–110.

Seo, K.-Y., Oh, S.-W., Suh, S.-H., & Park, G.-K. (2007). Intelligent steering control system based on voice instructions. *International Journal of Control. Automation and Systems, 5*(5), 539–546.

Setten, W. v., & Sanders, P. (2009). *Citizen alert with cell broadcasting: The technology, the standards and the way forward*. Retrieved October 18, 2009, from http://www.chorist.eu/index.php?page=1&sel=1

Shahmohammadia, G. R., Jalilia, S., & Hasheminejada, S. M. H. (2010). Identification of System Software Components Using Clustering Approach. *Journal of Object Technology, 9*(6), 77–98. doi:10.5381/jot.2010.9.6.a4

Shiode, N., Li, C., Batty, M., Longley, P., & Maguire, D. (2002). *The impact and penetration of location-based services* (pp. 1–16). London, UK: Centre for Advanced Spatial Analysis, University College London.

Shiyou, Y., & Ni, G. (1998). An universal tabu search algorithm for global optimization of multimodal functions with continuous variables in electromagnetics. *IEEE Transactions on Magnetics, 34*, 2901–2904. doi:10.1109/20.717676

Shneiderman, B. (1992). Tree visualization with treemaps: A 2-D space-filling approach. *ACM Transactions on Graphics, 11*, 92–99. doi:10.1145/102377.115768

Shortliffe, E. H. (1976). *Computer-based medical consultations, MYCIN*. Amsterdam, The Netherlands: Elsevier.

Shukla, A., & Tiwari, R. (Eds.). (2010). *Biomedical Engineering and Information Systems: Technologies, Tools and Applications*. Hershey, PA: IGI Global Publishers.

Shukla, A., & Tiwari, R. (Eds.). (2010). *Intelligent Medical technologies and Biomedical Engineering: Tools and Applications*. Hershey, PA: IGI Global Publishers.

Shukla, A., Tiwari, R., & Kala, R. (2010). *Real Life Applications of Soft Computing*. Boca Raton, FL: CRC Press. doi:10.1201/EBK1439822876

Shukla, A., Tiwari, R., & Kala, R. (2010). *Towards Hybrid and Adaptive Computing: A Perspective*. Berlin: Springer.

Shukla, A., Tiwari, R., & Kaur, P. (2009). Intelligent System for the Diagnosis of Epilepsy. In *Proceedings of the IEEE World Congress on Computer Science and Information Engineering*, Los Angeles, CA (pp. 755-758). Washington, DC: IEEE.

Shukla, A., Tiwari, R., Kaur, P., & Janghel, R. R. (2009). Diagnosis of Thyroid Disorders using Artificial Neural Networks. In *Proceedings of the IEEE International Advanced Computing Conference*, Patiala, India (pp. 1016-1020). Washington, DC: IEEE.

Si, Y., Gotman, J., Pasupathy, A., Flanagan, D., Rosenblatt, B., & Gottesman, R. (1998). An expert system for EEG monitoring in the pediatric intensive care unit. *Electroencephalography and Clinical Neurophysiology, 106*(6), 488–500. doi:10.1016/S0013-4694(97)00154-5

Sicilia, J. J., Sicilia, M. A., Sánchez-Alonso, S., García-Barriocana, E., & Pontikaki, M. (2009). Knowledge Representation Issues in Ontology-based Clinical Knowledge Management Systems. *International Journal of Technology Management, 47*(1-3), 191–206. doi:10.1504/IJTM.2009.024122

Simmonds, D. M. (2008). Aspect-oriented Approaches to Model Driven Engineering. In *Proceedings of the International Conference on Software Research and Practice*, Las Vegas, NV.

Simmonds, D. M., Reddy, Y. R., Song, E., & Grant, E. (2009). A Comparison of Aspect-Oriented Approaches to Model Driven Engineering. In *Proceedings of the Conference on Software Engineering Research and Practice* (pp. 327-333).

Simmonds, D. M., Solberg, A., Reddy, R., France, R., & Ghosh, S. (2005). An Aspect Oriented Model Driven Framework. In *Proceedings of the 9th IEEE International EDOC Enterprise Computing Conference* (pp. 119-130)

Simon, D. (2008). Biogeography-Based optimization. *IEEE Transactions on Evolutionary Computation, 12*(6), 702–713. doi:10.1109/TEVC.2008.919004

Simon, D. (2008). *The Matlab code of biogeography-based optimization*. Retrieved from http://academic.csuohio.edu/simond/bbo/

Simon, D. (2009). A Probabilistic analysis of a simplified biogeography-based optimization algorithm. *Evolutionary Computation*, 1–22.

Simon, D., Ergezer, M., & Du, D. W. (2009). Population distributions in biogeography-based optimization algorithms with elitism. In *Proceedings of the IEEE Conference on Systems, Man, and Cybernetics,* San Antonio, TX (pp. 1017-1022).

Simon, L. (2006). Managing creative projects: An empirical synthesis of activities. *International Journal of Project Management, 24*(2), 116–126. doi:10.1016/j.ijproman.2005.09.002

Smith, B. (2003). Ontology: philosophical and computational. In Floridi, L. (Ed.), *The blackwell guide to the philosophy of computing and information*. Oxford, UK: Blackwell Publishers.

Smith, B., Ashburner, M., Rosse, C., Bard, J., Bug, W., & Ceusters, W. (2007). The OBO Foundry: coordinated evolution of ontologies to support biomedical data integration. *Nature Biotechnology, 25*(11), 1251–1255. doi:10.1038/nbt1346

Song, J. D., Yang, B. S., Choi, B. K., & Kim, H. J. (2005). Optimum design of short journal bearings by enhanced artificial life optimization algorithm. *Tribology International, 38*, 403–412. doi:10.1016/j.triboint.2003.10.008

Sortino, F. A., & Price, L. N. (1994). Performance measurement in a downside risk framework. *Journal of Investing, 3*(3), 59–64. doi:10.3905/joi.3.3.59

Spiekermann, S. (2004). General aspects of location-based services. In J. Schiller & A. Voisard (Eds.), *Location-based services* (1 ed., pp. 9-26). San Francisco, CA: Elsevier.

Srinivas, N., & Deb, K. (1995). Multiobjective optimization using nondominated sorting in genetic algorithms. *Evolutionary Computation, 2*(3), 221–248. doi:10.1162/evco.1994.2.3.221

Stanley, K. O., & Miikkulainen, R. (2004). Competitive Coevolution through Evolutionary Complexification. *Journal of Artificial Intelligence Research, 21*, 63–100.

Stenzhorn, H., Schulz, S., Boeker, M., & Smith, B. (2008). Adapting Clinical Ontologies in Real-World Environments. *Journal of Universal Computer Science, 14*(22), 3767–3780.

Stephens, D. (2003). Protecting records in the face of chaos, calamity, and cataclysm. *The Information Management Journal*, 33-40.

Stillwell, M. (2010). Dynamic fractional resource scheduling for cluster platforms. In *Proceedings of the IEEE International Symposium on Parallel and Distributed Processing* (pp. 1-4).

Stojanović, D., Djordjevic-Kajan, S., Papadopoulos, A. N., & Nanopoulos, A. (2007). Monitoring and tracking moving objects in mobile environments. In Taniar, D. (Ed.), *Encyclopedia of mobile computing and commerce* (1st ed., pp. 660–665). London, UK: Information Science Reference. doi:10.4018/978-1-59904-002-8.ch110

Stone, R. W., Good, D. J., & Baker-Eveleth, L. (2007). The impact of information technology on individual and firm marketing performance. *Behaviour & Information Technology, 26*(6), 465–482. doi:10.1080/01449290600571610

Storn, R., & Price, K. (1995). *Differential Evolution-a simple and efficient adaptive scheme for global optimization over continuous spaces* (Tech. Rep. No. 12). Berkeley, CA: International Computer Science Institute.

Storn, R., & Price, K. (1997). A simple and efficient heuristic for global optimization over continuous spaces. *Journal of Global Optimization, 11*(4), 341–359. doi:10.1023/A:1008202821328

Stratopoulis, T., & Dehning, B. (2000). Does successful investment in information technology solve the productivity paradox? *Information & Management, 38*(2), 103–117. doi:10.1016/S0378-7206(00)00058-6

Studer, R., Benjamins, V. R., & Fensel, D. (1998). Knowledge engineering: Principles and methods. *Data & Knowledge Engineering, 25*(1-2), 161–197. doi:10.1016/S0169-023X(97)00056-6

Sung, M., Marci, C., & Pentland, A. (2005). Wearable feedback systems for rehabilitation. *Journal of Neuroengineering and Rehabilitation*, *2*, 17. doi:10.1186/1743-0003-2-17

Supreme Council of Information and Communication Technology. (2008). *Policy Intelligence Source Book*. Tehran, Iran: Iranian Information and Documentation Center.

Suresh, K., Kundu, D., Ghosh, S., Das, S., Abraham, A., & Han, S. Y. (2009). Multi-Objective Differential Evolution for Automatic Clustering with Application to Micro-Array Data Analysis. *Sensors (Basel, Switzerland)*, *9*, 3981–4004. doi:10.3390/s90503981

Surowiecki, K. (2004). *The wisdom of crowds*. New York: Doubleday.

Taghavi, M., Patel, A., & Taghavi, H. (2011). Web Based Project Management System for Development of ICT Project Outsourced by Iranian Government. In *Proceedings of the 2011 IEEE International Conference on Open Systems (ICOS2011)*, Langkawi, Malaysia (pp. 273-278).

Tan, L. X., & Guo, L. (2009). Quantum and biogeography based optimization for a class of combinatorial optimization. In *Proceedings of the 2009 World Summit on Genetic and Evolutionary Computation* (pp. 969-972).

Tan, Y.-H., & Thoen, W. (2001). Toward a generic model of trust for electronic commerce. *International Journal of Electronic Commerce*, *5*(2), 61–74.

Tanaka, M. (1995). GA-based decision support system for multi-criteria optimization. In *Proceedings of the International Conference on Systems, Man and Cybernetics* (Vol. 2, pp. 1556-1561).

Taxen, L. (2006). An integration centric approach for the coordination of distributed software development projects. *Information and Software Technology*, *48*(9), 767–780. doi:10.1016/j.infsof.2006.01.007

Telemedicine Project. (1998). *Mobile telemedicine testbed for national information infrastructure*.

Templeman, D., & Bergin, A. (2008). *Taking a punch: Building a more resilient Australia*. Retrieved February 2, 2009, from http://www.aspi.org.au/publications/publication_details.aspx?ContentID=165

Terashima-Marin, H., Moran-Saavedra, A., & Ross, P. (2005). Forming hyper-heuristics with GAs when solving 2D-regular cutting stock problems. In *Proceedings of the IEEE Conference on Evolutionary Computation* (pp. 1104-1110). Washington, DC: IEEE Computer Society.

The Australian Communications and Media Authority. (2004). *Location location location: The future use of location information to enhance the handling of emergency mobile phone calls*. Retrieved October 21, 2007, from http://acma.gov.au/webwr/consumer_info/location.pdf

The Australian Communications and Media Authority. (2009). *Australia's emergency call service in a changing environment*. Retrieved September 25, 2009, from http://www.acma.gov.au/webwr/_assets/main/lib311250/future_of_emergency_call_svces.pdf

The Australian Early Warning Network. (2009). *Townsville city council signs up to the early warning network*. Retrieved December 7, 2009, from http://www.ewn.com.au/media/townsville_city_council.aspx

The Australian Government: Attorney General's Department. (2008). *Privacy Act 1988: Act No.119 of 1988 as amended*. Retrieved August 2, 2008, from http://www.comlaw.gov.au/ComLaw/Legislation/ActCompilation1.nsf/0/63C00ADD09B982ECCA257490002B9D57/$file/Privacy1988_WD02HYP.pdf

The Australian Government: Attorney General's Department. (2009). *Rudd Government Implements COAG agreement on telephone-based emergency warning systems (Joint Media Release)*. Retrieved August 2, 2009, from http://www.ag.gov.au/www/ministers/mcclelland.nsf/Page/MediaReleases_2009_FirstQuarter_23February2009-RuddGovernmentImplementsCOAGAgreementonTelephone-BasedEmergencyWarningSystems

The Australian Government: Department of Broadband Communications and the Digital Economy. (2009). *Telecommunications amendment (Integrated Public Number Database) Bill 2009: Explanatory memorandum*. Retrieved August 6, 2009, from http://parlinfo.aph.gov.au/parlInfo/download/legislation/ems/r4062_ems_d2937505-3da9-4059-b9cb-e382e891dd23/upload_word/TelAm(IPND)_EM.doc;fileType=application%2Fmsword

The Australian Government: Department of Transport and Regional Services. (2004). *Natural disasters in Australia: Reforming mitigation, relief and recovery arrangements*. Retrieved February 18, 2009, from http://www.ema.gov.au/www/emaweb/rwpattach.nsf/VAP/(99292794923AE8E7CBABC6FB71541EE1)~Natural+Disasters+in+Australia+-+Review.pdf/$file/Natural+Disasters+in+Australia+-+Review.pdf

The Cellular Emergency Alert Systems Association. (2002). *Handset requirements specification: Reaching millions in a matter of seconds*. Retrieved April 2, 2007, from http://www.ceasa-int.org/library/Handset_Requirements_Specification.pdf

The European Commission. (2009). *The CHORIST Project: Integrating communications for enhanced environmental risk management and citizens safety*. Retrieved November 7, 2009, from http://www.chorist.eu/index.php?page=1&sel=1

The European Telecommunications Standards Institute. (2003). *Requirements for communication of citizens with authorities/organizations in case of distress (Emergency call handling)*. Retrieved May 20, 2007, from http://etsi.org/WebSite/homepage.aspx

The European Telecommunications Standards Institute. (2006). *Analysis of the short message service and cell broadcast service for emergency messaging applications; emergency messaging; SMS and CBS*. Retrieved May 10, 2007, from http://etsi.org/WebSite/homepage.aspx

The European Telecommunications Standards Institute. (2006). *Emergency communications (EMTEL): Requirements for communications from authorities/organizations to individuals, groups or the general public during emergencies*. Retrieved May 20, 2007, from http://etsi.org/WebSite/homepage.aspx

The European Telecommunications Standards Institute. (2010). *Study for requirements for a Public Warning System (PWS) service*. Retrieved February 10, 2010, from http://webstats.3gpp.org/ftp/Specs/html-info/22968.htm

The Federal Communications Commission. (2005). *Review of the emergency alert system*. Retrieved April 13, 2008, from http://www.fcc.gov/eb/Orders/2005/FCC-05-191A1.html

The International Telecommunications Union. (2007). *Compendium of ITU'S work on emergency telecommunications*. Geneva, Switzerland: The United Nations Agency for Information and Communication Technologies.

The Minister for Police and Emergency Services. (2005). *First calls made as part of early warning trial*. Retrieved June 4, 2007, from http://www.legislation.vic.gov.au/domino/Web_Notes/newmedia.nsf/35504bc71d3adebcca256cfc0082c2b8/4ae0fe91bdeb3e8aca25704d000729b0!OpenDocument

The United States Department of Homeland Security. (2008). *National emergency communications plan*. Retrieved October 6, 2009, from http://www.dhs.gov/xlibrary/assets/national_emergency_communications_plan.pdf

The Victorian Bushfires Royal Commission. (2009). *Interim report*. Victoria, Australia: Author.

The Victorian Department of Treasury and Finance. (2009). *Request for Information (RFI) for: Location based identification of active mobile handsets for emergency notification purposes* (RFI Number: SS-06-2009). Retrieved November 19, 2009, from https://www.tenders.vic.gov.au/tenders/tender/display/tender-details.do?id=87&action=display-tender-details&returnUrl=%2Ftender%2Fsearch%2Ftender-search.do%3Faction%3Dadvanced-tender-search-closed-tender

Theraulaz, G., Bonabeau, E., Sauwens, C., Deneubourg, J.-L., Lioni, A., & Libert, F. (2001). Model of droplet formation and dynamics in the argentine ant (linepithema humile mayr). *Bulletin of Mathematical Biology*, *63*, 1079–1093. doi:10.1006/bulm.2001.0260

Thimm, M. (2009). Measuring inconsistency in probabilistic knowledge bases. In *Proceedings of the Twenty-fifth Conference on Uncertainty in Artificial Intelligence* (pp. 530-537). Corvallis, OR: AUAI Press.

Togt, R., Beinat, E., Zlatanova, S., & Scholten, H. (2005). Location interoperability services for medical emergency operations during disasters. In P. v. Oosterom, S. Zlatanova, & E. M. Fendel (Eds.), *Geo-information for disaster management* (pp. 1127-1141). Berlin, Germany: Springer-Verlag.

Toigo, J. W. (1996). *Disaster recovery planning: For computers and communication resources*. New York, NY: John Wiley & Sons.

Toigo, J. W. (2002). *Disaster recovery planning: Preparing for the unthinkable* (3rd ed.). Upper Saddle River, NJ: Prentice Hall.

Tolnai, A. (2010). A virtualized environment security (VES) model for a secure virtualized environment. In *Proceedings of the International Conference for Internet Technology and Secured Transactions* (pp. 1-6).

Tsalgatidou, A., Veijalainen, J., Markkula, J., Katasonov, A., & Hadjiefthymiades, S. (2003). *Mobile e-commerce and location-based services: Technology and requirements.* Paper presented at the 9th Scandinavian Research Conference on Geographical Information Sciences, Espoo, Finland.

Tversky, A., & Kahneman, D. (1992). Advances in prospect theory: Cumulative representation of uncertainty. *Journal of Risk and Uncertainty*, *5*, 297–323. doi:10.1007/BF00122574

U.S. Department of Labor, Bureau of Labor Statics (BLS). (2009). *Nonfatal occupational injuries and illnesses from the Survey of Occupational Injuries and Illnesses.* Retrieved from http://www.bls.gov/iif/

Uhlirz, M. (2007). A market and user view on LBS. In Gartner, G., Cartwright, W., & Peterson, M. P. (Eds.), *Location based services and telecartography* (1st ed., pp. 47–58). Berlin, Germany: Springer-Verlag. doi:10.1007/978-3-540-36728-4_4

United Nations News Centre. (2010). *Earthquakes the deadliest of all disasters during past decade.* Retrieved January 29, 2010, from http://www.un.org/apps/news/printnews.asp?nid=33613

Van Laerhoven, K., Lo, B. P. L., Ng, J. W. P., Thiemjarus, S., King, R., & Kwan, S. … Yang, G. (2004, September). Medical healthcare monitoring with wearable and implantable sensors. In *Proceedings of the 3rd International Workshop on Ubiquitous Computing for Pervasive Healthcare Applications*, Nottingham, UK.

Vassis, D. (2008). *The Pamvotis simulator.* Retrieved from http://www.pamvotis.org

Vassis, D., Belsis, P., Skourlas, C., & Gritzalis, S. (2009). End to end secure communication in ad-hoc assistive medical environments using secure paths. In *Proceedings of the 1st Workshop on Privacy and Security in Pervasive e-Health and Assistive Environments, in conjunction with the 2nd International Conference on Pervasive Technologies related to Assistive Environments* (article 70).

Vassis, D., Belsis, P., Skourlas, C., & Pantziou, G. (2008). A pervasive architectural framework for providing remote medical treatment. In *Proceedings of the 1st International Conference on Pervasive Technologies Related to Assistive Environments* (Vol. 282, article 23).

Veld, C., & Veld-Merkoulova, Y. V. (2008). The risk perceptions of individual investors. *Journal of Economic Psychology*, *29*(2), 226–252. doi:10.1016/j.joep.2007.07.001

Venturini, G., Labroche, N., & Guinot, C. (2004). Fast unsupervised clustering with artificial ants. In *Proceedings of the Parallel Problem Solving from Nature (PPSN VIII) Conference,* Birmingham, UK (pp. 1143-1152).

Victorian State Parliamentary Offices. (2003). *Watching brief on the war on terrorism: Submission by the State of Victoria to the Joint Standing Committee on Foreign Affairs, Defence and Trade Hearing on Australia's Counter Terrorism Capabilities.* Retrieved January 18, 2009, from http://www.aph.gov.au/House/committee/jfadt/terrorism/subs/sub13.pdf

Vossen, G., Lytras, M., & Koudas, N. (2007). Editorial: Revisiting the (Machine) Semantic Web: The Missing Layers for the Human Semantic Web. *IEEE Transactions on Knowledge and Data Engineering*, *19*(2), 145–148. doi:10.1109/TKDE.2007.30

W3C. (2002). *Extensible Markup Language.* Retrieved June 5, 2011, from http://www.w3c.org/XML/

W3C. (2004). *Web Services Architecture.* Retrieved June 5, 2011, from http://www.w3.org/TR/2004/NOTE-ws-arch-20040211/

Wallace, A. (2005). *The Geographical distribution of animals.* Boston, MA: Adamant Media Corporation.

Walsham, G. (2001). *Globalization and ICTs: Working across cultures.* Cambridge, UK: University of Cambridge.

Wang, S., & Xu, X. (2005). Models for describing the Simplified building model for transient thermal performance estimation using GA-based parameter identification. *International Journal of Thermal Sciences*, *45*(4), 419–432. doi:10.1016/j.ijthermalsci.2005.06.009

Wang, Z., Xu, X., & Zhan, D. (2005). A Survey of Business Component Identification Methods and Related Techniques. *International Journal of Information Technology*, *2*, 229–238.

Weibull, J. W. (1995). *Evolutionary Game Theory*. Cambridge, MA: MIT Press.

Weiss, D., Kramer, I., Treu, G., & Kupper, A. (2006). Zone services - An approach for location-based data collection. In *Proceedings of the 8th IEEE International Conference on E-Commerce Technology and the 3rd IEEE International Conference on Enterprise Computing, E-Commerce, and E-Services* (p. 79).

Wellheiser, J., & Scott, J. (2002). *An ounce of prevention: Integrated disaster planning for archives, libraries, and record centers* (2nd ed.). Lenexa, KS: Scarecrow Press.

White, D., & Fortune, J. (2002). Current practice in project management – an empirical study. *International Journal of Project Management*, *20*(1), 1–11. doi:10.1016/S0263-7863(00)00029-6

Wireless Medicenter. (2006). Retrieved from http://www.wirelessmedicenter.com/mc/glance.cfm

Wolberg, W. H., Mangasarian, O. L., & Aha, D. W. (1992). *UCI Machine Learning Repository*. Retrieved from http://www.ics.uci.edu/~mlearn/MLRepository.html

Wood, T., Cecchet, E., Ramakrishnan, K. K., Shenoy, P., van der Merwe, J., & Venkataramani, A. (2010). Disaster recovery as a cloud service: Economic benefits and deployment challenges. In *Proceedings of the 2nd USENIX Conference on Hot Topics in Cloud Computing* (p. 8).

Wu, Y., & Offutt, J. (2003). Maintaining Evolving Component-Based Software with UML. In *Proceedings of the 7th IEEE European Conference on Software Maintenance and Reengineering* (pp. 133-142).

XACML. (2007). *XACML extensible access control markup language specification 2.0.* Organization for the Advancement of Structured Information Standards (OASIS). Retrieved June 10, 2010, from http://www.oasis-open.org

Xiao, J., Bai, Y.-F., & Yu, L. (2006). Overview of Fuzzy System Structure Identification. *Journal of Southwest Jiao Tong University*, *41*(2), 135–142.

Xu, W., Yin, B. L., & Li, Z. Y. (2003). Research on the business component design of enterprise information system. *Journal of Software*, *14*(7), 1213–1220.

Xue, F., Sanderson, A. C., & Graves, R. J. (2003). Pareto-based multi-objective differential evolution. In *Proceedings of the 2003 Conference on Evolutionary Computation (CEC'2003)* (Vol. 2, pp. 862-869).

Yang, B. S., & Lee, Y. H. (2000). Artificial life algorithm for function optimization. In *Proceedings of the 2000 ASME Design Engineering Technical Conference.*

Yang, B. S., Lee, Y. H., Choi, B. K., & Kim, H. J. (2001). Optimum design of short journal bearings by artificial life algorithm. *Tribology International*, *34*(7), 427–435. doi:10.1016/S0301-679X(01)00034-2

Yang, B. S., & Song, J. D. (2002). Development of an enhanced artificial life optimization algorithm and optimum design of short journal bearings. *Transactions of the Korean Society of Noise and Vibration Engineering*, *12*(6), 478–487. doi:10.5050/KSNVN.2002.12.6.478

Yang, J., & Peng, H. (2001). Decision support to the application of intelligent building technologies. *Renewable Energy*, *22*(1), 66–67. doi:10.1016/S0960-1481(00)00085-9

Yang, Z. Y., He, J., & Yao, X. (2008). Making a difference to differential evolution. In Michalewicz, Z., & Siarry, P. (Eds.), *Advances in Metaheuristics for Hard Optimization* (pp. 397–414). Heidelberg, Berlin: Springer-Verlag. doi:10.1007/978-3-540-72960-0_19

Yang, Z. Y., Tang, K., & Yao, X. (2007). Differential evolution for high-dimensional function optimization. In *Proceedings of the 2007 Conference on Evolutionary Computation* (pp. 3523-3530).

Yang, Z. Y., Tang, K., & Yao, X. (2008). Large scale evolutionary optimization using cooperative coevolution. *Information Sciences*, *178*, 2985–2999. doi:10.1016/j.ins.2008.02.017

Yao, X. (1993). A review of evolutionary artificial neural networks. *International Journal of Intelligent Systems*, *8*(4), 539–567. doi:10.1002/int.4550080406

Yao, X. (1997). A New Evolutionary System for Evolving Artificial Neural Networks. *IEEE Transactions on Neural Networks*, *8*(3), 694–713. doi:10.1109/72.572107

Yao, X. (1999). Evolving Artificial Neural Networks. *Proceedings of the IEEE*, *87*(9), 1423–1447. doi:10.1109/5.784219

Yao, X., Liu, Y., & Lin, G. (1999). Evolutionary programming made faster. *IEEE Transactions on Evolutionary Computation*, *3*, 82–102. doi:10.1109/4235.771163

Ying, H., & Sheppard, L. C. (1994). Regulating mean arterial pressure in postsurgical cardiac patients. A fuzzy logic system to control administration of sodium nitroprusside. *IEEE Engineering in Medicine and Biology Magazine*, *13*(5), 671–677. doi:10.1109/51.334628

Yu, J. (2006). CBR and ANFIS based Emergent Decision Support System of Intelligent Buildings. [Natural Science]. *Journal of Shenyang Jianzhu University*, *22*(2), 315–318.

Yu, Y., Yi, J.-Q., & Zhao, D.-B. (2008). Survey on Smart Spaces Research. *Computer Science*, *35*(8), 1–20.

Zadeh, L. (1965). Fuzzy sets. *Information and Control*, *8*, 338–353. doi:10.1016/S0019-9958(65)90241-X

Zadeh, L. (1975). Fuzzy logic and approximate reasoning. *Synthese*, *30*, 407–428. doi:10.1007/BF00485052

Zafeiris, V., Doulkeridis, C., Belsis, P., & Chalaris, I. (2005). *Agent-mediated knowledge management in multiple autonomous domains.* Paper presented at the Workshop on Agent Mediated Knowledge Management, Utrecht, The Netherlands.

Zhang, H., Li, H., & Tam, C. M. (2006). Particle swarm optimization for resource-constrained project scheduling. *International Journal of Project Management*, *24*, 83–92. doi:10.1016/j.ijproman.2005.06.006

Zhang, J., Chen, Y., Li, H., & Liu, G. (2009). Research on Aspect-Oriented Modeling in the Framework of MDA. In *Proceedings of the 2nd IEEE International Conference on Computer Science and Information Technology* (pp. 108-111).

Zhang, T., Ramakrishnan, R., & Livny, M. (1996). BIRCH: an efficient data clustering method for very large databases. In *Proceedings of the 1996 ACM SIGMOD International Conference on Management of Data* (pp. 103-114). New York, NY: ACM.

Zhang, W. (2009). On momentum and learning rate of the generalized ADLINE neural network for time varying system identification. In *Proceedings of the 6th International Symposium on Neural Networks* (pp. 1002-1013).

Zhang, Y. D., & Huang, S. B. (2005). On ant colony algorithm for solving multiobjective optimization problems. *Control and Decision*, *20*(2), 170–173.

Zheng, J. H. (2007). *Multi-Objective Evolutionary Algorithms and Their Applications.* Beijing, China: Science Press.

Zheng, W., & Fang, B. (2009). Structure-independent disaster recovery: Concept, architecture and implmentations. *Science in China Series F: Information Sciences*, *52*(5), 813–823. doi:10.1007/s11432-009-0095-8

Zhong, L.-S., & Song, Z.-H. (2008). Hierarchical Optimization Identification of LTI State-space Systems by Projected Gradient Search. *ACTA Automatica Sinica*, *34*(6), 711–715. doi:10.3724/SP.J.1004.2008.00711

Zimmermann, H. (1991). *Fuzzy Set Theory and its Applications.* Dordrecht, The Netherlands: Kluwer.

Zitzler, E., Laumanns, M., & Thiele, L. (2001). *SPEA2: Improving the Strength Pareto Evolutionary Algorithm* (Tech. Rep. No. 103). Zurich, Switzerland: Swiss Federal Institute of Technology.

About the Contributors

Mehdi Khosrow-Pour (DBA) received his Doctorate in Business Administration from the Nova Southeastern University (FL, USA). Dr. Khosrow-Pour taught undergraduate and graduate information system courses at the Pennsylvania State University – Harrisburg for 20 years where he was the chair of the Information Systems Department for 14 years. He is currently president and publisher of IGI Global, an international academic publishing house with headquarters in Hershey, PA (www.igi-global.com). He also serves as executive director of the Information Resources Management Association (IRMA) (www.irma-international.org) and executive director of the World Forgotten Children's Foundation (www.world-forgotten-children.org). He is the author/editor of over twenty books in information technology management. He is also the editor-in-chief of the *Information Resources Management Journal*, the *Journal of Cases on Information Technology*, the *Journal of Electronic Commerce in Organizations* and the *Journal of Information Technology Research* and has authored more than 50 articles published in various conference proceedings and journals.

* * *

Roba Abbas graduated with first class honours in Information and Communication Technology (majoring in Business Information Systems) from the University of Wollongong Australia in 2006, earning a place on the Faculty of Informatics Dean's Merit List, and finishing in the Top 5% in the Faculty. She is currently a PhD candidate and Research Assistant in the School of Information Systems and Technology at the University of Wollongong, working on an Australian Research Council (ARC)-funded project in the field of location-based services regulation. Ms Abbas has lecturing and tutoring experience in the Faculty of Informatics, and over five years industry experience in product management, corporate IT strategy, information architecture, consulting, and all aspects of web design and development.

Mutaz Al-Debei is an assistant professor at the University of Jordan, Department of Management Information Systems (MIS). He has also held posts at Brunel University – West London in the United Kingdom (UK) and Alahliyya University in Jordan. He is also a trainer for a number of professional certificates such as OCP for Oracle developer and Database Administrators (DBAs), MCSE, CCNA, Network+, Security+, and Credit Card Frauds. In addition to these technical training programs, Dr. Al-Debei is also a trainer of key business-related programs such as designing and managing innovations and technological artifacts as well as business model thinking for digital firms. Dr. Al-Debei has performed these training programs and given seminars in many local and global reputable training institutions, universities and conferences. Dr. Al-Debei also has about ten years of experience in the IT industry having worked in Jordan for the Royal Scientific Society and the Jordan National bank (Credit Cards Centre) as a network engineer and Database Administrator (DBA), respectively. Thereafter, he worked as an IT manager for Arab Radio and Television (ART) in Jordan Media City. Dr. Al-Debei is the founder of the V4 Business Model Ontology for designing and engineering technological artifacts. Even though it has been developed recently, this ontology has been adopted by researchers and practitioners given its perceived value and efficacy.

Ángel González Albo received his B. Sc. in Computer Science (2010) from the University of a Coruña, Spain. She has been a member of the Medical Computing and Radiological Diagnosis Center (IMEDIR Center) of the University of A Coruña since the year 2008. His main research interests include development of driver hardware devices, medical information systems and expert systems. She has participated in a project funded by the Department of Health Service of the Galician regional government to develop an expert system based on the use of ontologies for decision support in critical care medical environment of the Meixoeiro Hospital of Vigo which is part of the University Hospitable Center of Vigo.

Anas Aloudat (MIEE'09) holds a Doctor of Philosophy in Information Systems and Technology from the Faculty of Informatics at the University of Wollongong, NSW, Australia ('11); a Master of Science in Computing from the University of Technology, Sydney, NSW, Australia ('03), and a Bachelor of Science in Computing from the Faculty of Science at Mu'tah University in Karak, Jordan ('93). He is presently an Assistant Professor in the Department of Management Information Systems, at the Faculty of Business, at the University of Jordan, and has previously been employed as an associate lecturer and research assistant at the University of Wollongong, Australia. Aloudat has several publications, including in Proceedings of the IEEE, Electronic Commerce Research Journal, several book chapters in the national security domain in the Research Network for a Secure Australia (RNSA) series, *The Social Implications of National Security*, and one academic book chapter. Aloudat researches predominantly in the area of social implications of emerging technologies, and has interests in information systems innovation, adoption, diffusion and management.

Hanene Azzag is currently associate professor at the University of Paris 13 and a member of machine learning team A3 in LIPN Laboratory. Her main research is in biomimetic algorithms and data mining. Graduated from USTHB University where she received his engineer diploma in 2001. Thereafter, in 2002 she gained an MSC (DEA) in Artificial Intelligence from Tours University. In 2005, after three year Tours Lab, she received his PhD degree in Computer Science from the University of Tours.

Petros Belsis is currently a member of faculty at the department of Marketing at TEI of Athens. He holds a Diploma in Physics from the University of Athens, Greece, a Diploma in Computer Science from the Computer Science Department of Technological Education Institute, Athens, Greece, a MSc degree in Information Systems from the Athens University of Economics and Business, Greece, and a PhD in Information Systems Security from the Department of Information and Communication systems Engineering, at the University of the Aegean, Greece. He has published many journal and conference scientific articles, mainly in the areas of Information Systems security, policy based management in distributed environments, knowledge management, etc. His research interests focus on distributed knowledge management systems, policy based systems, and security in distributed environments.

Bendik Bygstad holds a PhD in computer science and a Master of Sociology. He worked 15 years in the IT industry. He is currently a professor at the Norwegian School of Information Technology. His main research interest is IT-based innovation and IS research methods. He has published articles in such journal as Information Systems Journal, Journal of Information Technology, International Journal of Project Management and International Journal of Technology and Human Interaction.

HongMei Cheng is a lecturer of school of management of Anhui University of Architecture. She is also a graduate student for Master of Business Administration of University of Science and Technology of China. Mrs. Cheng's research fields include financial engineering and data mining. Many of her research results were published in a number of information science academic journals and conference publications.

Ricardo Colomo-Palacios is an associate professor at the Computer Science Department of the Universidad Carlos III de Madrid. His research interests include applied research in information systems, software project management, people in software projects and social and Semantic Web. He received his PhD in computer science from the Universidad Politécnica of Madrid (2005). He also holds a MBA from the Instituto de Empresa (2002). He has been working as software engineer, project manager and software engineering consultant in several companies including Spanish IT leader INDRA. He is also an editorial board member and associate editor for several international journals and conferences and editor in chief of *International Journal of Human Capital and Information Technology Professionals.*

Deepak Dahiya is currently working as Professor in the Department of CSE & IT at Jaypee University of Information Technology (JUIT), Waknaghat, India. He has M.S. and PhD degrees in Computer Science from BITS Pilani, India. Deepak has over 18 years of extensive experience in IT Industry and Academics in India, Australia, US, UK and Oman. He has conducted senior executive training Programmes for both Private and Government sector. In the IT Industry, he has consulted for Corporate Clients in UK, US and India. Deepak is also a Visiting Researcher to RMIT University, Australia, Guest Faculty to Indian Institute of Management (IIM) Rohtak, India, Indian Institute of Management (IIM) Kozhikode, India and LNM Institute of Information Technology (LNMIIT) Jaipur, India. His interdisciplinary research interests span over software engineering and IT Management. He is a senior member of IEEE and Life Member of Computer Society of India.

HongBin Dong is a professor of School of Computer Science and Technology of Harbin Engineering University. Dr. Dong conducts active research in various computation intelligent related areas including artificial intelligence, multi-agent system, evolutionary computation, data mining, etc. His work was published in a number of computer science academic journals, conference publications.

Kevin E. Dow is an assistant professor at the University of Alaska, Anchorage. He received his PhD from the University of South Carolina. His research lies at the intersection of information systems and accounting and focuses on the design and use of accounting information for managing costs and evaluating business value. His papers have appeared in journals including Journal of Information Systems; the European Journal of Information Systems, Information Systems Research, Database for Advances in Information Systems, the International Journal of Accounting Information Systems, the International Journal of eCollaboration, Management Accounting Quarterly, Issues in Accounting Education, AIS Educators Journal, and the International Journal of Information Systems and Social Change.

Ángel García-Crespo is the head of the SofLab Group at the Computer Science Department in the Universidad Carlos III de Madrid and the head of the Institute for promotion of Innovation Pedro Juan de Lastanosa. He holds a PhD in industrial engineering from the Universidad Politécnica de Madrid (award from the Instituto JA Artigas to the best thesis) and received an executive MBA from the Instituto de Empresa. García-Crespo has led and actively contributed to large European projects of the FP V and VI, and also in many business cooperations. He is the author of more than a hundred publications in conferences, journals and books, both Spanish and international.

Gheorghita Ghinea received the B.Sc. and B.Sc. (Hons) degrees in Computer Science and Mathematics, in 1993 and 1994, respectively, and the M.Sc. degree in Computer Science, in 1996, from the University of the Witwatersrand, Johannesburg, South Africa; he then received the PhD degree in Computer Science from the University of Reading, United Kingdom, in 2000. He is a Reader in the School of Information Systems, Computing and Mathematics at Brunel University, United Kingdom. Dr. Ghinea has over 150 refereed publications and currently leads a team of 8 research students in his fields of interest, which span perceptual multimedia, telemedicine, semantic media management and technology adoption, human computer interaction, and network security.

Juan Miguel Gómez-Berbís is an associate professor at the Computer Science Department of the Universidad Carlos III de Madrid. He holds a PhD in computer science from the Digital Enterprise Research Institute (DERI) at the National University of Ireland, Galway and received his MSc in Telecommunications Engineering from the Universidad Politécnica de Madrid (UPM). He was involved in several EU FP V and VI research projects and was a member of the Semantic Web Services Initiative (SWSI). His research interests include semantic web, semantic web services, business process modelling, b2b integration and, recently, bioinformatics.

Stefanos Gritzalis holds a BSc in Physics, an MSc in Electronic Automation, and a PhD in Information and Communications Security from the Dept. of Informatics and Telecommunications, University of Athens, Greece. Currently he is the Deputy Head of the Department of Information and Communication Systems Engineering, University of the Aegean, Greece and the Director of the Laboratory of Information and Communication Systems Security (Info-Sec-Lab). He has been involved in several national and EU funded R&D projects. His published scientific work includes 30 books or book chapters and more than 200 journal and international refereed conference and workshop papers. The focus of these publications is on information and communications security and privacy. His most highly cited papers have more than 800 citations (h-index=16). He has acted as Guest Editor in 20 journal special issues, and has led more than 30 international conferences and workshops as General Chair or Program Committee Chair. He has served on more than 200 Program Committees of international conferences and workshops. He is an Editor-in-Chief or Editor or Editorial Board member for 15 journals and a Reviewer for more than 40 journals. He has supervised 10 PhD dissertations. He was an elected Member of the Board (Secretary General, Treasurer) of the Greek Computer Society. His professional experience includes senior consulting and researcher positions in a number of private and public institutions. He is a Member of the ACM, the IEEE, and the IEEE Communications Society Communications and Information Security Technical Committee.

Dennis C. Guster is a Professor of Computer Information Systems and Director of the Business Computing Research Laboratory at St. Cloud State University, MN, USA. His interests include network design, network performance analysis and computer network security. Dennis has 25+ years of teaching experience in higher education and has served as a consultant and provided industry training to organizations such as Compaq, NASA, DISA, USAF, Motorola, and ATT. He has published numerous works in computer networking/security and has undertaken various sponsored research projects.

Wei Hou is a Ph. D. Candidate of School of Computer Science and Technology of Harbin Engineering University. She is a lecturer of School of Agriculture Engineering of Northeast Agricultural University. Her main research include artificial intelligence, multi-agent system, evolutionary computation, data mining, etc.

He Jiang is an associate professor and Ph.D. supervisor of School of Software, Dalian University of Technology. Dr. Jiang received the B.A. degree and the Ph.D. degree in computer science from University of Science & Technology of China, Hefei, China in 1999 and 2005, respectively. He conducts active research in various information technology related areas, including evolutionary computation, heuristics, combinatorial optimization, and data mining.

Rahul Kala is an Integrated Post Graduate (BTech and MTech in Information Technology) student in Indian Institute of Information Technology and Management Gwalior. His areas of research are hybrid soft computing, robotic planning, biometrics, artificial intelligence, and soft computing. He has published about 35 papers in various international and national journals/conferences and is the author of 2 books. He also takes a keen interest toward free/open source software. He secured All India 8th position in Graduates Aptitude Test in Engineeging-2008 Examinations and is the winner of Lord of the Code Scholarship Contest organized by KReSIT, IIT Bombay and Red Hat.

Pavel Klinov is currently finishing his Ph.D. in Computer Science at the University of Manchester, UK. His research interests lie at the intersection of probability, description logic, ontology languages and automated reasoning. He has received an M.Sc. in Computer Engineering from the Moscow Engineering Physics Institute, Russia in 2004. He has spent 2.5 years working as a software engineer at the European Organization for Nuclear Research (CERN). Prior to transferring to the University of Manchester in early 2008 he started his Ph.D. studies at the University of Cincinnati, USA.

Angel Lagares-Lemos is a PhD Student at the SOC (Service Oriented Computing) Research Group in the University of New South Wales (Sydney, Australia). He worked as a Researcher at the Department of Computer Science in the Carlos III University of Madrid during one year. He obtained his MBA from the EAE Business School. He received a Msc. in Computer Science Engineering (Bilingual program) from the Carlos III University of Madrid. His current research interests include the Semantic Web, Semantic Web Services, Business Process Modeling, Software-asa Service (SaaS), Cloud Computing.

Miguel Lagares-Lemos is a researcher at IBIS group belonging to the University Carlos III of Madrid (Spain). Also He was working as a researcher for Philips Company allocated in High Tech Campus of Eindhoven (The Netherlands), mainly investigating about health care . He obtained his engineer degree on

Telecommunications at the University of Alcalá de Henares (Spain). He also holds an MSc in Biomedical Engineering from the University of Borås (Sweden). His current research interests include e-health, biomedical field, communications, Semantic Web, Semantic Web Services, Business Process Modeling.

Mustapha Lebbah is currently associate professor at the University of Paris 13 and a member of Machine learning Team A3 in LIPN Laboratory. His main researches are centred on machine learning (Self-organizing map, Probabilistic and Statistic).Graduated from USTO University where he received his engineer diploma in 1998. Thereafter, he gained an MSC (DEA) in Artificial Intelligence from the Paris 13 University in 1999. In 2003, after three year in RENAULT R&D, he received his PhD degree in Computer Science from the University of Versailles.

Olivia F. Lee is a marketing consultant and an Adjunct Professor of Marketing at Northwest University, USA. She has worked as an operation manager at two university hospitals and as a senior e-business market analyst in a business-to-business company prior to her academic career. Dr. Lee is a two-time Target Corporation teaching award-winner for her capstone strategic management courses. As an active researcher with multiple streams of research interest, her work focuses on technology practices in business environment, health care and service organization, and business resilience strategy. She has published her work and book articles on topics related to management, marketing and technology.

Javier Pereira Loureiro received his M.Sc. in Computer Science (1995) and Ph.D. in Computer Science (2004) from the University of A Coruña, Spain. He is an associate professor in the area of Radiology and Physical Medicine at the Department of Medicine at the Faculty of Health Sciences of the University of A Coruña, Spain. His current research interests include medical information systems, DICOM, PACS, medical informatics, accessibility in Information and Communication Technologies, disability and informatics and the development of technical aids. Since 1996, he has published multiple journal papers and book chapters on the above issues. He has led several projects funded by various Spanish institutions and/or companies. He is a member of the Medical Computing and Radiological Diagnosis Center (IMEDIR Center) from the University of A Coruña and belongs to several societies, such as American Telemedicine Association, Internet Society, ARPUF and SEIS.

Miguel Pereira Loureiro is Medical Specialist in the Anesthesiology Service Area of the Meixoeiro Hospital of Vigo (Complejo Hospitalario Universitario de Vigo which is part of the University Hospitable Center of Vigo, CHUVI since the year 2001. In 1997 he has graduated in Medicine and Surgery and he is currently a candidate for Doctor of Medicine from the University of A Coruña. He have a large number of publications in the field of using information technology in medicine and has participated in several research projects funded by public entities such as the University of A Coruña, Galician Department of healings or the Institute of Health Carlos III.

Marcos Martínez-Romero received his B.Sc. in Computer Science (2007) and M.Sc. in Artificial Intelligence and Computer Science (2008) from the University of A Coruña, Spain. He has been a member of the Medical Computing and Radiological Diagnosis Center (IMEDIR Center) of the University of A Coruña since 2006. He is currently a Computer Science Ph.D. candidate at the Department of Information and Communication Technologies of the University of A Coruña. His main research interests include ontology evaluation and recommendation, ontology based information integration, semantic annotation, semantic interoperability, semantic web services, semantic web rules, intelligent agents, ontology matching, systems integration and web based information systems. He is a member of several research projects, including the Galician Network for Colorectal Cancer Research (REGICC), the Galician Bioinformatics Network (RGB) and the IBERO-NBIC research network.

Katina Michael is an associate professor in the School of Information Systems and Technology and a member of the Institute for Innovation in Business and Social Research (IIBSOR) at the University of Wollongong. She is the IEEE Technology and Society Magazine editor-in-chief and also serves on the editorial board of Elsevier's Computers & Security journal. Michael researches on the socio-ethical implications of emerging technologies. She has also conducted research on the regulatory environment surrounding the tracking and monitoring of people using commercial global positioning systems (GPS) applications in the area of dementia, mental illness, parolees, and minors for which she was awarded an Australian Research Council Discovery grant. Michael has written and edited five books and published over 100 peer reviewed papers. She was responsible for the creation of the human factors series of workshops hosted annually since 2006 on the "Social Implications of National Security," funded by the ARC's Research Network for a Secure Australia (RNSA).

Hongwei Mo, born in 1973, Doctor of Engineering, Professor of Automation College of Harbin Engineering University. He is a visiting Scholar of UCDavis,CA, USA from 2003,10-2004,10. His main research interest includes natural computing, artificial immune system (AIS), data mining, intelligent system, artificial intelligent. He had published 30 papers and three books on AIS. He is director of Biomedicine Engineering Academy of Heilongjiang Province, commissioner of China Neural network committee, senior member of computer academy of China, secretary-general chairman and associate chairman of organization committee of 16th China Neural Network Conference and 1st conference of special topic on artificial immune system, which was successfully held from 5th Oct to 7th Oct in Harbin, China. He is a member of program committee of 2nd international conference on natural computing--fuzzy system and knowledge discovery(ICNCFSKD2006), 1st international conference on rough set and knowledge technology(RSKT2006), 6th international conference on simulation learning and evolution(ICSLE2006), BIC-TA 2008, GECS2009, ICSI2010,ICSI2011,ICNC'11-FSKD'11 and so on.

Rachit Mohan Garg has completed his post graduation from Jaypee University of Information Technology, Waknaghat in 2011. He has done his Master's Thesis under the guidance of Dr. Deepak Dahiya, Professor, Department of CSE & IT, Jaypee University of Information Technology, Waknaghat, India on Model Driven Architecture. At present, Rachit is working as a System Engineer with Infosys Limited, Bangalore, India.

Ana Torres Morgade received her B. Sc. in Computer Science (2010) from the University of a Coruña, Spain. She has been a member of the Medical Computing and Radiological Diagnosis Center (IMEDIR Center) of the University of A Coruña since the year 2008. Her main research interests include ontologies, expert systems and medical information systems. She has participated in a project funded by the Department of Health Service of the Galician regional government to develop an expert system based on the use of ontologies for decision support in critical care medical environment of the Meixoeiro Hospital of Vigo which is part of the University Hospitable Center of Vigo.

David Picado Muiño is currently working as a research assistant at the Technical University of Vienna on a project centered on the medical expert system CADIAG-2. He moved to Vienna in 2009 after finishing his Ph.D. in pure mathematics at the University of Manchester. His research interests are diverse. Up to now his focus has been mostly put on probabilistic inference and several issues related to inconsistency in databases.

Bijan Parsia is a lecturer in the School of Computer Science at the University of Manchester, UK. He has published extensively on various issues with ontology engineering using expressive description logics including optimisation of reasoning, the design of ontology languages, and explanation in description logic systems. He was involved in the standardisation of the second version of the Web Ontology Language (OWL 2).

Ahmed Patel received his MS and PhD degrees in Computer Science from Trinity College Dublin (TCD), specializing in the design, implementation and performance analysis of packet switched networks. He is a Lecturer and Consultant in ICT and Computer Science. He is a Visiting Professor at Kingston University in the UK and currently lecturing at Universiti Kebangsaan Malaysia. His research interests span topics concerning high-speed computer networking and application standards, network security, forensic computing, autonomic computing, heterogeneous distributed computer systems and distributed search engines and systems for the Web. He has published well over two hundred technical and scientific papers and co-authored two books on computer network security and one book on group communications, co-edited a book distributed search systems for the Internet. He is a member of the Editorial Advisory Board of the following International Journals: (i) Computer Communications, (ii) Computer Standards & Interface, (iii) Digital Investigations, (iv) Cyber Criminology, and (v) Forensic Computer Science.

Junying Qiu is a master student of School of Software, Dalian University of Technology. He received the B.A. degree in software engineering from Dalian University of Technology, Dalian, China in 2009. His research interest is hyper-heuristics.

M. Satpathy has his undergraduate, post-graduate and PhD degrees, all in Computer Science, respectively from Indian Institute of Science Bangalore, Indian Institute of Technology Kanpur and Indian Institute of Technology Bombay. He has taught at Indian Institute of Technology Guwahati and at University of Reading. He also worked as a post-doctoral researcher at UNU/IIST Macau and Abo Akademi University. Currently he is working as a staff researcher at General Motors India Science Lab, Bangalore. His research interests are Software Engineering and Formal Methods.

Anupam Shukla is serving as a Professor in Indian Institute of Information Technology and Management Gwalior. He heads the Soft Computing and Expert System Laboratory at the Institute. He has 20 years of teaching experience. His research interest includes Speech processing, Artificial Intelligence, Soft Computing, Biometrics and Bioinformatics. He has published over 100 papers in various national and international journals/conferences. He is editor and reviewer in various journals. He received Young Scientist Award from Madhya Pradesh Government and Gold Medal from Jadavpur University.

Christos Skourlas is a professor of Databases at the Computer Science Department of Technological Education Institute, Athens Greece. He holds BSc in Mathematics and PhD in Informatics from the University of Athens, Greece. His research interests focus on information retrieval, knowledge management, multilingual systems, disambiguation and natural language processing, and medical informatics.

Jin-Dae Song is a Senior Researcher at the R&D Institute of Hyosung Ebara Engineering Co., Ltd., South Korea. He recieved his MSc and PhD in Mechanical Engineering from the Pukyong National University, South Korea. His primary research interests are in intelligent optimum design and rotordynamics and applications.

Hamed Taghavi received his BSc degree in Computer Engineering and his MSc in Infotmation Technology Management (Advanced Information Systems) from Science and Research Branch, Islamic Azad Univerity of Tehran, Iran. His research interests topics are in the area of Strategic management, risk assessment of IS/IT, and Knowledge management. He worked as a Knowledge Management System develover in an IT consulting company and he is currently CEO of ISISCo (Iranian Strategic Information Solutions Company) in Tehran.

Mona Taghavi received her BS degree in Information Technology from Parand Islamic Azad University of Iran in 2007. Besides her involvement in several Iranian national ICT research projects, she had worked for an IT consulting and project managing company which was responsible for overseeing the Supreme Council of Information and Communication Technology (SCICT) of Iran programme. She was responsible for preparing some of the technical reports for this programme. Currently, she is pursuing her MSc in Management Information Systems and Network Security at University Kebangsaan Malaysia and undertaking research in cooperation with Prof. Dr. Ahmed Patel in advanced secure Web-based information systems. She has published 10 papers and she is a reviewer for the Computer Standards and Interfaces Journal.

Ritu Tiwari is serving as an Assistant Professor in Indian Institute of Information Technology and Management Gwalior. Her field of research includes Biometrics, Artificial Neural Networks, Speech Signal Processing, Robotics and Soft Computing. She has published over 50 research papers in various national and international journals/conferences. She has received Young Scientist Award from Chhattisgarh Council of Science & Technology and also received Gold Medal in her post graduation.

José M. Vázquez-Naya received his B.Sc. in Computer Science (2005), M.Sc. in Artificial Intelligence and Computer Science (2006) and Ph.D. in Computer Science (2009) from the University of A Coruña, Spain. He also received the certificate of Professional Expert on Information-Security in Computer Networks (2009) from the National University of Distance Education (UNED), Spain. He has been a member of the Medical Computing and Radiological Diagnosis Center (IMEDIR Center) of the University of A Coruña since the year 2000. He was a visiting scholar at the Artificial Intelligence Laboratory at the Polytechnic University of Madrid, Spain, and at the Simulation and Visualization Research Group at the University of Hull, UK. Currently, he is a teaching/research assistant at the Department of Information and Communication Technologies of the University of A Coruña, Spain. His main research lines include: Information Systems, Information Security and Ontologies.

Jeffrey Wong, PhD, CPA, is an associate professor at the University of Nevada at Reno. He received his PhD from the University of Oregon. Professor Wong has published work in journals including, Behavioral Research in Accounting, Database, International Journal of e-Collaboration, and Internal Auditor. His research interests focus on understanding how a firm's strategic decisions and actions ultimately map to financial results. This research focus has most recently examined how a company's information systems and investments in technology enhance the value of a firm.

Zhidan Xu was born in 1980. She is a Doctor candiate of College of Automation, Harbin Engineering University. She got her master degree of Science from Guizhou University, China in 2007. She is interested in intelligent control, natural inspired computing.

Jifeng Xuan is a Ph.D. candidate of School of Mathematical Sciences, Dalian University of Technology. He received the B.A. degree in software engineering from Dalian University of Technology, Dalian, China in 2007. His research interests include heuristics and software maintenance.

Bo-Suk Yang is the Director of the Intelligent Machine Condition Monitoring & Diagnostics Centre and the Dean of Academic Affairs at the Puyong National University in Korea. He received a Ph.D. degree in mechanical engineering from Kobe University, Japan in 1985. Presently he is a professor in mechanical engineering department at Pukyong National University since 1996. His main research fields cover machine dynamics and vibration engineering, intelligent optimum design, and condition monitoring and diagnostics in rotating machinery. He has published well over 170 research papers in the research areas of vibration analysis, intelligent optimum design and diagnosis of rotating machinery. He is a member of International Steering Committee for APVC and a director of International Society of Engineering Asset Management. He is listed in Who's Who in the World, Who's Who in Science and Engineering, among others.

GuiSheng Yin is a professor and Ph. D. supervisor of School of Computer Science and Technology of Harbin Engineering University. Dr. Yin research in a variety of information technology related areas including database system, virtual reality, data mining, etc.

ShuGuang Zhang is a professor and Ph.D supervisor of school of management of University of Science and Technology of China. Dr. Zhang's research fields include stochastic processes, random network, data mining and their application on financial engineering. Most of his research results were published in a number of mathematical academic journals and conference publications.

ZhenYa Zhang is an associate professor of school of electronic and computer engineering of Anhui University of Architecture. Now Dr. Zhang is the vice-dean of Key Laboratory of Intelligent Building of Anhui province and a post-doctoral of University of Science and Technology of China. His research fields include data mining, information retrieval, chance discovery, intelligent financial engineering, intelligent building and natural inspired computation, etc. Many of his research results were published in a number of information science academic journals and conference publications. In addition to his academic work, his engagements include providing expertise to a range of intelligent building, it audit and decision making.

Index

G

H

I

J

K

L

M

N

O

P

Q

R

S

T

U

V

W